# URBAN HOUSING

A VOLUME IN THE READER SERIES ON

URBAN PLANNING AND DEVELOPMENT

*Series Editors:* Martin and Margy Ellin Meyerson

*Edited by*

WILLIAM L. C. WHEATON

GRACE MILGRAM

MARGY ELLIN MEYERSON

# URBAN HOUSING

**THE FREE PRESS,** NEW YORK

*Collier - Macmillan Limited, London*

Library of Congress Catalog Card Number: 66–12082
FIRST PRINTING

# Introduction to the Series

Urban planning, the setting of policy for the development of cities, can only be accomplished well through understanding the functions of cities. This understanding requires a broad comprehension of the activities of the people who live in metropolitan areas: how and where they live and work; travel; spend their incomes and leisure time; raise their families; become sick and well again; worship; join groups; learn and teach; build, alter and replace structures and social institutions; see and are seen. These patterns of activities have become material for scrutiny and analysis by the urban expert, the city planner, and the student of cities. Just as the physician masters anatomy and physiology to understand human functions, so he who would comprehend the functions of cities must discern the physical form and structure and the changing way of life in urban concentrations. Along with the need of those concerned about the city to understand urban functions, is the need to understand the means by which urban malfunctions can be overcome, and the means through which the possibilities of urban life can be achieved.

The setting of urban policies assumes intervention into the normal activities of city living. Any intervention into an ongoing system should be undertaken with the same kind of awareness that a physician should have when he prescribes for a patient. The physician must check to see whether he is treating symptoms or the cause of the malfunction; he must judge the degree of effectiveness of the treatment in either case. Moreover, he must be alert to side-effects, which may be either beneficial or harmful. The urban specialist, too, must be aware of whether the remedies he advances are based on adequate knowledge and have been tested, at least in logic, if not in actuality.

Explicit in public intervention in complex issues should be a concept of reciprocity among the actions which might be taken. Since one kind of intervention might influence actions which another might not, scrutiny of the method of intervention and its consequences is as critical as comprehending linkages or patterning of urban functions.

City planning, as a relatively new formal field (the first degree program was started in this country at Harvard in 1929), and one more given to practice than scholarly activity (the first Ph.D. was granted in 1948), has perforce drawn heavily on the literature of other fields. While much information as well as insight may be obtained on the nature of urban functions from other disciplines – history, sociology, economics, geography, civil engineering, architecture, political science, management science – it is much more difficult to get such direct assistance from other disciplines on method. The literature by and for city planners, especially in recent years, has been expanding and increasing in quality. Now that there are over thirty university programs offering concentrations in or degrees in urban planning, the discipline of city planning may be expected to produce more and more of its own contributions in analysis, method and theory, and to make more syntheses of materials drawn from other disciplines.

The series of urban planning and development readers is primarily designed for students of city and regional planning. Since collections of essays have rarely been brought together on the subjects covered by the series, the separate volumes should also serve as introductory volumes for specialists; for example, the volume on planning law and zoning will be useful to the lawyer, the volumes on transportation will be of value to the transportation specialist. Furthermore, since the series is largely composed of analytic but not highly technical material, the separate volumes will also have considerable appeal for and be useful to the very many individuals and groups who are concerned with the solving of urban problems: civic leaders and government officials are among these.

This series of readers has been designed, as most readers have been, to collect materials which are presently not readily available to the many persons interested in the subjects they cover. Some materials are out-of-print, others are in publications of small circulation; some selections from recent publications have been included when they represent for the purposes of the volume the most pertinent views on the subject.

Those who have been involved in the preparation of this series have been fully aware that the volumes ought to be considered worthy more as stimulators to further efforts than as perfected works in themselves. In a field which is changing so rapidly, the editors assume that the volumes will become obsolete and they hope they will become rapidly obsolete. For the editors are in accord with Sir Francis Bacon's perceptive comment, when he urged in "A Proposition to His Majesty ... touching the ... Amendment of the Laws," that "books must follow sciences, and not sciences books." When the field of city planning has made further advances in functional analysis and method, it will be time for other volumes to replace these.

The editors of the volumes have tried to present an overview of subjects which are too frequently dealt with in a piecemeal or partial manner. Because the editors have sought breadth of coverage, sacrifices have been made in the choices of particular selections which do not necessarily represent the best work of each author nor even the best material on the subject,

for sometimes the best may be available in a readily obtainable source, or may be in a form which does not lend itself to excerpting. Attention is called to some of the omissions by their inclusion in the bibliographies. The editors have attempted to alert the user of the series to a variety of sources, to older as well as more recent materials, and to a variety of approaches. This breadth has been more difficult to achieve than a narrow focus: it would be easier for example to compile a reader on market analysis in housing than a reader which gives an overview of housing.

The series of urban planning and development readers was aided by a grant from the Ford Foundation to the University of Pennsylvania and by the resources of the Harvard Center for Urban Studies. The volumes have been tested in the classrooms of the University of Pennsylvania and Harvard University. The plan for the volumes was first conceived at the University of Pennsylvania; Professors Robert B. Mitchell, G. Holmes Perkins, William L. C. Wheaton and Martin Meyerson plus Margy Ellin Meyerson and Grace Milgram, who were on the staff at Pennsylvania, were involved in their preparation from the early days. After the initial setting of policies in Philadelphia and the decisions on the subjects to be covered and their general scope, the first complete drafts were prepared in Cambridge by Martin and Margy Ellin Meyerson. These drafts were then returned to the Institute for Urban Studies of the University of Pennsylvania for further refining.

The series is a unique effort at cooperation by institutions as well as individuals. For each of the persons involved, the work has largely been a labor of love.

MARTIN *and* MARGY ELLIN MEYERSON
*Series Editors*

# Preface

Housing is unique among consumer goods in the degree to which its quality can enhance or diminish the well-being of individuals and families, the impact its location has on the structure and financial health of communities, the role its production plays in the national economy, and the amount of emotionally charged discussion it provokes. Unlike other essentials, whose deficiency may not come to public attention, the failure of individual families to obtain adequate housing cannot be hidden. Poor housing is apparent to any passerby, blighting not only the individual, but the neighborhood and city as well. Housing, furthermore, is costly; a house is the most expensive single item most individuals ever buy, and except for food, expenditures for shelter take the largest part of the budget of most families. Finally, housing is extremely durable, and the inadequate house of yesterday continues to exist today and tomorrow.

The quality of American housing, if measured by possession of indoor plumbing and lack of dilapidation, has improved substantially in the past decade, yet the 1960 Census shows that, even by this crude criterion, about one-fifth of our housing units are still substandard. If the definition of substandard housing were enlarged to include dwelling units with inadequate space, hazardous heating and electrical equipment, and poor neighborhood facilities and environment, the proportion which would not meet our national goal of a sound house in a suitable living environment would be considerably enlarged.

This volume presents a selection of readings devoted to consideration of various facets of housing in the United States. It is divided into eight sections. The first attempts to provide a general setting, with discussion of the nature and extent of the problem of inadequate shelter, as it has been seen historically and currently, together with those aspects which require further research. Since the subject of housing refers not only to an individual dwelling unit, but also to a neighborhood, materials on the growth and desirable arrangement of neighborhoods are included in the second section. The third is devoted to consideration of the housing market, particularly those factors affecting consumer demand and expenditures. Special attention is given in the fourth section to groups whose needs for good housing pose particularly difficult problems: single and aged persons, minority groups, and those of low income. Following this, production of residential structures is examined, with a description of the industry and of problems associated with construction. Because of its particular importance in facilitating and expanding the construction and acquisition of residential property, the next group of readings is devoted to residential finance. The growth of housing standards is reported in the seventh section, together with methods of control by public agencies which have been developed in the effort to bring housing quality up to the adopted standard. Finally, the concluding portion of the reader deals particularly with the residential aspects of urban renewal, both the opportunities presented by renewal and the problems it creates. A selected bibliography of additional readings is included, arranged according to chapter subjects, except that its last section lists material on economic aspects of housing which could not be covered in the reader.

To anyone who examines the selections in this reader, or who follows all the material published in the field, it is clear that despite the long years of attention to housing problems, great gaps exist in our knowledge. Even the basic question of the extent of substandard housing cannot be answered, because of wide differences of opinion as to what constitutes a "substandard" dwelling unit. There is the further problem that our standards continually rise or, at least, change, so that what was acceptable when built may be considered substandard now because of obsolescence rather than physical deterioration. Partially this may be a matter of style, but more frequently it reflects changes in the technology of living – changed methods of heating, widespread ownership of autos and the need for garages, introduction of air-conditioning, and the myriad other ways in which our mode of living differs from that of even a generation ago.

There is, moreover, little knowledge of what types of houses and what arrangements of houses in communities best serve individual needs and social goals. Some isolated studies have been made of the effect of poor housing and slum conditions both upon individual physical and mental health and on the promotion of socially pathological behavior. Yet in spite of the development of more sophisticated approaches in recent years, there are great gaps in our understanding of these relationships. And the effect of different types of housing which are generally assumed to be adequate upon the well-being of presumably normal individuals and families remains almost completely unexplored.

Even the great movement of families from other houses and apartments in central city to new suburban, owner-occupied homes, which has so greatly altered the structure of our metropolitan areas, has been inadequately analyzed. We do not really know what families are looking for when they move, whether they find it, and what costs and benefits have accrued to society as a whole from this movement. And finally, although we recognize some of the areas of particular housing need among the low-income, aged, and minority groups, we have found few politically acceptable approaches by which to meet these needs.

In compiling this reader, selections have been taken from both well-known authorities in the housing field and those whose work is not so well known or whose major interest falls outside of housing. The volume includes a few early writings which made a major contribution at the time, and whose insights have been accepted and built upon. Selections are also included which represent current thinking, with several viewpoints presented, if possible, where consensus has not been reached.

It was inevitable that the selection process forced the elimination of many valuable writings. Whole areas of concern somewhat peripheral to planning interests have been omitted. Residential finance is limited to those aspects which are of concern to urban planners. There are no discussions of the role of the housing industry as a tool in economic stabilization or as a means of fostering economic development. Also excluded are technical studies on the operation and means of analysis of the housing market and on the physical design of residential structures. But even within those subject areas which are included, many interesting studies had to be omitted. This is particularly true in the case of lengthy analyses which could not be cut without destroying essential elements of description or logic. It is also certain that many persons will feel that some of the material which has been excluded is superior to that which has been chosen. Our hope, however, is that all of the material will be judged to be of high quality, and that in bringing the readings under one cover, we have provided a useful reference for both the beginning student and the more advanced scholar.

WILLIAM L. C. WHEATON
GRACE MILGRAM

# Contributors

CHARLES ABRAMS — Chairman, Division of Urban Planning, Columbia University, New York.

JANET ABU-LUGHOD — Sociologist, formerly associated with the ACTION Research Program.

DAVID M. BLANK — Chief Economist and Director of Economic Analysis, Columbia Broadcasting System, Inc., New York.

GURNEY BRECKENFELD — *Time* editorial staff, New York.

MILES COLEAN — Consulting Economist and Fellow of American Institute of Architects, Washington, D. C.

MARY EVANS COLLINS — Formerly associated with the Research Center for Human Relations, New York University, New York.

JOHN P. DEAN — At the time of his death, Dr. Dean was Director, Field Research Office, Cornell University, Ithaca, New York.

MARTIN DEUTSCH — Professor of Social Psychology, Teachers College, Columbia University, New York.

MARY MIX FOLEY — Formerly Associate Editor, *Architectural Forum*.

HERBERT J. GANS — Senior Research Sociologist, Center for Urban Education, New York.

JAMES GILLIES — Director, Real Estate Research Program, University of California, Los Angeles, California.

LEO GREBLER — Professor of Real Estate and Urban Land Economics, University of California, Los Angeles, California, formerly Director, Mexican-American Study Project.

WILLIAM G. GRIGSBY — Associate Professor of City Planning, University of Pennsylvania, Philadelphia, Pennsylvania.

JACK M. GUTTENTAG — Associate Professor of Finance, University of Pennsylvania, Philadelphia, Pennsylvania.

CHARLES M. HAAR — Assistant Secretary, Department of Housing and Urban Development, Washington, D. C.

JOHN P. HERZOG — Associate Professor of Economics, University of Wisconsin, Madison, Wisconsin.

HOMER HOYT — Planning Consultant, Homer Hoyt Associates, Inc., Washington, D. C.

REGINALD R. ISAACS — Professor of City and Regional Planning, Harvard University, Cambridge, Massachusetts.

RALPH J. JOHNSON — Chief of Housing Hygiene Activities, Division of Sanitary Engineering Services, Public Health Service, U. S. Department of Health, Education and Welfare, Washington, D. C.

BURNHAM KELLY — Dean of the College of Architecture, Cornell University, Ithaca, New York.

FRANK S. KRISTOF — Chief, Bureau of Planning and Program Research, New York City Housing and Redevelopment Board.

LUIGI LAURENTI — Economist and author of articles on real estate problems, formerly associated with University of California, Berkeley, California.

SHERMAN J. MAISEL — Member of Board of Governors, Federal Reserve System, Washington, D. C.

ROY O. McCALDIN — At the time of his study, Assistant Chief, Housing Hygiene Activities, Division of Sanitary Engineering Services, Public Health Service, U.S. Department of Health, Education and Welfare, Washington, D. C.

CARTER McFARLAND — Assistant Commissioner, Federal Housing Administration, Washington, D. C.

ROBERT K. MERTON — Chairman, Department of Sociology, Columbia University, New York.

MARGY ELLIN MEYERSON — Consulting planner, formerly associated with the Institute of Urban Studies, University of Pennsylvania, Philadelphia, Pennsylvania, and lecturer in city planning, University of California, Berkeley, California.

MARTIN MEYERSON — President, State University of New York at Buffalo, formerly Dean, College of Environmental Design, University of California, Berkeley, California.

GRACE MILGRAM — Research Assistant Professor, Institute for Environmental Studies, University of Pennsylvania, Philadelphia, Pennsylvania.

MARTIN MILLSPAUGH — acting General Manager, Charles Center Program, Baltimore, Maryland.

FRANK S. MITTELBACH — Assistant Research Economist, Real Estate Research Program, University of California, Los Angeles, California.

LEWIS MUMFORD — Author, *Culture of Cities, City in History,* and other works, Amenia, New York.

ROBINSON NEWCOMB — Consulting economist, Vice-chairman and member of executive committee of the Building Research Advisory Board, National Academy of Sciences.

CLARENCE A. PERRY — Deceased. Before his death, Associate Director of Department of Recreation, Russell Sage Foundation, New York.

THOMAS C. PINKERTON — Department of Biophysics, The Johns Hopkins University, Baltimore, Maryland.

CHESTER RAPKIN — Professor of City Planning, University of Pennsylvania, Philadelphia, Pennsylvania.

RICHARD U. RATCLIFF — Professor of Land Economics, University of Wisconsin, Madison, Wisconsin.

IRA S. ROBBINS—Former President, National Association of Housing and Redevelopment Officials, Washington, D. C., and Vice-chairman, New York City Housing Authority, New York, New York.

LLOYD RODWIN — Professor of Land Economics, Department of City and Regional Planning, Massachusetts Institute of Technology, Cambridge, Massachusetts.

ARNOLD M. ROSE — Professor of Sociology, University of Minnesota, Minneapolis, Minnesota.

ALBERT H. SCHAAF — Associate Professor of Business Administration, University of California, Berkeley, California.

ALVIN L. SCHORR — Acting Chief, Long Range Research, Social Security Administration, Washington, D. C.

JOHN R. SEELEY — Professor of Sociology, Brandeis University, Waltham, Massachusetts.

MATTHEW TAYBACK — Assistant Commissioner for Research and Planning, Baltimore City Health Department, Baltimore, Maryland.

BARBARA R. TERRETT — Consultant, Penjerdel, Inc., Philadelphia, Pennsylvania, formerly associated with the ACTION Research Program.

ALLAN A. TWITCHELL — Prior to his death, Mr. Twitchell had been Technical Secretary of the Committee on the Hygiene of Housing of the American Public Health Association, and subsequently Administrator of the Plan for Rezoning New York City on the staff of Harrison, Ballard, and Allen, housing and planning consultants, New York.

ROSABELLE PRICE WALKLEY — Associate Research Behavioral Scientist and Lecturer, School of Public Health, University of California, Los Angeles, California.

ROBERT C. WEAVER — Secretary, Department of Housing and Urban Development, Washington, D. C.

WILLIAM L. C. WHEATON — Director, Institute of Urban and Regional Development, College of Environmental Design, University of California, Berkeley, California.

HUNTINGTON WILLIAMS — At the time of his study, Commissioner of Health, City Health Department, Baltimore, Maryland.

DANIEL WILNER — Professor of Public Health, University of California, Los Angeles, California.

LOUIS WINNICK — Associate Director, Public Affairs Program, Ford Foundation, New York.

EDITH ELMER WOOD — Before her death, Dr. Wood was a leading authority on housing problems, serving, among other posts, as member of the New Jersey State Housing Authority and consultant to the Housing Division of the Public Works Administration, Washington, D. C.

CATHERINE BAUER WURSTER — Now deceased, Mrs. Wurster was active in housing and planning, serving as consultant to numerous governmental agencies, as well as professor of City and Regional Planning, University of California, Berkeley, California.

# Contents

Introduction to the Series *by Martin and Margy Ellin Meyerson.*   v

Preface to Urban Housing *by William L. C. Wheaton and Grace Milgram.*   vii

Contributors.   ix

## I. Background

A Century of the Housing Problem, *by Edith Elmer Wood.*   1

Housing Achievements, *by Ira S. Robbins.*   9

Housing and the National Economy, *by Martin Meyerson, Barbara Terrett, and William L. C. Wheaton.*   14

The Social Psychology of Housing, *by Robert K. Merton.*   20

Social Questions in Housing and Community Planning, *by Catherine Bauer Wurster.*   30

## II. Housing in the Neighborhood

The Structure and Growth of Residential Neighborhoods in American Cities, *by Homer Hoyt.*   53

The Theory of Residential Growth and Structure, *by Lloyd Rodwin.*   75

The Neighborhood Unit Formula, *by Clarence A. Perry.*   94

Attack on the Neighborhood Unit Formula, *by Reginald R. Isaacs.*   109

In Defense of the Neighborhood, *by Lewis Mumford.*   114

## III. The Housing Market

Housing Design and Family Values, *by John P. Dean.*   127

Family Housing Expenditures: Elusive Laws and Intrusive Variances, *by Sherman J. Maisel and Louis Winnick.*   139

Housing: Has There Been a Downward Shift in Consumers' Preferences? *by Louis Winnick.*   154

Winnick's Case for a Changing Attitude Toward Housing: Comment, *by Jack Guttentag.*   162

Reply, *by Louis Winnick.*   166

Rent–Income Ratio, *by Chester Rapkin.*   168

The Consumer Votes by Moving, *by Janet Abu-Lughod and Mary Mix Foley.*   175

The Filtering Process, *by William G. Grigsby.*   191

Components of Change in the Nation's Housing Inventory in Relation to the 1960 Census, *by Frank S. Kristof.*   202

## IV. Requirements of Special Groups

### A. Single and Aged Persons

Living Arrangements of Unattached Persons, *by Arnold M. Rose.*   217

Housing for the Elderly, *by the Subcommittee on Housing for the Elderly, U.S. Senate.*   223

Guiding Policies, *by the Committee on the Hygiene of Housing, American Public Health Association.*   226

### B. Low Income and the Ill-Housed

How the Poor Are Housed, *by Alvin L. Schorr.*   231

Housing of Low-Income Families, *by the Editors,* Journal of Housing.   241

The Dreary Deadlock of Public Housing, *by Catherine Bauer Wurster.*   245

Housing and Slum Clearance: Elusive Goals, *by William G. Grigsby.*   252

The Myths of Housing Reform, *by John P. Dean.*   255

Housing Environment and Family Life, *by Daniel Wilner, Rosabelle Walkley, Thomas Pinkerton, and Matthew Tayback.*   261

### C. Minority Groups

Where Shall We Live? *by the Commission on Race and Housing.*   269

Property Values and Race, *by Luigi Laurenti.*   286

Concerning Studies of Price Trends in Mixed Areas, *by Chester Rapkin and William G. Grigsby.*   292

Interracial Housing, *by Martin Deutsch and Mary Evans Collins.*   294

• The Urbanization of the Negro, *by Robert C. Weaver.*   298

## V. The Housing Industry

The Organization of the Construction Industry, *by Miles Colean and Robinson Newcomb.*   307

Classifications of the Construction Industry, *by James Gillies and Frank Mittlebach.*   314

Structural Change in the Housebuilding Industry, *by John P. Herzog.*   317

New Directions for the Housing Industry, *Editors of* House and Home.   324

VI.  **Housing Finance**

The Environment of Real Estate Finance, by *Miles Colean.*   333

Background of Federal Housing Credit, by *Charles M. Haar.*   347

The Growth of the Residential Mortgage Debt, by *Leo Grebler, David M. Blank, and Louis Winnick.*   357

The Subsidy and Housing, by *Charles Abrams.*   365


VII.  **Housing Standards and Controls**

Building and Land Use Controls, by *Burnham Kelly and others.*   373

Housing Standards, by *Richard U. Ratcliff.*   391

An Appraisal Method for Measuring the Quality of Housing, by *Allan A. Twitchell.*   394

The Quality of Housing " Before " and "After " Rehabilitation, by *Ralph J. Johnson, Huntington Williams, and Roy O. McCaldin.*   403


VIII.  **Residential Renewal**

The Slum : Its Nature, Use, and Users, by *John R. Seeley.*   409

Economic Aspects of Urban Renewal, by *A. H. Schaaf.*   418

Urban Renewal, by *Carter McFarland.*   428

Facts and Fictions in Urban Renewal, by *Louis Winnick.*   441

The Lessons Learned, by *Martin Millspaugh and Gurney Breckenfeld.*   451

An Evaluation of the Redevelopment Plan and Process, by *Herbert J. Gans.*   458


Notes.   475

Bibliography.   487

Index.   503

# URBAN HOUSING

# Background

## A century of the housing problem

*EDITH ELMER WOOD*

The housing problem is an inevitable feature of our modern industrial civilization and does not tend to solve itself. Supply and demand do not reach it, because the cost of new housing and the distribution of income are such that approximately two thirds of the population cannot present an effective demand for new housing. And while some of the older housing is acceptable enough, a great deal is shockingly inadequate.

It is not as though a wholesome circulation were established. If the worst of the old housing were automatically destroyed when and as new housing is built, one could look forward with some equanimity to the gradual elimination of slums. But that is not what happens. When the solid citizen builds himself a new house, he either moves farther from the center of the community to un-built-on land in search of more space and amenities, or he chooses a good built-up residence district and tears down a perfectly serviceable house which he or his wife feels is outmoded.

He certainly does not move into the slums in order to demolish a rookery. Slum districts stagnate with no new building undertaken and few repairs, while new residential districts are built up on the periphery, and ever-increasing rings of blight spread outward from the center. One of the commonest types of slum is the near-in formerly good residence district, invaded by business, but never wholly taken over, where large single-family homes are cut up either into makeshift apartments or makeshift offices, for neither of which they are adapted, and the one-time gardens are filled with temporary structures intended to pay for taxes till the district is absorbed by high-grade business. Meanwhile taxes are paid on high valuations, not because of present use, but because of hopes for the future in which owners and assessors agree.

Unfortunately, our business districts some years ago began expanding vertically instead of horizontally. Then immigration was ended, and

*Reprinted from a symposium, " Low Cost Housing and Slum Clearance," Law and Contemporary Problems, vol. 1 (March, 1934), pp. 137–147, Duke University Press, with permission of the publisher.*

with that, the period of rapid growth of population. The birth rate is down and still falling. The drift from farm to city has been turned back. And we all know, or should know, that we are arriving at a period of relatively stable population. The future growth of our cities must be qualitative, not quantitative. The word "must" is used advisedly. For if our communities do not face the task of clearing up the mess that has been heedlessly made and restoring to efficient use their areas of slum and their areas of blight, they are facing bankruptcy. No city of relatively stable population can go on giving city services of paving, street cleaning, sewer, water, lighting, police, fire, schools, and all the rest, to ever-widening new peripheral districts, while ever-increasing inner areas are maintained for their dwindling population at increasing loss.

A generation ago, Sir Ebenezer Howard and the English Garden City group began to preach the doctrine that existing cities and towns are too bad to be worth trying to save and that the road to salvation lies in drawing off population and industries together to new garden cities planned from the start for convenient and healthy living, the land on which they are built being held in trust for the benefit of the community. Letchworth and Welwyn were built as demonstrations of what life in such communities might be for families of all economic levels. The demonstration is convincing. Letchworth and Welwyn are charming towns. But the British are still trying to find ways to save London and Manchester and Liverpool and Birmingham and Glasgow and Edinburgh, and I suspect our American psychology will be found to work the same way.

There has always been bad housing, but the acute awareness of it, as well as the effort to do away with it, are modern phenomena. The stream of European immigration to this country after the Napoleonic wars caused great congestion in our seaports. The establishment of industries drew workers to various centers. Just a century ago, in 1834, Gerritt Forbes, city health inspector in New York, made the first American reference to the subject on record, in a report where he called attention to the connection between high death rates and bad housing conditions, and their relation to the spread of epidemics. His successor, Dr. Griscom, made more extensive and emphatic reports. The Association for Improving the Condition of the Poor (AICP) was founded as a result and conducted a housing survey, which, in 1847, reported that the tenements of the poor were defective in size, arrangement, water supply, warmth and ventilation, and that rents were disproportionately high. An investigation by the state legislature was made in 1857. But it was not till 1867 that the New York legislature passed the first tenement house law[1] for New York City, which was also the first exercise of the police power in this country to regulate the use of private property as tenement houses, in the interest of the health, safety and morals of tenants. For the first time, it became illegal in one American city to build a tenement house covering 100 percent of its lot. A 10-foot yard had to be left at the rear for light and air.* A wholly subterranean room could no longer be rented for human habitation. The ceiling must be at least 1 foot above curb level. City water must be somewhere on the premises, though a hydrant in the yard would do. It had taken 33 years of investigation and struggle to bring about this first step.

It took another third of a century of continued struggle to raise the standards of that first regulatory statute, by successive steps, to a comparatively adequate level, and to provide for its enforcement. The end of the period was marked by the report of the Tenement House Commission appointed by the Governor in 1900, the enactment of the New York Tenement House Law[2] for first-class cities in 1901, and the creation of the Tenement House Department to administer it in New York City, which began to function in 1902.†

---

* Not until 1879 was it required that new tenements should be built with a window to the outer air in every room. More than 350,000 windowless rooms had been built in what is now New York City before that date, and most of them are still in existence and in use, with no greater alleviation than a window cut in the partition of an adjoining room.

† Court decisions upholding tenement house acts have been numerous. A well-known case was that of Katie Moeschen, owner of a tenement in New York, ordered to remove school sinks from the yard and install water closets in the house in 1903 under the Act of 1901. The case was carried through the state courts to the Supreme Court of the United States, where the constitutionality

Other cities, such as Boston, Philadelphia and Washington, less acutely suffering than New York, began to be housing conscious during this period and made some beginnings in regulation.

Parallel, but by no means keeping pace with these regulatory steps, were sporadic efforts by philanthropists to build model tenements, by employers to house their workers, and, toward the end, by limited dividend companies.

The last third of a century of housing consciousness was marked, first, by a spotty effort over the rest of the nation to catch up with or to surpass New York in restrictive housing legislation, on the model of the New York Tenement House Law. This was followed by a wave of zoning, which also started in New York, but became widely popular. Zoning also is an exercise of the police power, intended to regulate the growth of our communities in matters of use, height and bulk of buildings.* It is preventive, not curative. We would have fewer blighted areas and less congestion on the land, had we started zoning sooner.

Meanwhile, we have witnessed the beginnings of a constructive approach to the housing problem, and with the opportunities now offered under the National Recovery Act as part of the Recovery Program, are, perhaps, standing on the threshold of a new era.

The more important American episodes along this newer constructive line may be listed as follows:

1. 1917. Massachusetts Homestead Commission was authorized to spend $50,000 in buying suburban land, building houses with gardens, and selling them on long-time payments to workers living in congested quarters.[3] This was a state public authority to build and sell at cost. Result, twelve houses on the outskirts of Lowell, sold to workmen.

2. 1918. The federal government undertook war housing for war workers.[4] Aside from temporary housing, the Emergency Fleet Corporation and the United States Housing Corporation of the Department of Labor completed about 16,000 family units, mostly single-family houses in neighborhood groups, or complete new communities, which were of excellent standard. Many times that number were planned or underway.

3. 1921–24. Milwaukee secured legislation permitting the city and county to subscribe to the shares of cooperative housing companies.[5] One such company was formed and 105 houses built on a well-laid-out site.

4. 1921. California enacted the Veterans Farm and Home Purchase Act,[6] and the Veterans Welfare Board was established to administer it and other matters. The purpose is to aid home ownership on the part of veterans of small means, without expense to the taxpayers. Homes of excellent quality have been acquired by over 11,600 veterans, who are paying for them over a twenty-year period. Serial bonds have been issued to an amount of $50 million. The veterans, not the taxpayers, pay principal and interest. Some 10,000 more approved applications awaited, at last accounts, authorization of the issue of further bonds.

5. 1926. The New York State Housing Law[7] was enacted and the State Board of Housing established to administer it. The bill, as originally presented, provided for a State Housing Bank to finance limited dividend housing projects under the supervision of the State Board. The bank feature was eliminated by opponents in the legislature. New York City is the only community which has operated under this act. To facilitate low-cost housing, it granted 20 years tax exemption to buildings in projects approved by the State Board. The result during the years 1927–1932 were the build-

---

of the Act was finally sustained. All decisions were unanimous. *Moeschen* v. *Tenement House Dept.,* 27 Sup. Ct. 781, 203 U.S. 583, 51 L. Ed. 328 (1906); aff'g *Tenement House Dept.* v. *Moeschen,* 179 N.Y. 325, 72 N.E. 231 (1904).
* Among the many court decisions concerned with zon-

ing, the most fundamental, perhaps, was that rendered by Justice Sutherland of the United States Supreme Court in the Village of Euclid (Ohio) case. *Ambler Realty Co.* v. *Village of Euclid,* 47 Sup. Ct. 114, 272 U.S. 365 (1926).

ing and operation of eleven garden-apartment projects, in various parts of New York City, housing just under 2,000 families, with average rentals in the several projects varying from $9.73 to $12.50 per room per month (heat included). Certain of these projects are cooperative. All are of high standard. Several involved small-scale slum clearance.

6. July, 1932. The Federal Home Loan Bank Act[8] and its developments, which have already put 299 federal savings and loan associations into localities previously weak in credit facilities, may prove to be of outstanding importance in financing the small home owner.

7 and 8. The big new opportunities born of the depression have been the offer of 4 percent loans to limited dividend housing companies under the Reconstruction Finance Corporation[9] (July, 1932) and the offer of loans and grants (June, 1933) under the National Industrial Recovery Act.[10] The only result of the first, beside preparing the way for the second, was the loan of some $8 million to the Fred F. French Company to demolish two slum blocks in the Lower East Side of New York and put up 1,600 garden apartments for white-collar tenants, renting at an average of $12.50 per month per room. Only three families previously on the site have any hope of living there. This project also is under the State Board of Housing.

Under NIRA, the possibilities open wider. Some $48,570,000 have already been allotted in loans to twenty limited dividend housing projects scattered over the country from New York to San Francisco and from Boston to the Virgin Islands. Rents in continental United States will range from $5 to $11 per room per month. Slum clearance is involved in a number of cases. Several of the projects are for Negroes, who are under particular difficulties in seeking for better housing. Eighteen of these projects provide homes for just under 10,000 families. In addition, $100 million are reserved for housing. Whether this will be expended by the recently created Federal Emergency Housing Corporation, organized to speed up action, but frozen into at least temporary immobility by a ruling of the Comptroller General,* or by the also recently created state, county and city housing authorities, is comparatively unimportant. In either case, it is expected to be used for slum clearance and low-rent housing. Public housing authorities are eligible for a 30 percent grant of cost of labor and materials, as well as for a 4 percent loan of the balance needed, and should, therefore, be able to offer substantially lower rentals than limited dividend companies. They will not be in competition, as they will cater to lower income groups.

It has been said that $20 to 25 million out of 100 are earmarked for use in New York City and $20 million for Chicago.

The potential importance of these recent developments would be hard to exaggerate. One hundred and fifty million dollars,† spread over the nation, can only produce demonstrations. But these demonstrations may have far-reaching results.

In looking back over our century of housing effort in the United States, it will be observed that approach to the problem has come from two directions, though one of them did not appear till quite recently. It was pointed out some years ago[11] that all attacks on the housing problem are either restrictive or constructive. They either forbid something bad and set up minimum standards of building or maintenance, which must be observed under penalty of the law, or they seek to provide adequate housing on a public utility basis for sections of the population for whom private business enterprise does not find it profitable to build. Both forms of activity are necessary for a comprehensive solution. They supplement

---

* On March 6, 1934, an opinion of Attorney General Homer I. Cummings was issued upholding the legality of the Federal Emergency Housing Corporation and ruling that it could acquire and convey title to real estate and that its acquisitions were not subject to review by the Comptroller General.

† In addition to this sum, $25 million is to be used for subsistence homesteads.

each other and are in no sense rivals. We cannot get on without requirements for running water, sewers, windows and fire escapes. And it was real progress when zoning curbed individual freedom to put up a filling station or a chain store or a skyscraper in a district of homes.

The value of restrictive measures depends on how high their standards are and how well they are enforced. But every additional requirement of larger yards or larger rooms, or more plumbing, or greater fire protection, adds to the cost of building, which is passed on to the purchaser or renter. Rising standards, therefore, necessarily mean higher costs and higher rentals and a decreasing proportion of the population able to live in new housing.

It must be remembered, too, that a standard which has been set for new building cannot be applied to already existing buildings – especially where there are a great many of them – if costly structural alterations would be involved. And yet such buildings may last for a great many years with continued injurious effect on the families living in them.*

In European countries, where their housing problems hit them earlier and harder than ours, they arrived many years ago at the realization that private enterprise was everywhere making a failure of housing the low-income groups, and, to some extent, the middle groups. Earlier than we, they were convinced that for its own sake, every child was entitled to grow up in physically wholesome surroundings, and that the state had a very real interest in seeing that he did so. The line of reasoning was much the same as that applied to free education or to social insurance. It was as often advocated by conservatives as by radicals, though usually with a different emphasis. Conservatives, for instance, have been strong for the encouragement of home ownership by government loans at low interest rate, long period of amortization, and small down payment. Radicals have generally preferred municipal housing. In other places, long-time loans to cooperative housing societies have been emphasized. For a generation or more, European housing of the working classes has tended to be handled as a public utility, on a self-supporting basis as far as possible, at the partial expense of the taxpayers where necessary.

It will be profitable to have a quick look back at the experience of Great Britain. The Industrial Revolution, which substituted steam power for hand power and factories for cottage work shops, drew the rural workers by tens and hundreds of thousands to the large towns in search of work. No housing was ready for them. No restrictive laws were in existence. Housing sprang up, mushroom-like, wretched in quality, jerry built, back-to-back cottages, crowded together, flat on the ground with no damp courses, lacking sewers, lacking water, with rents so high that the overcrowding was fearful. Some of that housing remains to this day, and forms the material for clearance schemes.

Harry Barnes, the historian of British slum clearance,[12] dates the first stage from 1830. The situation was already recognized as acute. Dickens and Ruskin used their talents to arouse public indignation. In 1830 Edwin Chadwick launched his first report on the sanitary conditions of the laboring classes in the metropolis. Years of great activity followed, marked by paving of unpaved streets, removal of refuse, installation of sewers, drains and water supply. In 1848 the first National Public Health Act[13] was passed. A series followed, ending in the consolidation of 1875. In these acts, and in the local by-laws made under them, we have the British equivalent of our much-later tenement house acts and building codes – the whole realm of regulation by statute. The fact that such regulation, under the British system, could be by national act, instead of requiring state laws of limited local application, insured more rapid and uniform compliance with the standards adopted.

Even more striking was their earlier recognition of the obligation of communities to supply housing themselves, if not otherwise satisfactorily provided, and to demolish slums if and where necessary.

The first principle was embodied in an Act of Parliament in 1851,[14] regarded by the Earl of Shaftesbury as the capstone of his series of

---

* For an example, see note * p. 2. The windows ordered cut in the partitions of existing dark rooms by the tenement house law of 1901 were realized to be wholly inadequate, but were all that was obtainable.

Factory Acts for the protection of workers. For, he argued, of what avail are good working conditions and shorter hours, or protection of women and children in the factory, if the worker and his family are at the mercy of the landlord in their home? So he authorized local authorities, in any community where working-class housing was inadequate, to build and rent working-class homes themselves. The idea was so far in advance of public opinion that for more than a generation the act remained a dead letter. Only one town, Huddersfield, built a few inconsequential cottages under it. During the 1880's, however, while a Royal Commission on Housing was in session, the aged author of the act convinced the Commission that it contained the principles necessary for the solution of the problem. It was accordingly embodied as Part III of the resulting Housing of the Working Classes Act of 1890,[15] which is still the foundation of British housing law.

During the 1890's British cities began to build working-class houses on undeveloped land in considerable quantities. In 1909, such action became obligatory, and the pace was speeding up when World War I intervened and building stopped.

Meanwhile, another line of activity had been developing – slum clearance. This was where the humanitarian impulse was strongest. Slums contained the worst housing and ought therefore to be dealt with first. Liverpool tore down some slums under a local act in the middle 1860's.

A series of acts of Parliament, the Torrens Acts (1868–82)[16] empowered a local authority to require owners to demolish single insanitary houses or small groups of houses at their own expense. This was useful, but too much like a confiscation of property to be used in a large way. The Cross Acts (1875–82)[17] on the other hand, permitted the compulsory taking of unhealthy areas by the authorities (after representations by the health officer and public hearings), with compensation, however, to the owners, accommodation at similar rentals to be provided for as many families as were displaced. Sometimes this led to rebuilding by the local authorities, sometimes by philanthropic societies, which put up model tenements. The Cross Acts became Part I of the 1890 Act, and the Torrens Acts, Part II. They also are still part of the basic law, though many times revised.

The expense involved to the taxpayers by condemnation awards always prevented any really large-scale application of Part I. In 1930, however, the Labor Government then in power thought the time had come for putting all the force of the National Government behind slum clearance, and enacted a law[18] for that purpose, making it compulsory on all communities of 20,000 inhabitants and over to make surveys of their housing, showing all insanitary areas, and to submit plans to the Ministry of Health for their improvement or clearance within a reasonable time. Since then, the government has changed, and although lip-service to slum clearance continues to be paid, no real energy is being shown. At this distance, it would seem that brakes are being applied rather than accelerators.

British municipal housing before the war, except where slum clearance was involved, was on what was called an economic basis. That means what our RFC and PWA call self-liquidating. The rents paid interest and repaid the principal of borrowed money. They also paid for management, repairs, insurance and local taxes (rates). This could not be the case in slum clearance, because the acquisition of the slum property, with compensation to the owner, always costs more than rents could cover, if the same economic grade of tenant was retained. It was considered quite an advance when a provision was adopted that the owner was not entitled to compensation for any income due to overcrowding his tenants. In 1925 and 1930, more drastic steps were taken, denying the owner's right to compensation for a house declared insanitary by the health officer. He was entitled to compensation for the land only, and if re-housing was to take place on it, he could recover only its fair value as a site for working-class housing. Whether any instances exist of these provisions being fully carried out, I do not know, but they have undoubtedly influenced the size of awards.

Before World War I, the London County Council had built some 10,000 flats and cottages, while all other local authorities had built between 20,000 and 30,000. Only a small fraction involved slum clearance. But public opinion had been growing in force. A decent home for every family had come to be accepted as a national requirement. The British system of volunteer recruiting during the war had led to widespread promises that the soldiers would have homes "fit for heroes" when they got back. It was not just a bonus offered to spur enlistment. It was a sincere expression of intention to right a great social wrong. The whole nation was behind the promise.

The task of fulfilling the promise was made unexpectedly difficult by the greatly increased cost of building at the close of the war. This was the reason for the use of subsidy in the 1919 Addison Acts.[19]

The housing shortage was estimated as around a million family units. There was no question, for the moment, of slum clearance, but only of building the greatest possible number of new houses of high standard, as rapidly as possible, to be let at rents working people and low-income white-collar families could pay. The 1,800 local authorities, urban and rural, in England and Wales, put up 176,000 cottages in garden suburbs, 8 and 12 to the acre, 5 or 6 rooms and bath. The houses were substantially built of brick or concrete, with slate or tile roof. Rents ran from $3 to $5 per week, including the local rates, or taxes, which in Great Britain are paid by the tenant.

The national subsidy was high. An economy wave and a Conservative Government called a halt to further building under the Addison Act in 1922. The next year, however, insistent public opinion forced the Conservative ministry to enact a housing law of its own (Chamberlain Act),[20] providing a new, though decreased, subsidy to local authorities and a lump-sum subsidy to private builders who would put up small houses to sell. This second provision produced over 400,000 houses disposed of to lower-middle-class purchasers including a few artisans. In 1924 a Labor ministry succeeded the Conservatives, and the Wheatley Act[21] was passed providing a more liberal subsidy to local authorities. A 15-year program was adopted to build two and a half million working-class houses. Altogether, about 723,000 houses have been built by local authorities in England and Wales since the war, and about 130,000 in Scotland. Adding the houses built for sale under the 1923 Act, it will be seen that about one and a quarter million homes have been built

with government assistance. Building costs dropped to the point where houses could be let at $2-$3 a week. In 1930, as already stated, a Labor ministry decided that the housing shortage had been sufficiently caught up with to permit the undertaking of slum clearance on a large scale.[22] Something like 100,000 houses a year for ten years was contemplated, and building under the Wheatley Act was to continue also.

Unfortunately for the continuity of the program, the present Conservative Minister of Health, Sir Hilton Young, under pressure of economy again, has brought about the repeal of the Wheatley Act,[23] and talks of clearing slums at the rate of 12,000 homes a year instead of 100,000, and having it finished in 5 years. It all depends on the definition of a slum. He is endeavoring to stimulate the building of working-class houses by private enterprise through government guarantees of mortgages held by building societies, the British equivalent of Building and Loan Associations.

This is not, of course, the end of British housing history, but it is the point reached at the present moment.

The legal obligation still rests on every local authority, urban or rural, to supply, itself, any deficit that may exist in adequate housing for the working classes, and to demolish and rebuild areas which endanger health. Liberal and Labor groups are pressing to speed up work again. They claim that 4 million houses ought to be replaced in the next 30 years, of which at least a million are urgent, and that about a million additional houses should be built at the same time to overcome the excess of families over houses.[24]

On the continent of Europe, there had been considerable housing activity before the war. There has been more since. Nearly every country has had some form of subsidized housing, some form of housing by public authorities. Nearly all have been building on new land. Slum clearance, though much talked about, has been practised very little. Germany has built about one and a third million working-class apartments since the war, but has not been clearing slums. This is true also of the 60,000 family units built by the City of Vienna.* It is true of the work in Nor-

---

* Some of the finest of these have been battered to pieces by artillery in the recent disorders.

way, Sweden and Denmark, in France, Italy and Belgium. It is true of the bulk of the work in Holland. But Holland and Great Britain are the two nations which have systematically attacked the problem of slum clearance. In proportion to population, Holland has done more post-war housing than any other country, having built for about one-fifth of her people. Her favorite method is by thirty-year loans, at the interest-rate of government bonds, to cooperative housing societies of working men or clerks, who are going to live in the houses when finished. She also has municipal housing for still lower-paid workers, but regards it as residual. When her new building caught up with the post-war shortage, in 1926, she began a systematic destruction of insanitary houses and groups of houses. As in Great Britain, there are alternate waves of housing energy and of economy. In both countries a well-developed public opinion insists on a wholesome environment for every child and therefore for every family, and enough has already been done to put the goal within reach of the generation now living.

In summing up this European experience, it may be said to prove that it is possible for public authorities to produce large quantities of good-standard housing on low-cost land to rent to fairly low-income groups at the expenditure of a moderate subsidy. Where slum clearance is in-

volved, the case is different. Slum clearance has been demonstrated up to a few thousand houses. It has never been carried out on a really large scale. It has been planned on a large scale in Great Britain only. The difficulties involved are very great. The much-quoted provisions of British law governing compensation for slum property do not seem to have overcome them.

For weal or woe, it appears to be at this most difficult and relatively untried point, that we in the United States have elected to begin our constructive activities. If we succeed, great will be our reward.* But the chances of non-success are undoubtedly multiplied.

So far, the State of Ohio[25] has passed a law permitting county housing authorities, and the counties which include Cleveland, Cincinnati and Toledo have organized under it. Michigan[26] has enacted a law which has given Detroit a municipal housing authority. Maryland[27] and New Jersey[28] have state housing authorities. Milwaukee is able under former legislation to carry on municipal housing.[29] New York State has passed an enabling act,[30] and the City of New York has just created a housing authority under it. All these and a number of others on the way† expect to do slum clearance and rehousing with funds supplied from Washington. The next thing, as the High Command is understood to have put it, is to make the dirt fly.

* The fundamental question of whether the taking of slum property for clearance by eminent domain is a public purpose is still to be tested in court. Where bad health or delinquency conditions can be shown to be involved, it seems reasonable to expect a favorable decision.

† Housing authority bills are pending in Delaware, Illinois, Massachusetts, South Carolina and West Virginia.

# Housing achievements

*IRA S. ROBBINS*

Active interest in bad housing was stimulated in this country with the publication of reports in the early nineteenth century which traced contagious diseases, particularly cholera epidemics, to insanitary conditions. Soon the interest changed from merely protecting the community against contagion to a genuine concern for the individuals who lived in filth and poverty. For years, housing reformers believed that the only hope lay in what they called "repressive" or "restrictive" legislation.

## "Philanthropy and 5 percent"

At the turn of the century, it was the predecessor of our limited dividend corporations which caught the imagination of the reformers. Model tenements and "basic" small homes were built as demonstrations of good housing, theoretically for the poor, but actually for middle-income groups. These demonstrations were sponsored in New York City by the City and Suburban Homes Company, Alfred T. White, and others. In Washington, D.C., the Sanitary Improvement Association followed suit. Cincinnati also had its model tenement movement and in New Haven, eight two-flat houses were built as demonstrations. By 1910, however, many of the models had become overcrowded and deteriorated and some had fallen into the hands of speculators.

In the battle against slums, philanthropic housing, with its higher standards of design and amenities, was a mere drop in the bucket. Voluntary rehabilitation of slums seemed to offer a possibility of benefiting the lowest wage earners.

The Octavia Hill movement, named for the famous Englishwoman who had invested her own funds in slum dwellings in order to rehabilitate them, gained much attention. Although many demonstrations of its effectiveness were philanthropically financed, slums continued to grow at an alarming rate.

It was the widespread interest in the New York State Tenement House Law of 1901 which gave impetus to organizing the movement for better housing on a national basis. At a meeting following the Conference of Charities and Corrections in Boston in 1911, the National Housing Association was formed.

## The first 10 years of the National Housing Association

Delegates from seventy-six cities, as widely separated as Ottawa, Seattle, and Savannah, gathered in Philadelphia in 1912 to attend the Second National Housing Conference. One of the delegates from New York City was Harold S. Buttenheim, who was especially interested in the address by Viscount James Bryce, the British Ambassador, on "The Menace of Great Cities."

At this second meeting of the new movement there were already leaders and heroes. Robert DeForest, who chaired the conference, and Lawrence Veiller, who became director of the new association, had worked together on the commission whose investigations resulted in the 1901 Tenement House Law in New York State. Jacob Riis provided the passion and publicity without which a movement cannot be born. From Indiana

Reprinted from The American Journal of Economics and Sociology, *Special Issue on " Municipal Progress During the Twentieth Century, Essays in Honor of Harold S. Buttenheim on the Occasion of his Eightieth Birthday," vol. 15 (April, 1956), with permission of the journal.*

came Mrs. Albion Fellows Bacon, secretary of the Indiana Housing Association, a feminist, a worker in child welfare, tireless in her efforts to secure legislation. Her speech succinctly stated the goal of the housing movement then: " Every building for human use or habitation should be required by law to be safe, sanitary and fit."

For 10 years, the conferences of the new organization were dominated by its dedicated founders. The housing of the lowest wage earners was their chief interest. Tightening up " repressive " legislation and extending it to one- and two-family houses were urged, and much time was devoted to strengthening sanitary inspection. " Remove all dirt and save life and health and one-half our social problems are solved," cried a Los Angeles lady at the 1912 conference. Another speaker rated the power of the sanitary inspector with that of Horatio and his friends at the bridge: " In yon straight path a thousand may well be stopped by three." The fact that the housing problem was basically economic was not mentioned.

Some of the discussion at the 1912 meeting would be timely today. Lawrence Veiller decried room overcrowding and described the nightly forays of sanitary inspectors into immigrant sections while roomers clambered shivering up and down fire escapes to avoid detection. He ascribed room overcrowding to the greed of heads of families and to a special " racial " solidarity among immigrants, to counteract which he proposed building dormitories for single workers of separate " racial groups." It was the representative of the New York League of Savings and Loan Associations who pointed out that " racial " division of workers was " not American " and would frustrate their assimilation into our country.

There was continuing interest in voluntary rehabilitation of slums, combining strict enforcement with education of tenants and janitors and beautification of backyards. John Ihlder, now one of the leaders in the movement for public and middle-income housing, was indefatigable for 20 years in campaigns to tear down back fences and to substitute small homes, instead of tenements, for workingmen.

By 1920 housing regulations similar to the New York law existed in ten other states. The establishment, in 1917, of the Massachusetts Homestead

Commission, which built and sold twelve houses to workmen outside of Lowell, and the California Veterans Farm and Home Purchase Act which provided government aid in the purchase of homes, was hardly noticed. The government-built war housing of 1917–18 was regarded as an anomaly, withal attractive, to be sold to private interests as quickly as possible. Rent control, a radical intervention of government in the housing market, made its first appearance during the same period.

## The housing movement in the 1920's

The National Housing Association lost much of its leadership effectiveness in its second decade. By 1923 the program of the conference was devoted to the problems of how to bring down the cost of small homes by reducing the charges for labor, materials, and financing. There was some discussion, too, of a housing cooperative movement for the members of the building trade unions. Mr. Veiller stated that it was impossible to find any person to advocate " government housing." He described the failure of the " British experiment."

The Conference of Charities and Corrections devoted much of its 1928 housing discussions to the building of small homes. Henry Wright was invited to discuss, " Is the low-cost small house a myth?" and answered with a strong affirmative. But his was a minority voice.

In 1923, New York's Governor Alfred E. Smith appointed the Commission on Housing and Regional Planning, with Clarence S. Stein as Chairman. Following the recommendations of the Commission, the 1926 Legislature enacted the first limited dividend housing corporation law in the United States, providing for partial real estate tax exemption and eminent domain in return for a limitation upon rents, all under the supervision of a State Board of Housing.

The last conference held by the old National Housing Association, in 1929, reflected the inflated dreams of that tragic period. The steel frame house, the concrete house, the modern kitchen were all described as ushering in the millenium. Edith Elmer Wood, who later became one of the great leaders in the public housing movement, proposed that the government aid in lowering financing costs, and she described this as the absolute limit of government intervention in housing. Government built housing, she said, could be found in Europe under socialistic conditions to which America would never submit. In his paper on "Slum Improvement by Private Effort," Harold Buttenheim made a more moderate statement: "Public effort of certain kinds is difficult . . . All – or almost all – of us would draw it this side of government housing." This was the first time in almost 20 years that any conference speaker indicated that among housing leaders, there was even a small group that advocated public housing.

The use of the police power as a means of clearing slums, and the idea of the scientifically conceived and developed neighborhood were both discussed in the 1920's. Compare this to 1911, when the president of the National City Planning Conference, Frederick Law Olmstead, asserted that "The hope of demolishing slum districts wholesale or arbitrarily converting a district of one kind into a district of a wholly different kind by any process of city planning may be dismissed as futile." In 1929, however, papers developing these approaches did not arouse as much interest as those which advocated glass for windows permitting ultraviolet rays to enter houses and cure the ills of the slum dwellers.

## The housing revolution

The great depression brought the demise of the first organized housing movement and the birth of a new one. With it came the first real effort to commit the government to a program which aimed to house the low-income families that could not possibly be housed by ordinary operations of private enterprises. Without the efforts of the early workers for housing reform, this change would not have been possible. It was they who roused the conscience of the nation. A few of them were on hand to usher in the new era.

Harold Buttenheim, Mrs. Albion Fellows Bacon, John Ihlder, Mary Simkhovitch, Edith Elmer Wood, and Lawrence Veiller were among those who attended the President's Conference on Home Building and Home Ownership in

1931. Although its purpose was to stimulate the private building industry, some significant sentences crept into the reports. The Committee on Large-Scale Operations suggested that if public works were undertaken, the money might better be put into housing than into roads and post offices. While expressing a firm opinion that private capital should be relied on, the report stated: "Still if we do not accept this challenge, the alternative may have to be government housing." The Business and Housing report asked that in research "we . . . approach with an open mind the proposal that the lowest wage earning group should be provided with homes at government expense."

In 1931, Mary Simkhovitch and others formed the Public Housing Conference, which later became the present National Housing Conference. Housing entered the state political arena for the first time in 1932, when the Republican Party platform in New York State called for the "immediate construction of low-rent housing to eliminate slums" without indicating the methods to be used. The Democratic state platform spoke even more vaguely of eliminating housing evils and encouraging limited dividend housing corporations. Nationally, the Republicans and Democrats alike in 1932 confined their platforms to some form of relief for homeowners faced with foreclosure.

The sudden blossoming of a bewildering variety of government housing programs in the early part of the 1930's is striking evidence of the effect of the depression upon previous thinking. It is in vivid contrast to the slow and tortuous progress of the first one hundred years of housing reform.

## Public housing

In 1933, the federal government ventured into public housing through the Public Works Administration. When an unfavorable court decision limited the power of the federal government to condemn property and threatened to halt the entire low-rent program, many states were added to those which already had legislation enabling local housing authorities to plan, build, own, and operate projects.

During the same period the federal government developed a program to eliminate sub-standard rural dwellings and undertook to provide housing for migratory farm labor. A very small but experimentally significant segment of this program was the development of the Greenbelt towns.

The Housing Act of 1937 created the United States Housing Authority and reflected the shift in emphasis from " pump-priming " to the promotion of the health and welfare of the people. In New York State a 1938 constitutional amendment permitted the state and its municipalities to use their own funds to aid public housing, setting a precedent for the few programs of state aid for housing and slum clearance that exist today.

By far the most extensive government intervention in the field of housing lay in the activities of the Federal Housing Administration. FHA was created in 1934 to stimulate construction and lower financing costs through federal insurance of mortgage lending by private institutions, and is responsible, to a large degree, for the vast increase in home building. Unfortunately, FHA's promotion of the concept of the racially exclusive neighborhood came just at a time when progress in breaking down racial barriers was being made in various parts of the country.

The Reconstruction Finance Corporation, and later the PWA Housing Division, offered liberal loans to limited dividend corporations for middle-income housing, but only seven projects materialized.

During World War II, the federal government again became involved in housing war workers. The intensified urbanization of Negroes when job opportunities opened for them in war industries made it impossible for many local communities to sidestep the question of segregation in public housing. A strong movement for the elimination of segregation in public housing forced concessions in many localities and now provide demonstrations of interracial harmony.

## Since World War II

The return of thousands of veterans after the end of World War II highlighted the dilemma of those in the no-man's-land between the rents in public housing and the lowest rentals or sales prices which private builders could achieve. The postwar boom, aided by the FHA and Veterans' Administration programs, took place chiefly on the outskirts of cities and in suburban areas. The only hope for middle-income families in cities lay in cooperative housing and the non-speculative developments built by insurance companies and savings banks. The results to date in numbers are not impressive, but precedents have been established. New York State again became a pioneer when the 1955 Legislature authorized both the state and cities to make long-term low interest loans to limited profit corporations, which with tax concessions, will be able to meet the needs of families just above the public housing eligibility limits.

The Housing Act of 1949 is a landmark in the advancement of thinking by Congressional leaders in the field of housing. The bill, sponsored by Senators Robert A. Taft, Allen Ellender, and Robert F. Wagner, Sr., established the goal of " a decent home for every family in a suitable environment." Governmental concern was widened to include housing for all, and not merely the lowest income groups. It was further widened by its concern for proper neighborhood environment and community facilities. Congress also recognized that a clear distinction exists between slum clearance and low-rent housing. It inaugurated a program of federal aid for urban redevelopment (Title I projects) so that substandard areas could be rebuilt for their appropriate purposes. Unfortunately, the program of public housing has since been whittled down to a gesture.

Racial integration in public housing is being achieved at a surprising rate with the aid of state legislation and the excellent work of the federal Race Relations Service. Urban redevelopment companies, too, are making progress in this field, again with legislative prodding. Private housing receiving FHA assistance is the latest field into which New York State has injected anti-discrimination legislation.

Despite the many changes that have taken place, it is startling to find so many similarities between the housing conditions of today and those of the first ten years of the " movement," but there is one amazing contrast – the most devoted advocates of the Baltimore Plan and its variations are the landlords' organizations and real estate boards who fought the early leaders of the housing movement tooth and nail.

## Unofficial housing organizations

Civic groups devoted to the improvement of housing conditions have increased in number, but they are far too few and lack widespread public support. The National Housing Conference does an effective lobbying job on the Washington scene and is of great assistance to local groups engaged in educating the public on the need for a comprehensive action program. The National Association of Housing and Redevelopment Officials, formed in 1934, does much to improve standards and the working relationship between federal and local agencies. The American Council To Improve Our Neighborhoods (ACTION), organized in 1955, is stressing the deplorable state of housing in American communities and the necessity for vigorous citizen participation in the movement for better housing. Notable among the local unofficial housing organizations are those in Baltimore, Philadelphia, Cincinnati, and Chicago. Led by Harold S. Buttenheim, a number of public-spirited citizens formed the Citizens' Housing and Planning Council of New York in 1937. Mr. Buttenheim has consistently supported and encouraged the directors and staff of the Council in their endeavors to make the organization a potent leader in the efforts to make New York a better city.

## Assets and liabilities

On the asset side of a half-century of housing experience we may list: the elimination in many communities of some of the worst of the unbelievable rookeries which existed at the turn of the century; the raising of minimum standards of construction and maintenance; the fact that in 1950, a new high was reached in the percentage of owner-occupied homes; the construction, each year beginning with 1949, of more than a million homes a year; the elimination of miles of slums through various public improvements; and public housing for more than a half a million families.

The liabilities are not pleasant to face: more than 15 million homes are substandard; many neighborhoods in large cities are deteriorating at an accelerating rate, often because buildings in good structural condition are badly overcrowded; the relocation problem is a serious impediment to slum clearance; despite progress in the struggle against discrimination and segregation, new economic and racial ghettos are appearing; shoddy and inadequate housing in outlying areas are incipient slums; and finally, the demand for housing in the future is far in excess of the rate at which we are producing it.

## The comprehensive approach

The most significant change in the last fifty years is the realization, by leaders in the field of housing, that the goal of a decent home for every family in a suitable environment requires a comprehensive approach, sometimes referred to as "urban renewal." Local codes with high standards for construction and maintenance can no longer be regarded as the only tools for improving housing or preventing slums. These codes still need strengthening and vigorous enforcement. There must be continued government aids for: the clearance and redevelopment of slum areas for their best social and economic purposes; the protection, conservation, and renewal of good and salvageable neighborhoods; low-rent public housing; private construction of middle-income housing; mortgage loan insurance to stimulate home ownership and to increase the supply of rental and cooperative developments. In addition, there must be more housing for single people, the aging, and large families, plus an understanding of the role of city planning, with special references to the need for schools, recreation spaces, and community facilities. Finally, the comprehensive approach takes into account the need for working out techniques to deal with those aspects of housing which are inextricably linked with the facts of metropolitan living. Just how this is to be done, is one of the most difficult of the many problems that face us today.

# Housing and the national economy

*MARTIN MEYERSON, BARBARA TERRETT, and WILLIAM L. C. WHEATON*

As an industry, housing is of major importance to the national economy because of its sensitivity to and influence on the course of business cycles, and because of its relationship to national economic development. As the product of an industry, housing is a vital welfare good; and our concerns about the housing industry and the housing market focus on their failure to provide a standard of living compatible with an expanding economy, and with growing personal and national income and wealth.

The importance of housing in the economy can be measured in terms of employment, production, investment, or consumer expenditures.

Residential areas provide at least 50 percent of the major source of local tax revenue, the property tax; and they are the largest single item of local capital investment. Nationally the value of residential land and buildings is well over twice the value of the country's 500 biggest manufacturing companies. Housing is almost the sole support of some industries. Two-thirds of all bricks, for example, go into housing.

In the peak postwar home-building year of 1950, according to the Bureau of Labor Statistics, 1,175,000 workers were employed on-site in new nonfarm residential construction alone. Off-site employment in the building materials and supply industries was nearly as great. A very large proportion of all private investments, whether in the form of equity or debt, goes into housing. New residential construction is half of all current new private investment in construction and a quarter to a third of total new private investment. Finally, in terms of family expenditures, and despite its decreasing share in their total, housing still remains second only to food in economic importance.

New homes generate demands for other types of construction and for other services, particularly roads, public utilities, and schools, three of the most important forms of nonresidential construction. School building lags several years behind residential building; but local roads and public utility services must be installed at the same time that new houses are built.

Residential building generates still other kinds of economic activity. Consumer durable equipment such as furnaces, hot-water heaters, dishwashers, washing machines, and air-conditioners make up an increasing proportion of residential construction costs, and the production of consumer durables rises or falls with the volume of residential building. There is also a link between housing construction and the output of other consumer goods, such as home furnishings.

## Fluctuations in housebuilding

The output of housing is exceptionally vulnerable to economic fluctuations. Sudden changes in family income or income expectations will alter the demand for housing more drastically than comparable changes in the economy will affect long-term investments in other fields. For example, the Depression of the 1930's reduced the production of various manufactured goods by anywhere from 20 to 50 percent, but it cut down the volume of housing construction

*Reprinted from* Housing, People, and Cities, *McGraw-Hill Book Co., 1962, pp. 19–31, with permission of the publisher.*

by more than 80 percent. The causes of the wide and violent fluctuations in the building and marketing of houses are complex. Housing is a capital good, but it is also a consumer product. Unlike factories or mines, which are developed by investors in anticipation of future nation-wide demand, housing is built in response to a fairly immediate and localized consumer demand.

The durability of housing also tends to accentuate cyclical fluctuations in residential construction. Because the supply of housing consists mainly of used homes, and new construction rarely amounts to more than 3 percent of supply in any year, a 5 or 10 percent decline in total demand, minor in other industries, can sharply reduce the demand for new houses. On the other hand a 10 percent increase in total housing demand cannot be satisfied by a 300 percent increase in production. In consequence, housing prices tend to rise faster than other prices in periods of rising income.

The demand for new housing can be postponed; this accentuates instability in the housing market. During periods of rising prices, families may seek to buy or build as soon as possible, even at prices slightly above current market levels. If buyers expect prices to increase substantially during the years ahead, as many did in the first few years following the close of World War II, they may decide to purchase at once even if it is necessary for them to pay a premium, since the debt they incur will be paid off in cheaper dollars in future years. This anticipation of price increases accelerates and increases demand on the upswing of the construction cycle. But if buyers expect price declines, home purchase may be deferred in anticipation of a lower price, thus accelerating a downswing in the construction cycle.

There are, however, other forces in the housing market that tend to soften the impact of cyclical influences. Housing markets are local in character, and the volume of building can vary widely in different metropolitan areas. Of course, in the depths of depression, such as that of 1929–1937, all areas suffer. But at other times some areas may experience a severe decline in residential construction while other areas enjoy a comparative boom. In recent years, the fast-growing cities of the South and West have had a far higher level of building activity than the older communities of the North and East. As long as cities continue to grow at a rapid rate, they are less vulnerable to sudden downturns in residential building.

Another corrective influence on the building cycle can arise from the expenditures made for additions to and alterations of existing dwellings. During the last half century, expenditures for additions and alterations amounted to an average of 11 percent of expenditures for new residential construction, varying from boom period lows of 6 percent to depression highs of 20 percent. Recent statistics which include repairs indicate that total maintenance, alteration, and repair expenditures may be as much as 75 percent of new construction volume, a stabilizing force. (Unfortunately, housing data suffer from errors and omissions in reporting the number of housing starts, the level of demolitions and other removals from the housing stock, and the expenditures for alterations and repairs.)

Fluctuations in new residential construction are shown in Chart 1. In the building boom following World War I, a peak was reached in 1925 when 937,000 new residential units were started. At the bottom of the Depression, in 1933, less than 100,000 new homes were put under construction. In the peak prewar year of 1941, residential construction climbed back to over 600,000 units. During the war, housing was cut back to a low of 139,000 in 1944. During the postwar building boom, residential starts reached a high of 1,352,000 new units in 1950. The wide variations are often described as " long building cycles." Since the Civil War these cycles have had their peaks in 1871, 1887, 1892, 1902, 1909, 1925, 1940, and 1950. Each has been succeeded by a trough in which building volume has dropped to low levels.

The cyclical pattern in residential building appears to accompany a similar pattern of prosperity and depression in the economy generally. However, residential building fluctuates far more widely; its peaks are higher and its depressions deeper than those of other industries. Some observers conclude that a decline in house-building, if not an important cause of the onset of business depressions, is certainly an important contributor to their severity.

## A shrinking sector of the economy

The cyclical swings in residential construction obscure secular changes which affect the present strength and future possibilities of the housing industry. Since the start of this century, a proportionately smaller part of the nation's resources has gone into residential building. Moreover, housing expenditures have declined in real terms, in relation to gross national pro-

In current prices, total annual outlays for new nonfarm residential construction during the early postwar years (1946–1953) were more than double those in the 1920–1929 decade, but when dollar values are made constant it is apparent that there was almost no change. Since there was a sizable increase in the number of dwelling units built during the later period, there was a long-run decline in the real average expenditure per unit.

Again, when prices are held constant, the startling fact emerges that the real value per dwelling declined by 37 percent from the start

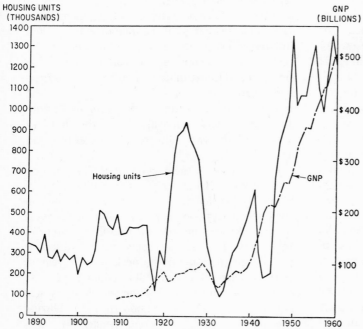

HOUSING UNITS (THOUSANDS)

GNP (BILLIONS)

Chart 1. New private nonfarm housing units started, 1889–1960, and Gross National Product, 1909–1960.

Sources: Housing units, 1889–1960: Housing and Home Finance Agency. *Housing Statistics*, March 1961. Table A–2, pp. 6–7. Gross National Product, 1929–1960: *Ibid*, Table A–30, p. 33; 1909–1928: J. F. Dewhurst, *America's Needs and Resources*, Twentieth Century Fund, 1955, Appendix 4–2, p. 958.

duct, capital investment, and consumer expenditures.

America's gross national product rose from an annual rate of $17.7 billion in 1900 to $503.2 billion in 1960. Investments in residential construction went from $800 million per year, during the early years of this century, to a peak of $24.7 billion in 1959. When measured in constant dollars, the proportion of national income expended on housing actually declined. For every $100 invested in new capital assets about $30 went into residential real estate in the early 1890's, and only $25 in the 1920's and about $13 in 1950.

of the century to the 1946–1953 period, even though average construction expenditures per dwelling more than quadrupled during that period. Because the drop in real value, shown in Chart 2, was accompanied by a decline in the average size of the household, per capita real investment changed very little. At the end of 1955, in fact, the per capita value of the nonfarm housing inventory was 7 percent less than at the beginning of the century.

The basic unit of demand for new housing is, of course, the household. A decline in the rate of population growth, in the rate of new household formation, and in the size of households thus becomes an important underlying factor in the long-run decline in the relative importance of housing. However, the absolute number of new families has increased by 7,700,000 or 18 percent between 1950 and 1959 and the rate of new household formation has fallen off far less than the rate of total population growth. Moreover, the size of the housing stock has increased through conversions of existing units, as well as through new construction. Population changes and conversions do not, by themselves, explain the marked downtrend in real capital per new dwelling unit.

Part of the decline in real expenditures since

consumer expenditures. As Chart 3 shows, average consumer expenditures for housing accounted for a decreasing proportion of total expenditures, from nearly one-fourth before World War I to a low of about 10 to 12 percent right after World War II, depending on which series of figures are used. Since then the proportion has gone up but to nowhere near the earlier ratios. Part of the reason for the decline undoubtedly is the upward change in family income over the period: as incomes rise, proportionate expenditures for housing and food tend to decrease. Another part of the reason is the great increase in housing costs since the war

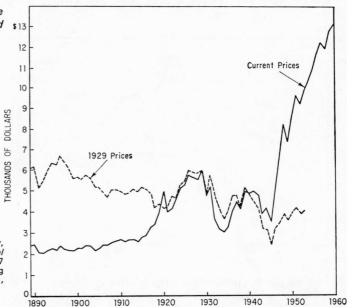

Chart 2. Average construction cost of private nonfarm housing units started, in current and 1929 prices, 1889–1960.

Sources: Current and 1929 prices, 1889–1953: Grebler, Blank, and Winnick, *Capital Formation in Residential Real Estate*, Princeton University Press, 1956, Chart 12, p. 107 and Table J–1, p. 426. Current prices, 1954–1960: Housing and Home Finance Agency, *Housing Statistics,* March 1961, Table A–3, p. 9.

the 1920's can be explained by construction changes. There has been a tremendous shift of residential building to the West and South and to rural nonfarm areas where, primarily for reasons of climate, the cost per unit tends to be smaller. Other forces that operate toward a reduction of real capital per unit include the historic decline in the average size of households, the trend toward lighter materials and construction, and, especially in the last fifteen years, the building of a larger proportion of smaller and therefore less costly houses.

Similarly, there is no single clear-cut explanation for the decreasing place of housing in total

compared with other consumer goods. Using 1947–1949 as a base, residential construction costs have increased far more than all consumer prices; the construction cost index for dwelling units stood at an all-time high of 139.7 in 1960 compared with 126.5 for all consumer prices. Rising costs mean that consumers get less house in real terms for the same outlay. Between 1929 and 1955, the real purchasing power of consumers increased by more than 50 percent. But, aside from some effect of mortgage credit changes, the purchasing power of the average family with respect to housing made no advance during the past generation and only a small gain over the past half century. In combination, those two facts help explain why consumers are reluctant to increase their proportionate expenditures for housing.

### Future trends

Although housing as an economic activity has failed to hold its own share of the American economy during the last three decades, several major forces suggest its steady growth in dollar output during the next two decades. Among them are the rapid population increase of the last twenty years, the rise in home-ownership in the years since World War II, and the trend toward suburban locations and densities. The

most important one. It is now fixed for the next generation.

Beyond this period – by 1980 – there may be more than 2 million new families entering the housing market each year. Estimates of the Bureau of the Census indicate that the population of the United States may reach 272 million by 1980, a growth of nearly 100 million in twenty-two years. In addition to the number of new families such growth implies, the expectation is that there will be more large families needing larger homes. At the other end of the scale, the extension of life expectancy combined with more ample social security and retirement systems will mean more older people in the population who will desire to maintain their

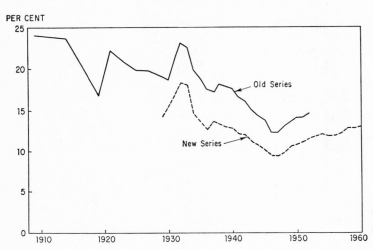

PER CENT

Chart 3. Housing expenditures as a percentage of total personal consumption expenditures.

Sources: Old Series: J. F. Dewhurst, *America's Needs and Resources,* Twentieth Century Fund, 1955, Table 33, pp. 102–103. New Series: Housing and Home Finance Agency, *Housing Statistics,* March 1961, Table A–42, p. 49.

first of these, population trends arising from war and postwar birth rates, implies a large absolute growth in building volume. The others may provide an opportunity for the housing industry to recapture some of its lost markets.

Beginning in 1940, the number of children born each year rose steadily – from 2.3 million in 1940 to 3.2 million in 1946, 3.7 million in 1951, and over 4 million in some of the years since 1954. This spectacular increase in the child population probably means that between 1960 and 1975 the number of young couples being married will mount steadily from about 1 million each year beginning in 1960 to over 2 million a year in the 1970's. Although the population reaching marriageable age is not the only factor that influences housing requirements, it is the

own houses or apartments. The population over 65 years of age is expected to increase from about 16 million in 1960 to over 20 million by 1985.

Another factor in the future demand for housing is the growing number of one-person households or households not consisting of husband and wife; in 1960 about one-fourth of our nonfarm dwellings were occupied by such households. By 1980 the rate of increase of these types of households will probably be more than double that of husband-and-wife families. Here again a change in population characteristics augurs a greatly enlarged demand for housing of certain types. These additions of single-person and aged families may continue to reduce average family size in keeping with the long-range trend even at a time when child population will be growing at unprecedented rates. More homes for larger families and more homes for smaller families, more for younger families and more for older couples, will probably raise the volume of residential building to unprecedented levels.

At the same time, some migration from rural and farm areas to cities will continue. Even conservative estimates suggest that virtually all of our population growth will continue to take place in urban areas. The growth of population in central cities is already being limited by overcrowding; in many of our older cities and in some new ones population is declining. Certainly there cannot be any great expansion of the central cities. But in the suburban areas population by 1975 may well increase by 75 percent or more and in the rural outskirts of metropolitan areas by 150 percent or more. Under these circumstances suburban areas will face investment requirements of unprecedented size for schools, highways, recreation and health, sewerage and water facilities.

The growth of population and household formation does not in itself assure that an equivalent effective demand for housing can be expected. The demand for new housing depends upon the level and distribution of income among families, consumer choices between housing and other expenditures, the cost, kind, and location of housing, and social and individual standards of housing adequacy.

Projections of national income and employment indicate that 86 million persons will be employed by 1975 and that per capita income will be 50 percent higher than it was in the late 1950's. A shorter work week will be offset by higher productivity. Women will constitute a higher proportion of the labor force. If these projections are realized, the number of families with incomes over $7,500 will double and the number of families with incomes of less than $3,000 will decline. As a result, it is reasonable to expect a large increase in the effective demand for housing.

If the trend toward lower proportional expenditures for housing can be arrested or reversed, demand might exceed 2 million new or newly converted homes per year by the mid-1970's. The tendency for housing expenditures

to decline as incomes rise may be offset by the shift in the population to higher proportions of white-collar workers who traditionally spend more, proportionally, for housing. To the extent that increased building efficiency can offset rising land and other costs, the building industry may obtain a larger share of an enormously enlarged national income.

The building industry will, at the same time, have to meet a heavy replacement demand, as our existing stock of housing grows old and deteriorates. Forecasts of housing requirements must include estimates of the number of substandard units to be replaced, the number of dwellings which deteriorate and drop out of use each year, the number which are demolished to make way for new land uses, and the number converted to nonresidential uses or lost through fire, storm, or other disaster. All of these are in addition to the estimated net total of new family formation. Defining housing requirements for the United States thus implies an estimate of the number of dwellings which are or will become so obsolete or deteriorated as to necessitate replacement or rehabilitation; and this estimate must be based on some assumption of a minimum standard of housing.

Estimates of future housing requirements made by both government and private agencies in the 1950–1960 decade vary from 1,200,000 to 1,800,000 additional new or converted units per year during the 1960's, and well over 2,000,000 units per year during the 1970's. These estimates assume that until new building and net new conversions (additional units created by conversion minus losses to other uses) exceed new family formation, the housing stock will continue to deteriorate at the rate of depreciation and other losses that occur annually. Since 1950 new building has met new family formation, but left little surplus to replace losses and deteriorating houses.

Can the gap between demand and the requirements of a rising standard of housing be closed in the years ahead? The answer depends largely upon the behavior of consumers, of the building industry, of the federal government in its credit policies, and of communities working toward comprehensive programs of renewal and development. If the expected growth of the economy is achieved, millions of consumers will have larger incomes with which to pay for better housing; others will still require some public aid for housing improvement. Any sizable expansion of housebuilding should provide the building industry with an unprecedented opportunity to improve its efficiency and to reorganize for greater service. How well the opportunity is realized, however, rests on the extent to which the industry, government at all levels, and consumers can devise better means for organizing and expressing their common interests or for overcoming their conflicting ones.

Any dramatic increase in the effective demand for new and improved housing will depend as much on the determination of the leaders of America's urban and suburban communities to solve some of their municipal problems as it will on changes in the industry itself. The housing industry has a right to question whether by making heavy investments in new designs, building processes, research, and financing and merchandising methods, it can overcome the historical ambivalence of the consumer toward its product unless at the same time the urban environment is recast in a more livable, efficient, and satisfying form. Also, national public policy must be implemented more consistently if residential construction and rehabilitation are to go forward at a high and relatively stable rate and if the housing industry is to be encouraged to provide a better product at a lower cost.

# The social psychology of housing

*ROBERT K. MERTON*

The social psychology of housing has a short, inglorious past and, I believe, a long productive future. In this fledgling field of research, it is more accurate to speak of emerging trends than current trends, for the long tradition of housing research has little to do with social psychology.

In its early phase social and psychological research on housing was virtually confined to social bookkeeping. During this phase, it was conventionally assumed that research comprised periodic audits of the proportion of substandard dwellings, meticulously described in terms of defective plumbing, defective structures, and consequently defective residents. It was devoted to gross and uncritical correlations between something called "bad housing" – typically meaning either slum areas with high frequency of substandard housing or household groups living in substandard housing – and a series of social morbidities: illiteracy, crime, juvenile delinquency, high mortality rates, poverty, public relief cases, illegitimacy, venereal disease. Yet the long and still continuing series of reports showing uniformly that slum areas, with their defective housing, are characterized by these social morbidities have seldom shown the role played by specifiable aspects of substandard housing.[1] Indeed, one of the very few studies attempting to locate the distinctive part played by substandard dwellings as such holds it "unmistakable that there is no relationship between

*Reprinted from " The Social Psychology of Housing," Current Trends in Social Psychology, Wayne Dennis (ed.), University of Pittsburg Press, 1948, pp. 163–188, with permission of the publisher.*

bad housing in its physical aspects and juvenile delinquency as revealed by court records."[2]

Yet so deep has been the concern of social movements for housing reform that they have sought to establish a " case " for adequate housing by citing often defective actuarial inquiries allegedly showing the social costs of bad housing, rather than by directly affirming an institutional right to decent housing in precisely the same sense that education was defined as such a right with the emergence of public education. It would seem that the doctrine of institutional claims to adequate housing can be supported without subscribing to the doctrine that researches purporting to show the disfunctional effects of bad housing are symptomatic of the more promising research trends in this sphere.

Nor is it to suggest that social bookkeeping serves no practical use,[3,4] to say that it has next to nothing to do with the science of social psychology or with the application of that science to practical problems of housing. The first effort of mind required to begin new and viable types of social-psychological research in housing is to think away the deeply-entrenched association of " housing " with " slum dwellings " and to abandon the implicit assumption that social psychology in this sphere deals solely with deplorable plumbing and social deviants.

### The hazards of research in housing

Having passed by the cul-de-sac of mistaking social bookkeeping for the whole of required research, the social psychologist entering upon research in the field of housing faces a formidable array of other hazards. These hazards, variously affecting the direction and content of emerging trends in the social psychology of housing, arise largely from two basic social facts: first, the social institution of housing is undergoing important changes, and second, housing involves the economic interests and social sentiments of important skill-groups and power-groups in American society. To assess current and prospective trends in the social psychology of housing, it is necessary to examine some of the more prominent of these hazards confronting the social psychologist who would focus his research interests on the substantive field of housing.

### The hazard of institutional cross fire

Housing is a social institution undergoing relatively rapid change. And, as in any institutional sphere subject to marked change, the field of housing is rich in conflict and controversy. The type of housing to be built, the amount to be built, how it is built, for whom and by whom it is built – all these are matters involving great conflicts of interests and sentiments rooted in economy, society, and culture. Some of the central issues have been joined : public housing versus housing privately financed in part or whole; ownership versus rental; the freestanding housing versus multiple dwellings; racial segregation versus nondiscriminatory neighborhoods – around each of these pairs of alternatives are ranged large and important groups, more concerned with satisfying their interests than with having research establish the sociological, economic, and psychological consequences of alternative policies.

The social psychologist bent upon entering into housing research, therefore, must know that he is forsaking the relative calm and peace of his academic laboratory for the strife and embroilments of the institutional battlefield. What is more, belonging to neither army, the social psychologist must be prepared to be caught in the heavy cross fire. Little if any of his research work will be taken for what he intends it to be : scientific analyses of the social-psychological consequences of alternative policies in housing. Instead, each research finding will be taken as a sign of abiding allegiance or of desertion from one army or the other. He may discover, for example, that the culturally imbued sentiment of the great value of home-ownership is meticulously reinforced by an unending flow of pronouncements by realtors, mortgage interests, builders, housing equipment corporations, university presidents, governors, mayors, and the only surviving ex-President of the United States. (The phrase " home " ownership rather than " house " ownership is perhaps itself symptomatic of the aura of sentiment which emanates from this *particular* form of property.) The social psychologist may find, further, that the sentiment attached to home-ownership operates to deflect the attention of many lower- and middle-income people from the great economic risks of homeownership for them under present institutional arrangements.[5] This quiet analysis of the role of sentiment in rational decision-making, one may be certain, will lead the social psychologist to be regarded as advocating the dangerous heresy of rental rather than ownership for some social strata or, worse still, as plumping for institutional rearrangements which reduce the element of risk not merely for the mortgage-holder but for the individual houseowner as well. In the arena of large decisions, some social-psychological findings are tagged as " dangerous thoughts " irrespective of the objectivity of the research.

Or, the social psychologist notes that under urban redevelopment laws, municipalities may aid private housing investors by exercising the power of eminent domain and by providing tax-exemption subsidies, and that, in some cases, this aid is conditional upon foregoing the practice of racial and ethnic discrimination. Seeking to have his research bear upon present and future developments in housing, he may set out to study the conditions promoting or hindering amicable social relations between Negroes and whites in neighborhoods which are biracial.

The social psychologist should be aware of the full import of his research decision. He may believe that he is merely engaging in socially relevant research, that, attuned to current changes in the institutional structure of housing, he is gearing his scientific inquiries to problems having both scientific and practical pertinence. In actual fact, he is doing much more. He is volunteering for a hazardous reconnaissance in a sociological no-man's-land, where he will be exposed to pitiless cross fire from all camps. Should he find some friction and conflict in biracial housing before mutual accommodation occurs, he will be accused promptly by many as a renegade from the ranks of those who support the American creed of equitable access to public opportunities. Or should he find that appropriate managerial decisions make for progressively amicable race relations in a biracial community, he will become the target of the day

for other economic and sentimental interests who insist on full segregation of the races. If our social psychologist happens to have studied a biracial *public* housing community, he may find policy-makers in the Federal Housing Administration becoming fearful lest his research call public attention to the fact that biracial communities do exist and that this be taken as grounds for further attacks on public housing by congressmen who identify voluntary biracial residence with a campaign for compulsory miscegenation. Or, at the extreme, representatives of both interest-camps may enter the fray to assure the social psychologist that *no* research is needed at all, since, " as everybody knows," the races can get along amicably in unsegregated communities or, " as everybody knows," it is impossible for the races to live in peace and harmony in biracial communities of equitable housing.

(This is no conjectural situation. Within the past six months, I have been assured by the research director of one national organization of Negroes that " no research is needed on the factors operating for or against friendly relations between Negroes and whites in residential communities, because the necessary facts are all at hand. It's only necessary to act and use pressure for equitable biracial communities." And, a spokesman for a large private corporation investing huge sums in housing developments asserts: " There's no point in any of this research on Negro – white relations in the same middle-class neighborhood. Negroes and whites just aren't ready to ' mix ' and that's that. Save your energies for research on questions where we don't have the answers.")

Caught in this cross fire and before he becomes worms' meat, the social psychologist may summon up enough strength to exclaim, " A plague o' both you housers, public and private."

Yet the social psychologist must be more stoic. When research bears upon large and important decisions, it has none of the privileges of neutrality. When his research is socially relevant, the social psychologist must expect to be alternately praised and damned, as his findings seemingly lend support to one or another interest group. Only if he violates his own professional code of full exploration of his problem and adheres to one or another of these opposed camps, can he fail, at some point, to be exposed to the hazards of the would-be neutral on the battlefield.

### The hazard of competing research demands

Let us suppose that the social psychologist performs the miracle of surviving these battles between the advocates of *opposed* housing interests. Then he has still to face attack from *diverse* (not necessarily opposed) special practitioners in housing, each with his own distinctive problems demanding systematic inquiry. If he confines himself to a range of research problems pertinent for the architect, he finds that the housing administrator regards his research as practically irrelevant. And if he orients his research toward the needs of the administrator, he is charged with the sin of irrelevance by the architect. For in this large and amorphous field of housing, so many are the specialisms and the specialized research problems, that one practitioner's relevance is another's irrelevance.[6] Since so much research requires to be done,[7] and there are, as yet, so few to do it, the social psychologist who would gear his research to the pragmatic needs of the field finds himself called upon to spin from one problem to another in an inevitably hopeless quest to have his researches be something to all housing men. Consider only a selected array of diverse problems awaiting disciplined research by both the sociologist and social psychologist:

The architect wants to know the diverse concepts of " privacy " among the several social strata that he may redesign space within the house to meet these changing needs for privacy as the family changes in size and composition;

The manager of large-scale rental housing developments wants to know how to motivate adequate maintenance by residents or how to avoid giving inadvertent grounds for the charge that he subjects residents to regimentation;

The private corporation investing in large-scale housing wants to know what to expect if race restrictions in the selection of residents are removed and how to minimize possible tensions between races in the community.

The public housing administrator wants to know the role of tenant councils and other organized groups in sustaining or vitiating resident morale, the social processes making for community centers as a social resource of the community or as a white elephant used only on ceremonial occasions;

The realtor wants to know the processes making for interest in rental housing and reducing the market for purchase of the free-standing individual house;

The urban planner wants to know something of the social and psychological consequences of one-class communities as compared with communities designed to harbor residents of several social and economic strata.

And the list may be indefinitely extended. Each of the numerous specialist groups diversely implicated in housing as a complex social institution has its own problems, each with its distinctive social and psychological aspects.

Of course, this immensity and diversity of problems awaiting investigation can be regarded as a definite asset, inviting the social psychologist to move into new and unexplored territory. It then remains only for him to exercise his professional prerogative to work on some rather than other problems, this decision to be based not only on the scientific nature of the research problem but also on the social uses to which this research will be put. This would be the case, were it not for another related hazard which awaits the intrepid social psychologist at work in the field of housing. This is the hazard of urgency.

### The hazard of urgency

Since research in the social psychology of housing is in its bare beginnings, there is relatively little by way of cumulative knowledge bearing upon the numerous decisions which must be made *now* by housing practitioners of every kind. It is not merely that the tempo of administrative and legislative decisions or of economic and architectural decisions in housing is more rapid than the tempo of applied research in social psychology.[8] It is, rather, that social psychology having only recently and belatedly trained its sights upon the field of housing has yet to accumulate a comfortable backlog of pertinent findings which can be taken into account by makers of policy. Consequently, when the social psychologist is called upon for pragmatic research, he is required to lead a hand-to-mouth existence; no sooner does he handle the data than he is expected to give voice to the tentative results.

The pressures for turning out results are insistent, sustained, and entirely understandable. Legislation on public housing is pending. Private housing developments are being built. Urban redevelopment is proceeding. All these are large-scale and long-term commitments. If you, the social psychologist, are worthy of your status in society, let us have your findings now, when they are needed, not in the indefinite future, when they will tell us only what we have learned through trial and error. The social psychologist must be prepared for an unyielding pressure, from all sides, to produce results, long before he is in a position to have warranted, adequately grounded results. Else, he will be subject to the charge that he fiddles with statistical tabulations and experimental designs while the home-planner yearns. For some time to come, the social psychologist's concern with putting his tentative hypotheses to adequate test will be at cross-purposes with the urgent pressures of housing decisions, here and now. It is almost as though Robert Louis Stevenson had had the plight of the social psychologist of housing in mind, when he wrote:

> This is no cabinet science, in which things are tested to a scruple; we theorize with a pistol to our head; we are confronted with a new set of conditions on which we have not only to pass judgment, but to take action, before the hour is at an end.

### The hazard of empiricism

The urgent demand for findings applicable here and now is linked with another risk for the social psychologist venturing into the field of housing: the hazard of empiricism.

He will find that housing practitioners are typically content with confirmed empirical results, however inconsequential and inconclusive these results may be from the standpoint of systematic science. The attitude of the practitioner is not unlike that of the patient suffering from malaria, some generations ago, who raised no further questions when he found that quinine was a specific remedy for the disease. It "worked" and that was enough. That more effective therapy might be achieved through basic research was a notion completely alien to him. He would have been incredulous if told by the medical researcher that next to nothing was known, by way of theory or by way of theoretically grounded therapy, when one knew only that some unknown constituents of quinine acted in some unknown way to affect a poorly known disease called malaria. Yet, it was only when Laveran discovered parasites in malarial blood and it was found that the life history of the parasite was correlated with the several stages of the disease and Ross discovered the anopheles mosquito as a carrier of the parasite and it was found that the bite of the anopheles led after a given interval to contraction of malaria and it was found that certain identifiable chemical properties of quinine affected conditions necessary for continued viability of the parasite – it was only when each and all of these detailed constituent elements and processes were identified, that raw empiricist application of quinine was transformed into skillful application of medical knowledge.[9]

But this difference between sheer empiricism and scientific research is not widely recognized in the field of housing (any more than it is in many other spheres of social practice). Here, empiricism still rules. Entering this field the social psychologist must be immunized against the tendency toward mistaking actuarial and wholly empiricist findings for research on relations between identified variables of psychology and sociology.[10] For he cannot expect the practitioners in housing to be interested in these theoretic explorations, any more than victims of malaria pressed for advances beyond the empirical use of quinine. Thus, in the current Columbia-Lavanburg researches,[11] we have found that residents in planned housing who are members of local voluntary associations and organized groups tend to be more deeply rooted in the community. They are more likely to plan to remain for the indefinite future. The housing manager concerned with ways and means of reducing tenant turnover may wish to " apply " this empirical finding by encouraging the formation of organized groups among tenants. He may see no occasion for further research. The fact remains that the theoretical variables in this finding have yet to be identified : do organizations of any type lead to rootedness? or are the organizations which *emerge* in response to the felt collective needs of tenants productive of social roots? If the latter, then the introduction of organizations by management staff will not necessarily have this consequence. All this may seem to the housing practitioner much ado about little. And this attitude will doubtless persist until the practitioner learns through repeated experience that empiricism does not pay, even in grossly pragmatic terms. One may venture the guess that only when a considerable fund of theoretical knowledge is available for application will tough-minded practitioners come to see that sheer empiricism does not provide reliable answers even to immediate limited problems.

Nor is this empiricist trend in housing research merely a response to practitioners' concern with immediately applicable findings. It is sometimes a consequence of social scientists being wholly concerned with meticulous methodological designs, often comprising ingenious controlled experiment, and failing to clarify theoretically the variables dealt with in the research. Several *methodologically* sharp and precise researches in the social psychology of housing suffer from any visible concern with *theoretical* and *substantive* content. Thus, in a series of excellently designed experiments on the " effects " of " slum clearance," " rehousing " and " good housing,"[12] Chapin exemplifies this combination of methodological sophistication[13] and complete substantive empiricism. An example will clarify the general issue. In one study[14] Chapin seeks to test the hypothesis : " The rehousing of slum families in a public housing project results in improvement of the living conditions and the social life of these families." He finds, through impeccable and difficult research involving experimental and control groups, a significant increase of " social participation," improved " conditions of furnish-

ings in the living room," and a decreased " use-crowding " of space among families in a housing project. Such findings are precisely on the plane of finding empirically that quinine is a specific for malaria. For what are the constituent elements, structures, and processes in " a public housing project " which lead to the observed effects of increased social participation? Are they identifiable elements in local managerial policy? the emergence of common purposes which can only be achieved collectively? nominal participation under pressure exerted by local group organizers? The folk phrase that " public housing projects " do or do not promote social participation is not a proposition in the *sciences* of social psychology or sociology. Nor does the finding provide clues to the distinctive complex of variables, masked by the blanket term " public housing projects," which are related to social participation. It is only when research is directed, with however rough an approximation, toward the study of determinate variables rather than the correlation of unanalyzed terms (such as " housing project ") that social science research in housing will move from the plane of raw empiricism to cumulative knowledge. And only when theoretically relevant as well as methodologically precise researches are instituted, will these findings be of maximum use to practitioners. It is no paradox to urge that the reliable application of social science to housing policy presupposes theoretically sensitized research rather than empiricist findings.

These considerations, I suspect, will be resisted by practitioners in housing. It is all the more necessary, therefore, that the social psychologist at work in this field not take the easy and empty path of quick empiricist findings rather than the more difficult and ultimately more productive path of empirical research oriented toward basic theory.

## The current promises of research in housing

In view of this uninviting prospect of numerous hazards, it might well be asked why the social psychologist should venture into the field of housing at all. Why seek out troubles, when there is so much to be done in fields tilled and cultivated by a generation or two of social psychologists. The pragmatic areas of mass communications, race relations, and intercultural contacts or the theoretic fields of social perception, attitude measurement, and sentiment-formation are available for study.

The point is well taken, but not compelling. Excursions into the field of housing have convinced at least one research worker that the scientific yield is worth the risk. The numerous and diverse items of human behavior encompassed by the term "housing" present a singularly productive sphere for inquiry by the social psychologist. The reasons for this certainly deserve some attention.

### Reciprocity of basic and applied social psychology

The "social psychology of housing" entails a reciprocal relation between the scientific discipline and a field of practical application.[15] Social psychology, as a science, has much to gain from the study of the substantive problems encountered in housing and, conversely, the field of housing, as social activity and social product, has much to gain from the application of basic research in social psychology.[16]

Housing provides a strategic area for putting many findings of social psychology to the test of further experience. Thus, in one biracial housing development, with a population divided equally between Negroes and whites, we found[17] that among those white residents hostile to Negroes, there occur marked anxieties concerning the future proportions of the races in the community. These anxieties give rise to the conviction that the proportion of Negroes will increase, thus disturbing the present social equilibrium. And responding to their own anxious expectations, they plan to move as soon as feasible. This interacting complex of attitude, anxiety, and behavior among the "racial illiberals" might thus initiate what the social ecologists have called a process of race invasion and withdrawal.

By locating the psychological dimensions of this process of invasion aid withdrawal, however, the social psychologist not only contributes to the science but provides a possible basis

for controlling the process. The housing administrator can make it wholly clear that there is an administrative stabilization of racial proportions among residents, such that the community will not be permitted to develop into a one-race and therefore segregated area. The planned assurance of preserving the present equilibrium could thus serve to curb anxieties regarding future inroads by the "other" race and set the stage for the continued mutual accommodation between the races now in process. The planned community, in contrast to the crescive community which lacks central management of such key decisions, can thus control the process of invasion and withdrawal which has been taken as "normal" under the special conditions of the unplanned community.

All too briefly, this may suggest a potential in the field of housing for reciprocity between basic and applied social psychology.

### A focus of collaboration between social science disciplines

The practical problems encountered by housing practitioners – architects, builders, community planners, administrators, project managers – cannot, of course, be solved by any one discipline (though decisions are sometimes made as though they were purely economic or architectural or sociological). Each practical problem in this field is many sided, open to study from the perspective of diverse disciplines. The problem of "privacy," for example, cannot be regarded as one to be settled by the architect who arranges for soundproofing of walls or enclosed outdoor spaces adjacent to the house or transit in the house without trespass upon intervening rooms. The conception of privacy among different social groups, the saliency of concern with privacy as a value, the various types of privacy and the respective degrees of importance assigned them in various social strata – these are questions calling for study by the sociologist and psychologist. So, too, the decision to build or not to build a community center is not wholly a matter for the housing economist to decide, unless he has at his disposal the facts on the potential role of this community center in tenant satisfactions and, consequently, in the rate of tenant turnover (once the temporary situation of an extreme sellers' market has moved into the limbo of sellers' markets of the past). Or, the legislative decision to enforce the removal of all restraints on occupancy based on race or religion or social station cannot be regarded *only* as a matter of law, but gives rise to the question of the optimum conditions under which these changes in race composition can be put into effect – conditions open to inquiry by the sociologist and social psychologist.

The sheer weight of practical problems in this field demands collaborative research among several social science and other disciplines. It is thus one of the major functions of research in housing to provide occasions and pressures for interdisciplinary investigation of a type which might otherwise not occur for some time to come.[18] Such collaboration is devoutly to be wished by those who look forward to the emergence of an empirically grounded and theoretically viable basic social science, in which the concrete whole analytically taken apart by the several sciences is put together again.

## A locus of basic social units

As a focus of social-psychological inquiry, housing has the further merit of directing attention to the territorial base of what the sociologist calls the "primary groups," that is, the groups involving face-to-face contact and fusion of sentiments among their members.

The dwelling unit is the locus of the initial socialization of the child: it is there that his character-structure is largely shaped. Not only are patterns of socialization typically enacted *within* the home; they appear in part to be oriented *toward* the house and its contents. With all the apposite observations on the effects of "overcrowding," there still remains an important area for investigating systematically the social-psychological consequences of overcrowding.[19] In the same fashion, there is place for continued inquiry into the effect of the multiple apartment dwelling as compared with the freestanding house in providing for free circulation or for restraints and controls exacted of the child.[20] To what extent is it the case that when housing authorities decide for fiscal reasons to build housing developments skyward rather than spread them outward in freestanding dwellings, they significantly influence the personality formation of the numerous children who grow up there? How does the friction of space in the small apartment enter into the friction between parents and children?[21] Questions of this order, seeking to relate the internal ecology of the dwelling unit to the socialization of the personality, are questions upon which many have strong opinions and few have the requisite facts.

But it is well-recognized that the dwelling unit, whether freestanding or encased in a multiple-dwelling structure, does not stand alone, either in the psychological or the sociological sense. The house and the family in it are unavoidably bound up with the neighborhood and the community in which they are found. Under which conditions does the individual establish roots in his local community and what are the psychological consequences of being rootless? Consider that the so-called social processes of ecological competition and distribution commonly result in local urban neighborhoods being very largely of one economic stratum and, not infrequently, of a single ethnic or racial group. What are the lasting psychological effects of living out one's early life in these "socially homogeneous" (or "socially parochial") areas, where contact with members of other groups is rare, casual, and conventionalized rather than frequent, ego-involved, and personal? Do these special expressions of group differences supply a firm psychological base for group cleavages and psychological distance difficult to bridge in later life, as one confronts a democratic credo with an unyielding conviction that the out-groups "just aren't real Americans"? Is the child in play groups composed solely of his "own" economic, social, and ethnic kind, father of the man who would keep "outsiders" from his organizations, neighborhood, and university?

In short, the very fact that housing, and all it entails, has only lately become a focus for research by social psychologists suggests that many of them are inclined to hold with the hare and run with the hound. They may hold to the general hypothesis that character structure is basically formed in the early years largely lived out in small primary groups of household, play group, and neighborhood, and yet they may run from the implication that the study of these small groups in their physical setting[22] is an essential part of their scientific task. Even if it is assumed, and this is a large and debatable assumption, that primary groups are only passive reflections of master social and economic trends, it is still necessary to see how these trends are wrought into the personality structure through the socializing agencies. To do other than this would seem to be an assertion of knowledge where there is still little more than unadmitted ignorance.

As for the local community, this is the one area where the sociologist and social psychologist have for some time explored the social consequences of different patterns of social organization. But even here, a great deal awaits further investigation. A major new pattern of community structure has evolved first in European countries and latterly in our own.[23,24] This is the "planned community" in which the number, size, distribution, and organization of the units comprising the residential community are more or less a matter of plan, rather than the casual by-product of uncontrolled accretions. Still new and consequently ready for continued improvement, the planned community, even in its most limited form of residential areas lacking their due share of local facilities – market place, workplace, places of recreation and social contact and planned organizational activity – even in this form, the planned community provides an exceptional laboratory for research in the social sciences.

(Throughout this paper we follow the usage of the National Resources Committee in treating the terms "planned community," "housing project," "housing development," and "housing estate" as loosely synonymous. Were it in point for present purposes, each of these would be distinguished from the others. Communities constructed in accordance with a comprehensive plan would of course provide not only for residential areas, but for the various facilities of production and consumption normally required in the ordinary routines of life. But all this raises questions not in issue here. This usage

also violates the taboo on the term "housing project," a taboo not uncommon among housing officials and residents in the field, who report that the term connotes "low income," "dole," and "charity." Since Veblen has so well analyzed the sources of the social equation of "high income" with "personal capacity" and since we do not subscribe to the implied equation of "low income" and "personal inadequacy," we shall venture the small risk of violating a word-taboo and adopt the term "housing project," whenever convenient.)

Since it is in varying degrees a moderately self-contained territorial unit, far more so than the unplanned communities, growing crescively in various directions, patterns of social interaction can the more easily be traced and investigated. Many personal relations, as preliminary investigation has found,[25] are located within a relatively limited area.

The flow of interpersonal influence,[26,27] a subject neglected by social psychologists partly because it is ordinarily so difficult to study in its context of social life, is a question at once of importance to those who are responsible for managing these planned communities and to the social psychologist who is concerned with the interplay of personalities.

The emergence of small, cohesive groupings within the large impersonal structure of the community, and the relations of these to the anchoring of the individual in groups with which he identifies himself is there to be studied.

And, as I have suggested, precisely because these communities *are* controlled, they represent experimental checks upon the many ecological findings of sociologists which have been almost invariably based upon crescive, unplanned areas. How does the social end product of innumerable private and unrelated decisions in the crescive community compare with the social end product of public and coordinated decisions in the planned community? Social ecology deals with allegedly impersonal processes in unplanned communities and has thus confined its studies to an unavoidably narrow range of observations.[28] Do comparable ecological patterns emerge in the planned community? Do we typically find, for example, ethnic and religious "islands" in the planned community as is so often the case in the crescive community?[29] And if these ecological formations of small, homogeneous groups do not develop, if, under central administrative direction, such patterns of deliberate or inadvertent segregation do not occur, what has this to do with the reciprocal attitudes and relations developing among members of diverse ethnic, religious, and racial groups? As we shall presently see, the planned community provides materials admirably suited for answers to questions of this order.

In any event, with continued growth in the number of planned communities and large-scale housing developments, as distinct from the accretion of individual units within and around pre-existing neighborhoods, contemporary housing provides an unparalleled near-experimental setting for the study of " what might be " rather than the continued observation of " what is " and " what has been " in human relations within the local community.

Surely there is no likelihood that the reader will interpret this to mean that " planned communities " or " large-scale housing developments " have solved problems of human conflict and social inequities. The text means only what it says at this point : however remote from the attainable, these developments with their central administrations are in a position to modify and curb some of the social processes of segregation, rootlessness, and conflict which, it has been alleged, are inherent in the ecological processes of the community. In any event, they depart sufficiently from the more familiar patterns of the unplanned, crescive community to provide limited test cases of alterations in community structure. For this reason, they are admirably suited to the research needs of the social psychologist who can otherwise seldom reproduce anything like these variations in community structure.

## Emerging trends in the
## social psychology of housing

Thus, if the social psychologist venturing into the field of housing may expect to en-

counter the hazards of institutional cross fire, of diverse specialized demands, of urgency, and of empiricism, he may also expect the rewards of working in a substantive field which permits a ready reciprocity of basic and applied social science, provides a focus for interdisciplinary collaboration and a laboratory for the study of social and psychological processes in the primary groups of society.

In turn, if the housing practitioners who tentatively accept the aid proffered by the social psychologist must put up with what may seem to them dangerous thoughts and occasionally irrelevant, agonizingly slow, and often abstract researches, they have the further assurance that here, as in other fields, they will reap the harvest of well-founded researches bearing upon the central decisions which must be made in this sphere of human activity.

Apart from the still-current research focus on social morbidities seemingly related to defective housing, a large variety of other foci of research attention have lately emerged. So numerous and varied are these that it is impossible to list them all, let alone subject them to even passing discussion. In varying degrees, the frontiers of research in housing are being advanced on problems of types of housing demand;[30,31] the " ecology " of the dwelling unit (that is, the internal spatial design of dwellings as a self-contained shelter for social relations and personality development);[32,33] resident morale in planned communities (ranging from mere inventories of complaints to explorations into the determinants of morale);[34,35] the social and psychological consequences of diverse managerial policies and practices;[36] the social relations between residents in housing projects[37] and the environing community;[38,39] factors involved in privacy,[40,41] resident turnover,[42] residents' feelings of spontaneity or regimentation,[43] emerging social organization of residents;[44,45] attitudes and relations between residents in one-class or one-race[46] communities and in multi-class, multi-ethnic, and biracial communities;[47] etc. And in several of these spheres, there are continuing advances in research methods and procedures.[48,49,50,51]

# Social questions in housing and community planning

*CATHERINE BAUER WURSTER*

## Introductory note: some qualifications

The purpose of this report is to set down some of the unanswered social questions that arise in the present-day process of housing and community development in America. It incorporates the suggestions of a fairly representative group of people professionally concerned with housing and city planning.* Although the detailed form and emphasis are necessarily the author's, there was remarkable unanimity as to the main issues that puzzle us. A number of recent proposals for research programs in the general field of housing and urbanism provide substantial added support.

In presenting this survey, which is essentially a plea for help from social scientists, certain qualifications sould be stressed:

First, the " social " issues here roughly outlined are by no means the only unanswered questions that confront housing and planning practitioners. A similar outline of the serious gaps in our economic knowledge, and another on the technical problems still awaiting solution,

could easily be put together. Indeed, they are already available in diverse forms. But the more deeply we get into economic and technical analysis, the more often we come up against social questions, issues that have hardly as yet been properly posed, let alone answered.

Second, what we seem to need is not just another group of independent specialists, a priesthood of " advanced social research," to get off by themselves and try to produce " answers " for us. Undoubtedly, basic contributions to long-term enlightenment will often be made in this way. But all our immediate practical problems cut straight across many different fields of expertise: social, economic, political, technical, aesthetic, administrative, etc. And their clarification and solution apparently requires a more integrated approach: continuous team work among the various research disciplines concerned, and active collaboration between researchers and " decision-makers."

Third, this report does not presume to outline a research program *per se*: it merely suggests some unanswered questions as they arise in our business, i.e., in relation to concrete

---

* A group discussion was held in Cambridge in 1949. Participating from Columbia was Robert K. Merton, sociologist. Participants from MIT included Victor Fischer, Roland Greeley, and Kevin Lynch, city planners; Robert W. Kennedy and William W. Wurster, architects; Lloyd Rodwin, economist; and Burnham Kelly, director of the Bemis Foundation. From Harvard there were G. Holmes Perkins, architect and planner; John Harkness, architect; William L. C. Wheaton, political scientist; Jesse Epstein, lawyer and housing administrator; and Catherine Bauer. Also participating were Louis Wetmore, planner of Providence, R. I., and William V. Reed, New York architect. Valuable suggestions were later received by letter from Robert B. Black, political scientist and student of British planning administration; Elizabeth Coit, architect with the New York City Housing Authority; Frederick A. Gutheim and Lewis Mumford, writers and critics in the field of human environment; and Coleman Woodbury, political economist and director of the Urban Redevelopment Study, Chicago.

Reprinted from Journal of Social Issues, *Special Issue on " Social Policy and Social Research in Housing,"* Robert K. Merton, Patricia Salter West, Marie Jahoda, Hanan C. Selvin, eds., vol. 7, Nos. 1 and 2, (1951) pp. 1–33, with permission of the journal.

decisions about buildings, streets, open spaces, housing management, financing methods, etc. For purposes of research, it may be that some of our problems should be sorted out on an entirely different basis. A classification according to the specific human needs to be provided for – child-care, privacy, leisure-time pursuits, for instance – might have much to be said for it in some cases.

Fourth, this outline of our problems does not imply any careful weighting as to their relative significance. All we claim is that the questions here posed are relatively " open ": they come at points in the housing and planning process where alternative decisions are frequently possible, and where good evidence one way or the other might have some influence.

And fifth, we do not expect research to answer all our questions overnight. Some issues may never lend themselves to scientific methods of social investigation; to tackle others, new techniques will undoubtedly have to be developed and tested. Premature judgments must be avoided; certain questions will require study under a wide variety of conditions to achieve dependable results, and few, if any, of our problems will ever be solved *wholly* by objective analysis. But it is up to us to ask the questions, not to decide the points where research will prove most fruitful here and now. And even where science fails to provide the answers, the personal judgment of experienced students of society, who understand the nature of housing and planning problems, might prove exceedingly valuable.

## The housing process

Two influences have been working great changes in home-production in the United States, as in the rest of the world. One is the trend toward large-scale building methods and " community " development, and the other is the marked increase in public intervention. Both trends open up enormous opportunities for improvement in human environment, to meet the needs and demands of modern society. At the same time, however, new questions are raised. The respective roles of the consumer, private enterprise and the government have undergone considerable change, and the responsibility of the " expert " has been greatly enhanced. Important social issues are involved in housing policy and design, but the basis for decision often seems confused and inadequate.

## The consumer and the housing market

Traditionally in America, the consumer was supposed to decide for himself how and where he would live. If he could not build his own home exactly the way he wanted it, then the automatic adjustments of demand and supply – the " market " – were expected gradually to satisfy his personal needs and desires, within the limits of physical possibility and his capacity to pay a profitable price.

This concept of the consumer's dominant role in the housing process has always been largely mythical, except for the fortunate few. When a frontiersman built his own house, the limitations of technique and material gave him little leeway in design. And the vast development of technical resources, although it certainly improved the housing of a great many families, has not automatically given them more direct personal control over their environment. Most new homes today are more or less standardized units in large developments, however well equipped or carefully laid out. The home-seeker buys or rents a packaged product, and even his whole neighborhood environment is largely predetermined, subject to little adjustment in use. There is little real knowledge of consumers' wants, even in general terms, and the user's reaction to innovation is seldom seriously investigated. Moreover, the selection available to a given family at a given moment is too narrow as a rule to permit much real choice, above all in a period of severe and continuing shortage.

The consumer's power to shape his environment is greatly influenced, of course, by economic factors: the price of available homes in re the amount he can pay for shelter. And for a great many years the vast majority of householders had little or no influence on home production, even in theory, because they were entirely outside the potential market for current building of standard quality. Since new homes were out of reach they had to be satisfied with whatever older dwellings were available (or self-built shacks), and for a large proportion of the population the only choice was sub-standard living conditions of one kind or another. Slums, blight, and the long-developing housing shortage are all largely traceable to the limited market for new homes.

In recent years, however, various public policies have been devised, intended to provide housing within reach of lower income families. But this means a new and entirely different kind of force helping to shape the decisions about our home and civic environment.

### Increasing public responsibility

As a direct result of slums, shortage, and general dissatisfaction with the housing situation, the consumer has stepped into his other role as citizen, and called for public intervention. All levels of government are concerned, and their activities take various forms for a wide range of purposes.

Local governments have long been responsible for restrictive housing standards to protect health and safety, and for the provision of various utilities and services that help to establish land-use and social patterns. But more positive zoning and planning controls are increasing, and many local governments now engage directly in slum clearance and public housing activities.

The Federal government's concern for housing developed through a series of emergencies: foreclosures and unemployment in the depression; housing for war-workers; veterans' housing and the general shortage after the war. There has also been a rising consciousness of slums and urban blight as a national issue. But piecemeal emergency measures have not solved the problems, and Congress has gradually enacted some important links in a " comprehensive long-term housing policy," including: (1) a variety of financial aids to grease the wheels of private home production; (2) subsidies for the construction of low-rent public housing by local authorities, to rehouse families from slums; (3) substantial aid for the clearance and redevelopment of slums and blighted areas by local agencies and private builders; (4) tentative encouragement

for broad local land-use planning and community development on a metropolitan or regional basis; (5) various aids for rural rehousing; and (6) research in the whole field of housing and community planning. Although no direct Federal initiative is involved, financial aid normally carries with it a considerable degree of Federal control.

Private home-builders and lending agencies have become almost wholly dependent on Federal financial aid and protection. Public housing for the lowest income group, however controversial, is firmly established with active programs in most big cities and hundreds of smaller communities. Special aid for cooperative housing, to serve " middle income " families who are ineligible for public housing yet cannot afford the product of speculative builders, is a lively issue. And public initiative will doubtless be required once more to meet the housing emergencies incident to defense programs.

This rapid increase in public responsibility results in two different but quite prevalent fallacies. On the one hand, many conservative analysts of building and land use tend to underestimate the role of public policy, hence the influence of political and administrative decision. And on the other hand, many liberal reformers tend to assume that once public responsibility is assured, with social purpose behind it and adequate funds to implement it, the consumer's interest will be served more or less automatically. But is this true?

### Housing policy involves basic social judgments

The implicit purpose of all housing legislation is to promote the general welfare, whether in terms of physical health, social and civic efficiency, national defense, protection of the family, maintenance of business prosperity and full employment, or the fulfillment of such social ideals as " equal opportunity " and " equal rights."

But these are very general goals, that must be translated into sites and buildings of the most specific, tangible and permanent nature. The Housing and Home Finance Agency is instructed by Congress to encourage and assist "the production of housing of sound standards of design, construction, livability and size for adequate family life," and also "the development of well-planned, integrated, residential neighborhoods and the development and re-development of communities." But how do we decide what kind of housing promotes adequate family life, or the exact nature of an integrated neighborhood, or what makes a real community? Housing legislation provides powerful instruments for the achievement of such goals, but little instruction as to what these goals are in three-dimensional terms.

And the consumer is hardly more potent or influential in the detailed operation of public policy than he is in the private market. As a citizen and voter, he can and does exercise enormous influence on broad public purpose, as reflected in the enactment of legislation. But he has little real control over the concrete administrative decisions which affect his own life most intimately: the size and appearance of his house, for instance, the convenience of shops and playgrounds, who his neighbors will be, how far he will have to go to work. Such questions cannot be settled by Yea and Nay. And yet it is the sum of small finite decisions that adds up to a satisfactory or unsatisfactory home and community.

## Who decides? The role of the "expert" as middleman

At every step in the complicated process of housing and civic development, however, somebody does have to weigh the possible alternatives, and make some sort of decision. And most of these decisions that determine the shape and quality of our environment are made neither by the consumer, by the builder reacting to known consumer demands, nor by elected representatives of the people. They are necessarily made, on the whole, by a long line of specialists, employed by public agencies and also by big builders and lending institutions. These middlemen translate the laws into standards, regulations and operating policies. They advise as to what will or will not be profitable. They design, construct and manage the housing projects. Their decisions are, of course, intermeshed;

no one individual is likely to have much power by himself. But together they are largely responsible for the home environment of their ultimate victims or beneficiaries, the people who need housing.

The American consumer has some ultimate check, of course. He can decline to live in a given development, if he can find something he likes better. And if the results of a law were very unpopular, it could eventually be repealed. But this would simply mean that the experts had failed to carry out satisfactorily the noble instructions they received by due democratic process. And the homes built in the meantime would have to be occupied for years in any case.

The big difficulty lies in the fact that every aspect of housing and city planning policy comes down, sooner or later, to qualitative *social* decisions, "value judgments" about individual needs and preferences, family and community functions, group relations and the whole pattern of civic life. Such judgments are peculiarly difficult to make in a society as varied and changing as ours, but they will nevertheless affect our everyday life for generations to come. And the typical experts currently employed in this field – builders, financiers, lawyers, administrators, economists, architects, city planners, engineers – are often exceedingly ill equipped to make such decisions.

The lack of positive instructions from the consumer, and the dearth of objective knowledge about people's housing needs and wants, is increasingly felt. "Who is our client?" says an architect. "We cannot design houses for faceless, statistical abstractions." Or as an eminent economist puts it, "There is no science of housing. There are only ad hoc cosmologies of prejudices, opinion, and convictions about housing."

## What we need to know: general view

Clearly, "social research" is needed: but what kind? Various branches of applied social science have been actively concerned with housing and city planning problems for some time. Economics, public administration and public health, for instance, are effectively established in

this field. And sociological survey methods provide most of the basic statistical data about
homes, families and cities that galvanized the
whole movement for housing reform and are
now utilized in all plans and programs.

But apparently none of these disciplines, as
currently applied, goes very far toward answering some of the questions that trouble us most:
these unavoidable judgments in the realm of
social values and human relations. To measure
" demand," in the traditional economic sense,
was one thing. But to measure " need " in
concrete qualitative terms is not just a matter
of adding a factor for slum replacement, based
on some obvious physical attribute such as the
lack of plumbing. It is an entirely different kind
of market analysis, requiring new criteria and
methods throughout.

### How do people live, and
### how does environment affect them?

To gauge needs, we should know a great
deal more than we do about people's behavior,
welfare and attitudes under different external
conditions. But even if it is known that certain
social phenomena are likely to occur in a given
type of milieu, this fact alone is not very helpful to the planner or housing designer. Man-
made physical environment is the sum of a
number of distinct and variable elements, and
what the planner wants to know is *the specific
effect of a particular factor in environment over
which he has some bona fide control*, and the
interrelation between one factor and another.

Also, he needs to know what to do, not merely
what to avoid. Even the most refined correlation
between slum conditions and an obvious evil
like juvenile delinquency is of little aid to the
designer of new housing. He won't be copying
the slum in any case: what he is interested in is
*the social effect of the kind of environment
produced, or capable of being produced*, today.
Moreover, he needs more constructive criteria
than the mere absence of juvenile delinquency.
As a distinguished health expert put it, health
must be interpreted in the broadest sense in
housing and neighborhood design, " to include
not only the avoidance of disease but also the

positive attainment of mental and emotional
well-being."

The effects of housing and planning policy
likewise extend into the field of *social organization and human relations*, at the community
level. Judgments that affect the whole future
framework of race and class relations are of
such significance today that they warrant the
most able and earnest analysis of their implications. Similarly, the geographic relationship
of homes to employment, schools, shops and
leisure-time pursuits calls for social investigations beyond the mere measurement of traffic-
flow.

Finally, since we are dealing with decisions
that affect the long-term future, research should
distinguish between average behavior and attitudes under Status Quo conditions, and *emerging trends in social values and activities*, which
may often require testing under new and experimental conditions.

### How do people want to live, and
### how can they achieve it?

" Needs," objectively determined, may or
may not be the same as what people " want."
But in America at least, the ultimate satisfaction
of consumers and citizens is the only real test
of success in housing and city planning. And a
great many experts would sincerely welcome
some means of sharing the responsibility for
decision with the people who will be most
directly affected.

To find out how people really want to live,
however, is no simple problem. Random opinion
surveys are useful, but they do not provide the
whole answer. For one thing, conscious consumer wants are limited by experience and
knowledge: by and large, you can only want
what you know. But entirely *new* kinds of
home, neighborhood, and civic arrangement are
possible today: indeed, they are almost inevitable, while on the other hand, some of the old
ideals about " home " now seem impossible of
achievement, at least in traditional form. What
we really need to know therefore is *what people
would want if they understood the full range
of possibility on the one hand, and all the
practical limitations on the other*.

Moreover, conflicting wants must somehow be resolved. Different individuals and groups often want things that are mutually exclusive. Personal desires are frequently in unavoidable conflict with standards and needs that are collectively determined. And even a single individual attaches so many different values to his home that his wants may be incompatible for all practical purposes.

And finally, what people want in houses and cities is not only a matter requiring objective research to illuminate expert decision. The basic challenge for "planning" in a democracy is how to transfer some of the actual responsibility for decision to citizens and consumers themselves. Two different aspects of this problem keep coming up in housing and planning discussions. How can the issues and alternatives be posed more clearly, not only for experts but also for laymen? And, how can we develop responsible citizen-consumer participation at the local level where such participation might conceivably be real and effective? The first question obviously calls for education, and the second for organization. But in both cases the planners, designers, administrators and civic leaders need the help of social scientists.

—

## The decision-making process:
## how does environment change?

The first step is to understand where and how decisions are made about housing and civic development. Useful research must be geared to the points of control, for one thing. And if responsibility is to be shared with sociologists and psychologists, or with citizens and consumers, it is essential to know where they can be brought into the picture most effectively.

The "experts" themselves should likewise come in for a little objective scrutiny: private builders and lenders, public officials, and the long line of specialists. They have to make all kinds of qualitative social assumptions in the ordinary course of their work: who are they? What do they conceive to be the goals of their activity? How are their judgments actually arrived at? In a simple stable one-class community perhaps the personal values of any one member might reflect those of the whole group

quite accurately. But the preconceptions and ideals of a middle-class professional man in Washington are likely to be quite different from those of the tenants in a public housing project in El Paso.

Behind the organization chart it is also necessary to get a better understanding of the outside pressures and how they operate. How *does* the consumer exercise influence, direct or indirect, on the private builder, the legislator, the public agency? How does the "market" respond to changing habits and social needs? And how do technological developments and economic conditions change the standard of consumer demand?

How does an experiment get started, for instance in home design, and by what process do innovations become accepted in ordinary practice? How do new civic goals get crystallized? When an idea apparently takes hold, such as "slum clearance" in the United States or "new towns" in England, how did it happen? What is the role of the reformer, the Utopian philosopher, the scientist, the artist, the politician, business interests, organized groups and unorganized public opinion?

What about the civic, business, labor, consumer, racial, religious, professional, welfare, political and other organized "interests" that are actively concerned with public policy in housing and urban planning? What are their motives and assumptions and how do they exercise influence? The recent Congressional hearings on the "Housing Lobby" provide interesting information: but how well do the leaders of pressure groups reflect the rank and file opinion of those they represent? What are the conditions that make housing reform and community improvement move forward rapidly in one area, while they are stopped in another?

The complicated present-day process of housing and urban development is an outstanding example of "mixed enterprise." Not only are "public" and "private" functions intermingled at every step, but the motives and values on both sides are equally mixed. A speculative builder, an insurance company, and a cooperative are all private enterprise: but their purposes in housing development may be entirely different. Public policy is devoted in part to stimulating private initiative, insuring profits and protecting property values, and in part to meeting social needs directly. This political-economic maze is a phenomenon of such basic significance in the Western world that it warrants refined analysis by all branches of social science.

Finally, the whole complex of forces that shape our environment should be better integrated at the theoretical level. Serious contributions to urban land use and building theory tend to be narrow in viewpoint, static in scope and method, and rare in any case. Much more attention should be focused on the dynamics of environmental *change*, along with the codification of existing patterns. The shifting roles of the consumer, the property owner, the producer, the lender, government, and experts of all kinds, under present-day conditions, need fuller recognition.

### Residential mobility: key field for research?

An important clue to environmental change, and the effect of environment on people, may lie in the fact that Americans move around so much. About three quarters of the population have changed their address since 1940, and a large proportion have made several shifts within the decade. Much of this movement is from one house to another in the same community but an infinite variety of longer jumps are made, and apparently the historic lines of flow from country to town, from east to west, and from city to suburb, are still predominant.

The incessant movement from one place to another is both cause and result of some of our most serious housing and planning problems. And at the same time this very mobility creates ever-new opportunities for improvement in living conditions, and also for testing the results of our housing and planning efforts. Here is a key field for research, almost untapped beyond superficial measurement.

When people move, they have reached a conscious decision strong enough to make them act. Their reaction to past conditions and their hopes and expectations for the future are relatively crystallized. Why they move is worth investigat-

ing. To what extent is geographic mobility related to social-economic mobility: a different job, or a change in social status? And to what extent, under what conditions, do people move primarily because of the way they want to live, in terms of physical environment? How compelling is the fact that people's housing needs may change at different stages in the family cycle?

Moreover, people who have moved from one kind of environment to another provide a kind of laboratory for comparative analysis. What is the effect on their habits, attitudes and social relations of specific changes in their mode of life? To what extent are their hopes and expectations fulfilled? Especially, we should know more about the effect of moving from old areas to new developments, including both the standard product of current housing and planning practice, and more experimental efforts. Some thought has been given to the effects of moving from a slum into public housing, but there are other important shifts to be explored and evaluated. The most hopeful and ingenious innovations have often been wasted, because no one tested them to see how they really worked.

### National policy and program: some basic questions

In the Housing Act of 1949, Congress declared that the national welfare requires " housing production and related community development sufficient to remedy the serious housing shortage," to eliminate " substandard and other inadequate housing," and to realize " the goal of a decent home and a suitable living environment for every American family." And all housing legislation requires adherence to positive " standards " of some sort as a condition of Federal aid. On the other hand, of course, there are cost limitations and numerous restrictions to promote economy and conserve public funds. And today the expenditure of money, materials and manpower for homes must also be weighed, in terms of demonstrable social need, against the requirements of military production.

Obviously a number of basic quantitative and qualitative determinations, supported by factual evidence, must be made in the course of translating national housing policy into specific programs. And this type of market analysis often requires social judgments that are outside the normal purview of economic or technological research, and little illumined by standard survey methods.

### Re qualitative needs:
### some social questions

The number of new homes needed within a given future period depends on estimates of the existing shortage of dwellings, the expected net increase in families seeking separate shelter, and the number of obsolete or otherwise unusable homes to be replaced. And all these determinations, which affect many other aspects of housing policy as well, are qualified by social factors about which we know too little.

The increase in households depends in part on demographic data, but apparently birth and marriage rates are difficult to predict. Part of our present shortage of homes and schools is due to the fact that the population experts of the thirties consistently warned us against over-expansion, and did not foresee anything resembling the present boom in new families and babies. Undoubtedly the net reproduction rate should be better understood in relation to social, psychological, economic and environmental conditions. Such understanding will be all the more important if the " population question " becomes a political issue in this country as it has in Europe, where housing policy and design have been greatly influenced by certain assumptions, largely untested, as to the direct effect of physical environment on the birth rate.

To estimate both the present shortage and future households, it is necessary to define the family group requiring separate shelter in terms of social as well as biological trends. The family homestead, which normally sheltered several generations (including maiden aunts) is apparently outmoded. Does this mean that most of the households that include more than a primary family group today are involuntarily " doubled up "? Does it mean that we should plan to provide separate homes for the increasing number of old couples and single adults? What is the effect of economic conditions – incomes, dwelling prices, employment – on this trend? The whole question of family size is directly related, of course, to the size and type of dwellings to be provided, as well as their number.

Moreover, the future housing needs of any given locality will be greatly influenced by in- and out-migration. And the dynamics of population mobility has already been mentioned as one of the great unknowns, fundamental to many aspects of housing and planning policy.

And finally, the establishment of criteria for the demolition and replacement of slums and blighted areas is an exceedingly difficult problem, involving some judgment as to the effect of housing conditions on health and welfare. Somehow a line must be drawn between the dwellings and areas which are at least potentially satisfactory, and those which are " substandard " or bound to become so. The rough measures of quality included in the Housing Census are inadequate, and an intensive local survey technique prepared by the Committee on the Hygiene of Housing of the American Public Health Association is often employed to supplement the Census. But complex social factors are necessarily involved in any such evaluation, and the methods and criteria should be subjected to constant critical analysis and refinement.

### New housing for whom? " filtering down " versus housing for special groups

The central issue in most of the debates about housing policy can be stated quite simply. Should we build practically all new housing solely for the upper income groups, on the assumption that it will gradually filter down to satisfy the needs of the rest? Or must we provide new dwellings directly within reach of low and moderate income families? Congress has decided that subsidized public housing for families from slums is necessary, but many local governments still disagree. Federal aids have broadened the market for speculative builders somewhat, but there is still the question of special encouragement for " middle-income " co-operatives, and the issue of public housing for defense workers looms once more.

The basic data required to clarify these questions are primarily of an economic nature: incomes, budgets, building costs in re acceptable standards, demand versus supply, etc. But there are some intricate social aspects as well. The circumstances under which houses handed down from one generation to another remain pleasant and livable, and the circumstances under which they become slums, cannot be wholly explained in terms of costs, incomes and physical obsolescence. The "filtering down" process cuts across the whole field of civic history, and relates to population movements, social mores, and the differing needs and habits of particular groups of people. The physical life of a dwelling has a great many social ramifications that ought to be explored in connection with present-day housing policy as well as the slum problem.

But if a "comprehensive" program of new housing construction is undertaken, this has some profound effects on social organization as well as health and welfare. For it tends to result in a series of more or less separate housing policies and home-production machinery, designed to serve special groups: low-income, middle-income, upper-income, veterans, families from slums, families with children, people in particular occupations, old people, working women, minority races, or whatnot. Strict rules of eligibility usually apply, and segregation by "projects" or larger areas is likely to result. What is the effect on class structure and consciousness, and on the relations between one group and another? If this trend is unhealthy, how can it be counteracted without sacrificing the benefits of a many-sided program?

In particular, the social effects of the rigid and detailed qualifications for tenancy in a subsidized public housing project should be explored. Are such families assumed to have the social status of "charity" dependents because the projects are subsidized: by themselves? by housing officials? by their neighbors or the city at large? What is the result of forcing families to move out of public housing whose incomes have increased beyond a certain fixed limit? What is the effect on community relations, individual initiative, and group leadership of large housing developments inhabited solely by low-income families from slums?

## Home tenure: ownership versus rental . . . versus cooperatives?

Most of the traditional arguments for ownership are of a qualitative social nature: security and independence, personal responsibility, family pride and status, civic participation, etc. And all of these arguments should be tested under the actual conditions surrounding the institution of home-ownership today, so unlike the frontier conditions which prevailed when these values were first attached to it. Buying a more or less standard product on a small lot with little or no cash investment, and with small likelihood of remaining there for more than a few years, is not the same thing as nailing together a homestead on a quarter-section of prairie.

Is the old concept merely a sentimental if persistent survival, bolstered by speculative building practice? Or should we try to achieve some of the old values and satisfactions by other means, cooperatives for instance? Or should we try to facilitate more bona fide individual initiative and responsibility, even under modern conditions? What is the effect on home tenure of our mobility?

Does a conscious preference for individual ownership still reflect a positive desire to own a piece of land and a house per se, for reasons of status, security and personal freedom? Or does it merely mean that most families want ground-level dwellings with private yards? Such homes have rarely been procurable in the past except by purchase, but they could also be provided on a rental or cooperative basis.

In any case, the official attitude toward tenancy has changed a great deal in the past generation. Private rental housing is promoted by FHA, large institutional investors are offered special inducements, and low-rent public housing is subsidized. How did this new trend come about? Does it reflect a real change in consumer demand, or changes in building economics and the production mechanism, or mainly the opinion of some top policy makers?

The trend toward big rental developments raises some new questions about management-tenant relations. When a single landlord selects all the people who will live in a large area, and controls not only home maintenance but also the use of all nearby open space and community facilities, the social effect is very different from the traditional American pattern of individual home tenure and responsibility. It is quite easy for over-zealous management to produce a distinctly institutional and paternalistic atmosphere, unattractive to many of the very people whom public housing authorities and insurance companies, for instance, intend to benefit, and quite different from the hopeful ideals of " community " planning.

Moreover, some degree of tenant maintenance is often desirable to help keep rents down. But can tenants be persuaded to do such work, even in their own economic interest, if they are not given considerable freedom and overall responsibility at the same time? Just where is the fine line between regimentation and the kind of restriction on individual freedom that is unavoidable in any close-planned development? How can tenant participation and a normal democratic community life best be encouraged? Every kind of management policy is being tried out in our big new housing projects, public and private, and we should know more about the results.

Finally, what about cooperatives? A considerable wave of interest has been developing in this country since the war. And, theoretically at least, co-op housing preserves some of the merits of individual responsibility and encourages more direct consumer control of the product, while eliminating speculative profits and reaping the advantages of large-scale production and maintenance. But very few Americans have the life-long education and experience in mutual endeavor that underlies successful cooperative housing abroad. Is this a serious obstacle, and if so, how can it best be overcome?

Also, the principle of cooperation can be applied at several different stages in the housing process. A group might construct a project, with ultimate ownership on either a cooperative or individual basis. Or they might purchase a completed development. Or a project owned by some other agency might be managed and maintained cooperatively by the tenants. Under what conditions will one or another form of cooperation prove most successful? Already there is a field for comparative investigation, in this country as well as in northern Europe.

## Qualitative controls:
### " minimum standards " and uniformity

Large-scale methods and local building restrictions both tend to promote uniformity in new home construction, but the trend toward standardization is greatly enforced by various Federal controls. FHA and PHA establish minimum standards and numerous other regulations as a condition of financial aid, and the local developer, private or public, usually finds it easier to conform to " approved " methods and patterns than to risk delay and argument.

Undoubtedly some of the worst types of land-sweating, speculative exploitation and jerry-building have been largely eliminated by public controls, and the average quality of new homes is probably better than it would otherwise have been. But " minima " tend to become " maxima." Enormous areas are covered with practically identical dwellings, and most subdivisions or apartment projects in a given general category tend to look pretty much the same, from coast to coast. The standard postwar house of moderate price, very small, with living room, tiny kitchen, two bedrooms and bath, is not a universal solution for all sizes and types of family. Yet inventive experiment to meet varying local conditions and individual needs is rare and hazardous. Two questions continually arise: Are the standards too low? And are they too rigid? Declining space standards are discussed in the next section, but some general questions on qualitative controls should be raised here.

The minimum level of housing quality established by public policy is influenced, of course, by all kinds of economic and political considerations. But the basic issue is nevertheless social: is the house too mean for " adequate family life " or isn't it? And the gap between the standards recommended by the American Public Health Association and those enforced by the federal agencies is so wide as to invite study from many viewpoints. Perhaps a history of housing standards, in relation to social and economic contions, might be illuminating.

The need for a greater variety of homes, to suit people with few or many children, differing occupations and cultural tastes, in different stages of the family cycle, living in different regions, is increasingly stressed. The National Conference on Family Life emphasized the changing housing needs of the young family, the expanding family, and the older people who now tend to live apart from their children. They also suggested that if varied accommodations were provided in the same neighborhood, families would not have to move around so much as their needs change. And sporadic efforts are made to overcome the normal inflexibility of public agencies, private builders and lenders, with respect to "mixing" different kinds of people as well as dwelling types, or any other kind of experimentation.

The fact is that rigid uniformity is not an inevitable result of large-scale building and public intervention: quite the contrary. We are beginning to build homes to reach different economic and social groups: there is no reason why we cannot encourage much greater physical and social variety of homes and neighborhoods. But it can no longer be left to accident and individual initiative. Within the present complex framework of the housing industry, variety can be achieved only by conscious policy. The fact that different types of housing are required by different kinds of households must therefore be demonstrated and documented. Also the specific effects of present regulations and building methods should be analysed, to discover how more flexibility can best be achieved. It might be argued that a wider range of "consumer choice" would be a more effective way to determine how people want to live than endless minute research. But more variety probably will not be provided, *without research*.

## Housing design

Design is primarily a process of juggling a number of different variables all at once, to meet certain relatively fixed conditions. If costs must be cut, for instance, the designer may have to decide whether to reduce the dwelling area, increase the density, lower the structural or aesthetic quality, eliminate some equipment, or erase the nursery school. And such a choice involves basic judgments about the whole related pattern of individual, family and collective activity.

A large volume could obviously be written on the social aspects of home design, studded with interrogation marks throughout. But the most urgent and puzzling questions tend to coalesce around a few fundamental issues: space standards and dwelling types in relation to varied family requirements, community facilities, aesthetics of housing design.

## Space standards

The average new home has been getting steadily smaller, on the whole, for some time. Not long ago, a house of 900 to 1000 square feet would have been considered about minimum. Today, FHA encourages the construction of "Economy Houses" for individual sale, at 650 square feet or less. Public housing standards are somewhat higher, but they have recently been reduced to offset high construction costs. However, household equipment is better, the home has lost many of its former functions, and the average family is smaller than it used to be.

But there is little proof of the social validity of these new standards, one way or the other. In a shortage, people take what they can find. And such surveys as have been made seem to indicate that most of the complaints and housekeeping difficulties of the people who live in typical modest homes are caused, directly or indirectly, by too little space. But a really comprehensive study geared to this basic question of policy has yet to be made.

Part of the money that formerly went into floor area now pays for equipment instead. And one crucial question is the comparative importance of dwelling space, beyond a certain point, and such equipment as refrigerators, automatic washers, television sets, automobiles, perhaps other items in the family budget as well.

The effect of family type, size, income and cultural background on desirable space standards, and also the influence of climate, should be explored. And the number of bedrooms required to meet varying concepts of "privacy" is an important aspect of the space problem. The more detailed problems of dwelling layout should also be tested in use. The "open" plan favored by modern architects – with everything but bedrooms, bathrooms and storage in one more or less continuous space – should be compared with the older type of plan that allotted separate cubicles for each function insofar as possible. The amount of glass, and the one-story versus the two-story house are also obvious current issues in design.

Exterior space in a housing development influences light, air, play space, " amenity," privacy, land value, and " density," and is often highly controversial. Open space standards per family range from practically nil on Park Avenue, even in new developments, to the acre-per-family minimum of an upper class suburb. Just how much adjacent open space is needed, by a given type of family, in a given type of building, and for what purposes, is a social question of basic importance to city planning as well as housing design.

One issue just coming over the horizon is the idea of making direct access to private outdoor living space a " minimum standard " for all new housing, particularly for families with children. This would take care of itself in a ground-level home with a yard, but it would mean adding balconies to our typical apartment plans, as has long been customary in most European countries. Would this feature, as claimed, simplify the problem of combining housework with child care in a tall building, and add to the amenities of city living?

### Dwelling types

The choice between high or low buildings, detached homes or a close-knit community development, is a far-reaching decision. It largely determines the suitability of the dwelling for a given kind of family use and also, as a primary factor in urban density, it greatly affects the entire pattern and extent of city development and communication. Even the most extreme and divergent Utopian theories about the " future of the city " (those of Frank Lloyd Wright, Le Corbusier, and Ebenezer Howard ·or Mumford, for instance) come down at base to different premises about the ideal type of dwelling.

In the past this choice was largely governed by location. Traditional ideals and zoning prac-

tice dictated free-standing houses in small towns and middle-class suburbs. Speculative land prices forced multifamily homes in central areas. But today there is much more freedom of choice in dwelling types. Various public measures make it possible to reduce central congestion very drastically. And on the other hand, " group housing " and apartments are not always automatically excluded in the suburbs. With more freedom, however, the responsibility of the decision-makers to choose the *right* type of dwelling for the people destined to live in it is greatly increased.

A big issue today in connection with slum clearance, public housing and redevelopment policy in large cities, is the decision between elevator apartments and low flats or one-family houses, particularly with respect to the needs of low- or moderate-income families with children. Although Federal aid makes low density theoretically possible, the trend is toward high buildings due to the combined pressure of central property and political interests, the housing shortage, and the frequent difficulty of finding suitable vacant sites within the city. Also, a great many designers like the concept of architectural urbanity and technological refinement expressed in tall buildings when properly spaced, and among the sophisticated there are those who feel that collective apartment living is more convenient, more efficient, and culturally more desirable than our old small-house pattern.

All the surveys of ordinary consumer opinion, however, seem to come up with the opposite answer. Almost universally, families with growing children (including most of those who have always lived in apartments) apparently want to live at ground level.

Are the consumers right, or do the experts know better? In addition to direct opinion surveys, there are various background factors to be considered. Are women going to work or stay home? What do people do with their leisure time? What kind of community facilities and professional services are favored, or essential, in a modern apartment development, and do they offset the advantages of ground-level entrance and a private yard? Which kind of environment is conducive to having children and raising them properly? Sooner or later, " population policy " is likely to influence this decision here as it has in Europe, but in which direction? The Swedes put their emphasis on efficient apartment dwellings with maximum services for child and mother, whereas the English favor one-family houses with yards.

But families with children are not the only group to be considered. The needs of older people, childless couples and single adults must also be better understood. Suitable housing for the aged is likely to become a lively public issue sooner or later. But again, in high or low buildings? And also, should such housing be provided in separate projects, or mingled with other types of homes?

The popular reaction to one particular dwelling type, the row or " group " house, deserves special study. From the designer's viewpoint, it has many merits: it provides a ground-level home with a private yard, yet is more economical of land, materials and utilities, and can be more conveniently served by community facilities, than detached homes. Properly planned, it can have sun, air, considerable privacy, and architectural distinction. But there is a strong prejudice against the row house in most sections of America. What we need to know is whether its unpopularity is due to inherent factors (such as closeness to neighbors, relatively small yards, lack of " individuality ") or to the fact that few people have seen or occupied a really well-designed up-to-date version as yet.


### Community facilities

Physically and socially, the modern urban dwelling is an integral part of its surroundings. Tied to a network of pipes, wires, pavement, transportation, and services, it must also have schools and shops nearby, at the very least. And the number and variety of community services and facilities required in residential areas seem to be increasing. It is no news to social scientists that many of the former functions of the home are now taken care of elsewhere on a commer-

cial or communal basis. Also, many services which used to be available only in the city center are now decentralized.

Large-scale housing development not only offers a chance to plan for community facilities: in most cases, they *must* be planned ahead if they are to be provided at all, since no vacant lots or old unused buildings will be available to meet such needs later on.

But what, actually, should be provided, under a given set of conditions? In what form, to serve how many people? Of the numerous experiments, which have proved successful? Which failed, and why? There are strong opinions as to what is needed, but they vary in the extreme. The guiding ideal may be " packaged services " to lighten housework, improved welfare via clinics and child-care centers, or a fuller social life and more responsible participation in public affairs. But there are obvious pitfalls in promoting such ideals from the top down.

Europe offers wide experience, from large community centers in England to all kinds of housekeeping and welfare services in Swedish cooperative apartments. American public housing frequently provides assembly rooms, indoor and outdoor recreation space, facilities for child care centers, clinics and libraries, etc. Experimental " model " projects have always stressed community facilities, and some of the larger commercial builders are now following suit. But we know very little about what happens in actual practical *use*.* And on the other hand, what about some new forces that may be restoring certain functions to the home: the automatic washer and television, for instance?

This is not merely a question of providing building space for specialized uses. Heightened group or community life might mean a closer form of development, different dwelling types, more public space even at the expense of some private space. It has been suggested that a basic approach to the problem of planning both homes and community facilities might be to analyse *all* the functions and activities that should be

---

* The United Nations' Department of Social Affairs recently sought factual reports from a number of countries on trends and experience with respect to community facilities in housing developments, but the lack of available primary data in the United States made it impossible for us to participate.

provided for, whether inside the house or elsewhere. By thus abstracting the functions and pooling the space needs of an entire community, instead of starting with the respective uses of kitchens, living rooms, assembly halls, etc., it might be possible to envision new and more effective forms and combinations of space and shelter.

It cannot be assumed, however, that there is always an either-or decision between what is enclosed in a house and what is transferred outside. The fact that small children attend nursery school does not cancel the need for play space at home, and many household services might be employed solely for occasional convenience. It may well be that the trend toward community facilities reflects mainly a desire for more flexibility, more choice, not an outright shift to a more collective mode of life.

### The art of " large scale housing "

New construction methods, new building requirements, new spatial arrangements, new human needs, require fresh aesthetic solutions. And since architecture is inherently a social art (if only because everyone has to live with it continuously) it seems reasonable to assume that housing developments should give pleasure and stimulation to the people who live in them, and express something valid about their life and the values of the community. Few architects would claim, however, that we really know how to achieve such solutions, despite a generation of serious effort and useful experiment.

The most obvious pitfall in large scale housing design is monotony: dreary repetition of identical units, a bleak and boring kind of orderliness. But monotony is not inevitable, and it is closely related to issues previously discussed: too rigid " minimum standards "; too little variety in dwelling types; the need for community facilities. In general, a more intimate knowledge and positive recognition of people's varied needs and desires would greatly help the designer. As long as the future occupants are faceless statistical categories – " slum dwellers," " veterans," " middle income group " – and as long as the goal is

merely " decent, safe, and sanitary " dwellings, over-simplified standardization is almost inevitable.

Most architects feel that they could do much more distinguished housing projects if they were given a little more leeway, and this further emphasizes the need to encourage experiment and innovation. But aesthetic expression is *itself* a big question, quite apart from functional refinement and administrative obstacles. And it is puzzling because the potential aesthetic virtues of large projects built by mass production methods are extremely different from the values most Americans associate with an attractive home or distinctive residential architecture. What is possible is urbanity: the balancing of mass and space for formal beauty, " civic design " in the classic sense. But instead of " urbanity " in residential architecture, most Americans seek " individuality," in the sense of unique and personal qualities pertaining to each dwelling, or the quaint charm that results from historic accretion and personal craftsmanship. But these are the very qualities that cannot be achieved successfully by a corps of hard-pressed planners, designers and building experts, operating through a system of standards and mass production, no matter how hard they try. Even a romantic isolated plot does not make a prefabricated house seem "individual": its aesthetic virtues are entirely different. And no modern housing project ever looked in the least like a quaint old village, whatever its name or however " Colonial " its detail.

Of course, experimentation with new architectural forms and values is an essential part of the cultural process, and nobody should expect innovations to be popular instantly. But we should know more than we do about the public reaction to modern architectural efforts. What is the initial attitude? How do people feel later when the novelty has worn off? Certain housing projects would generally be considered well designed, interesting or beautiful by progressive architects: do the occupants come to agree with them? Is it possible to distinguish between conscious attitudes toward modern design, and its effect on unconscious attitudes or behavior? Such questions are part of a very large and important general problem: the relation between

" experts " (or " artists ") and people in modern society.

## Social relations:
## segregation versus social mixture

Race relations is a major issue in America, and the question of racial discrimination and segregation is one of the most urgent and controversial aspects of housing and planning policy. From the viewpoint of those who are concerned with the process of housing and civic development, however, this is not an isolated issue, related wholly to racial prejudice : it is part of a general tendency to separate different kinds of people and different functions, with resulting standardization of land use over wide areas.

### The overall trend toward segregation

In the more or less feudal pattern of the old South, extreme racial discrimination did not result in wholesale geographic segregation. Quite the contrary. And today there are many northern cities where " white " or " Negro " districts are relatively larger and more concentrated, than in some Southern cities. Clearly, other factors than race prejudice per se must have some influence.

One of these influences is undoubtedly the strong trend toward economic segregation, which has been operating in most modern cities for the past century. Zoning and building regulations, large-scale enterprise, and restrictive covenants tend to standardize dwelling types, price and rent levels, and the social-economic class of the residents, over wide areas. Within this framework, it is very easy for the private covenant to become a major instrument for racial segregation as well, and for the large developer or landlord to establish with complete efficiency any occupancy restrictions he likes. But it should be noted that the trend toward class separation on a geographic basis has been fairly universal, not only in America but also in England with no race problem, and even in the Scandinavian countries with much weaker class distinctions than here. It was reinforced by the upper-middle-class flight to the suburbs, which tends to result in stratification not only by dis-

tricts but by whole communities and towns, and on the other hand by public housing construction in central districts, limited to " low-income families." Public and private projects restricted to " veterans " are a further example.

Moreover, the geographic standardization of dwelling types also promotes the segregation of families by size, type and age group. Families with small children gravitate toward individual homes where economically feasible, while adult households who prefer apartments must go elsewhere to developments where children are prohibited.

The functional segregation of land use that has been the primary goal of most official city plans should also be mentioned here : the trend toward vast areas that are wholly residential, wholly commercial, or wholly industrial, to the extent that " nonconforming uses " could be weeded out.

In this brief summary the picture has undoubtedly been cartooned. But the general past trend, however imperfectly realized, toward Everyone in His Place, in a standardized one-class, one-age-group, and one-color district devoted wholly to residence, can hardly be disputed.

This was not, however, the result of any conscious overall plan or public decision to encourage maximum social segregation. It came about more or less by accident, as a side-result of forces and policies employed for quite different and often distinctly progressive or idealistic ends, and because we were reluctant to assume any conscious collective responsibility whatsoever for the social pattern. In housing reform and city planning, we have been primarily concerned with plumbing and playgrounds, rent levels and rational building methods, and it was assumed that human relations would take care of themselves on the basis of personal choice. What we failed to recognize was that the powerful tools employed for civic development and home production *also* predetermine social structure to such an extent that there is little room left for free personal choice or flexible adjustment. The big social decisions are all made in advance, inherent in the planning and building process. And if these decisions are not made responsibly and democratically, then they are made irresponsibly by the accidents of technology, the myths of property interest, or the blindness and prejudice of a reactionary minority.

## The forces operating against segregation

The fact that racial separation is now inevitably a matter of public decision, one way or the other, is coming to be recognized. For an independent landlord or builder to say whom he will or will not accept in a building is one thing. But if he requires public finance or subsidy, and court enforcement of his racial policy on a neighborhood scale, then some responsibility also devolves upon government. Once the issue is clearly posed as a matter of conscious public policy, a policy that even has profound international implications, a great many people who took segregation for granted begin to question it. Throughout the North today, the color line is being seriously challenged, due to the new hope and political prowess of the Negroes and to the pricks of democratic conscience. The Supreme Court has outlawed the enforcement of race restrictive covenants in the courts. And even in the South, where the principle of segregation is still firmly established, in law as well as in custom, the potential effect of Supreme Court decisions and national policy is by no means disregarded.

Class segregation is somewhat less officially or dramatically questioned, but there is a growing feeling that a large area occupied wholly by people of identical social-economic status is alien both to our traditions and to our concept of social progress. The need for a greater mixture of age groups and family types, for reasons of convenience and social health, is increasingly recognized. The zoners' ideal of a pure unsullied " residential area " is being replaced by the notion that shops and community facilities should be located for maximum convenience, and that perhaps even some non-nuisance factories might be introduced. And finally, the desire to relieve the visual as well as social monotony of over-standardized land use is a factor of some consequence all along the line.

Once we become aware of the issues and alternatives, it is clear that our new housing and planning tools do not *inherently* produce social segregation. Indeed, they can be used to produce the opposite result quite as effectively. Even zoning laws can be drawn up and administered to encourage or insure diversity rather than uniformity. And a housing policy geared to reach all income groups is the primary requirement for the production of " balanced " communities, if that is what we want. There is no reason why public, private and cooperative projects of moderate scale and varied dwelling types cannot be combined in large development or redevelopment schemes. Also, a large project in single ownership can establish a pattern of *non*-discrimination just as effectively as it can enforce a color line. A number of public housing authorities in the North have demonstrated that " mixed " living can be entirely successful, and a few private developments are now taking the same step.

## Dilemmas for policy makers

Federal housing policies can influence all types of segregation, but it is the race question that has become a critical national issue, even though it is most difficult to resolve at that level. Sooner or later some decisions will probably have to be made among three alternatives, each of which raises certain questions that call for serious analysis:

a. Leave segregation or nonsegregation to local decision as in the past, merely trying to insure that minority groups benefit from Federal housing aid in proportion to their need. (Questions: Would this mean slow but solid progress toward nonsegregation? Or would it mean moving backward, on the whole? And how long will it be feasible politically and in the courts in any case?)

b. Make complete nondiscrimination and nonsegregation a legal condition of all Federal housing aid. (Questions: If enforced, would it merely slow down the improvement of housing conditions, particularly in the South where conditions are worst? If not fully enforced, what would be the effect of making segregation technically illegal but practiced in actuality?)

c. Insist on maximum progress toward nonsegregation in whatever terms may accord with local law, habit, and attitudes. (Questions: On what basis could such variable determinations be devised or enforced? Would it mean non-segregation in all FHA-insured private projects in the North, as well as in public housing? What is the next step in the South? Should there be some assurance that the scale of segregation, the size of the areas devoted to Negro or white use, is at least not expanded in the course of new development?)

In public housing outside the South, the trend is against segregation and there is now a considerable laboratory in which to study the effects of varied policies, and the conditions under which "mixed" living is apparently successful or unsuccessful. In some cities, the color line is ignored completely, and in others various patterns and proportions of mixture have been tried. One important issue is whether or not some sort of "quota system" is advisable, to allay the fear of minority inundation that underlies so much race hysteria. Also, what is the effect of having mixed public housing projects, while private developments are segregated?

The race-segregation issue is beginning to come up in connection with private housing also. Can the FHA refuse to approve a cooperative project sponsored by a mixed group? Can a private builder, profiting from public subsidies that enable him to reconstruct a valuable central slum site, refuse occupancy to Negroes, some of whom may have been living on the site previously? New York and San Francisco say No. And while most private builders and lenders are yet to be convinced about "mixed" occupancy, the rising opposition of Negroes to slum clearance and redevelopment will probably increase until they are assured that their future condition will really be improved thereby.

In some cities, notably Chicago, this issue is producing a state of political and psychological conflict which must somehow be resolved. As voters, the citizens seem to be increasingly opposed to discrimination in any form, while as householders and neighbors they are apparently as fearful and prejudiced as ever, or more so. Is this fear heightened by the housing shortage? by the recent influx of Negroes? by some presumed threat to property values? or by dislike of Negro neighbors per se? And if the color line is

erased by public action, as is more and more likely, how should the adjustment be handled at the level of everyday living? By clear-cut surgical operation, to remove uncertainties? Or by gradual steps, starting under favorable and carefully controlled conditions? The people responsible for housing and city planning policy need some sound and tested working assumptions on these questions, simply in order to make routine decisions and resolve day-to-day conflicts.

Even that citadel of segregation in all its forms, the "protected" upper-class suburban community, is being challenged at a number of points. Zoned for large individual homes, should it still prevent the construction of apartments even though some of its own citizens would like to live in them? Should it keep out a public or cooperative project serving lower income families, even though it has large areas of undeveloped land suitable for such a purpose? Will it prohibit a small non-nuisance industrial plant despite the potential tax benefit? And will it continue to exclude Negroes, and perhaps Jews also, despite the convictions of many of its citizens about "One World" and its implications for America?

One of the long-standing precepts that has furthered segregation of all kinds is that property values and neighborhood "stability" depend on social homogeneity. But it can also be claimed that rigidly guarded uniformity simply means a very inflexible community that cannot adapt to changing conditions and may therefore be highly unstable in the long run. These opposing hypotheses should be tested. Also, what is the relation between homogeneity or heterogeneity and the quality of neighborly social life? Which brings us to another large issue: the nature and purpose of "neighborhood planning."

## Social organization: the neighborhood issue

The idea that a residential district should be planned as a physical and social entity, a more or less self-sufficient community with a definite boundary and certain required components, has become widely accepted in city planning practice, but is also subject to frequent and bitter challenge.

The concept of neighborhood planning reflected a general reaction against the monotonous and wasteful gridiron pattern of city development prevalent in the 19th century. Simply to devise an efficient street system, with relative safety and quiet for residential areas, and to locate schools and shops and parks conveniently, required some planning unit larger than the standard lot and block. Also, the endless mechanical grid seemed to symbolize, and perhaps partly explain, the lonely rootlessness and civic irresponsibility that were widely felt to be characteristic weaknesses of urban society. The city was depersonalized, hence the restoration of neighborly communities would humanize it. The settlement house movement endeavored to provide a social focus for slum neighborhoods; and it came to be recognized that slums had a blighting social and economic effect on adjacent areas, necessitating complete " neighborhood " rehabilitation or reconstruction. At the same time, numerous suburban experiments in community planning were launched, with new street and land-use patterns that ultimately influenced ordinary building practice.

In America a neighborhood has usually been defined as the area and population served by an elementary school, and the detailed standards developed by the Committee on the Hygiene of Housing recommend a population range of 2,000 to 8,000 with 5,000 as a desirable goal, and an area of 50 to 250 acres. Outside boundaries should be marked by parks, main highways or other physical barriers, and no neighborhood should be crossed by a through road or railroad. Adequate community facilities for all everyday domestic and social needs should be provided. Such principles have had widespread influence, in Europe as well as America, and they are often reflected in official master plans.

But there is also some strong opposition to the neighborhood principle, on the ground that it is reactionary in effect and sentimental in concept. In actuality, it is argued, the neighborhood idea is more often employed to promote the antidemocratic practice of segregation than to further democratic ideals. And there is no question but that most of the " neighborhood " or " community " associations organized by property interests are dedicated to the exclusion of " undesirable " groups, and that many official plans reflect this attitude.

Furthermore, it is claimed that the whole concept is atavistic and false even when it reflects bona fide social idealism : that the healthy trend in modern society is *away* from localized " in-groups " and small parochial communities. True progress, made possible by modern methods of communication, means an ever broader and more varied pattern of social life, encouraging individual selectivity in friends and activities, and a freer kind of personal development. It has been suggested that the neighborhood ideal represents merely an escape, a rationalization of the real problem which we are afraid to face.

Here is a major dilemma for the planner, whose routine decisions require *some* assumption as to the proper organization of residential areas. And perhaps some of his questions can be stated in more specific terms.

### The physical pattern of social life : selectivity versus convenience

Every human activity has some sort of environmental pattern. And every facility used by more than one family has some sort of " catchment " area. A first step toward resolving the neighborhood debate would be to learn how people move around now, for what purposes, under varied local conditions, and with full recognition of age-group and cultural differentials. A useful distinction might be made between activities likely to be shaped by factors of proximity and convenience, and activities in which qualitative selection or special personal interest is more likely to dominate, which therefore may or may not take place within a given area however efficiently organized.

Convenience is probably a primary factor in most of the activities on which our present standards of neighborhood planning are based : everyday household shopping, children's education and recreation, access to rapid transit or main highways. And we already know something about how to plan properly for such relatively simple functions. But when it comes to the more selective types of social activity, and the whole field of interpersonal relations, we know very little about the geographic pattern or what determines it. To what extent are these activities, also, influenced by physical proximity and local conditions? Do most friendships grow out of neighborly contacts, and change when people move? Are cultural and recreational activities stimulated and localized if certain physical facilities are near at hand? Or have rapid transit and the automobile so greatly broadened the potential locus of such attractions that no "neighborhood" could confine them? What kind of people tend to move about freely over wide areas, and for what purposes? Who utilizes which facilities in central metropolitan districts? And who are the people who cling to one district, whether it has any apparent "advantages" or not? How does the pattern differ for different age-groups? If small children and their mothers are the most highly localized group, what is the scale of their activities, and when and for what purposes is their horizon extended?

### Should cohesion and self-containment be encouraged?

However refined our knowledge of the present pattern, the question of whether or not to promote a larger degree of local unity and self-sufficiency, and for what particular functions, must still be answered. Do people trek back and forth mainly because they "belong" nowhere? Is the cohesive group, identified with a well-defined area, an instrument for gossiping "small-town" complacency or is it, like the family and the home, a basic requirement for emotional security in our society? Does it require a high degree of social similarity, or can a strong neighborhood consciousness develop from a heterogeneous group? How does our high rate of residential mobility relate to the neighborhood question? Should we endeavor to provide an environment conducive to "settling down"? Some interesting evidence is beginning to accumulate. The important start made by the Lavanburg Foundation in financing Merton's studies should now be carried further to cover a wide variety of local conditions.

If some form of neighborhood unit *is* desir-

able, the conditions for its success should be explored: the social structure, the facilities to be provided, the size, the relation to the rest of the city. And how much should a neighborhood *seem*, physically, like a separate, enclosed unit? The sense of turning inward or outward, of being a distinct civic entity, or an overflow of the city, or wholly a part of it, can be greatly influenced by site selection, layout and architectural form. And this is one of the questions that puzzles the designers. Under what circumstances does enclosure produce a pleasant sense of intimacy, security and uniqueness, and when does it result in the unpleasant institutional "island" quality attributed to many housing projects? Such questions may seem vague and elusive to the social scientist. But the problems are real, the decisions have to be made, and examples of the whole gamut of "neighborhood" qualities and conditions could be found.

### What about the "face-to-face" group?

Some planners who approve the neighborhood principle think that the standard of 1,000 to 1,500 households is the wrong size: too small to permit real variety in function and facilities and social makeup, too large for genuine "neighboring." And much of the recent empirical research in human relations suggests that the primary or face-to-face group – at the scale of court, block or building complex – is often a significant social entity. Moreover it is this group whose social life is perhaps most directly affected by drafting room decisions, whose impact we know very little about.

In most modern site plans, homes are grouped around courts or cul-de-sacs, primarily for reasons of economy, quiet and traffic safety. But such arrangements quite arbitrarily establish the size of the "face-to-face" group, and the pattern of their everyday contacts. What should the site planner know about small groups? What kind of contacts and activities takes place at this scale, or would take place if properly planned for? The fine line between privacy and family self-sufficiency on the one hand, and casual group contact or cooperation on the other, a line that is constantly shifting in popular mores, has direct bearing on planning and design decisions at this level. Is there a trend toward neighborly cooperation in child care or other functions? What happens to nonconformers who don't want to know their neighbors, or whom their neighbors don't like? Should the families at this intimate grouping be fairly similar, perhaps self-selected, or would this merely result in isolated cliques? What is the influence of family income, age levels, cultural background, and other factors?

## Housing location and civic structure

The two poles of the urban problem are suburban spread and central blight. Those who can afford it tend to move out, shops and services follow them, and there is a separate trend toward industrial decentralization, now strengthened by defense considerations. Meanwhile, business offices, major cultural facilities, and many types of commerce and industry remain closely packed in central districts, ringed by ever-widening areas of slum and blight occupied mainly by those who have no other choice. People tend to live farther from their work, and traffic and transportation problems necessitate ever more costly and temporary remedies, less and less covered by local revenues. High property values have impeded reconstruction at the center, while the lack of any unified power at the metropolitan or regional level prevents comprehensive planning, and obstructs the rational development or preservation of outlying vacant land.

It would be hard to find anyone, least of all in the housing and planning professions, who would defend as positively " good " or " efficient " the present land-use patterns or administrative organization of a single big city or urban area. Invidious terms like " metropolitan sprawl " and " chaotic agglomeration " are almost universally applied, even in staid technical treatises. The remedies suggested are exceedingly varied, however, and our powerful new housing and planning tools could be used to further quite different ends.

The city planner's unanswered questions are legion, and only a few of the major issues that directly affect housing policy will be suggested here. But the home is a base point in the urban web, whose proper relation to other elements such as employment, open space, or the central district, is of key importance to city structure and functioning.

One vital question is the *journey to work*. The average distance covered, and the time, money and energy spent in commuting, have probably all been increasing steadily, but we have very little factual data about it. Now, however, confronted by gargantuan problems of traffic and transportation, and with millions of homes to be built and a great deal of employment shifting its locale, we are beginning to ponder the possibility of a more efficient relationship between homes and work. And numerous defense considerations give added emphasis to this issue. Economic analysis is a prime essential, but the social effects of the journey to work should also be explored. What value do people place on relative convenience to their jobs, by comparison with other values? What is the effect of a long, difficult or costly trip on working efficiency and on family and community life? What about the " weekend father " and the increasing segregation of residential areas from their economic base?

Another question, that cuts across the whole range of practical problems from dwelling type to regional planning, is the matter of *open space requirements*. If everyone wants a private yard, it means a spread-out low-density city, with attendant problems of communication. And if people should live within easy reach of big natural parks, farmland or wilderness areas, this fact is obviously a major determinant in any city or metropolitan plan. A great many planners and civic-minded people decry the " ravaging of the land " in spreading urban areas. There is a strong feeling that more open space should be set aside, and that the sprawl should be delimited by green belts. Do the habits and desires of average citizens support these convictions? Is there a conflict between the way people want to live, and their political-economic institutions with respect to land-ownership and land-use control? And what about the purely psychological effect of large open spaces? Would the " greenbelt " principle, as officially endorsed by the British, give people a pleasurable sense of enclosure and contrast, as well as convenient recreation facilities? Is part of the "amenity" of a park the fact that one *might* always use it for pleasant purposes even if one rarely does?

The *use of centralized "big city" facilities* is likewise a key question for city and metropolitan planning, as well as for neighborhood organization. To the extent that people's social, cultural and recreational pursuits depend on frequent and easy contact with the specialized resources and institutions that only a large metropolitan center can provide, this is a counter-force against extreme decentralization.

These issues and many others will affect decisions about the location of new dwellings. In relation to overall urban structure there are at least three distinct types of site theoretically available for housing development: a dormitory suburb, a reconstructed central site, and a complete new community. They will be considered here as "alternatives," simply to highlight their respective problems and implications and because different viewpoints tend to emphasize one or another. Almost any urban area might, however, find all three types of development going on concurrently.

### Location no. 1:
### the suburban fringe

Traditionally, most new housing is added on piecemeal at the edge of present built-up areas, and this is still the easiest and most "natural" location for the construction of middle-class homes by private builders. But if millions of additional dwellings are added in this way, it means an endless continuation of the "sprawl," and a still greater distance between central areas and open countryside. Also, since most white-collar and professional employment would probably still be concentrated in central districts, the journey to work would be greatly extended.

If these conditions are accepted as inevitable, however, it is only on the premise that a metropolitan area is a single urban entity, a social-economic hence a physical *continuum*. And the corollary, as agreed by most planners and public administration experts, is that some sort of unified control at the metropolitan level is absolutely essential, to replace the present anarchic struggle among dozens of wholly independent communities. But this is no simple problem. The movement toward metropolitan government, which once looked so hopeful, is now apparently quite dead in any effective sense. The central city and its several suburbs are more jealous and uncooperative than ever, as a general rule. But why? Aside from the political and economic obstacles, so easy to dispose of by rational argument, are there perhaps some basic social obstacles? Does the increasing degree of class segregation as between city and suburb foster political isolationism? Is there such a thing as a "metropolitan community," despite its obvious functional oneness? Is it perhaps too new and unstable, too big and too diverse, for the average person to identify his civic interests with it? Would it be possible to unify some governmental functions if certain others (e.g., school administration) remained in local hands?

### Location no. 2:
### central redevelopment

The wholesale clearance and reconstruction of slum and blighted areas has only recently been made possible in the United States, through Federal subsidy and State enabling legislation, and this offers a second major choice for the location of new homes. This program raises some new problems, however: conflicting goals to be resolved, and basic decisions about urban form and function.

The urban redevelopment movement is expected, variously, to improve the welfare of slum families, to remove civic eyesores, to stabilize central property values, to make old areas available for profitable building enterprise, and to "save" cities from the disintegrating forces of decentralization. But in any case it is a major civic operation. Substantial population shifts may result, with all kinds of social implications.

What will happen to the displaced families is one key question. Do they have strong neighborhood attachments? Will they live nearer their work or farther away? Will minority racial groups be better or worse off after the move? The forcible displacement of Negroes by public action in a crowded city full of color barriers raises the race relations issue in its most acute and turbulent form.

The welfare of badly housed families would often best be served by building an adequate supply of low-rent homes on vacant land before clearing the slums. But most local housing authorities can operate only within the city limits, where suitable vacant sites may be either nonexistent, expensive, or in middle-class residential areas opposed to the "intrusion" of public housing.

And what principles should guide the reuse of areas slated for demolition? The most routine decision about the kind of development to be encouraged, and about "density" or dwelling type if it is to be residential, involves some basic premise about the city's social, civic and economic requirements. In a number of cities new elevator projects house two or three times as many people as occupied the former slums on the site. But if few people really want to live that way, there is a serious question whether such methods can either solve the housing problem or "save" central districts in the long run. Other cities, particularly in Britain, are taking an opposite course and reducing the number of people living in central areas, in order to make the city better able to compete with suburban standards of amenity.

A drastic policy of central decongestion, however, often means that the "overspill" must move outside the city limits entirely. Will our traditional civic boosterism permit us to acknowledge that our cities are too big and must be thinned out? And where will the people go? Sooner or later, redevelopment raises all the other questions.

## Location no. 3:
### new communities

The third possibility, crystallized in British policy, is to group varied types of housing, industry, etc. together to form a new and relatively self-sufficient urban entity. The "new towns" hypothesis assumes that further decentralization is inevitable, if only to relieve central congestion, but that it can be better handled than by piecemeal attachments to the older urban fabric. The new community would be large enough to support adequate civic services and cultural facilities and provide varied employment, but it would be limited in size, and permanently protected from other built-up areas by a greenbelt of farms or parks. It might still be located, however, so that people could travel to the city or other communities with relative ease.

In America this alternative has been given little official attention until recently, but pressure for industrial decentralization and general dispersal as a defense measure is rapidly bringing it into public focus. But the power to encourage the development of complete new towns would put some heavy new responsibilities on housers and planners. The new British towns will have around 60,000 population: is this an efficient economic size under American conditions? A desirable social size? And just how self-sufficient could they or should they be?

The possibility of building a good-sized town *all at once*, to serve varied functions and a more or less cross-section population, likewise presents some special problems. Everyone living in it and all its institutions would be "new": how does a healthy community develop under such circumstances? Is it important to attract and organize a group of potential citizens, employers, etc. ahead of time, to participate directly in the planning and development? Despite our traditional "small town" idolum, which implies some degree of social mixture, would it be difficult to attract middle-class and professional families to such a community? Would it be better to start on raw land, from scratch, or with a small existing village or town?

## Conclusion

This is a long list of questions to put to the social scientists. And it could be a great deal longer. In presenting the problems posed so urgently by the small group of planners, architects, and housing experts consulted, the difficulty has been mainly a matter of selection and ruthless cutting.

And at best it is only a rough outline, suggesting the complexity and practical significance of numerous issues without explaining any of them fully. But it seemed important to emphasize the range and variety of questions that confront us, even at the price of superficiality, in order to demonstrate the wide field for fruitful social studies of all kinds.

Whatever its limitations, however, this article poses *real problems*. Every one of these questions has to be answered in some form in the ordinary course of our work, whether or not adequate evidence is available. To the extent that social research can enlighten our decisions, the essential framework for satisfactory family and community life will thereby be improved.

# II

# Housing in the neighborhood

## The structure and growth of residential neighborhoods in American cities

*HOMER HOYT*

An increase of population and new construction activity in any city tends to cause the settled area to expand and its neighborhoods to move, and the velocity of neighborhood change tends to vary with the rate of increase in the number of people in the urban community. The very next question that arises in the study of the dynamics of cities, however, is that of the direction and pattern of city and neighborhood growth. What is the shape of the path traced by the motion of growing communities? Faced with the fact that the addition of people and buildings to a city causes a change in its entire structure, students of city growth, property owners, or mortgage investors desire to know in what direction the city will grow and what areas will be affected by the process of neighborhood change.

In general, when a building boom is generated in a city, there are three ways in which new building may add to its supply of dwelling units. It may (1) expand vertically in areas already settled through the replacement of single-family by multifamily structures, (2) fill in the interstices in the existing settled area – *i.e.*, build on vacant lots in blocks already partially developed with structures, or, (3) extend the existing settled area on the periphery of the city by the erection of new homes on newly subdivided land.

The third method of growth – the lateral extension of urban areas – has been described by one writer[1] as growth about the central core, or growth in successive concentric circles around

Reprinted from The Structure and Growth of Residential Neighborhoods in American Cities, *Federal Housing Administration, 1939, pp. 96–122; Addendum from* Land Economics, *vol. 40 (May, 1964), pp. 208 and 209, with permission of the journal.*

the original settled nucleus. More recently,* the lateral extension of cities has been diagnosed as a phenomenon which occurs by (*a*) axial growth – the extension of buildings in radial lines from the main body of the city along fast transportation lines so that the city assumes a star-shaped appearance; (*b*) growth of isolated nuclei of houses beyond the periphery of the main urban area, and (*c*) growth of isolated nuclei until they coalesce with each other or the main body of the city.

These various types of growth are not mutually exclusive. In fact, all of them may be taking place simultaneously in the same city. In this chapter, however, we will discuss principally the lateral extension of cities in the several patterns outlined above. But first, we must set up a technique for the delineation of city growth. Just as the first step in the analysis of city structure showed the physical body of the city in one sweeping view at one period of time, the first step in studying the form of city growth is to compare a series of settled area maps showing the form of city structure at successive time periods. Settled area maps do not show vertical or interstitial growth of areas already settled. They do show, however, the pattern that cities assume at different time periods and thus reflect central and axial growth, the expansion and coalescence of existing outer nuclei, and the growth of new isolated nuclei on the fringe of the city.

The material for the construction of these settled area maps for different time intervals is derived from several sources. *First*, there are United States quadrangular survey maps of cities, showing the location of individual buildings for former periods of time beginning in the nineties. These maps do not cover regular time intervals, however, and vary considerably in the details presented. *Second*, Sanborn insurance atlases, showing location of individual houses are available for many cities for periods as early as the eighties. *Third*, in many cities such as Baltimore, Boston, and New Orleans, there are early maps, dating as far back as the period 1760 to 1800, that show the location of the individual structures. *Fourth*, early " bird's-eye " photographs of entire cities, such as Chicago in 1857, indicate the extent of the settled area at a given time. *Fifth*, from histories of cities, or from the files of newspaper accounts, information as to the building up of certain areas can frequently be obtained. *Sixth*, the record of building permits shows the age of the buildings in a given area. *Seventh*, from real property surveys showing age of structures, the period of time during which an area was first occupied by buildings may be derived. *Eighth*, the appearance and style of architecture of the oldest remaining buildings in an area tend to corroborate other records as to the age of structures. *Ninth*, the testimony of the oldest inhabitants as to the date when certain areas were first settled is useful in filling out gaps in the data or in corroborating other evidence.

When the material from these various sources is assembled, compared, and analyzed, a settled

---

* Fisher, Ernest M., " Speculation in Suburban Lands," *American Economic Review*, Vol. XXIII, No. 1, Supplement (March, 1933), p. 152.

" Around the fringes of all urban areas of any size, lies the territory into which the distinctly urban uses of land must expand as the community grows. This area has very appropriately been called the 'penumbra' of the urban community . . . Here and there patches are definitely withdrawn from the rural or semirural uses, platted in small units served by common means of access, and offered for sale as building sites. Frequently, the public utilities necessary for urban uses are at least partially installed and completely promised, plans are presented for the development of such community activities as schools and churches, and houses and business premises are built.

" These patches of development are widely scattered through the penumbra of the urban area, frequently without relation to one another or to the urban com-

munity as a whole. They are isolated nuclei which gradually grow by the process of accretion, absorbing more and more of the penumbra until their borders meet. When the whole of the area has been absorbed into one or the other of the nuclei, it becomes a part of the original community.

" Thus, the advance of urban uses into the penumbra is by no means a steady or uniform one; the urban uses do not, as might be supposed, creep out into the penumbra at an even pace. They sometimes leap over considerable stretches of territory to establish themselves at spots remote from the fringe of existing uses, leaving the intervening area to be filled in slowly.

" There are then two distinct phases of the growth of urban uses in the penumbra, one is the expansion stage during which the new nuclei are being established, and the other, the filling-in stage during which the interstices between nuclei are being absorbed."

area map of the city for a certain period of time may be prepared by filling in all areas where there is more than one house to the acre. All clusters of dwellings are included in the settled area. The urban mass, as thus defined, varies greatly in density of buildings and population, and these variations are not indicated on the settled area maps. These maps do indicate, however, the general shape, direction, and velocity of the lateral extension of the city as it increases in population.

The settled area maps may be presented in two forms. In the first, there is a series of maps, each one showing the settled area of the city at a given time. The growth of the city can be observed by comparison. In the second form, the growth of the settled area of the city is shown on one map which indicates the original nucleus of settlement and the growth added in each successive time interval. Both types are illustrated in Figure 1 which shows the growth of the settled areas in the Chicago metropolitan region.

History tended to repeat itself during the century that Chicago grew from a hamlet of a dozen log huts in 1830 to the fifth largest city in the world. As a result, several of the various types of city growth outlined above took place in Chicago simultaneously during each of the periods of growth mapped in Figure 1.

Thus, from 1830 to 1857, there was, at the same time, a filling in of partially developed blocks in the area of first settlement, axial growth along plank roads – Milwaukee Avenue, Madison Street, and Ogden Avenue, central growth between the radial lines of the plank roads, and the growth of isolated nuclei beyond the fringe of the main settled area.

In the period from 1857 to 1873, all these processes of urban growth continued. There was a growth of houses on vacant lots between existing buildings in the older settled area. There was continuation of axial growth along Milwaukee Avenue, Madison Street, Ogden Avenue, Blue Island Avenue, and the Rock Island Railroad, which caused the settled area to extend farthest along these fast transportation highways. There was central growth or filling in between the radial lines. There was the establishment of isolated nuclei of growth on the peri-

phery of the city. Finally, the earlier patches of settlement just beyond the fringe of the main body of the city of 1857 had coalesced with the central urban mass.

The period 1873 to 1899 witnessed a repetition of the process just described with the addition of another phenomenon – the replacement of single-family structures by apartments. Again, new radial lines of growth shot out; again, central growth filled in interstices between axial growths; again, isolated patches of growth sprang up on the periphery of the city; and again, the scattered nuclei just beyond the main body of the earlier settled area were absorbed in the central growth of the main urban community.

And in the period from 1900 to 1929, there was *first*, replacement of single-family structures and utilization of vacant lots in Hyde Park and Wilson Avenue and the near North Side areas by multi-family dwelling units. *Second*, there was a filling in of partially built blocks in many sections of the city such as Hyde Park and Wilson Avenue. *Third*, there was a radial extension of the settled area or axial growth in long streamers along fast transportation lines on the North Shore, and westward and northwestward. *Fourth*, there was central growth, or the filling in of vacant areas between the radial lines of growth. This filling in was facilitated by crosstown street-car lines on the northwest and southwest sides. *Fifth*, new isolated nuclei of growth were established in the penumbra on the fringe of the city. *Sixth*, there was an expansion of existing nuclei of growth until they coalesced with each other and formed continuous bands of growth. Evanston, Wilmette, Kenilworth, Winnetka, Glencoe, Highland Park, Highwood, Lake Forest, Lake Bluff, North Chicago, and Waukegan grew together on the North Shore until they practically formed one continuous streamer of urban growth northward along the lake shore. Similarly on the west along the Chicago & Northwestern Railroad, Oak Park, Forest Park, Maywood, Bellwood, Elmhurst, Lombard, and Wheaton tended to coalesce in a band of growth. Northwest, along another line of the Chicago & Northwestern Railroad, Norwood Park, Park Ridge, Des Plaines, Mount Prospect, Arlington Heights, Palestine, and Bar-

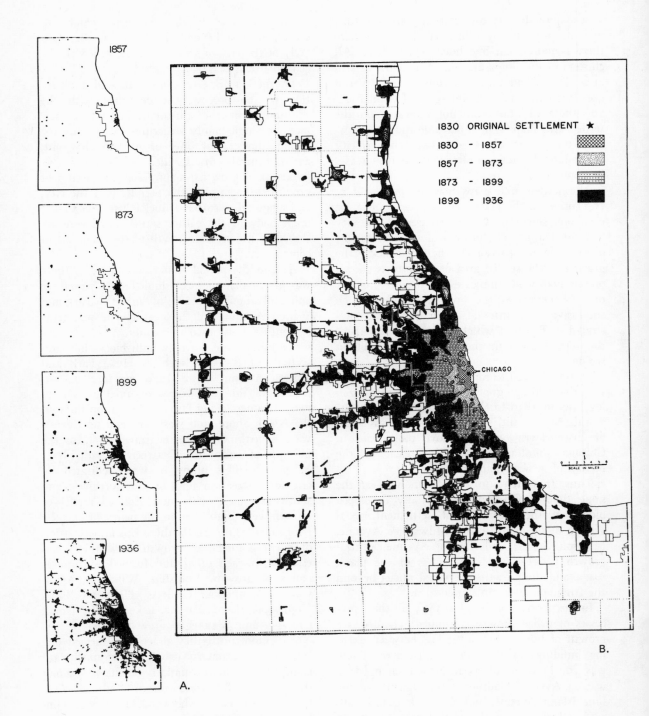

Figure 1. The Chicago metropolitan area.
A. Settled areas at different periods; B. Growth of settled areas 1830–1936.

rington tended to reach toward each other in their process of growth.

Thus, in Chicago's most recent period of growth, we had all the forms of growth simultaneously in evidence – vertical and interstitial expansion, axial and central growth, the expansion and coalescence of existing outer nuclei, and the growth of new isolated nuclei on the fringe of the city.

In New York City, the first settlement was at the tip of Manhattan Island; central and interstitial growth prevailed until the early 1800's. Only small tentacles of growth had stretched northward, and a few isolated nuclei had been established by 1861. By 1881, radial bands of settlement had grown north along the New York, New Haven, & Hartford Railroad. At the same time isolated nuclei of settlement had formed along the two lines of the Long Island Railroad. By 1903 these detached settlements coalesced to form continuous bands, and by 1934 they had spread on each side of the transportation system to cover a broad band of growth. Meanwhile, the detached settlements in the Bronx had coalesced between 1903 and 1934 to form a solid urban body. The present borough of Brooklyn originally consisted of a number of separate villages which gradually grew together into one urban mass. Thus, New York City expanded by axial growth, the flinging out of detached nuclei of settlements and the filling in by the process of central growth, and the growing together of isolated settlements. As the original detached settlements, like Greenwich Village and Harlem, were absorbed by the expansion of the main body of the city, additional independent settlements were developed in the Oranges and Maplewood, N. J., in towns like Pelham, Larchmont, Scarsdale in Westchester County, N. Y., and in Hempstead, Garden City, and other settlements on Long Island.

In Washington, D. C., the first areas of settlement were widely scattered over the four quadrants of the city, but the settlement in 1801 consisted of several nuclei along the axis of Pennsylvania Avenue from Sixth Street to Georgetown. By 1856 these settlements had grown together in irregular bands of growth that widened around the navy yard and the Capitol, and reached their greatest width be-

tween Sixteenth Street and New Jersey Avenue. There were large detached settlements of growth in the southwest quadrant and detached settlements beyond the main settled area but still within Florida Avenue in the northwest quadrant. By 1887, all of this stringlike growth and the isolated nuclei had become welded together and had bulged out beyond Florida Avenue to the northwest. From 1887 to 1917, there was growth on the periphery and radial extension in the northwest along Wisconsin Avenue and along Georgia Avenue. Finally, in the last period from 1917 to 1934, there were great radial extensions of the settled area along Connecticut Avenue and to the east of Sixteenth Street and northwestward, leaving vacant intervening spaces between the bands of radial growth in Rock Creek Park and in the area blocked off from direct access to the center of the city by Soldiers' Home. While the earlier isolated nuclei were coalescing in the main body of the city, other isolated settlements sprang up in Arlington County, Va., and in adjacent areas in Maryland, which in turn began to flow together.

Baltimore is a good example of central growth, particularly for the period prior to 1904, when it grew solidly in compact concentric circles around the starting nucleus north of the Patapsco River. After 1904, electric street-car lines enabled it to send out long streamers of growth northward.

Philadelphia grew mainly by central growth before 1840, but between 1840 and 1881 detached settlements grew up beyond the periphery. These settlements expanded in size by 1900, and finally had grown together into an almost solid mass by 1934. Meanwhile, additional nuclei of settlement were flung out beyond the main body of growth.

Charleston, W. Va., from the starting point on the east bank of the Elk River at its junction with the Kanawha River, grew first mainly eastward along the narrow river valley, and then from 1902 to 1912 expanded toward both the east and west. Westward growth continued from 1912 to 1922. From 1922 to 1933, some settlements spread into the hills as a result of improved concrete roads, and others grew across the Kanawha River. In the case of Charleston, the topography virtually compelled a stringlike growth along the narrow river valley, hemmed in by high hills on each side. There was no room for isolated nuclei to spring up until the way was opened by concrete roads.

New Orleans expanded along the bend of the river until 1906; but from 1906 to 1929, it flung out radial bands of growth toward Lake Pontchartrain and established a few settlements across the river from the main body of the city.

Thus, while some cities exhibit every type of growth simultaneously and spasmodically repeat the process, as did Chicago in its 100 years of growth, other cities tend to expand in more orderly fashion. In some cases, one form of city growth predominates and other types of growth are subordinated. Although the same forces are in operation in all growing cities, the intensity of the impact of those forces determines the type of growth that will predominate at any time. Examination of the maps of the 12 illustrative cities referred to in this chapter indicates that, generally, the more rapid the growth of the urban area, the more rapidly will axial lines of growth be extended and outlying satellite areas, or nuclei, be established, grow, and coalesce with the urban mass. Slowly growing cities will tend to fill out interstices and have greater central growth with sluggish axial growth and only little expansion of outer nuclei. On the other hand, rapidly growing cities like Chicago (see Fig. 1) will have active growth of all types – axial growth and the establishment, expansion, and coalescence of outer nuclei will proceed apace. The rapid growth of business and industrial activity at the central core with its consequent attraction of new inhabitants acts as a catalyst to the physical growth of the city itself and its outlying areas.

In the process of lateral growth, however, the topography of the urban area is a limiting factor. It is evident that hills, mountains, rivers, bays and lakes affect the form of cities located near them. Cities in narrow river valleys assume long stringlike forms like Charleston, W. Va. The configurations of rivers, bays, and ocean inlets affect the form of the settled areas of New York, Boston, San Francisco and other cities. Chicago's shape is influenced by the contour of Lake Michigan. Cities on one side of a broad deep river, such as New Orleans and Kansas

City, expand chiefly on the side originally settled. A swamp limits the growth of New Orleans on one side. Mountain barriers, arising out of a plain, limit the expansion of Salt Lake City.

Such natural barriers to growth are overcome only with difficulty. Man's ingenuity has enabled him to throw bridges across wide rivers, like the spans connecting Manhattan Island with Queens, Brooklyn, Bronx, and New Jersey and the Oakland and Golden Gate Bridges in San Francisco. He tunnels under rivers, as in the case of the Holland and Lincoln Tunnels under the Hudson River between New York and New Jersey. He reclaims land from lakes, as illustrated by the filled-in border of Lake Michigan forming Chicago's parkways between Sheridan Road and the lake. He fills in swamps, as in the case of the site of New York's 1939 World's Fair. He tunnels through mountains and levels off hills, as in Los Angeles. He fills in ravines, as in Washington, D. C. Numerous cases are known where streams have been diverted from their original courses.

All such cases, however, are limited by the benefits accruing from the expenditures necessary to alter or circumvent natural barriers. Generally, cities grow within the limits imposed by the topography of the terrain until the bursting growth makes large expenditures for such alterations or circumventions economically feasible. Thus, the principles of growth already discussed are generally applicable only within the limits imposed by nature.

The growth of these cities demonstrates that, except for growth facilitated by overcoming natural barriers, central and axial growth usually take place in broad, flat plains. On these, cities may extend built-up areas with equal facility in any direction. On the flat expanses of ground available about the core of the city, the chief force influencing city growth is the availability of transportation. Outer residential or business areas must have access to the central business and industrial districts.

*The growth of isolated nuclei* of houses beyond the periphery of the city is facilitated by suburban railroads with stations at intervals along the line, or by industrial plants furnishing employment to workers living nearby, or by prevailing automobile transportation which permits a wide diffusion of settlement.

*Axial growth* is the result of the existence of faster transportation from the center of the city to the periphery along certain main highways, elevated roads, or suburban railroads than in the intervening areas between these radial lines. The time required to reach the center of the city from all points of the periphery of the star-shaped city may be approximately equal. Of course, urban growth may extend farther in one direction in terms of time consumed in travel because of the superior attractions of one section of the city, or because of customary routes of travel.

*Central growth* is the result of forms of transportation that tend to be of approximately equal speed from the center of the city in all directions toward the periphery. It is not a question of absolute but of relative speed. Central growth may be as characteristic of automobile as of horse transportation. If the means of transportation is prefectly mobile and not tied to fixed routes or rails, urban growth may extend in concentric circles from the business center. Central growth also takes place as the result of a filling in of the interstices between radial lines of growth. There is a limit to the extension of settled areas along radial lines. After a certain point is reached, it is found that the time consumed in going to the most distant points on these radial lines is greater than the time required to take a slower crosstown line and to transfer to the main radial line at a point closer to the center of the city.

It is a noteworthy fact that the manner in which cities have grown has not changed with the evolution in the means of transportation during the past century. Chicago manifested the same types of growth during the horse car and early railroad era as during the electric street car and automobile ages.

While the various forms of city growth are not dependent entirely upon the form of transportation, it is true, nevertheless, that certain types of internal transportation within the city have favored one form of city growth rather than another. While there have been differences in the kinds of intraurban transportation in different cities, at the same time there have been certain major trends in the evolution of intra-urban transportation in the United States that have influenced the form of city growth in certain periods.

The evolution of internal transportation in American cities may be divided in three main periods. The first period, that prior to 1890, was characterized mainly by horse-car lines, with steam railroads and cable cars (after 1882) furnishing fast transportation on main routes in some cities. The period between 1890 and 1917 was the era of the electric surface car. In this period, also, elevated railroads and subways provided the most rapid transportation on some radial lines in a few large cities. Finally, the third period, from 1917 to the present, has been characterized by widespread use of the automobile.

The effect of the evolution in transportation upon the growth of cities is shown by the changes in the configuration of cities. Most cities had a very compact circular form until late in the nineteenth century. In Chicago, New York, and a few other cities, cable lines and suburban steam railroads permitted axial growth in long streamers, but Baltimore, and most other cities relying principally upon horse-car transportation, were concentrated as closely as topography would permit around the central business district. Central growth characterized this period prior to 1880 when horse stage-coaches or horse-car lines were the chief forms of internal transportation for all American cities.

Axial growth was promoted by cables that were installed on main trunk lines in a few cities like Chicago and New York beginning in the eighties. The cable-car lines, which roughly doubled the horse rate of speed, increased in the United States from 20 miles of track in 1883 to a peak track mileage of 632 in 1895. Elevated lines, operated originally by steam power, first appeared in New York in 1878 and in Chicago in 1890. Elevated lines still form a main internal transportation system for Chicago, but they are relatively unimportant elsewhere.

The revolutionary change in transportation that affected nearly all American cities and enabled them to spread out in far-flung lines was the advent of the electric surface lines about 1890. The rapid growth in the mileage of electric surface lines from 1,262 in 1890 to 10,363 in 1895, and to 40,808 in 1912 enabled American cities to grow in bands along street-car lines in the decades from 1890 to 1910. Meanwhile, animal traction disappeared, while subways were inaugurated and extended in the largest American cities.[2] The transportation lines in Washington, D. C., are shown in Figure 2 for four different periods of the city's history. Note, in each period, the settled area in the vicinity of transportation lines and the lack of settlement in areas not served by local public conveyances.

The last great revolutionary change to date in internal transportation in American cities was afforded by the automobile. Between 1900 and 1937, the number of registered passenger cars[3] increased from 8,000 to 25,500,000, and their use by all except the lowest income groups became almost universal. Street-car traffic declined; neighborhoods built along street-car lines were supplemented by neighborhoods that were reached largely by automobiles. Moderate elevations, made accessible by hard-surface roads or high-grade residential developments near automobile highways, became favored sites for a new type of development that was not tied to the fixed line of street-car rails. Since the area on the periphery increases with the square of the distance from the city, the automobile opened up extensive areas because it had a speed on open highways several times greater than that of electric street cars.

In congested cities, outer drives, as in Chicago, or elevated and express highways, as in New York, enabled the automobile to speed past congested areas. To most cities, the automobile opened up new areas on the periphery so that its effect was to add a section built during the automobile age to sections that were the products of street-car transportation. Some cities like Detroit, Los Angeles, and Miami had their most rapid growth during the automobile age.

The (a) continued development of superhighways and consequent easier access to rural areas from central parts of cities, and (b) possible future mass production of aircraft so that transportation by air may be common for large segments of the population, may become highly significant in the future growth of American

cities. What types of growth will such developments foster? What shape will cities assume? Will decentralization of cities become complete?

These questions cannot, of course, be answered with certainty. Possibly the same principles of growth, which applied in the three main periods just reviewed, may be depended upon in future years should superhighways and aircraft become common. Because of the fraternal nature of man, dwellings probably will not be scattered in helter-skelter fashion over the landscape but may continue to be congregated in communities. Dwellings may not be built so closely together but may still cluster. One school of thought holds that these clusters will not be isolated but will still be close to – rather than on – arterial superhighways radiating from cities in axial fashion. Distances from outer nuclei to urban centers may be greater, but may still be easily accessible by future forms of transportation. Although there is already a tendency for manufacturing plants to locate apart from large urban centers, the increasing complexity of modern life will probably continue to make it imperative that our main shopping, financial, and business centers be located in the inner portion of the urban organism. Increasingly rapid transportation forms hasten the tempo of life and allow for more far-flung urban organisms. Radial rather than central growth probably will be accentuated, and congestion will probably decrease in urban centers. Complete decentralization of cities, however, is extremely doubtful in any organized society.

### Changes in urban land uses

Dynamic maps may be cross-hatched to designate the different types of land use in any period, and comparison of succeeding periods shows the movement of business, industrial, and residential areas. They also show the lateral extension of the urban site to new areas but do not show two other forms of expansion. These are, namely, the filling in of vacant interstices in a built-up, or settled, area and the vertical expansion of buildings. Thus, residences may be erected on vacant lots between houses in established home areas; or large apartment buildings

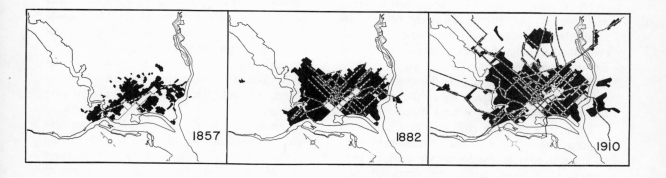

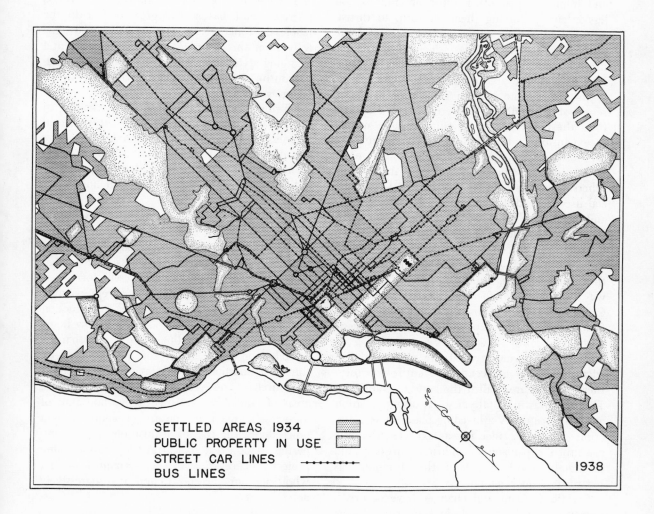

*Figure 2. Growth of settled areas and transportation lines, Washington, D. C., 1857–1938.*

may replace single or two-family structures; or large department stores covering entire blocks may occupy the ground formerly covered by small stores; or large office buildings may succeed smaller office buildings on the same site. Expansion of uses by increased intensity of utilization of the same area must be considered, as well as the lateral expansion or the shifting of location of given types of land uses.

Thus, in a growing city, changing land uses begin at the center with the expansion of retail or financial uses in the downtown area. In their process of growth, these uses press outward and impinge upon other types of land use of less intensity, forcing them, in turn, to thrust outward into the next encircling belt of land uses. Persons occupying residences near the heart of the city go farther out to live as business invades the area of their homes.

Just as a stone thrown in a pool causes a series of expanding circles, radiating outward from the point where the stone hit the water, so expansion of the highest land value uses at the business center of the city may impinge on other uses of less intensity and they, in turn, on others. Thus, in Chicago, as the retail commercial uses expanded from State Street to Wabash and Michigan Avenues, which were formerly occupied by residential and then by wholesale houses, they forced the wholesale uses southward on Wabash Avenue and northward across the Chicago River. Similarly, up to 1910 there was a tendency for factories located west of the Chicago "Loop" along the branches of the Chicago River, to expand on the near west, north, and south sides.

As the factories invaded the residential districts but failed to occupy the entire territory, there was an area called the zone of transition. This area was in a state of social disorganization and was frequently a breeding place for vice and crime. However, since it was expected that the continued expansion of industrial areas would ultimately absorb such land, this situation was regarded as only temporary.

Certain fundamental changes have occurred, however, which may slacken or stop almost completely this lateral expansion of commercial and industrial uses. In the first place, the introduction of the steel-frame skyscraper and the

invention of the steam and electric elevator beginning in the eighties, led to a vertical rather than to a lateral expansion of central business districts. As a result, there was much less lateral expansion in the area occupied by the central business district. The central business district also has been affected by another factor in recent decades, namely, the development of outlying business centers.

Secondly, the use of land for wholesaling may cease to expand because of direct purchases from factories in small quantities. Formerly large stores of goods were maintained in warehouses and wholesale houses near the central business district. There has been a great decline in the wholesale function as retailers buy goods directly from the factories. Quicker deliveries and changing styles have also caused increased hand-to-mouth buying from both wholesalers and factories.

Thirdly, there has been a great slackening in the expansion of industrial areas near central business districts. There are numerous factors already mentioned which tend to make it more economical for a factory to locate in a specialized industrial district or on an outer belt line rather than in the heart of the city.

As a result of the slackening in the expansion of commercial and industrial uses near central business districts, the so-called zone of transition surrounding the central business district has become a blighted area. In its present form, it is not wanted for any type of use except possibly for parking lots. New residential construction is discouraged because the value of a new home placed in slum surroundings may be less than its reproduction cost. On the other hand, to destroy slum neighborhoods would require the wholesale purchase and wrecking of buildings on wide areas of lands that are owned by thousands of individuals. Even by means of condemnation proceedings, the cost of acquisition of such properties is too great to warrant low-cost housing projects; hence, the area is reclaimed neither wholesale nor piecemeal, and it progressively deteriorates.

New homes for the middle and upper classes tend to be located as far away as possible from these deteriorated areas and are usually erected on vacant land on the periphery of cities. The movement of these types of residential areas will be discussed in the next chapter.

While the central business district has slowed up in its rate of expansion, it does, nevertheless, tend to move. The retail shopping center tends to be pulled in the direction of the best residential area. Thus the stores in New York moved up Fifth Avenue in the wake of the high-grade residential movement. The retail shopping center of Kansas City, Mo., moved southward from the river front to Third and Fourth Streets on Main Street, to Ninth on Main Street, and to Eleventh and Twelfth Streets on Walnut Street, as the high-grade residential area grew southward.

The central business district of Chicago moved southward on Michigan and Wabash Avenues, and State, Dearborn, and La Salle Streets when the trend of fashionable direction was south. When the Lake Shore Drive and the Gold Coast Belt developed on the near North Side, and finally when the Michigan Avenue Bridge was constructed in 1920, the office building area burst the boundaries of the "Loop" and grew northward up Michigan Avenue. Similarly, the development of Miami Beach and the northeast section of Miami has pulled the business section of Miami eastward on Flagler Street. In Seattle, the business district has moved northeast toward the higher grade residential sections. In Detroit, the business section has tended to move northward up Woodward Avenue as the result of the growth of the higher grade area northward; but there have been pulls also on the east and west which have tended to keep the central business district near its point of origin.

The growth of population, however, which causes shifts in residential neighborhoods, likewise changes the simple commercial structure of a city with one business nucleus into a more complex pattern. The rapid growth of the population on the periphery of the city and the decline in the number of persons living near the center lead to the development of satellite business subcenters in the area of new homes. There are three forms of commercial areas that tend to rise beyond the limits of the original central

business district as the city grows in population.*

The first is the line of stores strung out along the principal thoroughfares leading from the central business district. The main business center of the city may in fact move out along one of these principal highways as in the case of Euclid Avenue in Cleveland. The commercial uses along the main highways beyond the heart of central business districts are devoted to secondary commercial uses of less intensity than those in the downtown area. Thus in Charleston, W. Va., there is a growth of a line of stores along Washington Street.

A second form of commercial area is the outlying business center located at the converging point of two main automobile thoroughfares or at a street-car transfer point, at subway, elevated, or suburban railroad stations. Here there is a piling up or intensification of commercial uses. The growth of these embryonic clusters of stores, providing groceries or drugs, to adult business subcenters with full complements of motion-picture theaters, banks, restaurants, branch department stores, and specialty stores, is carefully described in Ratcliff's thorough study of the outlying business centers of Detroit.[4]

Finally there is the third form of commercial area, the isolated neighborhood store, or store cluster, in the middle of a block of homes or on a thinly developed traffic artery.

The central business nucleus, located at the converging point of the main highways leading into the city, is surrounded by satellite business centers at the intersections of highways along the periphery of the city. Lining the principal thoroughfares are also strings of stores, and in the midst of some home areas are isolated stores. The outlying commercial areas have grown rapidly at the expense of the central business district.

In all large cities, with the advent of the motor truck and the specialized industrial district served by belt line railroads, there has been a tendency for industries to move away from the congested area to locations on the periphery. It is no longer necessary for industries to locate

---

* For a thorough description of the various types of outlying business districts see Malcolm J. Proudfoot in

Weimer and Hoyt, *Principles of Urban Real Estate*, Ronald Press, 1939, pp. 94–97.

near the workingmen's homes, because such a large proportion of the employees have easy access to quick transportation or come to work in their own automobiles from a wide radius. Thus the factories on the outer belt lines enjoy the advantages of the city as the center of a network of transportation and as a pool of labor. They avoid the heavier city taxes, the limited land area, and the disadvantages of multistoried industrial buildings which break the continuity of the industrial process on each floor level. Industrial managers also prefer to build factories on tracts of land on the periphery that are specifically designed for industrial use and that permit direct switch track connections on the most efficient angles, rather than to locate in the heart of cities where rigid street layouts and city traffic impose barriers to extension of railroad tracks.

Hence, the danger of industries invading residential areas, once the bane of the city planners, has, to a considerable extent, become a thing of the past. In an earlier period, industries invaded home areas of cities, as in Detroit and Brooklyn, creating a jumble of factories and dwellings. Today, however, the preferred location for most industries is on the belt line on the periphery of the city. The vacant land there is cheaper and consequently permits the erection of one-story buildings affording the greatest economy of factory operations.

Even if not prevented by zoning, manufacturers do not often seek to establish large factories in well-developed home areas, because they would have to pay for residential structures merely for the purpose of wrecking them. Nevertheless, the protection by zoning of home areas from invasion by industrial establishments is a wise precaution because it bars small light manufacturing plants that might be started on a vacant lot in the midst of homes.

Usually existing residential structures deteriorate and become obsolete with the passage of time. They are occupied by successive groups of people of lower incomes and lower social standards with the result that the quality of the neighborhood declines with that of the buildings. Hence, the new single-family structures of a city tend to be erected on the periphery. The manner in which the rental neighborhoods shift

as a result of this new growth will now be considered.

## The pattern of movement of residential rental neighborhoods

Of the various shifts that take place in the internal structure of a city as a result of population growth, the movement of the residential rental neighborhoods most vitally concerns the home owner or the investor in residential mortgages. This monograph is primarily a study of residential areas; the other types of land uses are considered because of their influence upon the home sections of the city. Hence the technique for determining the pattern of movement of residential rental areas has unusual importance, and the formulation of the principles defining the path of neighborhood growth is one of the focal points of this study.

The manner in which the various residential neighborhoods are distributed in patterns according to rent was discussed in the closing chapter of part I. There the sector theory of residential rental areas was set forth. From the high rental areas that are frequently located on the periphery of one or more sectors of American cities, there is a downward gradation of rents until one reaches the low rent areas near the business center. The low rent areas are usually large and may extend from this center to the periphery on one side of the urban community. The high, low, and intermediate rental neighborhoods, however, did not always occupy these locations on the urban site. Their present positions are the points reached in the course of a movement taking place over a period of time. It is not a movement of buildings but a shifting and a change in the character of occupants that produces neighborhood change. New patterns of rent areas are formed as the city grows and adds new structures by both vertical and lateral expansion.

There is a need then for a technique for measuring the movement of the different types of rental neighborhoods so that the pattern of movement may be established. By tracing the course traversed by the residential communities of the various rental grades, principles may be formulated explaining the causes for neighborhood changes.

To measure the movement of rental neighborhoods over a period of time, a series of maps showing the average rent of dwelling units, block by block at different dates, would be desirable. Such maps are available for very recent years for those cities in which real property surveys have been conducted. Unfortunately, however, there is no *series* of real property surveys that will permit an exact comparison of rental areas at different time intervals. But the question of the shape and direction of movement of different rental areas is of vital importance, and it is necessary to use the best evidence available, even if it is not so accurate as real property survey data.

One method of showing the changes that have occurred is to compare a map showing the various rental areas today with a map showing the entire settled area at a previous period of time. When it is found, as in the case of Washington (Figure 3), that all the highest rental areas of 1934 lie beyond the limits of the settled area of 1887, it is evident that the best residential section has moved from some point within the area occupied by houses in 1887 to a new area that was entirely vacant at that time. Similar maps of five other cities indicate a similar shift of the best residential neighborhoods.

The use of dynamic factor maps, however, indicates the changes in the location of residential neighborhoods more exactly. These are constructed from evidence gleaned from old inhabitants. Those who have spent their lives in a city are often the only source of information on neighborhood changes. They have been eyewitnesses of the shifting character of neighborhoods. If a number of these residents are consulted independently and if they corroborate each other, much confidence may be placed in their evidence. To secure an accurate picture of the change, however, each of the residents should be asked to draw on a blank map of the city a line around the blocks in which the average rents of dwelling units were the highest in successive periods of time such as 1900 and 1915. Similarly, the same residents may be requested to draw, on another map, lines around the blocks in which the average rents of dwelling units were lowest at the same periods of time. Data for recent years are available, for a large number of cities, from real property surveys. In cities not surveyed, recent data may often be secured from local real-estate boards. Likewise the location of factory and commercial areas may be drawn for the same three periods of time.

In securing this type of evidence, it is desirable to ask only for the rental extremes – the most fashionable area on the one hand, the lowest rent area on the other. Persons depending upon memory might well fail to distinguish between intermediate gradations in rental areas that existed a number of years ago. It is desirable also to select time intervals a considerable number of years apart, so that there will be time for pronounced changes to have occurred that could easily be recalled.

The evidence of such witnesses may be further checked by an examination of the areas outlined. Old fashionable areas usually leave their traces in the form of a few obsolete mansions that are still standing. Frequently old photographic and historical records reveal the character of neighborhoods at an earlier period.

The technique of dynamic maps – used for the purpose of showing the location of the best residential neighborhood at different periods of time – reveals a striking principle of neighborhood growth in Bluefield, W. Va., Chicago Ill., Miami, Fla., Richmond, Va., and Washington, D.C.

*The high rent neighborhoods of a city do not skip about at random in the process of movement – they follow a definite path in one or more sectors of the city.*

Apparently there is a tendency for neighborhoods within a city to shift in accordance with what may be called the sector theory of neighborhood change. The understanding of the framework within which this principle operates will be facilitated by considering the entire city as a circle and various neighborhoods as falling into sectors radiating out from the center of that circle. No city conforms exactly to this ideal pattern, of course, but the general figure is useful inasmuch as in our American cities the different types of residential areas tend to grow

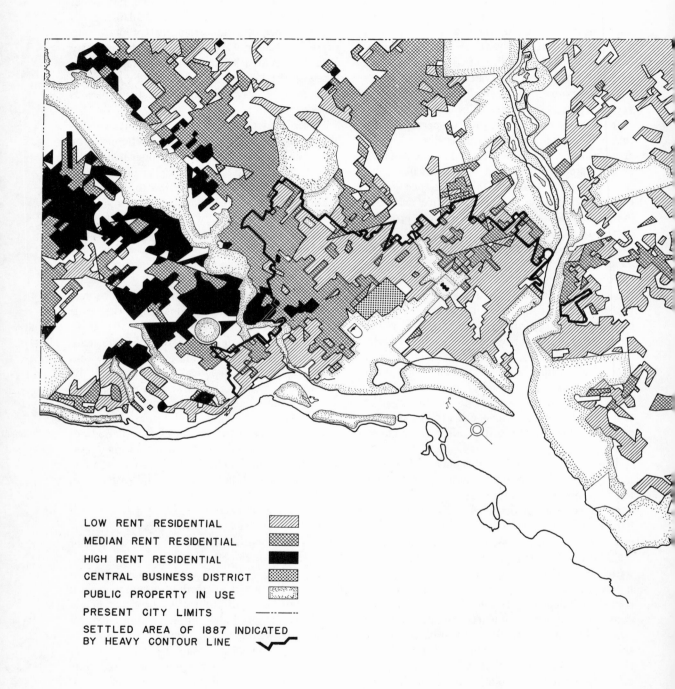

LOW RENT RESIDENTIAL
MEDIAN RENT RESIDENTIAL
HIGH RENT RESIDENTIAL
CENTRAL BUSINESS DISTRICT
PUBLIC PROPERTY IN USE
PRESENT CITY LIMITS
SETTLED AREA OF 1887 INDICATED
BY HEAVY CONTOUR LINE

*Figure 3. Distribution of rental areas, 1934, compared with settled areas of 1887, Washington, D. C.*

Source: Civil Works Administration, *Real Property Inventory for the District of Columbia, 1934.*

outward along rather distinct radii, and new growth on the arc of a given sector tends to take on the character of the initial growth in that sector.

Thus if one sector of a city first develops as a low rent residential area, it will tend to retain that character for long distances as the sector is extended through process of the city's growth. On the other hand, if a high rent area becomes established in another sector of the city, it will tend to grow or expand within that sector, and new high grade areas will tend to establish themselves in the sector's outward extension. This tendency is portrayed in Figure 4 by shifts in the location of the fashionable residential areas in six American cities between 1900 and 1936. Generally speaking, different sectors of a city present different characters according to the original types of the neighborhoods within them.

In considering the growth of a city, the movement of the high rent area is in a certain sense the most important because it tends to pull the growth of the entire city in the same direction. The homes of the leaders of society are located at some point in the high rent area. This location is the point of highest rents or the high rent pole. Residential rents grade downward from this pole as lesser income groups seek to get as close to it as possible. This high rent pole tends to move outward from the center of the city along a certain avenue or lateral line. The new houses constructed for the occupancy of the higher rental groups are situated on the outward edges of the high rent area. As these areas grow outward, the lower and intermediate rental groups filter into the homes given up by the higher income groups. In New York City the movement was up Fifth Avenue, starting at Washington Square and proceeding finally to Ninety-sixth Street in the course of a century. In Chicago, there were three high rental areas, moving southward along Michigan and Wabash Avenues, westward in the band between Jackson and Washington Streets, and northward along La Salle and Dearborn Streets to the Lake Shore Drive.

Sometimes the high rent pole jumps to new areas on the periphery of the city, as in the case of the development of Shaker Heights in Cleveland, Ohio, and Coral Gables in Miami, Fla.,

but usually these new areas are in the line of growth of the high rent areas. In Charleston, W. Va., the high grade neighborhood moved from the center of the city along Kanawha Street until it reached the river, and then the new high grade area jumped to new locations in the hills in the south and north. In Seattle, Wash., the high grade neighborhood started near the center of the city and moved northeast in one sector of the city – the location along the lake on the periphery. At the same time the high grade development sprang up to the northwest, jumping intervening low grade areas.

In Minneapolis, Minn., there was a movement of the high grade neighborhood to the southwest, starting at the center of the city and repeating the same type of growth until it reached the outer edge of the city in a lake region. In Richmond, Va., the sector of the city containing Monument Avenue first developed as a high grade area. The movement of the high grade neighborhood continued out along the line of Monument Avenue until it reached the city limits and then it expanded fan shape in a sector to the north and west. At the same time a high grade development started to the north in a sector which was bisected by Chamberlayne Street.

In Detroit, Mich., the growth of the high grade neighborhood proceeded eastward along Jefferson Avenue out to Grosse Pointe along Lake St. Clair. There was another band of high grade development west of the axis of Woodward Avenue. In Miami, Fla., bands of high grade development followed Biscayne Bay to the north and south and also to Miami Beach.

As a result of the outward movement of the high rent neighborhoods in American cities, present fashionable areas are mostly located beyond the earlier settled areas of American cities. Thus, Figure 3 shows that in Washington, D. C., practically all of the high rent area of today is located in a section that lies beyond the area occupied by houses in 1887. Similarly, in the 14 other illustrative cities referred to in this chapter, most of the high rent areas of today are located beyond the areas occupied by houses at a relatively recent period of time.

High rent or high grade residential neighborhoods must almost necessarily move outward

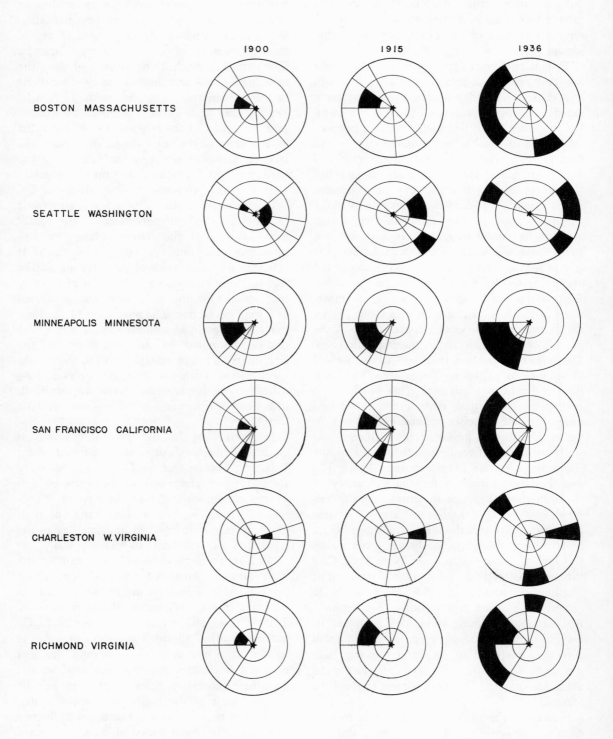

*Figure 4. Shifts in location of fashionable residential areas in six American cities, 1900–1936; fashionable residential areas indicated by solid black.*

toward the periphery of the city. The wealthy seldom reverse their steps and move backward into the obsolete houses which they are giving up. On each side of them is usually an intermediate rental area, so they cannot move sideways. As they represent the highest income group, there are no houses above them abandoned by another group. They must build new houses on vacant land. Usually this vacant land lies available just ahead of the line of march of the area because, anticipating the trend of fashionable growth, land promoters have either restricted it to high grade use or speculators have placed a value on the land that is too high for the low rent or intermediate rental group. Hence the natural trend of the high rent area is outward, toward the periphery of the city in the very sector in which the high rent area started. The exception to this outward movement is the development of de luxe apartment areas in old residential areas. This will be treated more fully on a following page.

What determines the point of origin of the highest rental areas of the city and the direction and pattern of their future growth? The answer to this question is of vital importance to all students of urban growth, for the high rent sector is the pole or center of attraction that pulls the other residential areas with it.

In all of the cities studied, the high grade residential area had its point of origin near the retail and office center. This is where the higher income groups work, and is the point that is the farthest removed from the side of the city that has industries or warehouses. In each city, the direction and pattern of its future growth then tends to be governed by some combination of the following considerations:

1. *High grade residential growth tends to proceed from the given point of origin, along established lines of travel or toward another existing nucleus of buildings or trading centers.* This principle is illustrated by the movement of the high grade residential neighborhood of Chicago along the main axes of the roads like Cottage Grove Avenue, leading south around the bend of Lake Michigan to the east, of main roads like Madison Street leading westward, and of roads following the lake northward to Mil-

waukee. In Detroit, Mich., there was a trend of fashionable growth along the radial line of Woodward Avenue, the main thoroughfare to Flint and Pontiac, beginning within the Grand Boulevard Circuit and later extending to Highland Park, Palmer Woods, Ferndale, Royal Oak, and Birmingham.

2. *The zone of high rent areas tends to progress toward high ground which is free from the risk of floods and to spread along lake, bay, river, and ocean fronts, where such water fronts are not used for industry.* The movement of high grade residential neighborhoods away from river bottoms to higher ground or to wooded hills is illustrated by numerous examples. In San Francisco, Calif., the wealthy moved from the lowland along the bay to Nob Hill which was less subject to fogs and smoke. In Washington, D. C., the high grade neighborhoods moved from the mud flats along the Potomac in the southeast quadrant and from the lowland in the southwest quadrant, to the higher land in the northwest section. In Springfield, Mass., the best areas moved from the lowland along the Connecticut River to rising land and to Longmeadow. In Kansas City, Mo., St. Louis, Mo., and Cincinnati, Ohio, there has been a movement of settlement away from the river bottoms to the higher land.

In cities located on relatively flat land near rivers, bays, lakes, or oceans, the high grade residential neighborhood tends to expand in long lines along the water front that is not used for industrial purposes. Thus in Chicago, the lake front on the north side is the front yard of the city and is preempted for high grade residential use for a distance of nearly 30 miles north of the business center. In New York City, a high grade residential area grew northward along the Hudson River on Riverside Drive from 72d Street to Riverdale in the West Bronx. In Miami, Fla., the high rent areas extend along Biscayne Bay to the north and southeast and along the ocean front on Miami Beach. In Detroit, Mich., a high grade development extends along Lake St. Clair at Grosse Pointe. On the New Jersey coast, there is a long string of resorts along the ocean front with the highest paid residential use confined to the strip along the beach. In Charleston, W. Va., one high grade residential area extends along the high bank of the Kanawha River.

Thus, where such lakes, rivers, bays, or ocean fronts exist and offer the attractions of bathing, yachting, cool breezes in summer, and a wide expanse of water with its uninterrupted view, rent areas tend to follow the contour of the water front in long, narrow lines of growth.

*3. High rent residential districts tend to grow toward the section of the city which has free, open country beyond the edges and away from " dead end " sections which are limited by natural or artificial barriers to expansion.* The lure of open fields, golf courses, country clubs, and country estates acts as a magnet to pull high grade residential areas to sections that have free, open country beyond their borders and away from areas that run into " dead ends." Thus the highgrade neighborhood of Washington, D. C., grows northwest toward expanding open country and estates. Thus, the expansion of high grade neighborhoods to the north of Baltimore, Md., to the south of Kansas City, Mo., and to the north of New York City in Westchester County is into areas with a wide expanse of country beyond them.

*4. The higher priced residential neighborhood tends to grow toward the homes of the leaders of the community.* In Washington, D. C., the White House; in New York, the homes of the Astors and the Vanderbilts were the magnets that pulled the members of society in their direction. One fashionable home, an outpost on the prairie, standing near Sixteenth Street and Prairie Avenue in Chicago in 1836, gave prestige to the section and caused other leaders of fashion to locate near the same spot.*

*5. Trends of movement of office buildings, banks, and stores, pull the higher priced residential neighborhoods in the same general direction.* The stores, offices, and banks in the central business district usually move in the direction of the high rent area, but follow rather than lead the movement of the high rent neighborhood. Sometimes, however, when an office building center becomes established at a certain point, it facilitates the growth of a high rent area in sections that are conveniently accessible to it. Thus the office building center in the Grand Central District in New York City has aided the growth of the de luxe apartment area in Park Avenue and also the exclusive suburban towns in Westchester that are served by fast express trains entering the Grand Central Station. The establishment of an office building center at Grand Boulevard and Woodward Avenue in Detroit, Mich., aided the growth of the high grade area to the north and west of it. In Washington, D. C., the northwestward trend of the office buildings, while the result of the pull of the high grade areas to the northwest, also favored the further growth of the northwest area because it made those areas more accessible to offices. Similarly, the trend of office buildings on North Michigan Avenue in Chicago favored the northward growth of the de luxe apartment area.

*6. High grade residential areas tend to develop along the fastest existing transportation lines.* The high grade residential areas in Chicago grew along the main plank road, horse car, cable car, and suburban railroad routes. In New York City, the elevated lines and subways paralleled Fifth Avenue. Fast commuters' trains connect New York City with the high grade suburban homes in Montclair, the Oranges, and Maplewood in New Jersey, in Scarsdale, Pelham, and Bronxville in Westchester, and in Forest Hills, Kew Gardens, Flushing, and Hempstead in Long Island. In Detroit, Mich., the high grade areas are located close to main arteries leading directly to the center of the city – Jefferson, Woodward, and Grand River Avenues. In Washington, D. C., the best areas are on the main transportation arteries – Connecticut Avenue, Massachusetts Avenue, and Sixteenth Street leading directly to the White House.

*7. The growth of high rent neighborhoods continues in the same direction for a long period*

---

* See Lynd, Robert S., and Helen M. *Middletown in Transition* (New York: Harcourt, Brace & Co., 1937), pp. 81–82, for an interesting example of how the northwest section of Middletown became the oustanding residential section as a result of the movement of the most prominent family to that section.

*of time.* In New York City, the march of the fashionable areas continued up Fifth Avenue from Washington Square to Central Park for over a century. The high grade neighborhoods in Chicago moved south, west, and north from their starting points in or near the present "Loop" to present locations – 7 to 20 miles distant – in the course of a century. In the century after the Revolutionary War, the high grade area of Washington, D. C., moved from the Capitol to the Naval Observatory. The high rent areas of Detroit, Mich., moved from points near the present business center to Grosse Pointe, Palmer Woods, and Birmingham, 6 to 10 miles away.

In Miami, Fla., Minneapolis, Minn., Seattle, Wash., Charleston, W. Va., Salt Lake City, Utah., and many other cities, this same continuous outward movement of high rent areas has been maintained for long periods of time. Except under the unusual conditions now to be described, there have been no reversals of this long continued trend.

8. *De luxe high rent apartment areas tend to be established near the business center in old residential areas.* One apparent exception to the rule that high rent neighborhoods do not reverse their trend of growth is found in the case of de luxe apartment areas like Streeterville in Chicago and Park Avenue in New York City. This exception is a very special case, however, and applies only to intensive high grade apartment developments in a few metropolitan centers. When the high rent single-family home areas have moved far out on the periphery of the city, some wealthy families desire to live in a colony of luxurious apartments close to the business center. Because of both the intensive use of the land by use of multiple family structures and the high rents charged it pays to wreck existing improvements.

Such apartments can rise even in the midst of a poor area because the tall building itself, rising from humble surroundings like a feudal castle above the mud huts of the villeins, is a barrier against intrusion. Thus, when the railroad tracks were depressed under Park Avenue in New York City and the railroads were electrified, that street, originally lined with shanties,

became the fashionable apartment avenue of New York City. In Chicago, the wall of apartments on the sands where Captain Streeter once had his shack is now occupied by the most exclusive social set. In both cases, there was a renaissance of an old neighborhood. It is only where intensive apartment uses occupy the land that such an apparent reversal of trend occurs.

9. *Real estate promoters may bend the direction of high grade residential growth.* While it is almost impossible for real estate developers to reverse the natural trend of growth of high grade neighborhoods, even by the expenditure of large sums of money and great promotional effort, it is possible for them to accelerate a natural trend or to bend a natural trend of growth.

Miami Beach, directly on the Gulf Stream in Florida, was favored by nature as the site for high grade resort homes. When it was a mangrove swamp, separated from the mainland by Biscayne Bay, it was almost inaccessible. Carl Fisher, by building a million dollar causeway and by pumping up 2,800 acres of land out of the bay and erecting thereon golf courses and hotels, made it possible for these natural advantages of Miami Beach to be utilized. Similarly, George Merrick acquired a great tract of land at Coral Gables, Fla., and, by spending millions of dollars in laying out streets, in planting flowering trees, and in establishing restrictions, gave the area a high grade character which it did not otherwise possess. So, likewise, did the developers of Roland Park in Baltimore, Shaker Heights near Cleveland, and the Country Club District of Kansas City take large areas in the line of growth and establish high grade communities by means of building restrictions, architectural control, community planning, and other barriers against invasion.

In all these cases, the high rent area was in the general path of growth; but which area of the many in the favored area became the fashionable center depended upon the promotional skill and the money expended by individual promoters.

As a result of some or all of these forces, high rent neighborhoods thus become established in one sector of the city, and they tend to move out in that sector to the periphery of the city. Even if the sector in which the high rent growth begins does not possess all of the advantages, it is difficult for the high rent neighborhood to change its direction suddenly or to move to a new quarter of the city. For as the high rent neighborhood grows and expands, the low and intermediate areas are likewise growing and expanding, and they are taking up and utilizing land alongside the high rent area as well as in other sectors of the city. When these other areas have acquired a low rent character, it is very difficult to change that character except for intensive apartment use. Hence, while in the beginning of the growth of the city, high rent neighborhoods may have a considerable choice of direction in which to move, that range of choice is narrowed as the city grows and begins to be filled up on one or more sides by low rent structures.

It is possible for high rent neighborhoods to take over sections which are marred by a few shacks. These are swept aside or submerged by the tide of growth. Negro houses have even been bought up and moved away in some southern cities to make way for a high grade development. This possibility exists where the houses are flimsy or scattered, where the land is cheap, where it is held by one owner, or where the residents are under the domination of others. It is extremely difficult otherwise. The cost of acquiring and tearing down substantial buildings and the practical impossibility of acquiring large areas from scattered owners, usually prevent high grade areas from taking over land once it has been fairly well occupied by middle or low grade residential uses.

Now that the radius of the settled area of cities has been greatly extended by the automobile, however, there is little difficulty in securing land for the expansion of high rent areas; for the high rent sector of the city expands with an ever widening arc as one proceeds from the business center.

The next vital question to be considered is how the various types of high rent areas are affected by the process of dynamic growth of the city and how the various types are related to each other in historical sequence.

The first type of high rent development was the axial type with high grade homes in a long avenue or avenues leading directly to the business center. The avenue was a social bourse, communication being maintained by a stream of fashionable carriages, the occupants of which nodded to their acquaintances in other passing carriages or to other friends on the porches of the fine residences along the way. Such avenues were lined with beautiful shade trees and led to a park or parks through a series of connecting boulevards. Examples of this type of development, in the decades from 1870 to 1900, are Prairie and South Michigan Avenues, Washington and Jackson Streets and the Lake Shore Drive in Chicago, Fifth Avenue in New York City, Monument Avenue in Richmond, Va., and Summit Street in St. Paul, Minn. The fashionable area in this type of development expanded in a long string in a radial line from the business center. There was usually an abrupt transition within a short distance on either side of the high grade street.

The axial type of high rent area rapidly became obsolete with the growth of the automobile. When the avenues became automobile speedways, dangerous to children, noisy, and filled with gasoline fumes, they ceased to be attractive as home sites for the well-to-do. No longer restricted to the upper classes, who alone could maintain prancing steeds and glittering broughams, but filled with *hoi polloi* jostling the limousines with their flivvers, the old avenues lost social caste. The rich then desired seclusion – away from the "madding crowd" whizzing by and honking their horns. Mansions were then built in wooded areas, screened by trees. The very height of privacy is now attained by some millionaires whose homes are so protected from the public view by trees that they can be seen from outside only from an airplane.

The well-to-do who occupy most of the houses in the high rent brackets have done likewise in segregated garden communities. The new type of high grade area was thus not in the form of a long axial line but in the form of a rectangular area, turning its back on the outside world, with winding streets, woods, and its own community centers. Such new square or rectangular areas are usually located along the line of the old axial high grade areas. The once proud mansions still serve as a favorable approach to the new secluded spots. As some of the old axial type high rent areas still maintain a waning prestige and may still be classed as high rent areas, the new high rent area takes a fan-shaped or funnel form expanding from a central stem as it reaches the periphery of the city.

The old stringlike development of high rent areas still asserts itself, however, in the cases of expansion of high rent areas along water fronts like Lake Michigan, Miami Beach, and the New Jersey coast. The automobile, however, has made accessible hilly and wooded tracts on which houses are built on the crest of hills along winding roads.

The fashionable suburban town, which had its origin even before the Civil War, has remained a continuous type of high grade area. Old fashionable towns like Evanston, Oak Park, and Lake Forest near Chicago, have maintained their original character and expanded their growth. Other new high grade suburban towns have been established. The de luxe apartment area has been a comparatively recent development, coming after 1900, when the wealthy ceased to desire to maintain elaborate town houses and when the high grade single-family home areas began to be located far from the business center. A group of wealthy people, desiring to live near the business center and to avoid the expense and trouble of maintaining a retinue of servants, sought the convenience of tall elevator apartments.

The high grade areas thus tend to preempt the most desirable residential land by supporting the highest values. Intermediate rental groups tend to occupy the sectors in each city that are adjacent to the high rent area. Those in the intermediate rental group have incomes sufficient to pay for new houses with modern sanitary facilities. Hence, the new growth of these middle-class areas takes place on the periphery of the city near high grade areas or sometimes at points beyond the edge of older middle-class areas.

Occupants of houses in the low rent categories tend to move out in bands from the center of the city mainly by filtering up into houses left behind by the high income groups, or by erecting shacks on the periphery of the

city. They live in either second-hand houses in which the percentage needing major repairs is relatively high or in newly constructed shacks on the periphery of the city. These shacks frequently lack modern plumbing facilities and are on unpaved streets. The shack fringe of the city is usually in the extension of a low rent section.

Within the low rent area itself there are movements of racial and national groups. Until only comparatively recently, the immigrants poured from Europe into the oldest and cheapest quarters on the lower East Side of New York and on the West Side of Chicago. The earlier immigrants moved out toward the periphery of the city. These foreign groups moved in bands or straight lines out from the railroad stations near the central business district. The Italian colony of Chicago moved westward along the area in the point between Harrison Street and Roosevelt Road and northwestward along Grand Avenue. The Poles proceeded northwest along Milwaukee Avenue and expanded southwest along the stockyards. The Russian Jews moved west between Roosevelt Road and Sixteenth Street. The Czechoslovakians shifted southwest from Eighteenth and Loomis Streets to Twenty-second and thence westward to Cicero. With the decline of immigration after the World War, new immigrants ceased to fill the old houses in the downtown area and this outward progression of foreign groups slackened. Many of the tenements in the lower east side were boarded up, and some of the oldest quarters near the central business district of Chicago were demolished.

During the World War and after, however, there was a great influx of Negroes into the northern cities to take the place of European immigration. The Negro neighborhood in Harlem, New York, expanded in concentric circles. In Chicago, the Negroes burst the bounds of their old area along State Street and the Rock Island tracks, Twenty-second and Thirty-ninth Street and spread eastward to Cottage Grove Avenue and south to Sixty-seventh Street. In this movement in Chicago, they spread into an area formerly occupied by middle class and some high income families. The area, however, was becoming obsolete and did not offer vigorous resistance to the incoming of other racial groups.

Thus, in the framework of the city there is a constant dynamic shifting of rental areas. There is a constant outward movement of neighborhoods because as neighborhoods become older they tend to be less desirable.

Forces constantly and steadily at work are causing a deterioration in existing neighborhoods. A neighborhood composed of new houses in the latest modern style, all owned by young married couples with children, is at its apex. At this period of its vigorous youth, the neighborhood has the vitality to fight off the disease of blight. The owners will strenuously resist the encroachment of inharmonious forces because of their pride in their homes and their desire to maintain a favorable environment for their children. The houses, being in the newest and most popular style, do not suffer from the competition of any superior house in the same price range, and they are marketable at approximately their reproduction cost under normal conditions.

Both the buildings and the people are always growing older. Physical depreciation of structures and the aging of families constantly are lessening the vital powers of the neighborhood. Children grow up and move away. Houses with increasing age are faced with higher repair bills. This steady process of deterioration is hastened by obsolescence; a new and more modern type of structure relegates these structures to the second rank. The older residents do not fight so strenuously to keep out inharmonious forces. A lower income class succeeds the original occupants. Owner occupancy declines as the first owners sell out or move away or lose their homes by foreclosure. There is often a sudden decline in value due to a sharp transition in the character of the neighborhood or to a period of depression in the real estate cycle.

These internal changes due to depreciation and obsolescence in themselves cause shifts in the locations of neighborhoods. When, in addition, there is poured into the center of the urban organism a stream of immigrants or members of other racial groups, these forces also cause dislocations in the existing neighborhood pattern.

The effects of these changes vary according to the type of neighborhood and can best be described by discussing each one in turn. The highest grade neighborhood, occupied by the mansions of the rich, is subject to an extraordinary rate of obsolescence. The large scale house, modeled after a feudal castle or a palace, has lost favor even with the rich. When the wealthy residents seek new locations, there is no class of a slightly lower income which will buy the huge structures because no one but wealthy persons can afford to furnish and maintain them. There is no class filtering up to occupy them for single-family use. Consequently, they can only be converted into boarding houses, offices, clubs, or light industrial plants, for which they were not designed. Their attraction of these types of uses causes a deterioration of the neighborhood and a further decline in value. These mansions frequently become white elephants like those on Arden Park and East Boston Boulevard in Detroit, Mich.

On the other hand, houses in intermediate rental neighborhoods designed for small families can be handed down to a slightly lower income group as they lose some of their original desirability because of age and obsolescence. There is a loss of value when a transition to a lower income group occurs, but the house is still used for the essential purpose for which it was designed; and the loss of value is not so great. There is always a class filtration to occupy the houses in the intermediate rental neighborhoods. Hence, a certain stability of value is assured.

Since the buildings in low rent areas are occupied by the poorest unskilled or casual workers, collection losses and vacancy ratios are highest. The worst buildings are condemned or removed by demolition to save taxes. Formerly these worst quarters in the old law tenements of New York or the West Side of Chicago were occupied by newly arrived immigrants. With the decline of immigration, this submarginal fringe of housing is being wrecked or boarded up as the residents filter up to better houses.

Thus, intermediate rental neighborhoods tend to preserve their stability better than either the highest or lowest rental areas.

The erection of new dwellings on the periphery of a city, made accessible by new circulatory systems, sets in motion forces tending to draw population from the older houses and to cause all groups to move up a step leaving the oldest and cheapest houses to be occupied by the poorest families or to be vacated. The constant competition of new areas is itself a cause of neighborhood shifts. Every building boom, with its new crop of structures equipped with the latest modern devices, pushes all existing structures a notch down in the scale of desirability.

## Addendum—1964

Apartment buildings, once confined to locations along subways, elevated lines or near suburban railroad stations, are now springing up in the suburbs, far from mass transit. Many families without children of school age desire the convenience of an apartment, involving no work of mowing lawns, painting and repairing, and with the comforts of air-conditioning and often a community swimming pool. Complete communities are now being developed in the suburbs, with a mixture of single family homes, town houses and apartments, and with their

own churches, schools, shopping centers and light industries, some even with a golf course and bridle paths, of which the 7,000-acre Reston development near the Dulles Airport in the Washington, D.C. area is an outstanding example.

The automobile and the resultant belt highways encircling American cities have opened up large regions beyond existing settled areas, and future high grade residential growth will probably not be confined entirely to rigidly defined sectors. As a result of the greater flexibility in urban growth patterns resulting from these radial expressways and belt highways, some higher income communities are being developed beyond low income sectors but these communities usually do not enjoy as high a social rating as new neighborhoods located in the high income sector. Thus the dynamic changes of the past quarter century make it necessary to review concepts developed from studies of American cities in 1925 and 1939.

# The theory of residential growth and structure

*LLOYD RODWIN*

There are many inadequacies in the prevailing theories of residential growth and structure. Prediction and policy making, therefore, cannot be very effective. Such a situation is particularly unfortunate today because of the need for guiding the emerging national policy of comprehensive urban redevelopment, a policy already spelled out by legislation and subsidies provided by Congress as well as by state and local governments. At the very least, it is important to understand the limitations of the

existing theories and the direction in which future changes may be expected.

In this discussion, two leading hypotheses, namely, the sector theory of Homer Hoyt and the socio-cultural hypothesis of Walter Firey, will be evaluated on the basis of a case-study of a specific city. Boston and its suburbs are selected as the testing ground for four reasons:

1. Major problems may be illustrated more concretely by reference to a specific city.
2. One of the leading theories of residential

*Reprinted from* The Appraisal Journal, *vol. 18 (July, 1950), pp. 295–317, with permission of the journal.*

growth and structure leans on the experience of Boston's development as a basis for broader generalization.

3. The age of the city permits the appraisal of historical experience as well as current trends.

4. There is no *a priori* reason for assuming that other cities would be more typical or suitable for this purpose.

## The prevailing theory:
## Hoyt's sector theory*

The " sector " theory of residential growth and structure is the leading hypothesis in the field. Influenced to some extent by earlier studies which noted the star-like projections of the city's borders, Homer Hoyt ventured the view that the pattern of residential land uses occurred largely in the form of sectors along the lines of transportation. High rent districts presumably shaped the trend by pulling " the growth of the entire city in the same direction."[1] Expansion tended toward the periphery largely because the development of " intermediate rental areas " adjacent to " the leaders of society " prevented expansion in other directions. The point of origin for the most fashionable area, according to Hoyt, was the retail and office center.[2] Many higher income groups worked there and it represented " the point farthest removed from the side of the city that has industries and warehouses."[3] And though not explicitly discussed, all of these adjustments presumably occurred through the normal operation of market forces.

## Firey's theory of cultural ecology

Hoyt's analysis has been sharply challenged by Walter Firey and an alternative formulation has been proposed.† Firey stresses the role of cultural and social systems‡ in conditioning land use. He attempts to explain this role using several recently developed concepts of sociological theory.§ Properties of space and the ends of the social system using the space, he explains, are derived from the cultural system. In some cases like Beacon Hill, the Boston Common and even the North End,** the society-space relationships may be " non-intrinsic," that is, the area has assumed certain symbolic qualities related to the cultural system. Activities are attracted to such space because of the significance of the symbol. The locational pattern is thus directly and actively determined by the values or ends of the cultural system. In other cases, space is not endowed with such qualities, and activities adapt themselves to the space on the basis of their " interests," as for example land used for business purposes; but here too, the relationship is indirectly but culturally conditioned since the use of the space reflects the rational adjustments of these activities to the requirements of a particular cultural and social system, such as the historically contingent " contractualistic " or market economy as contrasted with possible alternatives to such an economy. Where conflict may occur between both types of systems, the older system may wield a selective influence shaping the priority, types and patterns of new uses, as, for example, the better boarding houses or shopping facilities in the declining but still

---

* This summary is abbreviated since Hoyt's thesis will be analyzed in more detail later.

† W. Firey, *Land Use in Central Boston*. Harvard University Press, Cambridge, 1947, Chapters 1, 2 and 9. Firey's analysis refers to many other land uses, and his criticisms are also applied to the locational theories of Weber, Burgess, Predöhl, Park, Haig and others.

‡ Some of Firey's definitions ought to be noted. A social system is defined as the " organization of particular concrete persons and groups into regularized interaction," and a cultural system as " the integration of ends and meanings with respect to generalized types of persons and non-human externalities." (*Ibid.*, p. 32). The " non-intrinsic society space nexus " involves a symbolic relationship in which " the characteristics of of space are not those belonging to it as a natural object of the physical world but rather are those which result

from its being a symbol for a cultural system . . . the properties attaching to physical space and the ends by which a social system orients itself to space have their being in a cultural system. In contrast to this an intrinsic society space relationship would be one in which the properties of space were natural givens and in which the ends orienting a social system to space had their only being in the system itself, as a lone disparate unit seeking maintenance of identity." (p. 133).

§ Cultural anthropologists and psychologists also have been exploring these domains, and the contributions in these varying fields have become somewhat interconnected.

** Firey analyzes these and other areas in great detail, and much of his contribution lies in the skill and ingenuity with which he develops this point.

fashionable Back Bay area.* It is Firey's belief that this socio-cultural approach will clear away the discrepancies implicit in the prevailing economic or "deterministic" analyses and offer a more logically consistent and empirically satisfactory ecological theory.†

Firey's study is a curious anomaly. It is a model of correct methodology, thoughtful formulation of hypotheses, imaginative application of sociological theory, painstaking scholarship and keen criticism. These merits make it the more regrettable that the work is marred by misunderstanding or distortions of the theories he criticizes, incorrect interpretations of the data, lack of appreciation of the role of economic analysis, and a somewhat superficial and inadequate ecological "theory" of proportionality borrowed from the economists. It is nonetheless a sufficiently impressive contribution, as Hoyt himself observed,‡ to warrant close examination for whatever assistance it may offer for our own analysis.

Firey's initial insistence on the mechanism and determinism§ of Hoyt's thesis is inaccurate. Hoyt recognizes the role of noneconomic values. In fact, his principal thesis depends upon such a force, that is, the prestige of "leaders of society" to explain the cluster and development of housing in the direction of upper class environs.** Hoyt, moreover, is obviously describing

and interpreting past location tendencies and makes no claim for inevitability. One example of Firey's wrong insistence on this charge is seen in the following statement:

"The supposition of the idealized schemes has been that the outward extension of land uses is not only inevitable but is irreversible. Slums in particular have been considered as terminating phases in a unilateral cycle of residential land use, the outcome of which can only be commercial or industrial occupation. In point of fact, this uniformity has probably existed in most American cities during the period of expansion, but it can hardly be viewed as anything more than an historically relative rule of thumb. Uniformities of this kind are not material out of which a systematic ecological science can be built. Not only do they have exceptions, as our Fens case illustrates, but they are not stated in terms of variables that belong to a unified and logically closed frame of reference ... The failure of the idealized descriptive schemes to account for this variability cannot but qualify their explanatory adequacy."††

The supposition Firey mentions is unnecessary since economists can explain and justify such a reversal as an ordinary market phenomenon. Hoyt, moreover, in three separate parts of his study calls attention to circumstances where such a reversal can occur.‡‡ Firey cites

---

* Such selectivity undoubtedly existed for Beacon Hill – but Firey does not explain why an entirely different pattern held for an area like the South End when it started to decline.

† Firey's writing at best employs considerable technical sociological terminology and at worst is astonishingly prolix and obscure. The summary above is really a translation and interpretation; and though this writer reluctantly assumes responsibility for the statements, it may be wise for the more interested reader to consult the original source. It is a pity that much of what Firey has to contribute may well be lost or misinterpreted by his potential audience.

‡ Hoyt in reviewing Firey's book in the *Journal of the American Institute of Planners*, Vol. 12, No. 1, Winter, 1947 dubbed it "an outstanding contribution to urban land economics and human ecology." (p. 36.)

§ Firey limits his interpretation of determinism to "the premise that social activities, in their territorial layouts, always constitute the dependent, 'caused' variable, with physical space being the independent and 'causing' factor. It is only in this sense that the expression 'determinism' is to be used in the present study." A little earlier Firey also declares that most of the

ecological theories "ascribe" to space a determinate and invariant influence upon the distribution of human activities. The socially relevant qualities of space are thought to reside in the very nature of space itself, and the territorial patterns assumed by social activities are regarded as wholly determined by these qualities. There is no recognition, except in occasional fleeting insights, that social values may endow space with qualities that are quite extraneous to it as a social phenomenon. Moreover, there is no indication of what pre-conditions there may be to social activities becoming in any way linked with physical space. (W. Firey, *op. cit.*, pp. 1 – 2.)

** Firey does acknowledge in a footnote that Hoyt's analysis allows for many deviations and is not "doctrinaire," but contends that "the scientific adequacy of his idealized scheme may legitimately be evaluated and criticized," (*Ibid.*, p. 78, footnote 100.)

†† W. Firey, *Land Use in Central Boston*, Harvard University Press, Cambridge, 1947, pp. 69 – 70.

‡‡ See H. Hoyt, *op. cit.*, pp. 3, 118 and 119. One of these references is Number 8 of nine generalizations in Chapter 4, one of the most important discussions in the volume.

Hoyt only where he says that the central tendency is in the opposite direction which is true and which Firey does not deny.* Moreover, Firey seems to overlook the fact that for certain problems cultural phenomena can be treated as economic and price factors. Economists have frequently taken tastes, values and technology for granted. The simplication is useful and desirable. It does not mean that these factors cannot be treated differently for other inquiries.† The result, therefore, of Firey's misinterpretation of Hoyt's position is that he has failed to attack its strongest features and thus his own argument is essentially ineffectual.

Existence of a significant sector pattern either in Boston's past history or current housing patterns is likewise denied by Firey. Despite his detailed documentation, however, Firey's basic position may be questioned. He continually forgets that Hoyt indicated the possibility of several sectors.‡ Hence, when Firey finds several sectors in the early period he seems to argue that their existence contradicts the theory.⁴ The North End, Beacon Hill, Ft. Hill–Pearl Street districts at the time of the Revolution could be regarded as sectors in Hoyt's sense. But Firey contends the movement of these upper class districts was " from North to West, then from West to South following no consistent sector outward ..."⁵ Obviously topography was involved here. Ex-

pansion to the North was impossible; and Beacon Hill's growth was cut off by the still unfilled Back Bay. Thus it was logical that the southern Ft. Hill–Pearl Street area should be developed.§ Afterwards the line of growth continued in a southerly direction down Colonnade Row (Tremont Street) and later toward the South End.** Only after Back Bay was filled in did the Beacon Hill–Bowdoin Hill neighborhoods have an area for expansion and many families shifted from the South End to be closer to that neighborhood. True, scattered upper class families lived elsewhere and the sector is not entirely homogeneous; but it is astonishing even on the basis of Firey's own data and information to see him conclude that " The discovery of any sector of upper class residential distribution from such an arrangement appears to be quite impossible."⁶

When Firey finally discovers something that resembles a sector in 1865, he immediately reinterprets his conclusions. Attention is called to the fact that the Beacon Hill and Colonnade Row–South End neighborhoods – comprise two distinct non-contiguous concentrations which is true but perfectly consistent with Hoyt's thesis. As for the " direct linear succession outward from Colonnade Row to the South End which might confirm the dynamic aspects of Hoyt's theory,"⁷ Firey dismisses the pattern as an im-

---

* Several times, as a matter of fact, Firey commits the double injustice of choosing portions of Hoyt's text which do not correspond to Firey's views of what Hoyt should be saying and thereupon rebukes him for "deviationism." Thus, when Hoyt points out the practice of inflating land prices in order to maintain upper class development, Firey insists that neither the raising nor lowering of prices to limit or multiply sales was " an ecological necessity . . . To the extent that Hoyt relies upon this variable in his theory, then he is unwittingly introducing a volitional element which in its logical implications completely vitiates the determinancy of his scheme." (W. Firey, op. cit., pp. 64 – 65.) It is obviously not a necessity that merchants reduce prices on overstocked goods or raise prices for merchandise serving a special clientele. The effects and practice are still interesting subjects for economic as well as sociological analysis. Both subjects have been carefully analyzed by economic theorists under the theory of supply and demand and some interesting economic generalizations have been derived therefrom. Firey does not seem to realize that Hoyt takes the sociological aspects for granted and explores the economic mechanism and effects solely to see how the locational

characteristics emerge. Provided the limitations of the model are grasped, it is perfectly proper for the economist to explore the directions of economic forces alone. Failure of the economist to realize these limitations is a different kind of criticism and often more warranted.
† Hoyt, in fact, states at the beginning of his inquiry that " the techniques suggested and employed in this study, and the principles of urban structure and growth suggested are not set forth as the only method of attack upon the difficult question of the nature of the structure and growth of cities. There are innumerable roads by which the subject may be approached." (op. cit., p. 3.)
‡ H. Hoyt, op. cit., pp. 112 and 114. Firey, in fact, mentions this himself. (op. cit., p. 8.) Hoyt also indicates several sectors in his rent maps.
§ Hoyt also points out that in the early period of a city's growth, there is " considerable choice of direction in which to move but that range of choice is narrowed as the city grows and begins to be filled up on one or more sides by low rent structures." (op. cit., p. 119.)
** There was apparently another cluster along Summer Street from the Common to the river.

proper validation due to the peculiar, topographical configuration which forced development southward. It is only fair to ask why Firey detects here the role of topography whereas its importance for the earlier period in forcing a reversal of development in the North End and Beacon Hill completely escaped his attention. In any case, expansion of the upper income neighborhood need not have proceeded toward the "Neck" and South End as Firey maintains. An upper class residential district might have and almost did spring up in South Boston, something which many people anticipated and which Firey himself points out elsewhere.* Firey not only mistakenly charges others as tainted with determinism but assumes the mantle himself when it serves his purposes.

Later the Back Bay development is scrutinized from a variety of aspects all designed to show that it was not an inevitable development. Granting this is true, it was clearly a possibility that materialized. Nowhere, however, is there any mention of the obvious and undeniable sector appearance of Back Bay and its marked continuity with the Beacon Hill area. Firey's analysis of the role of prestige, precedent and values does help to explain why the rich live together in neighborhoods, factors that Hoyt in a sense took for granted. Little in Firey's approach accounts for the location, shape or direction of growth of areas such as Back Bay.

Contemporary trends, Firey discovers, indicate a clear-cut southwesterly high rental and/or upper class "band" extending outward from Beacon Hill which again would seem to confirm the sector hypothesis.† This cartographic misapprehension Firey immediately attributes to the existence of many upper class towns or summer resorts like Dedham and Weston where the rich had country homes. Their existence presumably antedated the radial development and thus are not accepted as evidence for Hoyt's thesis.[8] Quite the contrary could be argued, however. Hoyt specifically contends that "high grade residential growth tends to proceed from the given point of origin along established lines of travel or toward another existing nucleus of building or trading centers."[9] It is perfectly reasonable, or at any rate not inconsistent,‡ to find that the direction of growth was toward areas where the upper class had their summer homes or friends. However, Firey argues that within these broad sectors, considerable heterogeneity occurs so that the sector is really more apparent than real. As an example, he cites the working class and commercial areas lying between the Beacon Hill–Back Bay area and the fashionable Brattle Street residential section of Cambridge. Though the point has some merit, Hoyt could easily sidestep the charge by considering these areas as two separate sectors, as well they might be, since Brattle Street is not at all directly in line of development from the Beacon Hill–Back Bay area. The same argument holds for the Back Bay–Fens–Brookline development and the Dedham district to which Firey refers. Depending, therefore, on the period and the interpretation of a sector,§ Beacon Hill, Colonnade Row, South End, Back Bay, Brattle Street and still other areas might be regarded as upper class residential sectors from Hoyt's point of view and purpose.

---

* On p. 60, Firey says, "With business encroaching upon their homes, residents of the area lying south of the business district began to look elsewhere for places in which to live. Many moved to the suburbs. Others looked to South Boston. A writer in the Boston Almanac for 1853 wrote: 'South Boston from present appearance is predestined to be the magnificent section of the city in respect to costly residences, fashionable society and the influence of wealth.'" Yet on pp. 62 – 63 Firey says: "Hoyt does not mean to rest his case on such geographically determined processes . . . The imperious necessity of finding new land for residential expansion made the South End the only possible direction of growth. But this is not the kind of determinancy to which Hoyt would himself attribute his asserted radial extensions of land uses." (*Ibid.*)

† Firey includes in this band, in addition to Beacon Hill and Back Bay, the following communities: Brookline, Newton, Wellesley, Weston, and perhaps Dedham. (*Ibid.*, p. 77.)

‡ Actually the southward trend (Dedham, Dover, Medfield and Westwood) can be attributed to the increasingly advantageous location of the South and Back Bay Stations in relation to "big business" centers; and the West-Northwest trend (northern Wellesley, Weston and Lincoln) is correspondingly related to ease of access along the Charles by auto. To this extent, the sectors correspond to Hoyt's thesis, particularly the emphasis of the role of transportation routes in determining the shape of the residential pattern. The writer is indebted to Prof. R. B. Greeley, (Department of City and Regional Planning, MIT) for this point.

§ This problem will be discussed further.

Firey finally proposes that the community must serve as a " social system " with functional requirements set by the larger society, and the allocation of space for the various ends is to be achieved according to a criterion which he calls the " proportionalization of ends," that is, a point of maximum satisfaction or attainment of the various ends of the community.[10] This theory of " proportionality " does Firey a disservice in several respects. It is a close parallel to indifference curve analysis of economists and a comparison will quickly reveal its weaknesses. Specifically, the proportionality " theory " suggests that ends must be so served spatially as to minimize " end deprivation."* Firey explicitly indicates that it refers to more than costs, thus indicating he is thinking in economist's terms but wishes to broaden the elements included in the analysis. Firey's " theory " stops at that point.† Economists, however, go much further. Refined assumptions,‡ marginal analysis, use of the substitution principle, plus price ratios, are required to arrive at relatively significant and determinate conclusions rigorously deduced. In the absence of these or comparable elements, Firey's proposition is an empty, even if well-intentioned exhortation. The fact that he wants to extend the scope to noneconomic activities would further complicate the analysis – and here too there may be much that Firey could pro-

fitably learn from welfare economists who have been exploring social costs as well as those of the firm and industry.

Firey's conclusions, which are intended to serve as applications and implications of a cultural ecology, reflect all of these limitations. He favors central area redevelopment, long range planning, broadened urban boundaries, slum clearance, subsidized low rent housing, and more parks, all presumably as deductions from the theory of proportionality. One may or may not quarrel with these conclusions (and this writer personally favors them), but it would be easy to come to just the opposite conclusions if one so desired and if so amenable an instrument served as a guide. If, to cite some examples, a realtor claimed that in the long run the community would be better off with no public housing or if a " houser " favored peripheral rather than central area redevelopment, Firey would be assuming the proof if he argued that on the contrary it increased " end deprivation." At best his conclusions may be consistent with his principle but they are not in any way derived therefrom. Firey himself reflects uneasiness on this score in his last paragraph declaring that these conclusions " may not all be sound or feasible and they may not all have been properly deduced from our theoretical construct though every effort has been exerted to make them

---

* Firey describes the proportionalization of ends as follows: " Let us then imagine a city that is made up of certain ends defined for it by the value system of the society in which the city exists. We can postulate that there will be a hypothetical point at which the amount and 'kind' of space devoted to a particular end or function balances off with the spatial requirements of each other end or function comprising the city. At this point, the total deprivation of all the ends comprising the system is at a minimum. It is important to recognize that this 'end deprivation' is not synonymous with 'cost' in the economic sense of the word, since it refers not only to dearth of scarce goods but also to thwarting of intangible and nonempirical ends which are just as real functional requirements of a city. All of these ends and functional requirements must be attained, yet none of them can be pursued to an unlimited degree lest others be unduly deprived. That point along the 'deprivation continuum' of a particular end, at which point the degree of deprivation comports with a minimal deprivation of all other ends comprising the community may be called point x. Now by definition, any deviation away from x will entail increased deprivation to one or more of the other ends comprising

the community as a system. Thus an allocation of too much space to park and recreational facilities will obstruct certain other requirements of the city as a functioning social system, such as commerce or manufacturing. Likewise the allocation of too little space to park and recreational facilities will obstruct the 'best' functioning of the community as a system. Reasoning deductively, then, it may be suggested that departure from point x in either direction as to degree of a deprivation of a particular end is accompanied by a progressive increase in deprivation to the system as a whole – more specifically, to one or more of the other ends comprising the system." (Ibid., 326 – 327.)
† Firey also translates this into algebraic symbols, but, as he indicates, the significance of the proposition is not thereby changed.
‡ These include knowledge of ends, means to achieve them and maximum attainment. For a brief and elementary discussion of the analysis in economics, see G. J. Stigler, The Theory of Competitive Price, The Macmillan Co., New York, 1942, pp. 67 – 76; K. E. Boulding, Economic Analysis, Harper & Row, New York, 1941, pp. 501 – 517.

so."[11] His conclusions likewise indicate that Firey missed or dismissed part of the aim of Hoyt's analysis, namely to search for possible *locational* generalizations describing contemporary urban land use structure and growth. The explanation is simple enough: Firey does not believe such generalizations are possible.[12]

The purpose of this preliminary analysis is not to defend Hoyt's thesis. Account must still be taken of its shortcomings. But it must be clear, that an adequate substitute for Hoyt's basic generalizations on residential location has not been formulated. Firey's studies only graze Hoyt's empirical conclusions; and though Firey's emphasis on social and cultural systems is more complex and sophisticated than Hoyt's simple explanation, there is no necessary inconsistency between the two. In any case a satisfactory alternative or supplement must be able to introduce issues of public policy and social values without pulling solutions out of the air, or abandoning usable methodology and without ignoring either actual empirical tendencies or valid elements in existing hypotheses. If these limitations are noted, Firey's real contribution can be properly assessed.* His approach may be used to broaden and deepen the conceptual framework of Hoyt's empirical analysis and assumptions, especially by a more thorough appraisal of social structure and relationships. In particular, Firey's study suggests:

A. The historically contingent character of all our urban land uses and their reflection of cultural and social systems.

B. How values, purposes and community sentiments, as in the case of the Boston Common and Beacon Hill, may influence locational patterns and processes.

C. The importance of studying social systems and cultural values to understand adaptive behavior and use patterns *within*

defined areas or social systems such as the North and South End.

## The sector theory and Boston's housing patterns

Hoyt's generalizations do not have the rigor of a deductive system. Because they express empirical tendencies, it is possible for individual cities to reflect divergences without invalidating the central tendency. Noting such discrepancies in the case of Boston would not invalidate Hoyt's thesis as Firey supposed. Yet these deviations may indicate certain weaknesses and furnish clues for the formulation of a more adequate hypothesis. They may also help qualify some of Hoyt's narrow interpretations of the data which tend to distort applications of the thesis.

Several general tendencies characteristic of the pattern and movement of strategic high rent areas are submitted by Hoyt. In this section, the principal observations will be stated and their applicability to Boston appraised.†

1. "High grade residential growth tends to proceed from the given point of origin along established lines of travel or toward another existing nucleus of building or trading areas."[13]

As has been noted already, such patterns prevail in Boston in the westward movement from the Beacon Hill–Back Bay area to the Fenway and Brookline districts by way of Beacon Street or Commonwealth and Brookline Avenues; in the southwest movement to Dedham through Massachusetts and Columbus Avenues, and then along Washington Street; in the northwest movement to the Cambridge–Brattle Street section using Massachusetts Avenue, and on to Belmont through Concord

---

* Subsequent to the preparation of this article, the author's attention was called to the article by John James, entitled "A Critique of Firey's Land Use in Central Boston," (*The American Journal of Sociology,* Vol. 54, No. 3, November, 1948, pp. 228–234). Though the basic thesis is different in conception from the analysis above, several of the criticisms of Firey's study are surprisingly parallel. This writer disagrees with James' approach which is primarily designed to sustain

Hoyt's thesis and which overlooks some important possibilities in Firey's analysis.
† Hoyt's observations, in fact, are made with reference to the prevailing pattern of rent areas and movement of these rent areas. Most of the observations on the prevailing pattern are either touched on in paragraph 10 or in the subsequent section dealing with definitions. This condensation is necessary to keep the article within manageable scope.

Avenue; and in the westward movement to Newton along Commonwealth Avenue and Cambridge and Beacon Streets.*

2. "The zone of high rent tends toward high ground which is free from risk of floods and to spread along lake, bay, river and ocean ports, where such water fronts are not used for industry."[14]

Boston's experience has not been altogether consistent with this trend. South Boston in competing with the South End for upper class residential hegemony lost despite the fact it occupied a high bluff overlooking the ocean whereas South End and Back Bay were largely filled land. Better transportation routes seemed to be an important factor in the successful subdivisions on the peninsula plus the continuity which the South End offered with former and existing areas of high prestige. Present subdivisions in suburban areas, however, such as Belmont, Newton and Dedham seem to be in line with this trend, probably as a result of the increased importance of the automobile in overcoming transportation difficulties.

3. "High rent residential districts tend to grow towards the section of the city which has free open country beyond the edges and away from "dead end" sections which are limited by natural or artificial barriers to expansion."[15]

In the case of the North End and Beacon Hill, this generalization does not quite hold.† Barriers surrounded both developments: the ocean, Charles River and Back Bay in the case of Beacon Hill despite its suburban location when originally developed; and Boston's natural water boundaries and settled areas in the case of the North End during the period when it was the "court" district of town. Obviously, contradictory possibilities are involved since movement toward high ground and proximity to the new

State House which influenced the Beacon Hill subdivision were more important than prospects of expansion. Hoyt, however, qualified these generalizations by indicating that the pattern would be set "by some combination"[16] of these factors, thus imparting both flexibility and inconclusiveness to his generalizations.

4. "The higher price residential neighborhood tends to grow towards the homes of the leaders of the community."[17]

Bowdoin and Beacon Hill, South End and then Back Bay development seem to be evidence in favor of this proposition. High-priced homes emerge elsewhere, however: in East Boston, for example, from 1840 to 1860; in Dorchester, Jamaica Plain and West Roxbury, especially before 1890; and in suburban areas like Belmont, Milton, Melrose and Dedham. This generalization is a key element in the sector thesis but the evidence for it in Boston is equivocal and doubts emerge even concerning the meaning of the statement.

5. "Trends of movement of office buildings, banks and stores (sometimes) pull the higher priced residential neighborhoods in the same general direction."‡

The Fens apartment district largely built up during the twenties might be consistent with this observation. In Boston, however, only a movement of such activities toward the high rent area – the dominant pattern reported by Hoyt – rather than the reverse previously stated seems to be occurring. Its appearance is most obvious along Boylston Street and toward Copley Square.

6. "High grade residential areas tend to develop along the fastest existing transportation lines."[18]

South End's development along Huntington

---

* The route, according to this statement, need not be sited only through fashionable thoroughfares.
† Actually all of Boston was then surrounded by water with the exception of the narrow isthmus known as The Neck. There was relatively more prospect, however,

for expansion southward compared to other areas in Boston.
‡ H. Hoyt, op. cit., 117 – 118. The insert in the statement is based on Hoyt's important qualification made in the subsequent paragraph in the text.

Avenue and Tremont Street and Back Bay's munificent Commonwealth Avenue are evidence in favor of this pattern. South Boston lost certain advantages in competition with the South End partly because of its limited transportation services and the opening of a more efficient omnibus service to Roxbury.[19] Beacon Hill, however, is an obvious exception, being deliberately designed to avoid North–South traffic. Hoyt also notes that the new trend is in favor of secluded suburbs though the roads to these districts usually run through the old " axial high grade areas."* This penchant for privacy explains at least in part why Beacon Hill has been susceptible to revival.

7. " The growth of high rent neighborhoods continues in the same direction for a long period of time."[20]

Two possible meanings might be ascribed to this statement: (a) that the general area maintains its character for a long time; or (b) that the growth continues in that direction for a long time. The first interpretation, if intended, is not confirmed by Boston's experience. One upper class neighborhood after another collapsed, sometimes with considerable financial loss. Bowdoin Hill, Ft. Hill and Colonnade Row were soon absorbed by the rising tide of business. None of these areas survived more than a generation.† South End, initiated about 1840 to 1850, moved downhill rapidly after 1870–73.

South Boston had an even shorter period of glory lasting approximately from 1845 to 1855. Beacon Hill, after the completion of the development, stayed in favor less than two generations and then started to decline. Even Back Bay has not been the top residential area for much more than half a century. Though it still retains a slightly frayed distinction, by 1935 it was described as a potential slum.‡ Shops have invaded its precincts, and fashionable homes have been turned into " high class " rooming houses and professional offices.

On the other hand, the second interpretation as to the direction of development is partly true. Though there was a shift from the North End westward to Beacon Hill and then southward to Ft. Hill, geographical limitations partly account for these seemingly erratic movements. The shift, however, from the South End to Back Bay cannot be explained so simply. Even though the general direction was the same, there was a decided change in the locus of fashionable areas. If, however, the movement from Ft. Hill, Colonnade Row and South End is considered a relatively continuous line of development, and likewise for the Beacon Hill–Back Bay area, then the second meaning of the generalization is supported by Boston's experience.

8. " Deluxe apartment areas tend to be established near the business center in old residential areas."[21]

---

* H. Hoyt, *op. cit.* Hoyt explains that " the axial type of high rent area rapidly became obsolete with the growth of the automobile. When the avenues became automobile speedways, dangerous to children, noisy, and filled with gasoline fumes, they ceased to be attractive as home sites for the well-to-do. No longer restricted to the upper classes, who alone could maintain prancing steeds and glittering broughams, but filled with *hoi polloi* jostling the limousines with their flivvers, the old avenues lost social caste. The rich then desired seclusion away from the madding crowd whizzing by and honking their horns. Mansions were then built in wooded areas, screened by trees. The very height of privacy is now attained by some millionaires whose homes are so protected from the public view by trees that they can be seen from the outside only by an airplane.

" The well-to-do who occupy most of the homes in the high rent brackets have done likewise in segregated garden communities. The new type of high grade area was thus not in the form of the long axial line, but in the form of a rectangular area, turning its back on the outside of the world, with widening streets, woods, and its own community centers. Such new square or rectangular areas are usually located along the line of the old axial high grade areas. The once proud mansions still serve as a favorable approach to the new secluded spots. As some of the old axial type high rent areas still maintain a waning prestige and may still be classed as high rent areas, the new high rent area takes a fan shaped or funnel form expanding from a central stem as it reaches the periphery of the city." (p. 120).

† Note that Hoyt refers to upper class districts in New York as being in existence for more than 100 years. Three generations or more is the benchmark used here to judge existence for " a long time." Physically speaking, the houses may last 100 years or more.

‡ W. A. Ballard, and M. L. Rockwell (research assistant), *Proposals for Downtown Boston.* (A survey in respect to the decentralization of the Boston central Business District for the Urban Land Institute), Boston, 1940, p. 44.

Firey, it will be recalled, cited the Fenway's experience of replacing slum areas at the outer edge of Back Bay with upper income and park developments to show the inconsistency with Hoyt's hypothesis. Actually the experience might appropriately be employed to illustrate Hoyt's point. However, the observation is inaccurate for Boston at least to the extent that this "reversal" refers only to deluxe apartment areas. Beacon Hill's rejuvenation into single family homes occurred without substantial physical transformation because of the quality of the buildings. Similar remodeling might occur in the future for other conveniently located and well-built areas of Boston such as the South End and Back Bay.

9. "Real estate promoters may bend the direction of high grade residential growth."[22]

Beacon Hill, South End and Back Bay were all speculative enterprises. All three required extraordinary exertions, the first in reducing the hills, and the other two in filling the mudflats. Development on alternative sites could easily have occurred were it not for real estate promotion coupled with government assistance and subsidy for these areas. Not always do these schemes succeed as is evident in the frantic and unsuccessful efforts at bridge and road building in South Boston. Significantly enough, Hoyt completely overlooks or slights the role of government and public policy in shaping residential patterns. In Boston, at least, in reference to land and transportation policy, this influence was far from negligible.

Several other observations made by Hoyt

ought to be noted and checked. They are summarized and commented upon in paragraph 10.*

10. "The high rent neighborhoods do not skip about at random in the process of movement – they follow a definite path in one or more sectors of the city."[23]

Moreover, movement by the wealthy is seldom reversed because:

"On each side of them is usually an intermediate rental area, so they cannot move sideways. As they represent the highest income group, there are no houses above them abandoned by another group. They must build new houses on vacant land."[24]

Hoyt also notes that:

"Intermediate rental areas on the periphery of other sectors of the city besides the ones in which the highest rental areas are located are found in certain cities."[25]

Though the general trend is in line with these observations, particularly the formation of nuclei and definable patterns, Boston's experience indicates three interesting and possibly significant deviations. As many studies have pointed out, the north slope adjoining Beacon Hill throughout most of its history was occupied by low income and even socially disreputable groups. In other words, evidence for abrupt changes in land use is available,† at least as an exception to the general pattern. Secondly, the movement back to Beacon Hill following 1900 indicated the possibility of a special kind of second hand housing for the wealthy,‡ a pattern which could

---

* These statements include the substance of three of the five conclusions reached in Chapter 6 dealing with the static pattern of residential areas rather than the growth pattern. They are: (1) "The highest rental areas are in every case located in one or more sectors on the side of the city"; (2) "High rent areas take the form of wedges extending in certain sectors along radial lines from the center of the periphery"; (3) "Intermediate rental areas or areas falling just below the highest rental areas tend to surround the highest rental areas on one side"; (4) "Intermediate rental areas on the periphery of other sectors of the city besides the ones in which the highest rental areas are located are found in certain cities"; (5) "Low rent areas extending from the center to the edge of settlement on one side in certain sectors of the city are found in practically every

city." The fourth generalization is discussed herein and also in the section dealing with intermediate areas. The fifth statement is not discussed but it is confirmed by Boston's land patterns, especially the sector to the northeast.

† The same is true of the slums in the Fens prior to deluxe apartment building. Hoyt suggests it also may be true of Providence, Rhode Island.

‡ This point is partly anticipated by Hoyt in his introduction where he observed that "In years to come, continued eradication of slum areas or cessation of population growth may foster conditions favoring a double back of high grade residential areas rather than a continuation of growth in line with past experience." (H. Hoyt, op. cit., p. 3.)

assume more importance in the future. Finally, numerous and extremely broad intermediate areas may be found throughout Boston and its suburbs, notably in Dorchester, Brighton, Jamaica Plain, Malden, Medford, Arlington and elsewhere, with no *close* relationship to upper class developments. Absence of a close association raises important issues concerning the nature of intermediate areas which need to be explored.

The observed discrepancies, upon summary, indicate: (a) that upper income residential developments in the past have not always moved toward high ground or open country; (b) upper and middle income residential movements also occur in directions other than toward the homes of leaders of society; (c) upper class districts often have not lasted for long periods and though the same direction was generally maintained significant locational shifts are discernible; (d) return of the wealthy to the city's center has occurred not merely for deluxe apartment houses but for well-built older areas also; (e) the wealthy, under some circumstances, may find it feasible and desirable to use second-hand housing; (f) fashionable areas may be bounded by low income as well as " intermediate " areas; (g) government policy as well as real estate promoters may influence residential patterns; and finally, (h) housing of the intermediate groups covers such a wide swathe that a locational description only on the basis of relationship to the upper class district is probably inadequate.

The question arises whether these variations are peculiar to Boston or whether they evidence difficulties with the hypothesis itself. One or two items may be exceptional such as the co-existence of high and low rent areas or the relatively short life of fashionable areas in Boston. There is reason to suspect, however, that even if these cases are exceptional, they may be

important exceptions which an adequate theory must take into account.* Other items might still be fitted into the hypothesis and generalizations by slight modifications in formulation. For example, the return to the city's center can take place in older rehabilitated houses as well as deluxe apartments. Similarly, the evidence that upper income residential districts do not always proceed to high ground and open spaces may be explained by the fact that Hoyt's empirical generalization really stated the existence of a " force " which could be counterbalanced by the other " forces " described. The other items, however, seem to be attributable to certain ambiguities, oversimplifications and questionable assumptions which deserve careful, critical attention.

## Problems and assumptions of the sector theory

If the sector thesis† is scrutinized, three basic terms will be noted. These are: (a) the sector, (b) the leaders of society, and (c) intermediate income classes. Many of the issues raised with reference to Hoyt's analysis can be ascribed to problems surrounding their meaning.

### Sector

What is a sector? Would for instance, Back Bay alone qualify? Or must it include the whole southwestern trend of better residences? Firey does not raise the issue, yet tests both possibilities.[26] If the broader area were intended, then Firey would appear to be justified in calling attention to the slums, industrial areas and other land uses lying between districts such as Brattle Street and Back Bay. Apparently smaller groupings would allow more homogeneous areas, at least in this case. Perhaps the issue may be

---

* A partial explanation is possible for both items. Coexistence of high and low rent areas may often indicate the desire or need for servant or service classes near the upper income groups. Similarly, the short life of high income residential areas may reflect the termination of a family cycle, i.e., the departure of the children and the failure of new upper or high income groups to take up residence in this area.

† Note that this analysis is confined to the residential aspects. Moreover, though Hoyt also develops the thesis

with regard to other land uses, he was mainly interested in this aspect. He states, for example, that " having segregated the home areas from the general urban mass for study, the third major step in the technique differentiates the several types of residential areas on the basis of their essential housing characteristics. The analysis of these home areas and the formulation of generalizations apparently governing the distribution of the several types of residential urban areas are the main subjects of this monograph." (*op. cit.*, p. 4.)

clarified if the minimum elements that the concept was intended or ought to include are stated.

The sectors outlined on Hoyt's maps were based on rent classes. These classes range from less than $10, $10–$19, $20–$29, $30–$49, and $50 and more. Variations in rent areas within the corporate boundaries of cities were mapped. Each rent area represented the rent average within the district and block deviations within this district were ignored.[27] The maps indicated that the highest rental areas ($50 and more) were generally concentrated in one or several parts of the city. With the data, Hoyt was able to test the concentric circle hypothesis. The inadequacy of the latter was indicated by the fact that high rent areas were revealed only along one or several sides of the city – rather than in the form of a ring pattern. It was also possible to establish that various kinds of housing, particularly high rent areas, were not scattered throughout the city in random fashion. Up to the present, upper income families have lived in relatively homogeneous groups, thus creating a neighborhood with sufficient similarity of living conditions to mark an identifiable social and physical environment. Often, but not always, such an area had room for expansion, usually along or near an important transportation route. This characteristic is understandable since a new development usually begins with small numbers with other groups tending to follow. Few areas were or are completely built at the same time. These elements represent the essential basis for the sector, especially as it pertains to the upper income groups.

The sector then may be formally defined as a radial residential grouping, usually capable of expansion along or close to an avenue of transportation and comprising enough families able to afford a comparable type of housing to establish a pattern. If this interpretation is correct,

then it is appropriate to consider areas such as Beacon Hill, Back Bay and South End as independent sectors. Within these areas, a fairly homogeneous pattern is observable, though not necessarily a complete exclusion of alternative, perhaps even drastically different uses adjacent to and even within the sector.* Examples of the latter are the slum land uses characteristic of the Fens area before apartment building commenced or the type of housing still prevalent on the northern slope of Beacon Hill. The broader pattern, that is, the southwestern, western or northwestern suburban trends really reflect only a general direction of expansion, not a sector, though several sector clusters and higher average rents will also be found in the territory. This definition should help to clarify the idea of the sector and it should overcome or properly answer Firey's objections to the incongruity of substantial variations within such districts.

### Leaders of society

The notion of "fashionable" residential areas is equally troublesome. Hoyt's references vary from "leaders of society" and "most fashionable areas" to "high grade districts" and "highest rental areas." Contrary to Hoyt's supposition, these areas are not always synonymous.† Dealing with 142 cities made it necessary to find some relatively common denominator of several factors. Rent classes were used.‡ Implicit in Hoyt's approach, however, is an egregious oversimplification of class structure. In one sense this is curious. Though he deals with both the composition of urban inhabitants and minority groups in at least two separate portions of his study, the relationship of class and income pat-

---

* Hoyt believes zones should be so described. He indicated that "zones or sections are determined by the predominance of the one use, not by its exclusive presence." (Ibid., p. 5.)

† A recent study of Newburyport, for example, indicates that the lowest rent areas are "high in social prestige despite the low rentals. Their low rentals are in part due to their peripheral location." (W. Lloyd Warner and P. S. Lunt, The Social Life of a Modern Community, Yale University Press, New Haven, 1941, p. 232.)

‡ Firey also checked some of these prepositions by using names in the Social Register as an index and found considerable dispersion as well as concentration. (W. Firey, op. cit., pp. 56 and 75, Fig. 2 and 5.) Incidentally, it is somewhat surprising that Firey, as a sociologist, did not fundamentally challenge Hoyt's conception of class structure.

terns is overlooked.* Society is divided into three classes: the upper classes who pay the highest rentals, the lower classes with the lowest rentals and the "intermediate class" somewhere between the two. So gross an assumption of class structure in turn yields equally gross cartographical interpretations. This treatment is really the clue to the many limitations and discrepancies which Firey somewhat unfairly blames on cartography.

It is impossible to detail here the complicated class groupings found in most communities.† For most larger cities where mixed populations are encountered, it is clear that complex and multiple class relationships prevail. These intricate patterns apply particularly to ethnic, religious, and nationality groups which have not diffused throughout the urban area. In Negro, Italian, Jewish and other neighborhoods, strata will be found with upper, middle and lower classes running on economic and sometimes other lines.‡ Class movements within these groups tend locationally toward the upper classes of the group.§ Except for a small minority, there is little interest on the part of lower class members moving in a direction other than toward their own leaders. The bulk of the Jewish groups, for instance, have shifted from the North and West End to the South End, then to parts of Roxbury, Dorchester, Brighton and Brookline. Higher income Italians have moved from the North End toward areas such as East Boston, Somerville, Medford, Everett, Revere, Cambridge, Watertown and Newton. Higher income Irish groups shifted within a century throughout Boston's neighborhoods, that is, from the North, West and South End to South Boston, Jamaica Plain, West Roxbury, Brighton and even to some extent, to Back Bay. Negroes moved from the north slope of Beacon Hill to areas such as the South End, Roxbury and West Cambridge.

When a move is initiated and new nuclei are formed, the direction may tend toward upper income areas; but it is not necessarily toward the "highest" social class** of the community Because of this fact, it is quite misleading to confine the analysis to three simple categories. Quite different and significant theoretical and practical implications follow these distinctions, as shall soon be indicated. Hoyt's thesis, it therefore appears, is really more directly applicable to small, relatively homogeneous communities rather than larger metropolitan areas. If it is contended that possibly the whole pattern was really summarized in his simplified approach, the reply must be that not only is there no evidence of such an intention†† but also that allowance for the type or range of errors that would ensue was not made, assuming that it was at all possible.‡‡ Moreover, it would often be injudicious to act on the basis of this formulation, which in the last analysis was the reason why the study was undertaken.§§

---

* As an example Hoyt states: "Thus in many cities there is a circular or rectangular area of a few blocks in which is located the peak rental area from which rents of all other block slope downward. *Apparently each income group tries to get as close as possible to the next higher group in the economic scale.*" (p. 74.) Earlier Hoyt refers to the desire of people of the same nationality " to live together " and also of " the segregation of sectors populated by different races," but these facts are in no way incorporated in his analysis, (*op. cit.*, p. 62). When he comments on the movements of these groups, there is again no reference to class and ecological patterns within these groups. (*Ibid.*, pp. 120 – 121.)
† A very careful study of this problem for a New England community can be found in W. Lloyd Warner and P. S. Lunt, *op. cit.*, Chapters 6, 9, 20, 21 and 22.
‡ Warner and Lunt concluded that "On the whole . . . both class and ethnic factors operate in the ecological distribution of the Yankee City population." (*Ibid.*, p. 237.)
§ For example, divisions may occur on the basis of color, town, region of origin or other characteristics.

** A similar situation is reflected in Warner and Lunt's study, *op. cit.*, pp. 234 – 238.
†† Hoyt did suggest repeatedly that the research techniques must be adapted by different analysts to the problems under consideration, (H. Hoyt, *op. cit.*, pp. 57 – 58). The sector thesis however, is an interpretation based on the studies of the cities surveyed and this formulation presumably was not subject to such modifications.
‡‡ There may be some question whether such detailed data were available for the 142 cities studied. The 1940 census data could have been used to some extent supplemented by several more careful field studies for special cities. If that was not feasible, the study might have underlined the necessity for more refined analyses of individual cities to take account of these important variations.
§§ Firey reaches a similar conclusion using a quite different approach, (W. Firey, *op. cit.*, p. 86).

### Intermediate income groups

Uncertainty concerning the nature of intermediate groups likewise obscures the analysis. Whom do the intermediate groups represent? If the leaders of society are picked from the Social Register or arbitrarily defined as the highest rental groups, then many fairly well-to-do groups will still live outside the sector(s). A considerable number in this category probably serve as leaders within different class groupings and reside in excellently " groomed " neighborhoods, not necessarily near *the* " leaders of society."

The " intermediate class " is also a catch-all for other groups as well. For example, in Boston it presumably should include the broad middle income group who lived in or owned three deckers. The scope of the category is therefore significant: it forces a reconsideration of the notion of physical contiguity. Obviously only a small portion of the intermediate or even top income groups can live adjacent to the " leaders of society."* Sheer numbers would soon force many to live in closer association with other " intermediate " income groups. Under the circumstances, a considerable physical area of choice is possible. If it is impossible to live next to the nabobs, other alternatives may and probably will be explored. Wide areas, for example, are occupied by moderately wealthy and middle income groups in Boston, but not at all close either physically or socially to the fashionable areas of Back Bay and Beacon Hill or those of Brookline, Newton and Belmont, that is, upper class communities outside of Boston. If the North, West and South End plus East Boston, Charlestown, South Boston, parts of Roxbury and Hyde Park are eliminated as low income areas, there is still a wide physical range within Dorchester, Brighton and Jamaica Plain; and this range increases still further if other communities such as Cambridge, Watertown, Mal-

den, Medford, Arlington, Quincy and others are considered. To explain the patterns in these areas on the monistic principle of upper class polarity is to ignore the fact that not only leadership within groups but also other factors may be much more of an attractive force.

A simple explanation is still possible of the apparent " surrounding " of the " leaders of society." Having very high (if not the highest) rentals, their cluster is conspicuous, not only cartographically but visually as well, since the environs, both physically and socially, are as a rule very satisfying. Lesser socialites and income groups within this larger class will undoubtedly move to the area. Unless special factors intervene, a gradual shading off of high to moderate income neighborhoods will occur.† Allowing for this pattern still does not eliminate the need to explain the locational pattern of the overwhelming majority of the remaining intermediate groups; in short, to ascertain other directive influences which may affect spatial distribution.

### Market mechanism

Before possible changes in the sector thesis are considered, one unstated yet implicit assumption requires consideration. Throughout the analysis, Hoyt has been dealing with the operation of a relatively laissez-faire competitive economy. Past data were searched to discover emergent patterns. Since the conclusions, however, are intended to be extrapolated for practical decisions in the future, they might be misleading if the assumed conditions changed or were changing significantly.

What are the presumed bases of the free market economy? Theoretically ideal conditions include perfect knowledge and mobility, maximization of profit, many buyers and sellers, free entry and departure of productive factors, and homogeneous products. Allowances are usually made in practical problems for imperfections as

---

* Hoyt observed that in several cities intermediate income sectors were found on other sides of the city than where the " highest rental groups " resided. This fact should have indicated the need for some qualification or refinement of the hypothesis concerning the drawing powers of the fashionable areas.

† One exception illustrating the point may be the

frequent absence of " shading off " in central areas. High cost land frequently results in low cost slums adjacent to upper income residences. Most middle income families apparently prefer the advantages of better and cheaper suburban residences to the opportunity of living adjacent to Park Avenue or Beacon Hill socialites.

well as long and short run adjustments.* Real estate, however, is a notorious and oft-cited example of just such market imperfections. Housing, in particular, reflects an additional complication because its long production period and durability contribute to serious and prolonged marketing errors and maladjustments. Such dislocations tend not only to be perpetuated but to affect, perhaps alter, the resulting situation. Yet according to the theory of the market, efficient land uses, with exceptions for occasional distorting factors, are assumed.

Certainly, where the assumptions of the theory hold, such a relationship can in fact be logically demonstrated. Mounting evidence has been accumulating, however, to show that serious derangements have resulted or are occurring, thus indicating that the assumptions are often quite unreal. Traffic snarls, slums and blighted areas, inadequate open spaces, frozen subdivisions, oversupply in retail sites and in wholesale areas, and badly located railroad terminals and classification yards are some concrete examples. Some of these difficulties may be the result of swift, technological changes which cannot be avoided and which may eventually be ironed out. Nonetheless, the sluggish processes may still be an argument for appropriate types of public guidance and controls.

Other uses are doomed to neglect without public intervention because the fundamental requirements for market participation are absent. To compete in the urban land and housing market, uses must be income producing and rather high at that. Uses like playgrounds, parks and good minimum standard housing for low income groups cannot be or at any rate have not been adequately served under such a mechanism. Similarly, the traditional market theory presupposes that overall efficiency follows necessarily the tendency toward minimum costs for

independent decision making units. In point of fact, discrepancies often occur between individual and social costs as the classic factory smoke illustration† suggests. Public intervention is clearly required in such cases and already considerable inroads in the form of zoning and public housing have occurred with this underlying principle as one of the basic justifications. All of these conditions, plus a changing climate of opinion in favor of increasing public assistance, controls and positive planning, and construction and management programs, evidence the introduction of a new and powerful influence shaping land use patterns.

Hoyt's generalizations, on the other hand, tend to be conservative. Real estate promoters, new inventions and technological achievements will indirectly influence city patterns; and Hoyt does call attention to such forces. But men's ideas on what the city should be like are not noticed at all. To an increasing extent, however, these ideas will play a decisive role because of the expanding sphere of government and the obvious inadequacies of present urban and residential patterns. Objective and scholarly, therefore, as the sector analysis is, it is important to remember that its generalizations lean on past conditions, attitudes and ideals and that its bias† is in the direction of the past. Undiscriminating reliance upon its conclusions may produce negative attitudes toward policies or changes that were not examined in Hoyt's study.

## Toward a social interpretation of residential growth and structure

The sector thesis has provided a basis for a more systematic appraisal of the nature of urban land uses. Hoyt himself, however, anticipated the need for revision with further research.‡ Critical analysis and proposals for

---

* Other theoretical analyses have been developed for monopoly as well as for imperfect competition.
† In a statistical, not pejorative sense.
‡ Hoyt, in concluding his introduction, observed that ". . . modification of techniques and suggested generalizations set forth will doubtless prove necessary but at least the analytical method here suggested will provide a starting point and may serve as a basis for its own revision by the new evidence it will uncover." (Hoyt, *op. cit.*, p. 6.)

Actually the modifications proposed here are not based on Hoyt's procedures, though Boston's experience was used to check the analysis. Nonetheless, Hoyt's data can be further checked by other studies. Hoyt's cartographical and block statistics analysis also may prove more fruitful with tighter definitions and a more refined approach.

reformulation do not alter the fact that the study represents a pioneer inquiry and an obvious milestone in land economics theory.

Essentially, two crucial weaknesses characterize the sector thesis, if the previous analysis is correct. Oversimplification precluded certain vital insights despite the fact that useful data were unearthed and certain gross trends established. By assuming that the social attraction to leaders of society was the fundamental locational force, sectors were vaguely defined with principal emphasis placed on the highest rental area. Overlooked was the existence of multiple class relationships, the impossibility of social or physical contiguity except for a small minority and the influence of the other fundamental factors influencing residential location. The second limitation was the somewhat narrow perspective and problem which guided the inquiry. Preservation of investments of financial institutions was an important motivation of the study and the policies expressly or implicitly proposed serve this end. Improvement of general housing conditions was ignored as was the larger problem of preserving and protecting property values and public investments of the community as a whole. Neither were the inadequacies of the present market processes or the building industry considered. Yet, all of these factors may have strategic importance not only for wise public policy but even for the limited objectives Hoyt envisioned.

A more accurate appraisal of locational impulsions is required as a first step in eliminating these defects. A comprehensive approach would require the study of many factors: economic, sociological, geographical, historical, technological and others. Such an analysis cannot be undertaken here. However, the limitations of the existing approaches have been noted and a partial or preliminary basis for reorientation may be proposed. Undoubtedly, upper class attractions which Hoyt emphasized are a vital force;

but it is necessary to remember the complex affinities and selective differentiation for various groups in the community. As a consequence, many more upper class residential sectors may be shown to exist with some tendencies of gradation toward higher income and higher "class" locations. The study of these variant class relationships* within and between social systems, their ecological characteristics and their possible variations is still in the pioneer stage, and further study will probably yield many fruitful insights.†

On the other hand, it should be emphasized that most families particularly in the low and middle income groups also desire a *functionally adequate physical environment*. This physical environment will vary for different social and economic groups as well as different historical periods and stages of technology. Among the diverse conditions sought are adequate access to employment centers for the principal and secondary wage earners; convenient access to schools and shopping centers; and improved physical layouts providing adequate and attractive housing, open space, traffic safety and recreation areas. Others, of course, will think of additional items that might be placed on the list; and the importance of these factors will be shaped by changes in income, social organization, attitudes, technology, urban size, scale and function. Exploration of the range and relative significance of these variations would likewise merit a separate study.

Hoyt, it will be noted, placed special emphasis on the attractions of the upper income sector as the key dynamic locational force. Further analysis of the behavior of class structure and social systems will undoubtedly help to refine the explanation of the empirical uniformities he discovered and some of the unexplained discrepancies.‡ But neither Hoyt nor Firey have devoted much attention in their formulations to the rising income and status of varying groups

---

* Ethnic, national, religious and intellectual groups are included.
† Class attractions and complexities might be systematically explored with the theoretical tools elaborated in cultural anthropology and sociology. In addition to Hoyt's simple assumptions concerning the choice of areas by upper income groups and the tendency for

slightly lower income groups to gather around these nuclei, a clearer identification of the internal cohesions and repulsions of classes and groups can be developed – both for independent and interrelated social systems.
‡ The capacity of the upper and lower income group to live in directly adjoining areas is an illustration.

in the community, particularly low and middle income families; nor have they considered together with these changes the rising housing standards and the growing urge for these groups to live in a better environment where adequate housing in good *physical* as well as social surroundings is available. Significant readjustments of the sector thesis would follow if this additional variable were judged to be as important as class attractions in influencing land use change. Therefore, at the risk of some distortion and lack of refinement in analysis, it might be useful to explore the implications of such an additional assumption or hypothesis, namely that the desire particularly by low and middle income families for a satisfactory or improved housing environment (judged by contemporary standards) is as important a locational determinant as attraction to upper class groups. The differences obtained by comparing the results of this assumption with Hoyt's conclusions are of considerable interest and value in refocusing the sector thesis along normative lines.

### Residential location patterns

First, how much value does this assumption concerning physical environment have in interpreting Boston's residential history? The question might be approached by examining at the outset partially contrary evidence qualifying its application. South Boston, for example, because of its superior physical location might have proved to be a more satisfactory fashionable residential district than South End or Back Bay; and yet it was unsuccessful. Inferior transportation was an important reason for its failure plus the lack of continuity with an already existing fashionable area. The migration to Back Bay from the South End, likewise cannot be explained by prestige alone. Insufficient land sales, industrial and commercial infiltration from the north, plus the depression of 1873, resulted in forced liquidations and conversion to intensive and "inferior" uses. Prestige and status, however, were also important. These considerations account not only for the shift to Back Bay but

the hasty departure of many South End residents following the reduction of land prices and the building of relatively cheaper houses along Columbus Avenue. The shift at the same time from Beacon Hill to Back Bay was also as much of a reflection of status as superior environment. Despite the fact that other elements are involved, for these fashionable districts, the role of prestige was undoubtedly of considerable importance.

On the other hand, the flight from Ft. Hill to Colonnade Row and South End resulted from commercial invasion and profitable conversions of many of the houses into cheap slum quarters for Irish immigrants. The departure from Back Bay illustrated the shift to a new environment to a large extent because of dissatisfaction with the old town houses. Throughout Boston's history, movements of upper income groups in directions other than the southwesterly trends of the Beacon Hill, South End and Back Bay areas are likewise better accounted for by adding the touchstone of environmental adequacy; for instance, East Boston between 1845–60, Dorchester before 1890, and Belmont and Lexington today.

Even more important, a basis exists for interpreting certain locational patterns in areas where the influence of physical or social proximity to upper class districts was clearly minimized, namely the developments in Dorchester, Somerville, Cambridge, Watertown, Medford, Malden and other areas. The assumption is also particularly helpful in explaining movements of the middle and low income groups. Thus, there is evidence of a tendency of the low and middle income families of Boston to improve their housing status as real income rises by seeking more rooms and services and by escaping from the overcrowded "inner cordon."[28] The shifts of these same groups to suburban three deckers are likewise more suitably accounted for on environmental as well as class lines.

One of the virtues of *adding* this assumption lies in the fact that it builds upon rather than destroys the sector analysis: it simply sharpens and corrects a distorted focus. Class attractions (broadened for varying groups and social systems) are not dismissed; but other equally important factors are taken into account or emphasized and many discrepancies in interpretations are eliminated.*

### Policy and normative issues

Financial institutions and zoning agencies were expected to apply the conclusions of the sector thesis.† Presumably " good " expanding areas were to be identified for investment, and other " good " areas in which investments were made were to be guarded. Perhaps Hoyt may not have intended it as such, but there is a strong emphasis in the study in favor of preserving the better neighborhoods rather than improving the poorer ones. That suspicion is further supported by the fact that the study was made for the Federal Housing Administration whose interest and experience to date have been primarily to protect its insured loans and which has shown little interest in other points of view.‡

Avoidance of central areas further reflects the disinclination to tamper with the market mechanism. Inflated valuations based largely on false expectations and complicated by the jungle of blighted properties have created a situation which market adjustments alone can scarcely cure within any reasonable period of time. If, however, our central urban areas are to be reclaimed for many purposes including housing, government intervention and subsidy, it is generally conceded, are necessary. Instead of arresting existing trends, the emphasis on limiting investments only to good areas would intensify them. New investments in the older areas even under a rehabilitation program do not conveniently fit into the sector analysis. The community, however, has a strong interest in reversing or slowing down these unfavorable trends. Knowing, moreover, the needs and desires of many groups to live in the center, albeit in a satisfying environment, it is reasonable to suppose that new residential neighborhoods and other needed land uses could be successfully established. Obviously, most of the North, West and South End, East and South Boston, Charlestown and other areas might qualify for redevelopment for most, if not all, income groups.

The sector thesis, as formulated and applied, tends to encourage the exclusion of certain groups because of their alleged " inharmonious " characteristics. That they want to " get in " is taken for granted generally and in particular by the simple assumption of upper class attractions. Exaggerated emphasis of this desire would be corrected, however, by the correlative interest in decent housing and salutary neighborhoods which the second premise stresses. Satisfaction of these requirements may modify this other pressure, lessen the possibility of intergroup friction and misunderstanding and perhaps create a basis for greater social and group participation in common activities.

An important illustration of this principle is reflected in the housing of minorities. Negroes, for example, are denied decent quarters in many areas and cooped up in noisome slums; but there is still continual panic among whites lest these Negroes burst into a " good " area and destroy property values. Hoyt's analysis of the substandard conditions characteristic of Negro neighborhoods, his comments concerning the effect on rents of the presence of Negroes in twilight zones, plus the assumption of upper class attractions and the investment perspective perpetually chary of " racial mixtures," and " in-

---

* The emphasis on this factor may also be quite significant for Firey's analysis as well. The goal of a better environment tends to be greatly underemphasized in his study. That is because Firey, to develop his points more sharply, picks not altogether representative areas like the North and South End, Beacon Hill, Back Bay and the Common rather than middle and low income areas such as Dorchester, Brighton and parts of Jamaica Plain. Even for those areas selected by Firey, such as the North End and Back Bay, part of the explanation of the departure from the area is the desire to change the physical environment. The shift, of course, may be explained on the basis of the acceptance of new social relationships and ideals and can be described and analyzed as such. Nonetheless, it is important to emphasize that the merits of any analysis, even in terms of social and cultural systems, depends upon proper appraisal of the component elements within these systems.

† Hoyt also assumed the techniques could be used in demarcating slum areas as well as other purposes.

‡ In fact, it is a matter of common knowledge that its policies of encouragement of peripheral building have tended to intensify the decline of other areas.

harmonious groups " adds fuel to this hysteria.*
Were it equally clear that the desire of Negroes,
as of others groups, is also to find a decent
home and neighborhood and that frustration in
this direction too would push them with even
greater pressure toward " good " white areas,
the possibility of a more intelligent solution
might be explored. Better housing made available to these groups would lessen the pressures
and also, it is believed get rid of some of the
vicious myths associated with Negroes and housing. Movement of a few Negroes into white
areas would not imply mass entry, white mig-
rations and huge financial losses. Racial prejudice may not disappear, but surely a greater
possibility for accommodation and mutual understanding might then be encouraged.

Since many groups in the community cannot
be served through the economic mechanism,
either a solution calling for wholesale improvement of housing is idle speculation or else
" extra-economic " means are required. Unfortunately, ordinary market forces augur no sign
of improvement within a reasonable period. Nor
is it reasonable to anticipate a technological revolution in the building industry.† A variety of
possiblities, however, may be tapped through
government action including more subsidized
housing for low income groups, more and well-
distributed parks and open spaces, and reclamation of wasted or misused areas. None of these
positive, corrective measures are suggested by
Hoyt's analysis, even if only to preserve private
land values and investments. From a community
point of view, however, such a course of action
is mandatory if social conditions and values
throughout the community are to be improved
and organized on a sounder basis.

For Boston, in particular, such a program is in
line with its past policies. The local government
has been an active partner in land and housing
development as illustrated in the South End and
Back Bay operations. The objective then was to
encourage upper income residence within the
corporate boundaries. Today the loss of revenues
is even more serious, since in the past at least,
Boston continued to grow despite the steady
drift of population beyond its borders.‡ Present
programs will differ in that all income groups
must be served if losses to the community are
to be minimized. Criteria to judge these new
goals and balance them against costs, private
and social, are not easy to formulate or apply
and research and analysis are sorely needed. It
is of considerable importance that much of the
theoretical and empirical inquiries into growth
and structure be reexamined and extended in
directions where such a contribution may be
made.

## Summary

This discussion critically examines two leading hypotheses concerning residential growth
and structure. Walter Firey's critique of the
sector thesis is rejected on the grounds that the
position of Homer Hoyt is misinterpreted and
much of the contradictory evidence is either
faulty or consistent with the sector theory.
Though Firey's hypothesis that cultural factors
affect " spatial adaptation " may provide many
useful insights in the study of land uses and
" social systems," it is of little value in determining patterns of residential location and
growth.

Also Firey's " theory " of proportionalization
of ends, because of its vagueness and generality,
reveals itself to be a poor instrument for decisions concerning the best " allocation of space."

Serious defects in Hoyt's thesis were also
noted, namely: (a) its ambiguous formulation
and use of the sector concept; (b) its over-
simplified version of class structure; (c) its distorted dependence on upper class " attractions "
as a basis for interpreting shifts in residential
location; (d) the inaccuracy of some of the empirical generalizations; (e) its potentially mis-

---

* " It is in the twilight zone where members of different
races live together that racial mixtures tend to have
depressing effects upon land values and therefore upon
rents." (Hoyt, *op. cit.*, p. 62). Hoyt nowhere suggests a
policy of exclusion, yet this conclusion is inescapable
given these assumptions and emphases.

† Such a possibility is not denied; that it is a reasonable
probability is challenged, however.
‡ Many of Boston's suburbs were also within its corporate boundaries.

leading reliance on nineteenth-century free market residential trends; and finally, (f) the narrow perspectives resulting from the essential purpose of the inquiry.

As a corrective, broader and possibly more fruitful assumptions concerning the determinants of residential location are recommended. The factors influencing relocation trends of Boston's middle income groups indicate some of the *additional* forces that warrant consideration. Especially important is the need for a more refined analysis of class structure and greater emphasis on a functionally adequate physical and social environment. These additional criteria furnish a more illuminating guide to Boston's land use history as well as a basis for resolving moot and unsatisfactory points in Hoyt's hypothesis. They also furnish a more socially satisfactory guide for policy decisions designed to promote the most efficient use or reuse of all residential neighborhoods. Finally, a more satisfactory approach is thereby indicated for relieving the housing pressures confronting minorities, thus moderating group antagonisms and increasing the possibilities for mutual accommodation and tolerance.

# The neighborhood unit formula

CLARENCE A. PERRY

An instrument that is required to develop house building into a large-scale industry is a new form of cooperative relationship into which a municipality and a construction corporation could enter. By its terms the city would use its powers to place a large building plot within the reach of a corporation and, in return, the latter would erect upon the plot a residential development of a character yielding public benefits not attainable under existing real estate methods. Before the city could obtain from the legislature power to condemn land and turn it over to the corporation, however, the lawmakers would have to be convinced that the resulting benefits would be substantial enough to justify another extension of eminent domain powers. The only device that will meet this need is a formula defining the requirements which projects would have to meet in order to become the subject of this bargain. Such an instrumentality would enable a corporation to shape up the right kind of project and the municipality could use it as a yardstick in determining whether a submitted project would give citizens the stipulated benefits.

To be serviceable in the highest degree this formula should meet certain requirements:

1. It should not be a detailed plan of a model residential development, since there are many local conditions which a specific plan would not meet. Instead it should state principles and standards in definite, objective terms which the professional planner could apply in preparing a plan suited to the topography and other characteristics of a particular site.

2. It should be expressed in city planning terms, since it would deal with building plots, highways, recreation spaces, uses of land, loca-

Reprinted from Housing for the Machine Age, *Russell Sage Foundation, 1939, pp. 49–76, with permission of the publisher.*

tion of public buildings, and those public services which require structures large enough to involve site planning.

3. To be practical, it should describe a project sufficiently self-contained so that, with the boundaries fixed, it would be possible to go forward with construction without waiting for the planning of adjacent areas. Many an excellent project has failed of realization because there was no way of detaching it from plans relating to surrounding districts and dealing with the project by itself.

As to working out the content of the formula, the method of procedure seems clear. It should cover both dwellings and their environment, the extent of the latter being – for city planning purposes – that area which embraces all the public facilities and conditions required by the average family for its comfort and proper development within the vicinity of its dwelling. In this study that area is called the family's "neighborhood." The facilities it should contain are apparent after a moment's reflection. They include at the least (1) an elementary school; (2) retail stores; and (3) public recreation facilities.

The conditions surrounding the dwelling which a family most consciously seeks come under the head of residential character. This quality depends upon many and varied features. In an apartment house district, it may rest upon location of the site, architecture of the building, or the character of its courts. In a single-family district, harmony in the style of dwellings, amount of yard devoted to lawns and planting, and comprehensiveness and excellence of the entire development plan govern residential quality. Most important in this day of swift-moving automobiles is street safety. This can best be achieved by constructing a highway system that reduces the points where pedestrians and vehicles cross paths and that keeps through traffic entirely out of a residential district.

The formula for a city neighborhood, then, must be such that when embodied in an actual development all its residents will be taken care of as respects the following points: They will all be within convenient access to an elementary school, adequate common play spaces, and retail shopping districts. Furthermore, their district will enjoy a distinctive character, because of qualities pertaining visibly to its terrain and structure, not the least of which will be a reduced risk from vehicular accidents.

## Neighborhood unit principles

A formula which, it is believed, meets all the above requirements was elaborated and published in volume 7 – Neighborhood and Community Planning – of the Regional Survey of New York and Its Environs.[1] In that publication, " the neighborhood unit – a scheme of arrangement for the family-life community " is set forth in detail. Essentially, it consists of six principles :

1. *Size.* A residential unit development should provide housing for that population for which one elementary school is ordinarily required, its actual area depending upon its population density.

2. *Boundaries.* The unit should be bounded on all sides by arterial streets, sufficiently wide to facilitate its bypassing, instead of penetration, by through traffic.

3. *Open spaces.* A system of small parks and recreation spaces, planned to meet the needs of the particular neighborhood, should be provided.

4. *Institution sites.* Sites for the school and other institutions having service spheres coinciding with the limits of the unit should be suitably grouped about a central point, or common.

5. *Local shops.* One or more shopping districts, adequate for the population to be served, should be laid out in the circumference of the unit, preferably at traffic junctions and adjacent to similar districts of adjoining neighborhoods.

6. *Internal street system.* The unit should be provided with a special street system, each highway being proportioned to its probable traffic load, and the street net as a whole being designed to facilitate circulation within the unit and to discourage its use by through traffic.

The six principles above enumerated do not constitute the description of a real estate development or of urban neighborhoods in general. Together they do not make a plan. They are principles which a professional planner – if so disposed – can observe in the making of a development plan. If they are complied with, there will result a neighborhood community in which the fundamental needs of family life will be met more completely, it is believed, than they are now by the usual residential sections in cities and villages.

In this scheme, the neighborhood is regarded both as a unit of a larger whole and as an entity. It is not held, however, that in an ideal city plan the whole municipality could be laid out in neighborhood units. It is recognized that a city is composed of various areas each of which is devoted to a dominant function. There are industrial districts, business districts, and large areas used as parks and cemeteries. A neighborhood unit would have local retail business areas, but besides these there would also be downtown or main business districts, and subsidiary business centers serving large sections.

It is apparent that the unit scheme can be fully applied only to *new* developments. Thus it is limited to the unbuilt areas around the urban fringe and to central deteriorated sections, large enough and sufficiently blighted to warrant reconstruction. Nor is it expected that the whole of a residential section, in any practical plan, could be laid out in unit districts. There would generally be irregular areas set off by main highways, railways, streams, quarries, or parks, of a size or location that would make them unsuited for inclusion in a unit plan.

In more detail just what do the six principles of the neighborhood unit formula involve? Professional planners and other specialists may wish to refer to the original presentation in volume 7 of the New York Regional Plan. For the general reader the following condensation of that presentation will suffice.

### Size relations

A residential unit development should provide housing for that population for which one elementary school is ordinarily required, its actual area depending upon population density.

What, as to the number of residents, does this requirement really indicate? According to authorities in school administration, a public school equipped with an auditorium, a gymnasium, and other accessories, should have a capacity of from 1,000 to 1,600 pupils. Such a costly plant, they hold, should handle a sizable load. As a matter of fact, however, public schools are being built in small communities for 500 and even fewer pupils, while large cities, like New York, are constructing schools with 2,500 seats. The most practical procedure in determining the standard for a given city is to ascertain from the local school board the number of pupils it considers requisite for a model elementary school, and to adopt that figure.

The next question is: What proportion of the total population is represented by boys and girls in the elementary school age-group? This ratio varies greatly in American cities, but the average is about one-sixth. On the basis of the standard capacities given above, an efficient urban school district may range in population from 3,000 to 9,600 or say 10,000 persons. From the standpoint of educational service it is evident that considerable latitude is allowable in fixing the population standard.

There are, however, several other requirements that must be met, in which area or distance is a factor. Suppose we take a neighborhood of 6,000 people. Would the area of such a district be so great that children living at its border would have to walk too far in attending a school at its center? Obviously, the answer depends on how closely dwellings are placed. Let us take the density of 37.5 persons per acre, that is frequently found in single-family subdivisions. The requisite plot would contain 160 acres. If it were square, it would be half a mile, or 2,640 feet, on a side. A circle with a radius of a quarter-mile could be inscribed within it. Thus a school located at its center would be within a quarter of a mile of all its families except those living in the corners, outside the circle, and the farthermost of those would be only a third of a mile from the center.

Take an area less populous – that of 5,000

people in a 200-acre plot, a common suburban density of only 25 to the acre. Here the great bulk of the residents would be within a radius of only 156 feet beyond a quarter of a mile.

In these two examples we have dealt with probably the greatest travel distance that would be required by a commercial development or an efficient school administration. There might be sparser subdivisions, but there is no good reason why they should be greater than 200 acres, or indeed than 160 acres. When we move toward the center of the city higher densities are usually encountered. Even though school districts may contain more people, the congestion is so much greater that there is a net shrinkage in the size and the distance to be traveled. Pupils in slum sections seldom have to walk as much as a quarter of a mile.

Let us now see what educators say about the school radius. " Children of the elementary school grade should not be required to travel more than one-half mile to school."[2] The Com-

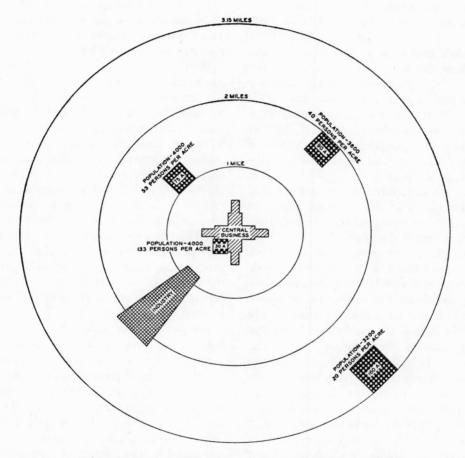

*Figure 1. Neighborhood unit scheme applied to a city of 200,000 population; size as affected by density and location.*

Source: Regional Plan Association, Inc, New York City.

mittee on School House Planning of the National Education Association made practically the same recommendation in these words: " In cities it is generally agreed that the contributing area for an elementary school may have a radius of one-half to three-quarters of a mile."[3] From these statements it is clear that the desirable population for a school, when housed at current densities, will live well within the travel distance which our educators say should not be exceeded.

Will a population size that meets the educational requirements fit the other neighborhood service radii? Among city planners it is a rule of thumb that families should be able to find a grocery or drug store within a half-mile of the home – the same maximum travel standard as the school. According to the unit formula, shopping districts are located in the periphery of the neighborhood, instead of, as in a village, at the center. There can be as many districts as the population's buying capacity requires and they may be located at points in the rim where convenience indicates. In the 160-acre plot, of a half-mile on the side, four districts at the corners would bring shopping facilities within a quarter of a mile for most families, while only two districts at diagonally opposite corners would place these facilities within a third of a mile for a majority of the residents. Thus our school district size comes within the travel requirements for retail shopping.

As to the playground service, wide experience shows that most children will not travel more than a quarter of a mile to use a playground. A large schoolyard at the center of a square 160-acre plot would be within this quarter-mile radius for the bulk of the children, and even the farthermost families would be only a third of a mile away. Many times it will be feasible to provide more than one play space, bringing this facility still nearer its patrons. In single-family districts, where home yards take care of small tots, a public playfield is more especially needed for the baseball and other large-space games of older youngsters. Under the topic "Open Spaces," the recreational service will be discussed in detail.

Size is a factor in two other aspects of the model neighborhood community – the achievement of a distinctive residential quality, and the possession of a rich associational life. Since both these points can be more appropriately discussed in detail later on, only an assurance need be given here that the unit formula does satisfy the two requirements as to area and as to desirable population.

## Boundaries

The unit should be bounded on all sides by arterial streets, sufficiently wide to facilitate its by-passing, instead of penetration, by through traffic.

The most important reason for wide highways as boundaries arises from their relation to street safety. The unit district is not too large, according to the opinion of an authoritative engineer,[4] to be treated as a partly closed cell in urban street systems, without doing violence to the highway requirements for general circulation.

With adequate express channels in the circumference of a unit, through traffic will have no excuse for invading its territory, and its own internal streets can fairly and deliberately be made inconvenient and forbidding for vehicles having no destination within the neighborhood confines. If any of the original boundaries of a unit district are not suited for through traffic, they should be widened by taking land, if necessary, from the unit area. Sometimes there will be temptation to use an existing park, a stream, or a railway as a unit boundary, in place of lining that side with a wide highway. It is not a safe thing to do, since the absence of a channel for through traffic on that side will generally force such traffic into one of the neighborhood's own internal streets.

Another value of wide and conspicuous boundaries is that they enable residents and public in general to see the limits of the community and visualize it as a distinct entity. Like a fence around a private lot, they heighten the motive for local improvement by defining the area of local responsibility; " Here neighborhood maintenance ends." Residential pride may also be stimulated by the erection of ornamental arches and architectural markers of various sorts.

## Open spaces

A system of small parks and recreation spaces, planned to meet the needs of the particular neighborhood, should be provided.

The large-scale advantage of unit planning shows up with special clearness in the ease with

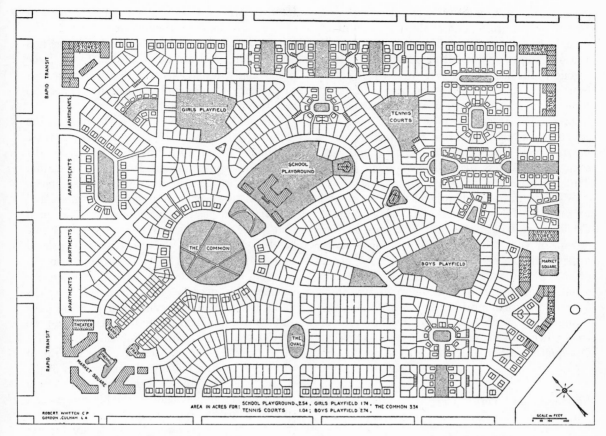

*Figure 2. A 160-acre neighborhood unit subdivision; liberal recreation spaces gained through comprehensive planning.*

Source: Robert Whitten, Architect, assisted by Gordon Culham, Landscape Architect.

which it makes possible abundant provision for play close to the family dwelling. Having a large area to draw on, and a definite and numerous clientele to provide for, the economies and efficiency of quantity production are attainable in a high degree. A few feet taken off from the depth of a number of lots and put together in a playground that will serve all the owners produces a valuable community asset without appreciable loss to anyone.

Again, the custom-made planning – which is inherent in the unit scheme – makes it possible to avoid the wastes incidental to undifferentiated subdivision layouts. These are especially

noticeable in the traditional rectangular street system, wherein two or three standard street widths are applied by a rule of thumb long before the mappers can know much about future traffic requirements. Under such circumstances it is not strange that many streets are found eventually to be of excessive width. In a unit project the function of each internal highway is determined at the time it is laid out and it can therefore be precisely adapted to its traffic load.

The layout of a 160-acre subdivision, accommodating 6,000 residents, developed in a study* of a district in the Borough of Queens, carried on by the late Robert Whitten, is shown on

---

* Originally presented in Neighborhood Unit, Monograph 1, New York Regional Plan, vol. 7, p. 36; and further discussed in The Economics of Land Sub-division, Part 3 of Monograph 3, p. 339 of the same volume. Its

research was based upon a planning study made of an actual tract of land located in a large unsubdivided area north of Jamaica in the Borough of Queens.

page 99. An examination of it will reveal that 10.6 (8.6 plus greens and circles 2.0) percent of its area is devoted to small parks, playgrounds, and other open spaces, all of which was gained through unit advantages over the standard gridiron system. Three-quarters of the gain came from savings in street area and the remainder from shallower lots. Because of the narrower streets it was calculated that the street improvements for this neighborhood plan would cost some $400,000 less than they would in a standard layout of the same size and character.

What part of a neighborhood unit plot should be set aside for small parks and playgrounds? Obviously no hard and fast rule can be laid down. In the Whitten study – a single-family district – the recreation areas covered 17 acres, or 10.6 percent of the total area. That suggests a flat 10 percent as a good figure to aim at in open or suburban unit subdivisions. Oftentimes it should be possible to exceed it. The kinds of uses which may be made of 16 acres – 10 percent of a quarter-section – are indicated in the following table:

*Recreation and Park Spaces in a Single-family Neighborhood Unit of 160 Acres*

| Kind of area | Acres |
|---|---|
| School grounds—building site and playgrounds for the younger children | 3.00 |
| Playfields—one for boys and another for girls | 5.50 |
| Tennis courts—12 courts | 2.25 |
| Common or civic square | 2.25 |
| Small parks—planted ovals and circles | 3.00 |
| Total | 16.00 |

Setting up a standard recreational allotment for apartment house units is a more difficult matter. Naturally these developments will vary widely in density and total area. The arrangement of structures and highways – governed by uncontrollable conditions surrounding the unit – will in certain instances permit larger play spaces than will be possible in others. Again it is not easy to draw a line between " space around the building" and a landscaped court which serves, or should serve, the purposes of a park.

The social objective to be kept in mind is plain. The practice of allowing city landowners to load their premises so heavily with apartment houses that no space is left on the plots

for the normal physical and moral development of tenants' children should be restricted. The neighborhood unit scheme furnishes a method whereby this evil can be avoided in future large multi-family developments with a minimum cost to property owners and a maximum benefit to society.

The guiding principle then is the need of the children and youths who are to live in these apartment house unit districts. Ordinarily, the larger the population the larger the recreation allotment, is the rule that should be applied. There is, however, a minimum allowance, and that has been passed when the space is so small that there is insufficient room for sports like baseball and football. Whether a neighborhood community covers 40, 80, or 160 acres, its youths will be much alike and have the same developmental needs. These large-space sports mean as much to the training of growing boys and youths in factories and offices as they do to those in high schools and colleges. Unless these facilities are accessible for the margin of work days and on holidays, large portions of the classes who most need them will never enjoy them. The large playfields in the big central and suburban parks, provided in most cities, are crowded on holidays and too far away for use at the end of a work day.

A distribution of recreation spaces is presented on page 101 which should be regarded as the minimum provision in an apartment house unit that is planned to meet the outdoor needs of its children and youths. It is too liberal for a downtown slum area.

It is probable, however, that even the above minimum provision will be found too spacious to include in a unit designed for the reconstruction of a central slum district in the larger cities. But there is a housing program which would meet this situation.

Rebuild these costly areas in, say, 20- or 30-acre neighborhood units. There is no physical reason why such developments should not contain spacious lawns, shrubbery, pools, handball courts, and gymnasiums. Through the use of such common facilities residents would become rapidly acquainted. People who could afford these apartments would be well able to enter into cooperative schemes for the recreational life of their boys and girls. For example, such a group would have little difficulty in arranging for a weekend, all-year rural camp for their children, to which every Friday afternoon they would be transported by bus.

*Recreation Spaces for an Apartment House Unit*

| Kind of use | Acres |
|---|---|
| Small children's playground, next to school | 1 |
| Older children's playground, next to school | 2 |
| Combined baseball and football field (300 feet by 435.6 feet) | 3 |
| Hockey field for girls (200 feet by 300 feet) | 1⅓ |
| Site of school building, landscaped area and grandstand | 2⅔ |
| Total | 10 |

Children of the higher income groups who enjoy a home in the country and one in the city, attend high or preparatory school, college, or university, and thus have superior advantages, do not need large recreational areas near their homes. They belong manifestly to the class for whom the downtown apartment units should be planned and constructed. For families that have less access to rural outdoor life, fuller recreational provision should exist within the neighborhood of their homes.

In apartment house units, landscaped courts may also serve certain play purposes. There may be lawns on which toddlers may romp and sand boxes where they may dig – under the eyes of nurses or mothers. Active or noisy play, however, in an enclosed court is generally objectionable. The chief enjoyment which courts can contribute is the delight to the senses that comes from lawn, shrubbery, and flowers. Is there any standard as to the amount which should be required in multi-family units?

A certain minimum requirement is set up by zoning ordinances. This usually is for the purpose of assuring to tenants adequate air and light, and belongs in a sanitary rather than an esthetic category. If an apartment house unit could not achieve more openness than municipal zoning ordinarily secures, it should be considered lacking in one of its chief virtues.

A standard of light which has been suggested by city planning authorities and which does automatically secure considerable openness requires that each structure be separated from its neighbor by a distance equal to its height.

When this is observed, each ground-floor window commands a view of at least 45 degrees of sky. While this standard should never be violated, it ought generally, in a unit project, to be exceeded. Within the large frame of a school district unit, it should be easy to stagger the dwellings, or arrange them in echelon or step form, thereby securing attractive vistas in great abundance. As an example, note how happily this effect has been achieved in Plan B, known as the Mathews Plan, for the World's Fair district.

Of course, the unit plan is supposed to provide only for the strictly neighborhood needs. These do not include golf links, sea beaches, zoological museums, woodland picnicking grounds, or any of the other opportunities usually associated with the large city or suburban park.

In a word, then, the unit scheme sets up the principle that every urban neighborhood catering to families should contain within its own boundaries facilities for a normal recreational life, shaped to fit local conditions. Furthermore, if play spaces can be incorporated in the neighborhood plan while it is being formed, they will not only be much more efficient but their cost will be hardly noticeable.

### Institution sites

Sites for the school and other institutions having service spheres coinciding with the limits of the unit should be suitably grouped about a central point, or common.

We now come to the organization of the neighborhood community center. Its structural components are obvious. First, is the elementary school. Next is a branch of the public library, unless as in some progressive cities this is included in the school plant. In well-to-do neighborhoods there might be a separate community building for social, club, and indoor recreational activities. There is no practical reason, however, why this structure should not be combined with the school. It would usually possess an auditorium equipped for stage productions; a gymnasium; a pool; and some smaller meeting-rooms. Located adjacent to the school, the pupils could make use of the auditorium and gymnasium without interfering very much with the adult and end-of-the-day, or holiday, occasions.

The difficulties encountered in a combined use of buildings are mainly administrative. A community clubhouse, in these modern days, must permit smoking, keep open until late hours, and altogether encourage an atmosphere of gaiety and freedom that is quite foreign to the traditional school. If local residents took an active part in the management of both institutions, however, it should be possible to make a practical cooperative arrangement. This might be worked out most satisfactorily with a community building equipped and administered pri-

A plot reserved for a community church could be used for residences or some other neighborhood institution if circumstances later prevented the carrying out of the original plan. A church whose members will come largely from outside the neighborhood should be placed at a street junction in the periphery of the unit. The weddings, funerals, christenings, and other ceremonies which take place in churches generally crowd the vicinity with motor cars. A neighborhood should not begrudge the street space required for the occasional ceremonies of its own residents. However, in selecting the components of the neighborhood community care can well be taken to avoid assigning central or interior

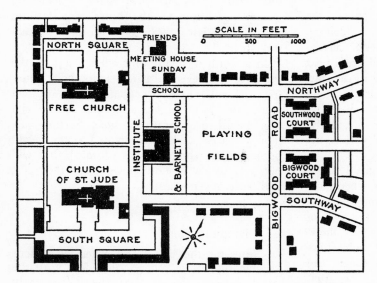

*Figure 3. Central square, Hampstead garden suburb, England.*

Source: New York Regional Plan, volume 7.

marily for its social and recreational purposes, but so arranged that pupils, entering through covered passageways, could make a scheduled use of the auditorium and gymnasium. Removing the clubhouse atmosphere would be simply a janitorial task. Instructors could bring the pedagogical atmosphere with them.

A place in the community center area should be reserved for a church, provided it is known in advance that its parish is to be generally conterminous with the neighborhood. Community congregations in which several denominations have joined for carrying on worship and other religious activities do exist, and it is obvious that such bodies would find the integrated neighborhood a congenial environment.

locations to any institution that frequently draws together large crowds of strangers.

For the same reason, and for its own intrinsic advantage, a commercial motion picture house, a fraternal lodge, or any other institution whose supporting population is ordinarily larger than that of a school-district neighborhood, should be located, not within a unit, but at the point where a cluster of neighborhoods comes together, generally a business center.

If school, library, community house, and church can be grouped around a common in the center of the unit, that will be the most convenient arrangement for the residents. Such a disposition will also make possible an architectural effect of great civic value. Fronting upon a square, the facade of each structure will be viewed from a greater perspective, and the motive for endowing it with a dignified design will be enhanced. As one of a group, there will also be reason to fit it into an attractive composition. Thus the square itself will be invested with a meaning, a symbolism, more significant than the mere sum of its parts. It will be a visible sign of unity. Obviously this effect, if it is to be nicely wrought, will have to be worked out by an architect or planner possessed of skill and taste. When the unit is constructed under a single comprehensive management, there should be no difficulty in securing adequate talent for this purpose.

The square itself will be an appropriate location for a flagpole, a memorial monument, a bandstand, or an ornamental fountain. In the common life of the neighborhood it will function as the place of local celebrations. Here, on Independence Day, the Flag will be raised, the Declaration of Independence be recited, and the citizenry urged to patriotic deeds by eloquent orators.

### Local shops

One or more shopping districts, adequate for the population to be served, should be laid out in the circumference of the unit, preferably at traffic junctions and adjacent to similar districts of adjoining neighborhoods.

Under this head we approach a municipal problem of great importance – the zoning of business and residential districts. That the present methods have not protected residential character to the degree that was expected is admitted by even the best friends of zoning. An explanation for this condition is offered by the Saint Louis City Plan Commission.[5]

When zoning was first undertaken, there were no scientific data as to the relative amount of land needed for various types of urban land use. Lacking such data and standards, it was but natural that the early zoning was unscientific and, consequently, failed to exert a beneficial influence in stabilizing population and in moulding the form and character of the city.

Residential property pays more taxes than all other classes of property combined, but zoning has failed to protect this huge investment. More than one-third of all residence property in Saint Louis is zoned for a lower classification, such as commerce or industry.

Commercial areas are 94 percent overzoned.

Further evidence of the same tendency is given by Edward M. Bassett – the "father of zoning" – in his recent authoritative work entitled Zoning:

It cannot be denied that municipalities of all sorts, especially towns, have been prone to place too much street frontage in business districts.

In some towns one hundred times as much street frontage has been placed in business districts as is likely to be used for business purposes in two generations.[6]

In view of the fact that the protection of residential quality from the depressing effect of nearby business was one of the foremost reasons for the institution of zoning, the above evidences of failure would at first sight seem highly discouraging. Such an attitude, however, would overlook the very substantial improvement in man's control of his environment which zoning has wrought. There are thousands of fine dwelling areas whose stability has been greatly strengthened by zoning. Most important of all is the fundamental principle that it has firmly established, viz., that the uses of property are matters of public concern, so vital that the state is justified in using its police power in a reasonable regulation of them. The device is sound. It is the method of applying it wherein improvement is needed.

The difficulties that surrounded zoning when it was first launched were great. Since zoning was a public regulative measure, there was a natural necessity, and desirability, to bring the whole city within its scope. Zoners began with the central districts and worked toward the periphery. They had no fixed pattern and had they possessed one they could not have applied it to the huge structural improvements of the downtown sections of our complicated commercial cities. An area that was dominated by dwellings they zoned as a residential district even though it contained some stores and factories. Non-residential structures could remain but no new ones could be erected. In a similar way they laid down business and "unrestricted" districts, factories or any type of use being permitted under the latter category. It was a workable method. It is difficult to see how, under the circumstances, a better one to begin with could have been devised.

In unbuilt areas, the task of the zoners was still harder. They had no existing structures to serve as a guide. It was plain that low land and land along railways or streams was suitable for industrial purposes, and that frontage on main highways was desirable for stores. Drawing the lines which determined the precise limits of those use-districts was not easy, however, and yet they were very important, since they also defined the residential zones.

The characteristics of business and industrial plots being so much plainer, and those uses being regarded economically as so much more important, it is not strange that in the allotment of land they were taken care of first and residential use given what remained. Furthermore, the central areas, where zoners first worked, were so largely devoted to business and industry that the experience with them yielded exaggerated notions as to the requirements of those uses. It was natural that the importance of these sections should govern the treatment of unimproved sections. May this not explain why the method has not more satisfactorily protected the character of residential districts?

When a zoner lays out use-districts in an unimproved area according to a zoning ordinance, he is allotting plots to specific functions. He is engaged in city planning. He must have not only a basis for determining what *kind* of land shall be devoted to a particular function, but also a notion as to how *much* of each kind of functioning is required per unit of population. Where now is he to seek these standards? Shall he take them from the wild, uncontrolled urban growth which zoning found when it came into existence? If not there, where or how shall he acquire the necessary standards?

It is here that the neighborhood unit scheme comes forward with a suggestion. Its offering does not directly deal with industrial districts

or existing business or residential districts, except where they need rebuilding for the use of dwellings. Its field is that of relating retail business to new residential districts. Its underlying principle is simple. The logical way to effect this relation is to break the new area up into more or less uniform divisions and then apportion to each part the number and kinds of stores which will be needed by the residents for whom that part will be planned.

The basis suggested for making such divisions is the neighborhood unit, that is, a public school district of from 3,000 to 10,000 people. The area occupied by the dwellings of such a population need not exceed a half-mile radius, which, city planners hold, is the maximum distance families should have to travel to reach a retail store. Also, within this same unit the dwellings – as has been stated – are conveniently located as respects not only the school but playgrounds and other neighborhood institutions. The unit is self-contained except as to places of work of its inhabitants and those services which ordinarily reach a city-wide clientele.

Coming now to the main detail – what is the number of retail stores which should be provided for a given population? Obviously no city planner, however proficient, has the final answer to this question. It is a problem that does not permit exact determination. Several studies have, however, been carried on which throw light upon the matter. Here it is sufficient to say that considering their conclusions, they have led the writer to the belief that *one* store per 100 of population to be accommodated is a fair working rule.

The truth is that we do not yet possess enough experience or data upon which to base a scientific determination. Consider then how much better off in this respect we should be if the planning and construction of neighborhood units were to become a recognized practice. In each case there would be somewhat similar conditions. The unit developments would have easily discovered characteristics, and their business data would be capable of more accurate interpretations. Furthermore such data, continually reinforced by new experience, would be more readily available for neighborhood planning because there would then be an agency, charged with the function of developing and publishing this scientific knowledge. The government would be called upon to participate in the shaping and supervision of the unit developments and public interest would require it to be concerned – as in principle it is now – in the business zoning of the neighborhood districts.

As to location of the unit business zone, several considerations demand a new principle. Villages, towns, and cities uniformly have business at the center. They grow up around commercial and industrial activities. The neighborhood contemplated by the unit scheme, however, is primarily a residential district and its workers go daily to occupations in other parts of the city, mainly downtown districts. The reasons for not locating its business zone in the center of the unit pertain to (1) the welfare of the commuiity, and (2) the intrinsic interests of business.

In the first place, the unit area is so compact that a collection of stores anywhere in its interior would extend their contact with dwellings and their blemish upon residential quality. Again, the supplying of goods for these stores would bring numerous trucks across the paths of boys and girls going to school and playfields, as well as occasion noise and traffic in an area where quiet and tranquility are desirable. Furthermore, the unit is too small to accommodate both a civic and a shopping group in its central region.

To understand what constitutes a good location for a store we must think about business practices. In selecting a site for a new chain store, the management sends out experts to make counts of the number of persons passing points which are under consideration. Those locations showing the highest rates are, other conditions being equal, the most desirable. Accessibility to population is a prime requisite in a store site.

It is one of the advantages of the unit scheme that it makes good business locations more definite and more easily found. Each neighborhood, being a concentration of families, whose workers pass daily through one, two, or possibly three main portals, the canalization of traffic is automatic. These portals are naturally located at the transit stations, or traffic junctions, in the main highways which bound the unit. Despite the telephone, the facile delivery services, and the automobile, residents frequently find it convenient to stop at a local store on their way to or back from " town." It is that convenience and the courses of the traffic streams which determine the neighborhood portals as the proper locations for local shopping districts.

Another advantage in having business in the periphery of a unit is that frequently it is only across the street from a retail district in an adjacent neighborhood. Sometimes four such districts, in the corners of their units, will be found in a cluster. Thus residents of those four neighborhoods will all enjoy a wider range of shopping opportunity. Such a collocation will not displease shop proprietors. Aggregations of similar lines of business take place spontaneously in a downtown district, each shopkeeper seeking to locate where customers interested in his line are most likely to be found. Even the disadvantage of greater competition does not counteract this commercial tendency.

The straddling of a main highway with business activity does, however, create a traffic problem. Shoppers on foot will not be so much bothered, since they will stream across the street anyway, and often with the protection of a traffic light. But motorists, not wishing to stop at that point, will complain. This difficulty will be still more vexatious in the case of a regional highway 200 feet wide. Even pedestrians would not like that condition, and a frequent stopping of the traffic would greatly reduce the value of an express channel.

The best solution of this difficulty would seem to be that of the bridge or the underpass. In a situation where the main problem would be to enable pedestrians – not vehicles – to get freely across a main highway, it might be possible to provide an underpass, accessible by stairs or a ramp, on each side of a street. The expense of this construction could be recouped, and funds for maintenance be provided, through the erection of underground stores, fronting on the underpass, thus creating a shopping arcade and extending the business facilities of the district.

Where it was desirable to provide a channel for vehicles across a main highway, in a business area, the same principle could be applied. Either a bridge or an underpass could be lined on both sides with stores. Of course, a larger layout and more extensive planning would be involved – especially in the case of an overpass – but there seems little question but that both shopping and traffic convenience could be served in this way. The new store sites thus created "out of the air" – literally *in* the air – would bring a revenue that would take care of both construction and maintenance. An overpass authority, the legal body similar to a bridge or a housing authority, could be set up to handle a number of such projects. The insertion of a 200-foot arterial highway in built-up sections does, after all, bring up problems for the neighborhoods which line them. Perhaps business opportunities will help us to cross them.

As to the shape of neighborhood business districts – that is a technical matter and planners are referred to the studies made by Clarence Stein, Catherine Bauer and others. Several principles, however, are apparent. Stores should be bunched rather than strung along a street. Parking space and rear service entrances should be provided. Frontage and depth of stores will vary according to kinds of merchandise or service. Chain-store experience on these points will be useful in planning. Special architectural consideration should be given to the business structure at the point where stores stop and dwellings begin. A flower shop, or store of equal attractiveness, at the edge of the district will soften the harshness of this boundary.

In the unit scheme, a business district is a custom-made product. To fashion shops for various purposes and provide them with parking spaces and service lanes it is clear that the planner must not be bound by use-zones which follow the traditional street and block lines. And, finally, the value of a business district is created by the purchasing capacity of its residents. A developer in a position to build both stores and dwellings has a broader basis for meeting price competition and making profits. Comprehensive developments are promoted by the unit scheme.

### Internal street system

The unit should be provided with a special street system, each highway being propor-

tioned to its probable traffic load, and the street net as a whole being designed to facilitate circulation within the unit and to discourage its use by through traffic.

When a residential district is laid out on a grid-iron street pattern there are no points, within it or on its border, in the reaching of which some residents would not have to travel two sides of a triangle. Through the unit scheme this inconvenience can be largely avoided. Before internal streets are planned, the principal destinations of residents in their daily movements will be definitely known. These will be the portals in the circumference where the traffic junctions and business districts are located, and the civic center where the school is placed. Channels for more or less direct movement toward these main destinations can be laid out and their capacities can be approximately adjusted to the volume of the streams they will carry.

In the pattern that will result from this process, there will probably be a combination of both radials and circumferentials. There may also be culs-de-sac. Obviously, the contours of the terrain will have to be considered, as well as the other factors of vista, economical lot subdivision, and street utilities. But there should be no necessity for making these interior streets continuous with similar streets in the adjacent neighborhood, or for even requiring their openings on the boundary highway to correspond with openings across the highway. Such a requirement would not only tend to invite through traffic into the unit but also rob it of its independence. In every way the principle should be observed that internal streets are to serve exclusively the purposes of residents of a particular district, and all of the planning and engineering ingenuity should be directed to that end. Since boundary streets are made extra wide to facilitate the by-passing of a unit by through traffic, a planner can feel free to shut traffic out from the interior, so far as his means permit.

The street pattern produced by this method may seem like a maze to stranger-visitors and department-store delivery trucks, but this difficulty can be met by posting maps of the neighborhood, under weatherproof frames, in police booths and at the portals of the district.

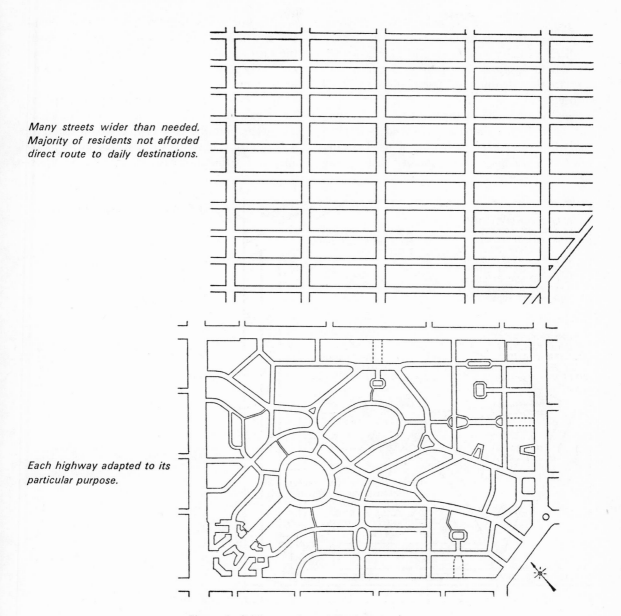

*Many streets wider than needed. Majority of residents not afforded direct route to daily destinations.*

*Each highway adapted to its particular purpose.*

**Figure 4. Gridiron and specialized street systems.**

Source: New York Regional Plan, volume 7.

If in the process of highway specialization we adapt parkways and boulevards to the needs of vehicles, why should we not fit neighborhood streets to the special requirements of pedestrians? Every thoughtful person, taking his car out of the garage, moves cautiously while in the vicinity of his neighbors. In a residential district, he is always near somebody's neighbors.

Why should he object to driving slowly for the few minutes required to reach the boundary highway where he will be able to speed? Suppose the neighborhood streets do seem like a labyrinth, and some of them are so narrow that, with cars parked at the curb, passage for other cars is a slow process – are not the safety and tranquillity thus obtained worth more than the convenience that is sacrificed? If we are going to do everything possible to reduce the present frightful casualty rate from vehicular accidents, we should apply a preventive principle of this sort to the planning of family-life residential districts.

Finally, we come to the matter of residential character. From what has been said it is plain that the unit scheme will not, of itself, confer upon a development the quality that comes

divided into many uniform lots, sold to whomsoever will buy, and built up in accordance with the tastes and means of different owners, it is not likely to have a character that is definite or outstanding.

By reason of its wide boundaries and special street pattern, a unit is almost certain to stand out geographically as a distinct community. It will probably have a special name. But appearance is not the only basis of distinction. A dis-

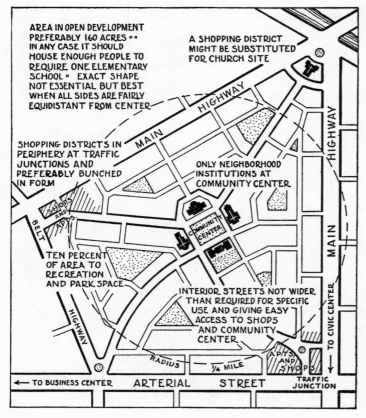

Figure 5. Neighborhood unit principles.

Source: New York Regional Plan volume 7.

from costliness of construction or wealth of landscaping. On the other hand, it enables a modest project to secure an amenity from parks and planted recreation spaces that is not ordinarily possessed by the average commercial development.

One important merit of unit planning consists in its ability to save a residential district from the miscellaneousness that characterizes most urban neighborhoods. When a tract is sub-

trict can be distinguished because of the affection which its residents have for it. When it has a complete equipment for the vicinity needs of its families; when the public services are nicely adapted to population requirements and all its component parts are integrated by a comprehensive plan – then you have a neighborhood community that is bound to be marked because of the esteem in which it is held by its residents.

If we will enable powerful special corporations

to construct family homes, we can make certain that there will be not only a large supply of reasonably priced *new* ones, but that each house will be built into its own neighborhood – an environment that will be right because it also will be planned and constructed, along with its dwellings, to specifications based upon family needs.

# Attack on the neighborhood unit formula

*REGINALD R. ISAACS*

" . . . Research is not an end in itself, but is justified to the degree that it contributes to sound . . . policy; and policies are useful in proportion to the degree that they result in action. But action depends on widespread public knowledge. In choosing subjects for investigation, the Fund (The Twentieth Century Fund) has sought out, rather than avoided, controversial issues, in the belief that controversy is an index of the public importance of a subject and of the need for its impartial treatment."[1]

In determining the "frontiers of housing research" many issues in housing and planning programs are frequently ignored on the tactical plea that they are controversial. There is no hesitation by redevelopers, housers, real estate groups and plan commissions to use the thirty-year-old neighborhood unit concept as a basis for planning for people. Yet even with wide and general acceptance of such a formula, the assumptions on which it is based should be re-examined.

Three of the basic questions which such examination might well include are: (1) Is it sociologically possible to create neighborhoods in the complex urban structure? (2) Is the neighborhood unit adequate as a physical concept for planning? (3) Should the concept be challenged on the basis that it lends itself to the purposes of discrimination since its most widespread application has been its methodical use for segregation?

## The neighborhood unit concept

The concept of the neighborhood as the basic unit in city planning gained wide acceptance following the formulation in 1926 by Clarence A. Perry for the New York Regional Plan Association. Perry defined the neighborhood unit as an area of a community usually bounded by main traffic roads with the elementary school as the focus of activities and containing all necessary recreational and shopping facilities. Roughly with a quarter-mile square in area to accommodate Perry's maximum of a half-mile walk to the elementary school from the farthest dwelling, the neighborhood would contain 5,000 to 10,000 persons. When related to the character of site and the prospective residents, it purported to give both form and stimulus to the common life of the area.

## The neighborhood unit as a sociological concept

Many planners are convinced that it is possible to import the physical and social amenities

*Reprinted from* Land Economics, *vol. 25 (February, 1949), pp. 73–78, with permission of the journal.*

of the rural and small town into the city through use of the neighborhood unit in which, they believe, " people can find friendliness, relaxation, convenience, and safety, as well as opportunity for self-expression and citizenship on a manageable scale."[2] The neighborhood proponents make much of the psychological and social advantages of creating a sense of belonging and of the use of neighborhood planning to eliminate the causes of social disorganization. They offer the neighborhood as a cure for the reputed " loneliness " of the city dweller and his induced nostalgic longing for a home away from the city. Yet the " flight from the farm " was motivated by more than the loss of rural economic opportunity. New contacts, anonymity and personal freedom were other attractions.

In earlier days neighborhoods were the fundamental areas of association for rural people, who constituted the great bulk of the population. Before good transportation, communication, industrial development and the growth of large cities, neighborhoods were usually economically self-sufficient and neighboring did take place. The families in the neighborhoods possessed so many traits in common that they constituted a cumulative social group of a high order of cohesion. Frequently, the families of a neighborhood were all related to one another. Nearly always they had known each other a lifetime. Differentiation along economic, religious, racial, occupational and educational lines was slight. Ordinarily there was one school and town hall government. The mores attained a high degree of homogeneity.

But is it possible for this kind of neighborhood to persist in the city of today? From observation, it is readily seen that people become members of groups larger than neighborhoods and merely reside in residential areas in contrast to living in rural or village neighborhoods as was true in the past.

The planner's concept of the neighborhood, as distinct from that of the sociologist,* has been described by one planner as follows:

" The purpose of neighborhood planning is to create an urban environment in which people will want to live, to recapture for American cities a quality of life that many small towns have kept but most large ones have lost ... There is an unfortunate tendency to call any new residential development a neighborhood unit, regardless of its size or composition. It is true that a group of as few as 50 or 100 families may enjoy a high degree of neighborliness, particularly if drawn together by relative isolation from other contacts. It would be rare, however, that a group of less than 500 dwelling units built within a major urban area would be large enough to maintain itself against outside pressures. The school is a good rallying point for the building and maintaining of neighborhood unity. A neighborhood too small to support such a rallying point is apt to prove too small to maintain its integrity in the surrounding city structures."[3]

## The neighborhood unit as a physical concept

Some planners recommend entirely homogeneous " neighborhoods," homogeneous as to both housing types and people. Other planners

---

* For example, T. Lynn Smith states: "Literally, the neighborhood would seem to mean the area within which *neighboring*, i.e., mutual aid, is extended or takes place among families. Small localities, in which country people live and know each other by their first names are neighborhoods ... The families tributary to a local institution such as an open-country church, a crossroads store, a one-room school, or an organization such as grange, club, etc., constitute genuine neighborhoods. Thus, for example, 30 or 40 families in an area of about five square miles may maintain a public school; and about this institution enough other activities may be polarized to make it a real neighborhood ... Unlike the situation in urban communities, the actual portion of rural society with which a given individual or family comes into contact exhibits little heterogeneity. The rural person's contacts are mainly with other farmers, who in turn are the sons of farmers. His associates generally are also members of his own religious group, neighbors of much the same economic and educational attainments, persons whose mores, traditional beliefs, language, and general behavior patterns are very similar to his own. The countryman's contacts are mostly with those who live in close proximity to him. It matters little that elsewhere in the nation there are other farmers with radically different cultural traits. For practical purposes the important thing is that each segment of rural society is highly homogeneous or very slightly differentiated." *The Sociology of Rural Life*. New York: Harper & Row, 1940.

and housers want mixed housing types but similar kinds of people. Still other planners want both heterogeneous housing facilities and people.

These easy formulae emphasize the immediacy of facilities to residences and attempt to force naturally overlapping service areas into a mold tightly lacing the resident to a rigid and precious pattern of the planner's making. There is a lack of coincidence in service distances and areas of necessary community facilities that has not been reconciled. There are nearly insoluble problems of planning with the same facile formulae for the extreme heavy density areas, the extreme light density areas, as well as for the average density areas. Sociologist Louis Wirth states:

"... It has been found that the settlement of human beings, the patterning of social institutions, the incidence of social problems, and the intricate network of social interrelationships does not, except by accident, conform to arbitrarily delimited areas and that hence administrative areas only rarely coincide with the ecological or natural areas. In the study of urban life, for instance, the types of land use and the types of residential areas to be found in the city do not conform to the neat lines of precincts, wards, and other political and administrative boundaries. Neither do crime, disease, family disorganization, and, for that matter, political alignments fit themselves into the static patterns of formally adopted areal units. They have patterns of their own, and they shift in accordance with the total conditions of life."[4]

A question is raised regarding location of schools. The formula is not readily applicable to areas of light density and is often ill-considered when traffic, topographic, industrial or other barriers interrupt the approved quarter-mile walk for children. What is to take place under this dogmatic formula in residual areas with too few children to efficiently use a school? What is to take place in areas with a 40 percent Catholic and 60 percent Protestant and other population? It has been reported that there has been a greater proportion of Lutheran than Catholic schools built since the war. Will there be both parochial and elementary schools provided with insufficient numbers of children

within walking distances? Which school is to be the focus of neighborhood activities? Which school is to have the neighborhood playground? Ruth Glass writes:

"Self-contained neighborhoods do not exist. The boundaries of neighborhood life vary for different activities. Secondly, there are also varied neighborhood boundaries for members of different age-groups. School areas, for instance, differ considerably from those of adult clubs, even where the school and the adult club are next to each other. Consequently, the school would not appear to be the natural focal point of a neighborhood."[5]

How can the church be planned in a tightly demarcated area since it is even less a common denominator than the school? Should not all faiths have equally convenient access for adults to church and for children to Sunday School? Isn't the average neighborhood too small to support several or even a few congregations?

A few planners have recognized that the shopping centers sometimes provide initial as well as continuing opportunities for the establishment of neighboring. Fewer planners have recognized the problems inherent in location, size, service areas, population density, purchasing power and competitive market requirements in the urban residential areas other than those encountered on their drafting board. One of these few planners writes, in description of his efforts to use the neighborhood unit concept as a base for planning: "... the thought here seems to be that the elements are so overlapping and heterogeneous that neighborhood lines just can't be drawn except in a few cases."[6]

### The neighborhood unit as a social concept

Even were the neighborhood theory a valid one in its physical and sociological aspects, it would be necessary to challenge it on another level – on the basis of its use as an instrument for segregation of ethnic and economic groups. Many city planners have also, deliberately in many cases, adapted the neighborhood for purposes far beyond the purposes embodied in the concept. Too often to be merely happenstance, the physical barriers and prescribed limits of service areas form gerrymandered boundaries as bases for the planned segregation of people by religious, racial or economic groupings. The neighborhood is an excellent device and framework for the organization and enforcement of covenants and deed restrictions and, today, the fear of minority group infiltration is substituted for a common denominator of neighborhood consciousness.

Has there been a definite and unconscionable effort toward the achievement of segregation? Over a period of years a pattern of action appears to have been developed by major proponents of segregation. Their methodology consists of the creation of *nostalgia* for the countryside, emphasis on *planned neighborhoods* as a panacea for satisfying that induced sentiment, the illusory promise of *community facilities* made easily accessible to toddler and adult alike; the stimulation of *neighboring*; the possibilities of *autonomous self-direction* and training for leadership of the city as a whole; and *associations* for preservation of the neighborhood against the onslaught of depreciating forces through use of isolating covenants. For example, a plan commission promises that " all of the longing of the city dweller for a ' house in the country ' can be realized in Chicago."[7] But how many urbanites want a " house in the country? " Over thirty years ago, a courageous planner questioned seriously the feasibility of establishing these rural characteristics in the city:

" ... the little garden, the croquet lawn, the grape arbor, and the happy privacy investing it all, form a charming picture of what does not exist in the city backyard. So primitive and wholesome a thing as the impulse to garden, which all men feel for a little time in the spring, no matter what their occupation or where they live, finds only abortive expression in the average backyard. City soil and city atmosphere are against it. Moreover, the Chicago man is not a gardener by instinct or tradition. His impulses are not pastoral, they are urban. The result is inevitable–the aver-

age garden on the average back lot is not successful."[8]

Neighborhood associations are part and parcel of the smoke-screen around the real objectives of many neighborhood proponents. A prominent real estater advises:

" All cities should, of course, through action of the planning commission be divided into neighborhoods for purposes of thorough study and to establish physical boundaries within which the local associations would act."[9]

Because of such recommendations, it is of significant interest to compare the boundaries (natural or unnatural) of ethnic groupings with those of the neighborhoods and communities proposed by planners for almost any city.

Even if it were a fact that perhaps a larger portion of these lines were the result of " natural " barriers, it is recognized that some of the boundaries are consciously emphasized to perpetuate the purposes of segregation.* Reinforcing this contention are the patterns of known covenants surrounding these areas, of gerrymandered school districts, of bombings and violence, and of areas of inadequate municipal housekeeping. Even were all neighborhoods of concentrated ethnic groups, it should be a task of the planner to break down the barriers and facilitate democratic integration.

The school has been regarded as the equalizing focus of activities for all people – white, Negro, Jew, Catholic, Lutheran and other Protestant, rich and poor, children and adults alike. Yet an avid proponent of the neighborhood states:

" ... Perhaps an even more important difficulty is the fact that heterogeneous city neighborhoods result in highly mixed racial, national, social and income groups served by the same schools. It is the rare big city school that does not have many such groupings, a fact which usually results in an unhappy situation for the children and is highly disturbing to their parents. Schools are, there-

---

* The conscious efforts of some cities to use such boundaries as first priority criteria for the insulation of neighborhoods by the aborting of highway, recreation and other plans should not be confused with the necessary demarcation of ethnic groups for purposes of planning research.

fore, the most important reason for the flight from the city . . . "[10]

He advises:

"In my own opinion a large, perhaps the major, part of the direction of local schools should be in local hands. In other words, the hiring of teaching personnel, the establishment of educational policies, and so on, in the neighborhood schools should be subject to the approval of the neighborhood improvement association and the local parent and teachers' association. In this way, the mediocrity of many big city schools could be alleviated in those better neighborhoods where the people were really interested in the problem."[11]

### Neighboring

Actually, many residential areas find their only bond is the fear of Negro infiltration; such fear is frequently injected into the consciousness of the community by the community organizer whose motives are directed to questionable preservative measures of fictitious real estate values. For example, one mid-western community organizer boasts that he brought five of his neighborhood councils into being by using as motivation the fear of Negro infiltration. He claims that nothing else would have brought them together to learn how to work together, to create a sense of "neighborliness" and solidarity, to feel effective. Establishment of "separate and equal" residential facilities discharges, in their minds, responsibility toward neighbors of another race or religion.

Yet Richard Dewey has pointed out that the major reason for purchase of a "house in the country" was expediency; those seeking "neighborliness" were about equal in number to those who sought a restricted area.[12]

### Neighborhood associations

To the romantic neighborhood concept, already burdened with the physical health of the city, and the physiological and psychological reformation of the citizen, is affixed the responsibility for the survival and advancement of democracy. Implied also is the belief that the

acceptance and promulgation of the concept will prevent chaos without the onus of being criticized for centralized planning. Yet government agency and private enterprise alike have provided cause for criticism. The prominent real estater advocates:

"There is no such thing as a neighborhood which does not need an improvement association. Such organizations, in addition to their effect on the neighborhood would have great value as educators in citizenship and democracy, and would give people a proper vehicle for approaching the city government on matters relating to their home territory."[13]

Covenants *are* the end product of these associations. Such groups have lost no time in marshalling their tactics to circumvent the Supreme Court decision outlawing judicial sanction of restrictive covenants. Their efforts include the fostering and spreading of rumors, falsehoods and racist propaganda. Gentlemen's agreements and clubs are abetted and property-buying associations are becoming common devices. It has already been found, given at least the tacit support of a few aldermen and indecision on the part of other city officials, that it does not take too much effort to foster mass hysteria to end in violence against person and property.

### A frontier of research

Although aware of undemocratic neighborhood planning and building, some housing planners have argued that the concept was not created for purposes of class discrimination, but that it had just been misused to that end. A questioning attitude on the part of social scientists must be part of the attack on the unknown areas beyond the "frontiers of research." It must be questioned whether there shall be a continued attempt to mold the urban family into an arbitrary and fixed pattern for its way of life and to strait-jacket our metropolitan areas to a rigid cellular concept. It must also be questioned whether there is sufficient evidence of the sociological, physical and social failure of the neighborhood concept. Should the planning of residential areas begin with fundamental thinking and not the embellishment of outmoded concepts?

Repudiating the neighborhood unit concept for its structural inadequacies, sociological impossibilities, and the fact that it lends itself as an instrument for implementing segregation, the question is raised as to what basis for the planning of residential areas is acceptable. However, the problem is not susceptible of facile solution and only a small portion of it can be answered immediately. And it is doubtful that a *fixed* answer can ever be determined, in view of our constantly changing ways of life. At this stage it would be presumptuous to present individual solutions until steps toward the goals of residential area safety, convenience and amenity are achieved by close collaboration among sociologists, social and political scientists, physical planners and architects, anthropologists, psychologists, economists – and the people whose lives are to be planned. Svend Riemer has decried the

narrow approach taken even by social scientists to this aspect of planning, saying:

" ... Whenever the need was felt to give a comprehensive picture of social inter-relationships, sociologists have availed themselves of a microcosmic approach; they explored the complex fabric of individual communities, not that of either state, region or the nation ... Even today the wider aspects of ... voluntary associations, of class lines and more specific interest groups remain largely white spots on our map of social investigation."[14]

Criticism of the limitations of the neighborhood concept cannot be an end in itself, but only a point of departure. It serves its purpose well if it presents evidence and evaluation and if it evokes thoughtful and intelligent response. It succeeds in its purposes if discussion results in questioning attitudes and collaboration toward solution. It fails, and democracy fails, if this frontier of research is ignored.

# In defense of the neighborhood

*LEWIS MUMFORD*

During the last two decades the idea of planning by neighborhoods has been widely accepted. But this has taken place more in principle than in actual practice, except in the British New Towns. At the same time, a counter-movement has come into existence; the critics of neighborhood planning identify it with many practices that have nothing whatever to do with the neighborhood principle, such as segregation by race or caste or income; and they would treat the city as a whole as the only unit for effective planning. This drawing up for

battle is somewhat premature, for there has been little opportunity to experiment with neighborhood units and less time to observe results. Strangely, the arguments for and against neighborhood planning have drawn together the most unlike kinds of people. Thus Mr. F. J. Osborn, a staunch advocate of garden cities of limited size, does not favor the physical definition of neighborhoods; while the planners of Amsterdam, though committed to increase the size of their city up to the million mark, have carried out their new developments on the same basic

*Reprinted from* Town Planning Review, *vol. 24, (January, 1954), pp. 256–270, with permission of the journal.*

lines as those of an earlier generation: namely, neighborhood by neighborhood, and up to a point they have equipped these neighborhoods as social units.

Much of the argument on this subject has served only to confuse the issues that should be defined; and my purpose in this paper is to clarify some of those issues and make it possible to take a more rational position on one or the other side. By accident, I began this paper in Paris and revised it in Venice. Within these two urban environments the recently posed question of whether neighborhoods actually exist, particularly within great cities, seems a singularly academic one, indeed downright absurd in their suggestion that neighborhoods are the wilful mental creations of romantic sociologists. Paris, for all its formal Cartesian unity, is a city of neighborhoods, often with a well-defined architectural character as well as an identifiable social face. The Parisian neighborhood is not just a postal district or a political unit, but an historic growth; and the sense of belonging to a particular *arrondissement* or *quartier* is just as strong in the shopkeeper, the bistro customer, or the petty craftsman as the sense of being a Parisian. Indeed, in Paris the neighborhood attachment is so close, so intense, so narrow that it would have satisfied the soul of Adam Wayne, Chesterton's Napoleon of Notting Hill.

This is not a subjective judgment or a hasty tourist's generalization; M. Chambert de Lauwe and his associates have just begun to publish the results of a careful survey of the movements of Parisians about their city, and have discovered that whereas professional people may move over a good part of it from one day's end to the other, the working people keep close to their own districts, where most of the facilities for life, the café, the dance hall, the church, the school, and not least the workshop or factory are found.[1] What is exceptional about Paris, I suspect, is not the facts themselves but the way in which the builders of the city, despite their efforts to achieve an overall unity, have nevertheless consolidated most of the daily activities of no small part of the population within a limited local area. As for Venice, it is a city of neighborhoods, established as parishes in relation to a dominant church or square; and by its very constitution it reminds us that the medieval city was composed on the neighborhood principle, with the Church serving as community center and the market place adjacent to it as " shopping center," both within easy walking distance of all the inhabitants. The very word " quarter " reminds us that, typically, the medieval city, up to the sixteenth century, though it usually contained fewer than 25,000 inhabitants, was divided into quarters: each quarter had its own section of the walls to defend, along with its own churches, workshops and minor markets.* In Florence, for example, each of the six " quarters " elected two consuls; so under a democratic regime the neighborhood even had a political aspect. These facts did not prevent the city from functioning as a whole, when some great feast or celebration sent the inhabitants into the central area, to worship at the Cathedral or to perform plays from its porch. The common size of these quarters must have been from about 1,500 to 6,000 persons, except in cities of abnormal growth, like Florence, Milan, or Paris.

## 1. The neighborhood as a fact of nature

Whether it is possible for a city, be it planned or not, to escape some sort of definition or at least local coloring by neighborhoods is problematic. Even in the undifferentiated rectangular plan of Manhattan, a plan contrived as if for the purpose of preventing neighborhoods from coming into existence, distinctive entities, like Yorkville, Chelsea, and Greenwich Village, nevertheless have developed, though they lack any architectural character, except that conditioned by the successive dates of their building. In a rudimentary form neighborhoods exist, as a fact of nature, whether or not we recognize them or provide for their particular functions. For neighbors are simply people who live near one another. To share the same place

---

* Up to 1450, according to one estimate, not more than twelve cities had more than 50,000 population; London still had 40,000 and the great majority of cities, including Lübeck and Cologne, had 25,000 or less.

is perhaps the most primitive of social bonds, and to be within view of one's neighbors is the simplest form of association. Neighborhoods are composed of people who enter by the very fact of birth or chosen residence into a common life. Neighbors are people united primarily not by common origins or common purposes but by the proximity of their dwellings in space. This closeness makes them conscious of each other by sight, and known to each other by direct communication, by intermediate links of association, or by rumor. In times of crisis, a fire, a funeral, a festival, neighbors may even become vividly conscious of each other and capable of greater cooperation; but in origin, neighborliness rests solely on the fact of local cohabitation. There is nothing forced in this relationship and to be real it need not be deep: a nod, a friendly word, a recognized face, an uttered name – this is all that is needed to establish and preserve in some fashion the sense of belonging together. Neither friendship nor occupational affiliation is implied in the give and take of neighborhood life, though in time such relationships may take form, along with intermarriage. Long-established residence, or the ownership of real property, cements this elementary bond.

At all events, neighborhoods, in some primitive, inchoate fashion exist wherever human beings congregate, in permanent family dwellings; and many of the functions of the city tend to be distributed naturally – that is, without any theoretical preoccupation or political direction – into neighborhoods. Marked topographic divisions, as in Pittsburgh, or old historic divisions, as in London, with characteristic modes of building, buttress this neighborhood consciousness. Neighborhood grouping, around certain common domestic and civic facilities, is complementary to another form of grouping, likewise ancient, in occupational association or zones, by means of which professions or industries of the same sort tend to form well-defined precincts, sometimes grouped along a single street, like Harley Street, sometimes forming an "island," like the Inns of Court in London. In defining the neighborhood unit, it is important to distinguish it from the occupational precinct or the caste quarter. In the latter, all the members of a trade or corporation are grouped together. In Indian cities, the quarter is composed of people of the same caste and occupation, and in American cities, during the last generation, caste quarters, based on race and income, have been created by zoning or deed restrictions, which equally narrow the basis of human association. In his well-founded distrust of this manner of organization, so hostile to the principles of democracy, Mr. Reginald Isaacs, one of the chief American critics of neighborhood planning, has attributed to the neighborhood principle the very vice of specialization and segregation that the modern concept of the "neighborhood unit" in fact attempts to break down. But the selective nature of these specialized zones should prevent a trained observer from characterizing them as "neighborhood units" even though the fact of cohabitation engenders neighborly relations.

How was it that spontaneous neighborhood grouping, so well-defined before the seventeenth century, tended to disappear in systematic new Plans, like those of seventeenth-century Amsterdam and nineteenth-century New York, though never entirely disrupted in the more organic growth of a great city like London? One of the answers to this is the segregation of income groups under capitalism, with a sharp spatial separation of the quarters of the rich and the poor; the other was a technical factor, the increase of wheeled vehicles and the domination of the avenue in planning.

The development of transportation caused the traffic avenue to become the dominant component in nineteenth-century design: the emphasis changed from facilities for settlement to facilities for movement. By means of the traffic avenue, often ruthlessly cutting through urban tissue that had once been organically related to neighborhood life, the city as a whole became more united perhaps; but at the cost of destroying, or at least of seriously undermining, neighborhood life. Where, as in the big American metropolises, the gridiron plan forestalled or overrode neighborhood development, the subordinate parts of the city came more and more to lack any character of their own. Though the successive times of building and the diversity of human purposes might still give a certain residual color to the growing urban extensions, in general the traffic avenue, abetted by other means of mechanical transportation, tended to break up, not just the rituals of local attachment, but the very sense, conveyed by street plans and architecture, of being part of an identifiable and often lovable whole. Even when the neighborhoods of the nineteenth-century city were identifiable, they were usually not lovable; so that, in a sense, it was only in the older quarters of the city or in the better suburbs that the neighborhood, as a cluster of visible and conscious domestic relationships, survived. Otherwise, the long uniform avenue, the random placing of public buildings, created a nightmare of the indefinable. It was easier to lose oneself in the city as a whole than to find oneself in the neighborhood.

## 2. The community center
## as neighborhood core

Thus things stood with the neighborhood at the beginning of the twentieth century; and so completely had the concept of the neighborhood disappeared that in the first attempt to design a complete, self-contained city, at Letchworth, Messrs. Raymond Unwin and Barry Parker, the town planners, made no effort to define or even suggest the neighborhood. The emphasis still lay on the city as a whole, treated as a single unit. But about this time a movement appeared in America that was to challenge this whole order of planning; and it came from two directions. On the scientific side, it stemmed from Charles Horton Cooley, who was to describe, in a series of books on social organization and social process, the part played by the intimate, face-to-face community, one based on the family, the common place, and general shared interests, rather than on specialized vocations and conscious affiliations. What the German sociologists called *Gemeinschaft*, as opposed to *Gesellschaft*, had its basis, Cooley pointed out, in this primary group, with its spontaneous, instinctual, largely "given" relationships. No matter how differentiated and directed the life of a great metropolis finally became there remained, at the core of its activities, the same processes and loyalties one discovers in the village.

But the discovery of the neighborhood as an important organ of urban life had two other points of origin. One was due to social impoverishment; the other to an attempt at social integration. In the East End of London, Canon Barnet and his associates discovered, there was a vast urban wilderness that lacked even the bare elements of social life and had sunk into a state of barbarism. In creating the social settlement, at Toynbee Hall, he provided a common building and meeting place where the residents of the neighborhood could come together for the purposes of play, education, or sociability. This social settlement (sometimes called Neighborhood House in America) answered so many of the needs of the great city, particularly those that grew out of its anonymity and loneliness, that it is hardly surprising that a parallel middle-class movement started in Rochester, New York, about two decades after Toynbee Hall, and became known as the Community Center movement. The advocates of the community center sought to animate civic life by providing a common local meeting place to provide a forum for discussion and to serve as basis for community activities that otherwise had no local habitation. One of the leaders of this movement, Clarence Perry, was led by his analysis of the local community's needs to give back to the neighborhood the functions that had been allowed to lapse, or had become unduly centralized, since the decay of the medieval city. That path led him from the neighborhood to the neighborhood unit : from a mere cohabitation to the creation of a new form and new institutions for a modern urban community. In planning the result of this was to change the basic unit of planning from the city block or the avenue, to the more complex unit of the neighborhood, a change that demanded a reapportionment of space for avenues and access streets, for public buildings and open areas and domestic dwellings : in short, a new generalized urban pattern.

The other movement that stimulated the consciousness of the neighborhood was the growth of the suburb, especially the suburb planned in a unified way by a development company. In the better suburbs, like Bedford Park and Hampstead Garden Suburb in London, Roland Park and Guilford in Baltimore, Riverside, Chicago, or Kew Gardens, New York, the flowing street plan, the fuller use of tree-lined streets and public open spaces, and the new romantic architecture, made people conscious of the neighborhood as an esthetic unit. Did not the first experiments in concentrated and planned shopping centres, usually adjacent to the railroad, take place in the suburb? Few suburbs were indeed mixed neighborhoods: segregation by income and social class characterized all of them, except perhaps those that had grown slowly out of an original country village; but in creating domestic quarters of a more ample nature than the city afforded, the suburb also prompted the beginnings of a civic consciousness, on a neighborhood scale. Though E. L. Thorndyke's rating for cities is not perhaps an infallible guide, the fact that suburbs stand high in the list is not altogether the result of accident or class bias. At least as identifiable neighborhoods they often have facilities that the disorganized and blighted metropolis, whatever its financial and cultural resources, lacks. (When the history of Town Planning comes to be written, it will be clear that most of the fresh initiatives in urban design – the open plan, the superblock, the differentiation of pedestrian and wheeled traffic, the parkway, the shopping center, and finally the neighborhood unit were first tried out in the suburb). From the suburb, as well as from historic quarters of the city, came the notion that the neighborhood should have a certain coherence of architectural expression, both through the general plan and through the individual design of buildings.

The community center movement seemed to collapse around 1920, along with another more ambitious effort, the Social Unit movement in Cincinnati, which likewise sought to rehabilitate democratic institutions at the neighborhood level. Yet both movements left their mark; for they brought forth a few simple concepts, long neglected, that have had, at least in America, a wide effect upon the minds of planners. The first is the recognition of the need for a definite building to serve as a meeting place for the local community; and the second, following from this, is the simple practical suggestion that the elementary school, the most ubiquitous of local

institutions, need only be provided with suitable halls, offices, and committee rooms to serve both children and adults, and to function both by day and by night. As a result, the minimum requirements for a community center have now become a standard basis for school design in almost every part of the United States; and in such buildings, even in cities otherwise as backward in civic design as New York, an endless round of neighborhood activities goes on. As an historic fact, then, the core of the neighborhood unit, its central nucleus, was projected and actually embodied before the idea of the neighborhood unit as such was defined, or a rational means of determining its boundaries suggested. That final act of clarification took place when Clarence Perry published his work on the subject, as a contribution to the Russell Sage Foundation's Regional Survey of New York and Its Environs.

Meanwhile, however, the notion of redefining and replanning the city on the basis of neighborhoods, had been broached in two other quarters. Perry himself was perhaps aided in his inquiry by the publication of the results of a now almost forgotten competition, held by the Chicago City Club, for the planning of a quarter section – 640 acres – of Chicago.[2] This is a much larger area than most students today would take as a neighborhood; but it brought forth, none the less, a remarkable group of designs; remarkable, at least for their time, and not without occasional hints and suggestions even to designers today. Published in the midst of the First World War, it has long been a forgotten item; but it focused attention on the process of integrating the domestic areas of the city and relating their housing to markets, schools, churches, and other institutions that serve the local area rather than the city as a whole.

Shortly after the publication of this report, Raymond Unwin, surely the most fertile urban innovator in his generation, published a paper on Distribution in the Town Planning Institute *Journal* (1920–1921) in which he asked: "How far is it possible for the growing city to secure an end so desirable as the greater localization of life?" And he answered: "I believe that the proper distribution of the parts of the city and the clear definition of its various areas would do much to secure this. Each area in which it is intended to develop a localized life must of course be provided with every facility for all the different branches of life that it is practicable to localize. There should be local work and occupation for as many as possible of the people living there; there should be local markets and shopping centers to provide for their daily needs; there should be educational and recreational facilities. It will not be practicable to have a university in every such locality but at least there should be high schools. You cannot expect to have your Albert Hall for great concerts or your Kennington Oval for international matches in each locality, but at least there should be the Hall of Music, the theater, and such ample provision of playing fields that no one need journey from the locality in order to enjoy the ordinary recreations." In this article, Unwin even anticipated the new uses of the greenbelt, which he had already foreshadowed in his Hampstead Garden Suburb, for he observed: "It will be found that the proposed distribution will largely depend on the proper apportionment of open space around each area, and that this open space will serve two main purposes. It will provide all the opportunities for recreation, gardening, and so forth, and it will give a degree of definition to the area and separation from other areas which will emphasize the locality as a defined unit. Referring to the importance of defining areas, I may perhaps quote what I wrote in 1919 that ' these belts might well define our parishes or our wards and by doing so might help to foster the feeling of local unity in the area.' "

## 3. Experiments with neighborhood units

When one is describing a movement as complex as this one, one is perhaps tempted to ascribe to one or two leading figures what was really the outcome of many minds, converging from different directions. But though Perry no more discovered the neighborhood principle alone than Le Corbusier discovered modern architecture, the work of each of them has had a dramatic value in crystallizing many diffuse efforts. In his thinking Perry certainly went no

further than Unwin, except in so far as he filled in the sketch with concrete details and proposals. What Perry did was to take the fact of the neighborhood; and show how, through deliberate design, it could be transformed into what he called a neighborhood unit, the modern equivalent of the medieval quarter or parish: a unit that would now exist, not merely on a spontaneous or instinctual basis, but through the deliberate decentralization of institutions that had, in their over-centralization, ceased to serve efficiently the city as a whole. He sought to determine what facilities and institutions were necessary for domestic life as such; how many people were needed to support an elementary school, a shopping center, a church, or other institutions; and by what rearrangement of the street pattern a coherent neighborhood could be created with every necessary local function within walking distance of the dwelling. With the aid of plans and elevations, Perry pushed beyond the work of the Chicago competition and attempted to describe an ideal unit, a fully equipped neighborhood. Some of the features of this ideal plan could not, perhaps, stand up under careful examination; but in the establishment of the proper distance from the remotest home to playground, park, or school, and in his suggestion that major traffic routes must be routed around, not through, a neighborhood unit, not least by dedicating 10 percent of the area to local parks and playgrounds, Perry made no small contribution to the reorganization of the modern city.

Even before Perry had published his work on the neighborhood unit, Messrs. Stein and Wright, in their plans for Sunnyside Gardens, Long Island, though confined by the existing gridiron street pattern, had created a neighborhood in which the playgrounds and open spaces and small meeting halls were treated as an integral part of the housing development; and in Radburn they carried this mode of planning, not without consultation with Perry and various school authorities, into their designs for the whole community.

Radburn, conceived in 1928 and largely built during the next three years, embodied in its planning the new concept of the neighborhood as a complete unit. The main traffic roads of the town went around, not through, the units: the movement of pedestrians was mainly along a spinal green that formed the inner core of the town, and, by its very constitution, furthered face-to-face acquaintance; at the center of each neighborhood was an elementary school, with its recreation field and its swimming pool; and the shops and services were gathered in a shopping center, with a parking place for cars, instead of being dispersed along a traffic avenue. The population of the neighborhood unit was calculated in terms of the number of families needed to support an elementary school. Because New York authorities consulted then favored big schools, elaborately equipped, from 7,500 to 10,000 was accepted as the normal population of a neighborhood; and this has led to a certain imitative rigidity as to the proper size of a neighborhood unit. Except where the density is unreasonably high, 5,000 would seem to me to be an upper limit, beyond which one should seek to create a new neighborhood; but there is no lower limit, except in terms of the facilities a smaller group can afford. As with the city itself, the main thing to recognize in neighborhood units is that there is an upper limit of growth and extension; and that, to define the unit and keep it in form, there must be both a civic nucleus to draw people together and an outer boundary to give them the sense of belonging together.

Perry's concept of the neighborhood unit carried a step further the earlier notion, first introduced in Germany, of dividing a city into specialized zones. Treating the domestic quarters of the city as a functional zone, to be differentiated in plan, because of its different needs, from the industrial or commercial zones, he established likewise the need for a nuclear treatment of the domestic zone, since the acceptable dimensions of a neighborhood depended upon such relationships as a quarter-mile walk to a local playground or a half-mile walk to the local school, to say nothing of such indeterminate though limited distances as those a housewife will willingly walk to do her marketing or shopping. All this seems like such elementary common sense that one wonders that anyone should seriously challenge it. Where such spatial relations are flouted – as they so often are in the

spotty, inconsecutive, irrational "planning" of our time – the members of the community pay for it in extra time and expense and inconvenience, in putting further burdens on the transportation system, in paying extra assessments for otherwise extravagant streets and traffic avenues, or in simply doing without facilities that properly belong within a residential quarter. The neighborhood is based, essentially, on the needs of families; particularly on the needs of mothers and children from the latters' infancy up to adolescence; as well as upon the needs of all age groups for having access to certain common cultural facilities; the school, the library, the meeting hall, the cinema, the church. To have all these institutions within easy reach of the home is a guarantee of their being steadily used by all the members of the family, while to have them scattered and unrelated, especially in distant parts of the city, is to discourage their constant use and often, when children must be cared for, to prevent their use entirely – except at the price of family neglect.

## 4. The extent of self-containment

In one of his attacks on the neighborhood unit principle Mr. Reginald Isaacs maps an area in Chicago covered by a typical family's activities: the map shows a theoretical self-contained neighborhood center devoid of any social facilities, apparently, except a school and a food shop, while most of the actual activities of the family (if the diagram has been drawn to scale) take place from two miles to twenty miles away from this area. On the basis of this diagram, he asks: Can any one neighborhood contain all the activities of a typical family? That is a naively specious question. As soon as one breaks down these activities one sees that they fall into two divisions. One consists of occasional activities, like a visit to a distant friend, or to a distant forest preserve on a holiday, or specialized shopping or daily work in an industrial plant necessarily outside the neighborhood – all activities which no one in his senses would propose to concentrate within a single neighborhood. But the other activities, the use of the health clinic, the library, the movies, a church, a park, a playground, a variety of shops, now found in every case outside the neighborhood, demonstrate how much of the time and energy of an urban denizen is wasted in unnecessary transportation, since there is not one of these activities that could not, with benefit, be relocated in a neighborhood unit. Even if no further advantages of face-to-face association and friendly intercourse and political cohesion followed from neighborhood planning, one could easily justify it on economic terms alone.

If the problem of urban transportation is ever to be solved, it will be on the basis of bringing a larger number of institutions and facilities within walking distance of the home; since the efficiency of even the private motor car varies inversely with the density of population and the amount of wheeled traffic it generates.

All this does not mean that the neighborhood actually is or ideally should be a self-contained unit. The fact is that no social organization, from the family to the state, is wholly self-contained or self-enclosed. The biggest metropolis, in fact, is no more self-sufficient than the neighborhood; for not merely is it dependent upon distant sources of energy, food, raw materials, and products, but, in the case of certain surgical operations, for example, even the biggest of cities may not provide the skill that has been developed in some smaller center. The only functions with respect to which the neighborhood unit is relatively self-contained are the domestic functions or those activities that spring from them. For neighborhood units are built around the home and they should be so designed as to give the fullest advantages of housewifely and parental cooperation and result in the greatest measure of freedom, pleasure, and effectiveness in meeting the needs of family life at every stage of growth.

In short the notion that the existence of a neighborhood unit presents an obstacle to the wider use of the city does not bear examination: rather it is only by the decentralization of as many activities as possible into local units that the centralized facilities can be kept from becoming congested and ultimately unusable. Sometimes this decentralization may be effected through a bit of mechanical apparatus, as when millions, with the aid of television, are present at a football match that could not possibly be watched by more than fifty thousand people; but at other times, the decentralization must take the form of creating and siting within the local area the appropriate organ of the common life.

From the nature of the case, neighborhood planning can be more easily achieved in new areas, where the whole site must be laid out, than in old quarters, where the very existence of established streets and property lines makes fresh planning difficult. Likewise, it is easier to achieve when the land is held by an urban authority or a development corporation than where it has already been broken into small individual parcels. But even in old neighborhoods, not yet sufficiently blighted or bombed to become "redevelopment areas" it is possible to take the first step toward neighborhood integration through the redesign of the central nucleus, partly through pulling together on a more adequate site plan institutions that had been set down more or less at random, partly by abetting the deliberate recentralization of institutions now available to the residents of a neighborhood only by going to a distant part of the city. The efficacy of many central institutions lapses, so far as the inhabitants of distant areas are concerned, because of the long journey their use demands: even when people are willing to make that journey – as they so long remained loyal to the big department stores – the very heaping up of facilities in the central organization often leads to inefficiency, if only because of the need for selling bulkier goods by sample and warehousing the product in a distant part of the city. In America, and first of all in the big cities, department stores have begun since the early 1930's, to distribute their activities in branch shops in the suburbs, though when I suggested this necessity to the President of Macy's in 1929, he dismissed it as an absurd dream, since the very basis of success, he believed, lay in having "everything under one roof." But what has begun to take place with department stores applies almost to every other important metropolitan activity: the same principle, of decentralization into communal and neighborhood units, applies to museums, libraries, hospitals – above all to hospitals and medical clinics. Except for highly specialized needs, all of these institutions should seek to multiply facilities scaled to neighborhood use. In the case of childbirth, for example, the neighborhood maternity unit would be preferable both to delivery within the dwelling house, already too cramped for space and often too insistent in the demands made on the mother, and the distant hospital, which, except in cases that promise surgical difficulty, provides nothing that a local institution could not give, and, on the contrary, presents many disadvantages for both the patient and the family. In all of these departments Perry's thinking, excellent as it was in the twenties, has now to be carried beyond the bounds of current practice. Neighborhood unit organization seems the only practical answer to the giantism and inefficiency of the over-centralized metropolis. To preserve specialized institutions for their unique and specific services, which should be available to the whole region, they must be relieved of the heavy burden of performing, in addition, purely parochial functions. There would be no place for the scholar in the Central Library in New York, if there were not local libraries, united into a metropolitan system, in every district in the city. This theorem has a wide application; and it justifies from the standpoint of the greater unit the principle of neighborhood decentralization.

The creation of a neighborhood involves something more than the planning on a different pattern than that which has hitherto characterized the undifferentiated big city; for it also demands the orderly provision and relationship in both space and time of a group of neighborhood institutions, such as schools, meeting halls, shops, pubs, restaurants, and local theaters. This calls for the continued activity of a public authority. It is the existence of a full complement of these latter facilities that transforms a spontaneous neighborhood into what one may properly call a neighborhood unit. Ideally, the neighborhood unit, then, would take an old form of association, never entirely suppressed even in the inorganic type of city, and reorganize it on a pattern that both amplifies and enriches daily activity. In doing this, so far from disrupting the functioning of the city as a whole, it rather makes more effective that

larger association, since the bigger unit need no longer try to combine the functions of the local community and the larger community, in one muddled, undifferentiated pattern. The fact – let me emphasize again – that many of the significant activities of the city are occasional ones, and lie outside the neighborhood, or that a large part of an adult's life may be spent far beyond his own domestic precincts, does not lessen the importance of neighborhood functions. Nor does the coming and going of the population of a big city lessen the formative result of good neighborhood design. Where in the city does the population come and go more rapidly than in the university, which turns over most of its population completely every four years? Yet who would deny that the orderly grouping of buildings and the concentration of student interests within the university precinct is itself a part of the educational process, and powerfully molds the lives that submit to it, even for a brief period? Universities whose separate departments were strewn over a great metropolitan area would lack both the economy and the *esprit de corps* a compact precinct gives.

## 5. The new problems of neighborhood planning

Needless to say, the acceptance of the neighborhood principle does not by itself solve the problems of design: on the contrary, it raises many interesting new problems. Perhaps the first question of importance is what degree of isolation should be accorded the neighborhood, apart from the inevitable separation made by major traffic arteries. In cities like Pittsburgh, whose strong topographical features have broken it up into well-marked neighborhoods, so unrelated that even the high school student finds his high school within his own neighborhood, one notes the danger of a spirit of "isolationism," and the more satisfactory the neighborhood, the greater the danger of the self-complacency and the psychological self-enclosure. (In Philadelphia this has even stood in the way of the multiple bridging of the Schuylkill, in order to join by direct highways the "Main Line" suburbs and Germantown and Chestnut Hill; each rather prefers to "keep itself to itself.") Messrs. Stein and Wright, in Radburn, designed their neighborhoods so as to overlap, with the shopping center serving as the point of fusion and intermixture, and by means of underpasses they bound together their neighborhoods by a continuous green core, which served as both park and pedestrian promenade. Both these devices seem preferable to the absolute isolation imposed by wide wedges of greenbelt in some of the British New Towns. When a greenbelt is employed to define a neighborhood, should it not be treated more economically and formally, so as to bring the neighborhoods, at the same time, into closer relationship?

The second problem is how far the tendency toward status and class affiliation should be permitted – abetted as they have been in recent years in the United States by zoning ordinance and deed restrictions – and how far should the neighborhood, as well as the city, be planned as a mixed community with housing for both upper and lower income groups? My own experience of living in a non-segregated community, at Sunnyside Gardens, with a wide range of income groups (from $1,200 to $12,000 a year) living side by side, has led me to believe that this is the best kind of community. In terms of educating the young and of making the institutions of democracy work, the arguments are entirely in favor of a mixed community. Here another principle may be invoked, which applies, it seems to me, to other parts of the design: the principle that the neighborhood should, as far as possible, be an adequate and representative sample of the whole. I would apply this notion so far as to question the soundness of creating residential quarters on such a scale that local shops and markets and public restaurants and taverns were more than a quarter mile distant from the center. In other words, most of the activities that, in more specialized form, enter into the adult's world should be represented, in simpler modes, in the local community. This would give a variety to the neighborhood unit that is too often absent in new housing developments. The mixture of social and economic classes within a neighborhood should have its correlate in a mixture of housing types and densities of occupation. One of the best examples of the architectural ad-

vantages of such mixture is in the Lansbury Neighborhood in London, which has a charm and variety, despite its 136 inhabitants per residential acre, that much more open schemes, at a flat 48 to the acre, often lack.

At the beginning, not every neighborhood can be fully equipped with all the social apparatus necessary for a full domestic and communal life. It would seem, accordingly, a matter of prudence to allow, in the areas set aside for local institutions, a certain amount of undetermined space, for later occupancy. Thus an occasional "island," in a local street plan, might allow space for a church, a cinema, or a group of shops, whose existence could not be provided for in the original layout. Until occupied such free space might serve for allotment gardens. Still another matter that should be a subject of experiment in neighborhood planning is the degree in which the interests of children and adults can and should be combined. The modern community, particularly in England and America, has drifted into the acceptance of age segregation: the young and the old, in their hours of recreation, have little to do with each other. But in France and Italy, on the boulevards or in the open squares, young and old coexist together. In the Piazza Navona at Rome, for example, the adults meet and gossip and eat together, while within sight of them, the young play their games and go about their own affairs, occasionally coming back to "home base" for comfort or reassurance or a bite to eat. In the Peckham Health Centre the custom that the families should share the same recreation center and be within sight of each other was established, as a step forward toward family integration; and this would seem to lead a much healthier relation, morally speaking, than one which either divorces the young from any kind of supervision, or gives the function of the family to a paid supervisor. There is room for fresh urban invention here: a new kind of urban open space, more completely liberated from wheeled traffic than the Italian piazza or the market place of Harlow, more intimate than the Parisian boulevard or the market place at Hemel Hempstead; but surrounded with the kind of facilities and institutions that would bring parents and children within sight and call of each other during their leisure hours, so that the parents need not be too strictly confined to the home, nor the children permitted to be completely on the loose. The re-integration of the family, in this fashion, should be one of the serious concerns in planning for the new neighborhood unit.

All these matters in turn raise further problems of architectural treatment: the height and scale of buildings, the relation of open spaces to occupied spaces, of exposure and enclosure. Here there is much fresh thinking to be done, as a basis for design; for in reaction against the congestion of the great city, our architects and planners now tend to sacrifice sociability and concentration to mere openness. In the effort to achieve roominess they have forgotten how, in urban terms, to create rooms, that is, public enclosures adapted to particular urban functions. In the neighborhood, if anywhere, it is necessary to recover the sense of intimacy and innerness that has been disrupted by the increased scale of the city and the speed of transportation.* Here the *cul-de-sac*, the court, even the cloister, have to be re-thought by the modern architect in new terms, and recaptured in original designs, adapted to our present needs. No mere sighs of admiration, however voluminous, for the Piazzo San Marco, will produce the kind of public space the modern city and the modern neighborhood need.

Let me sum up. The neighborhood is a social fact; it exists in an inchoate form even when it is not articulated on a plan or provided with the institutions needed by a domestic community. By conscious design and provision the neighborhood may become an essential organ of an integrated city; and the discussion of the problems raised by neighborhood design will lead to solutions that will carry further the movement begun theoretically in Perry's studies, carried out concretely at Radburn, and applied on a large scale in the British New Towns. Has not the time come for a much more comprehensive canvass of the social functions of the neighborhood, for a more subtle and sympathetic

interpretation of the needs of urban families at every stage in the cycle of human growth, and a more adventurous exploration of alternative solutions?

## Bibliography

Anything like a thorough bibliography of the idea of the neighborhood unit would take one far afield, beginning, possibly, with Thomas More's description in his Utopia, going on through schemes like those of Owen and Godin, to say nothing of Fourier, into such practical achievements as those in Amana, Iowa, a group of communities, self-contained but related villages, that successfully embodied all the principles of neighborhood association. Under Professor Franklin Giddings at Columbia there was an early Ph.D. study of the neighborhood as a social unit but we are still lacking in positive studies of well-integrated neighborhoods, though the Chicago school has justly made a name for itself by reason of its ecological studies of blighted and disintegrated neighborhoods. We need a whole series of fresh studies that will do justice both to the social pattern and the civic design, beginning with historic examples of the neighborhood plan. The following citations deal solely with the modern concept of the neighborhood.

American Public Health Association. Committee on the Hygiene of Housing. *Planning the Neighborhood.* Public Administration Service. Chicago: 1948.

Cooley, Charles Horton. *Social Organisation.* New York: 1909.

Dahir, James. *The Neighborhood Unit Plan: Its Spread and Acceptance; A Selective Bibliography.* New York: Russell Sage Foundation. 1947.

Isaacs, Reginald R. "Are Urban Neighborhoods Possible?" In the *Journal of Housing,* (July-August, 1948).

---

* See the analysis of the relation of speed to urban form in Hamlin, Talbot: *Forms and Functions of 20th Century Architecture,* Vol. IV. p. 775 ff.

Perry, Clarence. " The Neighborhood Unit : A scheme of arrangement for the Family Life Community." In *A Regional Plan for New York and Environs*; Vol. vii. New York : 1929.

Stephenson, Flora and Gordon. *Community Centres*. London : The Housing Centre, 1946.

Tyler, W. Russell. " The Neighborhood Unit Principle in Town Planning," *Town Planning Review*, (July, 1939).

Unwin, Raymond. " Distribution." In the *Town Planning Institute Journal*, (1920-21).

Yeomans, Alfred (Editor). *City Residential Land Development*. Chicago : 1916.

# III

# The housing market

## Housing design and family values

*JOHN P. DEAN*

For some years now, thoughtful architects and housers have puzzled about just what makes a house "work." By ingenious speculation on the implications of previous errors they have built up an impressionistic working knowledge of the "Do's" and "Don'ts" of housing design. Periodically they feel dissatisfied with their rules of thumb and turn hopefully to the social scientist for more reliable knowledge about family life so they can achieve a better running adjustment between houses-to-be and family activities.

For the most part, the social scientist has been of limited help. His efforts to be of assistance have generally taken one of four tracks, all of them with shortcomings from the architect's view point:

(a) The social scientist has asked families about their housing "wants" and "preferences." But, as Svend Riemer has pointed out,[1] the person being quizzed is likely to respond with whatever housing wants are cur-

rently on the top of his head. Wants satisfied by his current quarters will be overlooked in favor of the wants most keenly felt in comparison, say to what other families on his social range have acquired. And all sorts of intangible values such as owning one's own home or declaring one's status to fellow men are likely to intrude and muddy the waters.

(b) A second approach of the social scientist has been to tackle the problem from the negative side: what are the irritations and pet peeves induced by the house one is living in? This procedure succeeded admirably in getting at the obvious oversights of the architect and builder and has probably been in part responsible for such improvements as the increase in well-planned storage space. Housewives' articulateness about too few closets was beginning to become a market factor.

Comparisons of these two approaches disclose that, by and large, they yield two different types of data: (1) the "wants and preferences" ap-

*Reprinted from* Land Economics, *vol. 29 (May, 1953), pp. 128–141, with permission of the journal.*

proach gives clues as to sales appeal items that would attract home seekers' attention before *living in the dwelling;* (2) the "pet peeves" approach reveals obvious malfunctioning features *experienced while living in the dwelling.* Neither of these is satisfactory to the progressive architect; he may feel that the advantages of contemporary design are apprehended through experience living in the dwelling but, since few of his clients have such experience, about all he can do is dangle before their eyes living features that he hopes will counterbalance their spuriously derived "wants," and hope that by this process he can induce them to release him from the shackles of having to design a traditional house.

(c) To fill in the unchartered waters between "wants" and "pet peeves," the social scientists and architect took to asking families about their actual activities in and around the dwelling in hope that by analyzing these "use patterns" they could infer how well the current quarters "worked" and perhaps design more suitable quarters for other families. Do families actually eat in the kitchen? If so, let's not be middle-class, but frankly design kitchens with room for eating. Do working-class families have large overstuffed furniture that must be allowed for? If so, let's make allowance in our housing projects.

Even this approach has difficulties that stand out. Because of the infinite plasticity of human behavior, different family types seem to adapt their use patterns and housing habits to tremendous varieties of dwelling structures they happen to inhabit without experiencing serious dissatisfactions or deprivations. Let's face it; for most families the inadequate dwellings they now live in *do work* – not perhaps to a nicety or to a progressive architect's sharply focused eye. But it seems that the family's focus, being not nearly so sharp as the architect's, just picks up the crude blacks and whites and evaluates the house in rather gross terms. Much of the detail that goes into precise evaluations of housing operation seems to be below the average tenant's threshold of awareness. The housewife just doesn't know that not having stacking space on the right of the sink makes her take 21 percent more time to wash dishes.[2]

(d) To undercut this level-of-awareness factor, social scientists have introduced direct observation, inspection, and measurement. Time and motion studies are borrowed from industrial engineers and applied to operations in the kitchen. With this innovation, some of us felt that science had finally arrived on the housing scene. But this approach too readily adopts as its main yardstick *standards of efficient home management.* Tenant, architect, and social scientist will probably agree that this is too narrow. True, many aspects of house design and house furnishings are judged by all of us as to whether they aid or impede housekeeping. In the squirrel cage of endless household routines, the objectives of food preparation, dishwashing, bed making, housecleaning, etc. are all fairly explicit. As a workshop where the housewife is employed in daily chores, both house and housekeeper can be evaluated on technological efficiency, long a familiar norm in industrial operations. Rarely applied in the past to the sacred territory of family life, increased efficiency is today a moving spirit of home economics with its "time budgeting," space-and-motion studies, household hints, and time-saving gadgets.[3] One unpublished study pointed out that families with power-driven washing machines spend as much time doing the wash as those with no machines – because machines encourage women to do *more* laundry *more* often.

These studies are valuable; they steadily improve the standards for all sorts of household equipment. But if we were to accept them as the answer to house-family relationships, we would fall into the trap of adopting the standard of evaluation most easily made scientific in lieu of broader evaluations that we all feel are necessary but more difficult to specify.

Perhaps our greatest difficulty in trying to arrive at a more profound understanding of house-family relationships is the confusion we fall into when we try to specify more exactly (a), what it is about family life that we want to relate to housing and (b), what are the variations in housing design that we hypothesize would most affect those aspects of family life that we have specified.

We are faced with exceedingly difficult decisions when we try to choose which values in family life we should plan homes for. Let us assume that we would provide a tailor-made house for every family. To decide what would have to be included in a given house we would want to give consideration to each of the following:

(1) Those housing wants clearly recognized by a family as things they explicitly seek (e.g., an eating nook in the kitchen for breakfasts, lunches, snacks, etc.).

(2) Those taste preferences (hardly to be dignified as "needs") that would please the family (e.g., Dutch Colonial style with green shutters).

(3) Those dimly apprehended needs often overlooked entirely in the expression of housing desires (e.g., privacy for parental discussion, or a suitable study space for teen-agers).

(4) Those needs that the architect feels the family should have but of which the family is quite unaware (e.g., careful provisions for safety in the bathroom, on the stairs, and in the kitchen).

(5) Those needs that various scientific specialists feel essential to improved family living (e.g., the pediatrician's suggestions for improved infant care, the health specialist's suggestions for lighting).

Each of these various levels of needs may differ for each family member and sometimes will clearly conflict. If the society could provide for each family a fifteen- or twenty-room mansion on an acre of land, the majority of individual and family activities and psychological needs might be moderately provided for. But when it becomes necessary to collapse the twenty-room house into a four- or five-room bungalow to meet the needs of reality, we must choose arbitrarily among the various needs and interests and lop off things that penalize this or that family member and favor this way of life over that. If there is no ultimate arbiter among differences in values, we need, at least, intensive research on the way multiple needs *are* composed in order to squeeze them into a modest house and try to determine the differential impact on *which* housing values, and of *which* family members.

Such research would indeed be valuable. But it would still be rather limited. It would yield information on how housing design relates to the *housing values*. Evidence is beginning to accumulate suggesting that families are influenced by their living environments in all sorts of ways that neither the family *nor* the architect *nor* the social scientist was formerly aware of:

(a) Robert Merton found that the majority of residents of Craftown, a planned housing community, were more active politically in Craftown than in the community where they lived before.[4] I doubt if Dr. Merton attributes this change to any specific design aspect of the housing; yet undoubtedly it is related to the changes families moving into Craftown underwent in their new living environment – living environment conceived not narrowly as just the physical housing plant, but broadly as the total sociophysical environment they were exposed to by their change of quarters.

(b) The Massachusetts Institute of Technology study of the Westgate housing development shows that physical layout is clearly related to the patterns of group formation and the social pressures they exert on the residents.[5]

(c) The Collins and Deutsch research on intergroup relations in several mixed housing projects.[6] Merton's study of the racially mixed Hilltown project,[7] and our own researches on intergroup relations in mixed residential neighborhoods in an upstate New York community, all concur in finding that the residential environment has a marked influence on race attitudes and friendship formation between the races.

(d) These studies also agree in finding that residential propinquity is a major determinant of friendship formation, however unaware of it the residents may be.

(e) The importance of seeing the influence of the residential environment in these broad terms is pointed up by a consideration of a community we have been studying in our intergroup relations research. The community is composed of 400 or so families that interact closely. A community center promotes a local contact point for members of the community, especially teen-agers, and provides program activities that bring members of the community together. Social pressures operate within the community to bring about participation and conformity much as in a rural village. Over half of the members of the community belong to four organizations or more. Observers agree that it is a well integrated community.

From this description we can see that this community must have a housing layout that encourages social interaction, much as the Westgate or Craftown housing projects do. Actually, there is nothing of the sort. These are the 400 Jewish families in Elmira scattered as they are throughout the 18-20,000 families that make up the city. It is unusual for more than a few to live in any one neighborhood and even then Gentile families far outnumber them. For most of these families changing their place of residence from one neighborhood to another would have little effect on their social interaction or the social environments to which they are exposed.

Now what are the implications of these various findings? First of all, they suggest that we might pose the problem of relating housing to family life much more broadly. Instead of merely trying to relate *housing* design to *housing* values, we should relate the whole socio-housing environment to the residents' total scheme of values. We should ask what are the basic value patterns of individual family members and how, in this particular housing environment, do they become converted into a characteristic way of life? One finding emerging from our community studies seems rather patent when stated, but is of basic importance to these considerations of housing research: most people in patterning their daily activities develop a sort of "Indian path" that they tread from home to work, then back to home, then to lodge meeting, back to home; on Sundays to church and back, and then perhaps a visit to close relatives. Then the pattern repeats. Once developed, most persons stay on their Indian path and only once in a while get off into the forest where all the rest of the hustle and bustle of urban life takes place. Each person's Indian path is different from all the rest and there is all manner of variety in the range and types of Indian paths. But for the typical person, the Indian path is a rather narrow walk of life that exposes him to two or three, maybe four, different social environments; that's all. All of these environments bear down upon him with their social pressures, their group processes, their standards of attitudes and behavior. From time to time the Indian paths are modified by major transitions or crises in people's lives: births, deaths, changes of marital status, and changes of job. But perhaps the most frequent alterations in Indian paths take place as a result of changes in dwelling place, that in turn induce changes in the Indian paths of family members and the social environments to which they are exposed.

If these considerations hold true, the greatest influence of housing design on family life is the way it modifies the number and kind of social environments to which family members are exposed. A change of residential environment will usually alter the social interaction of family members not only among themselves but also most especially their social interaction in the surrounding neighborhood and in the community at large. Thus we would hypothesize that the following aspects of housing design are most crucial to family life:

(a) The location of the dwelling unit with regard to other major social environments where family members participate (or would be likely to participate). These include especially the play centers, the schools, the work place of the father, the church, social, economic, and political organizations, informal contact centers outside the neighborhood, close friends, and relatives.

(b) The orientation of neighborhood dwelling units to each other and to local neighborhood contact centers.

(c) The extent to which the housing design encourages or discourages performance of the living functions within the dwelling space or outside the home through congregate facilities or special *ad hoc* arrangements.

(d) The ways in which the style and plan of the house are related to the interaction of family members with each other and with their close personal contacts outside the home.

The remainder of this paper will be devoted to spinning hypotheses on (b), (c) and (d).

## Aspect (b)

*Tentative hypotheses about the influence on the family of the orientation of dwelling units to each other, and to neighborhood contact centers.*

Neither the internal organization of the dwelling unit nor the specific functions allocated to it is, probably, as influential in exposing family members to new social environments as the way the dwellings are grouped with regard to each other, to the local contact centers and to the prevailing ways of circulation. As Professor Kennedy has pointed out about the Westgate project, " these building relationships are of the greatest importance socially and ... are major determinants in friendship formation and thus social groupings."

In speculating about the implications of the studies that show the almost incredible influence of proximity upon friendship formation, we are drawn again and again to analogies reminiscent of gravitational theory. It almost seems sometimes as though two neighbors are attracted to each other directly in proportion to their common social characteristics and inversely as the square of their distance. If we could only reduce differences in social characteristics to a function of social distance we could derive our whole theory of neighboring from Kepler's law, pack up our things, and go home.

Unfortunately it's never that simple in social science. But it is worth speculating for a moment on the importance of neighborhood in drawing family members into new social relationships. We might hypothesize the following as of major importance:

(1) proximity of the dwellings to each other;
(2) the recurring contact opportunities that arise out of circulation;
(3) the location of casual contact centers that bring people together; and
(4) the existence of community facilities and leadership that encourage the formation of associations drawing memberships from the neighborhood.

Given these, residents with a normal quantum

of sociability, a lapse of time for recurring contact opportunities to bring residents together and we can guarantee that many family members will be drawn into new social environments. And as Festinger et al. have so well demonstrated, the social pressures of those groups may be a powerful influence in molding members' attitudes and behavior.

A few other hypotheses about this process:

(a) The more heterogeneous a neighborhood in the social characteristics of its residents, the more likely it is that friendship formation will depend most on organized associations, somewhat less on informal contact centers, and very little on sheer proximity.

(b) The absolute number of families in an area (above, say, fifty families) has little to do with the amount of friendship formation, since friendship is related to the number of recurring contact opportunities between families, not the number of families. London Terrace, the densest block in New York City, provides each resident recurring contact opportunities with just a few neighbors. The Elliott Lovejoy Houses just a few blocks away has many fewer families, but the recurring opportunities for contact for each family touch many more neighbors.

(c) Families with value orientation patterns and activity patterns " anchored " (to borrow Festinger's phrase) outside the neighborhood are less likely to be drawn into friendship formations by recurring contact opportunities.

(d) For family members in a given neighborhood setting, the recurring contact opportunities (for adults, anyway) and the social pressures of group formation sort out the congenial social environments to which residents will continue to be exposed. The cycle of social environments a person passes through during the course of his day-to-day living (i.e., his " Indian path ") tends to rigidify and limit the number of new, recurring contact opportunities and therefore the likelihood that the person will become exposed to new social environments.

How much a housing development becomes an isolated social island in the urban environment depends on (1), the differences in social characteristics between the housing tenantry and the residents of the surrounding neighborhood and (2), the ratio of the recurring contact opportunities tenants have to meet *each other* to the recurring contact opportunities they have to meet *residents nearby*. The housing design features that are most crucial are those that affect the differential availability of local contact centers to project tenants and nearby residents.

### Aspect (c)

*Tentative hypotheses on the effect of allocating various living functions to the dwelling unit or to congregate facilities outside the house.*

"Home" as a *locus* of family activities is frequently confused with "family" as a set of interacting loyalties and activities among family members *regardless of where they take place*. On the Cornbelt family-farm, this confusion causes no trouble. But as the twentieth-century developments in communications, mobility, special interest groups, technological innovations, and community services increasingly release activities of family members from a particular locus, it becomes possible, theoretically at least, to maintain family interaction without recourse to the traditional housekeeping dwelling. For many husband-and-wife families, affectional, companionship, recreational, aesthetic, and personal values within the home are balanced by a wide range of pursuits outside the home, such as occupational advancement, participation in community affairs, sports and other forms of recreation. Families with such value patterns might favorably evaluate living arrangements that involve shared or congregate facilities for many of the burdensome household tasks, with the functions of the dwelling unit per se ( – but not necessarily the space requirements) reduced to include only a privacy area for sleeping, dressing, toileting, sex relations, and personal care of the children; storage space for frequently used articles; and an immediate living area (preferably involving both indoor and outdoor space) for adult leisure and child play, for personal expression through decorating, arranging, and miscellaneous puttering, and for informal social life and entertaining. The major items of furniture and equipment could be furnished or built-in. Dwelling units such as these would satisfy family requirements only if good congregate facilities were provided for food preparation and its serving; call-for-and-deliver services of all kinds; housecleaning services; library and study areas; recreational facilities; community and clubrooms.

Like life on a college campus (sometimes deep in the city) congregate facilities would encourage informal social interchange among congenial persons of roughly the same age and status and would facilitate a wide range of contact, more casual " dropping in " and " visiting," softball, cards, or horseshoes, the casual chitchat of chance meetings while going to and fro, and the satisfactions of occasional impulsive "doing things together." Solitary walking, hanging around to watch, and just sitting and doing nothing would still be available to those who valued them. Today they are more often the symptoms of widespread social isolation and barren personal lives.

Congregate living arrangements are not generally considered satisfactory for promoting the values of family life, perhaps because we associate them with situations where there are inadequate provisions for intimate affectional needs (orphanages, poorhouses), insufficient personal freedom (prisons, mental hospitals), inadequate provision for a minimum plane of living (concentration camps, municipal lodging houses), or inadequate provisions for privacy (army barracks, college dormitories). Where these objections do not apply, congregate living arrangements could cater to a large number of customers among families such as the following : professional couples with husband and wife frequently engaged away from home; graduate-student couples; elderly couples; full-time working couples; husband-wife combinations active in community affairs; mothers who want greater freedom from the double task of housekeeping and child care; career wives; families with an indefinite future; cosmopolitan couples (citizens of the world); families wanting to "travel light," unburdened by accumulated possessions; transients; families with individuated life patterns (Bohemian or other); uncongenial mates with separate discourse groups; and finally, but not to be underestimated, wives whose value patterns just devaluate housework.

Many busy families undoubtedly look upon the traditional housekeeping tasks with distaste; an increasing number of them may wonder if housekeeping is a necessary burden. For most of them the answer is probably " Yes." Set firmly against any attempt to alter the home by emancipating *from* it some of the activities now assigned *to* it are numerous cultural sentiments that reaffirm the traditional housekeeping dwelling unit inherited from the family farm, the plantation, and the old homestead; the stress on family sanctity; the belief in family independence and self-sufficiency; the urge for ownership of property and possessions; and the need to protect the privacy of family life.

Where these values are deeply held, the traditional housekeeping dwelling will continue to fill the bill but, as the tug of war between " home " and the " outside world " becomes intensified, sharpened conflicts about the housekeeping functions of the dwelling will increasingly stand out. We can already see symptoms of this: (1) sentimental and not too cogent rationalizations in support of the traditional home; (2) halfway measures such as furnished apartments with maid service, frequent eating out, once-a-week cleaning ladies; (3) intermittent escapes into the luxury of congregate living in hotels, vacation resorts, shipboard life, and house parties. Experiences such as these may increasingly modify family members' evaluations of the labor standards and working conditions that prevail for full-time housewives. If a greater range of dwellings were planned with some congregate arrangements, we could perhaps find out how considerations of this sort fit into the values of American families.

Of course the allocation of the major clusters of family living functions to places outside the home can vary all the way from complete congregate facilities with little provision for privacy at one extreme, to the complete housekeeping dwelling unit at the other. In between lie all sorts of halfway measures that might be suited to families in special circumstances.

From the point of view of how housing influences family life, congregate facilities are important because they usually expose the user to a new social environment. Take the day nursery for instance. The World War II employment

emergencies forced many mothers to park their children in nurseries while they worked. Regardless of whether the nursery school was a good one with trained supervision or an *ad hoc* retention device to get Jimmy off mother's hands, the social experience with a significant peer group often was influential in the youngster's life. Likewise congregate arrangements such as joint recreational facilities, joint dining facilities, joint study areas, even joint bathing facilities – each of these could modify the social interaction of family members quite substantially and revamp their significant social environments. Conversely, installing in the dwelling unit an entire productive workshop for the housewife may reduce her social participation and bring about increased exposure to soap operas, television, or True Story. These, too, will have their impact.

Even though we are in agreement that the architect should try to understand the overall value pattern of family members, how shall we answer this query: " What can you do when the family members themselves are in conflict or in doubt about their own values?" Take the role of the wife in a modern family.[8] She may be pulled several different ways by the goals that her background and training have induced in her. American women are often caught among several incompatible roles that they expect themselves to play.

If, for instance, a wife values highly a *Hausfrau* role that stresses her functions as cook, waitress, chambermaid, cleaning lady, laundress, seamstress, social secretary, and general housekeeper, the home would be evaluated by her as a productive economic workshop where she would want to be employed as efficiently as possible. The full housekeeping dwelling unit would best suit her orientation. But if the wife values more highly her role as an up-to-date mother and accepts her biological destiny in order to contribute to the next generation, she would evaluate favorably those living arrangements that provided: nursery-gymnasium facilities, equipment to care for infants, arrangements easy for supervising child play both inside and out, durable furnishings to withstand rough treatment by her wild Indians, and protected areas for adult quiet and privacy. If the wife is

## Cluster of family values*

*Familistic type.* Strong in-group feelings and identification with the family name, family traditions. The integration of individual activities for the attainment of family objectives. Money and possessions conceived as family property, with understanding they may be used for the support of individual needs. Concern for family perpetuation and defense of members from outside attack.

*Integrated individualized type.* Cooperative furtherance of member's self-realization of his potentialities and objectives. Coordination of family activities for the attainment of individual ends. Some property family oriented, but also some emphasis on individual possessions. Individual rights given in return for individual responsibilities. Mutual concern for individual happiness.

*Emancipated type.* Personal pursuit of individual goals to the exclusion of (or conflict with) other family members. Coordination, if any, from individual realization of personal benefits from cooperation. Individual property with little or no obligation to family welfare. Heavy concern for self-interest, with the troubles of others conceived as their own responsibility.

*Status-striving type.* Pursuit of career success and secure social position, and the accoutrements of status and prestige. Activities of individual family members are scanned with an eye to how they reflect upon the family status, strong encouragement to competitive success in community affairs.

## Examples of use patterns flowing from this value orientation

1. The family is the basic social unit. Other social ties subordinated to family coherence.
2. Large families, much intradwelling unit interaction, heirlooms and possessions.
3. Many group activities, family occasions, special holiday celebrations and the family council.
4. Major housekeeping tasks performed in the dwelling unit. (a good bet for home ownership of the family homestead variety).

1. Frequent interaction of family members with other institutions.
2. Easy come and go, informal entertaining, segregated leisure activities.
3. The gearing of simultaneous individual pursuits, with appropriate privacy, space, and equipment.
4. Servicing the family at home with simplified economic tasks (a good bet for a modern house of contemporary design).

1. The integration of individual activities in social groupings outside the dwelling.
2. Minimum of activities in the home, which becomes primarily dormitory in function.
3. Maximum personal privacy, separate breakfasts, snacks and sleeping times.
4. Housekeeping service, delicatessen meals, call-for-and-deliver services (a good bet for congregate living facilities).

1. Activities of family members organized for the pursuit of extra-family goals.
2. Frequent social entertaining and much attention to well appointed house furnishings.
3. Planning by the social calendar, hospitality and the well-stocked larder and sideboard.
4. Maid service where possible (a good home with appropriate status symbols).

---

* Each of these types should be considered merely an *ideal* typical construct that is only more or less approximated in any real life setting.

a status striver who stresses her role as *socialite*, the acquisition of possessions, decor, manners, and mannerisms to induce favorable reactions in the eyes of significant others, the house would be appraised according to how well it met the social demands of decorum and partying. The wife who is a *careerist* has to subordinate some of the more traditional feminine duties in order to pursue her job goal full time. Her evaluation of the living arrangements might well stress the amount of personal and housekeeping services that could be shifted outside the home: and so on for the glamor-girl role, the companion-to-the-male role and all the other permutations and combinations of role emphasis that American womanhood reveals in its value patterning. Until value conflicts that are embodied in these incompatible roles are resolved, it is hard to know what activities the dwelling should be planned for. Meanwhile we need to study how different living arrangements facilitate or impede segmental role behavior and heighten or lower the conflict tension.

The wide variations in over-all value patterns are probably more important in determining levels of satisfaction and dissatisfaction with living arrangements than details about kitchen layout or plumbing. If we hypothesize that among the many different types of value patterns found in today's family life, the following type-clusters are frequently discernible; then it may be worth guessing at a few of the housing implications that flow from these value patterns.

Just a word about the status strivers. With the importance economic class carries in assigning family prestige in American society, it is natural that class competition enters into the evaluation of the home and its furnishing. Since major criteria of class status in urban America today are financial standing, occupation, and social background, the status-striving family naturally converts these into tangible assets that reveal their aspirations, if not their achieved goals. As a repository of family traditions and possessions, the home helps to peg one's social class at the highest economic level the family achieved in the past. This situation probably explains why many families claim higher social class than economic class.*

Through heirlooms a family can borrow heavily on the class standing of its forebears. And the active trading in antiques auction sales, and second-hand shops suggests that more than a few families have discovered that recently won purchasing power, through the home one presents to friends, can be converted into a beguiling bluff of social background. Perhaps these are among the reasons that status strivers cling to the symbolism of the traditional home and appear to be relatively unimpressed by the contemporary architect and his more functional wares.

Any such over-simplified picture of the relation of family values to housing use patterns can be no more than suggestive. The main point is that such value clusters are important in determining just what a family puts in and takes out of a given set of living arrangements. Just how value clusters align themselves in real life is a field task to be determined by empirical research.

## Aspect (d)

*Tentative hypotheses on the relation of intra-dwelling unit interaction to the values of family members.*

Interaction among family members is determined much more by the personalities and role patterns of the mates than by the physical house they inhabit. The major role patterns that gear interaction derive from emotionally-laden learning experiences that are deeply grounded in the past and resist modification. Hence, families will generally force their patterns of role interaction into a given dwelling unit and accept minor inconveniences and hardships in order to maintain their interaction patterns. In other words, the *use* patterns of family members are probably more important than the design per se in

---

* When people are asked with what income class they identify themselves and with what social class they identify themselves (upper, upper-middle, middle, lower-middle, lower); 54 percent give the same income and social class, 3.2 percent give an income group one or more steps higher than social class, 42.5 percent give a social class one or more steps higher than the income class they give. Hadley Cantril, "Identification with Social and Economic Class," *Journal of Abnormal and Social Psychology*, (January, 1943), (inpaged reprint).

determining how well the dwelling "works" for a given family.

In large part, the housing use patterns seem to be symptomatic and symbolic of family relationships and can be used as a diagnostic tool for understanding the family; but we can hypothesize that intra-dwelling unit variations probably have little significant influence on family relations unless they promote the exposure of one or another of the family members to a new social environment. This *does* occasionally occur – for instance, when overcrowding or other substandard living conditions induce members out of the house to the ball park, the street corner gang, or the barroom.

But, by and large, the architect in designing the individual dwelling unit is mainly concerned to plan for the maximum convenient housing of the family's established activity patterns (or " use patterns ").

Since families compress their multiple needs into houses that are limited in one way or another, they develop their patterns of use haphazardly and unreflectively. Frictions in the use of the dwelling unit are bound to arise. Being close to the scene and unsensitized to these problems, family members often have serious blind spots in understanding these frictions, especially when they are deeply related to personality needs.

Much of the friction derives from the different ways family members evaluate their homes and living arrangements because of differences in their value patterns. If the wife is especially sensitive to what her social callers will think of the living room decorum, but the husband is inclined to make use of it for his own spontaneous relaxing and cluttering, we are likely to see the fur fly.

On the basis of a pilot study[9] into the values of family members that are most frequently invoked in evaluating the living arrangements, the writer hypothesizes the following values as most salient:

(1) Does it (a given aspect of the living arrangements) promote or impede the *efficient operation* of household tasks? (See above.)

(2) How does it look to friends or relatives or others whose opinions matter? Household arrangements must frequently undergo the test

of "How would it look to others?" or "Is it presentable?" This *norm of decorum* regulates most rigorously and consistently those areas of the house most likely to fall under the scrutiny of outsiders.

(3) Does it hamper attempts to live up to accepted *moral standards about family living*, especially what family members expect of each other as mother or father, husband or wife, son or daughter? Quite naturally living arrangements provoke moral reactions whenever the touchy objects of sex, elimination, child training, and allocation of household responsibilities are involved. Differences in family background and early childhood conditioning frequently endow spouses with quite different reactions to nudity and exposure, dressing, and undressing, personal privacies, or property rights.

(4) Does it facilitate or inhibit the *spontaneous personal reactions and activities* of different family members? Individuals differ widely in personal interests, aesthetic tastes, habits of relaxation, reactions to dirt and cleanliness, tidiness and clutter. Yet these are the recurring standards of reference for many aspects of the living arrangements.

Today, despite serious overcrowding and doubling up, our house production machinery continues to offer more and more small houses and apartments. Within the limited universe of the dwelling unit, the concurrent application by family members of different value standards to the quarters, activates "household tensions"; i.e., conflicting evaluations of the different aspects of the living arrangements. As one respondent in the pilot study remarked : " My wife is an efficient housekeeper and keeps things a little neater than I do, although I also am rather intolerant of a ' messy ' house. My wife is more interested in keeping clean any part of the house that might be exposed to the public eye; on the other hand, I have to constantly clean out and rearrange our storage closets because of the lack of orderliness in putting things away." These differential reactions vary from minor preferences in personal tastes to deep and abiding rifts in personality needs. Because the home and the furnishings persist through time, differences about the living quarters are recurring sources of friction; the dwelling unit sometimes becomes a constant sniping ground for interpersonal hostility. Much of the friction in the dwelling unit can be explained by the various counter pulls among *efficiency, decorum, spontaneity, and morality.*

It may be worth offering a few tentative hypotheses as to what happens in an intra-dwelling unit when there are conflicting evaluations of the dwelling arrangements (and family tension of this sort is virtually universal).

(1) Where the conflict becomes intense, the use patterns tend to modify into a different space-time pattern that reduces the friction and is less destructive to family morale. There are at least four common types of patterns to resolve these household tensions: (a) spacial segregation, (b) time scheduling, (c) functional differentiation of occasions or objects, and (d) dominance and exercise of controls.

(2) Where family feeling is relatively harmonious, competing uses for space in the home will most frequently be resolved by scheduling different times for the competing uses. But where family conflict is more intense, family members tend unconsciously to "stake out area claims" and defend these territories as private domains. The allocation and defense of territorial boundaries frequently results from a test of power after which some bargain or balance may be achieved and maintained by "power politics." The greater the conflict, the more institutionalized and inviolate the delineated areas tend to become. Insofar as special segregation is institutionalized and accepted, the various family members expect and demand service from the ruler of the domain. It becomes "keep out and I'll tend to it" rather than "you know where it is, get it yourself." The bargaining process that grows up in such circumstances tends to instate a system of parallel rights and duties in the household.

(3) Where conflict prevails and space is seriously limited the husband may yield to the wife's traditional role as housekeeper, and delegate all matters of housekeeping and decorating to the wife. Or if the wife's emphasis on decorum is all-consuming, she may just "take over" and establish controls over neatness and decorum.

(4) A most tension-provoking value conflict that prevails in many of today's middle-class homes is the conflict between decorum and spontaneity. The living room of a small house is frequently given over to decorum and maintained in shipshape condition right around the clock. Family members, especially children, may be kept out, controlled, or inhibited against a free and easy use of living room. Under these circumstances the kitchen and bedrooms tend to become the casual living areas. In the Victorian house this rivalry between decorum and spontaneity was resolved by segregating a "parlor" as well as a "living room." Today's increasing demand for "rumpus" rooms or "playrooms" probably reflects the channeling of spontaneity away from the living room (today's "parlor") toward more flexible spaces.

(5) Many of the conflicts between spontaneity and decorum are resolved by differentiating "everyday" furnishings from "guest specials." This arrangement most commonly applies to furnishings that are breakable, soilable, or non-durable and therefore worth preserving in good condition to impress guests. Some families have special guest silver, guest dishes, guest towels, guest doilies, bathmats, guest everything. As guests get on a more familiar relationship with the family, the guest specials are gradually dropped. Where many of the household furnishings or arrangements are differentiated as "good" and "everyday," spontaneous entertaining of the "come-back-and-have-a-bite-with-us" or "let's-go-over-to-our-house" variety becomes inhibited because of the necessary changes that have to be made. Some families will maintain the living room constantly guest-oriented and if unexpected guests descend on them, make a few quick bathroom changes and then differentiate by using their "good" service ware. Where the differentiation is extreme, entertaining of any kind may become a major household chore. This guest-oriented decor is reflected *en famille* in the use of the "good" furnishings for family use only on special occasions or when the family members feel festive. Fear of breakage usually inhibits everyday use. The guest specials frequently symbolize new role and status relations to the children: "having company," being hospitable, learning to differentiate

what is acceptable *en famille* but not in the presence of company. Because the child doesn't discriminate well at first, the use of guest specials may call forth embarrassing comments from the children.

These speculations about family values and intra-dwelling unit interaction have been spelled out in some detail in order to suggest how varied are the ways in which personal values are engaged in the evaluation of living arrangements.

What are the possibilities of making research headway on these problems? In terms of the scientific techniques we have so far developed: excellent – depending primarily on administrative will to get the answers, and a modest budget to back up researchers in gathering and analyzing the data.

Architects and housing administrators deplore the lack of scientific knowledge that would help them make decisions on the location, size, and dwelling design of their projects. The architect can often advance equally cogent reasons for making decisions that are diametrically opposed. When such is the case – and doubtless it frequently is – the research imperative is clear: design half of the dwellings one way, the rest of them the other way and phone for the nearest social researcher.

Experimental opportunities like this are rare in the annals of social research design. The psychologist of family life cannot get half of the mothers to over-protect their children, half the mothers to be permissive; the race relations researcher cannot get half of his sample to mingle socially with Negroes, the other half to avoid contact. But in housing research we have research designs by the bushel. Half of the units of a project, half of the building structures, perhaps half of the projects under joint supervision, could often incorporate the experimental variables, the other half omit them and thus be the control group.

The objection may be raised: if the experimental way of design is better than the other, doesn't this just guarantee that half of the dwellings will have the inferior design? Casting research designs in reinforced concrete is a pretty expensive way to find out, isn't it? The answer is this: such research designs should be used only when there is genuine lack of knowledge as to which design practice is superior. When such is the case, the half-and-half research design at least guarantees that half of the dwellings will have the *superior* design – and strongly increase the chances that by the time of the next building operation, scientific findings will reinforce the superior alternative for *all* the dwellings.

Why is it that architects and housing administrators are so reluctant to experiment forthrightly in this way? Perhaps they are resting on the false assumption that all-or-none decisions based on guesswork are not experimenting. At least, the all-or-none procedure is reassuring in that it makes it impossible to ascertain the limits of architectural doubt. It also guarantees that the frontiers of that doubt will not be pushed back by the slow accretion of scientific knowledge.

# Family housing expenditures:
# elusive laws and intrusive variances

*SHERMAN J. MAISEL and LOUIS WINNICK*

## Some tentative conclusions

Our probe into the housing data of the *Study of Consumer Expenditures* yields one main conclusion: housing expenditures of American families are far too diverse to be explained by simple principles. Much of this diversity is real, i.e., inherent in consumer behavior. Choice of housing (which necessarily means choice of community and neighborhood) is a response to an extremely complex set of economic, social, and psychological impulses.

However, much of the variation which has been uncovered can also be attributed to the unsuitability of cross-sectional budget data for the derivation of "laws" of housing demand. Adjustments in housing arrangements to changes in individual circumstances are notoriously tardy and discontinuous. Budget data for housing therefore represent an amalgam of current attributes (age, occupation, income, etc.) with a variety of housing decisions made in the past, or which may, in varying degrees, anticipate the future.

Further, a large-scale survey of consumer expenditures must, as a practical matter, employ definitions and classifications which facilitate reporting and tabulation. However reasonable the adopted rules, they will not be equally useful to all investigators. In particular, the failure (a) to maintain a distinction between mortgaged and nonmortgaged homeowners, and (b) to re-

port the contractual mortgage repayments of indebted owners, gives rise to large if artificial differences. These affect not only the analysis of the housing sector but of other consumption relationships as well.

It is not that no connections can be traced between reported housing expenditures and socio-economic variables. Indeed, many distinct patterns in housing expenditures and choice of tenure emerge and are described in our paper. But when an attempt is made to measure the strength of these relationships, they are found to be feeble. They show up most clearly in group averages and tend to become progressively weaker when the data are disaggregated. In the ungrouped data (individual families) none of the independent variables tested accounts for more than a small proportion of total variance.

The main positive result of our negative findings is to point up the need for improvements in methodology. It is doubtful that reliable housing demand relationships will ever be formed until cross-sectional data are supplemented by longitudinal and attitudinal studies and until a more clear-cut definition of housing consumption is established.

## I. Problems in measuring consumers' housing behavior

It would be fair to say that recent discussions of demand relationships formed from

*Extracted from* Family Housing Expenditures: Elusive Laws and Intrusive Variances, *Reprint #25, Real Estate Research Program, University of California at Berkeley, pp. 359–368, 371–392, as taken from* Proceedings of the Conference on Consumption and Savings, *University of Pennsylvania, vol. I, 1960, with permission of the conference and program.*

cross-section data have centered on the choice and quality of independent variables. How valid a measure is current money income? How can life cycle be best introduced into regression equations? Should household inventories or liquid assets be included in the right-hand terms? Such questions are as pertinent for housing as for food or automobiles. But in the case of housing, more so than with other consumer goods or services, derived demand relationships are also seriously affected by the definition of the dependent variable and the manner in which the relevant data are reported and tabulated.

What constitutes the appropriate measure of housing consumption whose level and variations we are interested in explaining? Should we concern ourselves with the capital values of occupied dwelling units, or with current consumption flows? With economic measures of consumption or with cash expenditures? With outlays for reproducible shelter or for shelter and environment? With "pure" shelter or shelter plus various complementary goods and services? Such questions arise because of the many different interests in housing. Some are concerned with housing demand analysis primarily as a tool for forecasting residential construction or mortgage financing requirements. Others are concerned with housing as an index of welfare or standards of living. The attention of still others is fixed on housing's role in the allocation of family budgets among competing markets.

Our study was primarily directed toward measuring consumer's housing behavior in relation to general demand theory. We were interested in knowing what sacrifices of economic goods or resources a family is willing to make in order to meet its housing requirements. Because of the many unique economic and institutional factors associated with housing, it is difficult to determine which measurement of costs or expenditures comes closest to the concept of economic sacrifice. It also is hard to decide when a given outlay represents a sacrifice made for housing rather than for the satisfaction of other wants.

Housing is traded in both an asset market and a service market so that housing consumption may be measured either through capital stock and its changes or through current flows. Since housing is fixed in location, consumers buy, not merely a quantum of housing, but also a package of environmental and governmental services which often have little to do with shelter as such. Because of the extreme durability of housing and the large proportion of homes financed by debt, very sizable differences arise between the economic value of current housing services consumed and the amount of current cash outlays. Finally, legal arrangements and personal preferences permit wide variations in the amount and type of complementary goods and services included in housing payments.

Ideally, one could explore demand relationships for each alternative definition of housing consumption, compare results, and retain that relationship which offers the best explanation and has the greatest predictive value. In practice, however, available data restrict the choice of the dependent variable. Worse yet, available data, including the *Study of Consumer Expenditures*, do not provide consistent measures of housing consumption among individual consumers or groups of consumers. Inconsistencies in definition and classification, examples of which are summarized below, increase the dispersion of the dependent variable. Such "contributed" dispersion is added to the dispersion indigenous to consumer behavior and weakens the explanatory power of independent variables.

## Stock versus flow

As already noted, housing demand relationships can be obtained either from asset values of occupied dwelling units or by measuring current housing consumption as approximated, say, by rent or rental value. The derived results would presumably be similar but not identical. Similarity would be insured by the fact that the capital value of a dwelling unit is related to its current rent or rental value. Dissimilarities would be caused by the fact that rent or rental value does not form a constant ratio to capital value because of variations in (1) investment risks, resulting in differences in required yields which must be recovered from rent, and (2) real estate taxes and property maintenance.

Whether capital or rental values would give the best results is not now known. By either approach one important gain could be achieved – the combination of owner and renter families into the same demand equation. Separate analyses of each tenure group, now virtually unavoidable, may result in a misstatement of the true impact of important independent variables. For example, higher income is accompanied by higher homeownership rates. On the average, owners occupy larger and better dwellings than renters since, apparently, the change in tenure is associated with a desire to consume more housing. Consequently, an increase in income which brought a renter into homeownership would ordinarily be accompanied by a larger increment in consumption than if the family were merely to move upward in the rental housing scale.

The asset approach has never, to our knowledge, been attempted in budget studies. While values of owner-occupied homes are frequently collected in surveys, no similar data have ever been presented for renter-occupied units.*

Since the *Study of Consumer Expenditures* (referred to hereafter as SCE) was primarily concerned with consumption flows rather than with consumer assets, there was little reason to report data on house values. True, market values of owner-occupied housing were collected, but mainly for the purpose of measuring changes in net worth. The value data appear in none of the published volumes and were punched on the cards obtained by us only in stratified groups of "levels of housing," not readily useful for regression analysis or for comparisons with rental housing.

## Tenure and mortgage payments

Neither, unfortunately, did the SCE obtain consistent data on *current* housing consumption. The SCE set out not to measure consumption as such, but consumption expenditures. While for renters cash outlays and current housing consumption are closely related (subject to the qualifications listed below), the same is not at all true for owners.

An owner's economic sacrifice for housing is measured partly by the amount of cash he pays for such items as taxes, interest, and insurance. Even more important, however, are likely to be opportunity costs or those which require imputations such as interest on the equity and depreciation or appreciation in the capital value of the house.

Two owner families with identical homes will report entirely different cash expenditures depending on the amount of mortgage indebtedness and contractual mortgage terms.† It is known that the incidence of mortgage debt varies widely with such characteristics as occupation, location, income and especially age of head, (Table 1). In most income classes, for example, only one-third of owner families with a head 55 or more years old reported mortgage debt compared to more than 80 percent of heads under 35. This means that, when measured by current outlays, the actual housing consumption of the elderly tends to be understated relative to the young.

As seen in Table 2, the existence of a mortgage debt makes for considerable disparities in reported housing expenditures but not necessarily in housing consumption. Because of the size of these differences, we were led to subdivide homeowners into mortgaged and nonmortgaged

---

* On the grounds that (a) the values of rental real estate are determined in what are essentially investor rather than consumer markets and (b) it is difficult to allocate the total value of a multi-family property (the only values which can be observed) among individual dwelling units. The 1950 Census of Housing (Vol. IV, *Residential Financing*) reported data on values of mortgaged rental property. These data, however are rendered almost useless for consumer studies not only by the omission of unmortgaged rental housing (almost half of the total) but also by separation from the regular Censuses which contain the needed tabulations of household characteristics.

† A preferred datum would have been the rental value of owned homes. This would measure the consumption of housing services as the rental income foregone by an owner who chooses to occupy a dwelling unit rather than selling the housing services to a renter. Whether rental value is a fully valid measure of current housing consumption gives rise to questions which need not be discussed here. Residential appraisers are quite firm in their dictum that occupancy has greater utility for an owner than for a renter. As a result a renter-occupied house would be valued at a lower figure than the same house with an owner occupant.

groups, thereby foregoing any prospect of deriving a single demand relationship for all households combined.

The failure to report the full economic costs of consumption does not necessarily impair the usefulness of the data. For many kinds of inquiries, housing analysts would prefer to deal with the monthly or annual burden of cash outlays rather than with the economic concept of rental value. The cash concept often comes closer to the consumer's way of looking at housing. But SCE data fall short of a full cash budget since mortgage amortization, i.e., the portion of contractual debt service which goes toward the reduction of mortgage debt, is treated as a change in net worth rather than as an item of current housing expenditure. This fault cannot be corrected since the amount of mortgage repayment entered into the net worth account includes not only contractual amortization, but also voluntary prepayment (such as takes place when a house is sold). The omission of contractual repayment causes an understatement in the cash housing expenditures of mortgaged owners (estimated to be for most mortgaged owners between $100 and $300 a year).

## TABLE 1
### Percent of Owners without Mortgages by Income and Other Selected Characteristics

|  | Location | | | Education | | | Occupation | | | Family size | | | | Age of head | | |
|---|---|---|---|---|---|---|---|---|---|---|---|---|---|---|---|---|
|  | Cities and suburbs, North | Cities and suburbs, South and West | Small cities all regions | 8 years or less | 9–12 years | 13 years or more | a/ | b/ | c/ | 1 person | 2 persons | 3–5 persons | 6 or more persons | Under 35 | 35–55 | 55 or more |
| $ |  |  |  |  |  |  |  |  |  |  |  |  |  |  |  |  |
| 2,000–3,000 | 52 | 52 | 61 | 61 | 46 | 53 | 63 | 51 | 52 | 67 | 61 | 48 | 40 | 27 | 52 | 69 |
| 3,000–4,000 | 41 | 40 | 48 | 51 | 36 | 35 | 39 | 36 | 44 | 50 | 54 | 37 | 29 | 17 | 42 | 68 |
| 4,000–5,000 | 37 | 35 | 40 | 50 | 30 | 34 | 37 | 31 | 38 | 43 | 49 | 32 | 35 | 16 | 36 | 64 |
| 5,000–6,000 | 33 | 29 | 51 | 51 | 27 | 32 | 35 | 30 | 36 | 100 | 39 | 34 | 32 | 15 | 33 | 63 |
| 6,000–7,500 | 41 | 37 | 40 | 46 | 37 | 35 | 42 | 25 | 43 | 100 | 48 | 37 | 36 | 15 | 39 | 53 |
| 7,500–10,000 | 41 | 46 | 59 | 65 | 51 | 28 | 45 | 43 | 40 | 100 | 72 | 41 | 30 | 18 | 38 | 79 |

a/ Self-employed, salaried professionals, officials, etc.
b/ Clerical and sales workers.
c/ Skilled, semi-skilled, unskilled wage earners and not gainfully employed.

## TABLE 2
### Average Housing Expenditure by Tenure and Presence of Mortgage Debt

|  | Selected urban families* | | | All urban families | |
|---|---|---|---|---|---|
|  | Owners | | | | |
| Income class | Without mortgages | With mortgages | Renters | Owners | Renters |
| $ | $ | $ | $ | $ | $ |
| 2,000–3,000 | 388 | 528 | 520 | 456 | 491 |
| 3,000–4,000 | 444 | 580 | 590 | 547 | 583 |
| 4,000–5,000 | 515 | 656 | 650 | 657 | 671 |
| 5,000–6,000 | 559 | 716 | 709 | 732 | 742 |
| 6,000–7,500 | 594 | 822 | 826 | 810 | 869 |
| 7,500–10,000 | 675 | 879 | 921 | 947 | 941 |

Source: *Study of Consumer Expenditures.*

* Based on subset of approximately 8,000 families.

This means again that, as far as the reported data are concerned, the differences in housing costs between renting and owning as seen from the point of view of consumers become badly blurred.*

It also means that simple two-way tenure groupings, i.e., owners and renters, the usual way of classifying tenure in consumption studies, may result in serious biases. Owner expenditures represent mergers of two totally dissimilar groups, with mortgaged owners spending somewhat more on housing than equivalent-income renters and nonmortgaged owners spending less. The combined average expenditures of all owners depends on the relative proportions of the two groups in any major cell. Since (as Table 1 shows) these proportions vary greatly with other variables, observed differences frequently make little sense. For example, reported housing expenditures will be shown as differing by 5 percent for education groups and by over 15 percent among life-cycle groups. It is probable that actual housing consumption levels would diverge by much smaller amounts while cash outlays would differ by much larger sums.

### The problem of complementarity

A series of questions also arises in any effort to distinguish housing expenditures as such from expenditures on items which are complementary to the dwelling unit but which can be, and often are, purchased in separate markets. First, since current housing provides services only at fixed locations, housing expenditures must include a payment for what might be called "environmental factors." The consumer buys not only a given amount of housing, but a site as well, obtaining thereby varying mixes of access, convenience, municipal services and job opportunities.

Differences in housing expenditures due to variations in site values and local taxes are, to an important extent, disguised expenditures for other goods and services. Thus, a family which pays $100 a month for an apartment in the city's core rather than $60 in an outlying ring may actually be saving most or all of the difference in transportation costs.

Similarly, the real estate tax bill for municipal services contains payments for items which might be reported in accounts other than housing. One family may elect a community with high taxes because its school curriculum is enriched with music and dancing lessons. Another family may choose a low-tax community because its children go to private or parochial schools and take their music and dancing lessons elsewhere. The second family would be reported as having lower housing costs and higher education costs. Likewise, lower taxes may mean higher expenditures for insurance, garbage collection, or medical services.

The housing accounts in the SCE are also debited for a long but variable list of goods and services which are required for the effective utilization of living space. These items run the gamut of consumer durables, household operation, recreation, and transportation (employing the nomenclature of the SCE). According to long tradition, such utilities as cooking and heating fuels, electric power and water are generally regarded as part of housing expenditures. There is less agreement, however, with respect to the cost of kitchen and laundry equipment (washer, driers, stoves, refrigerators, etc.), furniture, garage space, cleaning materials, etc. Why, for example, should the outlay for a kitchen stove be included under equipment and cooking gas under housing? Is the cost of electricity for radio and television a housing or a recreation expenditure?

Questions such as these relate to a larger problem – whether consumption expenditures are best grouped by purpose or by object of expenditure, or, better yet, whether expenditures should be listed according to the goals the family is trying to achieve or by the means employed to achieve them. In other words, should family accounts, like fiscal accounts, be analyzed

---

* We should also like to add our warning that the distortions which arise because of failure to take account of the sizable differences in cash expenditures (or of economic costs and benefits) of mortgaged and nonmortgaged owners affect not only analyses of the housing sector but those for total consumption as well. Variations between identical consumers which can amount to hundreds of dollars are too large to be ignored, especially since the errors are not random.

as a program budget or a line budget? Under a family program budget the goal of "nourishment" would include not only expenditures for food and beverages, but also for kitchen equipment, dining furniture, cooking fuels, pots, pans, dishes, and vitamins now listed under a variety of other headings. A program classification would probably yield better insights into consumer behavior and motivation; "object" classifications are most suited to the analysis of markets as seen from the producer's viewpoint. To be sure, were consumption data subdivided as finely as we would like, the investigator could regroup all accounts by whatever principles of classification best served his hypotheses.

Arguments over systems of classification can easily become tedious. Logically flawless classifications are rare. Most people would be willing to accept a considerable degree of arbitrariness provided the groupings meet the test of internal consistency. That is, after a decision that utilities belong to housing and kitchen equipment does not, each family's accounts would be cast in the same way to avoid duplication and incomparability.

But SCE data do not entirely meet this test. Thus the rent paid by a family is listed under housing regardless of the items included in the legal contract. While a flat charge for gas and electricity is frequently included in the rent bill, the majority of renters and virtually all owners pay for them separately. Likewise, most apartment dwellers do not pay separately for heating, while the opposite is true for renters and owners of single-family homes. In our statistical analyses, we have reduced to some extent errors arising from this source by adding to housing costs all reported outlays for fuel, light, and refrigeration.*

We have, however, been unable to correct for inconsistencies in other types of housing-related expenditures. For example, in those cases where furniture has been included in rent, housing is being charged for an item listed elsewhere for

most families. Similarly, where a landlord supplied stove and refrigerator to his tenant, the annual charge appears under rent; if a tenant purchases his own, the full cost appears under equipment.†

Two final notes: First, the data on rents collected in 1950 are affected by rent controls which then covered perhaps a majority of urban renter units. Average expenditures on rent are therefore lower than would have been the case in a free market, but we have no sure way of knowing what distortions occur in elasticity coefficients and other parameters. The interaction among housing submarkets is so great that had a free market prevailed the rents on many units would have been reduced as the rent on most increased.

Second, we have been unable to deal with the physical characteristics of housing since such data were deliberately excluded from the SCE. Just what consumers got for their housing dollar in 1950, or how expenditures break down by quantity and quality of housing, cannot be related to budget data although a limited amount of information is cited from the 1950 Census of Housing.

It would have been desirable to have added fourth, fifth, or sixth variables of classification simultaneously in order to reduce still further the possibility of interaction. But this was not feasible because of the limited number of cases available. The addition of even a fourth variable resulted in a large number of small or empty cells. Instead, we combined or reclassified the data in whatever way seemed desirable for testing individual variables.

For the analysis of covariance, only families in the $2,000 to $10,000 income brackets were included. We also excluded certain groups of families with atypical housing arrangements, e.g., families with heads over 65, nonwhites, rent-free, nonhousekeeping, and families who shifted tenure during the year. Reported housing-income relationships of such families, who

---

* The dispersion around regression lines fitted to housing plus utilities was substantially less than for housing alone.

† The landlord supplying furniture or kitchen equipment is presumed to raise rent by an amount equal to the depreciation and maintenance costs of the durable plus a return on his investment. In New York City, the Rent Control Commission allows about $3.00 a month, or $36 a year, for a stove or refrigerator. Charges for furniture are more variable but may run to 30 percent or more of contract rent.

are distributed unevenly among the main sub-groups, are quite unusual and capable of biasing the results.

## II. The relationship of housing expenditures to income

The influence of income (without differentiating between permanent and transitory components) appears pervasive. Whatever the principle of classification, housing expenditures are seen to rise with income but at a lesser rate. As

(Table 3). For all families combined, the housing share was 14.1 percent before income taxes, 15.2 percent of income after taxes, and 15.7 percent of total current consumption expenditures.

The extreme negative slope of the average propensity curve is sharply reduced by omitting families with low and high incomes, i.e., under $2,000 and over $10,000, and still further reduced when housing shares are related to consumption rather than to income. In fact, for families with income of more than $5,000, housing as a share of total consumption tends to be

TABLE 3

*Average Housing Expenditures as a Percent of Current Income and Consumption Expenditures, U.S. Urban Families, 1950*

| Income class | Average housing expenditures | Housing expenditures as a percent of | | |
| | | Income before taxes | Income after taxes | Total consumption |
|---|---|---|---|---|
| $ | $ | % | % | % |
| Under 1,000 | 335 | 53.3 | 54.6 | 26.2 |
| 1,000–2,000 | 384 | 24.4 | 25.1 | 21.7 |
| 2,000–3,000 | 479 | 18.0 | 18.9 | 17.6 |
| 3,000–4,000 | 566 | 15.3 | 16.2 | 15.9 |
| 4,000–5,000 | 662 | 13.8 | 14.8 | 14.9 |
| 5,000–6,000 | 733 | 12.4 | 13.5 | 13.9 |
| 6,000–7,500 | 829 | 11.4 | 12.5 | 13.7 |
| 7,500–10,000 | 944 | 10.1 | 11.2 | 13.3 |
| 10,000 or more | 1,454 | 7.7 | 9.1 | 13.5 |
| All families | 596 | 14.1 | 15.2 | 15.7 |

Source: *Study of Consumer Expenditures,* Vol. XVIII. Housing expenditures include expenditures for fuel, light and refrigeration. In subsequent tables all income data are money income after taxes.

is clear from Table 3, average housing expenditures, including utilities and negligible amounts spent for vacation housing, show a clear tendency to increase for successively higher (measured) income groups. Thus, families with measured income of less than $1,000 before taxes reported $335 annual housing expenditures, families with $4,000 to $5,000, $662, and families with more than $10,000, $1,474. In proportion to measured income, housing expenditures decline from 53 percent for the lowest income group to 7.7 percent for the highest

fairly constant, ranging between 13 and 14 percent.

The inclusion of other variables of classification does not alter the overall form of the relationship. Average expenditures vary within particular groups but the values cluster about the averages found for all families.*

Mean expenditures in relation to mean income give indications of a clear relationship, whose form and magnitude can be examined more closely in simple regressions. Linear regressions were calculated of the form:

---

* The significance of differences in average expenditures as tested by an analysis of variance is discussed in the next section.

$$Y = a + bX \text{ and}$$
$$(\log Y) = a + b(\log X)$$

where Y was housing expenditures including utilties and X was income after taxes. In an attempt to improve the fit of the regressions we also tested the forms of:

$$\frac{Y}{X} = a + bX \text{ and}$$
$$Y = a + b(\log X).$$

However, neither of the latter gave an improved fit over the log-log equation which became our main tool for the analysis of covariance.

Before fitting regressions, the published data were combined into larger groups, no more than three for each variable. By merging comparable subgroups, not only are the data easier to follow but more observations are available for testing

relationships in later stages of analysis. As noted before, families with less than $2,000 and more than $10,000 income were omitted since examination showed that the fit of regression lines to the extremes of the income classes was quite poor.

The list of regression coefficients presented in Table 4 indicates, with one exception, that both the marginal propensities and income elasticities for housing expenditures of different groups of families are quite similar. Regressions fitted to mean income and housing expenditures of six income classes indicate a marginal propensity of .075 for all families, with a range for the 17 groups tested of between .068 and .093. The log-log regressions yield an elasticity coefficient of .605 for all families and a range of .490 to .721. The coefficients of determination ($r^2$) for all groups were, as might be expected, quite high for both the linear and log-log relations,

## TABLE 4
*Marginal Propensities and Income Elasticities of*
*Selected Groups of Housing Consumers, 1950*

|  | Log-log relations | | | Linear relations | | |
|---|---|---|---|---|---|---|
|  | a | b | $r^2$ | a | b | $r^2$ |
| *Tenure* |  |  |  | $ |  |  |
| Owners | .532 | .624 | .989 | 254.65 | .086 | .962 |
| Renters | .795 | .557 | .980 | 285.32 | .085 | .990 |
| *Occupation* |  |  |  |  |  |  |
| Self-employed, salaried |  |  |  |  |  |  |
| professionals, officials, etc. | 1.076 | .490 | .957 | 399.42 | .073 | .899 |
| Clerical and sales workers | .981 | .508 | .940 | 322.83 | .079 | .950 |
| Wage earners and not gainfully |  |  |  |  |  |  |
| employed | .776 | .550 | .950 | 255.51 | .077 | .958 |
| *Education* |  |  |  |  |  |  |
| 8 years school or less | .886 | .518 | .966 | 280.64 | .068 | .949 |
| 9–12 years school | .932 | .519 | .987 | 311.38 | .078 | .943 |
| 13 years school or more | .798 | .560 | .984 | 336.30 | .078 | .983 |
| *Family size* |  |  |  |  |  |  |
| 2 persons | .956 | .512 | .967 | 299.17 | .080 | .989 |
| 3–5 persons | .733 | .572 | .982 | 290.01 | .081 | .989 |
| 6 or more persons | .156 | .721 | .990 | 193.19 | .093 | .955 |
| *Age of head* |  |  |  |  |  |  |
| Under 35 | .653 | .591 | .989 | 266.06 | .083 | .943 |
| 35 to 55 | .726 | .574 | .995 | 279.28 | .084 | .987 |
| 55 or more | .994 | .497 | 1.000 | 325.90 | .069 | .970 |
| *Location* |  |  |  |  |  |  |
| Large cities and suburbs North | .821 | .551 | .984 | 296.29 | .083 | .966 |
| Large cities and suburbs |  |  |  |  |  |  |
| South and West | .742 | .565 | 1.000 | 271.08 | .079 | .978 |
| Small cities, all regions | .562 | .614 | .995 | 255.47 | .083 | .959 |
| Total all families |  |  |  |  |  |  |
| 9 income classes | 1.206 | .438 | .943 | 318.40 | .065 | .972 |
| 6 income classes | .591 | .605 | .938 | 283.00 | .075 | .990 |

Source: *Study of Consumer Expenditures,* Vol. XVIII.

with the latter form of equation offering, on the whole, the superior fit.

When regressions were fitted to smaller subgroups, the range of marginal propensities and elasticities of demand widened. However, the slopes of individual regression lines derived from subgroups did not differ significantly from the weighted average slope obtained from the major group. On the other hand, the average slope for the subset of families used in the analysis of covariance differs decidedly from that for all families as reported in the published volumes. For income classes between $2,000 and $10,000 the comparative regressions are:

$$Y = \$283 + .975X \text{ (full sample)}$$
$$Y = \$350 + .060X \text{ (adjusted sample)}$$
$$\log Y = .592 + .605 \log X \text{ (full sample)}$$
$$\log Y = 1.120 + .430 \log X \text{ (adjusted sample)}$$

The cause of these differences is clear. The full sample includes many groups with either zero or extremely low expenditures (rent-free, non-housekeeping, etc.). This leads to a relatively low height at the point of origin and a more pronounced slope. We feel, however, that this higher slope can mislead the analyst. Among the atypical families included in the full sample are many who cannot increase their expenditures with income in the form assumed by the theory of consumer demand. For this reason, the smaller coefficients found for the subset of families appear to be a better estimate of the underlying elasticities.

This important qualification aside, the coefficients of regression show no surprising results. The demand elasticities are in the range reported by other studies. There are no pronounced differences in reactions to increases in incomes among various subgroups. Variations in the income elasticities and marginal propensities of most subgroups appear to be almost random around the overall averages.

## III. The significance of other variables of classification

As noted, our procedure was first to examine the general two-way classifications as derived from the published data in the *Study of Consumer Expenditures*. This was followed by the preparation of additional three- and four-way classification tables from the individual cards. In all cases income forms one of the independent variables. Tenure (renters, mortgaged owners, and nonmortgaged owners) has been kept separate in all three- and four-way groupings. Other variables examined include race, family size, education, location, and age of head, taken singly or in combinations.

### Location

The largest average expenditures for housing ($717) were made by consumers in Northern suburbs and the smallest ($456) by the residents of small Southern cities. Geographical differences, though greatly narrowed, persist within income groups (Table 5) owing partly to regional differences in climate, type of structure and price levels. Thus, for families with $3,000 to $4,000 income, housing expenditures ranged from $471 in Western suburbs to $600 in the small cities and suburbs in the North.

In the three- and four-way tables of Appendixes C and D[1] some location groups are combined and the effect of tenure and education variables held constant. Differentials by location continue to be statistically significant, especially the higher level of expenditures in Northern large cities and suburbs (including the North Central cities), compared to the remainder of the country. However, the expenditures of renter families, particularly above the $3,000 income level, fail to reflect this locational difference. Perhaps rent controls were more widespread and effective in the Northern areas at the time of the survey. It is also possible that in large Northern cities, where there are more highly organized rental markets and a wider choice of units, renters were better able to fulfill their needs at a lower cost.

Another geographical finding worth citing is that, according to SCE data, suburban families in 1950 were not notably "homogenized" with respect to age or income. The exodus of child-rearing families to the suburbs had apparently not yet resulted in the high degree of uniformity in social and economic characteristics reported in new subdivisions such as Levittown and Park Forest. In the North and West, for example, average age of family heads was identical in suburbs and large cities, and the difference in proportions of heads aged 35–44 was negligible. There were, moreover, similar distributions of income. Large cities did contain somewhat higher proportions of low-income families and lower proportions of high-income families, but in the middle-income range ($3,000 to $6,000), the proportion of all families in large Northern cities (52 percent) was only slightly less than in the outlying suburbs (55.6 percent). Continued migration since 1950 has probably accentuated city and suburban differences but

## Family size

As family size increases, the housing decisions of consumers are placed in conflict. More living space is needed at the same time as urgent needs are imposed on the budgets for food and clothing.† And, other things equal, larger dwelling units cost more money.

The evidence indicates that the large family attempts to meet its need for larger dwelling units and more of every other necessity simultaneously. According to Census data, average size of dwelling unit – measured by number of

### TABLE 5

*Average Housing Expenditures by Income and Location,*
*U.S. Urban Families, 1950*

| Income class | Large cities | | | Suburbs | | | Small cities | | |
|---|---|---|---|---|---|---|---|---|---|
| | North | South | West | North | South | West | North | South | West |
| $ | $ | $ | $ | $ | $ | $ | $ | $ | $ |
| 2,000–3,000 | 506 | 435 | 476 | 518 | 507 | 475 | 511 | 369 | 430 |
| 3,000–4,000 | 570 | 553 | 568 | 599 | 560 | 471 | 600 | 538 | 536 |
| 4,000–5,000 | 680 | 628 | 662 | 687 | 602 | 579 | 700 | 620 | 619 |
| 5,000–6,000 | 733 | 747 | 688 | 813 | 789 | 683 | 753 | 707 | 696 |
| 6,000–7,500 | 806 | 841 | 794 | 941 | 823 | 663 | 950 | 843 | 728 |
| 7,500–10,000 | 946 | 869 | 900 | 1,035 | 933 | 1,005 | 917 | 1,005 | 827 |

Source: *Study of Consumer Expenditure,* Vol. IV.

the middle class is even now far from extinct in the core of the metropolis.* The statement that the central city is becoming a place only for the rich and the poor (a statement which can be found as far back as the 1870's) requires the utmost qualification. Often overlooked is the fact that a high proportion of city dwellers without children and child-rearing families in minority groups fall into the middle-income group. Exodus to the suburbs has doubtless been far more selective with respect to family type than with respect to age or income.

rooms – increased with each increase in family (household) size. Thus, in 1950, five-person households occupied an average of 5.40 rooms compared to 4.39 rooms for two-person households. At the same time, SCE data show that, within given income groups below the $5,000 level, very large families tended to spend less on housing than did two-person households. Obviously more space for less money implies some sacrifice in housing standards. Census data indicate that in 1950 large households occupied relatively high proportions of dilapidated hous-

* At the start of 1957, the Census's 1956 National Housing Inventory showed that 52.5 percent of the households who reported income in central cities were within the brackets of $3,000 to $7,000. In the remainder of the Standard Metropolitan Areas 53.8 percent were in these brackets.

† In fact, except perhaps for refrigerators and some types of furniture, few consumer durables bear such a close size relationship to the number of people for

whose use they are intended. There is a much wider range, as well as a more continuous distribution, in the sizes of dwelling units offered on the market than in the sizes of automobiles (measured in terms of seating capacity), washers, driers, vacuum cleaners and so forth. There is a greater likelihood that two-person and five-person households will buy the same size car than they will buy or rent the same size dwelling unit.

ing. Large households also accounted for the bulk of overcrowding, i.e., dwelling unit size does not increase as fast as household size, resulting in a more intensive utilization of space.

### Age of head

Tabulations by age of head show that housing expenditures, like total consumption, follow the cross-section life cycle of rising and declining income. The housing life cycle, however, has smaller amplitude. For all income classes combined, expenditures for housing averaged $469 for heads under 25, were at a peak of $654 for heads aged 35 to 44 (the age interval in which both family size and total consumption expenditures were at a maximum) and de-

the case for many other forms of consumption. This is because of the greater costs and frictions of adjusting housing arrangements to changing family circumstances. In the later stages of the life cycle, for example, shrinking family size results in almost automatic reductions in food and clothing expenditures and usually in reduced purchases of durables, but much less often in contractions of housing consumption. Neighborhood attachments, the desire for extra space for family visits, the relatively low cash cost of maintaining a house with little or no mortgage debt, and the difficulty of finding inexpensive rental units all make for maintenance of the *status quo.*

When atypical consumer groups are omitted

### TABLE 6

*Average Housing Expenditures by Income and Family Size,*
*U.S. Urban Families, 1950*

| Income class | Number of persons | | | | | |
| | 1 | 2 | 3 | 4 | 5 | 6 *or more* |
|---|---|---|---|---|---|---|
| $ | $ | $ | $ | $ | $ | $ |
| 2,000–3,000 | 426 | 508 | 493 | 459 | 464 | 406 |
| 3,000–4,000 | 518 | 569 | 578 | 565 | 579 | 520 |
| 4,000–5,000 | 613 | 668 | 686 | 656 | 647 | 608 |
| 5,000–6,000 | 778 | 719 | 763 | 732 | 679 | 733 |
| 6,000–7,500 | 618 | 840 | 794 | 839 | 854 | 858 |
| 7,500–10,000 | 790 | 977 | 911 | 965 | 955 | 913 |

Source: *Study of Consumer Expenditures,* Vol. XVIII.

clined to $472 for heads 75 and over. Omitting the youngest and oldest age groups within a given income class, the range in housing expenditures among age classes from 25 to 64 averaged only about $24 a year or less than $2 a month, much narrower, relatively and absolutely, than the range among these classes in income and total consumption. In relation to measured income and consumption, the cash housing expenditures of the elderly (65 or more) were quite high.

Although age-expenditure data shown here are strongly affected by the interaction of other variables, housing expenditures over the family life cycle tend to be much "stickier" and affected by more discontinuous changes than is

and the remaining families are analyzed by a four-way classification of income, tenure, age, and family size, many of the apparent differences narrow or disappear. A major share of the variations between age and size groups as reported in the published data appear to reflect the high preponderance of nonrent or nonmortgage paying consumer units among both the very young and aged and in single-consumer households.

### Race

Negro families spent less on housing in 1950 than white families of the same size and with the same measured income (Table 8). The differences were most evident among lower income groups and in the South compared to the North. Lower spending on housing on the part of Negroes was accompanied by high savings and, in relation to total consumption, larger outlays for food and especially clothing. Among families with $4,000 or more income, racial differences in spending were not consistently in the same direction.

part. Other studies reveal that Negroes have a preference for existing over new housing even when the latter can be obtained at moderate prices. There is also a tendency even among middle-class Negroes to reduce family housing space by sharing with lodgers. At the same time, some of the effects of racial discrimination are disclosed in Census tabulations which show that Negroes live in housing of inferior quality even

### TABLE 7
*Average Housing Expenditures by Income and Age of Head,*
*U.S. Urban Families, 1950*

| Income class | Age of head | | | | | | |
| | Under 25 | 25–35 | 35–45 | 45–55 | 55–65 | 65–75 | 75 or more |
|---|---|---|---|---|---|---|---|
| $ | $ | $ | $ | $ | $ | $ | $ |
| 2,000–3,000 | 432 | 472 | 488 | 487 | 486 | 476 | 490 |
| 3,000–4,000 | 526 | 559 | 584 | 559 | 566 | 568 | 612 |
| 4,000–5,000 | 578 | 662 | 657 | 682 | 663 | 668 | 623 |
| 5,000–6,000 | 708 | 738 | 745 | 722 | 719 | 733 | 755 |
| 6,000–7,500 | 674 | 814 | 863 | 844 | 760 | 883 | 774 |
| 7,500–10,000 | 1,115 | 863 | 1,011 | 950 | 878 | 858 | 1,900 |

Source: *Study of Consumer Expenditures,* Vol. XVIII.

### TABLE 8
*Average Housing Expenditures by Income, Family Size and Race,*
*U.S. Urban Families, 1950*

| Family size | Income | | | | | | | |
| | $1,000–2,000 | | $2,000–3,000 | | $3,000–4,000 | | $4,000–5,000 | |
| | White | Negro | White | Negro | White | Negro | White | Negro |
|---|---|---|---|---|---|---|---|---|
| | $ | $ | $ | $ | $ | $ | $ | $ |
| 2 persons | 414 | 324 | 520 | 425 | 574 | 512 | 666 | 737 |
| 3 persons | 443 | 333 | 510 | 387 | 578 | 577 | 685 | 686 |
| 4 persons | 400 | 297 | 476 | 392 | 568 | 530 | 661 | 564 |

Source: *Study of Consumer Expenditures,* Vol. XVIII.

Housing expenditures of Negroes are, of course, so affected by racial discrimination as to make it difficult to interpret the data. (For this reason we have excluded Negro families from the main body of our analysis.) Do Negroes have poor quality housing – as shown in Census data – because they choose to spend less or do they spend less because only inferior housing is available? Probably both factors play a

when paying the same rent or price as whites.

### Occupation and education

Judging solély from simple group averages, white-collar workers and the self-employed within the measured income classes of $2,000 to $10,000 tended to spend more on housing than blue-collar workers. For example, in the $3,000 to $4,000 income group, salaried professionals spent $658 and the self-employed, $619, compared to $552 for skilled workers, $514 for the semi-skilled, and $525 for the unskilled (Table 9). Housing expenditures for those not gainfully employed also tended to be quite high. This last group, however, is comprised mainly of the retired whose current housing expenditures are determined largely by housing decisions made at earlier stages in the life cycle.

Tabulations by education yield a pattern consistent with that for occupation. In given income classes, housing expenditures were higher for family heads with the most schooling. In the $3,000–$4,000 income group, heads with 13 to 16 years of school spent $627 on housing compared to $576 for those with 9 to 12 years and $521 for those with schooling of 8 years or less (Table 10).

When the effects of education and occupation are tested by the analysis of covariance, significant differences are found. For example, in the analysis of education (income, tenure, and location constant), variances significant at the .01 level are found in seven of nine cases. The remaining two are subgroups of owners without mortgages whose residual variance is extremely high, but even so they nearly meet the .01 test. The test of occupation with tenure and family size constant again shows significant divergencies.

When education and occupation are separated from each other however, the result is extremely interesting. A clear example of intercorrelated variables is demonstrated. The apparent influences of education and occupation, each of which have been cited as major forces in other studies, turn out not to be independent or addi-

TABLE 9

*Average Housing Expenditures by Income and Occupation,*
*Expenditures, U.S. Urban Families, 1950*

| Income class | Self- employed | Salaried Professionals | Clerical and sales workers | Skilled wage earners | Semi- skilled | Un- skilled | Not gainfully employed |
|---|---|---|---|---|---|---|---|
| $ | $ | $ | $ | $ | $ | $ | $ |
| 2,000–3,000 | 538 | 510 | 531 | 474 | 453 | 430 | 494 |
| 3,000–4,000 | 619 | 658 | 589 | 552 | 514 | 525 | 616 |
| 4,000–5,000 | 728 | 787 | 663 | 627 | 600 | 612 | 678 |
| 5,000–6,000 | 745 | 795 | 805 | 696 | 674 | 607 | 781 |
| 6,000–7,500 | 781 | 916 | 875 | 786 | 737 | 775 | 808 |
| 7,500–10,000 | 959 | 1,032 | 943 | 814 | 784 | 612 | 1,165 |

Source : *Study of Consumer Expenditures,* Vol. XVIII.

TABLE 10

*Average Housing Expenditures by Income and Occupation,*
*Expenditures, U.S. Urban Families, 1950*

| Income class | 8 and under | 9–12 | 13–16 | 16 or more | 13 or more |
|---|---|---|---|---|---|
| $ | $ | $ | $ | $ | $ |
| 2,000–3,000 | 439 | 513 | 499 | 650 | 516 |
| 3,000–4,000 | 521 | 576 | 627 | 707 | 635 |
| 4,000–5,000 | 625 | 659 | 726 | 759 | 731 |
| 5,000–6,000 | 631 | 745 | 824 | 819 | 823 |
| 6,000–7,500 | 698 | 877 | 897 | 934 | 904 |
| 7,500–10,000 | 860 | 888 | 963 | 1,366 | 1,051 |

Source : *Study of Consumer Expenditures,* Vol. XVIII.

tive. More education and a high job status both lead to somewhat higher housing expenditures. When either education or occupation is considered with the other variable constant, their apparent influence is considerably reduced.

What this indicates is a joint status as might appear on a more complete sociological scale. Higher status can be reached either through education or occupation. However, if a family attains higher status through occupation, differing educational levels will have but slight influence on its expenditures. Similarly, the more highly educated groups show housing tendencies which are independent of their reported occupations. These data may furnish a further interesting sociological lead. Since occupation and education are measured with income held constant, they point to status effects which are independent of current income. However, the divergencies caused by these status variables, though statistically significant, are relatively small in comparison to the effects of family income.

### Tenure

Despite the widespread existence of rent control in urban areas in 1950, annual housing expenditures for renters, as reported in the SCE, tended to exceed those for owners. At $2,000–$3,000 the comparable figures were $491 and $456; at $4,000–$5,000, $671 and $657; at $6,000–$7,000, $869 and $810 (Table 2). As noted earlier, much more crucial are the differences between mortgaged and other owners. Even omitting contractual repayment of mortgage debt, encumbered owners had cash outlays at least 25 percent higher than unencumbered owners in the same income class. The differences in payments by tenure were highly significant in all cases. Were a rough allowance made for annual contractual debt repayment, housing expenditures for mortgaged owners would be measurably higher than for renters of the same income, a fact more in accord both with common observation and with Census distributions of dwelling unit rents and values by income. As we noted, this disparity in reported housing consumption of homeowners, which stems from the definitions employed in the

SCE, greatly weakens the interpretative value of both the published tabulations and the results of our regression analyses.

## IV. The variability of housing expenditures

A source of constant perplexity throughout our analysis was the relatively small share of total variation in housing expenditures that could be explained by seemingly important economic and social variables. While, as the preceding section makes clear, housing expenditures reflect the play of a number of independent variables, the degree of each relationship appears to be weak. This is true despite the exclusion from the sample of groups which would have added greatly to total variance. Income, the most significant factor, accounts on the average for only 10 percent of the total variance in housing expenditures. Tenure, the next most important variable, accounts for about 6.6 percent of the residual variation. The influence of other variables is even smaller. Education (including its intercorrelation with occupation) explains 3.5 percent, location 2.0 percent, while other variables have even lesser explanatory roles. Holding four variables constant simultaneously in an analysis of variance enables us to explain 23 percent of the initial variance around the mean of the logs of expenditures.

Two reasons can be advanced for these rather disappointing findings. One is the tremendous magnification in variance when original observations are substituted for the grouped data most commonly used in previous explorations. The second involves a long overdue recognition of an innately wide range in the housing arrangements of seemingly identical types of families.

### Possible reasons for the high residuals

What implications arise from the primarily negative results of our statistical tests? That is, why should the influence of seemingly important variables prove to be so weak? One possibility, of course, is that our methods have been too crude and that more significant results might have been obtained by better and more complex statistical techniques. This we doubt.

As a check on our results, we subdivided large groups into the most homogeneous subgroups consistent with sufficient observations for statistical reliability. We utilized cells classified by all selected variables simultaneously. Thus we had cells in which all families were white, mortgaged owners, with heads from 35–55, wage earners, having between 9 and 12 years of education, with families of 3, 4, or 5 persons, located in large northern cities and suburbs. Moreover these groups had already been adjusted for rent-free families, and those who changed tenure, making each cell the equivalent of at least an eight-way tabulation.

Analysis of the relationship between changes in expenditures and income in these homogeneous groups produced little improvement over the findings previously cited. The residual variance of expenditures on housing was still enormous. Less than 14 percent of the total variance was accounted for by income. The income elasticities were of the same magnitude as those obtained from individual observations in the larger and more heterogeneous groups.

Some reasons for the failure to find higher correlations have been developed earlier. It is quite possible that better explanations of differences in housing consumption would have been obtained if the reported expenditures came closer to either the cash flow or economic concept of consumption and if all housing payments were tabulated in accordance with a more clearly defined package of services.

Another possible explanation is the unsuitability of a single year as a basic accounting period for housing. Maintenance and repair costs may vary widely from year to year. As a result some families will have significantly more expenditures of this type in one year than will others. This is probably one of the reasons why the variance among families in houses without mortgages averages nearly 50 percent more than for owners with mortgages. One type of payment-mortgage interest is absent from the reports of nonmortgaged owners with the result that irregular expenditures on repairs and main-

tenance, even if of the same average amount for all owners, will cause greater relative variance in the nonmortgaged group.

The sharp difference in expenditure variances, with ratios of 1.0 for renters, 1.3 for owners with mortgages, and 2.0 for owners without mortgages, indicates a still more basic reason for weak correlations. The housing expenditures will not adjust to changes in income (or other characteristics) as rapidly as will other types of expenditures. There are significant loyalties to one's home, neighborhood, schools, etc., which are not lightly broken. Such frictions, added to the heavy costs of transferring properties, cause decided discontinuities in any family's housing demand curve. The average family makes only a few moves over its life cycle. During the period between moves many changes will happen. Income and occupation may alter. The head will age. Family size will fluctuate. Even if these shifts were to cause movements in the family's utility function, adjustments to the new situation would occur only at relatively long intervals.

The large variances, therefore, may simply reflect the fact that a family has changed its characteristics since the time when it last made a basic housing decision. This would account for the rising variances as we move through tenure groups. The group which adjusted its housing arrangements most recently (i.e., renters) has the least variance and the group with the longest occupancy (unmortgaged owners) has the most.*

While all of the foregoing are logical reasons why housing expenditures are so diverse, they may not be the best explanation. It might be equally correct to assume that, because of the wide choice of housing available to the average family, tastes can be expressed in a tremendous variety of ways. As a result any family's utility function may have only a slight relationship to economic variables. They may depend far more on family history, on the characteristics of the local market, on psychological makeup, and a host of other elusive factors.

---

* This suggests that better relationships might be derived by concentrating on recent homebuyers. Two difficulties, however, with such an approach are (a) recent homebuyers constitute so small a proportion of effective housing demand that the results cannot have widespread application, and (b) the credit rules of mortgage lenders "artificially" restrict the variance which would be found in a perfect capital market.

# Housing: has there been a downward shift in consumers' preferences?

*LOUIS WINNICK*

## I. Residential housing since 1890

In any economy characterized by substantial long-term increases in the standard of living the production of necessities does not generally keep pace with the total output of goods and services. Consumer expenditure patterns are altered as new products emerge and luxury goods become more widely distributed. Kuznets has shown that the output of goods which can be classified as "old" and "indispensable," taken as a proportion of total consumer goods, has declined, at least since the latter part of the nineteenth century, while the share of "new" and "dispensable" goods has risen.

Similarly, residential construction outlays (including expenditures for additions and alterations but not repairs and maintenance) measured as a proportion of either gross national product or gross capital formation have experienced a marked decline since about 1890 in addition to the more familiar major swings. Even the current housing boom has not attained the relative strength of the 1920's and falls considerably short of the relative levels achieved during the 1890's. Since residential capital formation is closely geared to increases in population and households, the declining rate of population growth in itself would provide a sufficient explanation for its diminishing relative importance without further examination of the role of the consumer.

But the burden of this paper is that the decline of nonfarm housing construction in total output, rendered inevitable by demographic trends, has been powerfully reinforced by changes in consumer behavior. For not only has housebuilding declined in relation to total production, but the per capita real value of the standing stock of housing has failed to show any marked trend during the first fifty years of this century, and the average real value per dwelling unit standing has declined perceptibly (Table 1). These phenomena suggest, at least, that there has been a downward shift in consumer preferences for housing.

### TABLE 1

*Value Per Capita and Per Dwelling Unit of Residential Capital, 1890 to 1950 (1929 Dollars)*

| Year | Per capita value | Per dwelling unit value |
|------|------|------|
| | $ | $ |
| 1890 | 658 | 2,651 |
| 1900 | 793 | 3,355 |
| 1910 | 792 | 3,320 |
| 1920 | 747 | 3,119 |
| 1930 | 870 | 3,135 |
| 1940 | 770 | 2,662 |
| 1950 | 740[a] | 2,381[a] |

Source: Grebler, Blank and Winnick, *op. cit.,* and Table IV. A summary explanation of the derivation of these estimates is given in the Appendix.

[a] The maximum estimates, based on the wealth total derived from the 1950 Census of Housing would be $775 and $2,491. These estimates undoubtedly err on the high side. At any rate the main line of the argument would remain unchanged if the higher values were substituted.

Reprinted from The Quarterly Journal of Economics, *vol. 69 (February, 1955), pp. 85–97, and vol. 70 (May, 1956), pp. 314–323, with permission of the publishers. Copyright 1955, 1956, by the President and Fellows of Harvard College. This article had its origin in research leading to the monograph* Capital Formation in Residential Real Estate—Trends and Prospects *by Leo Grebler, David M. Blank, and Louis Winnick, a study by the National Bureau of Economic Research, published by Princeton University Press, 1956.*

A moderate rise in per capita value took place between 1890 and 1910 followed by a decline during the World War I decade, a sharp rise resulting from the housing boom of the twenties, and a pronounced drop since 1930. The per capita value of housing in 1950 falls considerably below the 1900 value. Though it may be astonishing to find the 1950 value below 1940 in spite of an impressive postwar residential construction boom, it should be recalled that new construction was severely limited during the war years and that a very large proportion of new households even in the years following 1945 was accommodated by conversion of existing houses; conversions represent an extremely economical method of adding to the stock of dwelling units. It is probable that there has been some understatement in estimates of construction expenditure for the decade of the forties which, together with some minor technical differences in definition and coverage, lead to some understatement in the 1950 values. It is unlikely, however, that any reasonable adjustment for these two factors would cause the 1950 per capita value to approximate the 1900 level, and thus leave the inference that we have not increased our use of housing resources over the past half-century.

As Table 1 shows, real value per dwelling unit has performed even more poorly than per capita value, primarily because of the long-run decline in household size which permits a smaller dwelling unit. The decline in average real value per dwelling unit standing reflects in part the fall in the average real input of *newly constructed* dwelling units. Average real input declined approximately 40 percent during the past six decades.*

In interpreting both per capita and per dwelling unit figures, one must bear in mind that the average age of the housing inventory has been slowly increasing. The annual depreciation charge (described in the Appendix) increases proportionately with the stock of housing but value increments have been declining relative to stock. The result is that capital consumption has become a very large and increasing offset to gross residential capital formation.

The findings on average real values per capita and per dwelling unit are astonishing in view of the rise in per capita real income over the past fifty years and (1) the consumption trends for other necessities and (2) the income and price elasticities of housing. While the shares of other necessities have diminished, rising standards of living have called for increased per capita expenditures on them. Thus, the share of perishables (of which food is a major component) has declined but per capita outlays have increased substantially from $127 (in 1929 prices) in 1884–1893 to $233 in 1929–1938.[1]

Second, it is a well-known fact and observable in cross-sectional data, that capital expenditures on housing have positive income elasticity. That is, the average value of a purchased home rises with the income of the purchaser though at a slower rate. This relationship is illustrated by FHA data in Table 2. Because per capita real income has more than doubled since 1890, it would be entirely reasonable to expect some discernible rise in the per capita use of housing capital.

Table 2 offers a clue to the size of the income elasticity coefficient. It may be noted that with a roughly doubled income from $1,000–$1,499 to $2,000–$2,499, from $1,500–$1,999 to $3,000–$3,499, and from $2,500–$2,999 to $5,000–$6,999 the percentage value increase of existing homes ranges from 42 to 67 percent. From data in the 1950 Housing Census[2] coefficients ranging between 38 and 60 percent can be derived, testifying to the stability of the income value relation. In other words, if consumer reactions to income had been similar to that which might have been expected from cross-sectional data, a substantial increase rather than stability in the per capita values might have been expected.

Obviously the deterrent effects of price elasticity cannot be ignored. The rise in both house prices and residential construction costs has been quite striking over the past six decades, substantially higher than in the case of other

---

* Because this finding came as a surprise, the construction cost index used for all deflated series was tested for a productivity bias. Although attempts to measure errors in cost indexes due to productivity can never be conclusive because of the complexity of the problem, the available evidence brought to bear indicates no serious long-term bias.

goods and services. On the basis of nine-year moving averages, the price index implicit in constant and current dollar gross national product series[3] rose by 160 percent from 1889 to 1945 (central years of the moving average); the residential cost index rose by 340 percent over the same period, or more than twice as much.

## TABLE 2

*Relationship Between Average Property Valuation and Borrowers' Annual Income, New and Existing Single-Family Owner-Occupied Houses with FHA-Insured Mortgages, 1941[a]*

| Income class | Existing houses | | New houses | |
| | Average Value[b] | Ratio of Value to income | Average Value[b] | Ratio of Value to income |
| --- | --- | --- | --- | --- |
| $ | $ | % | $ | % |
| Under 1,000 | 2,531 | 312 | 2,904 | 329 |
| 1,000–1,499 | 3,134 | 240 | 3,158 | 269 |
| 1,500–1,999 | 3,765 | 216 | 4,247 | 244 |
| 2,000–2,499 | 4,463 | 200 | 4,976 | 223 |
| 2,500–2,999 | 5,072 | 189 | 5,507 | 205 |
| 3,000–3,499 | 5,538 | 177 | 5,989 | 191 |
| 3,500–3,999 | 6,208 | 169 | 6,506 | 177 |
| 4,000–4,999 | 7,105 | 161 | 7,122 | 162 |
| 5,000–6,999 | 8,465 | 148 | 8,327 | 148 |
| 7,000–9,999 | 10,398 | 130 | 8,890 | 112 |
| 10,000 and over | 13,435 | 98 | 11,461 | 82 |

Source: Federal Housing Administration, *Annual Report*, December 31, 1941, p. 34 reproduced in Ernest M. Fisher, *Urban Real Estate Markets: Characteristics and Financing* (New York: National Bureau of Economic Research, 1951), pp. 84, 87.
[a] Similar data are available in FHA annual reports for somewhat earlier periods and for the war and post-war periods. All show the same general picture. Data for 1941 are presented here on the view that this year was characterized by relatively normal relationships in the housing market.
[b] Including land. The series would rise somewhat more sharply if value were defined exclusive of land, since other FHA data show that the ratio of land value to total property value rises with the increase in property value.

Hardly any data exist on the size of the price elasticity coefficient for housing. Duesenberry and Kistin[4] have estimated the elasticity with respect to *relative prices* for rental expendi-

tures (paid and imputed with real income held constant) to be .078. If this value is applicable, the relative price increase for housing of about 113 percent may have caused about a 10 percent shrinkage in housing demand. While more direct data would be highly desirable, it is extremely doubtful that any price coefficient would even approach the income coefficient. If this be so, the presumptive case for a change in tastes would appear quite strong.

Why has the per capita use of housing capital failed to show any marked increase over a half-century? Complete understanding of why the flow of resources into the residential real estate sector has been so insensitive to gains in real income may never be attained. But a few observations are offered.

First, consumers have chosen to spend part of their increments in income not directly on shelter but on many kinds of consumer capital related to the house and considered a vital part of household operation. Statistical measures of residential capital formation are dependent upon an arbitrary definition of items to be included or excluded in measuring outlays on construction, a definition which falls increasingly short of the full outlay for a dwelling unit as seen from the consumer's point of view. Thus, while certain consumer durables, such as oil burners and bathtubs, are captured by the construction data, others, like mechanical refrigerators, washing machines, garden equipment, venetian blinds, etc., are not. An expansion of the definition of residential capital formation to embrace items of this kind might possibly lead to a different conclusion; namely, that per capita use of housing resources has increased.[*]

Thus, while the proliferation of consumer durables has offered serious competition to all other goods in the consumer basket, the outlays for these durables – so many of which have become complementary to the dwelling unit –

---

* The increase would not seem marked enough, however, to vitiate the inference that some displacement of housing—more broadly defined—has occurred. Per capita consumer capital other than housing increased from $218 (in 1929 prices) in 1900 to $452 in 1948. Raymond W. Goldsmith, "A Perpetual Inventory of National Wealth," *Studies in Income and Wealth*, Vol. XIV (National Bureau of Economic Research, 1951). A large part of the increase in consumer capital is accounted

for by automobiles. Because of suburbanization, the automobile has become increasingly associated with home ownership and reduces the "amount" of house a family will undertake to buy. To make a reasonable guess, the average family, if it wished, could afford twice as much house as it now uses if the costs of the automobile (operating and capital) were removed from the family budget.

appear to have been substituted for construction expenditures as currently defined in greater measure than for other forms of consumer outlays.

Second, the size of the capital outlay a family is willing to make for a house is not independent of the annual level of carrying costs. To the extent that the latter increase, the former may shrink. If annual costs may be measured by the aggregate rent bill (imputed rents for home owners plus contract rents for tenants), the evidence points to a more rapid rise in rents than in capital values. Rent charges seem to have kept pace with income; that is, in spite of variations from decade to decade, there does not appear to have been any substantial long-run change in the ratio of rent to income; in the meantime the ratio of residential capital to income has been declining. The relatively greater increase in rents is attributed to the proliferation of services other than pure shelter, such as heat, light, janitorial and municipal services, and to the relatively greater amount of depreciation stemming from electric wiring, central heating, and kitchen equipment – all shorter-lived than the shell of a house. A larger and larger proportion of the annual rental bill is occasioned by services other than pure shelter, the costs of which are imputed or actually paid in the form of rent.*

Third, the apparent refusal of consumers to allow their rising income to be reflected in larger increases in space per person is also understandable in view of the housekeeping problems created by the large house calling for expensive domestic and maintenance services. At the same time the need for more housing space was becoming less urgent as many activities, recreational and domestic, were shifted from the household as a result of the automobile and the trend towards increased purchase of commodities and services traditionally produced in the home.

Nor need stable per capita values imply that no groups in the community were improving their housing standards in terms of real capital. Many observers feel that the lower income classes have substantially bettered their living accommodation, an observation perfectly compatible with the fact that easy mortgage terms have propelled the relatively poor into the new single-family home ownership market more readily than in earlier decades. It is probably among the middle and upper classes that housing has suffered its greatest decline. The ostentatious (and expensive) town house of the 1890's has no modern counterpart. And in any house rent and value distribution one can always find a surprisingly large proportion of families whose housing standards hardly correspond to their income position.

Those who hold the opinion that houses have become increasingly "shoddier" and that the modern house is a poor imitation of the solid structures of yesteryear will be inclined to interpret the data as demonstrating a deterioration of housing quality, at least over the more recent past. Indeed, one could even find a modicum of support in entertaining such a view when it is considered that per capita space increased between 1940 and 1950 while the average value per new dwelling unit decreased, and that rent (which includes repair and maintenance) has been rising relative to capital. But technological advances in material and design interfere with any such interpretation.

It would be erroneous to conclude that consumer satisfaction from housing changes *pari passu* with changes in the quantity of input. A change in fashion which substitutes a fireplace for a foot of ceiling height can raise consumer satisfaction though leading to a net reduction in input. Second, there is no evidence of any decline in the per capita use of space. The size of dwelling units (average number of rooms) has decreased but, apparently, no more rapidly than average household size. While the room is admittedly not the best unit for measuring the quantity of shelter, it is nevertheless significant that the average number of persons per room

---

* Since residential rent, the value of the current output of houses, has been rising more rapidly than residential capital, a declining capital-output ratio can be inferred. This is not the place to discuss this measure. It suffices to say that a residential capital-output ratio does not have the same interpretative or predictive value attributed to the capital-output ratios of other sectors because of problems in valuation and the large imputed component of rent.

declined slightly (4 percent) between 1940 and 1950. Third, even if the per capita use of space (by any reasonable measure) had decreased, how does one balance the effect of greater efficiency in design which may yield more net living space from a smaller gross area by eliminating staircases, useless corridors or dead corners?

Similarly, the lightening of the structural frame of the dwelling lowers real input but need not significantly affect the durability of the structure. Lighter walls may be cheaper than heavy ones but not necessarily less durable. And does it really matter that an eight-inch hand-hewn beam will last for 1,000 years if a two-inch beam will last for 200?

## II. Implications for the future

It is clear that some future revision of consumer preferences in favor of housing would serve as a powerful lever in raising the level of residential construction. Such an alteration in consumer standards could, demographic trends aside, arrest or even conceivably reverse past trends in the share of output absorbed by residential capital formation. Among the factors involved in any radical shift in tastes would be a willingness on the part of home owners and tenants to change old for new dwelling units at a more rapid and continuous pace. An accelerated exchange of old for new products would involve a more rapid decline in prices for old dwellings relative to those for new dwellings, with the ultimate prospect of displacing the least desirable part of the housing stock altogether because it would become worthless, or of making it available to groups which otherwise could not afford separate dwelling units.

A change in consumers' attitudes toward housing could conceivably be induced or strengthened by product innovation. Larger numbers of households might trade old for new units if the latter were vastly superior in design, style, location, or quality, and if the process of innovation could be kept alive so as to be sufficiently persuasive. In such an event, builders would develop a " replacement market " akin to that for other durable goods, in addition to the market hitherto served.

In the light of historical experience, this would be a revolutionary change in the character of the market for new residential construction. For the study of capital formation in residential real estate suggests that the market for additional residential facilities from 1890 to 1950 has been primarily a growth market with accretions to stock equalling approximately the growth in the number of households. Substantial innovations in style, design, and quality have occurred in the past, and yet they failed to generate a " replacement market."

Plotting the future course of consumer behavior with respect to residential construction is no less hazardous than the projection of aggregate consumer spending. But the probability of an autonomous change in favor of housing on the part of the consumer within the next generation must be questioned. It can hardly be anticipated that there will be no further development of new goods and services which will compete for a place in the family budget. Moreover, the position of housing in the budgets of large numbers of consumers may have suffered from rent control during and after the war. Tenants living in controlled apartments have become accustomed to paying a much smaller proportion of income for rent than was customary before the war and have adjusted their expenditures to this pattern. For these households, a spectacular change in consumers' preferences would be required to induce a demand for new housing that could only be satisfied at rents or carrying charges much greater than the controlled rents they have been paying for many years.

As to product innovation, the question is whether recent and prospective technological advances and style changes are of an order different from those experienced during the past sixty years. Is the new house of today and tomorrow, designed as it is for highly mechanized household operations, preferably on one floor, so different in kind from older houses that consumers will be induced to trade old for new units in any quantity and on a continuous basis? Will air-conditioning in new dwelling units become a decisive factor in their favor? Is the housebuilding industry developing production and marketing methods substantially different from those in the past? And at what price and rent levels relative to those of old houses will the new products be injected into the market?*

In the absence of public action the one factor now visible that portends a possible reversal of past experience is the suburbanization movement. It is conceivable that an intense repugnance towards city residence may lead to absolute declines in central city population. The resulting increase in vacancies and fall in rents and prices might fail to check new construction in the suburbs because the competitive relation between city and suburban housing markets will weaken. Also, suburban living tends to become centered on family and home and may bring about larger and more expensive houses. But the modern suburbanization movement is at least thirty-five years old and, thus far, no such changes have come to pass.

### III. The role of government

Finally, the profound and increasing interest of government in housing must be taken into consideration. In a broad sense the concern of government with housing and its financing, while it originated in depression emergencies and was intensified by war and postwar dislocations, must be viewed as a lasting and probably increasing influence on residential construction. This concern, by no means limited to housing conditions of the poor and indigent, expresses deepseated social forces which cause

housing to be clothed with substantial and probably growing public interest, although the scope and means of government action may differ in varying political and economic climates. Continued and probably intensified use of federal aids for residential construction is likely not only because they are tools in a broad program to improve housing conditions but also because they fit in with full employment policies.

Thus, the level of residential construction during the next few decades will depend on political as well as on the market-oriented decisions which were controlling before the thirties. Government activity will attempt to maintain a high volume of housebuilding taking the form not only of new dwelling units but of qualitative improvement or renewal of the existing inventory even in the face of declining market demand. To an important degree, the community at large through the federal government as its agent will attempt to revise the allocation of real resources to housing – a revision which consumers individually seem to have been unwilling or unable to undertake. Even without a " grand design " in allocating national resources, the rapidly growing interest of the federal government in the support of residential construction may broadly be interpreted as an effort to counteract the results of the historical forces that have led to a relative displacement of housing in the nation's total product.

Past experience is not conclusive as to the effectiveness of such an effort, particularly under adverse conditions such as contractions in em-

---

* So far as cost and price reduction of new construction is concerned, a basic difficulty has been pointed out by Ramsey Wood, " Housing Needs and the Housing Market," *Housing, Social Security, and Public Works*, Postwar Economic Series No. 6, Board of Governors of the Federal Reserve System, June 1946, pp. 18 – 19:

" Proposals to reduce cost to the occupant by reducing particular component costs overlook the important role played by capital values in regulating the amount and kind of new housing added to the supply. It has already been pointed out that new building takes place when the prices of existing houses are higher than the cost of building new houses which consumers regard as comparable, and also that, when building is under way, costs tend to rise to absorb the difference between the market value of existing houses and the sum of the prices of the component resources used in building comparable new houses. This behavior of the market, it has

been shown, stops building fairly soon because, when values have risen as high as incomes will permit, and costs have caught up with values, builders cannot operate profitably.

" This process goes on whether the techniques of building and the conditions on which houses are bought and paid for are changing or standing still. The introduction, at strategic times, of techniques and conditions which enable builders or landlords to make new housing available at lower prices than would otherwise be possible may give rise to building which would not have taken place under the earlier circumstances, but the very process of making use of these advantages tends to eliminate them. The market evaluates such advantages against the existing stock of housing and the incomes prevailing in the community; comparable houses command comparable prices; and the cost of building approaches market value."

ployment and income. Consumers' reactions to further liberalization of credit is uncertain, although it is fairly well established that housing demand responds much more to income than to price changes (including changes in the cost of borrowing). This much of a conclusion seems warranted, however: Government policies that result in a larger proportion of total resources being devoted to housing will probably involve great changes in institutional arrangements for the creation and management of the residential mortgage debt – more drastic perhaps than the changes brought by federal insurance or guarantee of mortgage loans. Liberalization of residential mortgage credit terms under these devices has already gone so far that there are narrow limits

to their use for further substantial increases in the ease of borrowing. Thus, demands for "stronger medicine" in the way of federal credit assistance will undoubtedly develop.

The future level of private residential construction will also be affected by government aids to urban redevelopment, which have but recently come into operation on a small scale. In the past, demolitions of residential structures have been so few in relation to the housing stock that their influence on the volume of new housebuilding has been negligible. But government programs to assist in urban redevelopment involve demolition of existing housing and its replacement on a scale far greater than has ever been experienced.

## TABLE 3

*Comparison of Cumulated and Census-Type Residential Wealth Estimates, Various Dates 1890–1950 (billions of current dollars)*

| Date | Cumulated wealth estimates[a] | | | Date | Census-type wealth estimates | | |
|---|---|---|---|---|---|---|---|
| | Structures (1) | Land (2) | Total (3) | | Structures (4) | Land (5) | Total (6) |
| | $ | $ | $ | | $ | $ | $ |
| 6/1/90 | 9.0 | 6.0 | 15.0 | 6/1/90[b] | 6.7 | 7.7 | 14.4 |
| 12/31/00 | 14.6 | 8.3 | 22.9 | 6/1/00[b] | 9.5 | 10.5 | 20.0 |
| 12/31/12 | 27.3 | 12.8 | 40.1 | 6/1/12[b] | 20.7 | 18.5 | 39.2 |
| 12/31/22 | 51.1 | 20.2 | 71.3 | n.a./22[c] | 30.0 | 34.9 | 65.0 |
| | | | | 4/1/30[d] | 98.1 | 24.5 | 122.6 (107.6) |
| 12/31/29 | 80.6 | 27.9 | 108.5 | n.a./30[c] | 51.6 | 56.1 | 107.7 |
| 12/31/38 | 75.1 | 21.7 | 96.8 | n.a./38[c] | 44.0 | 48.0 | 92.0 |
| 12/31/39 | 77.4 | 21.8 | 99.2 | 4/1/40[e] | — | — | 87.4 |
| 12/31/49 | 173.6 | 38.9 | 212.4 | 4/1/50[f] | — | — | 260.0 |

[a] Grebler, Blank and Winnick, *op. cit.*

[b] Simon Kuznets, *National Product Since 1869*, pp. 201–7. The estimates are derived by successively subtracting from the total taxable real estate estimates made by the various wealth censuses, estimates of agricultural, mining, and manufacturing real estate. The residual, comprising other industrial (commercial) and residential real estate is further subdivided by use of an estimated ratio of residential to the combined residual. The separation of land and structures is performed by dividing each of the categories, total taxable, agricultural, mining, and manufacturing real estate by estimated land ratios. Land and structures for the combined category, other industrial and residential, are then derived as residuals. The effect of this procedure is to assign to residential real estate the same land ratio as other industrial which is not in accord with available data.

[c] Robert R. Doane, *The Anatomy of Wealth*, pp. 213, 224, 251. Doane's procedure is essentially similar to that of Kuznets. Apparently as a result of a typographical error, a 1922 estimate of $67 billion is given on page 116. Subsequent discussion indicates that $65 billion is the total actually intended. "n.a." indicates month not available.

[d] David L. Wickens, *Residential Real Estate*, p. 3. His assumed land ratio is given on p. 4.

[e] Bureau of the Census, "Housing—Special Reports." Series II—1943, No. 1, Sept. 11, 1943.

[f] Derived as follows from *1950 Census of Housing*. Preliminary Reports, HC-5, No. 1.

| | |
|---|---|
| 15.6 million occupied dwelling units in one-family structures, average value $10.800, total value .. | $168.5 |
| 17.1 million tenant-occupied dwelling units, estimated average value $3,900, total value (Average monthly rent of $39 multiplied by a factor of 100 to obtain average value)  ..  ..  .. | 66.7 |
| 3.9 million owner-occupied dwelling units in other than one-family structures, estimated total value (The number of such units represents the difference between all owner-occupied units and owner-occupied single-family houses. The average value was assumed to be equal to the average value of a tenant-occupied unit, namely $3,900.)  ..  ..  ..  ..  ..  ..  ..  .. | 15.2 |
| 2.8 million vacant and other dwelling units, estimated total value  ..  ..  ..  ..  .. | 9.6 |
| Total  .. | $260.0 |

## APPENDIX

### Derivation of residential capital estimates

The residential capital estimates upon which the per capita and per dwelling units figures depend were obtained by forming a residential wealth estimate for 1890 to which annual estimates of net capital formation were successively added. The starting estimate of $15.0 billion (current), inclusive of land, represents the product of the total number of nonfarm dwelling units (taken from Wickens' *Residential Real Estate*) and the average value per dwelling unit. The average value per dwelling unit was assumed to equal $1,800 or 55 percent of the average value of an owner-occupied mortgaged home reported by the 1890 Census. In 1940 the known ratio was 63 percent.

Because both the starting estimate and all independent benchmark estimates include the value of residential sites, some estimate of the

### TABLE 4

*Derivation of Per Capita and Per Dwelling Unit Residential Wealth (all dollar figures in billions)*

| | Resid. capital (current dollars) | House cost index | Deflated capital | Nonfarm Population (millions) | Nonfarm dwelling units |
|---|---|---|---|---|---|
| | (1) | (2) | (3) | (4) | (5) |
| | $ | | $ | | |
| 1890 | 8.6 | 39.0 | 22.1 | 33.5 | 8.3 |
| 1900 | 13.7 | 38.5 | 35.5 | 44.8 | 10.6 |
| 1910 | 24.4 | 51.4 | 47.4 | 59.9 | 14.3 |
| 1920 | 50.9 | 92.1 | 55.3 | 74.1 | 17.7 |
| 1930 | 80.6 | 100.0 | 80.6 | 92.6 | 25.7 |
| 1940 | 77.4 | 98.0 | 79.0 | 101.5 | 29.7 |
| 1950 | 173.6 | 204.3 | 85.0 | 114.8[a] | 35.7[a] |

Source : Grebler, Blank and Winnick, *op. cit.*
Note : Values in Table 1 are derived from unrounded data and are therefore not precisely reproducible from this table.
[a] The Census totals were reduced by 10 percent to adjust for population and dwelling units not covered in the wealth total.

latter was required in order to convert a wealth estimate to an estimate of capital and vice versa. Existing annual FHA data indicate the average ratio of land to the total value of a house for the period since 1936. Benchmark ratios were also discovered for 1907 and 1929. An annual land ratio series was derived from these fragments starting at 40 percent in 1890 and declining gradually to 18 percent in 1950. The declining trend in land ratios which is in accord with

independent observations is due, primarily, to the opening of vast new areas made possible by the new forms of transportation and, secondarily, to the apartment house which is land economizing. The division between land and structures in the independent estimates, given in Table 3, does not appear plausible either in level or movement. Comparison of the cumulated and independent wealth figures is, therefore, made only inclusive of land.

The annual estimates of net residential capital formation represent the difference between gross capital formation and capital consumption. The annual series of gross capital formation (the sum of expenditures on new private nonfarm housekeeping dwelling units and the expenditures on additions to and alterations of such units) combine the new estimates – constructed by David M. Blank[5] for the period 1890–1920 and the official Commerce estimates beginning in 1921. A rough allowance for additions and alterations was added to Blank's series.

The annual capital consumption charge represents the sum of an allowance for basic depreciation and obsolescence and an adjustment for the remaining value of demolished units. The basic depreciation charge, over 90 percent of the capital consumption allowance, was derived by the declining balance method at a rate of 2 percent per year. Both the form of depreciation and the specific rate adopted were tied to FHA data in which the current value and reproduction costs of a large sample of single-family houses distributed by age were estimated. The sample houses showed a relatively greater value decline in earlier than in later years at an average rate of something under 2 percent. Certain minor biases in the sample, however, suggested a small elevation in rate. Since this rate was applied to the stock at the beginning of each year, an additional half-year's depreciation was charged to current gross capital formation. Finally, a separate charge for demolished units was obtained as the product of the estimated number of units demolished and the average value of such units.

The cumulated residential wealth estimates are compared with independent estimates of residential wealth in Table 3. When Wickens' estimate for 1930 is reduced by $15 million because of an error in the census reports of that year and a bias in the multiplier he employed to convert average rents of tenant-occupied units into average values, it is seen that there is a large measure of conformity in all years but 1940 and 1950. It is believed that in both 1940 and 1950 a large part of the discrepancy is caused by differences in valuation. The independent estimates for these years are based on owners' estimates of value (and transformation of rent of tenant-occupied units to value figures) while the cumulated series is tied to the movements of a construction cost index. Although our study shows a long-run conformity between the movement of residential construction costs and house market prices, there are many instances of short-run divergences. Furthermore, owners' estimates of value may be less than completely reliable. The cumulated series was preferred to the census-type estimates because the latter vary greatly in origin and derivation. However, one adjustment in the per capita and per dwelling unit values, given in Table 1, seems warranted. The cumulated value estimates for 1950 exclude: (1) The value of publicly financed housing, and (2) the value of private housing not arising from capital formation, i.e., the transfer of houses from the farm to the non-farm category between 1940 and 1950 because of a change in the census definition of a farm or an actual change in use. Both the affected dwelling units and the population residing in them ought to be subtracted from the denominator of each of the two measures. In 1950, it is estimated that about 1,200,000 units out of a stock of 39,000,000 warrant exclusion. On this account both the per dwelling unit and per capita value measures would be raised by 3 percent (assuming that the average number of persons per dwelling unit in the excluded categories was the same as the overall average). On the further assumption that official construction estimates were substantially understated during the 1940–1950 decade, the cumulative estimate for 1950 might be raised by an additional 5 or 6 percent. Combining these two adjustments, the 1950 values might well be 10 percent higher than those given in Table 1.

# Winnick's case for a changing attitude toward housing: comment

## JACK GUTTENTAG

Louis Winnick's argument in this *Journal*, that there has been a long-run downward shift in consumers' preferences for housing, rests on two basic assumptions:

1. Consumer behavior is appropriately analyzed with reference to capital outlays rather than carrying costs.

2. The demand for housing is much more elastic with respect to income than with respect to price.

Both of these assumptions are subject to question. With reference to the first, although Winnick does concede that "the size of the capital outlay a family is willing to make for a house is

*Reprinted from* The Quarterly Journal of Economics, *vol. LXX, No. 2 (May, 1956), pp. 314–319, with permission of the journal.*

not independent of the annual level of carrying costs," this is only a parenthetical qualification on his part. However, if qualification and assumption are interchanged, the argument can be reversed; it can be contended that over the years there has been an *upward* shift in consumers' preferences for housing. Consider the following line of reasoning.

Budget studies show that persons with high incomes spend a smaller proportion of their income on annual housing costs than do persons with low incomes. From this we should expect that for the community as a whole the ratio of carrying costs to income would decline as income rose. In fact as Winnick points out, the ratio of carrying costs to income has remained relatively unchanged. If changing relative prices can be assumed to have had a negligible effect (as Winnick argues), we are justified in inferring an *upward* shift in consumer preferences for housing.

Clearly, then, it is a matter of first importance whether consumer behavior is more appropriately analyzed in terms of carrying costs or capital outlays, since the implications drawn with regard to consumer preferences are diametrically opposed. There is no unequivocal answer to this problem; the assumption employed largely depends on which consumers we are talking about. Tenants are concerned only with carrying costs. Home buyers must consider both factors, with the point of balance between them depending largely upon financing arrangements. Where required down payments are high and no provision exists for regular amortization payments, the capital outlay is the important factor. Where there is no down payment required at all, or only a very small one, but provisions are made for regular amortization payments, decisions may be framed almost entirely in terms of carrying costs.

Over the period 1890–1950, there were more tenant than homeowning families. Moreover, the trend in financing home buying has been toward smaller down payments and regular amortization payments, so that the weight of

the two factors influencing decisions has probably been shifting in the direction of making carrying costs a more important determinant for homeowners also. Thus, if we are making a global analysis covering all consumers, and for the entire period 1890–1950, carrying cost would appear to be more important than capital outlay as an influence on consumers' decisions.

The second problem has to do with the relative magnitudes of the price and income elasticities of the demand for housing. Real income per capita more than doubled between 1890 and 1950; however, during the same period, the price of housing increased more than twice as fast as the composite price of all items entering the GNP. Even if we accept the capital stock measure rather than the carrying cost measure of the significance of housing, a downward shift in preferences can be inferred only if it is assumed that the demand-stimulating effect of the increase in income exceeded the demand-deterring effect of the rise in price.

Winnick argues that the income coefficient is of fairly substantial magnitude (a figure of about .5 is suggested by budget studies), but that the price coefficient is quite small; the Duesenberry-Kistin study is cited to this effect. Winnick appears to recognize that the results of this study may not be completely applicable to the problem at hand since he states that " more direct data would be highly desirable ..."* However, he concludes that "... it is extremely doubtful that any price coefficient would even approach the income coefficient." Although it cannot be certain, his choice of words appears to suggest that he feels that there are grounds other than the cited study for expecting that the income coefficient is substantially greater than the price coefficient. What these grounds are, however, is not indicated.

This is a serious omission. For although there is no more direct evidence available, presumptive considerations suggest that, at least over the long run, the price coefficient has been no lower than the income coefficient. The following considerations would appear to be relevant.

---

* As suggested below, one reason the Duesenberry-Kistin study is not applicable to the question at issue is the fact that it abstracts from the income effect of a price change. Whether Winnick had this in mind or not is uncertain.

A. Modern indifference curve analysis has accustomed us to think of a price change as having two distinct consequences; it changes the relative terms of acquisition between different commodities and it changes real income. The latter consequence provides an obvious overlapping between the income and price coefficients.

Assume that the demand function for a commodity is homogeneous and of zero degree. It can then be shown that the following relationship will hold.*

$$Expx + Expy + Exm = O$$

where

$x$ = commodity in question
$y$ = all other commodities
$m$ = income
$Expx$ = price elasticity of $x$
$Expy$ = cross elasticity of $x$ with respect to $y$
$Exm$ = income elasticity of $x$

Both $Expx$ and $Expy$ have income components, so that the above expression may be written

$$\left[ -\left( \frac{xPx}{m} \right) Exm - R \right]$$
$$+ \left[ \left( \frac{yPy}{m} \right) Exm + R \right] + Exm = O.$$

R is the substitution component of price elasticity and must be O or positive.† Hence, the price elasticity will be equal to *at least* a fractional part of the income elasticity, the fraction representing the importance of the item in question in the consumer's budget. If the amounts of $x$ and $y$ purchased change when their relative prices change at the same time that real income is held constant, then R has a positive value and there is price elasticity stemming from the substitution effect (in addition to that arising from the income effect).

Thus, if housing comprises 20 percent of the consumers' budget and the income coefficient is .5, the price coefficient will be *at least* .1. To the extent that housing is also a substitute for other goods, the price coefficient will be greater than .1.

B. There do in fact appear to be many possibilities of substitution between housing and other goods and services, notwithstanding the oft-expressed notion that housing is something of a "unique" service. The "unique" aspect of housing appears to be associated with the vague idea that it constitutes a "necessity," that "everyone must have a roof over his head"; however, the amount of roof can be varied within such wide limits (including changes in quality, which in this context must be thought of as changes in quantity) that the above consideration implies no substantial limitation on the possibilities of substitution.

It can be argued with some force that habit is a powerful factor which tends to reduce substitutability between housing and other goods. However, if this is the case, it seems reasonable to suppose that income elasticity also will be effected. Moreover, as we extend our time perspective, the influence of habit must become progressively less. Whereas in the short run the effect of a change in price comes up against established habits, in the long run habits *are formed* under the influence of relative prices.

C. There is a well-established community sentiment to the effect that one's housing expense should be fairly closely related to one's income. This is not only the approach adopted by many consumers but it is also a rule of prudence used by mortgage lenders (and by the Federal Housing Administration). Note the implication of this. If a *fixed* ratio is maintained between housing expense and income, the implied price elasticity is −1. There is no fixed ratio, to be sure, but the tendency of most consumers to think in terms of some such relationship does suggest a price coefficient of fairly substantial magnitude.

D. With reference to homeowners, the relationship between income elasticity and price elasticity is partly dependent upon the terms on

---

* The proof is given by Stigler, *Theory of Price* (rev. ed., 1952), pp. 299–300. Note, however, that his statement following the proof is incorrect.
† Where there are only two goods upon which the consumer divides his income, and the income effect of a change in price is already taken account of, the relationship between the goods must be one of substitution. The quantities purchased of the two goods cannot vary in the same direction (real income being given) unless there is a third group of items at whose expense this can occur. Cf. Hicks, *Value and Capital* (2d. ed.), p. 44.

which mortgage credit is available. It seems reasonable to suppose that the larger the required down payment, the greater will be the price elasticity relative to the income elasticity. When the down payment is large, the change in down payment resulting from a given change in price is also large. Conversely, when the down payment is small, the mortgage amount is correspondingly large and consumers think in terms of carrying costs and the relationship between carrying costs and income; hence, they probably are relatively more sensitive to changes in their income. Since we are thinking in terms of extreme cases, it can be assumed that only in the second case, where mortgage amounts are large, is provision made for systematic amortization.

Let us, then, consider the second case, assuming no down payment at all is required, where the ratio of income elasticity to price elasticity probably is at its highest. It is also assumed that there is a typical value : annual income ratio of 2 : 1, an interest rate of $4\frac{1}{2}$ percent and that carrying costs (which include payments on principle and interest only) are calculated on a uniform monthly payment basis. It is now possible to calculate income-price equivalents, i.e., the percent change in income required to support the change in carrying costs (at various terms and ratios of carrying cost increment to income increment) resulting from a given percent change in price (here assumed to be 10 percent). This is shown below :

| Ratio, increment of carrying cost to increment of income | Term of years | | |
|---|---|---|---|
| | 10 | 20 | 30 |
| ·33 | 7.4 | 4.6 | 3.6 |
| .25 | 10.0 | 6.0 | 4.8 |
| .20 | 12.4 | 7.6 | 6.1 |

The table may be interpreted as follows : at a term of 20 years, a consumer who spends 20 percent of an increase in income on housing would have to obtain a 7.6 percent increase in income to support an increase in carrying costs equal to that obtainable from a 10 percent change in price. Stated somewhat differently, a given percent change in income would permit him to assume an increase in carrying cost about 30 percent greater than that obtained from a price reduction of the same percent magnitude.

Thus, if there is no down payment, if consumers are responsive to changes in carrying costs, and if terms of 20 years or more are available, income elasticity probably will be greater than price elasticity. Even under these very restrictive assumptions, however, the ratio between the respective coefficients would only be of the order of 2 to 1.

Recall, now, that we are considering the entire period 1890–1950. Prior to 1933, few loans were extended for periods exceeding 10 or 12 years, and systematic amortization was not the common practice. Moreover, it has only been in the post-World War II period that we have had any no-down-payment loans. There is thus nothing to suggest that for the entire 60-year period, the income elasticity (with respect to home purchasers) was substantially greater than the price elasticity.

The two premises of Winnick's case for a downward shift in consumer preferences are thus shaky, to say the least. No such shift is in evidence when consumer behavior is analyzed in terms of carrying cost, which appears to be a more appropriate frame of reference than capital outlay. Moreover, there is no reason to assume that housing demand during the period 1890–1950 was more responsive to income than to price changes. Thus, if a general tendency for consumers to increase housing outlays prevailed because of rising incomes, it is likely also that a countering tendency to reduce such outlays prevailed as a reaction to the relatively rapid rise in house prices which occurred.

If the above statement is true, our perspective on the so-called replacement market will be quite different from Winnick's. The failure to develop this market in the past can be attributed to the rapid rate of increase of construction costs and to the relatively slow rate of technological advancement which has long been characteristic of the building industry. These problems are remediable, even though subject to no easy solution. Winnick's explanation, that demand is insensitive to price changes and that there must have been a downward shift in preferences, leaves much less scope for remedial action, and much less hope that a substantial improvement in housing conditions will ever be effected.

# Reply

LOUIS WINNICK

First, to clear up one fact – there *has* been a long-run decline in the ratio of aggregate *space* rent to disposable income. In 1909 the ratio was 20.4 percent;[1] in 1940, 12.3 percent;[2] and in 1953, 11.0 percent.[3] The stable rent-income ratio mentioned in my article had to do with a grosser measure of rent (paid and imputed) – one that included the cost of many kinds of utilities and services. Space rent is more nearly equivalent to the annual costs of the services flowing from housing capital as such. Indeed, it was stated that one of the reasons why the per capita amount of housing capital had not increased significantly was the competition between outlays for shelter and outlays for other housing services. The consumer buys relatively more electricity, gas, and municipal services (measured by real estate taxes) and relatively less housing.* The long-run reduction in the ratio of space rent to income is therefore consistent with (though not necessarily proof of) a shift in tastes.

The main difference between Guttentag and myself is his belief that the price elasticity for housing is appreciably higher than is suggested by the Duesenberry-Kistin study. If price elas-

ticity with respect to housing is higher than income elasticity there is no need to introduce a change-in-taste argument. Guttentag, however, is unable to produce any empirical evidence for a high price elasticity nor does he tell us why the Duesenberry-Kistin coefficient of .1 is unacceptable to him. Instead, Guttentag proceeds to *deduce* a high coefficient. But the deduction process turns out to be somewhat faulty since he succeeds in proving (1) that the coefficient must be zero and (2) that it is equal to $-1$.

There is, first, a demonstration that price elasticity must be high since housing is subject to an income effect. That is, a rise in the price of housing (measure in annual carrying costs)† causes a decline in real income and shrinkage in the demand for housing as well as for all other goods. With this point I am in hearty agreement. But Guttentag fails to see that the Hicksian income effect requires not only that the commodity in question form a large part of the consumers' budget but that it must be a commodity for which demand is quite insensitive to price change. In fact, as the reader can readily see for himself, Guttentag's derivation of a .1 "income effect" must rest on an assump-

---

* In terms of current dollars a downward drift is discernable even in the ratio of gross rent to income when the data are extended to 1955.

† I do not completely disagree with Guttentag's contention that price elasticity should be measured in terms of the annual carrying cost of housing rather than in terms of its supply price. An increase in the mortgage repayment period becomes then equivalent to a reduction in the price of housing. I do not think that the consumer is so indifferent to the price of housing that he would shift from a $14,000 to a $28,000 house even if no rise

in monthly payments or down payments were required. It would be preferable, therefore to treat changes in credit terms as shifts in demand curves rather than as movements along a single curve. The point is, however, that the rise in "price" of housing has been very much smaller in terms of monthly outlay than in terms of market price, making the case for a change in tastes even stronger. Between 1940 and 1950 as house prices more than doubled, monthly outlays on mortgaged homes rose by only 59 percent.

*Reprinted from* The Quarterly Journal of Economics, *vol. LXX, No. 2 (May, 1956), pp. 319–323, with permission of the journal.*

tion of *zero* price elasticity; the consumer continues to buy the same physical quantum of housing whatever the rise in its price, but ultimately decreases his purchase slightly as he realizes that his real income has declined. Since my analysis was carried out in terms of real income the " income effect" of a rise in the price of housing was accounted for as fully as available price indexes permit.

Second, Guttentag establishes a coefficient of — 1 by arguing that the ratio of annual housing outlays to income is fixed by " well-established community sentiment." The statement is made despite the fact that this ratio has varied greatly over time, varies widely during the life cycle of any family and, at any moment in time, varies greatly with income, household size, location and many other factors.

Moreover, an elasticity coefficient of — 1 would have a number of unbelievable consequences: First, we are given to believe that the consumer allots a fixed amount of money for housing which he proceeds to spend regardless of shifts in the price of housing services. If rent doubled, for example, the consumer would still maintain a given money rent expenditure and, therefore, would continue to spend the *same amount of money* for all other goods and services. Would Professor Hicks still recognize his income effect?

Second, a doubling in the price of housing services would lead to a 50 percent reduction in the physical quantum of housing purchased. Since the quality of existing housing is already fixed, consumers could adjust only by buying less space. Apart from conversions this adjustment could be effected solely by an enormous rise in both the vacancy rate and doubling-up rate – to levels approaching 50 percent. This seems incredible. As far as we know the doubling-up rate (except when construction has been administratively restricted) has varied between 4 and 6 percent over the period 1910–1954 and the vacancy rate from 1.5 to, perhaps, 8 percent despite wide changes in income and the cost of housing.

Admittedly, my brief for a change in tastes is " shaky " (*vide* the interrogatory title of my

article). Adequate documentation of changes in tastes is notoriously difficult when only aggregate data are available. I would like, however, to add the following important evidence. Between 1934 and 1950 in Philadelphia renter households in each household size class reduced their housing space (number of rooms) by amounts ranging up to 20 percent despite the fact that money incomes more than tripled.* The rise in the rent index during this period, marked by rent control, was less than 25 percent. Unless price elasticity were several times greater than income elasticity something must have happened to weaken consumers' preferences for housing space. But if the price elasticity of housing were in fact very high one should have expected that home owners, faced with a more than 150 percent rise in the market price of homes (and perhaps a 75–85 percent rise in terms of annual carrying costs), would have reduced their space holdings *more* than renters. Instead, as the table shows, owner households of the most typical size showed *a smaller* decline than renters. Owners are, of course, less mobile than renters but it is difficult to derive an important price reaction from these data.

*Average Number of Occupied Rooms, Philadelphia, 1934 and 1950*

| Household | Renters | | Owners | | Percent decrease | |
|---|---|---|---|---|---|---|
| Size | 1934 | 1950 | 1934 | 1950 | Renters | Owners |
| 3 persons | 5.00 | 4.17 | 6.98 | 6.25 | 16.6 | 10.5 |
| 4 persons | 5.63 | 4.65 | 7.14 | 6.45 | 17.4 | 9.7 |

Source: Louis Winnick, *The Distribution of Housing Space* (John Wiley & Sons Inc., forthcoming, 1956).

Important economic phenomena usually have more than one cause. Unquestionably, the steep rise in the price of housing served as a significant and, perhaps, even as the single most important deterrent to demand. But the weight of evidence suggests that price is not the only villain in the piece. A greater willingness (which may be now expressing itself) on the part of consumers, particularly in the upper income

---

* A similar phenomenon could be shown to have occurred for the country as a whole over the 1940-50 decade but a longer, more laborious discussion would be necessary.

groups, to channel more of their income gains into housing would go a long way to improve national housing standards. In 1950 nearly 200,000 households with incomes over $10,000 a year (22 percent of all such households) occupied owned homes valued at $9,999 or less or rented quarters for which they paid under $60 a month. Housing is no longer the guide to social and economic status that it used to be.

Finally, I do not agree with Guttentag's clos-

ing remarks that it is necessarily more difficult to change consumers' tastes than it is to reduce production costs. American businessmen lay out several billion dollars each year for advertising in the fervent belief that the opposite is true. The housing industry, partly because it is local and atomistic, has never seen fit to match the intense selling efforts of other consumer durables industries which have won for themselves a higher level of replacement demand.

# Rent-income ratio

*CHESTER RAPKIN*

Recently there has been an increase in the rate of turnover and in the vacancy ratios of public housing developments. At the same time, there has been a pronounced decline in the number of new applicants. In light of these developments, it has been proposed that the competitive position of public housing could be improved if the ratio of rent to income, which now stands at 20 percent, could be reduced to a lower figure.

Any revision of the rent-income ratio for public housing developments in the United States is not to be undertaken lightly. Decisions on this matter will not only affect the budgets of over 400,000 families who reside in these developments, they will also alter the disposition of substantial amounts of public funds and seriously influence the future of a major public program.

In approaching this question, three separate phases have been considered. First, there is an examination of various characteristics of the rent-income ratio for renters at all income levels,

then an analysis of the ratio as it relates to public housing, followed by a brief concluding section in which several additional questions are raised.

### Rent/income " folklore "

No discussion of the rent-income ratio can begin without a reference to the familiar belief that one month's rent should approximate one week's salary. It has never been quite clear to me whether this statement purports to be a statistical observation or whether it is a " folkloristic " exhortation to husbandry. At any rate, 12 weeks salary for rent out of 52 weeks earnings yields a ratio of 23 percent – slightly in excess of 20 percent, a figure now cloaked with the dignity of the law.

How this homily has survived in the minds of men, despite a century or more of statistical research on the patterns of consumption, is for others to determine. Long ago Schwabe pronounced an economic law that states that rent

*Reprinted from* The Journal of Housing, *vol. 14 (January, 1957), pp. 8–12, with permission of the journal.*

expenditures tend to rise with income, but at a slower rate. Hence the proportion of income spent on rent is not constant but declines, on the average, as income increases.

### Statistical studies

Scores of statistical studies have corroborated the negatively sloped rent function. One of them, the survey of consumer expenditures conducted by the bureau of labor statistics in 1950, provides an illustration of this relationship. According to this study, the proportion of money income before taxes expended by urban consumers on housing and utilities declined from 47.4 percent for income groups under $1,000 to

tenant, which may or may not include utilities, services, or furniture.)

The data show that in every class there is a strong tendency for families to cluster in certain rent-ratio brackets. In the group under $1000, 83 percent spent more than 30 percent of their income on rent and roughly the same proportion of the income groups between $5000 and $10,000 paid less than 15 percent of their income for rent.

Thus within each income class there is concentration within certain rent-ratio intervals. At the same time, it is apparent that there is a considerable amount of dispersion, more in some income classes than in others. For example, according to the census, 3 percent of nonfarm

### TABLE 1

*Percent of Nonfarm Families and Individuals in Each Income Class Having Designated Ratio of Gross Rent to Income; Renter-Occupied Dwelling Units in the United States: 1950*

| Gross rent as percent of income | Income in 1949 | | | | | | | |
|---|---|---|---|---|---|---|---|---|
| | Less than $1000 | $1000– 1999 | $2000– 2999 | $3000– 3999 | $4000– 4999 | $5000– 5999 | $6000– 6999 | $7000– 9999 |
| Less than 10 | 1 | 5 | 8 | 12 | 21 | 32 | 43 | 57 |
| 10 to 14 | 2 | 9 | 18 | 30 | 41 | 43 | 38 | 31 |
| 15 to 19 | 3 | 13 | 26 | 32 | 25 | 18 | 13 | 9 |
| 20 to 29 | 10 | 30 | 35 | 22 | 11 | 7 | 5 | 3 |
| 30 percent or more | 83 | 43 | 13 | 4 | 2 | 1 | 1 | 1 |
| Total | 100* | 100 | 100 | 100 | 100 | 100 | 100 | 100 |

Source: U.S. Census of Housing: 1950 Volume II, Nonfarm Housing Characteristics.
* May not add to 100 percent because of rounding.

15.0 percent for those earning between $3,000 and $3,999, and drifted down to 10.7 percent in the $7,500–$9999 group.

The rent-income function, regardless of its slope, can only have meaning if the average describes a behavior pattern that reflects a significant concentration around the central tendency in the distribution of rent expenditures (or rent ratios) in each income class. The housing census of 1950 provides data (see Table 1) that enable us to examine the extent of such concentration or dispersion in a tabulation of the percent of income spent on gross rent within each income class. (Gross rent is a computed figure that is comparable for all dwelling units, while contract rent is the amount paid by the

families with incomes under $1000 per year paid rents in excess of $75 a month, representing a rent-income ratio greater than 100 percent (see Table 2). Diagonally across the statistical table, we find that one out of eight renter families with incomes between $7000–$9999 pay less than $30 a month for rent, as do 6 percent of the renter families with incomes in excess of $10,000 a year.

### Variations: why?

A number of factors help explain the variation in the amount spent on rent within each income class. It is difficult to rank their relative importance but that they are significant in aggregate is without question. The statistical correlation of rent and income based upon 1950 data yields a coefficient of .41, which means that income alone only explains one-sixth of the variations in rent expenditures. Thus to account for the major portion of the variation, we must look beyond income differences.

The first factor of significance is the size of family. Within any income class, large families tend to allocate less for housing than smaller families. The heavy claims resulting from food and other prior expenditures make it necessary for large families to economize in housing. Since their space requirements are relatively larger, the smaller absolute rent expenditure results in

larger than for most other commodities. Thus for families that have recently moved to a higher income bracket, the rent-income ratio is likely to be below the average, while the reverse tends to be true for families whose income has declined.

Higher than average rent expenditures can be made by some families in each income group by virtue of their ability to draw upon accumulated assets. Other families, conversely, spend less than the average because of their need to repay debts. Thus the wealth position of a family also plays a role in explaining its housing outlays.

Then there is the simple fact that housing is

## TABLE 2
*Percent of Nonfarm Families and Individuals in Each Income Class Having Designated Monthly Contract Rent; Renter-Occupied Dwelling Units in the United States: 1950*

| Contract monthly rent | Income in 1949 | | | | | | | | |
|---|---|---|---|---|---|---|---|---|---|
| | Less than $1000 | $1000– 1999 | $2000– 2999 | $3000– 3999 | $4000– 4999 | $5000– 5999 | $6000– 6999 | $7000– 9999 | $10,000 or more |
| Less than $10 | 12 | 7 | 3 | 1 | 1 | 0* | 0* | 0* | 0* |
| $10–30 | 48 | 47 | 39 | 29 | 23 | 18 | 15 | 12 | 6 |
| $30–50 | 27 | 33 | 41 | 45 | 43 | 39 | 35 | 30 | 16 |
| $50–75 | 9 | 11 | 14 | 20 | 25 | 30 | 32 | 33 | 26 |
| $75–99 | 2 | 2 | 2 | 3 | 6 | 9 | 12 | 15 | 20 |
| $100 or more | 1 | 1 | 1 | 1 | 2 | 3 | 5 | 10 | 32 |
| Total | 100** | 100 | 100 | 100 | 100 | 100 | 100 | 100 | 100 |

Source: U.S. Census of Housing: 1950 Volume II, Nonfarm Housing Characteristics.
* Less than 0.5 percent.
** May not add to 100 percent because of rounding.

housing quality standards substantially below those of the income group as a whole.

By an ingenious juggling of four variables – income, rent, household size, and housing space – Louis Winnick has been able to show in a recently published study (*The Distribution of Housing Space*) that "at given income levels large families spend less on rent and obtain more rooms, but the increase in space is less than the increase in family size, resulting in higher densities."

The length of time that a family has been at a given income also influences its rent expenditures. There is a lag in the adjustment of consumer expenditures to a change in income and, in the case of housing, the delay appears to be

more important to some families than to others. Many families are willing to restrict expenditures on other commodities in order to have what they consider to be a proper home, while others prefer to spend their incomes on automobiles or vacations, or to accumulate savings.

Any analysis of the rent-income relationship for the nation as a whole must take account of the significant variations among cities in the rent expenditures within any income class. These variations are dependent upon city size; on differences in the number and type of utilities included in rent; on relative location, which affects land values; and upon local custom. Table 3 presents median monthly rents in each of three income groups for 10 large cities.

In the $1000–$1999 income class, median monthly rents ranged from $21 in Atlanta to $45 in Washington, D.C.; in the $4000–$4999 group, rents spread from $32 to $53; and in the $7000–$9999 bracket, the low and high median rents were $41 and $64 respectively.

### TABLE 3

*Median Monthly Contract Rent of Renter Occupants in Three Income Classes in Ten Selected Metropolitan Cities, 1950*

| City | Income Class $1000–1999 | $4000–4999 | $7000–9999 |
|------|-------------------------|------------|------------|
| Atlanta | 21 | 45 | 56 |
| Boston | 32 | 38 | 45 |
| Buffalo | 28 | 34 | 43 |
| Chicago | 39 | 44 | 54 |
| Detroit | 41 | 44 | 50 |
| Los Angeles | 40 | 49 | 61 |
| New York | 36 | 45 | 58 |
| Philadelphia | 30 | 41 | 46 |
| St. Louis | 24 | 32 | 41 |
| Washington, D.C. | 45 | 53 | 64 |

Source: U.S. Census of Housing: 1950 Volume II, Nonfarm Housing Characteristics.

### Definitions and concepts

In addition to the many factors that influence the rent-income ratio, the analysis of this measurement is complicated by ambiguities in the definitions of both rent and income. Rent has been taken variously to mean space

rent, contract rent, gross rent, or total housing expenditures. For owner occupants, the problem is even more intricate.

Many questions also arise regarding the proper or comparable definitions of income. Shall income be measured before or after personal taxes? Should income data be adjusted for changes in the general price level, especially when different time periods are studied? Shall only money income be considered, without regard to income received in kind? If other than money income is permitted to enter the income data, the effect will be to reduce the slope of the function, since lower income groups tend to have a higher proportion of nonmonetary income.

Table 4 presents a number of schedules, each of which represents a housing expenditure ratio. In the BLS study from which these data have been taken, disbursements for housing include rents for tenant-occupied dwellings, lodgings away from home, and current operation expenses for homeowners. Principal payments on mortgages are excluded. Housing expenditures have first been taken alone and then in combination with expenditures for fuel, light, refrigeration, and water. Income has been defined in two ways – as money income before and after taxes. To complicate the matter further, each of the two housing expenditure series has also been computed as a ratio of total consumer expenditure on the assumption that for

### TABLE 4

*Expenditures for Housing and for Housing Plus Fuel and Utilities as a Percent of Income Before and After Taxes and of Total Consumer Expenditures for Urban Consumer Units, 1950*

| Income class | Housing expenditures as a percent of | | | Housing plus fuel and utilities as a percent of | | |
|--------------|------------------|------------------|------------------|------------------|------------------|------------------|
| | *Income before taxes* | *Income after taxes* | *Total current consumption* | *Income before taxes* | *Income after taxes* | *Total current consumption* |
| Under $1000 | 34.7 | 37.1 | 19.3 | 47.4 | 50.9 | 26.5 |
| $1000–1999 | 18.3 | 18.9 | 16.7 | 24.4 | 25.2 | 22.3 |
| $2000–2999 | 12.7 | 13.4 | 12.6 | 17.1 | 17.9 | 16.9 |
| $3000–3999 | 11.0 | 11.7 | 11.8 | 15.0 | 15.9 | 15.8 |
| $4000–4999 | 9.5 | 10.2 | 10.7 | 13.0 | 13.9 | 14.6 |
| $5000–5999 | 9.0 | 9.8 | 10.2 | 12.2 | 13.2 | 13.8 |
| $6000–7499 | 8.6 | 9.4 | 10.2 | 11.4 | 12.5 | 13.6 |
| $7500–9999 | 8.0 | 8.9 | 10.4 | 10.7 | 11.9 | 14.0 |
| $10,000 and over | 7.2 | 8.4 | 11.9 | 8.6 | 10.1 | 14.4 |

Source: Survey of Consumer Expenditures in 1950, Bureau of Labor Statistics; data presented in *Characteristics of Low Income Population, etc.*, Joint Committee on the Economic Report, Washington, D.C., 1955, pages 35–36.

most families expenditures tend to be more stable than income from year to year.

On the basis of these calculations, the rent-income ratio can be shown to range from 34.7 to 7.2 percent, or from 19.3 to 11.9 percent, or from 50.9 to 10.0 percent, depending upon the definition that is chosen. The variation in definition has the greatest influence in the lowest income range, where a twist of a tongue can shrink the housing expenditure ratio from 50.9 to 19.3 percent.

For the lower income groups, an additional conceptual problem is present. How shall rent received from a lodger be treated? Is it an addition to income, or is it a subtraction from rent? Take the case of a family that earns $200 per month and spends $40 of that amount for an apartment – a rent-income ratio of 20 percent. Permit the family to rent one of the rooms for $10 per month. If this amount is deducted from the rent, then the rent-income ratio drops to 15 percent. But if $10 is added to income, then the rent ratio remains virtually unchanged, merely declining from 20 to 19 percent.

### Long-term trends

In the budget of the average American family, it appears that housing's competitive position has been losing ground over the years. For the nation as a whole, housing expenditures have declined both as a percent of national income and as a proportion of total consumption expenditures, despite an average increase in real income of 2 to 3 percent a year since the early 1900's. In 1909, $24 out of every $100 spent by consumers went for housing; by 1930 the ratio had dropped to 19.5 percent; in 1952 it stood at 14.6 percent.

Moreover, the average value of a new dwelling unit (adjusted for changes in cost of construction) has shown a marked long-run decrease – a decrease that cannot be explained by any substantial gains in construction productivity.

Housing expenditures have declined not only in relative terms but also in absolute per capita measures, at least during the last two decades. Thus, even when corrected for the reduction in average size of household, this decline is still visible. While a nation marked by a rising standard of living tends to spend a smaller proportion of its income on necessities, housing is the only necessity that has shown an absolute decline. This fact is even more startling when it is remembered that the house of today contains a large amount of equipment that was not present in the dwelling at the turn of the century or later.

The downward displacement of housing in the consumers' scale of preference is the result of families' decisions to spend their incomes on refrigerators, television sets, automobiles, vacations, etc., instead of devoting their funds to increasing their housing standards. It has been found, for example, that family expenditure on automobile transportation equals or exceeds the amount spent on housing.

In view of the complexity of the rent-income relationship, it would be extremely difficult to argue for a reduction in the public housing rent-income ratio on the basis of a comparison with existing ratios in the private housing market. The major conclusion that one draws from an analysis of the ratio is that no single figure presents a satisfactory summary of the relationship. In a minor way, this fact is recognized in the public housing formula, which exempts $100 of income for each child.

Thus if we attempt to compare the 20 percent ratio with rent expenditures made in comparable income groups, we must first standardize our data for size of family and the many other variables previously discussed. Moreover, we must also correct the quality of unit. In the private market, a family may be paying a low rent for a dwelling in poor condition, a situation that cannot be contrasted with the rental of a public housing unit of more than adequate quality. But even after all of the local factors have been considered, geographical differences will make it virtually impossible to draw an unequivocal conclusion for the nation as a whole.

It is more tenable to argue for the reduction on the basis of the long-term decline in the rent-income ratio in the private market. The public housing rent-income ratio has remained virtually unchanged since 1937, when the United States Housing Act was passed, while consumers at large seem to have reduced the percent of income spent on rent. It may be argued that this shift constitutes a structural change in consumption patterns that should be acknowledged in the administration of public housing.

### Possible changes

The heart of the problem consists of examining the economic, legal, and social implications of a change in the ratio. Since there are various combinations of rent and income levels that reduce the rent-income ratio, each is presented and analyzed in turn. A reduction in the ratio can be achieved in the following ways:

1 – By reducing rent but permitting income levels to remain unchanged.

2 – By maintaining current rent but increasing income levels.

3 – By reducing rent and increasing income levels to points somewhere between items 1 and 2.

4 – By reducing both rent and income levels but reducing the latter to a greater extent than the former.

5 – By increasing both rent and income levels but increasing the latter to a greater extent than the former.

1. – *Lower rent, maintain income levels.* Here are some of the possible consequences of lowering the rent without changing the income limit.

It is not likely that there would be an appreciable increase in demand as a result of a rent reduction. The price elasticity of housing is extremely low, which means that even a large relative decrease in rents would only result in a small relative increase in the number of units demanded.

A sharp reduction in revenue would be a virtual certainty under these circumstances. For example, if the rent income-ratio were reduced from 20 percent to 16-2/3 percent, all existing rents would be cut by one-sixth and, in the absence of any change in occupancy, gross revenue would shrink by one-sixth. A rise in occupancy could, of course, compensate for all or a part of the revenue loss, depending upon the occupancy ratio at the time of the rent

reduction. If the existing occupancy ratio were in excess of 83-1/3 percent, then a reduction in gross revenue would be inevitable. If the occupancy ratio were exactly 83-1/3 percent, then all vacant units would have to be rented if gross revenue were to be returned to its original level. If occupancy were less than 83-1/3 percent, then total revenue could be increased if occupancy were augmented by one-fifth or more. But to improve gross revenue in this situation, it would be necessary for a 16-2/3 percent decline in rent to induce a 20 percent rise in occupancy – a demand response that is totally inconsistent with the observed price elasticity in housing.

Since it seems certain that gross revenues would decline under these conditions, an increasing proportion of the maximum annual federal contribution would have to be used to compensate for the additional deficit. Although these annual contributions have always been less than the allowable amount, they have in fact been moving toward the maximum in recent years. Since 1949 this proportion has risen from 16 percent to 66 percent in 1954.

The sharp increase in this ratio is due to the fact that capital costs are considerably larger, that the bond amortization period has been reduced from 60 to 40 years, and that interest rates are higher for the housing constructed under the act of 1949 than under the original 1937 act. As units built under the 1949 act become a larger proportion of the total, more and more of the maximum contributions will be paid. Several years ago it was estimated that the actual contribution would level off at approximately 75 percent of the maximum but it now appears that this figure was an underestimate. A number of cities have already reached the 90 percent mark and, in some, the ratio is expected to go even higher.

Thus there is a serious likelihood that a reduction in rent without any increase in the income limit would make it necessary to use the full maximum annual contribution. If gross revenues were too drastically reduced, the deficit might even exceed the maximum contribution. Under these circumstances, it would then be necessary to increase the maximum allowable federal contribution to include a portion of the operating expenses. To do so, would, in effect, constitute a major revision in the public housing formula, which limits the federal contribution to capital rather than operating subsidies. If operating costs are not to be subsidized, then these charges act as a floor below which aggregate rents cannot fall.

But even if the maximum annual contribution were not exceeded, an increase in the deficit would be reflected in a rise in the subsidy per unit. According to calculations made in 1953, the average annual contribution per dwelling was $22.57 or 40 percent of total economic cost, and for units built under the 1949 act, the annual contribution amounted to $26.90 per unit. The higher the subsidy per unit is permitted to rise, the fewer units can be supported with any given amount of national resources. Since the housing needs of the lower income groups are still enormous, it is proper to question the economy of increasing the subsidy for a group that is already satisfactorily housed in public dwellings.

Just one more point. Payments in lieu of taxes are 10 percent of shelter rents. Any reduction in shelter rents not compensated by increased occupancy would diminish tax-equivalent payments to municipalities. Cities that have had large public housing programs would thus suffer a decline in municipal revenues without any concomitant reduction in costs.

*2. – Maintain rent, increase income levels.* Increasing income limits without altering rent levels would result in a substantial increase in demand for public housing units. The present upper limits of income eligibility touch the dense sections of the income distribution and a small increase in the income level would result in a large increase of the number of eligibles. In 1951, roughly 10 percent of all persons with money income fell into each of the three $500 income intervals from $2000 to $3500, so that an increase in income limit of $100 would bring an additional 2 percent of the *total population* into the eligible group.

Since the demand would increase, there is little doubt that occupancy and gross revenue would rise. The amount of the subsidy per unit would remain unchanged, or decline, and it is

very likely that the ratio of payments to maximum annual contributions would stabilize between 75 and 80 percent, reflecting the experience of the units built under the 1949 act.

This picture is indeed a rosy one and the only cloud may be the fact that, to achieve the described result, it might be necessary to raise income limits to levels at which it would be undesirable to extend a public subsidy. At these levels, family income might be sufficient to acquire an adequate dwelling in the private market.

*3. – Moderate reduction in rent, increase in income.* This change represents a compromise between alternatives 1 and 2. It simultaneously provides for a moderate reduction in rent and a tempered increase in income levels. Via this combination, the increase in demand and occupancy arising from the addition to the number of eligibles would compensate for the contraction in revenue that would accompany the rent decline. Moreover, if the income limit were extended moderately, the chance of subsidizing a sector of the population that might be able to provide for its own needs is reduced. Carefully calculated, this combination may provide the most satisfactory alternative.

*4. – Reduce both rent and income limits.* Quite obviously, both of these adjustments would be in the wrong direction, for they would bring about a simultaneous reduction in rent and occupancy.

*5. – Increasing both rent and income limits.* In the situation in which rents would be increased, income limits would have to be raised appreciably if the rent-income ratio were to be reduced. Under these circumstances, it is questionable whether public housing would continue to serve its functions of providing low-rent dwellings to families in the lower sector of the income distribution. Moreover, if rents were raised too much, it would be impossible to maintain the statutory requirement of a 20 percent gap between the rents for public and private units. The problems raised by a substantial increase in income limits have been discussed earlier.

### Conclusion

In the previous discussion, I have attempted to analyze the problem by assuming that basic price, income, and quantity relationships operate within the public housing market as they do in the private housing sector.

Let me now raise a disquieting question. Is public housing encountering a special type of consumer resistance that is not present in other sectors of the housing market? Has public housing lost its sex appeal? An analysis of recent admissions shows that roughly 60 percent of the new tenants pay the same or lower rents in public housing than they did in their previous slum quarters. Aside from the cases in which exorbitant rents were extracted from slum dwellers, this figure would seem to indicate that public housing must not only present a unit of superior quality but it must also be of lower rent before residents of substandard homes will seek admission.

Can it be that the public housing consumer has experienced growing resistance to the aspects of public housing about which our planners and sociologists cautioned us years ago? Does the potential public housing tenant find that the massive developments are too institutionalized and that they tend to segregate economic, social, and racial groups? Do potential public housing tenants or their adolescent children prefer the anonymity of the slum to the public badge of charity that may be associated in their minds with residence in low-rent housing?

If there is an element of truth in this picture, then perhaps we are ill-advised to seek the solution of a complicated social problem by means of a mechanical device. It may be a propitious time now to re-examine the entire public housing formula, the problems it purports to solve, and the methods by which it strives to achieve its ends.

# The consumer votes by moving

*JANET ABU-LUGHOD and MARY MIX FOLEY*

Mobility occurs when the occupant of a dwelling vacates it to establish residence in another one. By moving, the consumer adapts his housing to his changing needs and also expresses his preferences and values on the housing market. The degree of residential turnover can therefore be a sensitive index to the rapidity with which consumer needs and preferences are changing, and – less sensitively – to the efficiency with which the housing stock is satisfying these demands. In attempting to make such inferences, however, it is important to differentiate between mobility which is the result of actual housing dissatisfaction and that which has other causes.

About 20 percent of the United States civilian

*Reprinted from Nelson Foote, Janet Abu-Lughod, Mary Mix Foley, and Louis Winnick,* Housing Choices and Housing Constraints, *McGraw–Hill Book Co., 1960, pp. 134–166, with permission of the publisher.*

population changes its address annually.* Of this group of movers, nearly two-thirds (or about 13 percent of the total population) travel only short distances, remaining within the same community or county. These movers are trying primarily to adjust housing to household needs and preferences. The remaining one-third (or about 7 percent of the population as a whole) go longer distances, migrating to another county or even to a new state or region. Although a change in housing is a by-product of these latter moves, it is seldom the motivating factor. Most long-distance migrants are moving in hope of better working opportunities, as a result of actual job transfers or offers, or (especially if retired or in ill health) in search of a pleasanter climate.

The rates of both types of mobility are important in estimating housing demand and in describing the pattern of growth experienced by metropolitan areas. Statistics on long-distance mobility are of particular value in relation to migratory movements. High mobility into a specific region requires a larger housing stock than does regional stability. Thus the regions of in-migration (traditionally the West Coast) may experience housing shortages out of proportion to the situation in other parts of the country. Since this long-distance mobility is related primarily to job or climate considerations, it has little to do with satisfactions or dissatisfactions of a housing nature and reveals little about housing preferences.

Short-range mobility, on the other hand, and the stated reasons for the change in residence, do reflect consumer attitudes toward housing. But even within this group there are exceptions. Of the approximately 13 percent of the population which makes short-distance moves each year, some 2 to 3 percent can be classified as involuntary movers. Their dwellings have been taken away from them through fire, demolition,

forced sale, or eviction. Another 1 percent or more move because a new family desiring an independent household has been formed out of members of previous households. Perhaps only 8 percent of all families are actually moving voluntarily this year because of dissatisfaction with their current dwelling. Thus, it is clear that, although 20 percent of the population moves each year, only about two-fifths of this number can be considered as an index to changing consumer needs and preferences which are strong enough to produce mobility. Without any inherent dissatisfaction with the dwelling occupied, a certain amount of mobility is both logical and necessary.

Abnormal conditions also diminish the direct logical consequence of dissatisfaction. A housing shortage lowers mobility rates even when dissatisfaction is high. This situation was typical of the war and early postwar period. Rises in cost of better dwellings can also reduce mobility. This is quite obvious in the case of the low-income consumer who cannot afford to improve his housing. But cost inequities can occur even when the desired housing is of objectively lower value, as under rent control. There have been many instances of small "uncontrolled" apartments costing much more than larger "controlled" ones, thus distorting the normal tendency of families to adjust their space requirements. Another example is that of the aging homeowner who, having paid off his mortgage debt, is restrained from seeking smaller quarters by their higher out-of-pocket costs.

Even when opportunities offered by the housing market are quite adequate, a time lag may occur between dissatisfaction and an actual move. In periods of normal vacancy, there is ample evidence that less than half the consumers who are dissatisfied with their housing actually translate their desire to move into action.† Although these restraints on mobility

---

* Since 1947, the Bureau of the Census has published annual statistics showing the number of civilians who, at the end of the year, lived in different dwelling from that occupied when the year began. These statistics have shown such remarkable uniformity over a ten-year period that it seems plausible to accept close to 20 percent as a normal rate of postwar mobility. However, the census figures underestimate the number of *moves* as opposed to the number of persons moving,

since they fail to record more than one move per year per mover.

† George Katona and Eva Mueller, *Consumer Expectations 1953 – 56*, University of Michigan, 1956. About 70 percent of the renters and 34 percent of the owners in 1954 expressed a desire to move, although actually only 33 percent of the renters and probably 10 – 12 percent of the owners did move.

may obscure the housing discontent which exists, extreme mobility clearly indicates consumer dissatisfaction. High rates of mobility may arise from rapidly changing consumer needs and standards which outstrip the ability of the housing market to provide appropriate dwellings. Or they may be the penalty for a previous era of insensitivity to the desires of consumers. Mobility in its most exaggerated form – for instance, the rapid turnover of dwellings in a declining neighborhood – is in itself destructive, wasting resources, speeding deterioration, and disorganizing the community.

From the above examples it can be seen that some forms of mobility play a positive role in the appropriate allocation of housing, whereas other forms of mobility (or barriers to it) may have a negative effect. In a rational operation of the housing market, logical change of dwelling to meet changing family circumstances should probably be facilitated. Ideally, also, some attempt should be made to lessen change of dwelling due to shortcomings of the housing stock or its environment.

Since this study is limited to existing surveys and since these deal primarily with mobile consumers, the chapter will concentrate on defining those groups within the population who do move and on isolating the most important causes of their mobility. However, some studies have been undertaken which measure "mobility potential," the number of families who wish to move or are contemplating a move. In this way, at least some of the latent housing dissatisfaction can be gauged. The various mobility patterns – both long- and short-distance – will also be considered as they affect the different parts of the metropolis, specifically the city proper as against the suburbs.

## The mobile housing consumer

As has been stated previously, approximately 20 percent of the civilian population moves each year. If a different 20 percent of the population moved each year, a full 100 percent of the population would have changed residences by the end of five years. Instead, over a five-year period, 50 to 60 percent of the population change their address. After ten years, approximately 75 percent have moved; by the end of twenty years, 90 percent of the population are no longer living in the homes they occupied at the beginning of that period (see Figure 1).*

For the purposes of this study, the five-year interval has been selected. Individuals and families who have moved once or more during that period are classified as "mobile," the remainder as relatively stable. However, a further refinement can be made by isolating the multiple mover. Only one study of a national urban sample contains the information needed to estimate his role.[1] This poll found that 53 percent (1,320 persons) of the 2,490 interviewed had moved once or more during the preceding five years, to produce a total of 3,290 moves for the survey group. A small minority, 15 percent of the total interviewed, made three or more moves during the time period and accounted for over half of the total moves made by the entire

---

* Works Progress Administration, Division of Social Research (prepared by Peyton Stapp), *Urban Housing: A Summary of Real Property Inventories Conducted as Works Projects 1934 to 1936*, 1938; see especially p. 21, U.S. Summary (yearly and five-year mobility rates for the mid-1930's–24 per cent and over 55 percent respectively).

U.S. Bureau of the Census, *Population and Housing— Families—General Characteristics, United States, Cities of 100,000 and Metropolitan Districts of 200,000 or More*, a separate volume, but issued as part of the *Sixteenth Census of the United States*, table 18, pp. 50–51. (Five-year net mobility rate for 1935–1940, 61 percent.)

Melville C. Branch, Jr., *Urban Planning and Public Opinion*, Bureau of Urban Research, Princeton, N.J., 1942. (Five-year net mobility rate between 1935 and 1940, 53 percent.)

U.S. Bureau of the Census, "Internal Migration in the United States: April, 1940 to April, 1947," *Current Population Reports, Population Characteristics*, ser. P.-20 no. 14, Apr. 15, 1948; see table 4, p. 16 for nonfarm migration. (Seven-year mobility rate of 58.8 percent; from this estimate, a five-year mobility rate of 50 percent.) Decline partly due to change in unit of mobility: from a household count in earlier studies to an individual count in this study. Also most young men—the most mobile group within the population—were serving in the Armed Forces.)

Federal Reserve Board, *Survey of Consumer Finances*, selected issues from 1948 to 1958. (Family mobility information is available for selected years and varying time intervals in the *Federal Reserve Bulletin*. These data indicate that by 1955, the five-year net mobility rate had reached 57 percent.)

Projection for ten- and twenty-year mobility rates are based on the preceding statistics.

group. This restless minority can be termed extremely mobile.

Translated into numbers of population rather than percentages (and transferred from a sample group to a national level and from a 1940 population to a 1956 one of 170 million)*, this means that some 90 million people in the United States move one or more times within five years and that of these, 25½ million move three or more times. On the other hand, nearly 80 million persons do not move at all.

between owners and renters. Rates for renters are in every case substantially above those for owners. In no case do the rates come within 20 points of each other.

Several reasons for this differential are obvious. Renters are, on the average, younger than homeowners and are therefore less likely to have achieved what they consider to be a permanent housing solution. In Branch's study, nearly four-fifths of respondents under thirty years of age expressed a preference for owning,

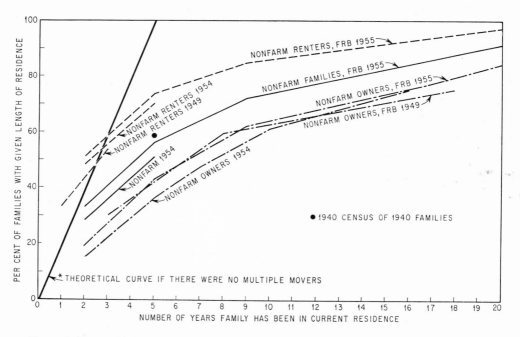

Figure 1. The multiple mover. Actual duration-of-occupancy curves compared with theoretical curve. Note: Per cent above line are stable; per cent below line are mobile.

The characteristics of the mobile 90 million, accentuated by the very mobile 25½ million, are roughly sketched below.

### The characteristics of movers

*Renters are more likely to move than owners.* Mobility rates for renters are, on the average, twice to three times as high as those for owners. This difference is evident no matter what data sources are consulted. Figure 2 combines all national mobility rates which distinguish

but only a little more than one-fourth of this group had translated desire into mortgage payments, as compared with two-thirds of those over fifty. Since their rental quarters are often considered little more than a temporary expedient, these are quite likely to be exchanged for more suitable accommodations if such become available, whether the new dwelling be another rental unit or owned housing.

In general, also, the consumer believes that the rental dwelling is less suited to family needs than is the owned home. The reason for this

---

* Because of this shifting of the base of estimation, the figures are only the roughest kind of estimate.

belief is at least partly founded in fact. Owned housing is predominantly the single-family detached house with a yard, but two-thirds of all rental units are in multifamily structures. Figure 3, which gives yearly mobility rates for housing of various types under different tenure forms, shows that families who own homes are least likely to have moved to them within the year. On the other hand, families renting apartments in multifamily structures are most likely to have moved to them recently (one-third of such families have occupied their dwellings for under a year). The higher mobility rates for renters can therefore be partly explained in terms of the type of housing which renting implies.

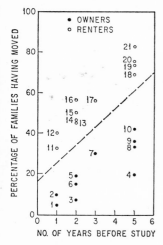

Figure 2. Percentage of U.S. nonfarm owner and renter households or families which had moved to present dwelling less than one, two, three, four, or five years before survey date.

However, if this were the only reason, those renters who do not live in apartments, but rent single-family houses, should be no more likely to move than homeowners. Instead, they show a mobility rate exactly midway between that for apartment renters and single-family homeowners. Therefore, there must be other differences between the rental and owner groups beyond the type of housing which they occupy.

Of first importance among these residual differences is doubtless the predilection of Americans for homeownership. Ninety percent of the nonfarm population considers owning the preferable form of tenure, and fully 70 percent actively desire it for themselves. Thus, when homeownership is achieved, a goal has been reached and one impetus to move is dispelled. Conversely, the renter who wants to own (and this is approximately 25 percent of the total population) tends to be restless and dissatisfied regardless of the objective quality of his rental housing.

Although of less basic importance than the ideological preference for homeownership, the mere fact that it is easier to move from rented quarters undoubtedly influences mobility. When a renter decides to move, he finds a new place, gives his notice, packs his belongings, and usually spends less than $100 on the move. Little time, money or effort is expended. When an owner decides to move, he often is unable to negotiate for new housing until he has sold his present home. This may take months in time and heavy costs in legal fees. In addition his cost of moving runs substantially higher, about $1,000. The expense, time, and trouble associated with a move made by a homeowner often may be enough to inhibit mobility even though the motivation to move exists. That is, homeownership in itself may be an obstacle to mobility and, indeed, is so recognized by some homeowners.*

Although overall mobility rates have not altered substantially during the past twenty-five years, and although renter mobility consistently remains higher than owner mobility, Figure 2 does reveal one interesting and significant change: the discrepancy between mobility rates of renters and owners has decreased steadily. That is, over the years, renters have become more "stable" in their market behavior, and owners have become more "mobile."

---

* A study of a Buffalo sample of 788 homeowners reported in the *President's Conference on Home Building and Home Ownership*, vol. IV, 1924, revealed that 12 percent of those owners interviewed reported that homeownership had interfered with moving to another community to take a better job; 7 percent felt that ownership kept them from adjusting their hous- ing to changed family needs; 5 percent said that it had interfered with moving closer to work or to the children's school, etc. Cited by R. Dewey and W. Slayton. "Urban Redevelopment and the Urbanite," in Coleman Woodbury (ed.), *The Future of Cities and Urban Redevelopment*, University of Chicago Press, Chicago, 1952, p. 326.

It is not difficult to find an explanation for this phenomenon. The period of greatest discrepancy was the Depression. During that period, home building all but ceased and few families shifted from rental to owner tenure; in fact, the movement was in the opposite direction. There were few "recent buyers" among homeowners to raise the mobility rate. Those who did own, and who managed to avoid foreclosure, tended to remain in the same house, rather than buy a second one. Among renters, however, there were both previous renters adjusting their housing expenditures to curtailed incomes and families who had lost their homes by foreclosure. The one-year mobility rate for

can be explained only by the fact that homeownership and home buying have been sustained on a very high level. About 10 percent of all owner families bought houses in 1956. Over a five-year period, some families purchase two houses, thus yielding a five-year net mobility rate of 40 percent.

It seems safe to predict that if economic prosperity continues and homeownership continues to rise, the discrepancy between the mobility rates of renters and owners will continue to diminish. It will never disappear, however. As previously outlined, rental housing is less suited to what the consumer perceives his needs to be; also, renters are in a stage of family growth

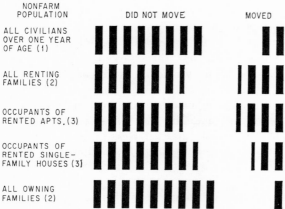

NONFARM
POPULATION                    DID NOT MOVE                 MOVED

ALL CIVILIANS
OVER ONE YEAR
OF AGE (1)

ALL RENTING
FAMILIES (2)

OCCUPANTS OF
RENTED APTS. (3)

OCCUPANTS OF
RENTED SINGLE-
FAMILY HOUSES (3)

ALL OWNING
FAMILIES (2)

EACH FIGURE REPRESENTS 10 PER CENT

*Figure 3. Percentage moving each year, by tenure class.*

Source: (1) U.S. Bureau of the Census, computed average 1948–1955, from annual figures appearing in selected issues of *Current Population Reports*. (2) "Survey of Consumer Finances," *Federal Reserve Bulletin*, reprinted from selected issues. (3) Theoretical estimate derived by applying a mobility rate 50 per cent higher for apartment renters than for single-family-house renters. The values were selected to average the known mobility of nonfarm renters in 1949 (Source 2). Justification for this assumption is found in the only study distinguishing between these two rental types. See T. Earl Sullenger, "Social Significance of Mobility," *American Journal of Sociology*, vol. 55, May, 1950, pp. 559–564.

renters in the mid-thirties was ten times the one-year rate for owners. By 1940, this gap had narrowed slightly, coinciding with the slow recovery of the late thirties.

Then during the war and afterwards the situations first of the renter and later of the owner were reversed. The gap between owner and renter mobility was narrowest during the period between 1940 and 1947, partly because rent control inhibited renter mobility. The postwar period, especially in the fifties, is characterized by relatively higher owner mobility rates (about 40 percent of the owner families residing less than five years in their current homes) and by relatively lower renter mobility rates (about 70 percent to 75 percent of the renter families occupying their current quarters for less than five years). The high mobility rate for owners

which requires more rapid change of housing accommodations.

*Movers are younger than nonmovers.* Age is directly related to mobility. Individuals aged between twenty and twenty-four are more likely than any others to move during a given year. Between 1954 and 1955, 42 percent of all persons within that age group did move. Mobility gradually decreases with each year of age until, after sixty-five years, less than 10 percent of the age group move within a year's time.[2] (See Figure 4A.)

The same relationship is evident in family mobility. The younger the head of the family, the less likely it is to be living in the same residence it occupied five years earlier. Families with heads aged below forty-five have higher than average mobility rates; those with heads over forty-five have rates lower than the average.[3] (See Figure 4B.)

This relationship between youth and mobility accounts for part of the association between stability and homeownership, since owners, on the average, are older than renters.

The 1955 *Survey of Consumer Finances* shows that, in the age group between eighteen and twenty-four years, only 16 percent are homeowners. This rises to 45 percent in the group aged twenty-five to thirty-four; to 61 percent in the group aged thirty-five to forty-four; and to 69 percent for the group aged fifty-five to sixty-four.

The relationship between age and mobility

their high rate of homeownership but partly also to the fact that they are no longer subject to the various pressures (job changes, family expansion, rises in social status with increased income) which motivate younger families to move. As explained in a preceding chapter, the one motive which they do have – reduction in family size – is not a pressing one and often is overbalanced by a fear of losing their independence. Hence the tendency on the part of the elderly to cling to their owned homes even after maintenance has become a taxing and too costly chore for curtailed energies and incomes.

At the opposite end of the scale is the high mobility of young men and women aged be-

Figure 4. Age and mobility. (A) *percentage of civilians moving between 1954 and 1955, by age of individual;* (B) *percentage of husband-and-wife families moving between 1935 and 1940, by age of husband;* (C) *percentage of families potentially mobile in 1954, by age and tenure of family head.*

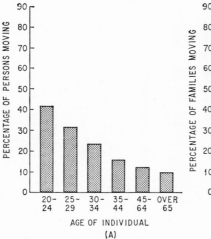
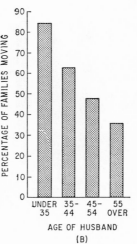
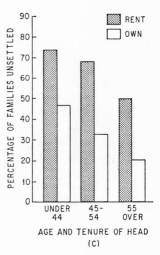

operates not only among those who have moved, but among those who plan to move. The *Survey of Consumer Finances* found this to be true in measuring mobility potential among families with heads of varying age and tenure. Renters were far more likely than owners to be anticipating a move, but younger renters had a higher mobility potential than older renters. Among owners, 47 percent of families in which the head was under forty-five years were planning to move, as compared with only 33 percent of owner families headed by men aged between forty-five and fifty-four, and 21 percent of owner families in which the head was fifty-five years old or over.[4] (Figure 4C.)

Lack of mobility in the oldest age group – that over sixty-five years old – is due partly to

tween twenty and twenty-four. This is partly explained by the fact that these are the ages when marriage and the establishment of independent households are most usual and when migration from farms to cities or from one region or city to another is most likely. At these ages, mobility is primarily individual rather than family mobility. It is expressed in the housing market as a demand for small rental units, often furnished, and often of relatively low cost.

On the other hand, mobility between twenty-five and forty-five years is predominantly family mobility and is explained primarily by growth in family size. The presence of young children in a family, which changes the nature of its housing requirements, is perhaps the single most important cause of mobility during the middle years. In fact, families with young children make up the most mobile group within any age level, and it is among this group that the largest proportion of renters who want to own are found.

Figure 5 shows the relationship between family composition and mobility. Full families, consisting of both parents and their young children, show the greatest tendency to change their residences. When only one child is present, a larger proportion of their moves are to other communities and counties. With the addition

marriage, the average family makes some two-thirds of all the moves it will make during its entire history. Rossi cogently summarizes why this should be so:[5]

The housing needs of a *young* household are most likely to be " out of balance," as it were, with its actual housing. This is the period in the family's life cycle where the greatest amount of change in household size and composition takes place. It is also the period in which the household, because of the financial demands made upon it by these rapid changes in size and composition, is

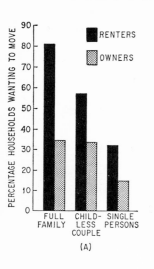

(A)

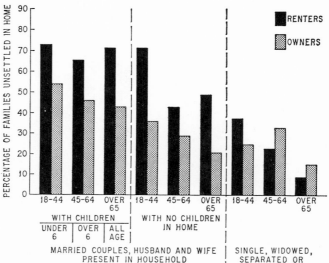

(B)

*Figure 5. Relationship between family status and mobility. (A) Mobility potential, by family status and tenure, Philadelphia sample, 1950; (B) mobility potential by family status, age of head, and tenure, U.S. nonfarm families, 1955.*

of more children, the tendency is to concentrate moves within the same community or county. Single individuals and, to a lesser extent, childless couples are far less mobile, when age is controlled.

Not only is mobility highest for young families with children, but the desire for mobility is also greatest for this group. Measures of mobility potential* show that the consumers most anxious to alter their housing are young families still growing or just reaching maximum size. Indeed, during the first decade of

least likely to be able to bring housing into line with its needs.

Obviously, then, the demand for housing expressed by the mobile family groups, whose heads are under forty years of age, is for larger quarters, owned homes, and usually suburban locations. In addition there is a latent demand for such housing which is not expressed on the market because of lack of resources. To look only at the demand expressed by persons actively seeking a different dwelling gives a somewhat distorted image of the total distribution

* Figure 5A defines mobility potential as that percentage expressing a desire to move within a year. Peter Rossi, *Why Families Move.* New York: The Free Press, p. 72. Figure 5B defines mobility potential as the

percentage stating that they feel that they are not settled in a satisfactory home. Federal Reserve Board, *op. cit.,* 1955.

of housing demand and the total distribution of housing consumers.

*Movers have lower income than nonmovers.* Between 1949 and 1950, the median income for nonmovers was $42 more than the median for the entire male civilian labor force over fourteen years of age ($2,578 as opposed to $2,536). The median income for those who moved within the same county was $2,356 or $80 less than the overall median. The median income for those who migrated to other counties or states was a full $465 less than the overall median – a low of $2,071.

However, this relationship between low income and mobility can be partly explained by youth, since the young are more mobile (particularly to different counties or states), and income is then at its lowest. Confirming this interpretation is the fact that expectation of higher income (again typical of youth) predisposes the consumer to move more than does the prospect of stable or diminishing income.

A survey undertaken in the early 1950s showed that some 45 percent of nonfarm, owner families who expected their income to be higher in the immediate future also expected to be moving; only 25 percent of the owner families who expected no substantial change in their incomes planned to move. Among renters the same relationship exists, but in more extreme terms. Of renter families, 80 percent of those optimistic about future income increases were planning to move, as contrasted with only 52 percent who expected no substantial change in their economic circumstances.[6]

Although undoubtedly much of the apparent relationship between low income and mobility can be explained by youth, some part of it cannot be so explained, since, for every age group – except the unusual interval between fourteen and twenty-four years – mobile workers have lower incomes than nonmobile workers. This residual mobility difference between income groups is probably partly due to the migration to the cities of unskilled rural labor and to the rapid turnover of rented dwellings in slum or declining neighborhoods.

Another factor may be the differential mobility rates for specific occupations. In 1955, for example, census figures showed that workers in the primary industries of agriculture, fishing, and mining, and the secondary industries of construction and manufacturing had higher than average mobility rates. On the other hand, male workers employed in transportation, communication, and other public utilities, professional men and those in related services, and the self-employed in nonagricultural industries had mobility rates substantially below the average (19.1, 18.8, and 12.0 percent, respectively, having moved between 1954 and 1955).[7] It would seem self-evident that the latter group of occupations would pay more than the former. Statistics for the year 1954 show this to be true, in general. In that year the low-mobility group of occupations uniformly showed substantially higher incomes than the high-mobility group ($8,854 for professional and technical people as compared to $1,867 in agriculture, for example), with the one exception of transportation-communication, in which earnings were, however, roughly comparable to those in manufacturing, the highest-paid of the high-mobility group ($4,932 in manufacturing as compared to $4,676 in transportation-communication).[8]

A case has also been made for the correlation of mobility with high income. William H. Whyte, Jr., in *The Organization Man* writes:[9]

> ... the experience of direct mail people indicates that address changes are more frequent in the $5,000 and over bracket. There are also indications that address changes are becoming more frequent in this group. In 1953, 14.8 percent of *Fortune's* subscribers changed addresses during the year. In 1954, 16.6 percent, and in 1955, 17.4 percent.

Although these figures would certainly indicate that mobility is increasing in the middle- and upper-income groups, it is quite possible that young adults and transient workers, with low incomes but with the very highest mobility rates, seldom order by mail. Moreover, these highly mobile consumers do not subscribe to an expensive business magazine.

*Movers have more education than nonmovers.* It has been found that mobile persons have more formal education than do those who display stable behavior in the housing market.

In general, however, this education-mobility relationship is probably another facet of the youth-mobility tie. It is well known that the average years of schooling completed by young persons is higher than the average for older persons – a testimony to the dramatic gains in mass education over the past generation.

In some measure, however, it may be true that education per se induces mobility. Advanced training increases the job potential and therefore those with higher education may be expected to range farther afield in search of employment. In particular, those who have gone away to college, especially from small towns, tend to take jobs in other cities after they graduate, rather than returning home again. According to recent census figures and the *Time* study, *They Went to College*,[10] only 27.3 percent of high school graduates aged between twenty-five and thirty-four were interstate migrants. Of those who had had at least one year of college, 45.5 percent crossed state lines. Of those who had completed college in another state, and who had worked their way through, 69 percent did not return to their original home town.

Furthermore, these college-educated young people, even after the start of their careers, may be more likely to receive offers which take them to another city from that in which they first obtained employment. Recruiting for the higher-status jobs in large national corporations, for teaching positions, for government service, for publishing, and similar fields which require a high educational level, is not limited to the local community. A possible confirmation of this lies in the fact that professionals and those in related services, in marked contrast to every other occupational group, are most likely to make an *intercommunity* move when they change residences. Although their overall mobility is not high (18.8 percent having moved between 1954 and 1955), 55 percent of these moves were to other communities or counties.[11]

Professional employment, like college training, is still far from typical of the population as a whole. Indeed, education-linked mobility might be more than counteracted by the mobility of rural migrants with comparatively little formal schooling. The education-mobility association must therefore, in the overall picture, be counted as another function of youth.

*The mobility profile.* From the preceding discussion of mobility factors, a fairly accurate picture of the mobile consumer can be drawn. The typical mover is a young person (or family) with a comparatively low income, who is currently renting an apartment. If this renter expects a rise in salary, or if he wants to own his own home, or if young children are part of the household – or all three – the mobility potential is increased. As possibly portentous deviants from this general mobility profile, it appears that the incidence of moves (at least long-distance moves) is quite high, and may even be increasing, among consumers of middle to high income, with a high educational level, particularly those in corporate or professional employment.

## Why people move

*Intercommunity as opposed to intracommunity mobility.* As was pointed out at the beginning of the chapter, there are two distinct types of mobility: the long-range or intercommunity move and the short-range or intracommunity move (Figure 6). Whereas the former is primarily job-motivated, the latter is chiefly housing-motivated. Furthermore, long-range moves are dominated by the attractiveness or positive " pulls " of the new location; short-range moves are dominated by dissatisfaction with the previous residence.

*Intercommunity moves.* Among a randomly selected sample of in-migrants to Kalamazoo, Michigan,* for example, 57 percent of

---

* Ralph Turner, " Migration to a Medium-sized American City: Attitudes, Motives, and Personal Characteristics Revealed by Open-end Interview Methodology," *The Journal of Social Psychology*, vol. 30, 1949, pp. 229 – 249. Turner studied 200 family heads over twenty-one years of age who had moved to Kalamazoo from a distance of over 25 miles during the period four to ten months before survey date. Of these respondents, randomly selected from a master list of all in-migrants to the community, there were 161 men with families; 9 unmarried men; 16 unmarried women; 5 widows and 1 widower; 5 divorced women and 1 divorced man.

the reasons given for moving were related to economic or job considerations. Almost two-thirds were related to the attractive influences of the new environment, which included, in addition to economic opportunity, the desire to lead a better life, to escape from undesirable large city conditions, or to live in a healthier climate. Only 4 percent of the reasons given were directly related to housing. Furthermore, the higher the level of education and socio-economic status, the more likely were attractive "pulls" to dominate the motives for moving.

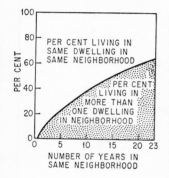

Figure 6. *Percentage of individuals residing in more than one dwelling unit in the same neighborhood by length of residence in that same neighborhood.*

Source: Special tabulations prepared for ACTION from data collected in Gallup poll, Ballot 453k, Feb. 24, 1950, questions 26a and b. *(Data were made available through the courtesy of the American Institute of Public Opinion.)*

Confirmation of the overwhelming importance of economic considerations in intercommunity mobility is found in comparable data for the town of Norristown, Pennsylvania.* A study of migrants into this community revealed that 63 percent of the men who moved there from outside the general area had been motivated by job reasons. Of the women, almost half had moved because their husbands had changed jobs; another 22 percent had migrated as brides of husbands already residing in Norristown.

*Intracommunity moves.* Conversely, perhaps three-fifths of those who move within the same community are seeking primarily to better their housing. The remaining two-fifths have either been forced to move or have done so as a by-product of some other decision. In a 1940 study which analyzed the reasons given for mobility within the preceding five-year period, 59 percent concerned voluntary attempts to obtain more suitable housing.† Similar distributions of stated motives appear in studies of Flint, Michigan, and Philadelphia.[12]

*Housing dissatisfaction: a "cause" of mobility.* Not all dissatisfied housing consumers move (even locally) and not all movers are dissatisfied with their previous dwellings. Low-level discontent coupled with inertia may keep some householders in unsatisfying quarters. At least twice as many households are not satisfied with their housing as move in any year. Still others may have their moving plans frustrated by conditions in the housing market or by economic incapacities to achieve a different standard of housing. In addition, moving does occur in the absence of conscious dissatisfaction and planning, as when some change in circumstances forces a move (sudden loss of income or of the dwelling itself by fire or flood) or when an appealing opportunity presents itself almost accidentally.

Nevertheless dissatisfaction with current housing does underlie the majority of decisions to move within the same community. As shown in various studies, slightly over 60 percent of intracommunity movers are so motivated. The major sources of discontent which lead them to move can be summarized in descending order of importance : ‡

1. Space within the dwelling (usually too little, occasionally too much).

---

* Sidney Goldstein, *Patterns of Internal Migration: Norristown, Pennsylvania, 1910–1950,* preliminary report issued by University of Pennsylvania Behavioral Research Council, July, 1953, vol. II, p. 60. (Hectographed.) In comparing these figures with those of Turner, it should be borne in mind that Turner interviewed only heads of households, whereas Goldstein interviewed all movers.

†Branch, *op. cit.,* p. 21. The answers have been regrouped somewhat for this analysis. Total adds to more than 100 percent because multiple reasons were given by many respondents. The reasons, in order of descending importance, were to secure better quarters of a better location, 18 percent; to build or buy a home, 16 percent; to obtain more space in the dwelling, 13 percent; to reduce costs or space, 12 percent. The remaining reasons were forced to move because of a change in, or destruction of, previously occupied dwelling, 13 percent; to be closer to job, 10 percent; as by-product of marriage or household formation, 5 percent; miscellaneous, 30 percent.

‡ In this and the following discussion, the authors are indebted to the material collected and analyzed by Rossi, *op. cit.,* on 273 Philadelphians who moved voluntarily between 1945 and 1950 in an attempt to better their housing conditions.

2. The neighborhood surrounding the dwelling (particularly the social composition of the neighborhood; secondarily its physical characteristics).

3. Cost of housing (invariably too high, or too high for value received).

4. Secondary sources of dissatisfaction, such as poor design or layout of the dwelling; difficulties with the landlord; tensions within the household not necessarily related to the quality of the dwelling; and other more vague and amorphous causes of discontent.

Such dissatisfactions may be accepted temporarily during a period of housing shortage or until slim family earnings increase. They may also be more permanent irritants, as in the case of the low-income consumer who has little hope of bettering either earnings or housing. On the other hand, actual deterioration of the dwelling and its surroundings may render previously satisfactory housing unsuitable.

It is interesting to note that cases in which discontent develops later are far more common than those in which it is present from the beginning of occupancy. Note further that dissatisfaction with housing is as much or more the result of changing family needs as it is of changes in the quality of the dwelling itself or of its environment.

This is particularly true of space complaints. Enlargement of family size is the most frequent cause of space dissatisfaction, almost independently of objective density of occupancy. Families seem to adjust to a particular level of density (whether it be high or low), but the addition of a new person tends to create feelings of overcrowding even when objectively there is enough space for all. Rossi found it to be true that more families living at densities exceeding one person per room registered space complaints as a primary cause of moving than did less crowded families. But fully twice as many families who had expanded in size cited space complaints as did those families whose size had remained constant.

Dissatisfactions with neighborhood are also often the result of changes in family status. A neighborhood environment which is suited to the needs of the young couple becomes inadequate when children reach school, or even toddling, age. A working wife finds her previously satisfactory neighborhood location undesirable when she ceases to work. Obviously, a major shift in job location can render a previously convenient dwelling quite unsuitable.

Of those movers who complained about their previous neighborhood, half were disturbed by its social composition. Less than one-quarter cited the physical structure of the previous area and an even smaller percentage the inadequacy of community or municipal services. In almost three-fifths of these cases there had been no discernible change either in the neighborhood or in the family's objective needs. Where changes had occurred, changes in needs were equally as important as actual deterioration of the area.

Cost complaints, although widespread, tend to be incidental, or somewhat ineffective in precipitating a move, unless they are felt in conjunction with other dissatisfaction. For instance, a young couple paying a moderate rental for a small city apartment may not feel the price too high for the small space until after children arrive. Then they would tend to seek larger quarters elsewhere, in a section of the city with lower housing costs.

As a general rule, renters register more cost complaints than do owners, not necessarily because their financial burden is heavier, but because it is somewhat less flexible than that of owners. On the other hand, owners are more sensitive to neighborhood inadequacies, which, it might be presumed, could indicate a concern with cost as " property value."

Obviously, then, dissatisfaction with housing contains a subjective element. There is some uniformity between level of satisfaction and objective characteristics of the dwelling, its cost and its surrounding environment and location. But correlation is not complete, since satisfaction is always partly a subjective phenomenon, varying from family to family, and depending upon the different standards by which they judge, as well as the different goals which they look forward to achieving.

Nevertheless, the major reasons for housing dissatisfaction do point to a general area of agreement and to one particular housing consumer. Space, neighborhood, and cost motives for moving all corroborate the finding that young families in the expanding stage of the family cycle are the most mobile type of household within the population.

## The changing patterns of mobility

The preceding pages have charted the mobility of housing consumers according to age, tenure, income, and education. Also defined were the major housing dissatisfactions which tend to precipitate a move. Still to be answered is the question of where the various consumers are going, and how their moves (or non-moves) affect the pattern of the metropolitan area. With this question, job-oriented mobility, as well as those moves made in order to obtain better housing, assume civic importance. Long-range trends in mobility become strategically relevant. And the movements of special groups within the population are of particular interest.

*Intercommunity movement trends.* In 1850, 25 percent of the native-born white population were living in states other than those in which they were born. By 1890, this interstate mobility had dropped to 20 percent of the native white population, and it continued to fall until 1920. But from 1920 onward a counter-trend set in, and long-distance mobility began to rise once more. Today, interstate migration of the native white population is roughly comparable to 1850, with somewhat more than 25 percent of the population living in states other than where they were born. Interregional migration rates have followed the same pattern, dipping between 1900 and 1920 and then rising again to an earlier level of over 10 percent.[13]

Although these figures can mean that interstate and interregional mobility rates have not increased substantially over the past one hundred years, they reveal the extraordinary phenomenon of a completely settled country in which interstate and interregional moves are even more frequent than they were while settlement was still taking place. Furthermore, 25 percent of an 1850 population of 23 million meant a movement of 5¾ million people. Twenty-five percent of today's 170 million population means a movement of 42½ million people, or 7½ times as many as were living in other states in 1850.

This is a different kind of mobility from that which was dominant during the settlement of America. It reflects partly the general rural-urban shift which, over the years, has brought farm and small-town residents to the larger cities; partly, increased job mobility which takes workers from one city to another across the country.

Of particular interest within this general trend is the recent Southern shift, including the agricultural movement away from cotton, which has been displacing low-income rural workers, white and Negro, sending them to the city and often to the North. Nor should one overlook the moves made in search of a pleasanter climate, notably to the West Coast, certain Southwestern states, and Florida, which have given these regions such dramatic population rises, preponderantly of older people. However, since World War II an unprecedented industrial boom has drawn also a great many younger families with children, particularly to California, somewhat less dramatically to Florida. Migratory farm workers, such as the "Okies" moving into California during the Depression, have also contributed to the western shift.

In contrast to the ebb and flow of white migration is the interstate migration rate of the nonwhite population (mainly Negro), which follows a quite different pattern. Since 1850, it has increased almost steadily, until today it exceeds that of the white population. These moves are, and always have been, mainly a migration from rural areas into the larger cities and, in the case of the Negro, from the South to the North.

*Intracommunity movement trends.* But the intercounty, interstate, and interregional moves, whether white or Negro, represent only about one-third of all the moves which occur in any given year. The other two-thirds are local moves, the majority of which are housing-motivated. Of this type of mobility in the nineteenth century almost nothing is known. However, it is unlikely that many moves in 1850, and even somewhat later, were primarily concerned with a change in housing. In 1850, 85 percent of the population lived in rural areas, and farm families are seldom motivated to change residences in order to obtain more suitable housing. Their homes are a part of the farm and may be neglected, improved, enlarged, or even replaced without any mobility being recorded for the farm family. When urban population was an insignificant part of the total, housing-motivated mobility must have been much less important than it is today, when more than 4 out of 5 Americans live in nonfarm communities. In earlier days, there could not possibly have been the dominant pattern of housing mobility seen in the foregoing analysis of the median housing consumer: from small rented apartment to larger rented apartment, to owned small home, to owned larger home.

their own dwellings at once, and the three-generation household has become an infrequent and undesired occurrence. Higher mobility rates undoubtedly result from this family pattern.

That housing-oriented mobility has increased in the past half century, we have no doubt. However, the only available direct evidence of this increase comes from the sample study of Philadelphia families in 1950 (Figure 7).* The findings of this study indicate that families founded before 1910 moved less frequently during their first decade of existence than did families of more recent origin. Seventy-one per-

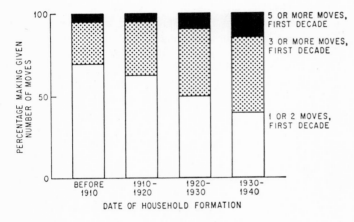

Figure 7. Distribution of households making a given number of moves during the first decade of duration.

Source: Unpublished draft of a study on mobility by Peter Rossi. The published version of the study (*Why Families Move*. Free Press, Glencoe, Ill., 1955) unfortunately omits these exploratory data. Figures are derived from a subsample of 632 families residing in four small areas of Philadelphia in 1950.

Today, this pattern has been further emphasized by the change in the American family from a three- or even four-generation household to a one- or two-generation household. When children remain in the parental home during their adult years, early marriage years, and even beyond the time when they have children of their own, mobility rates are low. This was the typical family pattern of earlier decades. Today, many unmarried children establish independent households, newly married couples move to

cent of the families formed before 1910 had low mobility records, making only one or two moves during the first ten years of existence. Of families formed in 1940, only 40 percent made as few as one or two moves between then and 1950. Three times as many of the latter families made five or more moves during their first decade as did families founded before 1920. Figure 7 also shows the relation between the date of family formation and the number of moves made during the first decade.†

---

* Data were collected by Rossi in connection with his research on *Why Families Move*. These figures appear in a hectographed prepublication draft but have not been incorporated into the published version.

† Nevertheless, since the new mobility pattern was established, counter-trends have appeared which decrease mobility, thus preventing a continual, overall rise: for example, an increasing percentage of persons in the older age brackets; an increase in homeownership; the widespread ownership of cars, and the improvement of the highway system, which allows workers to change jobs without changing residences.

Over the past twenty-five years there has been little net change in overall mobility. During the 1930's, when housing was easily obtained and jobs were not, mobility remained at a fairly constant level of 55 to 60 percent over a five-year period. The early 1940's saw a dip to about 50 percent, due to housing shortage and the absence of young men—traditionally the most mobile group—who were serving in the Armed Forces. By 1955, the five-year mobility rate had risen once more to 57 percent, a point roughly equivalent to the early 1930's.

*Population shifts.* Both these new types of mobility, job-motivated and housing-motivated, are important, but for different reasons. These become apparent when the population movement each year is broken down in its component parts, roughly as follows:

*Interstate, intercounty, or interregional.* Of the approximately 7 percent of the population making long-distance moves each year, the white majority are moving predominantly:

1. From rural area or small town to city or suburb.

2. From city to city.

3. From the suburbs of one city to the suburbs of another.

4. From the city to the suburbs of another city.

5. From central city to suburbs, where these are in a different state or county.

6. To the North, South, and West.

The nonwhite (mainly Negro) minority is moving predominantly (1) from rural area to city, (2) from South to North.

*Intracommunity or intracounty.* Of the approximately 13 percent of the population making short-distance, house-motivated moves each year, the white majority are moving predominantly (1) within the city proper; (2) within the suburbs; (3) from city to suburb, where these are in the same county or state. The nonwhite minority is moving predominantly within the city proper.

The nonwhite shift, although smaller in percentage of total population, is concentrated mainly in one direction, into the city. The white shifts are made in a great many different directions. But the net result is a shift away from the central city. Thus, the significant job-motivated mobility is that which brings the Negro and other nonwhites into the city. The significant housing-motivated shift is that which takes the white to the suburbs. What these moves mean in relation to each other can best be seen in specific examples of both large and medium-sized cities.

In 1957, New York City (population: 7,812,509) gained 311,000 Negroes and 304,000 Puerto Ricans. It lost 720,000 whites. By that time 20 percent of New York City residents were either Negro or Puerto Rican. Although the city showed a net loss since 1950 of 79,448 persons, its New York and New Jersey suburban areas gained 1,278,078, the Connecticut suburban gain being uncounted.[14]

From 1950 to 1956, the Negro population of Syracuse, New York (population 214,000), rose by nearly 100 percent. In that period, the city gained 4,767 Negroes and lost 10,767 whites. Although the city showed a net loss of 6,000 people, the suburbs gained 60,000, all except 400 of them white. Of the Syracuse city population, 4.3 percent is now nonwhite; of the nonwhite group, almost all are Negro (there are a few Indians and a negligible number of Orientals).[15]

From 1950 to 1957, Chicago gained 197,000 nonwhites, mostly Negro. It showed a net loss of 93,000 whites. The loss would have been much greater were it not for the very large (although uncounted) gain in rural Southern whites, congregating, like the Negroes, in the central city.[16]

Since 1940, Indianapolis, Indiana (today's population 450,000), has experienced an industrial and birth rate boom which has increased the population by over 63,000 people, most of them in the suburbs. The Metropolitan Planning Commission expects that within the next eighteen years, the eight suburban counties surrounding Indianapolis will be entirely filled up, tripling the size of the metropolitan area. Unlike the other cities cited, the Negro population has increased by only 3 percent. The majority of newcomers are workers drawn from the Indiana farm and small-town population, white workers from the rural South, and executives from all over America. In 1940, Indiana had a 60:40 farming to industry population ratio; it is now 65 percent industrial to 35 percent agricultural.[17]

Although the increase of nonwhites may be much slower in some cities than in others, and indeed may be outweighed by white gains in some sections of the country, it is nevertheless evident in most of the larger cities.

There is no reason to expect that the migration of nonwhites and rural whites to the city and to the North will stop, although it may be temporarily slowed or halted by unforeseen factors. Indeed, in the long run it can be expected to increase as agriculture in general becomes more mechanized and larger in its scale of operation. Coupled with the net shift of whites away from the city and of Northern whites toward the South and West, this means, over the years, a redistribution of population which must have profound effects upon metropolitan areas in all sections of the country. Within this pattern of mobility cities today must plan for the future. And within this pattern the shift to the suburbs is of primary importance.

## How are the suburbs expanding?

The mobility pattern which creates the suburban shift is not a simple move like that of rural migrants to the city, but a complex of different moves (and even nonmoves). The phrase "flight to the suburbs" used so confidently today conjures up a picture of a mass exodus from the city which is actually far from accurate. It also implies the use of the suburbs almost entirely as residential "bedroom communities," an equally inaccurate concept.

A great many suburban communities have developed around existing small villages or industrial towns. Thus some sizable proportion of suburban residents have simply remained in their communities of origin and the suburbs have engulfed them. For the most part (and except for established industrial towns), these people are older families, usually retired from farming or from small proprietary business.

Second, another segment of the suburban population has been drawn, not from the central city itself, but from other regions: from small towns and farms, or from the suburbs surrounding other large cities. Their flight is not out of the city, but part way into it. Although their choice of the suburbs is a housing choice, they exhibit the job-motivated mobility which today moves certain segments of the population about the country. This group includes both factory workers drawn by expanding suburban or near-suburban industry and commuters in higher-status occupations, such as corporation executives, either transferred to the new community,

or arriving in response to better job offers. Their incomes range from median to very high, and they may be either commuters or part of the noncommuting suburban population.

The consumer who moves outward from the central city itself, however, is not altogether a fictitious character. From all the milling, moving, shifting, and sifting of population within the entire metropolitan area, the net result – obvious over time – is a redistribution in favor of the peripheral areas. But this outward movement appears to be much slower and smaller than the phrase "flights to the suburbs" would indicate.

A Minneapolis mobility study,[18] found that, of all moves made by a sample over an eight-year period, only 1 out of 16 actually contributed to the dispersal of the city's population. This represented but 6 percent of the entire sample and only 13 percent of all the movers. This seemed so trivial a displacement that it led the author of the study to raise the question of "whether the visible growth of peripheral urban areas does not often represent the addition of new family units, created by marriage or migration, to a much greater extent than it reflects the displacement of the existing family population."

Moreover, those who move out of the central core of the city rarely move directly to the suburbs. They move usually to an adjacent district only a mile or so farther away from the center. Those who do move from city to suburb do so from the outermost part of the city's residential area, that section of the city immediately adjoining the suburbs. For most urban residents then, the suburbs are not reached by one flying leap, but by a series of short hops, each one a little farther out from the center of town.[19]

Among the families who move to suburban locations, not all are moving in order to become commuters, an assumption which is often made by students of decentralization. Some persons classified as suburbanites are actually moving closer to their jobs by their ostensible decentralizing. This is becoming more often the case as industries take up peripheral locations and as commerce and service trades follow residents into newer areas of settlement.

Obviously there is little chance of either holding in the city or attracting back again the resident who both lives and works in the suburbs. On the other hand, the commuter, whether drawn from the central city or other regions, is a much more likely prospect.

# The filtering process

## WILLIAM G. GRIGSBY

The various housing market relationships with which this volume is concerned can be viewed as ramifications of what is often referred to as the filtering process. It might seem more logical and analytically fruitful, therefore, for filtering itself to be the theme and focus of the study. This, however, would be inadvisable for a number of reasons.

First of all, although the concept of filtering is widely recognized, there is not universal agreement on a definition of the process. Since the definition that is used virtually determines the selection of factors to be examined and influences the types of measurements to be made and conclusions reached, there are obvious difficulties in choosing but one of several that are widely employed.

Second, the term filtering, because of its historical association with some violent arguments over national housing policy, might conjure up in the minds of many readers certain predilections which would make their evaluation of purely theoretical arguments rather difficult.

Finally, as will be shown in more detail below, the traditional concept of filtering and the one which should really be used in any extensive treatment of the subject encompasses several separate and analytically distinct pheno-

mena.[1] These tend to become merged and confused in most discussions of the subject, and in addition raise barriers to empirical research.

For all these reasons, none of the various definitions of filtering has been accepted as an organizing concept in this study and except for the discussion in this chapter the term itself is used sparingly. Nevertheless, we must inquire into the process somewhat more thoroughly before discarding the word in favor of other terminology. For after all, filtering in its broadest sense *is* the dynamic aspect of the housing market, the one aspect about which we know so little and must know so much if we are to have effective housing and urban renewal programs. Moreover, the concept of filtering represents a first crude attempt at macroanalysis of the housing market, an approach still lacking, unfortunately, in current policy formulation. Examination of the process, therefore, seems an appropriate part of the study.

### Definitions of filtering

As already pointed out, there are several different views of what filtering actually is. The disagreement, if it may be called that, is really over the question of which of several housing

*Reprinted from* Housing Markets and Public Policy, *University of Pennsylvania Press, 1963, pp. 84–110, with permission of the publisher.*

market processes – changes in occupancy, values, and housing standards – should be incorporated into a definition of filtering. It is interesting that despite the various meanings given to the term, there seem to be no semantic difficulties when it is used in casual conversation. The problems of definition have been associated with attempts to adapt the general concept to varying analytical and empirical requirements. Four different usages of "filtering" will be described here in an effort to provide a better understanding of the term.

*Change in price or rent – Change in occupancy.* Of the various definitions of filtering, the one which expresses the most common and widespread understanding of the concept is contained in a thorough and penetrating discussion of the subject by Ratcliff: "This process ... is described most simply as the changing of occupancy as the housing that is occupied by one income group becomes available to the next lower income group as a result of decline in market price, i.e., in sales price or rent value."[2] The Ratcliff definition may be used to describe the filtering down of dwelling units or the filtering up (percolation) of families. Usually, it is assumed that the two occur simultaneously and are simply opposite sides of the same coin, but this need not necessarily be so, as will be seen in the following paragraph. It may be noted that there are two separate and distinct elements to the definition: change in value, which Ratcliff describes elsewhere as gradual, and change in occupancy. But the key feature is the latter. It is this which provides the analogy to filtering in the physical sciences.* Shifting value is only a permissive factor. Subsequent definitions by other analysts have completely reversed this emphasis.

*Change in position of dwelling unit on the value scale.* The first departure, and a major

one, from the traditional view is the Fisher-Winnick definition.[3] The dual elements of value change and shifting occupancy described by Ratcliff are shown by Fisher and Winnick to result in a confusion between downward price movement, which they regard as the actual filtering process, and change in occupancy, which they view as the effect of this process. They demonstrate that a price decline among a group of dwelling units may or may not be associated with a complementary change in residency. With generally rising real incomes, it is quite possible for a group of dwellings to be occupied by successively higher income groups as the relative values of the units decline. Thus, the same data could support an argument for either filtering up or down. The difficulty stems from the incorporation of the two separate factors – occupancy and price – into a single concept, when the relationship between the two is not uniform.

Equally, there is the problem of even detecting price declines when the process of depreciation spans such a long time and is obscured by broad inflationary movements and a changing product mix in the consumer market basket. In addition, there is an even more basic objection. "This change in the real value of a rental is not at all synonomous with filtering.... Deflation of rents cannot measure filtering, and definitions of filtering which explicitly or implicitly rest on price deflation are not logically meaningful."[4]

To solve these theoretical and empirical difficulties, Fisher and Winnick simplify the definition. Ratcliff's key element – change in occupancy – is dropped. "The succession of occupancy by lower income groups is not part of the definition of filtering. Only the relative change in rent or price is a necessary and sufficient condition.... Filtering is a movement of dwelling units, and the test for filtering is in rent and price, not income."[5] The index pro-

---

* The analogy itself is interesting. Although filtering is used to refer to both dwelling units and families, it is the former to which the term is usually applied. Yet since it is the families who in a sense pass through the structures which are physically stationary, it is really the families that filter, not the houses. Thus, in applying the term to the housing market, the metaphor has been reversed. It is also reversed in yet another

way. Filtering in the physical sciences implies a cleansing process in which the superior (more pure) elements usually are those which pass from one stage to the next. The waste materials remain behind. In the housing market, however, the inferior dwelling units filter while the better ones stay at their original level. The families with rising incomes filter up; those with declining earnings tend to filter down.

blem is solved by making all prices relative to each other. Filtering is defined as " a change over time in the position of a given dwelling unit or group of dwelling units within the distribution of housing prices and rents in the community as a whole."[6] Regardless of changes in absolute value, or in occupancy, dwelling units filter if they move from, say, the upper third to the middle third of the value spectrum.

On the surface, the exclusion of the occupancy factor might seem to be the more important of the two changes by Fisher and Winnick. In some respects, however, measuring the filtering of one group of dwelling units in terms of another group or all units, rather than against prices generally, represents an equally significant change. It is an obvious aid to empirical studies. Whether housing prices and rents as a whole move up or down does not matter, for a median figure at the new price level can easily be calculated and the changed position of various groups of dwelling units noted.

The empirical simplicity, however, is not the crucial innovation. Rather, as the authors point out, it is the standard of measure itself. For example, of all the various definitions of filtering, only theirs yielded a measurement indicating downward filtration in New York's Lower East Side from about the turn of the century to 1940, even though this was generally regarded as a period of decline for the area. Why their result should differ can be seen more clearly if we examine the definition in somewhat greater detail.

It follows from the definition that " As newer units are added (generally at higher than average rents), the community standard is raised; and statistically the mean or median of the distribution is shifted to the right; most existing units are further to the left. Demolition of the lowest-priced (and presumably the poorest) housing will have a similar effect by raising the average quality of the housing inventory."[7] If, for example, the median house price in an area in 1950 were $10,000 and the supply between 1950 and 1960 experienced a huge increase through the construction of houses priced only at $15,000, the new median, barring a drop in the general price level, would almost certainly

be above $10,000. As a result of the concentration of new construction at higher price levels, all units under $10,000 would, in the absence of improvements extensive enough to raise their value substantially, stand relatively lower on the value scale of units in existence in 1960, and thus, by the Fisher-Winnick formulation, would have filtered down. Demolition of some of the lowest-quality units would cause the filtering of additional units, as well as greater filtering of the same unit.

But suppose that all this new construction had been in response to population growth and that the number of new households exceeded the number of units produced, the excess families all being in the lower-income groups. The pressure of this population increment on demand for units under $10,000 might raise the prices (in constant dollars) of these units and push up prices throughout the entire stock without materially shifting the position of any units on the value spectrum. In this situation, the traditional view would hold that the lower-priced units would probably have a tendency to filter up, the amount of such filtering being a reflection of the relatively greater difficulty faced by lower-income groups in their search for adequate living accommodations.

The Fisher-Winnick measure, however, would indicate substantial filtering down and suggest improvement in housing conditions at the same time that families of modest means were finding it increasingly difficult to obtain accommodations at prices or rents they could afford. Clearly, such a definition is not intended to be used to answer the question of whether the filtering process is bringing dwellings within the reach of lower-income groups, nor whether housing conditions are generally improving or deteriorating. But this is not necessarily a limitation of the definition, since the ability or inability of the private market to meet the requirements of households that cannot afford new construction is best gauged by direct reference to the volume of occupied substandard housing and to the amount of overcrowding. The definition is most useful in revealing differential rates of depreciation or appreciation within the stock and thus the varying effects of rising incomes, changing tastes, public improvements, etc., on each of the housing submarkets within a total market area.*

Perhaps the main virtue of the Fisher-Winnick formulation is that in all respects it is a "clean" definition. Not only has it the advantage of avoiding the problem of the changing price level, but it sanitizes the entire concept by neutralizing it with respect to the main issue with which it has been so long concerned. No longer are we burdened with the argument of whether filtering works, i.e., supplies lower-income groups with decent housing, for it is now only a statistical measurement incapable of illuminating this question. For this very reason, however, it could hardly be expected to receive universal acceptance since the original issues concerning public housing and other governmental aids are still with us in modified forms. Hence, still another definition has been developed, one which lies between the Ratcliff and Fisher-Winnick formulations.

*Change in price or rent (constant dollars).* This definition has been used by Lowry to examine theoretically whether filtering can provide adequate housing for lower-income groups.[8] It differs from simple depreciation or appreciation only in that the measurement is in constant rather than current dollars. It may be distinguished from Ratcliff's concept by its exclusion of the notion of changing occupancy and from the Fisher-Winnick statement by the standard against which filtering is measured. This standard is outside the housing inventory itself. If prices and rents of a particular group of houses and apartment units do not advance as much as prices generally, they have filtered down; if they advance more than prices gene-

rally, they have filtered up.† The definition, it may be seen, is not confined to *downward* movements of prices and rents. It reflects the fact, recognized by analysts and investors alike, that the value or rent of a unit may rise over time, beyond general inflationary price movements.

The practical distinction between the Fisher-Winnick and Lowry measures is greater than may first appear to be the case. It is not simply a question of index numbers. Construction of low-cost housing, for example, would cause units of higher price or rent to filter up on the Fisher-Winnick scale. Simultaneously, however, it might cause absolute value declines – *downward* filtering on the Lowry scale – among dwelling units which were of roughly equal quality to the new units but which had been renting or selling at a slightly higher level until the injection of the additional supply into the inventory. The likelihood of the two measures producing opposite results in other situations can be readily demonstrated. For this reason, the Lowry definition, even though it excludes the occupancy factor, can be regarded as conceptually closer to the Ratcliff than to the Fisher-Winnick view.

In excluding the element of shifting occupancy, but at the same time clearly implying that shifts will indeed occur, Lowry ignores a conceptual problem which Fisher and Winnick are neatly able to avoid altogether. This is the difference between what might be termed market and nonmarket filtering. To illustrate, a house built fifty years ago for $10,000 and which today would command a price of $9,000 is not considered to have experienced market filtering unless sometime during its life it

---

* When the concept is used for this purpose, the comparison must be confined to dwelling units in existence at both the beginning and end of the period over which measurement is made.

† Logically, the price index used to deflate house prices and rents should exclude housing itself, for residential prices and rents should not be part of the standard of value against which changes in the values of dwelling units are themselves measured. On a practical level, moreover, one could argue that housing is such an important element (roughly one-fifth) of the total price index that its inclusion might materially change the movements of the index relative to housing itself. Apparently, however, this has not been generally so for most areas in recent years. In Philadelphia, for ex-

ample, the consumer price index advanced about 12 percent from April, 1950, to December, 1956, while the rent index moved up 14 percent, and the total housing index, including home purchase and other homeowner costs, 14 percent. The consumer price index exclusive of housing would have increased about 11.5 percent. Thus, it would make scant difference which standard was chosen, and the simplest, i.e., the total consumer price index, might be favored. A more important question, but one which cannot be dealt with here, is whether the rent index itself is accurate. See Sherman J. Maisel, "Have We Underestimated Increases in Rents and Shelter Expenditures?" *Journal of Political Economy*, LVII (April, 1949), 106 – 117.

actually is sold for less than $10,000 or is rented at a figure that does not reflect the original price. There would be no doubt that nonmarket filtering had occurred. The lower value of the structure would be immediately recognized by tax assessors as well as the casual observer. The quantitative difference between market and nonmarket filtering is of negligible importance among rental units because contracts are typically renegotiated every one to three years. In the ownership sector, however, a large portion of the stock goes for years without being revalued in the market place.

Downward nonmarket filtering, unlike market filtering, does not provide low-income families with housing. It must not be overlooked, however, in any analysis of this problem. A good many low-income families owning "filtered" homes may actually have acquired them at a time when the units were competitive with new construction and when the income or asset position of the family was much higher. Thus, they did not have to rely on filtering to bring adequate housing within their reach.* This suggests, as also do the more sophisticated income studies, that the measure of the number of families not served by the new construction industry should be based on the income – asset – family-size characteristics, not of the entire population, but of the group actually in the market.

The most interesting contribution of Lowry is not the definition itself, which is not an integral part of his analysis, but rather his separation of the causes of filtering into those which are either exogenous or endogenous to the market process. The former include such variables as real incomes, tastes, and the supply price of new construction, whereas the latter include items such as deterioration which are internal to the market itself. In Lowry's view, only the endogenous variables can be included in an examination of whether filtering provides ade-

quate housing for low-income groups. If, for example, rising incomes cause filtering and result in an improved living environment, it is the increment to earning power, not the intermediate market consequence, which should be given credit. When filtering is viewed in this light, a question can be raised as to whether the process ever has taken place to any great extent, much less furnished lower-income families with socially acceptable dwelling units. For in the housing market, virtually all the variables are exogenous. Even the rate of deterioration is highly controllable and much more a function of underlying demand factors than of time and climate. Nevertheless, for some purposes, the Lowry classification is a useful one.

In summing up the differences and similarities between the Ratcliff, Fisher-Winnick, and Lowry definitions, it may be noted that all three would apply rather well to other consumer durables. Take, for example, automobiles. New popularly priced cars could be purchased in 1950 for around $1,700. A decade later, despite the general inflationary trend, virtually all of those vehicles still in existence sold for under $200, and most of them for much less than that. Many of them had declined all the way to junk value and passed out of the stock completely. They dropped in value both absolutely and relative to the automobile stock as a whole, and in the process became available to lower-income groups.† Thus, in the car market either the traditional view of filtering or the Lowry concept or that of Fisher and Winnick would present the same picture. It is because a group of dwelling units, unlike cars, may not filter relative to the housing inventory in the same direction as it filters relative to general prices that the Fisher-Winnick definition yields different results from the other two concepts.

*Improvement in housing conditions.* The fourth, and to my knowledge only other, con-

---

* If nonmarket filtering were viewed as simply a decline in quality, whether accompanied by a value decline or not, then it could also be regarded as one of the precursors of market filtering. The movements of value and quality, however, are not always in the same direction, as will be shown in a later section of this study.

† This does not necessarily mean that the car market and the automobile industry function better, in relation to the needs of the low-income population, than the housing market and the construction industry. The acquisition and maintenance expenditures may be greater for a used car, relative to its remaining useful life, than for a used home.

cept of filtering departs quite radically from all of those discussed thus far. It might be described as a social formulation to contrast it with the other three, which are essentially market concepts.

It could be argued that, considering the high initial cost of a house, there is an economic need for it to be durable and to retain its usefulness for a long period of time. Consequently, an extremely gradual rate of value decline is to be expected. Because of the very slow rate at which dwelling units depreciate, most house prices may at any one time be moving upward as rapidly as prices generally. Investors, interested only in seeing which houses – by age, location, or price level – are not keeping pace, could use one of the market measures of filtering. But if one wanted to see whether our economy is making inroads on the problem of housing the entire population at a reasonable price or rent, and insofar as filtering would shed light on this question, the most appropriate definition of filtering would be something quite different from those discussed thus far. It would instead incorporate some measure of improvement in housing conditions.

In fact, the term filtering has already frequently been used in such a way as to suggest that the process, when it works, typically produces better housing standards. None of the previous definitions includes this assumption, but it has crept into much of the thinking on the subject. It is particularly apparent in the early part of Ratcliff's analysis, although at a later point he takes a somewhat different position. The argument is that if filtering can only be stimulated, housing conditions will be raised. This view follows from one or both of two implicit notions about filtering which have not been proven and which may not be correct. The first is that a more rapid rate of depreciation would have no adverse effects on quality.* The second is more complicated for it embodies the fallacy of composition. Since "filtering does not begin until one or more householders at a lower income level discover that the used housing that

is released represents an advantageous alternative to the housing that they are presently occupying,"[9] individual moves obviously result in better housing for the families concerned. This suggests improvement in residential accommodations generally. Looking at the whole population and the entire housing stock, however, this movement to improve individual situations occurs continuously, no matter whether aggregate housing quality is static, rising, or declining.

Since the idea that increased filtering would indeed raise standards does seem to have some acceptance, there is perhaps added reason for a definition with this element as a specific ingredient. Such a definition would hold that filtering (changes in house prices and rents) must be measured while holding income, quality, and space per person constant, or in more relaxed form, that filtering occurs only when value declines more rapidly than quality so that families can obtain either higher quality and more space at the same price, or the same quality and space at a lower price than formerly.

In empirical studies, the measure could show simply whether *incomes* were rising faster than housing costs. If house prices and rents were rising faster than all prices, i.e., filtering up by the Lowry definition, but incomes were rising even more rapidly than house prices, then in one sense filtering down would have occurred. In the actual measurement process, the index problem would be solved by the use of current rather than constant dollars. There would, however, be the problem of deciding whose income to use as the standard against which to measure what price movements, particularly if the focus is on housing for low-income families, for, as will be shown later, incomes may rise faster than residential values as a whole, but slower than prices and rents within specific categories of dwelling units. There are also problems stemming from changes in quality and in utilization of space,[10] but if measurements are made over fairly short periods of time, these difficulties are not serious.

---

* Lowry strongly disputes the thesis that more rapid value declines will bring better housing within the reach of lower-income groups.

*Summary*. The filtering process is viewed variously as a change in home values and rents relative to (1) all residential prices and rents, (2) consumer prices, and (3) consumer income. It is frequently either assumed or specifically stated that the shift in value is accompanied by a change in occupancy, but it is not always clear whether this is a necessary part of the process. It is doubtful whether there is one definition which is better than the others. Each is fitted for a particular purpose. Having several concepts does, however, tend to be confusing. In this volume, formulations (1) and (3) are examined empirically, but the theoretical discussion revolves more often around matters which are closely identified with (2). For this reason and because of the general confusion surrounding the concept, we use the term minimally in subsequent chapters and try to keep it well identified with respect to whether it refers to the traditional view, the Fisher-Winnick concept, the value-decline definition, or the income – housing-standards definition. In its place we have substituted such phrases as " price change," " depreciation," and " shift in occupancy," all of which relate to specific aspects of the process. Also used is the term " stock flow," borrowed from general economics to indicate both change in value and change in occupancy as dwelling units move from one submarket to another in the course of their lifetime. This may seem on the surface to be a step backward in that some of the significant contributions to housing market theory have been made as a result of a shift in emphasis from a flow to a stock concept,[11] but much can be learned about the dynamic aspects of housing markets by examining the flows of dwelling units and of the people who occupy them.

## The mechanics of filtering

As already mentioned, filtering is, in a sense, the subject of the entire book since, broadly speaking, it is the principal dynamic feature of the housing market. Nevertheless, it may be well as a preface to later discussion to sketch some of the forces behind filtering in rough outline, and to suggest some of the problems that confront the analyst seeking to probe into the subject more deeply.

In general, the concept of filtration accepted in the past differs in essence very little from that of simple depreciation and thus could be applied to most of the things we buy or use. Were it not the fact that filtration frequently implies a change of user as well as in value, housing would be ranked among the least filterable of consumer goods, preceded only by jewels, rare coins or books, paintings, and other works of art. The high initial cost of construction and the role of housing as a consumer necessity militate ·against rapid declines in value even in the most wealthy of societies. This characteristic of the housing supply has extremely important social, economic, and financial implications. Of equal importance is the fact that although the overall downward movement is slow, the rate of decline varies considerably among different sectors of the housing supply. In fact, some sections of the stock may even appreciate in value for extended periods of time because demand has been powerful enough to overcompensate for physical depreciation.

*What causes filtering?* According to Lowry, filtering is associated with technological obsolescence, style obsolescence, and deterioration.[12] He hints at but does not specifically recognize site and locational obsolescence as well.* Style and technological obsolescence, but not deterioration, cause higher-income groups to insist periodically upon *new* housing. Their former dwellings enter the used market, create an excess of supply over demand and a depressant effect upon prices and rents throughout the market. In the rental market this results in a lower level of maintenance and gradual decline in physical quality as the landlord seeks to preserve the same return on his annual expenditures: " Undermaintenance is an eminently reasonable response of a landlord to a declining market." Thus, style and technological obsolescence start the process and deterioration keeps it

---

* Site obsolescence might be caused by small yards, lack of off-street parking, etc., whereas locational obso-lescence might stem from shifting employment locations, shifting composition of local population, etc.

going. In the ownership market, where the consumer and investor are one and the same person, the result is quite different. The owner does not benefit either by realizing his loss through a sale or by reducing his expenditures on maintenance. The dichotomy between the rental and ownership markets has important policy implications which are pursued in more detail later.

Ratcliff explains the process differently. While mentioning the importance of deterioration and obsolescence, he points out that these factors alone are not enough to cause filtering. "Quality is a relative matter, so that these forces lie dormant until some better housing value appears."* Within a particular stratum of the stock, better housing values will result from a surplus of dwelling units, created either from a change in demand or supply, sufficient to cause a weakening in prices. For the entire housing inventory this surplus, except in areas of declining population, results largely from new construction. Although some surplus can result from conversions and doubling up of existing households, these factors contribute relatively little to the total.

Clearly, the greater the surplus, the greater the amount of filtering. The surplus itself, however, tends to check the rate of filtering. Because of the pyramidal shape of housing values, production near the top of the spectrum will be retarded by only a small absolute excess of units. The farther down the scale that new construction can be injected, the larger the excess, absolutely, needed to check further building, and the greater the ultimate effect at the bottom of the market. Equally, the effect of low-priced construction will be felt much sooner at the bottom since the impact is transmitted a shorter distance. Regardless of the initial level, the impact will be felt much more rapidly in the rental market since more frequent occupancy changes cause the influence of new construction to travel faster throughout this sector of the supply.

Ratcliff is aware that filtering is not proportional to the rate of deterioration and may in fact move in the opposite direction, as during a period of housing shortage. Like Lowry, however, he does not hold out much hope of raising the rate of depreciation above the rate of quality decline, in some measure because our land-planning policies have attempted to strengthen, not depreciate, values. He points out that if the rate were raised, however, it might be quite costly to owners. Filtering can, he says, be speeded up somewhat by removing the surplus dwelling units once they reach the bottom, but he observes that this seldom is done. There seems to be some doubt in his mind, though the point is not stated in quite this way, that the rate of filtering has very much to do with the problem of substandard accommodations. A large percentage of units classified as substandard have not arrived at this condition through a process of decline. Rather, some are substandard because they were inadequate when constructed. In other cases, our concept of adequacy has changed. Sometimes the structure itself may be entirely satisfactory, but placed in a substandard category because it is occupied by too many people.

Fisher and Winnick do not differ importantly from Ratcliff or Lowry in their explanation of the general causes of filtering. Filtration will result from "change in relative desirability of a dwelling unit as compared to available alternatives."[13] Relative desirability will be altered by differences in the rates of deterioration, changes in taste, changes in the area in which the dwelling unit is located, and new construction. As to exactly how these underlying forces affect different structures and various areas, little is known.

*The depreciation curve of housing.* Demand constant, the value of a home, like that of any asset, is a function not only of the current relative quality and size of the stream of services that it provides, but also the expected size, quality, and duration of this stream. The predicted duration of the stream is in turn a function of current relative quality and the expected life of the unit. Although it is possible that in the housing market the latter variable

---

* Ratcliff, *op. cit.*, p. 325. It should perhaps be mentioned that unlike obsolescence, deterioration is not relative and does *not* lie dormant, but instead leads to the introduction of better housing values.

is of no practical importance, its distinctive role in determining value should be pursued, if only briefly, on an analytical level.

To see the independent effect of changing quality on value, imagine houses built with materials having a perpetual physical life. Now suppose that each year a new and better house were produced and marketed at no increase in price. This would gradually reduce the value of the earlier models to zero.* Both the depreciation curve and the quality curve for houses would have negative slopes, as in Chart A-1.

To see the independent effect of life expectancy on value, imagine houses built like the one-horse shay, as good as new until the day they disintegrate. Assume further that successive models of houses contain no improvements over earlier models. Thus, old and new houses are of equal quality. The quality curve for dwelling units would be rectangular (Chart A-2) but the value curve (Chart A-3) would have the same general downward slope as houses of declining relative quality but everlasting physical life.

Insofar as filtering is concerned, however, the situations depicted in A-1 and A-3 would evoke a completely different market response. A price decline occasioned by reduced life expectancy but no quality decline would not result in occupancy by lower-income groups, since families with higher earnings would still find the units acceptable and prices per year of remaining life would not change.† Conversely, a price decline stemming from a relative drop in quality would almost certainly cause the dwelling unit to pass on to a family of lesser means. Clearly, a definition of filtering as simply a drop in value is misleading in the social context in which the term is most often used.

Since houses are not built like one-horse shays and since quality is not completely independent of age, it is useful to make the analysis somewhat more realistic by trying to construct a representative depreciation curve for housing as a combined function of the two variables. In the early years of most new houses, life expectancy is indefinitely long and declines in quality are minimal if they occur at all. Consequently, no drop in value would occur over this portion of the depreciation curve (Chart B). Somewhere between ten and twenty years, depending on the house, portions of the structure may show deterioration or start becoming obsolescent.‡ The depreciation curve starts moving downward, though remodeling efforts by homeowners may retard its descent.§ At about twenty years, mortgage lenders may, depending upon the availability of funds, commence attaching a limited life to the home and anticipate quality decline even though none is currently evident. Thus, as twenty years turn to thirty, thirty-year financing disappears and is replaced by twenty-year instruments, which reduce prices without bringing the dwellings within reach of families of lesser means since carrying charges remain the same (Chart A-3). Simultaneously buyers, regardless of the attractiveness of the structures, are also reminded of their age. They may not think in terms of limited life expectancy but do ponder the possibilities of higher than normal repairs sometime in the foreseeable future. This reaction to age alone forces the depreciation curve down more steeply.

Once a decline in relative quality has begun, a continuous downward trend would seem to be a reasonable forecast for most houses. The amount of relative decline, *when translated into reduction in price*, diminishes in the later stages of the life of the structure. This is because at each lower value level, a larger number of families can afford to occupy the unit, and since many will choose to do so, there is increasing pressure against further price reduction. The inability of the home-building industry to expand directly the supply of low-priced housing intensifies the pressure. The result is that the depreciation curve for most homes can be expected

---

* Barring the emergence of value as an antique.
† Most people would prefer to buy houses they can stay in as long as they wish. Thus a short life expectancy of a house reduces its attractiveness, and, in the real world, would no doubt cause its price per year of remaining life to fall.

‡ Witness, for example the huge change in kitchens in the last ten years.
§ Whether an owner modernizes his home to keep it at a higher value or does not improve it and sells at a lower figure, he has absorbed a loss due to depreciation.

to flatten out even though decline in quality, measured in some social or physical sense, may actually accelerate. Put somewhat differently, a 10 percent difference in value represents a greater gap in "pure" quality at the lower end of the scale than at the upper end. The curve in the chart depicts, therefore, what obtains because of inventory shortages toward the lower end of the value spectrum. It should be emphasized that the curve does not indicate physical deterioration or obsolescence in the sense of the amount of money required to restore the unit to some higher value or quality level.

Unlike housing quality, which declines, if sometimes imperceptibly, with age, the expected remaining life of a residential unit does not diminish with each passing year, and this fact materially affects the shape of the depreciation curve. After a structure reaches a certain age, say fifty years for illustrative purposes, the market again gives it an indefinite physical life. Regardless of its age, the investor reasons that it should last at least another five or ten years. Transactions are made with this in mind. The result is a further flattening of the depreciation curve.

Assuming the dwelling unit is not converted or demolished before the end of its potential economic life, the entire depreciation curve is, then, an inverted S, or the mirror image of a growth curve. The precise shape will of course vary considerably from structure to structure,

but empirical evidence supports this conclusion in its general characteristics.* One interesting feature of the curve is its suggestion that filtering may take place at a perceptible rate during less than one-half of the life of a dwelling unit. This is due in part, however, to the fact that many owners take depreciation losses in the form of higher expenditures for maintenance and modernization instead of lower sales prices.

*Vacancies and filtering.* To understand fully the concept of filtering, it is also necessary to appreciate the relationship of the filtering process to vacancies. Filtering and changing vacancy rates are more or less complementary phenomena. As demand for units at a given price (or rent) declines relative to supply, the units will either fall in price (or rent) or the proportion that stand vacant will rise, or both. Thus, the same factors which create a *potential* for filtering create a *potential* for increased vacancies. Given an excess supply of units at a given price or rent, however, factors which facilitate filtering will minimize vacancies and, conversely, factors which motivate owners (homeowners or landlords) to let units remain unused inhibit filtering. At some point, depending on the type and location of the structure, filtering can continue no longer, either absolutely or relatively, and vacancies must result. This concept is important to grasp because one of our main purposes in studying the dynamics

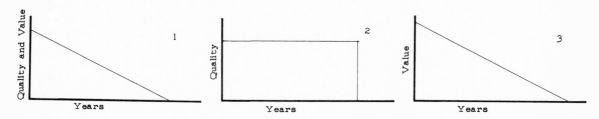

*Chart A. Hypothetical quality and depreciation curves.*

* For somewhat contrary evidence as to the shape of the curve during the early years of a dwelling unit, see Leo Grebler, David M. Blank, and Louis Winnick, *Capital Formation in Residential Real Estate*, National Bureau of Economic Research, Princeton University Press, 1956, Appendix E. Also William Hoad, "Real Estate Prices: A Study of Residential Real Estate in Lucas County, Ohio," unpublished doctoral dissertation, University of Michigan, 1942. The depreciation figures in both studies indicate a sharp decline in value in the first few years after construction, but since in each instance the new homes to which the figures refer were built during the depression, this result would be expected.

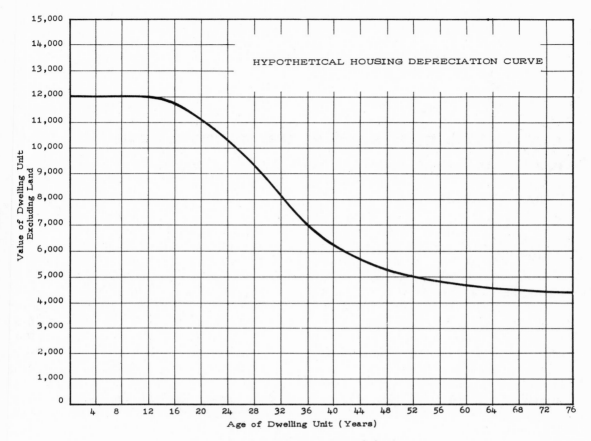

Chart B. *Hypothetical housing depreciation curve.*

of the housing market is to see to what extent and by what means the market might be manipulated to produce a surplus of homes and a decline in prices in excess of that which would ordinarily deter new construction.

*The termination of the flow.* Quite obviously the downward filtering of a particular dwelling unit stops permanently when the unit has reached the lowest value stratum and is vacated or abandoned. The process also stops when the original dwelling unit ceases to exist. Thus, if the unit is converted to two or more dwellings or is merged with another unit, filtering ends insofar as the original unit is concerned. It might be argued that the conversion process is simply a continuation of filtering, that it is indicative of a value decline for which the owner is trying to compensate; and that through conversion the owner may increase the value (cause filtering up) of the entire property. However valid such arguments are, they result in analytical difficulties. It would seem better, therefore, to regard conversions as independent sources of housing supply that sometimes result from, but are not equivalent to, filtering.

# Components of change in the nation's housing inventory in relation to the 1960 census

*FRANK S. KRISTOF*

## Introduction

In the short period of 25 years we have observed the transformation of the residential construction industry from a purely private activity of the economy to one of our most publicized, analyzed, and legislated industries. The residential construction industry had constituted an important segment of the nation's economy before it became clothed with a public interest. However, when it was seized upon, during the 1930's, as both a means of stimulating a lagging economy and of raising the American standard of living, our housing industry moved to the forefront of political and legislative activity. Again, when the unflagging pace of housing construction helped shore up the economy during the recession of 1953–54, the Cinderella-like quality of the industry was further enhanced.* Today, with the problem of urban blight plaguing every sizable community in the nation, housing problems associated with slum clearance and urban renewal have become almost a daily topic of discussion.

It is no coincidence that during this same quarter of a century that statistical knowledge about the housing field has jumped from almost nothing to a fairly well documented aspect of American life. The real property inventories of the 1930's, followed by the 1940 and 1950 Censuses of Housing provided the basis for this major statistical breakthrough. Data provided by the censuses actually preceded the existence of agencies able to exploit fully this information – particularly at the local community level.†

During the early 1950's pressures developed from several sources for more sophisticated and useful data on the dynamics of housing than that provided by the Housing Census. The first major recognition of this need was a joint project of the Housing and Home Finance Agency and the Bureau of the Census. The housing experts of these agencies undertook the task of defining concepts to express these needs. Techniques for collecting the necessary data were explored and developed, and the results of the project were reported in a formidable 200 page document.[1] The culmination of this work was a

---

* The favorable terms of the 1954 Housing Act probably contributed materially to the high level of residential construction through this recession.
† Major exceptions to this point were some local and regional planning agencies, and local housing authorities which were compelled to undertake serious study of available statistics to justify requests for public housing subsidies. The recent success of the Bureau's contract block statistics program indicates that this pressure still is strong. Some 250 places below the

50,000 population level are under contract for 1960 housing statistics by blocks. The willingness of local governments to expend funds for these statistics, plus the ability to read, understand and carry out the Bureau's meticulous directions for preparation of adequate block maps is not only a sign of growth in statistical sophistication in the Nation's communities, but an indication of the extent to which small communities now are participating in federally subsidized urban renewal programs.

*Reprinted from* Components of Change in the Nation's Housing Inventory in Relation to the 1960 Census, *a paper presented at the annual meeting of The American Statistical Association, December 28, 1959, with permission of the association.*

two sentence congressional appropriation in 1956 for $1,000,000 for "expenses necessary for conducting a survey of housing." Shortly thereafter the Bureau of the Census created a separate Housing Division to carry out the 1956 National Housing Inventory – the first systematic attempt to measure changes in the nation's housing inventory.

The National Housing Inventory was undertaken in the fall of 1956 and preliminary results were released in the fall of 1957; the first of twenty-one reports was issued in May of 1958 and the last appeared in April 1959. Despite the time lapse in producing them, these reports were well received in housing circles, and during the planning for the 1960 Housing Census many requests were received by the Bureau to incorporate a Components of Change survey within the Housing Census program. In response to the urging of the Bureau's Housing Advisory Committees and the Federal Housing Agencies, the Housing Division included within its census program plans for a Components of Change survey.

When the Director of the Bureau of the Census affirmed a decision to undertake a Components of Change survey in the fall of 1959, it marked a milestone in the field of housing statistics in the United States. This decision was the green light for a project which would provide the first complete explanation of the changes in the housing inventory which occur between decennial censuses. Enumeration was undertaken this fall and is nearing completion. With good fortune we should have our results by the end of next year.

The Components of Change program has been designed to utilize the total inventory figures to be obtained from next year's Housing Census to increase the reliability of the new construction estimates. And through the Bureau's Post Census Evaluation Program, we hope to link the 1959 dwelling unit inventory figures with the 1960 Housing Census results obtained from use of the new unit of enumeration – the Housing Unit. The linking process should account for the differences between the inventory figures obtained from the two programs attributable: (1) to the differences in definition of the unit of enumeration, and (2) to the time lapse between the 1959 and 1960 enumeration.

Before further discussing the interrelationship of the Components of Change and other phases of the 1960 Housing Census program, it would be useful to review the nature and objectives of the Components of Change program as it was developed in 1956.

## Major subjects of inquiry

What is the character and significance of the changes which were to be measured? These may be classified under the following major categories:

*New construction.* What is the rate of new additions to the housing inventory? Despite two housing censuses and Bureau of Labor Statistics monthly housing starts data,* no really accurate measure of this statistic existed. BLS housing starts data, even when placed in the most favorable light, have been shown to understate nonfarm new construction when compared with Census results.† The "year built" data of both the 1940 and 1950 censuses were widely at variance with the BLS estimates. However, the census "year built" data could not be accepted as conclusive because this information was subject to response error. As a result, users of data have remained dissatisfied with available estimates of new residential construction. A corollary question in connection with new additions to the inventory is: What is the rate of "other additions" to the housing

---

* Collection of accurate data on housing starts was hampered by what we now see were inadequate funds.
† Grebler, Blank and Winnick, *Capital Formation in Residential Real Estate*, Princeton University Press, Princeton, N. J., 1956, p. 373. The authors quote a "Reconciliation of the Net Change in the Nonfarm Housing Inventory, 1940 – 1950, [reported by Census] and New Construction as reported by the Bureau of Labor Statistics" labeled as a "preliminary report of

an interdepartmental committee of federal agencies (to be published)," which indicated that BLS underestimated new construction by 6 percent for this period. The "Reconciliation" quoted was prepared by the Bureau of Labor Statistics members of the Interdepartmental committee, but it neither was accepted as official by the committee nor was its publication authorized.

inventory, i.e., the shift from nonresidential to residential use? With respect to this question, virtually no information was available.

*Conversions and mergers.* These types of changes within the housing inventory long have been the subject of deduced estimates, but of little certain knowledge. During the depression 1930's, about a third of the additions to the housing inventory were attributed to conversions – the division of existing dwelling units into smaller units. During the war and immediate postwar 1940's a somewhat smaller proportion of the net additions was credited to this source. Housing analysts believed that this phenomenon had become a declining influence on the housing inventory by the 1950's, but there were no figures to demonstrate it. Correspondingly, they also suspected that mergers, or the combining of dwelling units into fewer units were becoming an increasingly important source of losses from the inventory. It is, of course, recognized that conversions and mergers add or subtract virtually nothing from total living space, but merely change the existing supply into a larger number of smaller units or smaller number of larger units. Nevertheless, no analysis of the housing inventory would be complete until this phenomenon can be measured.

*Demolitions and other losses.* Possibly the most distressing gap in housing knowledge was in data on withdrawals from the housing supply. How much of the nation's inventory is lost annually through demolition, fire, flood or the shift from housing to nonresidential purposes?

Direct information was of the most fragmentary nature. Some estimates had been made on the basis of the overall changes in the total inventory measured by the 1940 and 1950 housing censuses. But even these were subject to varying assumptions about the other components of change, i.e., new construction, other additions, conversions and mergers.

*Qualitative changes in the housing inventory.* In what direction is the quality of the existing housing inventory changing over time? Although new construction tends to improve overall housing quality, what are the characteristics of the housing being removed from the inventory? More important, what is happening to the remaining inventory? And at what rate?

These questions are particularly relevant in any discussion of " housing needs " for America. This subject probably has generated more heat in the housing field than any other as a result of the widely disparate estimates of " housing needs " that have been developed over the years. Glenn Beyer notes that " when the 1949 Housing Act was being considered in Congress, leaders of the home building industry set a range of 600,000 to 900,000 per year " as the annual need for new construction.[2] For the ten year period 1956–1965, Beyer places the need between 1,300,000 and 1,900,000 annually depending upon the assumptions used.[3] At the other extreme, estimates by William Wheaton placed annual need at 2.0 to 2.4 million units annually.[4] Although much of the differences among these estimates stemmed from disagreement among analysts over the rapidity and methods by which the substandard inventory was to be eliminated, a part of the difference is attributable to different guesses about the direction and rate of qualitative changes in the housing inventory.

*Household formation.* The annual rate of new household formation is another statistic that eludes accurate measure between censuses. True, the Bureau of the Census now publishes annually a total household figure obtained from its monthly Current Population Survey, and from this has been derived an annual change in number of households. The latter figure, however, is subject to such a large variance that it is of little utility in making year to year estimates of household increase. As long as more precise data on this subject are lacking, analysis of market demand for housing based upon the rate of household formation cannot be undertaken.

*Mobility and housing demand.* The mobility of the American population has created problems for housing analysts in estimating the ability of local markets to absorb new construction. Some analysts believe that, by itself, " sheer mobility alone tends to increase the quantity of housing demanded even if net migration is zero."[5] The various types of population mobility further complicates the problems of analysis, e.g.:

(1) The general movement from the central city to the suburbs;

(2) the continued shift from rural to urban areas, including the shift of nonwhites from the rural south to central cities of the north, and the migration of Puerto Ricans to New York City.

(3) The regional movement to Florida and the West Coast (particularly California).

(4) Growth and mergers in American industry have created large industrial aggregates and established thousands of new branches in suburban and rural areas, resulting in the movement of tens of thousands of business managers, engineers and other scientists in a constant cross-current of movement.

One aspect of our population movement which has been well noted is the increase in home ownership from 55 to 60 percent of all households since 1950. Other aspects of this movement are less well known. For example, what are the components of the net shift in tenure? Who are the people that move – are they a typical cross-section of the population or not? Do they have special characteristics which will help predict the impact of future movement on housing demand? Does sheer movement, per se, increase the demand for housing? What effect do household moves have upon the relative expenditures of income for housing?

## The results of the 1956
## National Housing Inventory

The information yielded by the 1956 National Housing Inventory provided direct answers to many of the questions raised in the preceding paragraphs. Some of the results and

experiences associated with obtaining them are worth reviewing.

*NHI results – new construction.* Since new construction represents the largest change in the housing inventory, these figures were of most interest. Staff members of the Housing Division had made national estimates of new construction for the 6¾ year period ranging from 9.6 million to 11.5 million or annual rates of 1.4 to 1.7 million. These figures were higher than any existing published estimates because of a conviction that BLS starts were continuing to understate the volume of new residential construction. The first UNIVAC runs on new construction were dismayingly low. Of the nine SMA's, five actually were slightly below BLS estimates. The national figure was 9.1 million compared to a comparable BLS estimate of 8.1 million for this period. On the surface, the national new construction figure was not unreasonable even though it was below the lowest staff estimate. The extent to which some of the SMA figures were below BLS estimates was more disturbing. This, plus a " red light " warning of a control figure built into the tabulation program, led to a complete review of the processing procedures. Parenthetically, it might be observed that not only was the NHI conceptually a new program, but it was the first major survey to use the new FOSDIC device.* Consequently, there were serious fears that something untoward had developed in processing. These fears were realized when a print-out of an SMA output tape was compared with the original schedules and it was discovered that FOSDIC had only intermittently transcribed the new construction mark from the microfilms to the magnetic tape.†

Time and cost factors prohibited any consideration of " refosdicing " the microfilmed data. Since the tracked down difficulty affected only the simple count of new construction, it was decided to obtain these figures for the nine

---

* FOSDIC is a device, developed by Bureau of Standards' engineers, designed to eliminate punch cards and card-to-tape operations by a process of transcribing marks from 16 to 35 millimeter microfilm to magnetic tape. This requires a specially designed enumeration form although it is marked by ordinary pencil. The

document is microfilmed and then fed through the FOSDIC device. The magnetic tape output of FOSDIC then is ready as input to UNIVAC.
† The difficulty eventually was traced to inexact printing of the schedules where accuracy is measured up to the thousandth of an inch.

SMA's and the United States by a hand count. The final verified hand counts largely closed the gap between the BLS and NHI figures in the SMA's, nevertheless, it left four SMA's with slightly lower totals than the BLS estimates since the overall count was increased by only 4 percent. The significant change as a result of the hand count occurred for the U.S. total which was raised from the original UNIVAC figure of 9,100,000 to 10,900,000, an increase of about 20 percent.*

Although Housing Division personnel involved in processing NHI spent several anxious weeks before finally obtaining a valid new construction count, the experience carried an important lesson. No matter how marvelous and efficient are the complex electronic devices available to us, they will perform no better than the quality of the personnel responsible for their operation. Although they need not be responsible for operations, subject matter people must understand the workings and monitor the output of our electronic equipment. In this instance, had the subject matter people been unfamiliar with operations, the warning provided by the check incorporated within the UNIVAC program might have been rationalized or even ignored. But with operational knowledge, housing personnel were alerted by the warning, and coupled with their intuitive conviction about the magnitude of new construction figures to be expected, the figures obtained from the original UNIVAC run were immediately investigated.†

It was many months before the significance of the new construction data provided by NHI had any public impact. And when it came, the reactions were understandably adverse. The possibility that the United States had been adding new housing at an average rate of 1,600,000 units annually since 1950 seemed incredible. It is not surprising that the figure was branded as incorrect by many analysts. Many months of checking by staffs of the Bureau and other

interested government agencies, however, failed to reveal any significant source of error in the NHI findings.

Only recently, a leading daily newspaper headlined a story that the government was looking for 2 million houses " lost " somewhere between 1950 and 1956 – referring, of course, to the BLS-NHI disparity.[6] This time, however, Federal administrative processes moved rapidly. While some readers were learning for the first time in November 1959 that the nation had built far more homes than it suspected between 1950 and 1956, the responsibility for collecting housing starts data had rested with the Bureau of the Census since July 1, 1959. Henceforth, inconsistencies between housing starts statistics and future components of change data will be the headache of a single statistical family. But with the responsibility for both sets of data so centralized, the pressures for clarifying concepts and improving methods of data collection to close the statistical gap will be multiplied manyfold.

*NHI results – conversions and mergers.* The intuitive feeling among housing analysts that conversions had become a declining influence on the nation's housing inventory was confirmed by NHI. Approximately 700,000 units became 1,400,000 between 1950 and 1956. This average of one unit gained from each one involved in conversion is the lowest that normally might be expected from this process and it signalizes the end of the era of large old single family mansions being cut up into four, six, or ten units. The evidence in Table 1 indicates that this type of conversion, since 1950, no longer has been an influence of significance in the housing supply.

Almost as interesting is the manner in which mergers have completely nullified the effect of conversions on the housing inventory. The picture presented in Table 1 demonstrates that this

---

* The problems in obtaining NHI new construction figures turned out to be the only major processing difficulty the Housing Staff experienced. In retrospect, it can fairly be said that the processing and tabulation job accomplished by FOSDIC and UNIVAC was an amazing accomplishment. In addition, the Bureau's engineering staff gained invaluable experience in pre-

paring the new FOSDIC's for processing the coming 1960 Census.

† The memory of this experience has carried over into preparations for processing the 1960 Census. Both operations and subject matter staffs have combined to incorporate into the final program sufficient checks to assist in the detection of processing flaws.

occurred in each of four regions as well as inside and outside standard metropolitan areas. Again, the average loss of one unit from each two involved in merger is the exact reverse of the results obtained from conversions.

*NHI results – demolitions and "other losses."* The loss from all sources of $2\frac{1}{2}$ million units in $6\frac{3}{4}$ years, an average of nearly 400,000 annually, was somewhat higher than most analysts' estimates. That less than half of these were classed as demolitions might seem a little surprising, but the demolition figure probably is a conservative estimate because some units actually demolished were incorrectly reported as "other losses" by enumerators. The "other losses" component of

"other losses – about 400,000 units – was classified as "moved from site." This is essentially a segment concept rather than an inventory concept, that is, it is associated with the data collection technique. The concept "moved from site" has real meaning to an enumerator seeking a house which has moved out of the way of a road-building project, or trying to explain a trailer which has left the site in the segment. This concept has a counterpart within the category "units added through other sources," and is usually labeled "moved to site."

Although these two concepts literally are examples of housing mobility, they are not, strictly speaking, housing inventory concepts since they really do not represent additions or subtractions from the nation's housing inven-

## TABLE 1
*Conversions and Mergers in the Housing Inventory: 1950 to 1956 (In thousands of dwelling units)*

| Area | Conversions | | | Mergers | | | Net change from conversions and mergers |
|---|---|---|---|---|---|---|---|
| | From | To | Net gain | From | To | Net loss | |
| United States | 668 | 1,376 | 708 | 1,321 | 649 | 672 | +36 |
| Inside SMA's | 422 | 880 | 458 | 765 | 371 | 394 | +64 |
| Outside SMA's | 246 | 496 | 250 | 556 | 277 | 279 | —29 |
| Northeast | 199 | 412 | 213 | 349 | 170 | 179 | +34 |
| North Central | 215 | 452 | 237 | 422 | 216 | 206 | +31 |
| South | 184 | 378 | 194 | 431 | 204 | 227 | —33 |
| West | 71 | 133 | 62 | 120 | 60 | 60 | + 2 |

withdrawals from the housing inventory, which numbered 1,400,000, probably is conceptually the weakest figure produced by NHI. A significant proportion of "other losses," about 400,000, consisted of units recorded by enumerators as "abandoned." This proved to be a poor concept in that if offers to less conscientious enumerators an easy disposition for vacant units in rural areas when no one is conveniently nearby to furnish information on the dwelling. Post enumeration investigation of "abandoned" units suggests that some proportion of them should have been classified as vacant. For this reason the term "abandoned" has been discontinued for both the 1960 Housing Census and the 1959 Components of Change program.

Another and equally large component of

tory. However, even this statement must be qualified. For example, a vacation trailer which is sold and moved from a backyard to a lot where it is used as a permanent residence actually is an "other gain" to the housing inventory.* A house that is moved out of the way of a road-building project to a "used house" lot or to another site where it is used for non-residential purposes actually is an "other loss." Some of the houses moved out of a segment may subsequently have been demolished. It is not known to what extent this occurred. For this reason it was decided to record all units moved into, or moved out of a segment as "other gains" or "other losses." Since these two factors essentially are opposite sides of the same coin, they should be self-canceling except

---

* Trailers comprised about 150,000 units "moved to site" and nearly 100,000 units "moved from site."

for the type of examples cited above. Actually, about 400,000 units were recorded as moved out of segments and slightly less than 500,000 were recorded as moved into segments.

Of the remaining 600,000 units ascribed to "other losses," nearly 200,000 represented shifts from dwelling units to quasi dwellings, i.e., rooming houses, boarding houses, transient hotels, etc. It is probable that some large old former single-family structures have continued to disappear into this category. Another 250,000 units shifted to nonresidential use and the remaining 150,000 were ascribed to fire, wind, storm, and "torn down," i.e., demolitions inaccurately recorded in this category.

It is probable that the rate of demolitions and "other losses" will continue to increase in the years to come. The full impact of urban renewal and our highway construction programs has not yet been felt. Although the future rate of withdrawals from the housing inventory is a matter of speculation, there is little evidence to justify a recent estimate that "new permanent construction for the next decade will have to be 1,250,000 units greater than the net increase in households and vacancies in order to replace those units lost from the inventory."* An estimate of twice this size would not be unreasonable.

*NHI results – qualitative changes.* The NHI figures on condition and plumbing facilities showed a significant decline in substandard dwellings between 1950 and 1956. About 3,000,000 units, which were recorded in 1950 as dilapidated or lacking some or all plumbing facilities, in 1956 were recorded as not dilapidated, with all plumbing facilities. Upon consideration, this change is not too surprising since the nation's level of living has moved upward in every respect during the 1950's. According to the definition of substandard housing generally accepted today, two-thirds of the nation's rural housing, much of which was sound in construction, but which lacked running water and inside plumbing facilities was classified as substandard in 1950. Since the nature of urban life makes a facility like running water a necessity, whereas this is not necessarily the case in homes in rural areas, application of the term substandard to some of our rural housing probably is questionable. Nevertheless, nearly 2,000,000 of the 3,000,000 units which changed from substandard to standard between 1950 and 1956 were outside standard metropolitan areas, where much of the housing is rural.

Nothing in these figures, however, should give cause for any complacency about the problem of substandard housing. It is to be expected that housing should participate in the general rise in our level of living, and presumably only the lack of adequate data on expenditures on private residential repairs and rehabilitation justifies surprise at the extent of improvement in housing quality recorded since 1950.† On the other hand, it is reasonable to presume: (1) that major expenditures on improving existing housing most frequently occur

---

* U.S. Senate Subcommittee on Housing, *Study of Mortgage Credit*, Dec. 1958, Sherman J. Maisel, "Importance of Net Replacements in Housebuilding Demand," pp. 32–42. The analysis in the Maisel paper on this point is open to question. Table 16, the core of his argument, is a combination of estimates and extrapolations that can be accepted or rejected depending upon the assumptions one is willing to make. For example, I would reverse his projection of 40,000 units gained from conversions and mergers in 1961 – 70 to an annual net loss of nearly the same magnitude. The 1950 – 56 figure of 210,000 net from "demolitions and other changes" used both in Tables 16 and 17, and attributed to NHI, apparently is an arithmetical error. Maisel cites the stock of nonfarm housing shifting from farm to nonfarm status as an important "source of supply" although partly a "statistical illusion." He then proceeds to use in Table 16 an extrapolated figure of 45,000 such units annually as an offset to his estimate of withdrawals from the nonfarm inventory during the 1960's. Effectively, this means a shift from farm to nonfarm usage of 45,000 units annually augments the supply of nonfarm housing. Maisel is using these 45,000 units twice–once to house the farmer Jones' who are now nonfarmer Jones', and second to house 45,000 households who have lost units through "net from demolition and other changes." This is very efficient use of the housing inventory but it would require a very sharp increase in "doubling"–at a rate of 45,000 units annually. Maisel also includes seasonal units as an offset to losses from the inventory. This, too, is a statistical illusion, since seasonal units by definition either are vacant or are occupied by households who have a permanent residence elsewhere; they therefore cannot be classified as offsets to losses in the inventory.
† It is hoped that work of the Bureau of the Census' new Construction Office will, in the near future, fill the gap in data on expenditures on residential repairs and rehabilitation.

in urban neighborhoods that are not rundown and in rural housing that does not require major rehabilitation; and (2) that the largest proportion of repairs and improvement expenditures was not major rehabilitation but the installation of inside plumbing facilities, particularly running water and water heating equipment – a relatively less expensive means of shifting units from substandard to standard status than major rehabilitation work. This would argue, then, that the rapidity of the improvement in housing quality from 1950 to 1956 is attributable to the completion of the easier and less expensive improvements required to remove housing from substandard status. If this is true, it means that continued improvement in quality of the existing stock during the 1960's will come harder and more slowly. It also means that the hard core of the substandard housing problem – namely homes of low income owners in deteriorated neighborhoods who are unable to improve their housing and rental properties in slum areas whose owners are not financially justified in investing in improvements or unable to obtain financing when they are willing – basically is not touched by this type of upgrading.

Consequently, it may be unwarranted to utilize a projection of the 1950–56 NHI results to justify the conclusion reached by Reinhold Wolff that repair and rehabilitation will upgrade as many as 4,600,000 substandard units during the 1960's, unless there is substantial increase of local and Federal activity in the form of code enforcement, urban renewal, and subsidies to accelerate the removal or improvement of substand housing.*

*NHI results – household formation.* In March 1957, the Census Bureau published a CPS household figure of 49,543,000 which, compared to the CPS household figure of March

1950, gives an annual rate of household increase of 856,000 for the seven year period.[7] The 1956 NHI figures for occupied dwelling units (households) was 49.9 million compared with the 1950 Census figure of 42.8 million, or an annual rate of increase of about 1 million for the 6¾ years. Although dissatisfaction has been expressed with this variance in household figures emerging from the same agency, it is a danger inherent in the measurement of the same concept by separate surveys with different orientations. The primary task of CPS is to identify employment status of persons in the labor force. True, in the process, households are defined and an attempt is made to obtain their proper definition, but it is not the primary emphasis. In NHI, on the other hand, great stress in the training and induction of enumerators was placed upon the definition of the dwelling unit.† As a consequence, it is reasonable to expect that the NHI enumerators did a more thorough job in this area than is done by the CPS. Although it is regrettable that such differences occur, it should be remembered that before the NHI results became available, CPS was the only source of any information on households. Even though Bureau statisticians had reservations about the use that might be made of the annual CPS household figure, it was published upon the urging of many users that some information on households was better than none at all.

*NHI results – mobility.* Some aspects of the amazing mobility of American households were measured by NHI. The dimensions of this mobility were familiar, but its characteristics were not well known. For example, it was well established that owner households tended to move less than renter households, but it was not known that over half (57 percent) of the renter households (as of 1956) had been in their

---

* U.S. Senate Subcommittee on Housing, *Study of Mortgage Credit*, Dec. 1958, Reinhold P. Wolff, "Substandard Units and Their Replacement, 1961 – 70," pp. 43 – 58. Wolff overstates the NHI 1950 – 56 figure for "substandard units rehabilitated and now standard" by 1.1 million units in his Table 20. It is not clear how he arrived at this result. This error may have contributed to his projection of 4.6 million units to be shifted from substandard to standard during the 1960's

which is, I judge, too optimistic. If this gross figure reaches 3 million the nation would be fortunate.
† In an effort to improve the quality of enumeration, Bureau personnel accompanied each new enumerator in the nine SMA's through his first few interviews. NHI was the first major Bureau survey in which a systematic attempt was made to induct new enumerators in the field under supervision.

present unit betwen two and three years while about half of the owner occupants had been in their units six years or more. The instability of the renter population was least marked inside central cities – 47 percent of the households outside SMA's had moved into their present unit within the past two years; for SMA's, the corresponding figure was 44 percent and for central cities 41 percent.

Information obtained on present tenure, previous tenure, and "year moved into present unit" permits analysis of the increase in owner-occupancy from 55 to 60 percent of all households between 1950 and 1956. About one quarter (14 million) of the nation's 55.3 million households moved into their dwelling unit during 1955 or 1956. Twelve million of these were households with the same head, of which 9 million were former renters and 3 million were former owners. Although most renter movers remained renters, 2.7 million or 30 percent shifted to owner-occupancy. Only three quarters of a million former home owners became renters; however, they constituted 27 percent of all former owners who moved in these two years. During this same period, about 2 million moves involved a change in household composition, a large part of which represented a new household formation. Three-quarters of these 2 million movers whose previous tenure was not investigated, became renter households.

Not too much can be said from our tabulations about the distance of moves. For example, 10 percent of all households who moved crossed State boundaries. But we do not know what proportion of this group merely crossed nearby borders, such as the Hudson River from New York City to New Jersey or vice versa, and what proportion made cross-country moves. The flow to the suburbs, however, is indicated in the moves of households formerly residing in central cities. About one-third or 1.3 million of nearly 4 million central city households who moved in 1955 and 1956 left the city.

The majority of households who moved from

one owner occupied single family unit to another paid more for their new homes. The median value of the house they moved from was $10,000 compared to a median value of $13,100 for their new house – a 30 percent increase.* There are also significant differences between households which have moved from one owned home to another and all owner households. For example, their median household size was 3.5 compared to 3.1 for all owner households; their median income was $5,400 contrasted to $4,800 reported for all owners.† The quality of homes acquired by these movers also improved significantly. Whereas 16 percent of all owner occupied units in the United States were dilapidated or lacking plumbing facilities (substandard), only 9 percent of the units occupied by recent owner to owner movers fell into this category.

In contrast, the characteristics of households who moved from renter-occupied units to other rental units are not very different from all renters. In terms of household size, median number of persons for renter to renter moves was 3.0 compared to 2.8 for all renter households; median incomes were about the same, $3,700 for renter to renter movers compared to $3,600 for all renters. Similarly, there was virtually no change in the quality of housing of this group of movers, although there was a slight but possibly not significant increase in median contract rent from $54 in the previous unit to $58 in the new unit.

A comparison of the average value of homes occupied by former renters with the average rents they used to pay shows a correlation of +.48, but the dispersion is wide. In short, previous rents would be poor predictors of the value of homes presently occupied.‡ The median contract rent of households which shifted from renting to owning in 1955 and 1956 was $61. Although this was higher than the $54 median for renters who moved to other rented units, many of the new home owners came from the low rent brackets. About a sixth previously paid less than $40 a month rent. The wide

---

* Value information for recent owner to owner movers probably is the most reliable of the NHI value data collected, since it represents, for the most part, actual prices received and paid for homes in the two years, 1955 and 1956.

† The median value for all owner-occupied nonfarm 1-unit structures was $11,400.
‡ Nevertheless, the generalization may be made that the higher the previous rent, the higher is the value of the home subsequently purchased.

spread in value of homes purchased by these previously low rent payers is shown in the following illustration:

### TABLE 2

*Value of One-Dwelling Unit Nonfarm Structures for Recent Movers from the $30–$39 Rent Category: 1956*

| Percent of recent movers from the $30–$39 rent category | Purchased homes valued at: |
|---|---|
| 27 | $6,000 or less |
| 27 | $6,000 to $10,000 |
| 26 | $10,000 to $15,000 |
| 19 | $15,000 or more |

Source: Unpublished 1956 NHI tabulations.

Only one cross-tabulation was obtained for recent movers who shifted from owner to renter occupancy (Table 4). The data show a correlation of +.46 between value of previous resid-

higher than the median contract rent for all renter-occupied units. This fact seems to be significant relative to the demand for rental units. If the shift from owner to renter occupancy increases appreciably, the demand for better quality and higher rent units may be strengthened. Even today, this may be a factor in the recent resurgence in the rental market discussed by Louis Winnick's ACTION report.[8]

*NHI results – some conclusions.* The 1956 NHI results answered many questions that have been raised about the housing market in recent years. Even the cursory discussion in the preceding paragraphs, however, indicates the endless possibilities that exist for more intensive mining of these data. Nevertheless, we now have a basis for evaluating an approach commonly used by housing analysts in estimating future

### TABLE 3

*Contract Monthly Rent of Present Units by Value of Previous Properties, for Units Occupied by Recent Movers: 1956 (In thousands)*

| Contract monthly rent—nonfarm renter units occupied by recent movers | Total | Under $6,000 | Value of previous property: owner-occupied nonfarm 1-unit structures | | | | | | | |
|---|---|---|---|---|---|---|---|---|---|---|
| | | | $6,000 to $7,999 | $8,000 to $9,999 | $10,000 to $11,999 | $12,000 to $14,999 | $15,000 to $17,999 | $18,000 to $19,999 | $20,000 or more | NR |
| Total | 510 | 124 | 43 | 73 | 57 | 67 | 46 | 14 | 54 | 30 |
| Less than $30 | 31 | 20 | 4 | 2 | — | 2 | — | — | — | 3 |
| $30 to $39 | 31 | 10 | 3 | 4 | 3 | 2 | 4 | — | 3 | 2 |
| $40 to $49 | 51 | 18 | 4 | 8 | 8 | 2 | 4 | — | — | 6 |
| $50 to $59 | 71 | 27 | 9 | 21 | 4 | 1 | — | — | 10 | — |
| $60 to $69 | 73 | 10 | 8 | 10 | 15 | 16 | 7 | 1 | 1 | 6 |
| $70 to $79 | 61 | 17 | 6 | 7 | 9 | 10 | 4 | 3 | 2 | 2 |
| $80 to $99 | 69 | 10 | 5 | 9 | 7 | 14 | 14 | 1 | 7 | 2 |
| $100 or more | 97 | 3 | 4 | 7 | 8 | 16 | 14 | 9 | 29 | 8 |
| Not reported | 25 | 9 | — | 4 | 3 | 3 | — | 1 | 2 | 2 |

*Same head in present and previous unit*

NOTE: Due to independent rounding, figures may not add to totals.
Source: Unpublished 1956 NHI tabulations.

ence and the present rent paid by former owner-occupants indicating that the higher the value of the previous residence, the higher will be the present rent paid by former owner-occupants. The median value of their former homes was the same as that for all owner-occupants who moved in 1955 or 1956 – $10,000. But the $68 median contract rent of former owner-occupants was $10 higher than that of movers from renter-occupied units and $15

"demand" for new residential construction. This method begins by making assumptions or estimates for the period ahead about:

(1) The state of the economy – employment, incomes, etc.

(2) Net new household formation.

(3) Units lost and units added in the existing inventory.

(4) Change in gross vacancies.

The analysis of "(1) The state of the economy ..." is used in making estimates of net new household formation, losses and gains in the existing inventory, and the expected direction and magnitude of change in vacancies. These estimates then become factors in the following equation:

"(2) Net new household formation" + "(3) Units lost and units added in the existing inventory" + "(4) Change in gross vacancies" (i.e., + increase or − decrease in gross vacancies) = "need" for new construction.

The resulting "need" for new construction

and high incomes even though encompassing the recession of 1953–1954. For the United States as a whole, 178 units were provided for each 100 households added. Of this total, 155 were new units and 23 were additions from other sources. Losses in the inventory amounted to 46 units for each 100 households added. The surplus of 32 (178 provided, less 46 lost) represents additions to the vacancy supply – although only 14 of these were in the form of available vacancies. The other 19 units were either held off the market, owned or bought and awaiting occupancy, or dilapidated.

When the national figures are classified by

## TABLE 4

*Value of Previous Contract Monthly Rent by Value of Present Property, for Units Occupied by Recent Movers: 1956 (In thousands)*

| Value of present property—owner occupied nonfarm 1-unit structures | Total | Contract monthly rent—nonfarm renter units occupied by recent movers | | | | | | | | |
| --- | --- | --- | --- | --- | --- | --- | --- | --- | --- | --- |
| | | Less than than $30 | $30 to $39 | $40 to $49 | $50 to $59 | $60 to $69 | $70 to $79 | $80 to $99 | $100 or more | NCR or NR |
| Total | 2,214 | 142 | 205 | 293 | 346 | 391 | 242 | 248 | 195 | 152 |
| Less than $6,000 | 227 | 50 | 56 | 52 | 6 | 20 | 2 | 2 | — | 19 |
| $6,000 to $7,999 | 208 | 21 | 27 | 57 | 34 | 39 | 18 | 5 | — | 7 |
| $8,000 to $9,999 | 273 | 25 | 29 | 47 | 64 | 50 | 15 | 18 | 9 | 16 |
| $10,000 to $11,999 | 291 | 12 | 21 | 37 | 66 | 66 | 37 | 27 | 8 | 18 |
| $12,000 to $14,999 | 501 | 20 | 33 | 63 | 87 | 114 | 82 | 53 | 26 | 23 |
| $15,000 to $17,999 | 312 | 10 | 22 | 15 | 35 | 64 | 35 | 53 | 55 | 22 |
| $18,000 to $19,999 | 117 | — | 2 | 3 | 17 | 13 | 31 | 32 | 10 | 8 |
| $20,000 or more | 257 | 2 | 16 | 16 | 13 | 24 | 22 | 56 | 83 | 25 |
| Not reported | 29 | 2 | 1 | 4 | 3 | — | — | 2 | 4 | 13 |

Source: Unpublished 1956 NHI tabulations.

theoretically can be translated into effective demand if certain conditions about the price and mortgage credit terms of new construction are met.

Table 5b fills in the variables of the above equation from data obtained from NHI for the period 1950–1956.* Table 5a provides the background of absolute change against which these relative changes may be examined. The relationships derived for this period were obtained from an economic climate of full employment

inside and outside standard metropolitan areas, relationships change sharply.† The first and most obvious fact is that relative growth inside standard metropolitan areas was twice that outside standard metropolitan areas (Table 5a). More important, however, only 146 units were needed to accommodate each 100 households added inside standard metropolitan areas compared with nearly twice this figure (275) outside standard metropolitan areas (Table 5b). A similar ratio held for the number of new

---

* Analysis of the relationships shown in Table 5b was suggested by Miss Beulah Washabaugh, Chief of the Housing Division's Occupancy and Utilization Branch.

† Although the dichotomy is not at all clear cut, housing inside standard metropolitan areas is essentially urban while virtually all rural (as well as much urban) housing is located outside standard metropolitan areas.

units constructed for each 100 households added – 128 inside standard metropolitan areas and 233 outside standard metropolitan areas. It is clear that, inside standard metropolitan areas, the relationship between net new household formation and new construction (between 1950 and 1956) was close enough so that the measure of one would have provided a good basis for predicting the other, whereas this was not true outside standard metropolitan areas.*

Since standard metropolitan areas are frequently treated as analyzable housing markets, and since most forecasts of new construction are made for local housing markets, the NHI figures showing the relationship of new construction to increase in number of households for the nine standard metropolitan areas are of particular interest. These relationships range from a low of 105 new dwelling units per 100 new households in the Los Angeles SMA to 144 per 100 in the Dallas SMA. The average for the nine SMA's was 124, close to the figure of 128 recorded for all SMA's of the nation. This suggests that the variation in the ratio between new construction and net new household formation for individual SMA's is not so wide as to vitiate the usefulness of the average in predicting demand for new construction for individual SMA's. The relevant question is with respect to the stability of this ratio for the near-term future, i.e., can it be used for prediction?

Examination of the composition of this ratio indicates that there is basis for expecting it to be stable over the next decade for SMA's which continue to grow at approximately their 1950 to 1956 rate. Internal changes† in the housing inventory of these areas are small and largely offsetting relative to net household growth. However, for those few standard metropolitan areas which are growing only slowly, internal changes will be large relative to net household change and the relationship between new construction and net household increase will fall apart.‡

What are the implications of a close relationship between new construction and net increase in households? To the realtor, the builder, and the supplier of mortgage funds, a close relationship between these two variables probably is desirable because it indicates a stable housing market. From a purely social standpoint, a close relationship between these variables is not necessarily desirable. When the housing market starts from a position of tightness – a very low available vacancy rate – as in 1950, a practically one-to-one ratio between new construction and net new household formation precludes any easing of the market and the efficient operation of the filtration process – one means whereby the quality of the housing supply may be improved.§ Thus, the construction of 281 new units for each additional 100 households in Philadelphia theoretically would mean that improvement in the quality of housing occurred through operation of the filtration process to the extent that new units replaced substandard units which shifted to the available vacant category or completely disappeared from the housing inventory. However, no such conclusion can be deduced. Although about one-quarter of the increase in Philadelphia's vacancies and three-quarters of the units removed from the inventory were substandard, the city's experience was similar to that of SMA's whose new construction-household increase ratio approached one.

---

* The construction of 233 new units for each 100 households added outside SMA's has virtually no analytical significance because of the diverse composition of this part of the Nation. About half of the housing outside SMA's consists of urban places of 2,500 to 49,999; the other half is classified as rural and includes farm and other isolated housing, small settlements below 2,500 population, and the suburban housing outside of places of 2,500 to 49,999.
† Conversions, mergers, demolitions, other losses, additions other than new construction, and changes in vacancies.
‡ Indirect evidence on this point exists from data about this relationship for two NHI cities. In Chicago

where the percent increase in number of households from 1950 to 1956 was 4.2 percent, 183 new construction units were provided for each 100 households added. In Philadelphia, with a household increase of 2.7 percent, the ratio was 281 new construction units provided for each 100 households added.
§ The essence of the filtration process is in the production of a surplus of new housing—a new construction-net new household formation ratio substantially greater than one—permitting poorer quality housing to be released to successively lower levels of demand until the effect reaches the bottom of the market, where the poorest housing will remain vacant or be removed.

## TABLE 5A
### Number and Increase in Households: 1950 to 1956

| Area | Number of households 1950 (thousands) | Increase in households 1950 to 1956 Number (thousands) | Percent |
|---|---|---|---|
| U.S. | 42,826 | 7,048 | 16.5 |
| Inside SMA's | 24,514 | 5,264 | 21.5 |
| Outside SMA's | 18,312 | 1,784 | 9.7 |
| REGIONS | | | |
| Northeast | 11,228 | 1,780 | 15.9 |
| North Central | 12,972 | 1,618 | 12.5 |
| South | 12,633 | 1,852 | 14.7 |
| West | 5,994 | 1,797 | 30.0 |
| SMA's | | | |
| Atlanta | 191 | 66 | 34.6 |
| Boston | 646 | 50 | 7.7 |
| Chicago | 1,607 | 268 | 16.7 |
| Dallas | 187 | 52 | 27.8 |
| Detroit | 829 | 199 | 24.0 |
| Los Angeles | 1,440 | 600 | 41.7 |
| N.Y.-N.E.N.J. | 3,774 | 654 | 17.3 |
| Philadelphia | 1,018 | 185 | 18.2 |
| Seattle | 236 | 42 | 17.8 |

Source: 1956 National Housing Inventory, Volume I.

## TABLE 5B
### Changes in the Housing Inventory per 100 Households Added: 1950 to 1956

| Number of units added | | | Minus all losses[b] | Equals net additions | Minus increase in gross vacancies | Equals increase in number of households |
|---|---|---|---|---|---|---|
| Total | By new construction | From existing inventory[a] | | | | |
| 178 | 155 | 23 | 46 | 132 | 33 | 100 |
| 146 | 128 | 17 | 32 | 114 | 14 | 100 |
| 275 | 233 | 42 | 86 | 188 | 89 | 100 |
| 153 | 133 | 20 | 32 | 121 | 21 | 100 |
| 179 | 150 | 29 | 50 | 130 | 30 | 100 |
| 231 | 203 | 28 | 70 | 161 | 61 | 100 |
| 149 | 131 | 17 | 30 | 118 | 18 | 100 |
| 139 | 129 | 11 | 23 | 117 | 15 | 100 |
| 182 | 138 | 44 | 44 | 138 | 40 | 100 |
| 134 | 115 | 19 | 27 | 106 | 5 | 100 |
| 156 | 144 | 12 | 38 | 117 | 17 | 100 |
| 136 | 124 | 12 | 23 | 113 | 14 | 100 |
| 117 | 105 | 12 | 16 | 102 | 2 | 100 |
| 128 | 113 | 16 | 25 | 104 | 4 | 100 |
| 143 | 127 | 16 | 21 | 122 | 22 | 100 |
| 138 | 121 | 17 | 33 | 105 | 5 | 100 |

[a] Includes units added through conversion and from other sources.
[b] Includes units lost through merger, demolition and other means.
NOTE: Because of independent rounding of figures, detail may not add to totals.
Source: 1956 National Housing Inventory, Volume III.

Without further evidence, the most that can be said is that the occurrence of a high ratio of new construction to net new household formation in a housing market creates the condition for an improvement in the quality of housing by providing scope for the operation of the filtration process. So long as such a development does not continue to the point where vacancies become a glut on the market and react negatively on construction activity, a high ratio of new construction to net new household formation may be regarded as desirable.

Part of the preceding discussion alluded to the reversibility of the new construction/net new household formation ratio, i.e., one can attempt to estimate new construction if estimates of household formation are available, and occasionally, estimates of net new household formation for the recent past are made on the basis of new construction figures. The NHI data indicate that the foregoing types of estimates could have been made with reasonable accuracy for the early 1950's. The difficult task for individual SMA's is a forecast of net new household increase which, for the nine NHI standard metropolitan areas, ranged from 8 percent for Boston to 42 percent for Los Angeles. It is obvious that it would be difficult to use the new construction/net new household formation relationship to forecast the demand for new construction unless techniques for obtaining good estimates of net new household formation in local areas are developed. If the new construction/net new household formation relationship for the nation has any stability, it can be useful for forecasting national demand for new construction since aggregate household growth is more easily predicted than that for a single standard metropolitan area.*

## Extrapolating the NHI results to 1959

It will soon be possible to check the stability of the relationships shown in Table 5b and thus their usefulness for prediction. What kind of figures will the 1959 program yield on the basis of the 1956 relationships? Since economic conditions for 1956–1959 basically were similar to the earlier years of the decade, it is reasonable to assume a rate of net new household formation of 1,000,000 per year for the past three years. This would give a net addition of 4,000,000 units and a total inventory figure of 59,300,000 dwelling units; the figure for new construction would be 4,650,000.† As a forecast, the figure for new construction seems reasonable, but the total inventory figure appears high.‡ At any rate, the results of the 1959 Components of Change survey will permit an evaluation of the stability and usefulness of these relationships.

## The 1959 Components of Change program and the 1960 Census

The 1959 Components of Change program will mark the climax of a decade of research in the dynamics of housing statistics. Basically, the program is identical with the NHI which has been discussed in some detail in the previous pages. The experience gained from NHI proved valuable in planning the present survey and some of the problems that arose in 1956 have been eliminated. The information obtained for the United States and the nine standard metropolitan areas in the 1956 sample segments has been transcribed to schedules used in the current survey. This information will be compared with the 1959 status of dwelling units in the same segments. In order to obtain measurement of

---

* This is true because migration into or out of standard metropolitan areas, which causes wide variations in household growth rates of individual SMA's, does not affect such estimates for the nation.

† Column 5 of Table 5b gives a relative of 132 for net additions to the housing inventory and column 2 a figure of 155 as the relative for new construction. Thus:

  3,000,000 added households × 132 = 4,000,000 net addition of dwelling units
  3,000,000 added households × 155 = 4,650,000 newly constructed units
  Total inventory = 55,300,000 + 4,000,000 = 59,300,000

‡ If any modification is to be looked for in the U.S. relationships in Table 5b, one might expect a decline in units added from the existing inventory and an increase in all losses, which would tend to drop the figure for net additions. I would estimate that the relative of 132 for net additions thus might decline to about 124, which would yield a total inventory figure of about 59,000,000 dwelling units as of December 1959.

new construction since 1956, an added group of new construction segments have been delineated and will be enumerated throughout the United States.

The 1959 Components of Change enumeration will be carried out independently of the 1960 Housing Census. However, the total housing inventory figure obtained in the 1960 Census will be used for ratio estimating to obtain a more accurate new construction figure, which is the largest single change in the inventory. This will require re-enumeration of the components of change segments immediately after the 1960 Census to obtain the count of housing units – the new unit of enumeration to be used in the 1960 Housing Census – in those segments. The count of housing units in the sample segments, and the total count for the nation will provide the 1960 factors for the ratio estimating equation.

At an earlier stage it was planned to utilize the 1960 re-enumeration of the Components of Change segments to obtain a complete reconciliation of the 1959 dwelling unit figures with the 1960 housing unit figures – including accounting for changes that occurred in the time lapse between the survey and the census. Time and cost factors have led to a shift of this objective to the Bureau's 1960 Census Evaluation program, which will provide such a reconciliation on a national basis. Information about several housing characteristics and about family income were left off the 1959 schedule because these data will be obtainable from the 1960

Census. Consequently, tabulations for the 1959 program will be essentially limited to those provided in Volume I of the 1956 NHI plus some tabulations for recent movers that appeared in Volume III.

The sample for the Components of Change program was expanded in 1959 to include eight additional standard metropolitan areas – all those of 1,000,0000 or more inhabitants in 1950. Budgetary limitations, however, require use of a smaller sample for the newly added standard metropolitan areas. The method of making the 1950–1959 comparison will be essentially the same as that used for the 1956 National Housing Inventory. Enumerators will compare the status of dwelling units in their segments with the information reported on the 1950 Census schedules.

When all phases of the 1959 Components of Change program are complete, components of change statistics in terms of dwelling units will be provided for the $9\frac{2}{3}$ years since the 1950 Census, permitting a virtually complete explanation of all the housing changes which have occurred during the intercensal period; estimates will be available to link these dwelling unit data with the housing unit results obtained from the 1960 Census of Housing; and housing and household characteristics from the 1960 Census of Housing will provide the information not available from the Components of Change program. This will make available to analysts the most complete set of housing statistics ever provided – in this nation or any other.

# IV

# Requirements of special groups

## A / Single and aged persons

## Living arrangements of unattached persons

*ARNOLD M. ROSE*

Social problems receive differing degrees of attention from those who are affected by them and from the general public. The seriousness of the problem – measured either by the number of persons affected or by the degree of the need – is not necessarily an index of the amount of interest in the problem. This paper will describe a social problem – the inadequacy of housing for unattached persons – and suggest its degree of seriousness. This problem is not being given the degree of public or expert attention that would seem to be merited by its seriousness, although the closely-related problem of housing for families is being given a large amount of public and expert attention. A companion article will describe the variations in interest in the problem for the unattached and attempt to get at some of the reasons for the variations and the general lack of interest. By means of these two articles, we hope to demonstrate the lack of correlation between the existence of a social problem and the amount of interest in it.

In 1940 there were at least 12,285,000 unattached persons in the United States.* They constituted about 9.3 percent of the total population or about 14.2 percent of the population 20 years of age and over. It is probable that there were many more unattached persons during the depths of the depression in the 1930's (when it was estimated that there were 1½ million homeless, mostly unattached),[1] and in the midst of the war boom of the 1940's (when

* This figure includes lodgers in private households, one-person families, members of quasi households (such as lodging houses and hotels), servants and hired hands living in private households. The figure is a minimum estimate because it does not include related persons living with families (no matter how remote the relationship), those who had no place of residence at all, transients who were unknown to their neighbors and thus were missed by the Census.

*Reprinted from* The American Sociological Review, *vol. 12 (August, 1947), pp. 429-435, with permission of the journal and the author.*

it was estimated that 30 to 50 percent of those who migrated to boom cities were at least temporarily unattached).[2] For the purposes of this paper, an unattached person will be regarded as one who does not have parents, collateral families, spouse, or children living with him and who has not joined an institution which incidentally provides living arrangements. Although this definition is occasionally unsatisfactory in deciding whether certain marginal persons are unattached or not, it is the one used because it is desired to examine the living arrangements of those persons in urban American society who do not live either as a member of a family or in an institutional home.

The existence of large numbers of unattached persons is a modern phenomenon, a consequence of the Industrial Revolution that came to England in the late 18th century and to the United States in the middle of the 19th century. the requirements of industry and the attractions of cities, as well as the relative inability of rural areas to support all the persons born in them, brought unprecedented numbers of single, young people from farms to cities, and from small cities to large cities.[3] Most of them ultimately got married, but for awhile they were unattached, and some never got married at all (almost 10 percent of the population never gets married).[4] A special type of these migrants were those who emigrated from Europe: beginning with the new immigration from southern and eastern Europe about 1880, the proportion of unattached immigrants rapidly rose until immigration was all but cut off by the first World War and the restrictive laws of 1921 and 1924.[5] The Industrial Revolution also brought the business cycle and increased seasonal and casual employment.[6] Since these had the social effect of reducing the marriage rate and breaking up families, they irregularly increased the number of unattached.[7] There are other miscellaneous types of unattached whose numbers were relatively stable: the "homeless men," the temporarily unattached (including some traveling salesmen), and some prostitutes.

Although large numbers of unattached persons have been in American cities for almost a hundred years, few suitable living arrangements for the bulk of them have developed. The " Y's," the Eleanor Clubs, the Arlington Farms, and other organized residences built to meet their housing needs serve only a small proportion of the unattached. Most of the unattached live in what might be termed the cast-offs among residences: they live in rooming houses or lodging houses that have been converted from family residences; they live in spare rooms rented out in family homes. The problem can be conceived of as one of cultural lag. It would seem that society still considers the condition of being unattached as either a temporary or an unusual condition. This would help to explain the fact that few residence structures, with the exception of hotels that are usually too expensive for permanent residence, have been built to meet the special needs of the unattached, either by private capital or by the federal government. It has been shown, by the example of the Mills' Hotels in New York City, as well as by other lodging houses built about the same time in other cities, that even the cheap lodging house can be made adequate for the residents and profitable for the owners. But although the Mills' Hotels are over forty years old, practically no other private capital has entered the field of building houses for the unattached poor, and not much more for those unattached who earn fairly good wages and salaries. There are some exceptions, of course, but apparently even most of these date back to pre-World War I days, and many have a philanthropic motive behind them. The federal government has, during the last fifteen years, concerned itself with clearing slums and providing adequate housing for the underprivileged, especially in cities. But, until the need for labor in war industries practically forced the government to start building dormitories in 1942, it paid no attention to the housing needs of the unattached in cities.* This was true even when the well-motivated slum-clearance projects drove lodgers out of family housholds and razed room-

---

* The federal government through C.C.C. camps and F.S.A. labor camps, did provide some very inexpensive barracks for certain types of unattached persons in rural areas during the 1930's. Also the government entered the housing field briefly during the first World War to build some temporary barracks for unattached war workers.

ing houses. City planners and students of housing have tended to ignore the unattached in their studies and plans for the past twenty-five years.[8] All these facts suggest that there is a blind spot in the thinking of the experts as well as of the general public when it comes to the housing of the unattached.

The income of the average unattached person is half to two-thirds as large as that of the average whole family,[9] and if the indigent unattached were eliminated from consideration, and age of income earners held constant, this discrepancy would be even less. Further, since families always have more than one member, and usually not all the members are income-earning, the average family member has only a little over one-third the income available to him of the average unattached person ($411 compared to $1151 in 1935–36).[10] Considering these facts, the income of the average unattached person could not be said to be so relatively low that he could not afford adequate housing.

At any given income level, the average unattached person spends a greater proportion of his income for housing than does the average family.[11] The average urban tenant family paid a monthly rent of $25.22 in 1940, while the average urban tenant person living by himself paid $19.47.[12] Considering what the unattached person got for his money, and the smaller number of his needs that could be satisfied by his housing (for example, he can seldom have food preparation, laundering, sociable amusement, minor recreation, carried on in his one room that families can have in their homes or apartments), the rent for unattached persons could be said to be relatively high. Available studies[13] of rooming houses – taken as the currently single most important form of living arrangement for self-supporting unattached persons – show that the furniture in furnished rooms is often cheap and insufficient, the sanitary facilities are frequently outmoded and insufficient, the presence of vermin is frequent, the rooms are often not kept clean, there are seldom any common rooms or other facilities for the entertainment of guests. These facts make the relatively high rents for furnished rooms seem even higher. The greater turnover of population in furnished rooms also does not justify high rents,

since vacancies are of shorter duration in furnished rooms than they are in unfurnished apartments for families, so that the vacancy rates per year are about the same.[14] Alternative explanations do not seem to stand up therefore, and we are obliged to seek the conditioning factors of inadequate living arrangements for the unattached in lack of public and expert interest or knowledge.

The actual living arrangements for the unattached can best be considered under the three historical types of unattached persons who made most use of them, the immigrants, the hoboes and other indigents, and the native-born, self-supporting migrants to cities. Unattached immigrants lived mainly as roomers and boarders in the homes of families of their own nationality. Other living arrangements developed logically out of this: The boarding boss system was one in which a single man or a couple took in boarders as a business. The cooperative non-family group was one in which a number of unattached persons got together to rent a house or apartment, buy furniture and hire a house-housekeeper (or sometimes do their housekeeping themselves). The labor camp had a boarding boss system where the " boss " was an employee of the company rather than an independent entrepreneur. Mainly for immigrant women, there were charitable or semi-charitable boarding homes sponsored by religious, ethnic, or philanthropic groups. Immigrants also lived in regular lodging, boarding and rooming houses. There were grave inadequacies in all these types of living arrangements, the most important of which were extreme overcrowding, poor sanitary facilities and lack of cleanliness, invasion of the privacy of families, and lack of opportunity for recreation and social contact. After the laws restricting immigration were passed in the early 1920's, the number of foreign-born in the United States began to decline, and the proportion of unattached declined still more rapidly, so that their living arrangements are no longer a major problem. A similar problem exists today, however, for Negroes who have migrated from the rural South to the urban North.

The chief type of residence for unattached " homeless men " and the unemployed is the common lodging house. Although some of these call themselves "hotels" they are very cheap, and are the poorest form of living arrangements for the unattached. Most of them can be classified under one of three types: the room-type lodging house (where several beds are put in a single room, which is otherwise like a room in a rooming house), the cell-type lodging house (where each lodger has his own small cell, very scantily furnished and not separated at their tops from similar cubicles), the "flophouse" (which is usually simply a bare room where lodgers sleep on boards, sometimes covered with thin mattresses and sometimes with piles of rags or newspapers). In addition to the common commercial lodging house, there are the model lodging houses built by philanthropists (the Mills' Hotels, for example), the missions sponsored by religious groups, and municipal lodging houses built by cities for men and women who are completely without funds. These indigent persons devise all sorts of other living quarters for themselves: they sleep in taverns, in all-night movies and restaurants, in police stations, on park benches, in doorways and hallways, in vacant lots and abandoned buildings. During the depression of the 1930's, they even built whole villages, commonly called "Shanty-towns," for themselves in public grounds. Among the unemployed during the depression, families were better off than unattached persons, since they were less often evicted and more often supported in their homes by relief payments.

Single young people who came from rural areas to cities to earn their living and make their fortunes in expanding commerce and industry at first lived in boarding houses. These were usually quite adequate to satisfy the social and recreational needs of a home for the unattached as well as their physical needs (for a place to sleep, eat and do laundering). But these did not have enough flexibility with respect to time for eating and coming home at night, and did not have enough privacy, to be popular. When the restaurant and the rooming house came into existence, the boarding house declined, until by the year 1900 they were very few in number in large cities.

Living in rooming houses, or as a roomer in a family home, is now the most popular form of living arrangement for unattached persons. Most of the available evidence indicates that rents in rooming houses are high for the services rendered, and that furniture and other facilities tend to be inadequate. The unattached person who comes from a given social level or who has a given income sinks a step or two in the quality of furniture he uses when he lives in a rooming house rather than in a family home. The roomer in a family home, on the other hand, has as wide a variety of quality in his living quarters as families do, since families of all income levels – except at the very top – take in roomers.

The organized boarding home and the residence club also exhibit a wide variety as far as their quality is concerned, but they are non-profit making and sometimes even partially supported by philanthropic groups so that their rents are not high in comparison to what the renter receives. They have also become more popular in recent decades, since their restrictions have been reduced and since some of them have eliminated the practice of charging for meals whether they are taken or not. Such homes are not numerous, relative to other forms of living arrangements, and the number of rooms in them has not kept pace with the increasing demand. It requires a fairly large accumulation of capital to build and maintain an organized boarding house or residence club.

Insofar as private capital has gone into providing housing for the unattached, it has gone into the building of hotels. Hotels are not for the unattached alone, of course, but cater in large measure to transients and moderately well-to-do families. Hotels provide a fairly satisfactory living arrangement for high salaried unattached persons, but they are too expensive as a permanent residence for the bulk of the unattached. A development of the last several decades, which combines some of the desirable features of both the hotel and the family home, is the apartment hotel. Is it used by unattached persons as well as by families. The apartment hotel also tends to be expensive and sometimes requires a high initial outlay of money for furniture and other household essentials.

The rooming house and the lodging house,

which together provide housing for a very large proportion of unattached persons are usually converted structures.* That is, they were originally constructed to serve functions other than those which they are now serving. Few, if any, buildings are built with the intention of making rooming houses out of them. Thus, rooming houses tend to be old buildings, and not always suited for their purpose. Their sanitary facilities are old-fashioned and perhaps worn out. The rooms are not spaced properly for individual living. There may be no fire exit, and if there is one it is likely to be through someone's private room, which is usually kept locked. In various other ways, the rooming house in a converted structure is an undesirable place to live.

The most rapidly growing cities, region of country held constant, are the ones which have the largest proportions of unattached. Rapidly growing cities have many advantages, but their housing facilities probably tend to be insufficient in number. The areas within a city in which the unattached can find furnished rooms tend to be the poorest ones. They are areas from which upper and middle class families have moved, and which industry and commerce are invading. Or they are along noisy arteries of transportation. The areas of Chicago in which the unattached are concentrated have been found by correlation,† to be areas of economic blight, of commercial and industrial invasion, of old structures in poor condition, of dwelling units lacking such facilities as inside bathrooms and central heat, of overcrowded residences owned by absentee landlords. These areas also have well-defined social characteristics: relatively few children in the population, a high sex ratio,

proximity to red light districts, high venereal disease rate, high schizophrenia rate. Thus, the areas are characterized by a high degree of social disorganization to which the unattached contribute after they have been there a while. They have two main advantages for the residents: (1) They tend to be near most of the places of work. (2) They tend to be near the centers of amusement,‡ and have characteristic service institutions which especially cater to the needs of the unattached.

World War II increased the disadvantages of unattached living. The pressure on living quarters for the unattached increased so markedly that they were living in all the odd corners that unemployed men found for themselves during the depression of the previous decade.[15] The federal government belatedly went into the field of building housing for the unattached 15 months after it began on war housing for families.[16] But the dormitories were insufficient in number,[17] and generally not nearly as adequate as the war housing built for families. Private owners of furnished rooms raised rents markedly for the unattached, despite O.P.A. price ceilings because the O.P.A. could not adequately police the large number of furnished rooms and because the new rooms or "improved" rooms put on the market were not subject to O.P.A. control for their initial pricing. The O.P.A. even hurt the unattached as far as hotel rooms were concerned, because hotels found it more profitable to charge daily rates rather than weekly rates and so forced their guests to move every 5 days. This situation continues after the war, but, of course, there is an acute shortage of housing for families also.

The overall picture, then, is one of inadequate

---

* The rank-order correlation, for the community areas of Chicago, between the proportion of units in converted structures and the proportion of roomers in the population is +.69.
† Coefficients of rank-order correlation, for the community areas of Chicago, have been worked out between each of the indicated characteristics and the proportion of roomers in the population. The data have been taken from a variety of sources: (1) Chicago Plan Commission and Work Projects Administration, *Residential Chicago*, Vol. I of the *Chicago Land Use Survey* (Chicago, 1942); (2) Arthur J. Todd et al, *The Chicago Recreation Survey, 1937* (Chicago: The Chicago Recreation Commission, 1937); (3) U.S. Bureau

of the Census, *Sixteenth Census of the United States: 1940, Population and Housing: Chicago, Ill.* (Washington, D.C.: Government Printing Office, 1942); (4) Chicago Department of Health, *Health Data Book* (Chicago: Dept. of Health, 1939), pp. 85–86; (5) R. E. L. Faris and H. W. Dunham, *Mental Disorders in Urban Areas* (Chicago: University of Chicago Press, 1938), Appendix B.
‡ The rooming house areas in Chicago (1937) have a disproportionately large number of liquor establishments, billiard halls, carbarets, penny arcades, movie theatres. They have a low number of bowling alleys and dance halls.

living arrangements for the great bulk of the unattached population in American cities. There has been little interest, either on the part of private capital or on the part of the general public (as manifested through goverenment) in remedying the situation. It is not mainly a matter of charity, since most of the unattached have relatively more money than do family heads to spend upon their living quarters. It is largely a matter of getting either government action or of getting private capital together to finance large projects. The new projects can be modeled after the existing residence clubs, if the aim is to provide adequate living arrangements to meet the needs and desires of the unattached. The various occupational groups will need somewhat different facilities.

The very poor among the unattached need housing badly also. It is questionable whether private enterprise would find it profitable to build for this group, although the Mills' Hotels and other philanthropy-sponsored lodging houses built around the turn of the century made regular profits. Today, because of increased building costs and higher land values, housing for hoboes and the unemployed would probably have to be a matter for philanthropic or government support. New building would not be necessary if remodeling went along with conversion of older buildings. It might be that some social service functions should be given along with board and lodging for indigents, in order to increase their capacity for self-support.

Some of the unattached persons themselves will continue to prefer to live in rooming houses, lodging houses, or one of the other forms of living arrangements now predominant. There are aspects of privacy, anonymity, cheapness, about some of these places which they prefer, and certainly no one should try to force them to live elsewhere. But the United States can do what Great Britain had accomplished by the 1920's – give these places a continual and thorough inspection, and require them to meet certain minimum standards of cleanliness and completeness.

# Housing for the elderly

*THE SUBCOMMITTEE ON HOUSING FOR THE ELDERLY, U.S. SENATE*

### The outlines of the problem

While the Nation's nearly 17 million older citizens are a heterogeneous group with an endless variety of individual characteristics, they tend to have certain problems in common which bear on their housing needs.

*Incomes of the elderly are low.* Most people over 65 are retired from the work force and live on reduced incomes. As Henry D. Sheldon has remarked:[1]

Since ours is a money economy, income is generally regarded as the best single index to welfare. . . . Food, shelter, clothing, medical care – in many contexts, self-respect – may all be had for a price.

While there is not always a direct relation between income and well-being, too many older

Reprinted from Housing for the Elderly, *a report of the subcommittee on housing for the elderly to the Special Committee on Aging, of the United States Senate, Government Printing Office, 1962, pp. 2–5.*

persons live in the economic cellar. In 1960 the median personal income of men aged 65 and over who were family heads was about $1,900, and the median income of persons 65 and over who were living alone was $1,050.[2] At that low an income level, people can hardly buy the first two of the everyday necessities, food and clothing, to say nothing of securing adequate housing.

*Income declines as age advances.* Senior citizens, whose incomes have already declined because of retirement from the work force, may expect still further reduction of income as the years go by. When one partner of an elderly couple dies, the other partner's income is cut. It is typical of aged widows that they receive about half the income of aged couples. The average social security benefit to widows in 1959 was $56 a month, as compared with $119, for couples.

*Income cannot be increased.* An elderly person is not only retired on a reduced income, but he is rarely able to augment his income through employment. The proportion of older male workers in the labor force has been decreasing steadily since modern industrialization began, partially because their skills tend to become obsolete and partially because of the trend toward earlier retirement. Over the past half century, participation of older men in the labor force has declined by about 50 percent.

*The elderly have limited liquid assets.* Most of the savings of older people are tied up in homes and in life insurance rather than in forms readily convertible to cash. According to a Federal Reserve Board survey, 46 percent of spending units* with heads 65 years of age or more had liquid assets in 1959 of $500 or less. Moreover, as might be expected, liquid asset holdings decreased with income. Among those aged spending units with less than $3,000 of annual income, almost half had liquid assets of $200 or less.

A survey by the Bureau of Old-Age and Survivors Insurance in 1959 of a sample of its beneficiaries shows a similar picture. Among couples, 28 percent had no liquid assets at all and another 12 percent had liquid assets of less than $500. Among the single elderly (widowed, divorced, or never married), 43 percent had no bank deposits or savings and an additional 13 percent had some but less than $500.

*Only a very few have any substantial property assets.* Contrary to the traditional notion that older people tend to own property, few, in fact, own real property with any substantial value and even fewer own marketable securities.

The Federal Reserve Board found in a 1957 survey that only 11 percent of the aged spending units owned corporate stocks and bonds or Government securities. Virtually all of those owning such assets were in the group which also had $2,000 or more in liquid assets.

Most of the savings of the aged are represented in equity in their homes and for most this equity is their only substantial asset. Data from the 1960 census show that the median value of homes owned and occupied by persons 65 to 74 is $9,900. Those owned by persons 75 and over had a median value of only $5,600. Typically these properties are old homes, often located in areas no longer considered to be desirable residential areas and frequently run down and neglected because of the physical and financial inability of their owners to maintain them. Thus, these assets often are difficult to convert to cash, and when sold do not yield enough to provide suitable new housing.

*Retirement lasts a long time.* The trend toward increasingly early retirement, coupled with increasing longevity, means that the retirement period will tend to be longer and longer. A 65-year-old today has a life expectancy of 14 years. If we were considering only the problems of the relatively young retirees in vigorous health, providing housing for the elderly at prices they can afford would be less difficult.

---

* A spending unit is defined as a household in which income is pooled for the use of all members with one member substantially in control of its expenditure.

But such housing must be suitable not only for the earliest phase of retirement, but for the latter stages, when frailty, disability, accident proneness, weakened vision and hearing difficulties are liable to accelerate and multiply. Housing design and location must take these potential disabilities into account.

*The elderly are clustered in the decaying cores of cities.* The elderly are harder hit than any other age group by urban renewal and other community redevelopment programs. Because the elderly have low incomes and because they tend to be residual occupants of old and deteriorating urban neighborhoods, their concentration in such neighborhoods is particularly great.

Their removal from these neighborhoods is especially fraught with personal and social problems. Even if their housing is substandard, it is nonetheless situated in an area of longstanding associations and familiarity, the values of which are compelling. If the elderly must be relocated, the psychic cost to the elderly person of change itself cannot be disregarded.

*Household size is usually reduced.* Housing designed for families is not necessarily suitable for retired persons. By the time parents reach age 65 their children have generally established homes of their own, leaving the parents as a two-person household. But even by this time widowhood has overtaken many, and by age 75, fewer than half are living with their spouse in their own household. If the older persons remain in their original family homes, they are liable to have more space than they can utilize, maintain, or afford. Specialized housing for the elderly, therefore, needs to be designed for one-person and two-person households.

*Yet many older people live with their children.* According to 1960 census data, 2,300,000 elderly people live with their children or other adult relatives. The oft-heard complaint that children have lost their sense of filial responsibility appears to have little basis in fact.

The cherished belief that in the past grandparents always had a home with their children also has been challenged. Prof. Robert W. Kleemeier of Washington University, who testified before the subcommittee, said:

> There is ample reason to believe that in the past it was characteristic for children to leave the parents at home while they went forth, frequently to the frontier, to set up homes of their own. Living in the extended family of grandparents, children, cousins, uncles, and other relatives was ... simply not the common rule. Nor do we have any evidence from earlier times that having the grandparents live with their children and grandchildren was better accepted then than today. The romanticized larger houses of former times ... which remain today [are] relics or monuments of the past; the one-room cabins are gone and forgotten.[3]

In any case, there is solid evidence that many of the millions of older people who live with adult children would prefer not to have to do so. For a great many the arrangement cannot help but be unsatisfactory – both for the older person who has lost command of his own household and for the child who must struggle to meet the needs of the elderly parent as well as those of his own children and spouse. Dr. Kleemeier and other witnesses pointed out that the desire to be independent of their children is very strong among the elderly.

In addition, it must be remembered that the number of four-generation families in the United States is increasing rapidly. Since 1920 we have experienced a ninefold increase in the number of persons 85 years and older. A million Americans are in this category; 5.6 million are 75 or more. So the question arises: If a 65-year-old retiree is expected to live with his children with whom do his 86-year-old parents live?

*Most elderly persons live where they have always lived.* The extent to which older people move to warmer climates upon retirement is vastly overestimated. Florida, California, Arizona, and other "sunshine States" have some "retirement communities" settled mainly by northerners, but compared to the total of 17 million older people the number in these communities is negligible. California and Arizona actually have a smaller proportion of persons over 65 than does the United States as a whole. Of all the States along the southern border of the country, only Florida has a percentage of elderly higher than the national average, and even Florida has fewer old people in relation to population than do five Northern States – Iowa, Missouri, Nebraska, Vermont, and New Hampshire.

The fact is that few elderly persons have both the financial means and the desire to spend their retirement years in a locality other than the one in which they spent their working years. The problem of housing for the elderly is a universal one, shared by every State and every community.

*Older people differ in what they want and need.* While housing of 17 million older people has to be considered as a national problem, and one of great magnitude, it must also be regarded as 17 million individual problems. The aged and aging differ widely in their needs and desires. Some prefer to live in "projects" or "retirement colonies" confined to their age group, while others prefer to live in close proximity to younger families. Some prefer apartment living; others are not happy without a separate house with a lawn and garden to care for. Some want to live downtown with ready access to community activities and services; others prefer to live on the edge of town or in the suburbs. Some are sufficiently vigorous to live independently; others can maintain their households with a minimum of help, if they live in the kind of housing that is easy to maintain; still others require medical care or supervision in varying degrees.

A visitor to housing projects for the elderly in Sweden and Denmark is particularly impressed with the variety of accommodations and services offered, and the care with which housing and health services are related. In downtown Copenhagen, the chairman of the subcommittee visited a project which encompassed the four sides of a city block surrounding a pleasant park. The compound provided apartment units with cooking facilities for those able to take care of themselves, community dining facilities for those who were ambulatory but unable or unwilling to do their own cooking, and a nursing home for those no longer ambulatory. Similarly, a high-rise building in downtown Stockholm designed for the very aged provided apartments in the lower five floors for persons capable of some degree of independent living, with nursing home and hospital facilities on the higher floors. An apartment development for retired workers in suburban Stockholm provided cooking facilities in each unit but prepared in a central kitchen a choice of hot meals which could be ordered and sent in to the individual units.

The program developed in each American community for housing of its elderly citizens should include a variety of types of accommodations and offer each individual or couple a range of choice.

# Guiding policies

THE COMMITTEE ON THE HYGIENE OF HOUSING, AMERICAN PUBLIC HEALTH ASSOCIATION

Other changes that occur as a population ages pose more problems than the mere increase in the proportion of older people, and housing requirements must differ with changes in family size and composition. A rational housing policy encompasses all groups of the population and a practical program is a flexible one which incorporates the aging; increases the general supply of low- and medium-cost dwelling units of acceptable standards, suitable either for the vigorous or those who may be handicapped by age or disease; and recognizes the very small household, and also the larger-than-average household since the three-generation family is often a necessity. Housing for older people is a problem, not for want of specific plans for the aged, but for lack of plans that include them as a part of the community.

Housing patterns tend to mirror existing conditions and these change. The average dwelling size now and 50 years ago reflects the change in the average size of the family. Increased use of multi-family buildings in part reflects decline in the average size of the family as well as the change to an urban civilization. Present sanitary standards were unthinkable not too long ago, and gas-jet lights were once the symbol of modern innovation. Diversification in building practice is always possible and housing patterns will continue to change.

In the wake of an increasing proportion of older people, the two- rather than the seven-person family is most prevalent and the relatively rapid aging of the population is simultaneously changing the composition of families. Many households are one-person and more household heads are aged, or aging and in need of housing which will continue to be suitable as physical strength and general ability diminish. It is incontrovertible that an older person will be a member of the family, in some capacity, at some period in every family cycle; many families will have a chronically ill person whose housing needs are almost identical to those of older people; and many families will have a member physically handicapped by war injuries or civilian accidents who has problems of locomotion and protection from fatigue similar to the aged.

The housing problem cannot be solved by piecemeal attempts to take care of various small groups. In countries where segregated housing has been tried, the error has been acknowledged in such extremes as housing projects designed exclusively for families with children, for artists, unmarried working mothers, slum families, problem families, or the aged. Experience has shown that special housing is not only expensive but unwarranted, and new policies are based on flexible, long-term programs toward better housing conditions for everyone. Supplements to housing manuals have become necessary.* The

---

* Special groups are listed as older people, other small households, especially large households, disabled people, higher income households, and those who need special facilities because of the occupation of one of their members. Since it is now emphasized that each of these special groups should be housed " as an important and integral part of the population, there should be no segregation and their houses should be built among

Reprinted from Housing an Aging Population, Committee on the Hygiene of Housing, American Public Health Association, 1953, pp. 54–56, 59–63, with permission of the publisher.

social and medical surveys on the problems of aging and care of old people undoubtedly influenced the change in policy in Great Britain. It was concluded that the importance of building special houses for old people is easily exaggerated. " Among other reasons, a great many do not want to live in houses built specially for them, and the most urgent need of the aged is for more accommodation on a permanent basis, the greatest single requirement for their welfare at the present time, and the living problems of old people are primarily domestic, rather than institutional."

At best there is confusion about " special housing for the aged," undoubtedly because of technical differences. Many features recommended in the United States have been arrived at, or based on, methods in other countries. They are special or unusual where, for instance, central heating, or plumbing facilities, considered minimum in this country, are not general. The practical difficulties in providing different facilities for a small group wthout some degree of separation has led to the erroneous assumption that special housing and segregated housing are the same. There is a tendency to emphasize that certain facilities are essential for the aged at the same time their desirability for all housing is not only acknowledged but advocated. The focus has been too much on the afflicted older person to the exclusion of natural aging in spite of the fact that nearly 95 out of every 100 old people in the country spend their entire lives in conventional houses which can be suitable even if the occupants suffer some disability.

In a Joint Statement of Recommendations on Planning for the Chronically Ill, it was maintained that wide expansion of housing programs could have important effects in decreasing the incidence of chronic ailments, which often originate in mental and emotional stresses of family life and appear related to bad housing and sanitary conditions. Housing for those who are handicapped by physical or mental disability should be an integral part of a housing program for an aging population.* Well-designed dwelling units are satisfactory for a large proportion of the seriously handicapped of all ages and for most older people.

A well-designed dwelling suitable for an older person is not basically different from any other and dwellings for small families´cannot vary fundamentally, only in degree. Important details of design, however, make the difference between good and bad housing and all dwellings should be so built that anyone, including those handicapped by age or disease, can live in them comfortably and safely. Any increase in an improved supply is all to the total good.

There have been a few specifications for location and design of housing units for older people, so often repeated that they may be considered standard. These add up to just two things – that aging people should be maintained in their accustomed environments, and that their homes should be as accident-proof as possible. Objective basic standards, previously formulated for all healthful housing, are entirely applicable to the aged.

The only notable special provisions suggested to make a dwelling unit completely suitable for the aged or the handicapped are doors, about two inches wider than present standards, to admit a wheel chair. Slightly wider doors would be desirable in any dwelling except for their greater cost, but they still would not suffice since the 35 square-foot bathroom standard in all designs for low-cost housing will not accommodate a wheel chair. Neither will elevator doors and corridors in many apartment houses. Changes of dimension in halls and bathrooms,

---

the houses built for the general population," one is entitled to speculate if the general population is represented only by the unemployed poor. (See Scottish Housing Advisory Committee. *Housing of Special Groups*, 1952.)

* The American Hospital Association, American Medical Association, American Public Health Association, and American Public Welfare Association. During World War II, 265,000 men were permanently disabled as the result of combat injuries but in the same four years 1,250,000 civilians were permanently disabled as the result of disease and accidents and 350,000 become disabled through illness or injury every year. Prior to World War II an estimated 23 million people in the United States were handicapped to some extent by disease, accidents, maladjustments or injuries from former wars. These 23 million disabled civilians include the estimated 1.3 million disabled aged and the 2 million known physically handicapped children.

corridors and elevators, possible in new building, are completely impractical for existing structures. It would be more fruitful to redesign the wheel chair. Furthermore, the private home without steps or equipped with a ramp to permit easier access for an aging person or a wheel chair would be better justified if public buildings did not have flights of outside steps still in vogue from a day when life expectancy at birth was only 22 or 23 years.*

Many of the features recommended for healthful housing are missing in many existing dwellings because good housing has never been a complete reality. If there were enough good housing at prices or rents that could be afforded, there would be no serious problem of housing older people. The housing problem has been long in the making and the current shortage of desirable dwelling units has been accumulating over many years. Available .data demonstrate the need for improvement of substandard units as well as for increased new construction†

If it is recognized that housing the aged is a part of the total housing problem, the most important question is how the aging may share in the general program. Even now, the "two-bedroom" unit fits only two-fifths of the population. More general acceptance of this fact and appropriate action would result in more dwelling units suited to the aging; and revision of the regulations under the National Housing Act would eliminate discrimination against them in federally-aided low-rent housing projects.‡

Since 1930 there have been more two-person households than any other size and these increased by 45 percent during the 1940 decade, and there was a 55 percent increase in one-person households. Among people 65 years and older, 43 percent represent two-person families and one-fourth constitute one-person households.

Many of these single households and some two-person families could be, or would like to be, or might have to be parts of larger households if accommodations were adequate. These various types could be fitted into public housing if the definition of "family" were broadened to include other associations than those of blood relatives or married couples, and to include the "one-person household," which has been completely disregarded. Originally, public housing was set up for low-income familes with young children, relegating the childless couple to a position of minor importance. At present, limits are based on room costs rather than on household-unit costs, so that the small household becomes relatively more expensive and small units are discouraged. Some tenants in early projects are now older couples, but the survivor must be evicted upon death of one. In slum clearance projects a few former site tenants in the older age group have been admitted to new developments not necessarily intended for them but they may stay only as a couple.

Except for high cost apartment buildings in large cities, the one- or two-person family has been almost completely ignored by the private builder who tends to provide, not too many dwellings for the "average" family, but too few for the small household characteristic of older people; and too few for the larger household which oftentimes represents the three-generation family.

A realistic proportion of housing units suited to childless couples, to individuals and to the five- or six-person family would substantially ameliorate the continuing problem of accommodation for older people. Young couples are accustomed to move to larger houses or apartments as the family increases, thus releasing smaller quarters for older people. Conversely,

---

* See American Institute of Architects. *Buildings for the Handicapped and/or Aged*, concerning ramp or stepless access to buildings used both by the active and the handicapped.
† Estimated, in the study of *America's Needs and Resources* published in 1947 by the Twentieth Century Fund, to bring all housing up to standard from 1946 to 1960 and provide for new families would require an annual average for 15 years of 363,000 rehabilitated and 1,312,000 new units.
‡ The National Housing Act defines "low-rent hous-

ing" as decent, safe, and sanitary dwellings to be available solely for "families" whose income at the time of admission does not exceed a specified proportion of the rent (including heat, light, water and cooking fuel). But administrative regulations under the Act define "family" as a group of persons regularly living together, which consists of two or more persons related by blood, marriage or adoption. A group of unrelated persons living together or a person living alone is deemed not to constitute a family, nor may lodgers be included in a family.

more available accommodation for small households releases larger quarters for larger families.

Semi-dependent old people have been virtually ignored by both public and private builders. The evidence shows that most older people prefer to live independently although it is impossible to establish whether the 15 or 20 percent now living with children or other relatives wish to do so or whether they are wanted. For many, if space permits, this is a satisfactory arrangement and for some it is and will continue to be the only feasible one. Apartment units can be designed flexibly to permit adding or subtracting a bedroom from one apartment to another, and interchangeable units are possible in detached houses if zoning regulations permit. Over 25 years ago, Henry Wright designed a flexible duplex house for the City Housing Corporation of New York, which built twelve of them at Sunnyside Gardens. The two-story building contained one four-room flat and one two-room flat on each floor, separated by the stairwell. These could be used as two- or four-room units, or combined to make six-, eight-, ten- or twelve-room units as needs varied. The owner could rent out the units not required for his own use.

Once it was considered a startling innovation that every dwelling should have a bathroom. Eventually, it may be accepted that many dwelling units can be designed with space to be used as a nursery for young children, as a small apartment to be let at a later period, and still later as living quarters by older people. Such flexible units also reduce shelter cost. Recently a builder in San Antonio, Tex., reported that he has under construction five " flexabilt " houses which are designed to " meet the needs of families from newlywed days through old age." Only the exterior walls and those around the bathrooms and kitchen are permanent. Other walls can be shifted (by the owner without any knowledge of carpentry and without any expense, it is claimed) to provide from one to four bedrooms or to convert the house into a two-family unit. The builder suggests that a young couple could first occupy the efficiency apartment and rent the other unit. After the arrival of a child they could rent the apartment and occupy the larger unit. As the family grew they could take over the entire house and as the children left home the process could be reversed.[1]

These American equivalents of the Swedish flexible flat, the duplex house and the duplex house in reverse are all possibilities for taking up immediate slack with units for small households, adaptable to different uses later. Small houses or apartments for small households are not an excuse for cramped quarters.* Inadequate space always contributes to accidents, makes care of the ill difficult and housekeeping more arduous. Maximum comfort and convenience within relatively small space are possible with good planning.

Large flexible dwellings can accommodate the three-generation family and small, flexible dwellings the two-person household. For the independent older individual, the " plus-Granny " flat is a recent British proposal, although Eugene Gardner, planning houses for special purposes in 1875 in Boston, designed efficient " one-room houses for old maids."[2] Hillside Homes, the limited-dividend apartment project designed by Clarence Stein in the Bronx, includes a number of small garden apartments, entered from the interior courts, each with its own private outside space. Mr. Stein considered the smaller ones suitable for older people to live independently of their families and some were used in this manner.

The indicated modifications in definition and building would provide an adequate basis for housing people of all ages with one exception. For old people who are unmarried, or widowed, or without children, there can be no solution within the family and if they are unable to fend for themselves even in efficient one-room apartments, their problem is crucial. Except at high income levels the old person alone and unable to do any housekeeping cannot find desirable accommodations and many of the aged, particularly in large cities, live in undesirable room-

---

* Careful analysis of space standards essential for healthful living indicates the need for 400 sq. ft. for a single person and 750 sq. ft. for a two-person family.

ing or boarding houses. The Housing Association of Metropolitan Boston has considered the needs of these people carefully in the plans for apartment houses with 20 percent nonhousekeeping units and three-fourths of all units for single persons.

If special housing were to be built it would be years before any effective proportion of the aged could be rehoused. Ashley points out that the often quoted three million increase during the next decade in the population over 65 years of age is not a reliable measure of the magnitude of the housing problem for the aged during that period, since some considerable number of old families are well housed in their own homes and neither need nor want to make a change. This limitation of the scope of the problem can continue only with a substantial general increase in dwelling units of acceptable standards. Otherwise, the housing difficulties of older people will become more acute with time because the proportion of the aged who are well housed in their own homes will inevitably be reduced as their numbers increase and because of the simultaneous impact within the next

decade on the entire housing situation of the increase in families composed solely of aging adults, and the anticipated increase in new households. As long as medium- or low-income families with small children cannot find suitable houses, completely adequate housing for older people in corresponding income groups is unlikely, and housing costs for older people can be lowered only if housing costs are reduced.

Suitable shelter for older people will be attained only as the housing problem for all age groups is solved. Aging is a process which begins long before the age of 65, and housing the aged must be considered in relation to people many years under the age of 65. There is a lesson from the false starts which have been made when the focus was limited. It is worth repeating that " the aging process affects and relates to all human beings at all stages of their lives and not solely to the aged. Hence, the challenge of the aging population is faced everywhere and at all times and the problem is not solvable by any single formula, such as social security, old-age pensions, geriatrics, or the cottage system for aging couples."[3]

# How the poor are housed

*ALVIN L. SCHORR*

In arguments about the adequacy of public relief, occasionally someone is heard to say : " But where are these people who are in such difficulty? After all, no one starves in the United States." It is approximately as ambiguous to say that everyone in the United States is, after all, under a roof. Some are malnourished, as some are malhoused. In order to examine the question how families get under a roof, it will be useful to visualize the income that they require.

Analysis by Warren Jay Vinton of income and new housing in the years 1947 to 1958 shows that it was, on the whole, those families with over $6,000 a year* who were served. Families with less than $6,000 account for 88 percent of the substandard housing in the country, suggesting that they are not served very well by existing housing either. Many have adequate housing, especially if they are close to $6,000 income or if the income supports one or two people rather than four or five. But it seems clear that income of at least $6,000 is required to assure adequate family housing.[1] A similar analysis brings Joseph P. McMurray to the conclusion that, in standard metropolitan areas, an income of $5,000 a year is required to rent or purchase decent housing. In smaller communities, an income of $4,000 is required.[2] That McMurray's estimate may be on the conservative side is suggested by the city worker's family budget of the Bureau of Labor Statistics. Designed to establish an amount necessary to maintain a family of four at " a level of adequate living," the total budget in 20 large cities ranges from $5,370 (Houston) to $6,567 (Chicago). The amount needed for rent and utilities ranges from $871 (Scranton) to $1,386 (Chicago).[3] It is evident that the family to which we are addressing our attention, with income equivalent to $2,500 or less for a family of four, will have to make adjustments of some kind in their housing expenditures.

How do poor families pay for housing? The question has dimensions that are private and public. As a private matter, the question is answerable in terms of budget management and family arrangements. As a public matter, one answers in terms of specific public programs or of the concept that housing filters down to the poor as those who are better off move on to better housing. All national programs intended to sustain income and insure against such risks as old age are, in a certain sense, devices to provide housing (et cetera) to those who might otherwise be poor. However, most of these programs place in the beneficiary's hand money which he has, in one manner or another, earned. He is in the same situation as any wage earner, so far as housing is concerned. (If his benefits are inadequate, he is in the same situation as other poor people.) Two national programs, public assistance and public housing, incorporate a means test and intervene directly in the housing of the poor. They will merit special attention when we come to the public dimension of the provision of housing to the poor.

---

* Dollar figures used in this paragraph are for years from 1956 to 1959. They are not adjusted here, as they are being used to establish the magnitude of income that is necessary rather than a precise amount.

*Reprinted from* Slums and Social Insecurity, *U.S. Department of Health, Education and Welfare, 1963, pp. 98–137.*

## The private dimension

The poor pay for housing, first, in its poor quality. Reflection will show that this is a theme that lies just under the surface of most of our discussion. Whether they own or rent, it is the poor families who tend to occupy the country's substandard housing. In 1956 half of those with income less than $2,000 lived in housing that was dilapidated or lacked plumbing.[4]

This is a rough measure. We have not taken into account size of family. Moreover, current income counts several kinds of people as if they were the same: the rich man who has taken a temporary loss, the retired man who once had more income, and the man who is chronically poor. The first man is likely to be able to spend out of savings and conceivably the retired man too, but hardly the man who has never had a decent income. Nevertheless, the rough measure makes it clear that some who are poor acquire standard housing. They do not acquire it by accident. Analysis of the Chicago population shows that the poor in standard dwellings "typically" pay more rent than those in substandard dwellings.[5] Even those who do not manage standard housing make sacrifices for the quality that they do achieve.

One step that poor families take is to allocate a high percentage of their income to housing. We have already noted a tendency for those who relocate from cleared areas to spend more for improved housing. In 1956 the great majority of families with incomes under $2,000 spent 30 percent or more of their income on rent. On the other hand, of families with incomes between $8,000 and $10,000 the great majority spent less than 15 percent.[6] We have suggested that current income is not always a good indication of a family's financial circumstances. However, relating the amount a family spends to the cost of its housing gives a similar picture. In 1950 urban families with incomes under $1,000 a year spent 26 percent of their total outlay for housing. Families from $1,000 to $2,000 spent 22 percent; from $2,000 to $3,000, 18 percent; and so on.[7]

One possibility is clear – to pay for adequate shelter by settling for inadequate food and clothing. In many cases, the family must be governed not by a deliberate choice to favor housing but by the way inadequate money gets spent. Under sustained pressure, costs that are fixed and regular are met and those that seem stretchable or postponable – food, clothing, recreation, medical care – are not met. In any case, the consequences of spending more than 20 percent for housing do not seem healthy. It is anybody's guess how much lower than 20 percent a rule of thumb for poor families ought to be. Certainly, so far as public decisions are concerned, 20 percent should be regarded as a maximum rather than an average housing expenditure for poor families.

Income for income, naturally, the pressure to make some adjustment to housing needs is felt most by large families. What steps do the large families take? Reviewing the 1950 *Survey of Consumer Expenditures*, Louis Winnick concludes about the average large family: "They obtain more housing space and, at the same time, maintain or even increase the budgets devoted to other consumer goods."[8] However, poor large families are not able to bring this off. They spend more in total for food and for clothing. To balance the increase, they spend less in total for housing, household operation, and medical care.[9] (This confirms a conclusion we had already reached.) How do the higher income families manage to maintain their spending for other items while obtaining more space? Apparently they do it by sacrificing the physical quality of the housing. (We have seen that poor families are familiar with this tactic too.) So far as ownership is concerned, for example, small families tend to have houses that are worth more, compared to their incomes, than large families.[10] Thus, relative values are lower for the larger families despite the fact that they have more space. Larger families generally try to gain some advantage by purchasing rather than renting,[11] but lower incomes tend to close off this possibility. Poor large families do not, like other large families, show a markedly higher tendency to own than smaller families.

To return to speaking of poor families in general, an additional strategy has now been suggested. Any family, large or small, may think of purchase as a way to secure more housing for its money.* Obviously, however, low income restricts the opportunity to buy.

The purchase of housing, though it is not usually thought of in the same terms, is a form of going into debt. Poor families may not receive more short-term credit than families with more income (because it will be refused), but the struggle to buy on credit or borrow money is an everyday fact of life. Borrowed money may be applied directly to rent or it may buy clothing because clothing money went for rent – the effect is the same. The use of credit to pay for housing produces the problems that have just been noted – a future commitment to sacrifice something tomorrow to pay for today's housing and limited flexibility in the face of emergencies. Moreover, the poor family pays a premium for credit.

The strategies that are open to poor families are not limited to trying to shift about small sums of money. Analysis of the living arrangements of the aged in the United States indicates that, when help for the old person is needed, the poor tend to pool living arrangements. The plight of the poor " is so difficult that they must select the most efficient way of sharing, which is living together."[12] In sum, one tactic for providing housing is to share space beyond the immediate family and to pool available money.

As a private matter, then, poor families get and apply money wherever they can. They use a variety of strategies, some because they come to hand and some in which there is a measure of choice. An aged widow will make different adjustments from a young father, for example. But few of the deliberate choices that are open seem attractive. Families can go without standard housing. They can borrow from food to pay housing. Few who are poor will have saved money; those who have, can use it. They can struggle to buy on credit or to borrow. They can try to buy instead of rent. Those who manage to bring this off may make out better in the end. Others will face additional difficulty because they are borrowing from other budget

items and are leaving themselves less room to maneuver in the next emergency. They can extend the size of their households, trading crowdedness and tension for shelter and a measure of financial flexibility. Families can break up or at least give up children. Throughout, they can seek ways to improve their income. Some poor families try all of these. For some but not for others, purchasing a house and sending additional members to work, when they are possible, are constructive steps. For the rest of it, the avenues that are open go around in a tight little circle, enmeshing families deeper and deeper in deprivation.

### The public dimension

Broadly speaking, the first line of action in providing housing to those who are poor lies in the normal operation of the economy, stimulated and secured by the Federal insurance programs. Clearly, there have been gains in housing poor families that result from the operation of economic forces not directly concerned with them. The number of substandard units in the country has declined steadily in the past two decades, though the total housing inventory has increased by over 50 percent.† On the other hand, substandard housing or crowding is still the common and not the exceptional fate of 32 million Americans who live in modern poverty. The normal operation of the economy is not dealing adequately with the housing of the poor while it deals with them incidentally.

Public housing and public assistance, in different ways, address themselves directly to the housing needs of poor families. How do they serve?

*Public Housing.* Public housing is not a single program, historically; it is a single vessel that has been used for diverse public purposes. In the 1930's, public housing was intended for families who voluntarily sought to improve their housing but could not afford private rentals. This group was not regarded as dependent.

---

* The question of ownership versus rental is not determined simply on financial grounds.
† Standards of housing do not remain static over 20 years, any more than other consumption standards.

Whether the housing of those who are poor has improved at the same rate as general standards of housing is not evaluated here.

Indeed, some housing authorities limited the number of public assistance recipients they would accept and others would not admit any.[13] In the 1940's, the program was redirected to provide housing for war workers. Following the Housing Act of 1949, public housing was oriented again to poor families – with a difference. Partly because postwar amendments gave priority to families having the most urgent housing need, to the aged, and to those displaced by urban renewal, this third generation in public housing contains a high concentration of depressed, untutored, and dependent families.

It would be misleading to speak of the development of the program as if all the crucial changes were made by Congress. If public housing is the vessel, perhaps Congress is the vintner, but one must ask about the grape and the palate of the taster. The recipe for populating a city, of which we have spoken, concentrates Negroes in public housing as in slums. Segregation is not entirely new, of course, but since 1954 it has become a more open insult. To the extent that public housing found its sites chiefly in land cleared for renewal, large areas were devoted exclusively to public housing (St. Louis is an example). To the extent that the growing suburbs successfully resisted public housing, they confined it to the city core. Meanwhile, as between 1935 and 1960, there was a greater proportion of Americans who had never experienced poverty personally or were trying to forget it. They contributed to a more critical, if not pious, public view of public housing. Thus, a conjunction of social and economic trends leads to the setting apart of families in public housing.

Public housing is faced with problems which go to the heart of its ability to remain solvent and shape the kind of housing, in the sense of total social and physical environment, that it is able to provide. Of a number of serious problems that are well known, perhaps the gravest is that public housing is not available to more than a small proportion of low-income families. From the minority who are admitted, there is a tendency to exclude those regarded as undesirable and those with the lowest incomes. Families with less than $1,500 income have half the chance of getting into public housing of those with $1,500 to $4,000.

Americans are often more attentive to the tempo and direction of a trend than to the underlying facts. Because we are preoccupied with the problems and movement of public housing, we may conceivably overlook the function it is performing. When they are asked, the majority of families who live in public housing say that they like it. They appreciate its facilities; their general morale is higher than it was in substandard housing.[14,15,16] One must, of course, take into account that those who would object most to public housing never enter it, or they leave.* Nevertheless, for those who take up tenancy, public housing represents a considerable improvement in physical surroundings. Moreover, the aspects of the environment which are offensive to some families may be secondary or even functional for others. Kurt W. Back finds that two types of people move into public housing, those who seek to use it as a vehicle for change and those who see it as an end in itself. Of the latter, he writes:

> In general, the tenants form the weaker and more vulnerable part of the [public housing] population. They have less income, less secure income, and are more likely to represent broken homes. In a very real way they need the protection afforded by government action, and many of them received some government aid. These people apparently look on government housing as a type of institutional support, which they need.[17]

Thus, public housing performs at least acceptably for those poor families who see it as an improved, somewhat protected environment. Presumably, it offers their children a better start than they might otherwise have had. Analysis of turnover statistics suggests that others use public housing as a way station to improved housing.[18] In this sense, too, public housing serves the prevention of poverty.

---

* The rate of moveouts, though it signals difficulty in some places, is not strikingly high compared with general population mobility. It is lower overall than the movement rate for rental housing insured by FHA.

Thus, strictly managed housing may suit one family – or at least not trouble it – and trouble others very much. Public housing is pressed, if it is going to serve families with any precision, to define its objectives and to alter policies to further these objectives. At least three choices are open : (1) A real estate operation for the respectable poor – the purely poor. (2) A rehabilitative program for the seriously dependent and troubled poor. (3) A greatly enlarged and altered program, at least in part deinstitutionalized, with a variety of kinds of housing opportunities. In the absence of a settled decision to seek the third course and of the legislation that would make it possible, local housing authorities are moving slowly, in most cases with pronounced reluctance, toward rehabilitative programs.* Under present circumstances the families who are entering public housing make such a course inevitable. Not only are the families isolated and segregated; increasing numbers are aged, many receive public assistance, and many are in broken families. They cannot be abandoned to their problems; they must be served. Moreover, when they are not served, buildings deteriorate, delinquencies occur, and deprived youngsters grow into disabled adults. It becomes plain that neglect is expensive.

Ambivalence about what course to take is reflected in the development of practices concerning the provision of health and social services. During most of its postwar third stage, public housing has been a real estate operation in theory if not in fact. Health and social services, except as they contributed directly to management, have been regarded by the Public Housing Administration as an inappropriate cost. At most, housing authorities might provide space to community agencies and employ staff members to direct tenants to appropriate community services. The rationale for this point of view has been clearly expressed by social welfare and housing organizations :

Public housing management is not equipped either by training, personnel, structure, or financing to assume full responsibility and direction of the social aspects of the program – nor would it be desirable to supplant the traditional reliance of management on public and voluntary organizations sustained by citizen support. United funds, community chests, welfare planning councils, public welfare agencies : these are the organizations through which the total community conscience is motivated and applied....[19]

The quotation implies another important argument for relying upon community services. That is, services offered internally might add to the degree of isolation that tenants feel.

This statement of principles was not intended simply to limit the services that public housing might offer. Rather, it was intended as an affirmation that would move public housing and community services at least to the point of full collaboration. There have been some encouraging demonstrations of what might be achieved by such a partnership.[20,21,22,23] But generally speaking, services have not been available – frequently not sought and, when sought, only sometimes provided. The principle of community provision of services offers only a temporary resting place and appearance of consensus. Those who wish to continue a real estate operation but perceive that they must take a new approach to new tenants, are hoping to do both at once. Those who perceive the need for a rehabilitative development see the opportunity to take a step forward.

The provision of direct services by public housing would, necessarily, raise the question whether the Federal subsidy is adequate to the current task of public housing. Generally speaking, the subsidy covers capital costs and debt service; operating cost must be met out of income. In effect, additional costs mean tenants must pay higher rent. Other considerations than providing health and social services suggest that the subsidy requires re-examination. We have noted, first, that management costs have risen more sharply than the income of tenants. Second, the lowest of the low-income families

---

* At one extreme, a rehabilitative program suggests therapeutic housing communities, planned to protect and teach families. Tried in a number of European countries, these smack of regimentation to Americans.

Though it may seem inconsistent with observations about management tendencies, distaste for excessive management responsibility is probably one factor that leads local authorities to resist the rehabilitative trend.

are finding it doubly hard to get into public housing. Third, almost half the families in public housing are paying 20 percent or more of their income for rent. Some are paying over 30 percent.[24] We have suggested that this is too much. Recent legislation provides a special additional subsidy for housing very low-income, aged persons. Thus, the problem has been recognized, but the problem is by no means limited to the aged.

Though less directly than public housing, to be sure, public assistance is the largest national program concerned with the housing needs of the poor. It is important, therefore, to ask about the quality of housing that assistance recipients secure and about the welfare department's influence upon it.

Although information about the quality of recipients' housing has not been systematically collected, it is clear that the quality is poor. Data about plumbing facilities in the following table suggest how the housing of recipients compares with that of the general population. It may not be surprising that assistance recipients, having the lowest incomes, are worse off than the average. However, it is an impressive figure that four out of ten aged recipients and three out of ten recipient families with dependent children manage without each of these basic facilities. One can guess at the proportions of their dwellings that are dilapidated and deteriorated. Measures of crowding suggest that over time assistance recipients are not improving

*Plumbing Facilities Available in 1960, to Total U.S. Population, to Recipients of Aid to Families with Dependent Children, and of Old Age Assistance*

|  | Total U.S. population, percent having | Aid to families with dependent children, percent of recipients having | Old-age assistance, percent of recipients having |
|---|---|---|---|
| Hot and cold running water inside structure | 87 | 70 | 60 |
| Exclusive use of a flush toilet | 87 | *72 | 59 |

* Includes a small number having a bath or shower but no flush toilet.

Sources: *1960 Census of Housing, Characteristics and Financial Circumstances of Recipients of Old-Age Assistance 1960,* and a national study of aid to families with dependent children.[25]

their housing at the same rate as the general population. In the decade from 1950 to 1960, the median number of persons per room in the AFDC household declined from 1.0 to 0.94. In the same period, the national median declined from 0.75 to 0.59. That the median number of persons per room in the AFDC household is now 0.94 means that almost half the families are crowded. One in five of the AFDC families are " critically overcrowded," living in households in which there are 1.5 persons or more per room.[26]

Special State and city studies provide a more intimate appraisal of the housing of public assistance recipients. Florida reviewed 13,000 cases of aid to families with dependent children to determine whether the homes were suitable for children. The study noted " excessively high rents for unspeakably inadequate slum homes."[27] A survey of recipient families with dependent children in the State of Maine found that four out of five did not have central heating. The report concludes:

> Over half [of AFDC families] do not have what most Americans take for granted: central heating and all three of the essential plumbing facilities; running water, bath, and exclusive use of a toilet. About a third ... are overcrowded and many others lack privacy because of a need to share a living arrangement with relatives and non-relatives.[28]

There are variations in the numbers and the degree of detachment with which other studies report. But the same basic situation has been documented for Chicago;[29,30,31] Atlanta;[32] Baltimore;[33] Washington, D.C.;[34] Philadelphia;[35] Westchester County, N.Y.;[36] and Alexandria, Va.[37] Occasionally a study inquires specifically into the housing of recipients who would have special difficulty in finding housing – for example, families with unmarried mothers. The findings are predictable. Of over 3,000 illegitimate children who were receiving AFDC, Cleveland reported that 10 percent were living in public housing. The remaining 90 percent lived in housing that was " overcrowded and substand.... The majority live in neighborhoods that are rooming house areas and slums."[38] A similar study in New York City found a quarter

of the married mothers and half of the unmarried mothers living in " rooming houses considered undesirable for family living."[39]

One has to ask how such conditions occur for
so many people in programs intended to maintain health and decency and to strengthen
family life. It goes without saying that, by the
nature of the problem that makes recipients of
them, some families are handicapped in finding
and maintaining decent housing. Old age, physical disability, and a broken marriage or no
marriage may each, in its own way, make a
family poor tenants. But there are simpler, more
powerful causes of the problem.

Fundamentally, the amount of money paid
to recipients of public assistance in most places
is not enough to pay for proper housing and
the other elements of a healthful and decent
budget. Payments under the Federal-State programs are, in all cases, based on an assessment
of actual need. In making the assessment and
determining the payment, however, a number
of policies and practices are interposed to reduce
the amount of assistance that is paid to a
family. First, the basic amounts allowed for
budget items are likely not to be realistically
related to costs. The cost of rent or mortgage
payments is not estimated in standard amounts
by States; it is budgeted in relation to the actual
payment.

Second, regardless of the amount of money
that States determine to be needed, they may
apply a maximum to the overall amount of the
payment.

We have already looked at the dilemma in
which the family with less than enough money
finds itself. In addition, recipients are more than
ordinarily likely to suffer [for housing purposes]
from being Negro, in broken families, and having several children. The fact of being a recipient may itself lead landlords to refuse to
rent. Less than enough money is, one might say,
sufficient handicap. The compounding of the
problem by other handicaps means that most
recipients will not find decent housing unless
they are somehow protected or aided. In fact,
welfare departments are moving to assist with
housing. Their motivations are several: the desperate circumstances of some recipients, the
patent exploitation of others, and the cost of

paying for hotels or institutional care simply
because reasonable housing cannot be found. In
general, three courses are open to welfare departments. They may provide counsel and other
aids to clients. They may turn to public housing for their recipients. They may ally themselves with other community forces to eliminate
substandard housing and superstandard charges
for it. Let us look at each of these possibilities.

Providing aid to recipients may be as simple
as counseling them about their housing and
suggesting where vacancies may be found. In
Cleveland, for example, special services were
provided to 600 AFDC families, including 180
who lived in " definitely substandard housing."
Within a year 119 had moved to better housing.[40] Departments that become deeply engaged
in improving recipients' housing tend to find
that the problem is too complex for social services alone. These departments establish units
which maintain contact with real estate agents
and landlords, develop special knowledge about
housing codes, and provide counseling as well.

The best of these programs represent a substantial service to recipients. At the same time,
they reflect the welfare department's view that
housing is not fundamentally its business. That
is, special units represent a device for responding to emergencies or outrageous situations.
They do not provide a continuing review of
recipients' housing. They usually do not help
the recipients whose situations are poor but
somehow short of desperate. We have noted one
reason for this approach: the welfare department's relationship is to its client and not to his
landlord. To be sure, the welfare department is
not barred from helping a recipient with his
housing. But its concern about quality is not
automatically aroused, as it would be if the
department dealt with the landlord.

Let us turn to the second course open to welfare departments – to arrange for recipients to
enter public housing. The proportion of recipients living in public housing has mounted
steadily; they are now about 25 percent of
tenant families.[41] The converse percentage is
more difficult to estimate; roughly, perhaps 7
percent of public assistance recipients live in
public housing. Obviously the policies of each
agency are important to the other.

Public housing and public assistance have much in common – their origin, in their present form, in the economic upheaval of the 1930's; their common purpose to assist the poor; and public skepticism about the methods and accomplishments of both. There are also differences between them. The same individual is a client of one agency and a tenant of the other. One may be more philosophical about a client's failure to pay rent than about a tenant's. The assistance agency sees itself as serving a range of family needs. The housing authority is more likely to see itself as providing a single commodity. The assistance agency is interested in finding housing for its clients, but the housing authority thinks of his effect on other tenants. Because of differences such as these a number of issues arise.

Perhaps the oldest, most prevalent issue concerns the rent that a public assistance recipient should pay. To pay according to his income, like those who do not receive assistance, would be meaningless for a recipient. The assistance he receives for rent is based on the amount he pays; the rent almost has to be established first. Public assistance agencies may want to pay little; they have many uses for every dollar. On the other hand, public housing authorities face difficulty in meeting their costs. They would want to be paid as much as possible. An agreement on principles, subscribed to by housing and welfare organizations, recommends that public assistance rentals should be high enough to cover the full operating costs of public housing (exclusive of debt service).[42] Public assistance recipients would pay more than most other tenant families. This may seem to some to take unfair advantage of assistance agencies. On the other hand, it represents recognition that shelter is a basic requirement and "public [assistance] funds must be made available in amounts that are realistically related to current costs of living."[43]

The issues that exist between public housing and public assistance are predictable byproducts of the convergence of two independent programs. The provision of more effective service by public assistance to its clients in public housing should assist in resolving these issues. But with or without issues, public housing is the one dependable resource to which public assistance may turn for acceptable housing for recipients. The help that it finds is limited chiefly because the quantity of public housing is limited.

The final course open in attempting to assist recipients is for welfare departments to ally themselves with other community forces to eliminate substandard housing and exorbitant rents. Though welfare departments are widely privy to violations of housing codes, they do not routinely press the appropriate municipal departments for enforcement. The studies of housing codes in Philadelphia and New York State that were touched upon earlier criticize welfare departments for failing to offer cooperation.[44] It is unlikely that the failure arises from a lack of concern. Whether they have wished to be involved in providing decent housing or not, it looms up as a major problem confronting welfare administrators. Moreover, with funds for assistance chronically short, it nags at one's nerves to know that a portion of the money that is available goes into the exchequers of profiteers. In their experience in reporting violations, however, welfare departments have discovered how little they can expect in the way of result. They discover, with a certain immediacy, the powerful forces that operate against code enforcement. Depending upon the local situation, they may abandon reporting violations entirely or report the more dramatic ones – but without hope or followup.

In the nature of the severity of the problem of enforcement, attempts to bring pressure on landlords, like attempts to counsel recipients, have been directed to the worst cases. There is no apparent alternative for welfare departments. But here we perceive still another effect of their lack of objective standards of housing quality: We know that assistance recipients live in squalor and are exploited. But so long as we do not know precisely how many, how squalid, and how costly, governments tend to seek remedies that deal only with what is visible.

Welfare departments face a heavy task if they are to develop devices for assuring decent housing more or less by themselves. In 1959, a Mayor's Committee of Inquiry in New York City commended the department of welfare for having performed "heroically" in the field of housing, though it did not have authority to use the resources of appropriate city departments. The Committee of Inquiry concluded that the responsibility was not properly located in the department of welfare. A municipal co-ordinator of housing was needed to direct the efforts of such departments as health, fire, housing and building, and welfare. The committee wrote:

> The City of New York must enter the situation to provide for safe and adequate housing so that no person within its limits is forced to live on a level below decent human standards.[45]

The committee states in organizational terms the point with which we set out in the introduction. Unless the policy of all city departments is shaped by a common purpose, charging one city department with the amelioration or prevention of poverty is unlikely to be effective. The illustration of confused purposes should not be left at the municipal level alone. As we have noted, the Federal Urban Renewal Administration requires evidence of enforcement of housing codes. And it is Federal money, in large quantities, that moves to States, to cities or counties, to welfare recipients, and in their turn to landlords who ignore housing codes.

How does public assistance serve in providing housing for poor people? It leaves many in poor housing and some in desperately poor housing. Basically, its failure is a failure to provide recipients with enough money to pay for decent housing. Because of this failure, public assistance is pressed to offer special aids and protection for its clients. These help, to some degree, but to larger degree are frustrated by limitations of available housing and inability to force legal maintenance of housing. Because public assistance has not historically regarded itself as a provider of housing, agencies may also fail to invest their fullest energies in the securing of housing.

Two old studies suggest the direction and pace with which public assistance has moved in relation to housing. A U.S. Children's Bureau study of Mother's Aid (a predecessor to AFDC) in ten representative communities in 1928 reports:

> Except in one large city, where housing conditions left much to be desired, the families were for the most part in decent, sanitary dwellings or flats in respectable neighborhoods; many were in comfortable one-family houses, and a considerable number had flower gardens. If families were found living in too congested quarters, under insanitary conditions, or in neighborhoods where morality was questionable, the courts required them – or the agencies persuaded them – to move to better locations.[46]

In 1940, the U.S. Housing Authority and the Social Security Board reviewed common areas of their programs. Among their conclusions:

> ... it is apparent that relief and public assistance families are inadequately housed.

> ... It is estimated that 50 to 90 percent of such families occupy the *worst* kind of shelter.

> ... Inadequate housing is related to inadequate income with but few exceptions.

> ... There are no *generally accepted* basic standards of the quantity and quality of housing considered a minimum essential for every family.[47]

So far as the housing of public assistance recipients is concerned, the direction between 1928 and 1940 was downward. The recommendations that followed from the findings of the 1940 study are obvious: adequate payments, applying objective standards to recipients' housing, regular reporting of the quality of recipients' housing, more public housing to use for assistance recipients. Prescriptions that were plain when the Social Security Act was new have yet to be acted upon.

### Can poor families be housed?

If one reflects upon the ways in which poor families pay for housing in their private lives and upon the ways in which public policies assist them, it is possible to perceive a discrepancy. The private and the public dimensions are out of balance. Poor people pay for housing as a total effort, out of their food and out of the fabric of their lives together. The effects of the struggle are experienced without Sabbath and without holiday. But public efforts to assist them are directed only to a minority. Out of those who are reached, many are helped meagerly, subject to conditions that may be relevant, irrelevant, or even self-defeating.

In public efforts to provide housing we have so far relied chiefly upon stimulation and subsidy of private industry. The results, for those with incomes over $5,000 or $6,000, have been respectable. Recent legislation attempts to extend the impact of such activity to lower incomes. The problem has so far appeared to be one of interesting builders and developers in such a market. It appears likely that some gains will be made. But it must be evident that the problem of the poor will not be met in this manner. We have referred to the reasons; they require only to be brought together.

First, though special incentives for low-income building and contraction of demand in the middle-income market may lead to more builder interest in low-cost housing than heretofore, it is unlikely that interest will reach down to the families with $2,500 incomes. High risks, limited profits, and other difficulties that have discouraged business from building for families with $5,000 incomes will seem insuperable at half those incomes.

Second, it is not unreasonable that builders and banks should take pause. A family of four with less than $2,500 income is not able to buy a house or pay a rent that provides a profit on it, no matter how low the interest rate on the mortgage. The family's income is not adequate to its need for food, clothing, and other necessary items – even if it were paying no rent at all.

Third, inducing low-income families to pay 25 or 30 percent of their incomes carries a heavy risk of its own and is not sound public policy. The housing that is bought at the expense of food or medical care is dearly bought.

This is not to say that we are unable to provide decent housing for all American families. Public housing and public assistance provide avenues for decent housing, providing that the serious limitations of these programs are corrected. Small-scale experiments of other sorts are being tried. A number involve public subsidy to those who provide housing for low-income families, with purchasers or tenants making such payments as they can afford. There has been recurrent consideration of the possibility of providing a direct subsidy to low-income families to be used for purchasing or renting standard housing. Such a proposal was considered by the Senate Subcommittee on Housing and Urban Redevelopment headed by Senator Robert A. Taft. Reporting in 1945, the subcommittee rejected direct subsidies, mainly because they might flow to substandard housing. There was also objection to channeling such funds through public assistance agencies. After more than a decade of experience with urban renewal, attention has been turning again to the possibility of providing a direct subsidy to poor families. A number of schemes have been put forward that provide protections against misuse; nor would subsidies necessarily be furnished through public assistance agencies.[48,49,50]

We can indeed shape a program that will provide "a decent home and a suitable living environment for every American family."[51] Such a program need not appear to be favoritism. On the contrary, aids that have so far been devised (income tax advantages, mortgage insurance) reach middle- and upper-income families with special effect. Resources and techniques are available to right the balance.

# Housing of low-income families

*THE EDITORS OF THE JOURNAL OF HOUSING*

The magnitude of the need for low-income housing assistance is in dramatic contrast to the past production of the public housing program. It is obvious that a national effort must be organized that will make a major impact on the total need. One of the key factors in achieving such a large-scale effort is a consistent commitment to low-income housing by public policy-makers and by all sectors of the private housing industry.

## Past production experience

Valuable insight can be gained by observing the place that the low-income housing effort has occupied in the total production effort of the past three decades. Public housing production has shown an extremely wide annual range since 1935, including a low of 1200 housing units in 1945 and a high of 86,000 housing units in the war year of 1941. Over the past five years, public housing (excluding Capehart housing for the armed forces) has averaged only 30,000 units annually. Public housing as a component of total residential construction has averaged only 2.8 percent since 1957. The full reflection of public housing's isolation from the main stream of housing effort is shown in Table 3, where the record of conventional private residential construction is contrasted with government-assisted programs under the Federal Housing Administration, the Veterans Administration, and the Public Housing Administration in five economic periods. Peak years for the conventional construction, FHA and VA pro-

grams were in the economic growth period of the 1950's; the peak year for public housing was during the defense housing build-up for World War II.

Public housing for low-income families has never been linked closely with national economic goals, with housing production goals, or with total housing market considerations. The primary rationale for determining public housing production has been the total number of substandard housing units in the national inventory. Thus, the 810,000 units authorized in the Housing Act of 1949 were scheduled for a six-year period and were aimed at making a considerable dent in the substandard housing inventory. Yet, the full amount of funds authorized in 1949 were not appropriated until 1961 and production under the 1949 authorization is some eight to nine years behind the original timetable. As noted above, the number of public housing units constructed has never been related to forces in the private housing market and in the total economy; rather, the volume of public housing units has depended on how many dwelling units congressional appropriations committees would approve, on a year-to-year basis.

Another factor that is a matter both of experience and import for the future is that the types of low-income families and their housing needs have changed since the 1930's. Such changes are to be expected as economic and social conditions change. Some reflection of this shift in the characteristics of low-income families is contained in the occupancy patterns of

*Reprinted from " Six Goals for a Program of Low-Income Housing," The Journal of Housing, vol. 20, No. 5 (May, 1963), pp. 259–265, with permission of the journal.*

## TABLE I
### Deficient Housing in the United States: 1960

| | |
|---|---|
| Total estimated population in deficient units* | 36,475,000 |
| Total population of the United States | 178,464,000 |
| Percent of population in deficient housing | 20 |

\* Estimated on the basis of the median size of households occupying the four categories of deficient housing.

| | |
|---|---|
| Total deficient housing units | 12,591,572 |
| Total housing units | 53,023,875 |
| Percent of total units deficient | 23 |

| | | Percent of total |
|---|---|---|
| Total deficient housing units *inside* standard metropolitan areas | 5,732,373 | 45 |
| Total deficient housing units *outside* standard metropolitan areas | 6,859,199 | 55 |
| Total deficient units | 12,591,572 | 100 |

#### Type of deficiency

| | Total units | Percent of total |
|---|---|---|
| Sound, lacking plumbing facilities | 3,379,784 | 27 |
| Deteriorating, with all plumbing facilities | 4,117,877 | 33 |
| Deteriorating, lacking plumbing facilities | 2,825,931 | 22 |
| Dilapidated | 2,267,980 | 18 |
| Total deficient units | 12,591,572 | 100 |

#### Housing deficiency and income

| Annual income, 1959** | Deficient units | Percent of total |
|---|---|---|
| Under $2000 | 4,924,460 | 39 |
| 2000–2999 | 1,814,987 | 14 |
| 3000–3999 | 1,576,081 | 12 |
| 4000–4999 | 1,345,056 | 11 |
| 5000–5999 | 1,058,988 | 9 |
| 6000 and over | 1,872,000 | 15 |
| Total deficient units | 12,591,572 | 100 |

\** Income of primary families and individuals.
Source: 1960 Census of Housing.

## TABLE 2
### Public Housing Production, United States: 1935–61

| | Thousands of dwelling units* | Percent of total housing starts | | Thousands of dwelling units* | Percent of total housing starts |
|---|---|---|---|---|---|
| 1935 | 5.3 | 2.4 | 1949 | 36.3 | 3.5 |
| 1936 | 14.8 | 4.6 | 1950 | 43.8 | 3.3 |
| 1937 | 3.6 | 1.1 | 1951 | 71.2 | 6.4 |
| 1938 | 6.7 | 1.7 | 1952 | 58.5 | 5.0 |
| 1939 | 56.6 | 11.0 | 1953 | 35.5 | 3.2 |
| 1940 | 73.0 | 12.1 | 1954 | 18.7 | 1.5 |
| 1941 | 86.6 | 12.3 | 1955 | 19.4 | 1.5 |
| 1942 | 54.8 | 15.4 | 1956 | 20.4 | 2.2 |
| 1943 | 7.3 | 3.8 | 1957 | 25.5 | 4.3 |
| 1944 | 3.1 | 2.2 | 1958 | 33.2 | 3.6 |
| 1945 | 1.2 | 0.6 | 1959 | 22.1 | 1.4 |
| 1946 | 8.0 | 1.2 | 1960 | 30.7 | 2.4 |
| 1947 | 3.4 | 0.4 | 1961 | 38.5 | 2.9 |
| 1948 | 18.1 | 1.9 | | | |

\*Exclusive of Capehart Housing, 1956–61.
Source: Housing and Home Finance Agency, *Housing Statistics,* Annual Data, April, 1962.

## TABLE 3

*Housing Production in Five Economic Periods, United States: 1935–61*
*(Average Annual Starts in Thousands of Dwelling Units)*

| | Conventional | Federal Housing Administration | Veterans Administration | Public Housing Administration |
|---|---|---|---|---|
| 1935–39—Depression | 261.9 | 80.0 | — | 17.4 |
| 1940–42—Defense build-up | 294.7 | 188.7 | — | 71.4 |
| 1943–45—War | 80.3 | 90.2 | 8.8* | 3.9 |
| 1946–49—Postwar | 510.1 | 239.0 | 103.5 | 16.5 |
| 1950–61—Growth economy | 734.9 | 277.1 | 175.5 | 34.8 |
| Peak year | 1959 | 1950 | 1955 | 1941 |
| Low year | 1943 | 1935 | 1945 | 1937 |

* One year only: 1945.
Source: Housing and Home Finance Agency, *Housing Statistics*, Annual Data, April, 1962.

the public housing program. A comparison of the characteristics of families in public housing occupancy over the ten-year period from 1952 to 1961 is shown in the several breakdowns of Table 4.

These tables reveal a number of significant trends on a nationwide basis:

*White* families in public housing occupancy are shifting from three- to four-person households, with heads in the 25 to 34 age group, to one- and two-person households, with the heads 65 years of age or older. There is a related shift in source of income from earned income to benefits provided by Social Security and private pensions.

*Negro* families in public housing occupancy have shown relatively less change in characteristics since 1952 than white families, although the number of large families of six persons or more has been increasing at the expense of the two- to three-person households. The median income of Negro families experienced a larger increase than income for white families in occupancy, reflecting, again, the change in characteristics of white families.

The median annual income of families in public housing occupancy between 1952 and 1961 increased by only 13 percent from $2124 to $2406.

The gross monthly rent in public housing increased by only 20 percent, from $35 to $42 per month, including utilities.

The significance of these trends can only be judged by viewing them in relationship to the changes that were taking place in the nation as a whole, particularly as such national shifts have affected the concept of what constitutes a low-income family under changed circumstances. A small indication of some of this relationship can be seen by noting that in the period when the median income of public housing households was increasing by 13 percent, the national median income gained by 44 percent, from $3467 to $5009. Average costs of private one-family houses constructed in nonfarm areas rose from $9475 in 1952 to $13,875 in 1961 – a gain of 46 percent. The economic ability of a family to locate satisfactory housing on the private housing market was changing at the same time that incomes were rising.

The result of all the shifts of the last decade is that the defining of low income in the 1960's (and in particular, the defining of the ability of a family to procure housing within its reach) needs to be carefully examined in terms of the types and characteristics of families who are most affected by lack of housing opportunity. The accommodation of the public housing program to the small-sized elderly household has, without question, identified one of the key areas of low-income housing need in the 1960's. There are indications, also, that the housing needs of the large low-income family of six persons or more is another area of prime need that is becoming increasingly acute and pressing for solution. The identification of the types of low-income families needing housing assistance in the 1960's has complex facets related to the size of family and its economic and social status.

Again, the 1960 census of housing can yield

# TABLE 4
## A Comparison of Federally-aided Public Housing – 1952 and 1961

|  | 1952 | 1961 |
|---|---|---|
| Families re-examined | 167,283 | 403,500 |
| Percent white families | 59 | 49 |
| Percent Negro and other | 41 | 51 |
| Percent servicemen and veterans | 34 | 28 |

### Characteristics of families living in federally–aided public housing—1952 and 1961

#### 1—Household size: Percent of total families

| Persons | White 1952 | White 1961 | Negro and other 1952 | Negro and other 1961 | Total 1952 | Total 1961 |
|---|---|---|---|---|---|---|
| 1 | 4 | 17 | 2 | 8 | 3 | 12 |
| 2 | 23 | 22 | 23 | 16 | 23 | 19 |
| 3 | 21 | 15 | 21 | 16 | 21 | 15 |
| 4 | 22 | 15 | 19 | 17 | 21 | 17 |
| 5 | 15 | 12 | 15 | 15 | 15 | 13 |
| 6+ | 15 | 19 | 20 | 28 | 17 | 14 |
| Median household size | 3.79 | 3.56 | 4.02 | 4.40 | 3.89 | 4.00 |

#### 2—Age of family head: Percent of total families

|  | White 1952 | White 1961 | Negro and other 1952 | Negro and other 1961 | Total 1952 | Total 1961 |
|---|---|---|---|---|---|---|
| Under 25 | 8 | 7 | 8 | 8 | 8 | 8 |
| 25–34 | 31 | 22 | 35 | 34 | 33 | 28 |
| 35–44 | 27 | 21 | 29 | 27 | 28 | 24 |
| 45–54 | 14 | 14 | 15 | 13 | 14 | 14 |
| 55–64 | 8 | 10 | 7 | 8 | 7 | 9 |
| 65+ | 12 | 26 | 6 | 10 | 10 | 18 |
| Median Age | 39.1 | 44.7 | 37.6 | 38.1 | 38.5 | 40.9 |

#### 3—Number of Minors: Percent of total families

|  | White 1952 | White 1961 | Negro and other 1952 | Negro and other 1961 | Total 1952 | Total 1961 |
|---|---|---|---|---|---|---|
| None | 21 | 35 | 18 | 17 | 20 | 27 |
| 1 | 21 | 14 | 22 | 15 | 21 | 15 |
| 2 | 24 | 16 | 21 | 18 | 23 | 17 |
| 3 | 17 | 14 | 16 | 17 | 17 | 15 |
| 4 | 9 | 9 | 10 | 11 | 10 | 11 |
| 5+ | 8 | 12 | 12 | 20 | 9 | 15 |
| Median no. of minors | 2.02 | 1.91 | 2.24 | 2.75 | 2.11 | 2.34 |

#### 4—Number of Adults: Percent of total families

|  | White 1952 | White 1961 | Negro and other 1952 | Negro and other 1961 | Total 1952 | Total 1961 |
|---|---|---|---|---|---|---|
| 1 Adult | 27 | 38 | 29 | 39 | 28 | 39 |
| No minors | — | 17 | — | 8 | — | 12 |
| with minors | — | 21 | — | 31 | — | 27 |
| 2+ Adults | 73 | 62 | 71 | 61 | 72 | 61 |

#### 5—Source of income: Percent of total families

|  | White 1952 | White 1961 | Negro and other 1952 | Negro and other 1961 | Total 1952 | Total 1961 |
|---|---|---|---|---|---|---|
| No assistance or benefits— | 68 | 48 | 74 | 59 | 71 | 54 |
| Benefits only— | 13 | 27 | 6 | 13 | 10 | 19 |
| Assistance with or without benefits | 19 | 25 | 20 | 28 | 19 | 27 |

#### 6—Anticipated annual income**: Percent of total families

|  | White 1952 | White 1961 | Negro and other 1952 | Negro and other 1961 | Total 1952 | Total 1961 |
|---|---|---|---|---|---|---|
| Under $1000 | 10 | 10 | 11 | 6 | 10 | 8 |
| 1000–1999 | 32 | 31 | 40 | 29 | 35 | 29 |
| 2000–2999 | 31 | 25 | 32 | 31 | 32 | 28 |
| 3000–3999 | 19 | 17 | 13 | 20 | 17 | 19 |
| 4000–4999 | 8* | 10 | 4* | 10 | 6* | 10 |
| 5000–5999 | — | 5 | — | 4 | — | 5 |
| 6000+ | — | 2 | — | 2 | — | 1 |
| Median income | $2252 | $2317 | $1965 | $2472 | $2124 | $2406 |

*Indicates total percentage over $4000.
**Definition of family income was slightly different in 1952 and 1961.

#### 7—Median annual income by family size**

| Persons | White 1952 | White 1961 | Negro and other 1952 | Negro and other 1961 | Total 1952 | Total 1961 |
|---|---|---|---|---|---|---|
| 1 | — | — | — | — | $ 847 | $1083 |
| 2 | — | — | — | — | 1432 | 1815 |
| 3 | — | — | — | — | 2002 | 2360 |
| 4 | — | — | — | — | 2376 | 2713 |
| 5 | — | — | — | — | 2588 | 2966 |
| 6+ | — | — | — | — | 2747 | 3259 |

** Definition of family income was slightly different in 1952 and 1961.

#### 8—Gross monthly rent: Percent of total families

|  | White 1952 | White 1961 | Negro and other 1952 | Negro and other 1961 | Total 1952 | Total 1961 |
|---|---|---|---|---|---|---|
| Under $20 | 10 | 3 | 15 | 3 | 12 | 3 |
| 20–29.99 | 22 | 21 | 25 | 18 | 23 | 19 |
| 30–39.99 | 25 | 23 | 28 | 21 | 26 | 23 |
| 40–49.99 | 24 | 20 | 19 | 20 | 22 | 19 |
| 50–59.99 | 19* | 13 | 13* | 15 | 17* | 15 |
| 60–69.99 | — | 11 | — | 15 | — | 13 |
| 70+ | — | 8 | — | 8 | — | 8 |
| Median | $37 | $41 | $33 | $44 | $35 | $42 |

* Indicated total percentage over $50.

Source: Report 225.1, *Families in Low-Rent Housing*, "Families Re-examined during Calendar Years 1952 and 1961"; Statistics Branch, Program Planning Division, Public Housing Administration.

some meaningful insights through examination of data on the concentration of low-income families living in deficient housing by income group and household size. Table 5 shows that almost half of the households with incomes under $2000 live in deficient housing but, also,

### TABLE 5
*Concentration of Deficient Housing,*
*United States: 1960*

| | Number of households | Percent in deficient housing |
|---|---|---|
| *By Income* | | |
| Under $2000 | 10,071,920 | 49 |
| 2000–2999 | 4,729,952 | 40 |
| 3000–3999 | 5,090,040 | 31 |
| 4000–4999 | 5,631,544 | 24 |
| 5000–5999 | 6,049,493 | 17 |
| 6000 or more | 21,450,926 | 8 |
| Total households | 53,023,875 | 23 |
| *By household size* | | |
| 1 person | 7,074,971 | 36 |
| 2 persons | 14,858,746 | 20 |
| 3 persons | 10,007,178 | 19 |
| 4 persons | 9,130,447 | 17 |
| 5 persons | 5,878,067 | 21 |
| 6 persons or more | 6,074,466 | 36 |
| Total households | 53,023,875 | 23 |

Source: 1960 Census of Housing.

that significant proportions (24 percent and 17 percent) of households in the income groups from $4000 to $6000 occupy such housing. Again, the census tables reveal that while 36 percent of one-person households live in deficient housing, an identical percentage of households of six persons or more occupy such housing.

Even the comprehensive 1960 census of housing does not contain published data that shows the interrelationships of income, household characteristics, employment, health, and educational status that would yield meaningful guides for a large-scale low-income housing effort. Some of this data could be made available through special cross-tabulations of information from the housing and population census: a meaningful first step. But, even beyond this, the understanding of the most effective kind of housing assistance for low-income families in the 1960's involves more than the collection and analysis of statistical data. It involves an intelligent effort to match statistically-defined need with effective programs that will assist a variety of types of low-income families and will encourage initiative among families themselves to achieve the most adequate housing within their reach.

# The dreary deadlock of public housing

*CATHERINE BAUER WURSTER*

Low-rent public housing has not followed the normal pattern for reform movements in modern democratic countries. Every social experiment starts off as an abstract idea, frequently in an atmosphere of violent theoretical debate. But after it has been tried out for a while, one of two things usually happens. Either it dies off, an acknowledged failure, or it "takes" and is accepted as an integral part of the ordinary scheme of things. The original theories, meantime, become modified and adapted to actual conditions. In the United States, public attitudes about social security, collective bargaining, and national economic controls have all

*Reprinted from* Architectural Forum, *vol. 106, No. 5 (May, 1957), pp. 140–142, 219, 221, with permission of the journal and author.*

followed the classic steps outlined years ago by George Bernard Shaw: (1) it's impossible; (2) it's against the Bible; (3) it's too expensive; and (4) we knew it all the time. But public housing, after more than two decades, still drags along in a kind of limbo, continuously controversial, not dead but never more than half alive.

No obituary is yet in order for the U.S. Housing Act of 1937 " as successively [but only in minor respects] amended." It is more a case of premature ossification. The bare bones of oversimplified New Deal theory have never been decently covered with the solid flesh of present-day reality. Even among public housing's most tireless defenders, many would welcome a fresh start if they did not fear that in the process any program at all might get lost.

If the dreary deadlock is to be broken, it is first necessary to figure out what really ails the program. If it is purely a matter of selfish reactionary obstruction, we who want to rehouse slum-dwellers will just have to go on fighting until we win. But if there are inner weaknesses as well, it is high time we faced up to them.

Unquestionably private builders, lenders, and property owners have been increasing in political power ever since the mid-thirties, when Uncle Sam rescued them from ruin. And it is equally obvious that they have been all-out in their opposition to public housing.

In general, however, their tactics have been so arrogant, and most of their claims so wild, that they have often tended to backfire. In recent years, moreover, some of the National Association of Real Estate Boards' allies (notably the National Association of Home Builders) have become more sophisticated about the slum problem, and highly vocal about the need to remedy it. The current slogans are " renewal " and " rehabilitation." But gradually it becomes clearer that Operation Fix-Up is no cure-all, and that outright clearance and redevelopment bring relocation problems that cannot be glossed over. The great national spread of anti-slum propaganda by ACTION (The American Council to Improve Our Neighborhoods) probably tends to favor the cause of public housing, however inadvertently.

The most serious effect of all the controversy has been more subtle. Public housing officials,

Federal and local, have been kept continuously on the defensive, and the neuroses that come from chronic fright and insecurity are translated into excessive caution, administrative rigidity, and lack of creative initiatve. Everybody tends to sit tight, clinging desperately to the beleaguered formula, instead of trying to improve it in the light of experience and public attitudes. Sporadic efforts to broaden or modify the program have usually met with as much opposition from professional public housers as from opponents of public housing. Moreover, the hostility has probably tightened management controls, making " project " housing more and more institutional.

But even so, despite the millions they have spent in a vain effort to kill it, the real estate interests can hardly be held wholly responsible for the program's failure to take hold.

## Solid support is lacking

If the public housing program in its present form had managed to achieve real popularity with the general run of ordinary citizens and their leaders, and above all with the people who live in slum and blighted areas, the real estate opposition would by now have lost its political force. The idea of public housing would be taken for granted, like old-age pensions or FHA mortgage insurance.

But this has not happened. The program has never called forth the kind of pervasive and persuasive popular support that oils the wheels of change in democratic countries. The lot of public housing tenants has undoubtedly been improved in many ways. But the fact remains that only a small proportion of the people eligible for occupancy (by legal definition, low-income families living in substandard homes) actually apply for low-rent dwellings in public housing projects. And of those who do, most appear to be desperate for shelter of any kind: minority families about to be thrown on the street by clearance operations, " problem " families sent by welfare agencies, and so on.

Moreover, general local support by civic-minded groups, such as one might reasonably have expected for such a program, has seldom developed. The United States Housing Act has been kept alive by the earnest annual efforts of the Washington offices of national labor, welfare, veteran, municipal, civic and religious organizations, held together by the National Housing Conference and sparked by the genius and devotion of its executive vice president, Lee Johnson. But despite considerable prodding, the local branches and members of these organizations have on the whole been apathetic, sometimes lending their names in a crisis but rarely showing much continuing interest. Where there are established citizens' housing organizations, they tend to be kept gong by a few devoted individuals with little general backing.

### Why isn't the program popular?

This question has never been seriously investigated, but in general terms, the answer seems quite clear. Life in the usual public housing project just is not the way most American families want to live. Nor does it reflect our accepted values as to the way people should live.

In part the weaknesses are inherent in the physical design. As architect Henry Whitney said in the first (and still one of the best) critiques by an experienced housing official:

> The typical publicly subsidized dwelling is deficient in interior space, in outdoor privacy, and in true American residential character. ... Families with children generally want to live in individual homes.... A yard, a porch or a terrace is almost universally desired.

While everybody who had any choice was moving into a one-story home, the housing authorities were busily erecting high-density high-rise apartments, with no private outdoor space whatever. Significantly, perhaps, public housing is most accepted in the one American city where apartment living is also most taken for granted – New York. But even there, opinion surveys show that most tenants would prefer ground-level living if they could get it.

There are also more subtle social reasons for the lack of enthusiastic acceptance. Public housing projects tend to be very largely and highly standardized in their design. Visually they may

be no more monotonous than a typical suburban tract, but their density makes them seem much more institutional, like veterans' hospitals or old-fashioned orphan asylums. The fact that they are usually designed as islands – " community units " turning their backs to the surrounding neighborhood which looks entirely different – only adds to this institutional quality. Any charity stigma that attaches to subsidized housing is thus reinforced. Each project proclaims, visually, that it serves the " lowest income group."

The resulting degree of rigid social segregation is difficult to align with traditional American ideas. And in addition, if a tenant manages to increase his income beyond a certain point, out he goes, a restriction which also results in the continuous loss of natural leadership among the tenants themselves, and a trend toward problem families as the permanent core of occupants.

On the other side of the ledger has been the considerable success of nondiscrimination and mixed racial occupancy in northern public housing projects. But even this great gain is being lost. Owing to the preponderance of minority families in the lowest income group, and in the areas slated for clearance and relocation, the proportion of minority occupancy tends to rise above the line where mixture is successful, and more and more projects become virtually all-Negro.

And finally, there is the question of management policy and practice in itself. Because of legal requirements, high densities, problem families and sensitivity to continuous political attack, local authority landlordship tends to be rigid and heavy-handed, with all kinds of rules and regulations unknown in ordinary private rental management and unthinkable in a pattern of individual ownership. Sometimes special welfare services are provided which, under these peculiar conditions, may be admirable and necessary. But even at its best, this type of concern by one's landlord seems paternalistic in American terms, and hardly adds to the popularity of project living for normal families.

These are the issues that keep coming up in critical analyses by housers, in conversations with all kinds of people all over the country, and in the few random studies by social scientists. And alongside these criticisms is the patent fact that, with all its drawbacks, the program is so expensive. I doubt that the fact of subsidy in itself is very important in the general public reaction, or in any stigma that may attach to public housing occupancy at present. With all their profound and well-justified faith in private enterprise, Americans have never been purists in the matter of accepting public aid where necessary to achieve something they want. The idea of subsidy is part of the American system, whether for shipping or public education, irrigation projects, redevelopment schemes or housing. Had we not enjoyed a steadily rising market, the FHA-VA system of mortgage aid would have cost the taxpayers far more than the most tremendous public housing program ever envisioned. And certainly no stigma attached to accepting the costly aid of HOLC [Home Owners Loan Corporation, created in 1933 by the Home Owners Refinancing Act to refinance home mortgage debts for nonfarm owners]. But subsidies must look reasonably sensible in terms of value received. And the fact that high-rise apartments (which no one likes very much anyway), erected by local housing authorities, tend to cost more than the price of a modest FHA-insured tract house, even allowing for a substantial speculative profit, just does not look sensible on the face of it. So the unattractive aspects of the program cannot even be justified on the grounds of economy.

And finally, with all the hullabaloo and all the expense, the program still does not meet even the most obvious immediate need of families displaced by clearance or renewal operations, let alone the need in outlying areas for families whom FHA cannot serve. The legal income limits are so low and the other limitations so rigorous, including the territorial jurisdiction of municipal housing authorities, that only a small portion of the need can be met through public housing aid.

## Premises: true or false?

How do the assumptions that shaped the public housing program stand up today under quite different economic conditions and in the light of more than twenty years of experience?

Clearly the basic premises are as sound today as they were then. Even after a long period of high prosperity, there are just about as many insanitary, congested and dilapidated homes in the United States as there were in the middle of the Depression – probably with more people living in them! And today almost everyone recognizes their existence, and admits that these conditions must somehow be remedied. It is also as true as ever (if more reluctantly recognized) that you cannot get rid of slums just by tearing them down, or fixing them up. Somewhere, in reasonably suitable location, there must be better homes available to the slum occupants, at prices they can afford to pay. And although prosperity, FHA, VA and more efficient homebuilding techniques have expanded the effective market for new private housing, it is still true that practically no slum dwellers can afford new, privately-built homes, and the few who can are often minority families who would not be accepted. There is some "filtering up" [moving from one rental or housing category into a slightly higher one when income permits and better accommodations are available] now that the postwar shortage at middle and upper price levels has been relieved. And if there were no vast backlog of outright slums, and little or no urban growth, and no racial discrimination, then a strong program of enforcement and rehabilitation might actually do the job of housing low-income families adequately. But the situation is far different. Millions of existing slum dwellings should be torn down as soon as possible; millions of additional low-income families are certain to migrate to urban centers (a large proportion of them Negroes). And in the light of this, how can filtration possibly be expected to solve the slum problem, now or in a thousand years! Even a slight stepping-up of the process, if it is not merely to produce a lot of new slums by stuffing several families into a dwelling intended for one, would mean a rate of devaluating decent older property that would disrupt the real estate market more than any amount of public housing. FHA financing, also, is geared to steady or rising values for the life of the house, not a reduction in monthly payments that would permit it to "filter down," however gradually.

Apparently it is still as true as it ever was that we need some new housing within reach of families now outside the effective private market. Prosperity only makes the continuance of slum living conditions less excusable, the need for effective solutions more urgent. And the rising significance of the racial aspects of the housing problem adds to the urgency. So does the relocation problem growing from the desire to revitalize central blighted areas and from the tremendous displacement of homes for freeways and other public works.

The basic problem we tried to tackle in the United States Housing Act is still with us. What was wrong with our efforts to solve it?

In the light of 1957 conditions, it now seems there were two fundamental fallacies in the original approach, one a matter of basic policy formulation and administration, the other a matter of physical planning and design. The 1937 approach was natural, valid, and even necessary at the time, and it represented progress in relation to what had gone before. But it jelled too soon, became too rigid, without allowing for flexible adaptation to American values and conditions.

The most questionable assumption was the notion that slum rehousing should be established permanently as an independent program, with its own separate legislation and administrative machinery at both Federal and local levels, quite apart from other housing policies and the overall housing picture. This insured the segregation of the low-income slum-dweller, and fortified his isolation as a special charity case by permitting only public initiative and public landlordship, with narrow rules of eligibility, for any form of subsidized housing that might be needed. This also contributed to the segregation of upper-income families in FHA schemes, and to that lily-white suburbia that now presents such a critical problem. And it is just as much public housing's responsibility as the National Association of Home Builders that there is such a vast gap between the two narrow, entirely separate types of Federal housing policy, with no real responsibility at any level of govenment to determine overall housing

needs – whether on a national basis or for any given community – and to see that policies are adjusted to meet those needs.

This came about because Federal housing aids were all initiated on an *ad hoc* emergency basis during the Depression, with little thought for long-term needs or goals. But Depression-mindedness continued too long : it was a fallacious element in much postwar planning, particularly housing. Vested interests grew up and were institutionalized around each separate fragmentary program, with the result that all three groups – lenders, builders, and public housers – have been about equally opposed to the kind of coordination that would permit more flexibility and realism in meeting the full range of local needs.

Similarly, while the early crusade on behalf of local initiative and responsibility was fine, and the establishment of local housing authorities (or something of the kind) was a necessary step, their permanent role should never have been defined and jelled so narrowly. We now have a proliferation of special-purpose local agencies concerned with slums and housing, with no responsibility anywhere to view the housing picture as a whole, least of all at the metropolitan level where this is most essential. The result is a few expensive, high-density, over-controlled municipal projects, mostly on central sites, and a vast chaotic flood of middle-class individual homes in the suburbs. With all our complicated housing machinery we cannot solve either the relocation problem in central areas or the equally urgent problem of balanced development out on the fringe.

Viewed in retrospect, it would have been worthwhile, for the sake of better integrated, more flexible tools, to make some real concessions. Not the principle of subsidy, for this is absolutely essential to any solution of the slum problem. But if necessary, public landlordship might have been given up and in any case it should have been possible to subsidize various forms of private housing enterprise, including suburban tracts for individual ownership, in order to meet a wider range of need and popular desire (and, incidentally, to bring some private building interests over to advocacy of public housing).

## Misapplied " community planning "

Having established machinery that could only produce a type of residential development quite alien to any American ideal of community, we then proceeded to dramatize this extreme form of paternalistic class-segregation architecturally, in the name of " modern community planning."

The basic ideas that stemmed from the British garden city planners, and were rationalized by the Bauhaus school of modern architects, contributed vital concepts to American housing. [The Bauhaus school was established in Weimar, Germany, in 1918 by Walter Gropius to create a functional experimental architecture utilizing all the resources of art, science, and technology. Long under academic and political pressure it was closed by the Nazis in 1933. – Ed.] The reaction against chaotic individualism and the wasteful crudity of the ubiquitous gridiron street pattern was long overdue. But in grasping for modern principles of large-scale community design, we embraced too wholeheartedly functionalist and collectivist architectural theories that tended to ignore certain subtler esthetic values and basic social needs. To experiment in this direction was healthy and necessary. The mistake, again, was to jell both policy and practice in rigid formulas that prevented further experimentation to adapt and humanize these principles in suitable terms for the American scene.

The public housing project therefore continues to be laid out as a " community unit," as large as possible and entirely divorced from its neighborhood surroundings, even though this only dramatizes the segregation of charity-case families. Standardization is emphasized rather than alleviated in project design, as a glorification of efficient production methods and an expression of the goal of " decent, safe and sanitary " housing for all. But the bleak symbols of productive efficiency and " minimum standards " are hardly an adequate or satisfactory expression of the values associated with American home life. And all this is, in addition, often embodied in the skyscraper, whose refined technology gladdens the hearts of technocratic architectural sculptors but pushes its

occupants into a highly organized, beehive type of community life for which most American families have no desire and little aptitude.

There is no room in such schemes for individual deviation, for personal initiative and responsibility, for outdoor freedom and privacy, for the type of small-scale business enterprise that plays such an important social role in most slum areas. Management domination is built in a necessary corollary of architectural form.

A fresh start is badly needed to bring this frustrated effort to effective maturity. And the time may at last be ripe. Until recently there were only a few lonely critics within the ranks of the " housers " themselves. But now some local housing authorities are beginning to question the old formulas. The big push for redevelopment and renewal has also performed an important service in forcing all kinds of civic groups and agencies, including real estate interests and local housing authorities, to face up to hitherto insoluble problems and get together to find solutions. In some areas local and metropolitan planning agencies are beginning to assume some responsibility for determining overall housing needs, and for fitting the bits and pieces of Federal aid and private and public initiative together. In several cities, the mayors have appointed housing coordinators for this purpose. And alongside central redevelopment, a new issue is just coming over the horizon officially in fast-growing regions such as California : how to encourage better balanced communities with a wider variety of homes in the fringe areas, to meet the needs of the lower-income and minority families who are more and more likely to find their employment in outlying plants and offices.

All this broader-based civic effort and sharper awareness tends to make the weaknesses in narrow, overcompartmentalized Federal housing policy more apparent. Sooner or later there will be a grass-roots demand for greater flexibility and better coordination, strong enough to overcome the special-interest lobbies, each trying to maintain its own little preserve. And this is the only effective and healthy way to bring about the necessary changes. For it is only when cities and metropolitan areas know what they need and want in terms of Federal housing aid that greater flexibility will be justified.

It is not a matter of substituting a new legal-administrative formula for the old one. Under certain conditions the old formula is still the best answer, perhaps the only possible solution. But what is primarily needed, not only for low-income slum dwellers and minority groups but for the great mass of middle-income families in all their infinite variety of taste and need, is more choice in location, dwelling type and neighborhood character. The kind of home best suited to a given American family can never be decided by officials. Their highest responsibility, rather, is to make sure that public policies keep the " effective market " broad enough to provide some real selection at all economic and social levels.

Freedom and flexibility are probably the hardest things to achieve with public policy. But a country that can devise the insured mortgage (in all its different forms), Fannie May [Federal National Mortgage Association], the modernization loan, the annual contribution, the local authority bond, redevelopment and renewal grants, and ingenious methods for local governments to contribute their share, should certainly be able to find some way to make these excellent tools work more freely and more effectively.

### The Wurster proposal:
### begin a Federal/local pilot program

A great many communities are not prepared to take on the job of deciding what their overall housing needs are, or how they might best be met. But some are, or would be in short order if they thought they had half a chance to guide their own housing destinies with sympathetic Federal support. It should be prime national policy to encourage these progressive communities as an example for the rest.

Therefore I propose that the HHFA [Housing and Home Finance Agency] be empowered to initiate a pilot program, in cooperation with qualified communities, to tackle housing problems on an experimental basis, subject to local guidance rather than to establish Federal policies and procedures.

The qualifications for local participation would be: (1) the existence of a thorough over-all analysis of housing needs and the current housing market; (2) the existence of a comprehensive, general, long-term plan for the physical development and redevelopment of the community, advanced enough in preparation so that the main outlines are clear, widely understood and officially accepted; (3) any proposal for Federal aid – whether for public or private housing, rehabilitation, land acquisition, community facilities, or whatnot – to be clearly justified by the housing study and related to the local plan.

Under such conditions HHFA would be empowered to make available any of the forms of assistance administered by its agencies – mortgage insurance, mortgage purchase, yield insurance or other devices for attracting capital, as well as direct loans, annual contributions and grants – subject only to controls for insuring that the desired ends are achieved with reasonable efficiency and economy. In short, performance standards.

Experimental projects, instead of being turned down on principle, would be favored in such a program, particularly in cases where Federal aid might help initiate programs which could later be expected to continue, if successful, without any special Federal assistance. Cooperatives, self-help projects, housing for minority families or mixed groups, housing suitable for old people, might fall in this category.

Such a program would be worth trying, even as a strictly administrative experiment within the framework of existing legislation. All our housing laws are much more flexible on paper than they have ever been in practice.

Ideally, however, this pilot program would be initiated under special authority from Congress, with maximum freedom within a limited period and a total expenditure, and with instructions to make a detailed report later.

# Housing and slum clearance: elusive goals

*WILLIAM G. GRIGSBY*

The general antagonism toward and conflict over housing goals and programs for low-income families have led many observers to conclude that elimination of substandard housing in the near future is both politically and financially impossible and that reliance must be placed on a continuation of the progress of the 1950's to eliminate the problem gradually over a period of three or four decades.

It is not necessary, however, to wait so long. There are already in existence several programs which have found acceptance as devices to help middle-income families and which in combination could bring the cost of housing within reach of the low-income population at very little public expense. These include tax abatement, mortgage loans at below-market rates but above the cost of borrowing to government, and the Title I write-down provision of the Act of 1949. To implement them would require very little change in existing legislation. The major barrier seems to be the extremely inadequate data regarding the occupants of substandard accommodations. It is not known how many of these families have serious problems other than housing and, hence, how many can or cannot be helped through particular housing programs.

In fact, almost fifteen years after the passage of the federal legislation, there still has not been a single study which explores this question in order to determine the specific programs and public expenditures necessary to bring the housing inventory and residential environment up to an acceptable level.

Without this information on costs and possible consequences, it is difficult to defend a given set of priorities or programs. For example, although the drift away from the legislative intent of the Housing Act of 1949 has been opportunistic, it is conceivable that this departure either will bring about the realization of housing goals sooner than would otherwise be the case or will facilitate the achievement of national objectives of higher priority. Regardless of the position taken in this matter, however, it is time to re-evaluate national housing and renewal goals with respect to the low-income population and to develop new methods to facilitate implementation of these goals at the local level. The Housing Act of 1949 and subsequent amendments have created an admirable mechanism for demolishing slum housing; they have not produced an instrument that assures the replacement of these structures with decent living accommodations.

## Middle-income housing

One of the most controversial issues in housing and residential renewal concerns programs for families whose incomes are too high to qualify them for public projects but too low to permit them to purchase or rent new homes. Various approaches have been tried to enable a larger proportion of this group to be served by the home-building industry. All of the plans provide for some form of direct or indirect subsidy, such as tax abatement or mortgage loans

*Reprinted from* The Annals of the American Academy of Political and Social Science, *Philadelphia vol. 352 (March, 1964), pp. 111–114, with permission of the publisher.*

at below-market interest rates, not requiring a cash supplement by the sponsoring agency or public construction and ownership of housing developments.

The issue concerning middle-income housing is only partly a conflict over ends and means. It stems also from the lack of a more precise definition of middle-income families and from differing interpretations of the same statistics. The definitional problem will be examined first.

The conventional description of the middle-income housing problem in terms of the families unserved by either new private construction at the one end of the scale or public accommodations at the other implies that the housing needs of all of the population except this in-between segment are already being met. Actually, however, public housing supplies very little low-cost shelter relative to the total need – half a million units as compared with 5,000,000 families in substandard quarters. Thus, there is perhaps nothing to distinguish the middle- from the low-income housing problem unless perhaps it is that the former is much less severe.

This possibility highlights the fact that the conventional definition tends to confuse objectives. Within the broad classification of middle income, there are actually two analytically distinct groups. Members of the first cannot afford *new* homes or apartments but do have the resources to acquire *decent* housing. Members of the second cannot afford either new or decent accommodations and, in addition, are not eligible for public units. Housing assistance for the second group could probably be justified on purely humanitarian grounds, assuming that some form of subsidy other than housing was not preferred. Aid for the slightly more affluent families, however, would seem warranted only if it could be demonstrated that total housing production was completely inadequate and also that it was politically impossible to raise levels of construction by providing equivalent assistance to lower-income families who actually needed it. For, certainly, any housing subsidy which is suitable for a group that already has adequate shelter is even more appropriate for many families with greater need for assistance if provided in larger doses. If

3.5 percent mortgage loans and 50 percent tax abatements are deemed necessary for the one group, then surely 2 percent loans and complete tax exemption are justified for the other. The argument against this view is that the lesser subsidies are, in effect, costless, but there is no equity in arbitrarily limiting aid to forms and amounts that require no out-of-pocket costs or absolute losses in ratables by the local community.

Moreover, any subsidy for the entire middle-income range constitutes an admission that the home-building industry has failed to meet the shelter requirements of an extremely large segment of our society. Not all analysts are yet ready to concede that over one-half of the population must receive a subsidy from government if the nation is to be adequately housed. If, however, the point has indeed been reached where such a huge proportion of the families in the United States must be given special assistance to solve national housing problems, separate programs for middle-income groups will no longer suffice. It will be necessary to institute basic changes in federal housing policy and to develop mechanisms for applying assistance equally across the board to all families.

The arguments have been rejected both in federal legislation and in housing programs of a few states. The distinction between adequately and inadequately housed middle-income families is not made, possibly because all available statistics indicate that only a very small proportion of middle-income families do have a pressing shelter problem. It is simply asserted that the middle-income group, as defined, is so large and the proportion of the total population served by new construction so small that special housing assistance programs to fill this gap are urgently needed.[1] Within this framework, the most critical question, therefore, is a statistical one. Is it really true that prices and rents of new construction are so high relative to family income that home builders are able to serve only a small proportion of the population?

Most statistics seem to suggest that this is in fact the situation. For example, one recent study of ten metropolitan areas representing all geographical sections of the United States concluded that, in the single-family home market in seven of the areas and in the rental market in all of the areas, less than one-half of the families had incomes sufficient to acquire a new dwelling unit.[2]

Since these figures and others like them have been used to demonstrate the necessity for a middle-income housing program, they need to be explored in somewhat more detail. They are based primarily on the rule-of-thumb assumption that, on the average, a family should spend not more than 20 percent of its income for housing. Thus, if a household's annual earnings were $4,500, its gross rental expenditures should not, according to this rule, exceed $900. Quite apart from whether the 20 percent figure is the most appropriate, the rule itself can yield quite misleading results. This can best be seen with a simple illustration. If the cheapest new apartments rented for $1,400 annually, a $500 housing subsidy would be necessary to enable the family just described to enter the new construction market. In effect, the subsidy, regardless of its precise form, increases the family's yearly income to $5,000, and its housing expenditures to $1,400. As a by-product, however, the subsidy also causes the rent-income ratio to rise to 28 percent, suggesting that the family is now spending too much for housing, although quite obviously it is not.

A proper estimate of ability to pay for either new or decent housing, as opposed to willingness to pay, would require that housing be treated as a residual with all other expenditures which a family must make calculated first. Using cost-of-living data compiled by the Bureau of Labor Statistics, this principle was applied to five of the ten metropolitan areas mentioned above, and it was found that well over one half of the families in all of the areas had incomes sufficient to buy or rent new dwelling units.* In Boston, for example, whereas the rule-of-thumb estimate showed that only 35 percent of the population could afford new homes, the refined calculation indicated that 55 percent were in this category. In the other four areas, the "new" figures were all over 60 percent. In brief, the evidence indicates that most middle-income families can afford new construction prices and rents even though a smaller proportion may choose to spend this much of their income on housing.

It would seem clear that present middle-income housing subsidies can be justified only as the means to other ends, ends which have yet to be spelled out. Further, the disguises in which these subsidies are cast in order to win political acceptance reflect the widespread public opposition in the United States to subsidizing income per se. This opposition, as well as much of the conflict between residential and nonresidential goals, could be avoided by linking special housing assistance programs to the renewal process rather than to income. This would require modification of existing legislation to enable *all* displaced families, regardless of income, to obtain either below-market-rate mortgage loans and tax abatements on single-family homes or access to similarly financed and taxed rental accommodations. Such a plan would more fairly distribute the costs and benefits of renewal and, by stimulating new construction for persons who must be relocated, join the separate goals of increased housing production and slum clearance in a single program.

---

* Equally, it indicated a significant percentage who could really not afford to pay any money for housing at all. Among low-income groups, small differences in income make large differences in ability to allocate money for shelter. For example, for a retired couple with an annual income of $3,000, if a rent-income ratio of 25 percent or $750 were just right, then, for a similar couple with an income of $2,800, only $200 less, it would be considerable burden to spend one-fourth of income on housing.

# The myths of housing reform

*JOHN P. DEAN*

The story of housing reform is shot through with controversy, emotion, and pseudo-science. The smoke generated out of this controversy has concealed the economic and political manipulations of various groups seeking to maneuver the situation. The private housing industry has its folklore in terms of "Own-Your-Own-Homes," and "Filtering Down"; the chief medicine men of housing reform have now developed their own folklore; both groups make all the necessary passes and incantations before the public. In the meantime, the patient continues to sicken.

This situation arises from the recurrent dilemma of social reform movements: a set of conditions widely condemned is brought to public attention – in this case unhealthful and unsafe housing. But to remove these conditions would be to change established ways of doing things. L. K. Frank pointed out as far back as 1925: "The crux of the problem is to find some way of avoiding the undesirable consequences of established laws, institutions, and social practices, without changing those established laws, etc."[1]

Social reformers have long realized that restrictive municipal codes clinging to the margin where health and safety are threatened can change operating practices barely enough to achieve minimum protection for the family. To achieve broader social objectives, reformers embody these objectives in housing standards that would require considerable change in existing institutions.

Once codified, such housing standards give a point of leverage from which to pry at existing housing regulations. Much of the fight for better housing revolves around the battle to narrow the gap between currently enforced regulations and reformers' standards of social welfare. Any achievement results mainly in a reformulation of the welfare standards to give a new margin for "progress." In a double sense the reformers are the "standard bearers" in the battle of the slums.

Frequently, however, reformers are hard pressed to justify these higher standards, since they represent debatable value-judgments and difficult scientific analyses. Therefore, the fight for social welfare through housing reform appeals to science and business realities where it can, but readily falls back on emotional appeals and myth where its defenses are weak.

By and large, these nonrational defenses of housing reform are of four kinds: (a) appeals to the subjective evaluational roots of housing standards, (b) myths surrounding the complex relationship of slums to social disorder, (c) myths about the social effects of rehousing and (d) myths about the financial liability of slums to the municipality.

(a) *Appeals to the subjective evaluational roots of housing standards.* Beyond considerations of health and safety, a housing standard embodying social objectives is likely to represent some personal yardstick or subjective judgment among the professional and technical people who fight for better housing. A subjective criterion is of little help in justifying legislation in the political arena. So, to bolster their position,

*Reprinted from* The American Sociological **Review,** *vol. 14 (April, 1949), pp. 281–288, with permission of the journal.*

housing reformers naturally appeal to the sympathies of good-hearted people by devices such as dramatic photographs of the squalor of slum dwellings. These techniques frequently pull a few heart and purse strings. Photographs of this sort, statistics on the lack of plumbing, spot maps of social disorders, and other similar trappings have become institutionalized as standard paraphernalia of housing reports.

(b) *The myths surrounding complex relationship of slums to social disorder.* But since it is often considered "emotional" to dramatize the unpleasantness of the slums, attention is devoted to "proving" that slums impair other social values by causing crime and delinquency, ill health, or exorbitant municipal expenditures. These studies grew rapidly in the 1930's and helped to rally support for local housing reforms; they were quoted by high federal officials in the halls of Congress in support of legislation to implement slum clearance; they achieved a currency that entitled them to be quoted by the best authorities.

Most housing reformers probably believe that the effect of substandard housing on social welfare has been determined. But even with workable criteria for discriminating standard from substandard housing, an enormous amount of research time and effort would be needed to untangle the complicated causal relations. And one could probably never say "substandard housing contributes this much to delinquency, that much to poor health."

A number of commonly-used indices of social conditions and social pathology correlate with slum or blighted areas. By one or another study, the areas of most substandard housing have been found linked with:

- high population density
- high death rates
- high proportion of families dependent on social assistance
- high proportion of illiteracy
- high proportion of women employed
- high juvenile delinquency rates
- high rate of sex offenses
- high rate of gambling arrests
- more multi-family dwellings
- large average family size

- high proportion of males to females
- small proportion of owner-occupied homes
- high proportion of relief cases
- more unemployment
- more poverty
- high rates of divorce
- high rates of non-support cases
- high rates of illegitimacy
- high rates of venereal disease
- high rates of alcoholism
- low proportion of males married
- high proportion of foreign born
- high suicide rate
- high rates for various mental disorders
- low marriage rates
- high residential mobility
- more restaurants per 1,000 population
- low average educational level
- low proportion of radio ownership
- high rates of mental deficiency
- low proportion of telephones

In city after city – Buffalo, Birmingham, Cleveland, Denver, Detroit, Hartford, Indianapolis, Los Angeles, Milwaukee, Newark, Washington, and others – slum areas have been shown to be the areas of poorest health and the greatest personal and social disorder.[2] The implication is: "Remove the slums and you remove the social ills!" But it would be just as illogical to say that ills of slum areas are caused not by substandard housing conditions, but by the absence of telephone service, which also correlates with indexes of social disorder. Scientifically, we should not attribute causation to one or a few factors in an *area* which happens to be correlated with an overall *rate* of disorder. This blend of correlation does not explain why many families living in substandard conditions do *not* experience divorce, or delinquency, or alcoholism. It fails, further, to explain why in a given family in substandard housing one boy may be delinquent, or mentally deficient, or unhealthy, while his brother has remained free of these maladies. Beyond these few expected relationships between slum dwellings and health, the effect of poor housing becomes quite difficult to determine, especially where *social* behavior is involved. Goldfeld's study[3] tested one relationship with greater care than most studies. In the East Harlem slum area he held social factors constant where possible and compared the delinquency rates among families that lived in the superior structures with the rates among families that lived in inferior structures. He stated after careful statistical manipulation : " The one unmistakable conclusion that emerges from the study is that there is no relationship between bad housing in its physical aspects and juvenile delinquency as revealed by court records."

(c) *Myths surrounding Social Effects of Rehousing.* In their eagerness to get slum clearance legislation, housing reformers fought against the idea that slum conditions were the fault of the families that lived in the slums : How could the tenants be responsible for housing deficiencies such as lack of air, light, toilet, bath, or central heating? The reformers argued further that ill-health, uncleanliness, and delinquency are not *innate* characteristics, but are the result of life in the slum environment. Their conception of slum environment emphasized primarily the inadequate *physical* environment of the slums. It understressed the connection between the *social* environment of the slums and the disorders they wanted to cure. So it was easy to jump to the conclusion that slum clearance would remove the social ills – and the public housing program has been sold with that assumption.

Social reformers hoped that the U.S. Housing Act would introduce a new way of life for the slum family. They believed that many personal and social maladjustments would wither away in the new life of the housing community. But they failed to appreciate the problems of rehousing. Public housing developments, once completed, have provided a laboratory for testing out the housing gospel that " decent housing instead of slums means less crime, less juvenile delinquency, lower costs for police and fire protection; it also means better health, lower death rates, and lower costs of medical care."[4]

Studies in Gary, Newark, Philadelphia, and Pittsburgh[5] have shown that rehoused slum families have relatively low rates of tuberculosis, infant mortality, adult criminal offenses, juvenile delinquency, fires, home accidents, and communicable childhood diseases. But we cannot tell whether or not the families admitted to the projects were different in personal and social characteristics that would account for the lower rates. Low-rent public housing projects (where these studies took place) admit only families from substandard dwellings who are citizens of the United States, have low incomes, and no substantial assets. Single persons and oversized families are not accommodated. Tenant selection procedures draw proportionately more families with children or about to have them, more of the reliable or steadily employed and fewer trouble makers. Public assistance cases are accepted but kept to a limited proportion. Families that apply for admission are also " selfselected " according to their knowledge of available public housing and their willingness to move in, if approved. Some families are undoubtedly deterred by such considerations as : home ownership, satisfaction with present quarters, unwillingness to leave their present neighborhood, their preference for a store-dwelling combination, or misconceptions or prejudices against " Government housing."

The extent of self-selection in determining the " effective " public housing market is indicated in the results of a pilot survey in deteriorated areas of Aliquippa, Beaver Falls, and several other small steel towns in Beaver County, Pennsylvania, in May 1946. The 1,194 interviews revealed that the families eligible and willing to move in amounted to only 6 percent of the families interviewed, only 14 percent of the families in substandard housing conditions. Only 31 percent of all *eligible* families said they were willing to move in. This willingness of families to move into public housing varies sharply with condition of dwelling, tenure, and income, as the table shows. Compared with an equivalent number of dwellings in slum or blighted areas, public housing developments undoubtedly include fewer aged indigents, transients, single men and women, hobos, crackpots, criminals, panhandlers, prostitutes, alcoholics, bohemians, taxi-dancers, and other social misfits. Little wonder that indexes of social-welfare favor public housing.

A few studies have made thoughtful attempts to discover whether families transplanted from the slums to public housing developments improve in health and social life :

(1) Full medical data were secured for seventeen tuberculous families admitted to public housing in New Haven and resident there for three to seven years. They were matched with seventeen parallel families on the date of primary diagnosis, the status of the disease at the time of diagnosis, and, so far as possible, on age, sex, and racial characteristics. While only nine of the control group showed favorable progress, fifteen of the rehoused families progressed.[6]

(2) For 317 families resident in a public hous-

social status before the experimental families moved in in 1939 and a year later in 1940 after the experimental families moved in. The results showed no significant change in morale for either group. Both groups gained in social participation, but the rehoused group gained twice as much. Both groups gained in social status, but the rehoused group showed a greater gain. The scores on condition of living room showed a striking gain for the rehoused group, but a loss for the control group. Both groups im-

*Answers to the question:* " If you had the chance to move into a public housing project, and if you had to pay no more rent than you are now paying, would you move in or not? "

| | Owner–occupied | | | | Tenant–occupied | | | | |
| | Standard | | Substandard | | Standard | | Substandard | | |
| Weekly income $40 and over | Weekly income Under $40 | *1 | *2 and *3 | Rent $25 and over | Rent under $25 | *1 | *2 | *3 |
|---|---|---|---|---|---|---|---|---|
| Cases— | | | | | | | | |
| 206 | 72 | 191 | 68 | 119 | 52 | 198 | 102 | 29 |
| 100.0% | 100.0% | 100.0% | 100.0% | 100.0% | 100.0% | 100.0% | 100.0% | 100.0% |
| Yes— | | | | | | | | |
| 8.3% | 13.9% | 11.0% | 17.6% | 26.1% | 42.3% | 40.9% | 53.9% | 82.8% |
| No— | | | | | | | | |
| 81.0% | 73.6% | 79.1% | 57.4% | 59.6% | 48.1% | 40.4% | 30.4% | 13.8% |
| Don't know— | | | | | | | | |
| 10.7% | 12.5% | 9.9% | 25.0% | 14.3% | 9.6% | 18.7% | 15.7% | 3.4% |

Source: Special tabulation of the interview schedules of an income survey of small towns in Beaver County, Pa., conducted by the Housing Authority of the County of Beaver, in cooperation with the Federal Public Housing Authority.
* Depending on whether none, any one, any two, or all three of the following conditions were present:
————in need of major repairs
————without private bath for exclusive use
————more than 1.5 persons per room
The dwelling unit was considered:
standard       = none            substandard *2 = any two
substandard *1 = any one         substandard *3 = all three.

ing development in New Haven for 2½ to 4½ years, the rate of juvenile delinquency per 100 children per year was only 1.64 as compared with a rate of 3.18 for those same families during the seventeen years before entrance to the project.[7]

(3) Forty-four families about to be admitted to public housing were matched on ten characteristics with 38 families who were on the waiting list to be admitted and both groups were given tests on sociometric scales on morale, general adjustment, social participation, and

proved in percentage " use crowded," but the rehoused group improved three times as much.[8]

(d) *Myths surrounding the dollars-and-cents costs of slum dwellings to the municipality.* In all, about a dozen studies have been made to show that slums are a financial liability to the city. The methods for showing the deficit vary widely, but in every case (1) municipal expenditures must be allocated to substandard areas, and (2) assumptions must be made about the relation of bad housing to those expenditures. The cost of public baths may be counted against dwellings where bath facilities are lacking, but it may be impossible to tell how much was spent on patrons from a given area. Other costs, such as arrests for burglary or prostitution, are usually assigned against the slums where the offenders live, thus ignoring arbitrarily that this protection may benefit the people in better residential areas. Most studies assign to slum areas costs that might be attributed to the population composition of those areas. The well-known "Cost of the Slums in Newark" study, for example, assumes that the cost of educating a child is the same for a slum as for a good residential area. It then assigns to the slum area a per capita cost for education that is double the per capita cost for education in the good residential area on the grounds that in the slum area "20 percent of the population consisted of children attending public schools whereas only 10 percent of the population of (the good residential area) were in that category." Before assessing the costs of these additional school children against the slums, the Newark Housing Authority might have reflected on the figures in its earlier study showing that (1) the proportion of school age children and (2) the birthrates per 1,000 women 15–44 years of age are *both* substantially higher in its public housing projects than in substandard areas it compared these projects to.

If studies of the costs of slums were to throw out all expenditures that either are not allocable by area or are related to population composition rather than to substandard housing, much of the so-called financial deficit of the slums would disappear. And surely, any municipal contribution to the cost of rehousing (which in 1944 ran over $5.00 per unit per month in public housing nationwide) would overbalance any municipal expenditures chargeable directly to the substandardness of the dwellings.

With these myths, the humanitarian fight for housing reform has opposed the traditional mores that maintain "business-as-usual" attitudes toward the slums. Public housing, as a new reform institution, represents a sharp and unconventional departure in operation of residential real estate: "Government" on both

local and federal levels becomes directly concerned with the construction, financing, ownership, and operation of housing. But even though public housing has spread from community to community, it is clear that the battle for social welfare through housing is far from won. Without question, public housing has provided rehoused families with structures more comfortable and decent (Standard I) and more healthful and safe (Standard II) to live in; but the anticipated improvements in social welfare (Standard III) have failed to materialize. Studies that show striking gains in social welfare have generally fallen into some unwarranted manipulation of the facts; they are inconclusive at best.

This failure should not surprise us: public housing operations have been hedged in and hampered in the pursuit of social welfare objectives by several traditions: (a) the heritage of laissez-faire individualism, (b) the current practices of real estate, of local government, and of federal government, (c) housing reformers' confusion about the social effects of housing.

(a) *The heritage of laissez-faire individualism.* Public housing reflects the conditioning atmosphere of those aspects of protestant ethic and the spirit of capitalism that underwrite (1) the sanctity of private enterprise, (2) the debilitating effect of "charity," and (3) the moral qualifications for public aid. Each of these is reflected in the operation of public housing:

(1) The American faith in the sanctity of private enterprise is reflected in the increasing clarity with which public housing formulates its sphere of activity as non-competitive with private enterprise. Public housing permits occupancy only by families of low-income who are unable to afford decent available private quarters. "Low-income" has frequently been interpreted at levels well below the minimum budgetary requirements for working-class families (as defined in welfare assistance budgets). In New York City, the admission limits for veterans to a postwar project were originally set so low that many of the young families admitted found that without the assistance of the in-laws they had been doubled-up with, they were quite unable to make ends meet. A family that exceeds the income limits in public housing is

expected to vacate even though the increase in income is unlikely to continue. The breaking of local friendships and community ties makes stable community life an objective hard to achieve.

(2) Public housing has operated under the stress of the American folk belief that "any individual worth his salt can get ahead and raise his family out of the slums." By this reasoning a slum family is morally inadequate and must not be pauperized by public assistance which makes things too easy. This belief in "minimum charity" is translated into accommodations that are often pared to the bone in room size, equipment, noise insulation, cupboards, and floor covering. A government study reported that many units required about $85 to bring the dwelling up to tenants' standards.

(3) Public housing reflects the widespread American attitude that help should be given only to the "deserving." Thus benefits are limited to citizens and to families of more than one person. Since slum children, forced to live in the slums through no fault of their own, deserve a better break, tenant selection procedures generally cater to families *with* children. Few accommodations are provided for the aged and the proportion of public assistance cases is limited. And since those who help themselves are more "deserving" of help, the steadier, more reliable, less troublesome families are generally favored.

(b) *The current practices of real estate, local and federal government.* (1) Public housing operation reflects, too, private real estate customs. The rent in private dwellings is determined by the size and "quality" of the accommodations; public housing emphasizes that families should pay according to their ability. Many rent schedules in current operation in public housing are a curious amalgam of these two points of view; in some schedules the rent is determined by both *income* (ability to pay) and *number of bedrooms* (size of accommodations). Furthermore, the private landlord concerns himself only with property maintenance and rent collection; public housing following the example of private practice has concentrated on these

as its primary duties and left social considerations in the background.

(2) Public housing operation reflects its status as an adjunct of the local government. Local housing authorities were set up as organizations separate from the city administration proper to avoid political interference. And for the most part, graft or favoritism have been negligible in land acquisition, contract awards, tenant selection, and job-filling. Occasionally, the services for a project (such as utility contracts or orders for management supplies) have been manipulated in favor of one local son rather than another. Sometimes the top positions have been filled by political favorites, but sometimes, too, this guaranteed needed political support. But when local political connections have been emphasized at the expense of contacts with local social service organizations, the long-run social welfare objectives of public housing have been hampered. In dealing with these problems the supervising federal agency has walked a tightrope between local autonomy and a too-close supervision of – or "interference" in – local affairs.

(3) Public housing must gear itself to the practices of federal politics (and in New York, state politics). Since legislators are often under attack for over-spending and since their housing attitudes have usually been derived from private real estate practices, political experience has encouraged local housing authorities to emphasize the efficiency of its real estate operation rather than the extension of its achievements in social welfare.

(c) *Housing reformers' confusion about the social effects of rehousing.* The housing reformers themselves have frequently been taken in by their own myth: "Clear the slums and you remove the social ills." Those who are well trained in community organization and leadership have never thought of clearing the slums and providing in their place decent, safe and sanitary homes as the whole public housing job. But the vast bulk of housing officials are not well trained in the arts of organization and leadership. Faced with the concrete realities of rent collection, property maintenance, and budget balancing, they have not been in a position to make the most of the opportunity rehousing offers to inaugurate social relationships, to help families to participate in community life, to encourage the use of social services infrequently or never used, and to create leisure time satisfactions which exceed anything previously experienced. Until housing officials frankly face the rehousing of families as a *social* experiment in relocation and adjust policies and procedures accordingly, large-scale rehousing operations will frequently be accompanied by conditions falling far short of current objectives of social welfare.

Fortunately, a few scattered housing research studies point in this direction: both R. K. Merton's Studies of Craftown and Hilltown[9] and

M.I.T.'s Group Dynamics' Study of a Veteran's Housing Development for Students[10] approached housing developments as unusual opportunities to study social organization. The New School's Research Center for Human Relations has underway a study of intergroup relations in several housing developments with varying patterns of Negro-White occupancy. If a few studies such as these can demonstrate the decisive impact of haphazard architectural decisions and of operating policies and practices arrived at by loose judgment, then perhaps we can look forward to a widening circle of housing reformers who argue their case *not* in terms of myth but terms of housing's real possibilities for social reform and sociological experiment.

# Housing environment and family life

DANIEL WILNER, ROSABELLE WALKLEY, THOMAS PINKERTON, *and*
MATTHEW TAYBACK

This chapter provides the summary and conclusions for three principal components of a study of the effects of housing on physical and mental health. The study was carried out at The Johns Hopkins University in the years 1954–1960 and involved measurement of approximately 1,000 families (5,000 persons) over a three-year period of time (1955–1958).

The instigation to undertake the research arose from three principal considerations. First, is the scholarly general interest in the effects of man's physical environment on behavior, an environment which in our epoch is, of course, largely of man's own devising. Secondly, in a more pragmatic vein, is the belief and conviction among social planners and officials in public agencies that improved housing leads to an improvement in health and the amelioration of social ills. A third consideration to some extent bridges the first two. This is the need to gain experience in the conduct of the sort of systematic research on complex social variables that may lead to relatively unequivocal assessment of effects.

A review of forty representative researches revealed some demonstration of the relationship between housing and health, the direction of the relationship in most cases being: the better the housing, the better the health, and the fewer the social maladjustments. However, in

Reprinted from Housing Environment and Family Life, *The Johns Hopkins Press, 1962, pp. 241–252,* with permission of the publisher.

many instances, an equally plausible relationship could very likely be demonstrated between health and many correlates of housing quality, such as education, income, or general cultural level. In other words, because of the research design principally employed – the cross-sectional study – it has been difficult to rule out the effects of non-housing factors.

In an effort to provide more conclusive findings, a nearly classical study design was adopted in the present research. It involved two samples, each surveyed eleven times during the study: a test group originally living in the slum but subsequently moving to a new public housing project; a control sample matched to the test families on many characteristics and slated to *remain* in the slum. The housing development to which the test families moved consisted architecturally of both high-rise and low-rise buildings.

Both groups were surveyed initially *before* the test sample moved to good housing. Subsequently, a total of ten " after " surveys were conducted with each family in the home. Detailed assessment was made of housing quality, physical morbidity, and social-psychological adjustment. In addition, the performance of every child attending public school was assessed from school records.

Originally, the test group consisted of approximately 400 families (2,000 persons); the control group of 600 families (3,000 persons). Two problems arose which made necessary some adjustment of the two samples before the final analysis of the data began. The first problem was attrition in the samples over time. Such losses were not unexpected, and, in fact, unusually time-consuming measures were used to keep them to a minimum. In the course of the ten waves of morbidity and adjustment surveys in the " after " period of the study, the sample loss was approximately 1.3 percent per wave, or about 13 percent of the originally constituted matched groups.

The second problem was totally unexpected. It was found that control families were, in the passage of time, not only moving about in the city at the rate of approximately 10 percent per wave, but also that much of the movement was to improved housing – both public and private.

This development undoubtedly was due to the increasing availability of adequate housing in the period 1955–1958, while the study was being conducted.

In order to adhere to the experimental conditions required by the study design, the original samples were adjusted to take losses and moves into account. There resulted two reduced effective samples, well-matched on a number of demographic, initial health and initial adjustment characteristics: a test group of 300 families (1,341 persons), all in good housing after the initial move, and 300 control families (1,349 persons), who, despite some improvement in housing during the study, were in poorer housing on the average, than the test families. Both samples consisted of low-income Negro families. All subsequent findings were based on these adjusted samples.

**Physical health**

At the outset of the study, consideration of the ways in which the housing quality of test and control groups would differ led to a number of hypotheses and expectations regarding the role of housing in disease. Among important housing items considered were density and crowding, hot water and facilities for cleanliness, toilet, sharing of facilities, screening, rodent infestation, food storage and refrigeration. It was anticipated, for example, that variation in the quality of these factors would affect introduction of infective organisms into the dwelling unit and their subsequent transmission among family members either by airborne or contact means.

Beginning with initial over-all comparability on morbidity matters, it was expected that, as a consequence of subsequent differences in housing quality, test rates of the incidence of illness would be lower than control rates. The prediction of lower test incidence included both serious and less severe episodes of illness. There was, in addition, the expectation that rates of disability would be lower in the test group than among controls. Finally, it was expected that certain categories of disease might be particularly affected by the housing differences: acute respiratory infections, the communicable diseases of childhood, tuberculosis and syphilis, digestive complaints, and inflammatory and non-inflammatory diseases of the skin. The incidence of accidents in and about the home was expected to be influenced by housing dimensions such as space, maintenance and repair. It was thought, also, that the generally " harder " living in the slum might contribute to a higher rate of exacerbation of chronic conditions in the control than in the test population.

### Morbidity

*The morbidity data provided findings which, in general, confirmed the hypotheses for persons under 35 years of age, and especially for children, but there was little confirmation of the hypotheses for persons of age 35–95.*

*Persons under 35 years of age: episodes of illness and disability.* For persons under 35 years of age, general confirmation of the hypotheses was observed in the last two years of the study for serious episodes,* for less severe episodes, and for total days of disability. Several subgroups, distinguished by age and sex, varied in degree of confirmation of the general directional trend.

Males under 20 years of age as a group appeared to show the greatest effects, the magnitude of the test-control differences appearing larger for them than for girls, both in rates of episodes and days of disability. While all of the more refined age groups contributed to the general findings for persons under 20, the 5–9-year-old group, for both sexes, showed most consistently lower test than control rates of illness and of disability.

Among young adults ages 20–34, females showed far greater and more consistent effects than did males. Test rates among the females in this age group were lower than control rates in episodes of any severity as well as in days of disability.

*Persons under 35 years of age: types of illness.* Expectations regarding the categories of

disease that would be most affected by housing quality were only partially borne out. Among *children* (under 20 years of age), the findings indicated that in the final two years of the study, test rates were regularly lower than control rates in three illness categories : † infective and parasitic conditions (mainly the communicable diseases of childhood), digestive conditions, and accidents. The findings with respect to accidents are especially important and clear. Accidents were one-third lower in the housing project as contrasted with the slum. The data showed general confirmation of this fact among all age and sex groups under 20. In at least one of the two years, test rates were also lower than control rates in respiratory conditions, and allergic and metabolic episodes.

Among *adults* (20–34 years of age), hypotheses regarding communicable diseases, such as respiratory and digestive conditions, were in general not borne out. However, slightly lower test than control rates of episodes were distributed over a wide range of conditions, including some that were predominantly chronic in nature, such as allergic, endocrine and metabolic diseases, mental disorders, and circulatory conditions.

*Persons under 20 years of age: morbidity in the "interim" period.* The data for children during the "interim" period, approximately five months following the resettlement of test families into their new quarters, was of considerable epidemiologic interest. The findings showed during this period that test rates of illness and disability were *higher* than control rates for almost every age-sex category in the group under 20 years of age. Further examination of "interim" period data by classification of disease revealed that the higher test rates were entirely accounted for by three categories of conditions: infective and parasitic, respiratory, and digestive, all of which have communicability as a principal feature. The most likely explanation was that the test children, newly assembled into the housing project, were

---

* Serious episodes were those that involved either medical attention or had one or more days of attendent disability; less severe episodes were without either medical attention or disability.

† Disease classifications derived from the *Manual of the International Statistical Classification of Diseases, Injuries, and Causes of Death*, World Health Organization Geneva, 1949.

strangers to one another in more than just a social sense, and lacked group immunity to common communicable diseases. A similar phenomenon has been observed in the rise of infectious disease in other newly assembled groups, for example, new recruits in the armed services.

*Persons 35–59 years of age.* In contrast to the morbidity data for persons under 35, the findings for persons 35–59 years of age showed general nonconfirmation of the study hypotheses in the "after" period. In the final two years, test rates were higher than control rates, among males, for serious episodes of illness and days of disability; among females, for both serious and less severe episodes and for days of disability. The test-control differences, while not statistically significant, were of considerable magnitude. Investigation of the reasons for this unexpected direction of differences revealed the existence of a small but disproportionate number – more among tests than controls – of persons with a relatively large number of episodes in the "interim" period, and with a history of chronic illness at Wave 1. Adjusting the data to take this inequality into account resulted, for males, in lower test than control disability rates in the final year of the study, and for females, resulted in lower test than control episode and disability rates in the last two years.

## Mortality

It was found, unexpectedly, that 10 control deaths in contrast to 2 test deaths occurred in the "after" period of the study. The 2 test deaths were among children under 6 years of age. Of the control deaths, 5 were likewise very young children, and 5 were among persons 60 years of age and older.

Among the older persons, the finding of 5 control deaths compared to no test deaths was of interest in itself, although the numbers were too small to be anything but suggestive of the relationship of housing to mortality. One consequence of the control deaths among the older persons in the study was the necessity for removing the cohort of persons 60 years of age

and older from the morbidity analysis. The 20 test and 20 control persons who originally constituted this age group had the highest rates of episodes of illness and disability of any of the age categories in the study. To analyze the morbidity of this cohort would therefore have involved estimating the illness rates of the controls who had died, and it was felt that this could not be done properly.

## Freedom from illness

Wave-by-wave data as a percent of all persons in the test and control samples showed only small differences between the two groups in the proportions of individuals who experienced *no* illness. At most, there was a modest directional trend in which tests were more likely than controls to be free of illness in nine out of the ten "after" waves. Test persons of all ages tended to be freer of illness than control persons, more so for males than for females.

## Childbearing experience

The general childbearing experience of females in the study was described in terms of the outcomes of pregnancy and the morbidity of the mother. The data reported were for Waves 3–11, this time period being designated in order to insure that pregnancies of the test women began after the move into the project, and, therefore, that the prenatal experience took place under good housing circumstances.

The findings revealed little to suggest that differential housing affected, in any significant way, the outcomes of pregnancies. There was similarity between the test and control mothers as to the number of pregnancies that occurred and the ages of the women at outcome. There appeared to be a slight excess of perinatal mortality among the test outcomes, but there was evidence of somewhat greater incidence of prematurity among the control live births. Little difference occurred between the two groups in the incidence of either minor or more serious complaints during the pregnancies. A slightly smaller proportion of the test than of the control pregnancies were *free* of episodes of illness related to childbearing, the test-control difference being equally distributed among major and minor complaints.

## Social psychological adjustment

Test-control differences in the quality of housing were expected to play a role not only in physical health but also in matters of social psychological adjustment. Of the specific elements that distinguished test from control housing, it was expected that a few factors, such as space in the dwelling unit, would influence both morbidity and social adjustment. However, several elements of housing quality that were thought to affect social attitudes and behavior differed from those believed to influence morbidity. Among these were aspects of the larger housing environment such as architecture and community facilities, as well as the esthetic qualities of the dwelling unit.

It was also apparent that there was a difference between social-psychological adjustment and physical health or illness, in connection with their dimensional aspects. Whereas morbidity may be considered as consisting primarily of a unitary dimension, measured by episodes of illness and days of disability, attitudes and behavior in social settings, on the other hand, were thought of as multidimensional, consisting of a number of relatively discrete components. Six major social psychological content areas were therefore delineated, and measures were devised for each area which were felt to be suitable for testing the relationship to housing quality.

For each major area, hypotheses were formulated regarding the differences that would be likely to emerge between the test and control groups over time, following the move of the test families to good housing. Various housing elements, individually or in combination, were singled out as likely to be related to the subject matter of the particular adjustment area. Since some of the content areas more clearly involved interchange with the physical environment while others were more deeply rooted in the self, the degree to which confirmation of the hypotheses was expected varied according to the area. Thus, the areas, in their anticipated order of confirmation of housing-connectedness, were:

reactions to housing and space, relations with neighbors, personal and family relations, attitudes and behavior toward neighborhood and community, social self-concept and aspirations, and psychological state.

*The basic social adjustment findings indicated that a majority of the items in each area showed at least a directional trend confirming the expectations specified for the area.* However, in most of the areas, by no means all of the test-control differences confirming the hypotheses reached statistically acceptable levels of confidence. The anticipated order in which the areas would confirm the hypotheses was in general borne out, the one major exception being personal and family relations. The status of each area is indicated in the following brief review of the original expectations and the subsequent findings.

### Reactions to housing and space

It was expected that, due to the alteration in numerous physical aspects of their housing, test women would be more likely than controls to express " positive " reactions to specific aspects of the housing environment, and would in other ways indicate awareness of the improvement in their living circumstances.

The data showed marked confirmation of the expectations. A larger proportion of test than control women liked their apartments, commented favorably on the safety of their children's play places, felt they were getting their money's worth for the amount of the rental, indicated an increased likelihood for personal privacy, and reported less friction and dissension directly related to space.

### Relations with neighbors

Closer and more amicable relations with neighbors were expected to occur among test than among control families as a consequence of differences in their physical environments. Some of the factors in the housing project that were considered conducive to the formation of these relationships by the test group were: a dwelling architecture providing many opportunities for daily contact, a dwelling unit possessing some esthetic qualities and sufficient room space, and the existence of facilities used in common and under non-competitive circumstances.

The hypotheses of this content area were in general confirmed. Notably, the rehoused families, in contrast to the controls, underwent a marked increase in neighborly interaction of a mutually supportive variety, such as helping out with household activities, with children, and in time of illness. This heightened interaction was not viewed as infringing on privacy. The test women were more likely than controls to report both pleasant *and* unpleasant experiences with nearby women, but they were also more apt to have formed new, close friendships in the immediate neighborhood.

### Personal and family relations

Housing-related factors, such as greater space, and general practical and esthetic improvement of the dwelling unit were expected to be conducive to better personal relations within the test families, as manifested by an increase in mutually shared activities (in connection with both routine tasks and leisure-time pursuits), greater feelings of warmth and compatibility, and lessened friction among family members.

The data for this area showed directional trends confirming the hypotheses only in connection with common family activities and the mothers' reactions to, and discipline of, children. Other aspects of intrafamilial activities, cooperation, and affect revealed findings that were mixed or counter to the hypotheses.

### Attitudes and behavior toward neighborhood and community

The project and the slum neighborhoods were viewed as differing from one another with respect to general physical characteristics, availability and accessibility of community facilities, characteristics of the inhabitants, and quality of the individual dwelling unit. It was expected that these factors would give rise to differences between the test and control groups in feelings of allegiance to, and interest in, the neighborhood, extent of participation in community and neighborhood activities, and in other indicators of good citizenship.

The findings revealed that test-control differences in the expected direction emerged in a number of matters related to the immediate neighborhood. Test respondents showed more pride in their immediate neighborhoods than did control respondents, reported more activities devoted to keeping up the neighborhood, and gave far more favorable views regarding its adequacy as a place to live and to raise children. Other topics which pertained more to the " broader " neighborhood or community, such as satisfaction with proximity to various facilities, interest in " larger issues," and evaluation of Baltimore as a place to live, showed either no systematic test-control differences or only a slight advantage for the test group.

### Social self-concept and aspirations

Although change in perceived social status is customarily associated with altered occupation and income, it was anticipated that an alteration in housing quality, alone, and without attendant increment in income, might give rise to upgrading of self-perceived class affiliation, particularly for members of a socially and economically deprived group like the test families. This in turn led to the supposition that having achieved as self-concept the image of persons " on the way up," the test families might also acquire heightened aspirations: for themselves, in connection with such matters as home ownership or better jobs; for their children, in connection with schooling, future jobs, and other benefits.

In general, the findings revealed partial confirmation of the hypotheses. Test respondents, more than controls, were likely to indicate felt improvement in their position in life, and to report themselves as rising in the world. However, the expectation that heightened aspirations would accompany this perceived betterment was, with a few exceptions, generally not borne out.

### Psychological state

It was expected that the move from a generally depressed and deprived environment to good housing might result, for the test women, in some psychological alterations. These changes were viewed as probably involving intermediary processes rather than being directly relatable to the more tangible, physical elements of housing quality improvement.

Findings for the series of ten psychosocial scales consisting of variables pertaining to the *self*, revealed directional trends confirming expectations on all the scales. Those topics dealing with general morale (Optimism-Pessimism, Satisfaction with Personal State of Affairs, and Potency) were more likely than the scales involving stressful, inner feeling states (Mood, Control of Temper, and Nervousness) to show test-control differences confirming the hypotheses.

## School performance of children

Consideration of several direct and indirect outcomes of differences in test-control housing quality suggested the possibility of differential scholastic achievement of the test and control children. The housing variable expected to be most directly related to school performance was that of dwelling unit density which, being lower for the test children, was expected to provide greater opportunity to study and to do homework unhampered by interruptions from other family members. In addition, there was the possible advantage accruing to test children related to some other expected effects of good housing: better morale, increased parental aspirations for the education of children, and activities related to these aspirations. Finally, it was anticipated that illness rates, expected to be lower among test than control children, might also play a role in school performance.

To test these hypotheses, a total of 486 test and 510 control schoolage children were identified in September, 1956. Approximately 150 in each group were excluded in the interest of maintaining uniformity of school records and in view of the unavailability of data on initial comparability. After follow-up losses, the records of 293 test and 287 control children attending Baltimore city public schools were examined for evidence relevant to school performance.

Age, sex, and grade distributions showed a generally fair degree of comparability between the two groups of children, with test children tending to be slightly in excess in age 10 and under, and grade 5 and under.

Three types of tests were administered to Baltimore public school children: intelligence (Kuhlmann-Anderson and Otis), arithmetic achievement (Metropolitan and Stanford), and reading achievement (Iowa, Metropolitan, and Stanford). The data showed that these tests were administered fairly equally to test and control children, slight differences in pattern of administration being related to the age and grade differences.

Mean scores of the test and control children on the intelligence and achievement measurements were similar in the "before" period, thus indicating close initial comparability of the groups. *In the "after" period, mean test scores (adjusted for grade level of children tested) were also closely similar. Thus, the hypotheses regarding housing and one measure of school performance were not borne out.*

Examination of records of promotions showed that, in one-year "before" period, test and control children were comparable in the proportions experiencing normal promotions from grade to grade. *In a two-year "after" period, test children were considerably more likely to be promoted at a normal pace, control children being held back more often for one or more semesters. In connection with record of promotions, then, study hypotheses were confirmed.*

Efforts to reconcile the findings regarding test performance and promotions suggest several possibilities. One is that promotion standards varied systematically in schools attended by test children in comparison with those attended by control children. There is no evidence in the data to indicate such differential standards. In fact, many test and control children attended the same schools. Where they attended different schools, it is worth noting that "test" and "control" schools were under the same general school administration.

Another possible reason for the test-control promotion difference is suggested by the data on daily attendance at school. Corresponding to morbidity differences already described, mean daily attendance of test children was considerably higher than that of control children.

Improved housing quality may thus play an indirect role in school performance of children in a way not completely anticipated by the original hypotheses, by lessening illness and in turn making possible more regular attendance at school. School promotion, while undoubtedly affected by intelligence and intellectual achievement as in more general school samples, is evidently also related in a significant way to regularity of school attendance. The data suggest a modest but specific illustration of the interweaving of environmental, physical, and social variables.

# Where shall we live?

*THE COMMISSION ON RACE AND HOUSING*

### Housing demand factors

Many forces work to maintain the segregation of minority groups and to discourage their dispersion. Most important from the standpoint of civil rights are the pressures to exclude members of these groups from the general housing market. These pressures, exerted by government agencies, real estate brokers, builders, housing finance institutions, property owners, and others, constitute the compulsory aspect of residential segregation, but they are not, at least in the short run, the only factors supporting the actual concentrations of minority groups. In a number of reported instances, where housing opportunities have been offered outside the established minority areas, observers have been surprised to find no rush of applicants. Builders of new housing developments open to nonwhites have often commented on the thinness of the market among nonwhites for new housing, especially at a distance from existing minority communities. Developers of interracial housing projects have found that they could not take for granted a large waiting demand from nonwhites for their product. Minority communities, apparently, notwithstanding their generally unenviable living conditions, possess a considerable stability of their own, as will be shown in what follows.

Poverty is a major factor of residential stability. Because the incomes of minority families are generally low, their housing demand is mainly for the cheaper dwellings to be found most abundantly in the older and deteriorated residential areas. The economic position of the minority groups and consequently their ability to compete in the housing market have improved notably in recent years; nevertheless, the median income of nonwhite urban families is still about 40 percent lower than the median income of white families nationally, and the disparity is even greater in the South. In 1955 nonwhite families constituted about 9 percent of all American families but scarcely more than 3 percent of families with incomes of $5,000 or more per year. Obviously, a much smaller proportion of nonwhite than of white families can afford the price of good quality housing, new or used.[1] Moreover, a smaller part of the income actually received by nonwhite families, as compared to white families, is convertible into effective housing demand because of the frequent instability of income sources and the frequency of families without a male head. Builders experienced in marketing new housing to Negroes report one of their principal difficulties to be the inability of many would-be purchasers to qualify for mortgage loans according to the usual requirements.

The housing demand for nonwhites is further limited by their tendency to spend a smaller part of their resources for housing than do whites, regardless of income. Housing market analysts have commented on the apparent reluctance of many Negroes, especially in the South, to increase greatly their outlay for housing, although their incomes would permit them to do so. Statistics of the 1950 Housing Census indicate that nonwhite families tend to pur-

*Reprinted from* Where Shall We Live? *Report of the Commission on Race and Housing, University of California Press, 1958, pp. 10–42, with permission of the publisher.*

chase cheaper houses or pay lower rents than do whites at each level of income. This behavior is, of course, not characteristic of all Negroes, but it is a group tendency. The reason may lie in their long habituation to poor and cheap housing or perhaps in the restricted availability of good housing to them. It may reflect a lag in the adjustment of consumer behavior to recently improved incomes. Whatever the explanation, it seems evident that nonwhites as a group compete less strongly for housing than even their limited incomes would permit.

When members of any group share a common cultural heritage or common experiences or both, it is only natural that they should seek to live in some proximity to each other. When the larger world is strange or unfriendly to members of the group, their congregating tendencies are reinforced. The group then becomes a refuge and a shield to its members. To the members of many newly arrived groups in the United States, the ethnic colony has been a place where familiar language was spoken, accustomed ways of living were maintained, and where one was at home and among friends.

American Negroes, of course, are in no sense "foreigners." Few persons in the United States can claim to be more American than they. Immigrants to the United States have imported their foreign cultures and maintained them in some measure for long periods of time. The circumstances of the Negroes' involuntary coming and of their life as slaves cut them off decisively from their ancestral cultures. Negroes are not "Afro-Americans" in any cultural sense; they are wholly American. They share, however, a particular historical experience and status which has held them as a group apart from the larger society and compelled them to develop a group life of their own. Seldom accepted in white society, they must look to other members of their race for almost the whole range of associational opportunities. Negroes have developed various social institutions, above all the church, which serve them as a unifying force. Indeed, for them, perhaps even more than for other minority groups, the Negro community affords protection and release from the strain of relations with the unfriendly white world. It is the one place where the

Negro can behave naturally, use freely such facilities as are available, and avoid the immediate impact of prejudice and discrimination.

All these factors of group cohesion sustain the segregation of a group by leading its members to place a value on remaining in the colony as against moving in search of better living conditions elsewhere. This observed tendency of racial and ethnic minority groups to segregate themselves is sometimes used to justify the exclusion of minority persons from other areas. Thus it is said that Negroes, for example, prefer to live by themselves or that they will not be happy in neighborhoods occupied by white people. This rationalization overlooks the fundamental fact that group self-segregation is voluntary, whereas exclusion is compulsory. It is one thing for a person to choose to live adjacent to others of his color or cultural background. It is quite a different thing to decree that he *must* live there and not elsewhere.

Just as different groups vary in the strength of their internal cohesion, so do individual members of each group differ in degree of attachment to the ethnic community. So long as an ethnic group is homogeneous and markedly different from the general population in culture or economic status, its members are likely to manifest a high degree of identification with the group, particularly if prejudice against them is severe. The long-lasting, tightly segregated Chinatowns are a case in point. Given time and opportunities, minority populations in the United States have tended to become more differentiated within themselves. As their members have entered a variety of occupations and moved upward in the scale of socioeconomic position, a growing number have come to value the opportunities and goals of the larger society more than the solace of their ethnic group. This process has been accelerated in recent years by the unprecedented economic opportunities available to members of minority groups and the general lowering of discriminatory barriers. Again the Chinese afford a striking example. After two generations of immobile confinement in their ethnic slums, these people, following the last war, began an exodus which, by 1950, had substantially reduced the Chinatown populations of San Francisco and New York, notwithstanding a major increase in the total Chinese populations which occurred simultaneously.

The example of the Chinese also illustrates the importance of family structure for housing demand. Reference was made earlier to the depressing effect of the high proportion of female-headed families on the housing demand of Negroes. The Chinese, during their long period of segregated immobility, had a conspicuous absence of women and hence of families. The remarkable exodus from the Chinatowns followed the lowering of immigration barriers, which permitted the entry of thousands of Chinese women as wives of American citizens and the consequent formation of many new families.

The group cohesion or self-segregation of Negroes in cities of the North and West is currently affected by two major kinds of change. On the one hand, the number of Negroes with the incomes and cultural outlook of the middle class is increasing rapidly. At the same time, the ranks of the poor and culturally retarded Negroes are constantly replenished by migration from the South. Very different perspectives of housing characterize the two extremes. For the foreseeable future, the mass of poor and " unassimilated " Negroes will probably provide a large population for the " Negro ghetto." The growing middle class, with little in common with the lower group save color, will undoubtedly press with rising insistence for the opportunity to live like other Americans of their social level. A large and increasing proportion of white Americans, apparently, is prepared to see the minorities achieve this opportunity.

## Race attitudes and beliefs

Underlying the exclusion of nonwhites from white neighborhoods is the unwillingness of many white people to live in proximity to Negroes or other minorities. Those who make decisions for exclusion usually claim to act out of respect for public sentiment. Resistance of white to nonwhite neighbors has varied from mere avoidance to acts of violence such as dynamiting homes acquired by nonwhites. Not infrequently minority families have required special police protection to occupy their homes in disputed sections of a city. Short of violence, the residents of a neighborhood have, of course, a great many ways of discouraging a newcomer.

The race prejudice of which this behavior is a manifestation is a complex phenomenon. To treat it adequately is beyond the scope of the present report. Only some aspects of race prejudice especially relevant to housing can be examined briefly.*

In the first place, the pressure of whites to reject nonwhite neighbors is not universal or uniform. In virtually every large city with a biracial or multiracial population, and in many smaller cities as well, there are residence areas of racially mixed occupancy. Many public housing projects and military housing communities are open to eligible families of whatever race. In recent years, a few private builders have successfully marketed new housing developments of a wide price range to an interracial clientele. Thus, whatever may be said about white attitudes toward racial mingling, it is not a fact that whites always refuse to tolerate nonwhite neighbors.

Probably the most important aspect of racial attitudes in the United States is the conflict between attitudes on the levels of principle and of practice, respectively. The social ideals of the American nation, as embodied in its great political documents and its religious heritage, emphasize individual liberty, equal rights, and the fundamental equality of all men. These ideals are constantly reiterated in political speeches, sermons, judicial decisions, preambles to legislative acts, and elsewhere. In flagrant contradiction of these principles are race prejudice and discrimination which deny equal opportunity to members of certain racial and ethnic groups. American principles have never required equality

---

* This discussion is based upon research reports prepared for the Commission on Race and Housing by Claire Selltiz and Stuart W. Cook, *Studies in the Social* *Psychology of Race and Housing;* and Helen E. Amerman, *Studies of Attitudes Toward Housing and Race.*

of men in achievement. That people should be either handicapped or favored, however, by the condition of their birth has always been repugnant to the American ethic.

Unfriendly critics often call Americans hypocritical for professing equalitarian principles while simultaneously denying equality to various groups, but probably few Americans would accept this judgment. The truth is that a genuine conflict exists between two sets of irreconcilable ideas. It is not too much to say that the race problem exists because of this conflict. If the American nation could bring itself to settle decisively the status of nonwhite peoples by one standard or the other, there would be less controversy. But this has never been possible. The conflict, as other observers have pointed out, is not essentially between groups of people holding opposing views, but like the struggle between good and evil, it goes on in the hearts and minds of individuals.*

When people hold conflicting attitudes, they are placed under the psychological necessity of reconciling or rationalizing them in some way. In the past, the principal bridge between the creed of liberty and equality and the white's will to subordinate nonwhites has been the belief of the whites in the inherent racial inferiority of the darker-skinned. Modern science, however, has discredited the older theories of innate racial differences and directed attention to factors of experience and opportunity in explanation of group differences which actually exist. The spread of modern scientific views among the general population has undermined the factual basis for race prejudice and in so doing, accentuated the conflict of ideals and practice.

The trend of white attitudes toward racial questions is plainly in the direction of tolerance. This trend can be inferred from the growing readiness of state legislatures in the North and West to pass laws against racial discrimination. There is, in addition, direct evidence from public opinion polls. When the National Opinion Research Center, in 1942, asked a national cross section of the white population, "If a Negro family with the same income and education as you have moved into your block, would it make any difference to you?", 42 percent of the Northerners and 12 percent of the Southerners said it would not make any difference. The same question was repeated to a similar cross section fourteen years later, in 1956. At this date, the proportion stating no objection to residential proximity had risen to 58 percent in the North and 38 percent in the South. Replies to questions on racial integration in schools and transportation showed a similar shift. Indicative of a fundamental change in racial attitudes, both North and South, were replies in 1942 and 1956 to a question on the intelligence of Negroes: "In general, do you think Negroes are as intelligent as white people – that is, can they learn things just as well if they are given the same education and training?" The proportion of white persons interviewed who believed Negroes equally intelligent rose, in the North, from 50 percent to more than 80 percent, and in the South, from 21 percent to 60 percent.[2]

People vary widely in the intensity of prejudice toward minority groups. With allowance for shifts in the general level of prejudice and for regional differences, various studies support a conclusion that only a minor fraction of the population is strongly prejudiced. A correspondingly small fraction is strongly unprejudiced to the point of advocating racial equality. In between is the majority – probably 50 to 75 percent of the white population in cities of the North and West – who are somewhat prejudiced but who do not feel strongly about racial issues one way or the other. This large group, with no strongly fixed opinions, is capable of being influenced by education or pressures from either side.†

People vary also in their readiness to translate prejudiced feelings into overt discriminatory behavior. Feelings are not necessarily acted out.

---

* Gunnar Myrdal's classic treatise, *An American Dilemma* (1942), defines the Negro problem in America as a conflict between equalitarian ideals and discriminatory practice.
† The findings of some twenty studies, carried out between 1944 and 1956, on attitudes towards mixed neighborhoods are analyzed and compared in the research reports to the Commission by Claire Selltiz and Stuart W. Cook, and Helen E. Amerman.

Hence a person may have fairly strong racial prejudices but, for a variety of reasons, refrain from discriminatory conduct. Typical, perhaps, is the white housewife in a racially mixed neighborhood who told a social survey interviewer that she "didn't care for colored people" and was "upset" when a Negro family moved into her street. But she realized that Negroes "have to live somewhere" and did nothing to discourage the newcomers. Besides, she added, there was "nothing I could do about it, and if I said anything it would only cause unpleasantness." It is equally true that unprejudiced or slightly prejudiced persons may engage in discriminatory acts because of situational pressures. Instances are frequently reported, for example, of property owners refusing to sell their for-sale houses to nonwhites not because of personal feelings, but out of their wish not to offend the neighbors. Real estate brokers, as described below, are held in line by the policies of their boards, regardless of their personal attitudes.

Racial prejudice and discrimination do not exist in isolation but are always influenced by other factors and conditions. The operation of social institutions such as government and law often plays a major role in stimulating or weakening both prejudice and the disposition to express prejudiced feelings in discriminatory action. For example, race-restrictive housing covenants were originated by private real estate interests, but when the Federal Housing Administration put its approval on them and advocated their use, they acquired a status and a sanction which they had not had before. Some of the general factors which, in the past, have served to justify and sustain race prejudice have been discriminatory race laws in many states, certain government policies, segregation in the armed forces, and the judicial doctrine of "separate but equal." In recent years many of these supports for race prejudice have been removed. One obvious result has been to deprive race prejudice of moral sanction and social respectability. Rarely, nowadays, are sentiments of racial antagonism openly expressed in public. On the other hand, certain environmental supports for prejudice have been strengthened by recent trends. The mass migration into Northern cities of hundreds of thousands of poor and culturally retarded Negroes and Puerto Ricans and the increase of social problems in the areas of their concentration have served to stimulate prejudice. In the South, public appeals to white supremacy seem to have passed out of favor, but anti-Negro hostility has drawn fresh support from identification with the traditional cause of regional independence and states' rights.

In addition to generalized racial prejudice, white resistance to minority neighbors seems to rest upon a number of rather specific fears. Some of these seem to be status anxieties, fears of property value loss and neighborhood deterioration, fear of being inundated by minorities, and fears for personal safety.

*Status.* The central problem in practically all aspects of race relations is social status, and housing is no exception. The presence of minority persons in a neighborhood in the capacity of servants, caretakers, janitors, or the like rarely, if ever, attracts unfavorable notice from the whites. The latter become disturbed only when minorities come in under circumstances which imply equality of status.

Two considerations are basic: first, nonwhite color and certain ethnic origins are identified with low status in American society; second, a family shares to a large extent the status of its neighbors, and the neighborhood one lives in is a measure of his social position. Therefore, when minority people move into a neighborhood, the resident whites may feel that their own status becomes equated with that of a low-ranking group. Whites, who may themselves be relatively unprejudiced, may be sensitive to the opinion of others – their friends, relatives, or even strangers. For instance, a white woman, commenting on a Negro family's purchase of a house a few doors away, observed that it was "a fine family," the husband was a surgeon, and she had no personal objection to them whatever. But, she added, people driving by see the little boy playing on the sidewalk. "How are they to know that he is a doctor's son?"

Fears of racial intermarriage, it may be noted, are part of the status problem. Although racist ideology makes much of race purity and the evils of miscegenation, actually sex relations between whites and Negroes have provoked racial antagonism (often violent) only when the white partner was female. When whites express race-sex fears, it is practically always in relation to white women. The freedom of white men to court relations with Negro women, and the concomitant violent suppression of any Negro pretensions to white women, has always been, in the South especially, among the main symbols of white dominance. Marriage, moreover, implies an equality of status between the partners which nonmarital sex relations do not.

People vary, of course, in the extent to which they may perceive minority neighbors as a threat to their social status. The socially secure may be little concerned. But those who are striving for acceptance at a higher social level and are not sure where they stand are likely to feel threatened by the prospect of sharing their neighborhoods with members of groups to whom society attaches a stigma of low status. Thus, neighborhoods occupied by second generation ethnic groups have manifested some of the bitterest resistance to Negro entry. Many of the new suburban residents are just arriving socially on the fringes of the middle class; their anxieties about status doubtless contribute much to the determined exclusion of nonwhites from suburban housing tracts.

*Property values.* In the whole field of housing and race, probably no idea is more widely or firmly held than the belief that entry of nonwhites into a neighborhood causes property values to fall. Many real estate brokers, mortgage lenders, and property appraisers hold to this belief almost as an article of faith. In addition to whatever factual validity it may have, the belief can be an excellent rationalization of prejudice because the conservation of property values is an eminently respectable purpose.

The available evidence of the effects of nonwhite entry on property values is examined in one of the special studies prepared for The Commission on Race and Housing.[3] In this report only a few salient aspects of this complex subject can be touched upon. Inquiry has found cases conforming to the common belief, but in other observed cases the movement of

property values has run contrary to the popular belief. The outcome is affected by various factors other than the actual movement of nonwhites into a neighborhood.

More often than not, residential areas which nonwhites are permitted to enter are older neighborhoods where the housing is already obsolescent or deteriorating. Declining values in those districts, coinciding with nonwhite entry, have furnished much of the " evidence " for the thesis that nonwhites injure property values. In reality, values in those areas would decline in any case; the demand of incoming nonwhites for housing, replacing the loss of white demand, probably tends more often to support rather than depress the housing market in older neighborhoods.

Much depends on the reaction of white residents to the coming of minorities. If the whites hasten to leave, the market may be glutted by an oversupply of houses offered for sale in a short period. Then, the expectation of a fall in property values becomes a " self-fulfilling prophecy." Whites predict that values will drop with the entry of nonwhites, and when the entry occurs, they act in a manner to make the prediction realized.

On the other hand, if white residents of an area are in no hurry to leave, but nonwhites are eager to come in, the pressure of nonwhite demand may bid up the price of houses. Several situations of this type have been observed, with market values of property rising during a period of racial transition.

In a third type of situation, whites may not rush to leave an area but nonwhite demand may be weak, and the presence of nonwhites may discourage demand from whites. In these circumstances a decline of house prices is probable. In some cases which have been studied, however, the presence of a limited number of nonwhites in a good residential district or housing development seems not to have discouraged seriously white interest in the area. Interracial neighborhoods have come into existence, with both whites and nonwhites active as both buyers and sellers, and values have remained stable.

In general, the conclusion seems warranted that nonwhite entry into residential areas does not necessarily depress real estate market values. Under certain conditions it may increase values. Among neighborhoods actually investigated for this Commission, in cities on both coasts and in midcontinent, the entry of nonwhites was found to have had either no effect or a favorable effect on property-selling prices in the majority of cases.[4] Whether entry of nonwhites into a neighborhood will tend to support or depress property values, or have no effect, depends upon the housing market circumstances of the particular case. However, as a motive to action, facts are less important than what people believe to be facts; and as noted, the property-values belief, if widely acted upon, can produce its own validation.

"*Inundation.*" The arrival or prospective arrival of nonwhite families in a neighborhood frequently generates fears that more will follow and the neighborhood will become all nonwhite. Many whites can accept the presence of a small number of minority families, but even among the relatively unprejudiced, few would be willing to live in a predominantly nonwhite district. Hence, fear of being inundated by nonwhites is often a significant motive, first, to exclusion, and second, to white evacuation of areas entered by nonwhites.

This fear has a basis of experience in the seemingly inexorable process of racial transition around the edges of existing nonwhite residential areas. Away from these areas, new all-minority communities are likely to develop only under special conditions – when they are actively promoted by commercial interests, or when various factors combine to produce exceptionally strong minority demand for housing in some particular area. In many cities there exist a considerable number of neighborhoods which have received one or a few minority families and no more.

Two principal factors conducive to racial transition in neighborhoods are the restricted supply of housing available to nonwhites and the pressure of a growing population for more living space. When a particular area is opened to nonwhites, they tend to crowd into it because of their need and lack of alternatives. However, where the supply of housing open to nonwhites is relatively adequate, tendencies to inundation of additional areas are greatly reduced.

For a neighborhood to shift from white to nonwhite occupancy, it is obvious that not only must there be a sufficient nonwhite demand, but whites must be willing to abandon the area. In many cases, areas involved in racial transition had largely ceased to be attractive to the white population even before the entry of nonwhites; nonwhite interest has provided more of an opportunity than a pressure for the resident whites to leave. As for nonwhite entry into neighborhoods still competitive in the white market, evidence indicates that whites will often remain or continue to buy into the area so long as the nonwhite proportion of the population is relatively small and does not lead to expectations that the neighborhood will become all nonwhite. If the nonwhite population increases beyond some point, the neighborhood is usually written off by the white market and tends, sometimes rapidly, sometimes slowly, to become wholly nonwhite. The turning point cannot be precisely defined but varies with different circumstances.*

*Personal safety.* Connected with white fears of inundation is fear of being exposed to the unhealthful social conditions frequently characteristic of racial transition areas in large cities. The prevalence of juvenile crime, gang activity, and other social pathology in many areas of minority concentration is attributable to social conditions in those areas rather than to race or ethnic origin as such. The existence of undesirable social conditions is, nevertheless, a powerful motive to exodus of the remaining whites and a stimulant to race prejudice in other areas.

---

* Housing market characteristics of mixed neighborhoods and interracial subdivisions are examined in several of the special studies edited by Nathan Glazer and also in the research reports by Eunice and George Grier, Luigi Laurenti, and Chester Rapkin and William G. Grigsby.

## Housing industry practices

The group prejudices of the white population provide a basis and support for the segregation of minority groups, but the actual controls and sanctions are administered largely by the housing industry. It is the real estate brokers, builders, and mortgage finance institutions which translate prejudice into discriminatory action. Not all members of these large and diversified business groups discriminate against racial minorities; some are scrupulously nondiscriminating and some are even crusaders for equal rights. But in the main, the services of brokers, builders, and mortgage financiers are extended to nonwhites only in limited measure and under special conditions. Spokesmen for the housing industry usually disclaim responsibility for their discriminatory practices, asserting that their actions are dictated by the prejudices of their clientele or the general public, or by the imperatives of profit and loss. There is unquestionably some basis for this defense, but it is also true that members of the housing industry often lead rather than follow the public in matters of housing discrimination. Whatever their motivations, members of the housing industry have the power to make important decisions concerning access to housing. Virtually everyone must depend in some degree upon the industry to satisfy his housing needs. The unwillingness or inability of the housing industry to make its services fully available to the members of minority groups has had the effect of creating, for those groups, a separate housing market in which only a limited quantity and quality of merchandise is offered for sale.

## Real estate brokers

Real estate brokers, with occasional exceptions, will negotiate the sale or rental of property to minority persons only in areas considered appropriate for minority residence, usually areas where minorities are already living.* To do otherwise is considered among brokers an unethical practice. Until recent years, the Code of Ethics of the National Association of Real Estate Boards contained a provision specifically enjoining realtors from being instrumental in introducing a minority person into a white neighborhood, and many local boards had similar provisions. The references to race or nationality have been removed from the National Association's Code and some ambiguous statements substituted, but from all indications the restatement has made little change in actual practice. The intent of the " ethical " provisions is, of course, to enforce uniformity of action by real estate brokers, regardless of their individual attitudes.

There is no reason to believe that real estate men are either more or less racially prejudiced, on the whole, than any other segment of the American population. However, the controls exercised by the business group over its members lead them to consistent practice of discrimination, whether or not it represents their personal choices. Real estate men are typically convinced that to " break " white neighborhoods would bring serious harm to their business. Damaging reactions are expected both from neighborhood residents and from colleagues in the real estate business. It is the latter which serves to maintain a high degree of uniformity in practice. Granted the frequently strong pressures from neighborhood residents, it is not for the individual broker to assess the situation and choose a course of action. If he desires to be considered reputable and to hold the esteem and cooperation of his associates, he must adhere to the prescribed racial practices of the real estate business. On occasion, members who violated the racial code have been expelled from real estate boards. Sanctions of this kind are not favored, however, because they risk bringing into the open the contrast between real estate ethics and public ideals in regard to race. Other sanctions are available to hold individuals in line.

Supplementing group control of the individual, real estate brokers tend to hold in common certain theories which sustain discrimination. One

---

* More detailed analysis and documentation are presented in *Residence and Race*, Chapter 14 : " Real Estate Brokers," and the special study by Rose Helper.

of these is a belief in the social and economic virtues of the homogeneous neighborhood. For many years, real estate dealers and appraisers have been taught to value homogeneity and avoid the hazards of "incompatible groups." In the same doctrinal family are equally traditional and widely held beliefs that entry of nonwhites into a neighborhood damages property values, and that the presence of nonwhites, particularly of Negroes, places a neighborhood on an inevitable descent toward a slum. Real estate businessmen generally regard the entry of a nonwhite into a white neighborhood as an unmitigated threat to the economic and social status of the neighborhood. As an organized business group, laying stress on "ethics," realtors have assumed some responsibility to guard the racial homogeneity of white neighborhoods.

It is sometimes asserted that brokers do not initiate discrimination but only follow the wishes of their principals, the sellers, and that if the latter were willing to accept minority buyers, the brokers would be equally willing. The evidence indicates, however, that brokers generally take a more independent view of their responsibilities, and will refuse to participate in transactions which they consider improper, regardless of the wishes of individual sellers and buyers. There is no record of any real estate board's having announced that introduction of a minority buyer into a white neighborhood was permissible if the seller were willing.

Moreover, beyond the sphere of business transactions, real estate boards have occasionally taken the lead in defending racial segregation in the arena of public policy. The Los Angeles Real Estate Board, for example, urged a constitutional amendment to reverse the Supreme Court's decision against judicial enforcement of race-restrictive housing covenants. In New York City, the real estate boards led the opposition to a proposed municipal law against discrimination in private housing.

Still another way in which real estate brokers help to maintain segregation is by expediting and guiding the process of neighborhood racial transition. When an area is likely to be entered by nonwhites, brokers usually try to hold the line against them, but only up to a certain point. After a number of nonwhites have en-

tered the area, real estate agents often reverse their tactics and work to bring in as many nonwhites as possible, while stimulating the whites to leave. This practice is considered unethical by many real estate boards, but the prospect of a turnover in ownership of all the properties in a neighborhood within a short period of time offers a tempting opportunity to real estate agents which many are unwilling to forego. By restricting minority access to many neighborhoods and actively promoting white-to-nonwhite transfers in other areas, the real estate brokers often exercise considerable influence on the racial pattern of residence in the direction of intensified segregation.

A further aspect of the race relations of the real estate business that merits notice is the exclusion of nonwhite real estate brokers from the professional associations of real estate men, the real estate boards. Only a very small number of nonwhite brokers have been admitted to these associations in a few cities. Their exclusion testifies to the racial attitudes of the real estate fraternity and symbolizes the separate housing market for minority groups. Exclusion is regarded by these groups as an arbitrary denial of opportunities for wider business and professional contacts and facilities which the trade associations provide for their members.

There are consequences for the general public as well. One result is the absence of communication between white and nonwhite interests in the real estate field. Many of the problems constantly arising around race in the real estate field might be susceptible of easier adjustment if the interests involved had the opportunity of communicating with each other. From the standpoint of preserving the *status quo* in race relations, however, communication would probably be a disadvantage, since it would lead necessarily to the posing of alternatives. The real estate boards, by excluding nonwhites, insulate themselves from the possibility of having to listen to the minority point of view. Another consequence of exclusion is to remove nonwhite real estate agents from the scope of ethical practice controls which the real estate boards endeavor to exercise with respect to their members and the real estate business generally. Real estate boards place considerable emphasis on their functions of raising standards in the real estate business and protecting the public from unethical practices, but this protection is not extended to those sections of the public served by brokers who are not white.

### Builders

Racial segregation is much more complete in new housing developments than in established neighborhoods. Among the latter, though barriers to nonwhite entry are often strong, they are seldom absolute because no one has complete control of the situation. Even in the most exclusive neighborhoods there may be some nonconformist seller or broker who will refuse to hold the line. In a new housing tract, on the other hand, a single management controls, at least initially, the occupancy of all houses in the tract. Except as limited by law in certain states and cities, the vast majority of private builders[5] in all sections of the country maintain a strict policy of racial segregation. These builders permit nonwhites to buy or rent only in developments specifically intended for minority occupancy. Since there are comparatively few of these, the result is to exclude nonwhites from the larger and better part of the new housing supply.

Changes in the house-building industry during the past twenty years have magnified the power of private builders to shape the character of communities. So long as house building was small-scale business, no single builder could greatly affect the nature of residential districts to which he might add a few units. With the transition of house building to a large volume, mass-production industry, the modern tract developer builds not just houses but communities. He has acquired the power to determine, for whole communities, not only the racial pattern but many other aspects of community life. Throughout the country, many new communities have come into existence into which no single Negro has been admitted, by policy of the private builders. In creating thousands of housing developments exclusively for whites, and some scores of others wholly for nonwhites, the private building industry has done much to intensify racial segregation.

The expanded power of private builders and the use of their power in the manner described go far to explain the paradox of increasing residential segregation during a period of generally weakening racial prejudice and discrimination. Builders, no doubt, are on the whole no more prejudiced racially than they were twenty years ago, but changed conditions in the production and marketing of housing have given greater scope to their racial decisions.

In sales housing, of course, builder control of occupancy usually terminates with the initial sales. Resales in most developments are at the discretion of the individual homeowners. However, once a pattern of racial exclusion has been established through an entire community, many interests solidify in its support, and it becomes extremely difficult to change.

The rationale of builders in the North and West for racial exclusion runs mainly in terms of business necessity. In the first place, many builders report that financial institutions and local governments insist upon racial segregation as a condition for their cooperation in homebuilding enterprises. According to these reports, a builder who proposed to admit nonwhites to a development in a white area would be stopped by inability to obtain financing or by the refusal of local government authorities to grant necessary permits and approvals, or by both. Actually, few builders have tested their assumptions in this area, but it is, nevertheless, a commonly stated belief.

Most builders share with real estate brokers and others the conviction that whites will not live in the same neighborhoods with nonwhites, or at least that the number of whites who will do so is not large enough to provide a sufficient market for a new housing development. For this reason, builders are generally convinced that to admit nonwhites would be a fatal handicap to sales. Builders point out that a successful housing tract operation requires a rapid rate of sales with a complete sellout. It is said that a builder makes his profit on a particular development from the last 10 percent of houses sold. Therefore, a development which sells slowly or fails to sell out completely within a reasonable time is a commercial failure. A nondiscriminatory policy is considered a business risk which the large majority of builders have determined not to undertake.

In addition to these business calculations, many builders undoubtedly favor segregation on principle. In the South especially, interracial housing is never considered except as an alternative to be fought. Some leading builders have publicly advocated expansion of segregated building for Negroes as a means of forestalling pressures for open occupancy in private housing.

A few builders, in various parts of the country, have ventured to challenge the racial assumptions and practices of the industry and offer their products to an unsegregated market. Their experience, reported elsewhere in detail,[6] has confirmed the existence of strong opposition to interracial housing by other builders, real estate and financial interests, and local government. Opposition has been focused against the introduction of nonwhites into areas considered to be for whites only. Mortgage lenders, in addition, have questioned the existence of a sufficient market for interracial housing. Nondiscriminatory builders have usually met the opposition, not by collision, but by seeking sites where the presence of nonwhites would meet with least objection. There is evidence of some moderation of the opposition to interracial housing, particularly by financial institutions, but there is still a long way to go in this direction. Lenders have been encouraged to a more receptive attitude toward interracial housing by the change in policy of the Federal Housing Administration, discussed below.

With respect to the salability of housing in interracial developments, experience to date has not provided a wholly unbiased test because of builders' enforced frequent use of less attractive sites. Sales have often been somewhat slower than in comparable (but better situated) all-white developments, but with few exceptions, open-occupancy builders have been able to sell out profitably to an interracial market. Where a good housing value has been offered, together with evidence that the community was genuinely interracial and not a Negro development euphemistically called interracial or open, whites have proved willing to buy.

## Financial institutions

Mortgage-lending institutions have provided major support for racial segregation by their common policy of lending to nonwhites only in certain areas and refusing to finance the purchase of housing by nonwhites in white neighborhoods. Most lenders insist that they make no racial or color distinctions in the granting of loans, and as evidence many can show substantial portfolios of loans to nonwhites. The restriction of nonwhite borrowers to certain racial districts, nevertheless, is a serious form of discrimination. Not only does it serve to sustain segregation, but it disadvantages nonwhites in the terms of mortgage credit because the properties in the areas where they are permitted to buy are generally inferior risks from a lender's standpoint.

A "racial areas" policy is not universal among lending institutions, and there are variations in the strictness with which it is applied. Two principal justifications for the policy are advanced by lenders who adhere to it. One is the belief that nonwhite entry into white neighborhoods damages property values and hence the security of real estate investments. The other is public relations, a desire to avoid the wrath of property owners, brokers, depositors, and policy holders, and other lenders for helping to "break" a white neighborhood.

In recent years, lenders' belief in the property-values theory seems to have weakened considerably and, in consequence, the public relations motive has become, for many lenders, the chief basis for withholding loans to nonwhites in white neighborhoods. The shift of emphasis is important because factors of public relations do not exert a uniform force in all areas nor upon all lenders. Moreover, there is usually room for differing judgments about the extent of adverse reaction to a particular loan and probable consequences for the lending institution. As a result, lender policy on the issue has tended to become vague and variable.

## Government

The policies and actions of government agencies and public officials must be counted among the principal influences sustaining racial segregation in housing. As the United Nations Subcommission on Prevention of Discrimination and Protection of Minorities has said, "The most serious forms of discrimination are those embodied in laws and regulations ... [and] those practiced by authorities and public officials."

*Federal housing agencies.* The Federal government, through its mortgage credit aids, public housing, and slum clearance programs, has come to exercise a large measure of control over housing. Both directly and indirectly, the Federal housing programs have strongly influenced the racial patterns of residence, mainly in the direction of increasing racial segregation. During the first dozen years of its existence, the Federal Housing Administration operated explicitly on the real estate doctrine that mingling of racial groups in residence areas was socially undesirable and a threat to the financial stability of neighborhoods. Its appraisal manuals stressed the importance of protecting neighborhoods against invasion by "incompatible racial and social groups." For "surest protection" against such an eventuality, FHA recommended blanketing all land in the vicinity of a mortgage-insured housing development with race-restrictive covenants, particularly in undeveloped or partly developed areas. It is fair judgment that FHA's influence contributed largely to the spread of race-restrictive covenants (subsequently declared unenforceable by the Supreme Court) and hence to the exclusion of minority groups from wide areas.

In the postwar period, FHA has abandoned its earlier racial policy and declared for "equality of opportunity to receive the benefits of the mortgage insurance system ... irrespective of race, color, creed, or national origin."[7] The agency now officially encourages open occupancy in housing developments, but it does not attempt to control the discriminatory practices of private builders or lenders.

The public housing program has always insisted, and in the main successfully, on minority groups' receiving an equitable share of publicly subsidized dwellings. With respect to the racial pattern, Federal policy has been to leave the decision for open or segregated occupancy to local housing authorities. The latter, in all sections of the country, elected initially for segregation, with one or two notable exceptions. In the South, compulsory segregation remains, but in the North and West, many local authorities have shifted to policies of open occupancy, some by their own decision, others under court order. In this movement, public housing has been and remains far in advance of the private field. The earliest, and still the majority, of planned housing communities open to qualified tenants without racial barriers are public housing projects. Notwithstanding open-occupancy policies, however, the recent trend has been running strongly toward concentration of minority groups in public housing. Among the major factors contributing to this trend are the frequent location of projects in areas mainly occupied by minorities, the wider opportunities of whites than of nonwhites to obtain housing in the private market, and statutory preference in tenant selection to families, largely minority, displaced by slum clearance operations. Without discounting the earnest efforts by some local housing authorities to develop racially integrated patterns, but considering all factors, the conclusion seems justified that public housing has served, on the whole, to sustain and probably intensify racial segregation.

Beginning during World War II, the Federal government has become increasingly sensitive to the housing disadvantage and needs of the minority groups. It has moved to assist these groups to obtain housing but has tried to do so without interfering with the segregation practices of the private housing industry. In wartime, housing for nonwhite (as well as white) war workers was programmed, and a share of materials priorities was allocated to it. Special staffs of "Race Relations Advisors" have been set up in the housing agencies. Special credit assistance has been provided through the Federal National Mortgage Association and the Voluntary Home Mortgage Credit Program. The result of these provisions has been to stimulate a volume of new construction for minorities, not large, perhaps, in relation to the need, but much greater than private industry would otherwise have provided. A high proportion of all postwar new dwellings built for minority use has been financed by mortgages purchased by the FNMA, that is, by government credit. These new houses have been built, with few exceptions, in segregated projects. The special assistance measures, therefore, like public housing, have been both a source of housing and a force for segregation.

Indirectly, Federal policies have stimulated segregation in two important ways. The changes in the housing industry which have so largely increased the power of private builders to determine community patterns, as described above, have been made possible by the Federal mortgage insurance systems. The FHA and VA policies of giving commitments to insure the mortgages on entire housing tracts in advance of construction provide the necessary basis for corresponding advance commitments of financing by lending institutions, thus enabling builders to construct hundreds and even thousands of houses for subsequent sale. FNMA advance commitments to purchase mortgages have supplemented this system, providing assurance of financing for housing projects at a disadvantage in the commercial money market. Without Federal mortgage aids, housing tract building operations could not have developed to anything like their scale in the postwar years.

The other indirect Federal support of segregation has been the moral sanction given to the racial discrimination practices of private business. As Myrdal has said, " It is one thing when private tenants, property owners, and financial institutions maintain and extend patterns of racial segregation in housing. It is quite another matter when a Federal agency chooses to side with the segregationists." Government, as an expression of the public will, is one of the sources of moral as well as legal authority. If the government sees nothing wrong in racial discrimination, how can private persons be censured for practicing it? In some fields, notably the armed forces, the government has actively moved to abolish segregation. In the housing field, the Federal government, in recent years, has withdrawn from any explicit endorsement of housing segregation. Federal agencies, however, aside from verbal pronouncements for equality, continue to tolerate the discriminatory practices of those who distribute Federal benefits.

*Local governments.* Municipal governments, in the past, have repeatedly endeavored to enforce segregation upon racial minority groups by law. All such measures, whenever they could be brought under judicial review, have been declared unconstitutional. Racial zoning ordinances were invalidated by the Supreme Court in 1917, but at least one large city – Birmingham, Alabama – nevertheless continued to pass and enforce racial zoning laws in the 1950's.[8]

Local housing authorities in many cases, both in the South and elsewhere, have enforced by administrative procedure a more rigid racial segregation in public housing than existed in private neighborhoods. In many southern cities, New Orleans for example, whites and Negroes have historically lived interspersed throughout a considerable part of the city, but in public housing the local authorities have established complete segregation.[9]

In ways not accessible to judicial review, local public agencies and officials, particularly in suburban communities, frequently use their discretionary powers over land use and building to prevent the entry of minority groups into areas reserved for white occupancy. Zoning classifications may be changed, land may be condemned for public use, or necessary official approvals may be withheld. In the South, these official actions are often quite open, although illegal, but in the North and West the discriminatory purpose is customarily concealed behind other announced motives. Because the motives are concealed, it is not possible to know exactly how extensive the practices are, but there is evidence of frequent abuse of governmental powers to restrict the housing opportunities of nonwhite minorities. Builders who have attempted or considered projects either for open occupancy or for minorities consistently describe the policies of local governments as one of the major factors restraining the use of land for those purposes.[10]

### Addendum

Implications that real estate brokers,

builders, and financial institutions, as a group, favor and promote discriminatory practices in housing may be justified in regard to individuals but are not warranted in regard to those occupational groups as such. These people do not originate policies, discriminatory or otherwise, in the operation of the projects they negotiate or finance.

The value of anything, including land and buildings, is subjective. If real estate investors believe, rightly or wrongly, that integrated occupancy does impair values, that belief, widely enough held, will of itself impair values. That this is now true, no one who looks at the situation fairly and is competent to judge will deny.

Brokers, builders, and lenders handle their businesses in ways which reveal that in some areas the belief in the possibility of such impairment is widely enough held to be an obstacle to negotiations and a threat to the stability of values.

Except in those cases where real estate brokers affirmatively encourage, rather than reflect, the belief that integrated occupancy impairs values, they cannot fairly be held responsible for a situation which might better be handled by changing the thinking of a community, which is after all, the basis of opposition to integrated occupancy.

## Social and economic consequences of residential segregation

The exclusion of persons from residence areas because of their race, color, creed, or ethnic attachment is a deprivation of personal freedom of a particularly vital kind – the liberty to move and to choose a place of residence according to one's needs, tastes, and ability to pay. There is, of course, no absolute freedom of residence choice for anyone. Individual choices are always limited by law and by economic considerations. But racial or ethnic discrimination imposes on the subject groups special and additional restrictions. These restrictions violate fundamental principles of American democracy and Judeo-Christian morality. Compulsory racial or ethnic segregation is, therefore, inherently wrong, regardless of the consequences which can be traced to it. However, segregation does

have many damaging consequences, both for the segregated groups and for the general public and nation.

### Consequences for the segregated groups

*Residential and other forms of segregation.* The residential segregation of a minority group leads directly to segregation in other areas of life: schools, churches, hospitals, places of public accommodations, recreation, and welfare and civic activities. Although compulsory segregation in public schools has been declared unlawful by the Supreme Court, many schools in the North and West are actually segregated, not by law but in consequence of the racial pattern of residence.

Segregated social institutions restrict personal contacts across racial lines between persons of similar interest. Professional workers and businessmen of the segregated group, limited to clients in the "ghetto," are turned inward toward their racial group rather than outward toward their occupational and business groups. Of all factors tending to isolate nonwhite minorities and impede their participation in the general community life, residential segregation is without doubt the most important.

*Segregation and discrimination.* Compulsory segregation is itself discrimination, but it also exposes the segregated group to other forms of discrimination. When a group is set apart spatially, it becomes very easy to neglect their needs or to discriminate against them. The facility of discrimination is accentuated when, as in many parts of the South, the segregated group is also disfranchised and has no way of influencing public policy or public officials in the normal democratic way. One of the outstanding characteristics of minority residential areas is the inferior quality of public services including police protection, sanitation, street and sidewalk maintenance, and housing code enforcement. The public neglect of Negro districts is notorious in the South and is common throughout the country.

*Housing market effects.* The restriction of minority groups to limited areas and, in cities of the North and West, the accompanying increase of minority populations, together result in chronic, severe scarcity of housing available to segregated groups. This leads in turn to overcrowding of dwelling space, doubling of families, and the subdivision of dwellings into smaller units (conversions). Moreover, the housing in the areas where minorities are permitted to live is in great part old and of poor quality. A striking consequence is that segregated groups receive less housing value for their dollars spent than do whites, by a wide margin. Census statistics indicate that at every level of rent or market value, nonwhite renters and homeowners obtain fewer standard quality dwellings and frequently less space than do whites paying the same amounts.[11]

Nonwhites purchasing homes receive, on the whole, less favorable terms of mortgage credit than do white home buyers. This is due not so much to direct discrimination by lending institutions as to the poorer quality of the nonwhites' properties, a handicap deriving from segregation. Many mortgage lenders will not loan at all in blighted areas. Those who do ordinarily demand higher interest rates, larger down payments, and shorter repayment periods than in good quality districts.[12]

For similar reasons, segregation also deprives nonwhites of equal participation in the benefits of government housing programs. Housing conforming to FHA insured loan standards is very scarce in the slums and blighted areas, and nonwhites are not permitted to live in the areas where most government-aided housing is being built.

*Barriers to social progress.** The traditional individualistic response of Americans to an undesirable situation has been to move away from it. The migration of Negroes from rural areas and away from the South is in this tradition. But when they find themselves caught in a city slum, their avenues of escape are blocked by segregation. Not just in a negative but in a positive sense, mobility has always been one of the principal avenues in America for individual advancement. Its denial to nonwhites, as concerns residence, greatly handicaps the efforts of individuals to improve their circumstances.

In even more basic ways, segregation tends to obstruct the avenues of advancement for segregated groups. On the way to fuller participation and higher status in American life, the members of these groups have a great deal to learn. In addition to a low level of general education and a limited development of occupational skills, large sections of the Negro, Puerto Rican, and Mexican-American populations are unfamiliar with many of the values, standards, and accepted ways of behaving in the urban environment. In a phrase, like many immigrant groups before them, they are culturally unassimilated.

To develop culturally is a learning process, but learning depends upon experiences, contacts, and opportunities, as well as on the motivation of expected rewards. Formal education is, of course, crucially important, but social learning comes from many sources other than the schools. People learn ways of behaving by example and, above all, by participation. The isolation of a group from the larger community both deprives its members of learning opportunities and insulates them against pressures to learn, thus retarding the normal processes of cultural development.

*Psychological effects.* Psychologists are generally agreed that compulsory segregation has harmful psychological effects on the segregated groups. Arbitrary interference with an individual's pursuit of what he considers, and is socially encouraged to consider, a legitimate goal (such as better housing) produces feelings of frustration, hopelessness, and hostility. When minority families are prevented from moving into better homes and neighborhoods as their incomes rise, a normal incentive to self-improvement is taken away. They become habituated to a low standard of housing, and their aspirations for something better are curtailed.

---

* This discussion of social and psychological consequences of segregation draws heavily from a research memorandum prepared for the Commission in the Department of Social Sciences, Fisk University, summarizing the findings of pertinent research. Jitsuichi Masuoka and Preston Valien, *Social Consequences of Racial Residential Segregation.*

As an unceasing reminder of inferior status, segregation and the discrimination that goes with it are damaging to the personality development of minority children. Many, particularly adolescents, develop feelings of inferiority and doubts of their personal worth, and they fail to develop strong motivations to achievement.

Disorganization of family life, common among Negroes of the lower class, results from a historical complex of factors of which housing conditions are only one. However, one of the consequences of segregation has been to compel many Negro families to occupy quarters poorly adapted to family needs. The crowded conditions in many Negro households and the lack of suitable space and facilities for family living have unquestionably contributed to the instability of Negro family ties.

### Consequences for the
### general community and the nation

*Loss of potential skills and talent.* Segregation handicaps the members of minority groups and obstructs their economic and social progress. When individuals are denied opportunity or stimulus to develop their potentialities, it is not they alone who suffer, but the whole community as well, because it is deprived of contributions which the disadvantaged persons might otherwise make. The community's interest in the development of all its members lies at the basis of the public school system and the large expenditures of public funds for education at all levels. In the present world, few will deny that the security and welfare of the United States demand realization of the potential of its human resources to the fullest extent. Hence, racial segregation and related conditions which impede the development of a large section of the population – one-sixth of the total – impose a handicap on the nation which cannot with safety be ignored.*

*Segregation and slums.* One of the principal social problems confronting American cities is the persistence and growth of slums. Many cities are clearing and rebuilding their slum areas with financial assistance from the Federal program of urban renewal, but there is evidence that slums may be growing faster than they can be removed under this slow-moving program.

The problems of slum clearance and urban renewal are seriously aggravated by residential segregation. Urban renewal plans usually contemplate the reuse of slum areas, after rebuilding, by higher income groups than previously occupied them, or reuse for nonresidential purposes, or both. Sound planning, also, in many cases requires substantial reduction of population densities. The result is that all or part of the renewal area population must be relocated elsewhere. When the slum residents are minority groups, as to a large and increasing extent they are, their relocation becomes very difficult because of the limited alternatives available to them.

Municipal agencies in charge of urban renewal are seldom prepared to challenge racial segregation, although this is the main obstacle to finding alternative housing for minority groups displaced from slums. But to relocate the excess population in other slum or blighted areas intensifies the crowding there, while threatening an overall net reduction in the living space available to minorities.

Persons concerned with minority rights have been critical of urban renewal programs because of their tendency to remove minorities from certain areas without opening up adequate alternative opportunities for residence. For this reason, slum clearance is sometimes called " Negro clearance," and Charles Abrams asserts that urban redevelopment has been " deflected from its original social reform course and pointed toward ousting minorities."

---

* The words of one student of the problem of utilizing the potentialities of the Negro population are worth quoting. Concerned mainly with education and occupational preparation, this author writes: " It must be recognized that the Negro cannot suddenly take his place among whites in the adult world of work if he has never lived, played, and studied with them in childhood and young adulthood. Any type of segregation handicaps a person's preparation for work and life. . . . Only when Negro and white families can live together as neighbors, when Negro and white children can play together, study together, go to the same church—only then will the Negro grow up properly prepared for his place in the world of work." Eli Ginzberg, *The Negro Potential*, New York: Columbia University Press, 1956, pp. 114–115.

The problem has been pointedly stated by the Administrator of the Housing and Home Finance Agency, in the following terms:

Regardless of what measures are provided or developed to clear slums and meet low-income housing needs, the critical factor in the situation which must be met is the fact of racial exclusion from the greater and better part of our housing supply.... No program of housing or urban improvement, however well conceived, well financed, or comprehensive, can hope to make more than indifferent progress until we open up adequate opportunities to minority families for decent housing.[13]

Apart from urban renewal problems, the expansion of residence areas open to minority groups frequently takes place in a manner and under circumstances conducive to the formation of slums. Properties tend to be overused and abused, housing space is subdivided into smaller units, maintenance is neglected, public services and law enforcement deteriorate.

When a person acquires a home in a neighborhood, he typically moves into an established social situation and normally conforms to the neighborhood standards. A good neighborhood is usually an organized one, at least informally, and often formally with a property owners' association or similar organization. A family that fails to maintain its house or control its children according to neighborhood standards will be brought under social pressures to conform. The organized neighborhood is also usually alert to maintaining a proper standard of municipal services and to opposing unwanted types of building.

When occupants of a neighborhood are more or less completely replaced by a new group, the neighborhood's system of standards and social controls is likely to be swept away, particularly if the transition takes place rapidly. The new occupants may form their own system of social controls, but time is needed for this because they come as individuals, not as an organized group. In the meantime, the neighborhood may deteriorate slightly or greatly. If the incoming group is culturally advanced, the quality of the neighborhood is likely to suffer little if at all.

But if, as is more common, the newcomers belong to a lower socioeconomic group, a marked decline of housing standards is probable. Age and condition of the houses involved are, of course, also important factors in determining the outcome.

The deterioration of housing and neighborhood conditions which often occurs with racial transition is not racially caused but results from the nature of the transition process itself, the socioeconomic status of the groups involved, and the character of the properties. Where individual minority families have been able to acquire homes in good neighborhoods without setting in motion a process of racial transition, surveys indicate that they have been absorbed without disturbance to neighborhood standards.

*A stimulant to prejudice.* If racial segregation is sustained by race prejudice, it is equally true that segregation is, itself, a major stimulant to prejudice. Group prejudice is basically a habit of looking upon members of certain groups not as individuals but as groups, and attributing the same characteristics to all. Isolation of a group and consequent reduction of personal contacts between its members and others obviously reinforces this tendency. Most white people have very little opportunity to learn what Negroes, for example, are really like as persons. Contacts of whites with Negroes are nearly always limited and formal and usually involve unequal status, with the Negroes in the position of employees, servants, or service workers. Several studies have shown that interracial contacts on an equal status basis are conducive to a reduction of prejudice, especially when the contacts are based on common interests.[14] Under a regime of segregation, however, contacts of this type are rare.

The fact that segregation minimizes opportunities for experience with individuals almost inevitably leads to superficial group observation and judgments. It is easy to see, for example, that the worst housing sections in town are full of Negroes or Puerto Ricans or Mexicans. Since type of house and neighborhood carry fairly definite implications about personal worth and status, those who live in disreputable neighborhoods are readily judged to be low status people.

Also, in some specific ways, segregation stimulates group antagonisms. The pressure of a segregated group to expand its residence boundaries is perceived by the residents of nearby areas as a threat. Thus the competition of people for housing, which otherwise is an economic and marketing problem, is transformed by segregation into a source of social conflict.

*Foreign relations.* The problem of racial inequality in the United States is no longer a purely domestic issue; it vitally affects the foreign relations of the country. One of the stakes in the struggle between the free world and the communist bloc is the allegiance of the so-called "uncommitted peoples," almost all of whom are nonwhite. In this phase of the world contest, the United States is seriously handicapped by the continued practice of racial segregation and discrimination within its borders. The rising colored nations of Asia and Africa show extreme sensitivity about their status in the world. Any evidence that white people regard or treat nonwhites as inferiors is fiercely resented, and race relations in the United States and South Africa constantly provide that evidence. The fact that nonwhites are compelled to live apart from the white population, in separate and usually inferior districts, is a glaring example.

Few aspects of American life are more highly publicized throughout the world than racial discrimination. Communist anti-American propaganda plays tirelessly on the racial theme, and this attack is difficult to counter because of the element of truth in its allegations. Such dramatic episodes as the violent exclusion of Negro children from the high school at Little Rock do grave damage to the prestige of the United States abroad, as President Eisenhower stated; and every action that deprives individuals, because of their race or color, of rights and privileges enjoyed by others, in some measure burdens the nation in the world struggle.

# Property values and race

## LUIGI LAURENTI

The major statistical finding of the present study is that during the time period and for the cases studied the entry of nonwhites into previously all-white neighborhoods was much more often associated with price improvement or stability than with price weakening. A corollary and possibly more significant finding is that no single or uniform pattern of nonwhite influence on property prices could be detected. Rather, what happens to prices when nonwhites enter a neighborhood seems to depend on a variety of circumstances which, on balance, may influence prices upward or downward or leave them unaffected.*

These conclusions are at variance with the belief that nonwhite entry always provokes a

---

* The reference to prices in this paragraph, it will be understood, is to neighborhood price movements which can be connected with the racial factor and which are measured relative to price movements in all-white areas.

*Reprinted from* Property Values and Race: Studies in Seven Cities, *University of California Press, 1960, pp. 47–57, with permission of the publisher.*

fall in property values. Instances of such decline have been observed. But so have cases of rising values – and, as noted, these have appeared in the data of the present study much more frequently than the cases of decline.

### Influencing factors

To set these conclusions in proper light, and before looking at them in more detail, it is first necessary to examine briefly the factors that may influence prices when nonwhites move into a neighborhood as well as special factors affecting this study.

The major variables interacting in these local situations appear to be : (1) strength of whites' desire to move out; (2) strength of nonwhites' desire to move in; (3) willingness of whites to purchase property in racially mixed neighborhoods; (4) housing choices open to whites; (5) housing choices open to nonwhites; (6) absolute and relative purchasing power of nonwhites; (7) absolute and relative levels of house prices; (8) state of general business conditions; (9) long-run trend of values in areas involved; (10) time.

The first three variables, in addition to being influenced by the others, are affected by a number of further conditions, including at least the following : the way in which nonwhite entry is initiated and continued; the socioeconomic status of both groups; the "attitudinal flexibility" of both groups; the existing state of race relations in the community at large and in the particular area; the availability and character of leadership in the community, not only in religious and secular organizations, but in local government agencies.

*One extreme: the glutted market.* A combination of the foregoing conditions which would lead to abrupt and large price declines can be easily visualized. If the resident white owners regard the coming of the first nonwhites as a disaster to be escaped quickly at all costs, a great many properties will probably be offered for sale at the same time. Then, if few or no other whites are willing to buy into the area, and if the demand from nonwhites is not sufficient to take up promptly the houses offered for sale, the market will be glutted. The owners,

in their anxiety to leave, will be willing to accept "sacrifice prices" and probably will have to do so in order to attract a sufficient demand. Later, as whites achieve their desire to escape, the continued in-movement of nonwhites could operate to push prices up again, perhaps even to or above their pre-entry level.

This is the "classic" case. It sometimes happens, and is usually cited in support of the belief that nonwhite entry damages values. For the supposed outcome to occur, however, requires not only a "panic flight" psychological state on the part of the white residents, but an availability of alternatives. A generally "tight" housing supply, as existed during and for some years after World War II, will slow down racial transition independently of the attitudes involved, and probably operate to prevent prices from declining. On the other hand, an abundant supply of desirable alternative housing will stimulate whites to move out of transitional (usually older, less desirable) areas, even if the sellers are in no great anxiety to escape.

*The other extreme: short housing supply.* A different combination of circumstances will produce not falling but rising house prices when nonwhite entry occurs. This will happen when the white owners, for whatever reason, are in no haste to leave a neighborhood, but many nonwhites are eager to buy homes within it. In these conditions, the white sellers may be able to obtain premium prices from the house-hungry nonwhites.

Market situations of this kind have frequently developed during the years since 1940, particularly in urban areas experiencing population increases, both white and nonwhite, that tended to outrun the housing supply. Whites may be reluctant to move out because they do not see where they could move to with advantage or because they may be willing to accept some nonwhites in their neighborhood, or for both reasons.

*Intermediate: a variety of market conditions.* Between the extremes described, it is clear that there is room for a variety of market conditions and price effects depending on particular circumstances. One of the many in-between situations occurs when a rapid white exodus is offset by an equally rapid in-movement of nonwhites. Instances have been observed of virtually complete racial turnover in a neighborhood within a period of one or two years. Prices in these circumstances might drift either way depending on the precise "balance of forces," but the evidence suggests it is unlikely that they would move far from their original level.

Another fairly common case, which may well become more frequent in the future, is the neighborhood where a very few nonwhites gain entry but, for whatever reasons, are not followed by others. It seems logical to suppose that such a neighborhood would probably decline somewhat in attractiveness to the white market, relative to comparable all-white areas, but assuming no rush of the white residents to sell, there is no reason to expect any large price changes. A study of several dozen such "infiltrated" neighborhoods in San Francisco and nearby cities supported the conclusion that the presence of one or two nonwhite families in a neighborhood, after a period of time, usually went unnoticed.[1]

### Housing market conditions since 1940

Housing market conditions prevailing during the time period covered by the present study were generally such as to minimize the vulnerability of local markets to price dislocations associated with racial changes. This should be borne in mind in assessing the significance of the factual data and the conclusions based on them.

In general, the period was characterized by strong demand for housing and by rising real estate prices. The housing demand of nonwhites in northern and western cities was undoubtedly stronger than ever before, both because of improved economic conditions and the nonwhite's heavy in-migration to those cities. At the same time, racial restrictions on residence continued to be fairly tight in most cities, resulting in the concentration of nonwhite house purchases in relatively few "open" areas. Finally, there seems reason to believe that along with the general movement toward racial equality of

rights and the improving economic position of minority groups, white populations have become more "sophisticated" toward neighborhood racial change than in the past. While instances of violent resistance to nonwhite entry or panic flight from "invaded" neighborhoods have not been lacking, they appear to have been less frequent than in some past periods. More often than not, in recent years, racial transition of neighborhood occupancy has been a peaceful process.

### Summary of findings

#### Price behavior in San Francisco, Oakland, and Philadelphia

Basic information for the present original study came from these three cities. Price data over the period 1943–1955 were gathered for house sales in single-family, largely owner-occupied, residential neighborhoods.

A total of 5,417 individual sales prices was collected from 20 formerly all-white neighborhoods which underwent some degree of nonwhite entry during the time of observation. Another 4,495 sales prices were gathered from 19 closely comparable neighborhoods which remained all-white over the same period. Neighborhoods were deliberately selected to give as much diversity as possible in price class, degree of nonwhite occupancy, and other factors.

The movement of house prices in the neighborhoods entered by nonwhites (test areas) was compared with price movements in matching all-white neighborhoods (control areas). For each pair of neighborhoods, two types of price comparisons were made:

(a) *The relationship of test prices to control prices before and after nonwhite entry*. On the assumption that the relationship between test and control prices during the time when *both* areas were all-white is the normal one, it becomes significant to see whether that relationship continued in essentially the same fashion after nonwhite entry began in the test area. For this purpose, the percent ratio of average test prices to average control prices for the last four quarters of the observation period is compared with the corresponding ratio for the entire period preceding nonwhite entry.

(b) *The relative change in test versus control prices* from the average pre-entry level to the last four quarters of the observation period. In order to adjust for differing durations of the observation period, the percent change so obtained is divided by the number of quarters from the entry date to the end of the period. The result is a figure expressing the average rate of increase or decrease in price, per quarter, for the period following the date of nonwhite entry. For the control areas the figure is computed for the same time interval so that the test figure may be directly compared with it.

Studying these comparisons yielded the following principal conclusions on price behavior:

1. In 41 percent of the comparisons, test prices stayed within 5 percent of control prices over the observation period. This is taken as indicating no significant difference in price behavior.

2. In 44 percent of the comparisons, test prices ended relatively higher than control prices, by margins ranging from over 5 to 26 percent.

3. In the remaining 15 percent of the comparisons, test prices ended the observation period relatively lower than control prices, by margins ranging from over 5 to 9 percent.

4. From the date of first nonwhite entry to the end of the observation period, 59 percent of the comparisons showed larger percentage increases per quarter for test prices than for control prices. The remaining 41 percent showed larger increases per quarter for control prices.

5. Neither the price class of the test neighborhood nor its percentage of nonwhite occupancy showed any regular relationship to observed price movements. All ranges of price and nonwhite occupancy displayed both superior and inferior test price behavior, as compared with control prices.

Four of the twenty test neighborhoods had nonwhites living in them before the period for which adequate price data could be gathered. In these cases no " before-and-after entry " comparisons could be made. The price performance of these areas – compared with that in five control areas – was judged by using the first four quarters of available price data as a measurement base. The findings for these four test areas were found to be generally consistent with those for the sixteen for which pre-entry price data exist.

The findings for all areas place in doubt existing beliefs concerning the harmful effects of nonwhite occupancy on property values. Were such beliefs rooted in fact, the statistical evidence of this study would have shown downward shifts in test neighborhood price levels, relative to control prices, following changes in the racial pattern. Few such shifts took place in the areas studied, and where they did occur they were moderate.

Two broad conclusions stand out: *first*, price changes which can be connected with the fact of nonwhite entry are not uniform, as often alleged, but diverse. Depending on circumstances, racial change in a neighborhood may be depressing or it may be stimulating to real estate prices and in varying degrees. *Second*, considering all of the evidence, the odds are about four to one that house prices in a neighborhood entered by nonwhites will keep up with or exceed prices in a comparable all-white area. These conclusions are chiefly based on observations of real estate markets in a period of generally rising prices. This period, moreover, was characterized by unusually strong demand for housing, particularly by nonwhites who had been making relatively large gains in personal income. These conditions seem likely to continue into the foreseeable future, and therefore the main findings of the present study may be valid for many neighborhoods certain to experience the entry of nonwhites.

### Price behavior in Chicago, Kansas City, Detroit, and Portland

The findings for San Francisco, Oakland, and Philadelphia are generally consistent with those of other investigators studying similar situations in Chicago, Kansas City, Detroit, and Portland, Oregon. Because of procedural differences, none of these studies is strictly comparable with the San Francisco-Oakland-Philadelphia inquiry. All the former studies agreed, however, in the finding that nonwhite entry was usually associated with rising rather than falling prices. It should be noted, too, that all reported developments during periods when real estate prices were rising generally. It remains an open question in several of these studies whether prices rose as rapidly or to the same extent in the transitional areas as in comparable all-white neighborhoods, and in one (Portland) it definitely appears that they did not. Nevertheless, the general finding that prices in the transitional areas usually did not fall but rather increased is a significant one in the light of the common assertion that nonwhite entry brings large absolute declines in property values.

The highlights of the other studies are summarized below.

1. *Cressey's 1920-1930 study of Chicago's South Side.* In this early approach to the problem, based on the comparative land values in racially mixed and all-white neighborhoods, no definitive findings emerged. Cressey[2] found that values in some mixed areas fell behind those in comparable all-white districts, while they stayed even or moved ahead in comparison with others. Because of limitations in the data and the considerable lapse of time since the study was made, its findings do not contribute much toward understanding the present-day problem of race and property values.

2. *Schietinger's 1940-1951 studies in Chicago.* One of the most industrious investigators is Dr. E. F. Schietinger,[3] whose studies have examined the behavior of sales prices for nearly 900 properties in seven areas of Chicago's South Side. No all-white control areas were utilized, the prices in racially mixed areas being compared with base year assessed valuations and test area price averages. The study sought to determine the effect of nonwhite occupancy and threat of occupancy on values, and also whether the degree or stage of racial succession had an observable price influence.

Schietinger's main finding was that prices in areas entered by nonwhites were generally improved, especially where the typical residential structures were of two units or more. The exceptions seemed to be predominantly single-family areas which were either threatened by nonwhite entry or saturated by nonwhites over a considerable time period. A second major finding was that the degree of use potential in terms of owner occupancy or income, rather than whether occupancy was all-white or racially mixed, was the major price determinant.

3. *Gillette's 1949-1953 study in Kansas City.* Selling prices in two Kansas City neighborhoods were compared by Thomas Gillette[4] over a five-year period. One neighborhood was racially changing and had nearly 50 percent Negro occupancy by the end of the period; the other was a comparable all-white area. The major finding was that over the observation interval gross selling prices were higher for the test area in 67 percent of the comparisons, higher for the all-white area in 23 percent, and about equal in the remaining 10 percent.

4. *Wander's 1940–1950 study in Detroit.* In this investigation, Richard Wander[5] compared selling prices and assessed valuations in an area that reached 30 percent Negro occupancy during 1948–1950 with those in two similar all-white areas. The comparisons were carried through the entire 1940–1950 decade. He also examined test area prices between blocks with and without nonwhite residents.

The findings indicate that properties in the test area had been declining in value relative to the two all-white areas up to 1948, but that the entry of Negroes first checked and then reversed this trend. However, up to the end of 1950 when the study period ended, the reversal had not been sufficiently strong to bring the average test area price level up to that of the two control areas.

For selling prices *within* the test area alone, values for mixed blocks reached higher levels than those for all-white blocks.

5. *City of Detroit 1946–1950 study.* Observations were made by the Mayor's Interracial Committee[6] of selling prices in an area experiencing Negro in-migration as compared with those in an all-white area of comparable properties. The principal finding was that the racial transition area displayed consistently

higher selling prices than did the all-white area.

6. *Portland, Oregon, 1944–1954 study.* Conducted by the Urban League of Portland,[7] this study was limited to five small areas, each entered by just one Negro family. Selling prices were compared with those in similar all-white areas.

The findings are subject to some reservations as to sufficiency of price data and comparability of test and control areas. While all test area prices continued on an upward trend after the Negro family moved in, they did not rise as fast as those in the control areas. Out of four sets of comparisons, one set was about even, another showed a moderate advantage for the control area, and the other two displayed a markedly slower rise for the test areas.

### Financing characteristics

An analysis of financing data available for sales in the San Francisco neighborhoods revealed that:

1. Only half as many nonwhites paid all cash as did whites (one in sixteen as compared with one in eight).

2. Almost as many nonwhite buyers purchased for cash plus a first mortgage (no secondary financing) as did whites (48.4 percent as against 53.6 percent).

3. Resort to secondary financing was about the same: two out of five nonwhite buyers, two out of six white buyers.

4. For nonwhites, cash down payments were from 17 to 25 percent less than those made by white buyers.

5. First mortgages extended to nonwhites were as large or larger than those to whites and involved the same loan/price ratios.

6. Recorded interest rates were the same for nonwhites as for whites.

### Property maintenance

Evidence obtained while gathering neighborhood data for San Francisco, Oakland, and Philadelphia indicated that nonwhites were maintaining their properties at least as well as white homeowners in comparable areas. This conclusion is supported by Gillette's investigation of this point for Kansas City.

### Implications for the future

Discussions of race and property values usually assume that the demand for housing in a racially mixed neighborhood must come entirely or almost entirely from nonwhites – that few if any whites will consider buying property in such areas. Insofar as this is true (and it has doubtless been largely true in the past), it means that the price effects of racial changes in a neighborhood depend basically on the rate and urgency with which whites add homes to the housing supply in relation to the strength of nonwhite housing demand. The major threat to prices seems to be a too sudden and large addition to the neighborhood supply of housing available to nonwhites. Time, therefore, has a major influence on how racial change will affect values. Racial transition that is accomplished gradually is likely to have very different effects on house prices than a sudden shift.

In the neighborhood real estate markets investigated for the present study, the sellers were white and most of the buyers were nonwhite. The study findings signify, therefore, that in the time period and the areas covered, nonwhites were generally able to enter each local market fast enough to avoid the creation of a relative price slump.

As segregation barriers in housing continue to weaken, however, the important question for the future is probably not the ability of nonwhite demand to equal white supply, but the willingness of whites to continue buying into neighborhoods which have become racially mixed. To the extent that nonwhites gain opportunity to acquire housing in a variety of neighborhoods, their demand will be dispersed and they can no longer be counted upon to take all the houses in a particular area. The prospects for housing desegregation and its implications for the real estate market are outside the scope of the present study, but a few observations may be ventured.

There is evidence that resistance of white people to buying or renting in racially mixed neighborhoods is greatly reduced when the non-white group is not numerous and is not perceived as likely to become the numerically dominant element. Studies have revealed frequent instances of neighborhoods which have remained interracial over a period of years with a low percentage of nonwhites. In a significant number of cases private builders have successfully sold new tract houses on an interracial basis.[8] Several states and cities have adopted legislation prohibiting racial discrimination in housing developments built with public aid, and New York City has recently extended the prohibition to multiple unit and subdivision housing generally. To the extent that racial exclusion lessens, the number of neighborhoods containing small numbers of nonwhites will be multiplied. Opportunities to escape living near nonwhites by choosing exclusive neighborhoods will become fewer, and, as this process continues, race should gradually lose its importance as a consideration in the real estate market.

# Concerning studies of price trends in mixed areas

CHESTER RAPKIN and WILLIAM G. GRIGSBY

The popular conviction that nonwhite entry into an all-white residential area causes home prices to decline is regarded by many analysts as a major barrier to the goal of better housing for minority groups. It has been the view of these analysts that Negroes, in attempting to improve their housing situation by moving into neighborhoods occupied by white families, would meet with much less resistance were it not for the fear of homeowners that prices would surely fall. To combat this damaging and, presumably, erroneous conception, several major research efforts have been devoted to the investigation of the behavior of home prices in racially mixed areas. There is now a fair body of evidence indicating that prices often rise during, and perhaps because of, racial transition. Whether these findings will prove to be as useful as originally anticipated, however, may be questioned on several grounds.

First, it is small comfort to an institutional lender protecting other people's money, or to an owner intent on safeguarding his investment, to know that prices sometimes rise and sometimes fall when Negroes enter a neighborhood, particularly since the question seldom arises on the occasion of a white purchase. Unless predictions can be made in specific situations, the attitudes and practices of mortgagees, appraisers, brokers, and owners will not change materially, for these groups cannot be expected to take the very real risk of a possible decline. Lenders in particular are prone to take a cautious view of neighborhoods experiencing racial change until the likely long-term trend can be determined.

Second, almost without exception, Negro inmigration in the areas in which price studies have been made appeared to be associated with a visible reduction in white demand and, in many situations, an increase in the supply of houses for sale. The price reaction, therefore, was largely dependent on the extent to which Negro de-

*Reprinted from* The Demand for Housing in Racially Mixed Areas, *University of California Press, 1960, pp. 102–105,* *with permission of the publisher.*

mand filled this partial vacuum. Prices could rise above the general level in comparable all-white neighborhoods only if Negroes had both the buying power (liquid assets and credit) to absorb all the market supply of the areas at a higher price level and the willingness to pay premiums to purchase the houses offered for sale. But Negroes could be expected to pay premium prices only if they were experiencing a housing shortage as a result of having limited access to the market. Thus, the very argument (that prices actually rise when Negroes purchase into a neighborhood) used to reduce discrimination against nonwhite home buyers is valid only when precisely the same form of discrimination exists on a wide scale.* It is doubtful whether potential Negro home buyers view the phenomenon of a price rise with any degree of pleasure since its cause reflects the persistence of an unhappy circumstance.

An examination of the price studies reveals yet another curious twist. In the face of an attrition of white demand, prices in a mixed neighborhood can be maintained only if Negroes continue to buy into the neighborhood and at the original price level. Thus, at the present time white residents have the choice of declining prices or an increasing number of Negro neighbors, or both. There are few instances of firm or rising prices and a stable mixed neighborhood being achieved simultaneously.[1] In view of these facts, it could be argued that the effect of the price studies might be to solidify resistance to Negro entry or at best to assist white residents in deciding the most propitious time to sell.

In their zeal to show that Negro entry has a beneficial effect on the market, analysts have tended to overlook these aspects of rising prices. They have also glossed over the reasons for price declines. For example, one author states "It is the mass exodus that temporarily gluts the market with offerings that depresses prices, not the influx. It is like a bank run engendered by fear. The fears produce an unwarranted condition that could be avoided if people would stay

put."[2] Laurenti takes a similar point of view and expresses the thought that downward price movements may be largely a matter of the self-fulfilling prophecy.[3] Residents who think prices will decline try to sell their homes before the market weakens and thereby bring about the decline which they fear.

The limited applicability of these observations is readily apparent, both theoretically and in the market place itself. In sections of West Philadelphia and Strawberry Mansion white sales were substantial, yet there was sufficient Negro demand to sustain prices. In West Mount Airy, on the other hand, where the houses were expensive and nonwhite demand limited, a moderate price decline was observed in the face of no increase in the rate of white out-migration. If price declines occur in connection with a prophecy, it is more probably the unfulfilled prophecy. Many white families try to leave a mixed area in the expectation that it will soon become all Negro, rather than in anticipation of a dip in prices. If their prediction is incorrect, however, and the expected rush of Negro buyers does not materialize, prices may indeed move to a lower level.

In summary, it appears that the studies of price movements in racially mixed areas have fallen short of their basic objectives because they have focused on the price shifts themselves rather than on the full array of underlying causes of these shifts. In essence they have failed to provide any real foundation for a change in attitudes or practices toward Negroes by brokers, appraisers, mortgage lenders, and homeowners. If discrimination was good business prior to these inquiries, it is equally good business today. It is unfortunate, too, that this type of analysis carries with it the implication that the justification for a social objective such as equality of access to the housing supply must be evaluated primarily in terms of the criteria of the market place. In all fairness, however, it must be stated that the principal and permanent value of these studies may be in erasing the primitive folk notion that Negroes have an

---

* Or when most white buyers cease to avoid mixed areas. The argument—in milder form—that prices do not fall when Negroes enter a neighborhood would also be valid in the rare situation when the reduction in white demand is exactly offset by the increase in Negro demand and market supply does not increase or decrease.

inherent taint which inevitably causes house prices to decline in any area that they may enter. If this belief has fewer adherents as a result of these studies, then an important contribution has been made to the improvement of race relations and to the ultimate goal of equality for Negroes.

# Interracial housing

## MARTIN DEUTSCH and MARY EVANS COLLINS

Two integrated interracial low-rent, public housing projects in New York City were compared with two similar segregated bi-racial projects in Newark to determine the socio-psychological effects of the two occupancy patterns upon racial relations and racial attitudes. The projects in the two cities were selected so as to be matched in terms of Negro-white ratios and comparable in other relevant respects. Approximately 100 white and 25 Negro housewives were intensively interviewed in each of the four projects. In addition 24 children between the ages of 11 and 14 years, of both races and of both sexes, were interviewed in each of the two types of housing projects.

The integrated interracial projects in comparison with the segregated bi-racial projects were characterized by:

1. Many more instances of friendly, neighborly contacts between members of the different races.

2. A social atmosphere more favorable to friendly interracial associations.

3. A more closely knit project community.

4. More favorable attitudes toward the Negro people in the project and also toward Negro people in general.

5. More favorable attitudes also toward the Chinese, although here the differences between the two types of projects were smaller.

6. More favorable attitudes toward living in an interracial project.

### Interpretation

These behavioral and attitudinal differences between the tenants in the New York and Newark projects seem to result directly from the following differences between the two types of occupancy patterns:

1. The physical and functional proximity of Negro and white families is considerably greater in the integrated than in the segregated projects.

2. The social norms with respect to racial relations implicit in the official policy regarding the type of occupancy pattern by a public authority is more favorable to friendly interracial relations in the integrated than in the segregated bi-racial projects.

3. In a broader social milieu characterized by racial prejudice, the discrepancy between the social norms of the project and those of the broader community is greater for the residents in the integrated projects; it seems likely that this greater discrepancy has drawn the tenants in these projects closer together.

*Reprinted from* Interracial Housing: A Psychological Evaluation of a Social Experiment, *University of Minnesota Press, 1951, pp. 122–129, with permission of the publisher.*

In an *ex post facto* study, such as the present one, change is always inferred rather than directly observed. From the existence of the marked differences in racial attitudes and behavior between the tenants in the integrated interracial projects and those in the segregated bi-racial projects, we *infer* that a considerable number of tenants in the former have become less prejudiced. This inference is supported by the reports of the housewives about their own attitudinal changes: many more women in the integrated than in the segregated projects report favorable attitudinal changes. The findings of related research,[1] which indicate that equal-status contacts with Negroes are likely to reduce prejudices, also lend credibility to our inference. However, without an examination of alternative interpretations of the differences found between the two types of projects, we cannot be reasonably confident of the correctness of our interpretation.

We have reviewed the evidence that we could bring to bear upon the question of the comparability of the interracial experiences and attitudes of the tenants prior to their moving into the two types of projects. All of the evidence – the psychological situation of the low-income family with a dire need for housing, the low rate of refusals by applicants and the low rate of voluntary move-outs by tenants of the various projects we have studied, the reports of the housewives about their attitudes and experiences prior to moving into the projects, and our comparison of housewives in the two types of projects who are similar in education, religion, and political attitudes – all indicate that it is unlikely that the behavioral and attitudinal differences our data have revealed can be " explained away " in terms of an initial lack of comparability of the tenants in the two types of projects. Nor are the differences we found, so far as it is possible to tell, attributable to any idiosyncrasies in the projects we studied: tenant morale is high in all projects, no " special " efforts have been made to produce changes in attitudes in any of the projects, the projects in the two cities are similar in many respects (in ratio of Negroes to whites, in neighborhoods, in eligibility requirements, in age, in possessing interracial staffs, etc.)

Thus, factors other than the occupancy pattern that might explain our results, have been systematically examined and have been found to be inconsistent with the available data. It seems not unreasonable to conclude that *from the point of view of reducing prejudice and of creating harmonious democratic intergroup relations, the net gain resulting from the integrated projects is considerable; from the same point of view, the gain created by the segregated bi-racial projects is slight.*

## Implications

In examining the implications of our results we shall ask first about their meaning for interracial housing and then about their significance for intergroup relations in general. In what circumstances should we expect our results to hold for other comparisons of integrated interracial and segregated bi-racial projects? Under what conditions could we recommend the adoption of integrated housing in anticipation of results similar to those we found? From our results what can we conclude about factors affecting intergroup relations outside of public housing?

*Implications for interracial housing.* As a first step in considering the meaning of our results for interracial housing in general, let us examine the probability that our results would be confirmed in other comparisons of the two types of occupancy pattern. A study by Merton, West, and Jahoda of (in our terminology) a segregated bi-racial project in Pittsburgh reports results very similar to the ones we found for the bi-racial projects we studied in Newark. Our survey of housing officials experienced in interracial housing also supports the impression that the segregated bi-racial project does not afford enough opportunities for intimate interracial contact to produce major attitudinal changes.

While we have studied integrated projects only in New York, our interviews with housing officials in different parts of the country certainly suggest that New York is not the only place in which an integrated policy is possible. In such various cities as Hartford, Los Angeles, Philadelphia, Seattle, and Berkeley, integrated interracial projects exist and they are managed without difficulties. Though the population of New York (and of the projects we have studied) is undoubtedly more polyglot and possibly more tolerant than in other sections of the country, the residential segregation of Negroes (apart from public housing) has been more rigid than in many other cities. Integration thus, in a sense, represents in New York a greater break with community practices than would be true for many cities. Moreover, the integrated interracial projects we studied in New York are far from ideal choices to demonstrate the "workability" of integrated housing. Both projects contain a relatively high proportion of Negro families, and many housing officials believe that when a project contains a population as high as 40 percent Negro (both of the projects we studied had at least this proportion) it becomes more difficult for the white tenants to adjust to living in an integrated project. Both projects are also located in predominantly Negro neighborhoods, neighborhoods which are, in addition, rather deteriorated and characterized by considerable delinquency.

Further, although the tenant composition of the New York projects may differ from that to be expected in many other cities, it should be stressed that no matter what segment of the housewives we studied is considered, similar results are obtained with respect to changes in racial relations and racial attitudes. That is, Catholic, Protestant, and Jew, the politically liberal and politically conservative, and the well educated and poorly educated adjusted to living in an integrated project and became less prejudiced despite initial forebodings.

While we see no reason for believing that integration is workable only in New York, the favorable results we found might not be expected under the following types of circumstances: where an "integrated" project contains only a token representation of Negroes, or, in other words, if the proportion is too small to result in any considerable amount of interracial contact; where attitudes in the community are extremely hostile, perhaps violently opposed to integrated housing – so much so that it becomes impossible to live in the project without bearing the brunt of the active opposition of the community; where the housing authority and project management do not firmly support and execute a policy of integration without equivocation – where, in other words, "integration" can be subverted by "complaints," by manipulation of management, etc.; where the management staff are prejudiced; or where extremely inefficient management results in low tenant morale, with bickering and hostility characterizing the relationships among tenants of all groups.

In the light of these judgments about the conditions under which our findings might be expected to hold, what can we recommend concerning the use of integrated housing in other cities? Before attempting an answer to this question we should point out that there is the possibility of much confusion in the discussion of the relationship between research and policy decisions. Research can never dictate or be a substitute for basic value judgments; it can only determine, at most, which of several alternatives is likely to lead most effectively to desired objectives. The objectives themselves, except insofar as they are only "means" to further objectives, are beyond the purview of science. In his role as scientist, the social psychologist cannot assert whether, in and of themselves, the reduction of prejudice and the creation of friendly equal-status interracial relations are desirable (though in terms of objectives related to democracy or to international relations, it may be possible for him to make this assertion without violating his scientific role). He can, however, state that if these are desiderata, then under certain conditions, and not others, they will be attained.

Independently of research findings, every individual has the right to search his conscience and make a moral judgment about the desirability of an integrated or a segregated policy. Of course, research results, by extending the factual context and by pointing out consequences, may influence this judgment. However, even if research findings were to indicate that the integrated pattern, under conditions such as exist now in the Deep South, results in "trouble," the ethical principles of many would still lead them to favor the integrated pattern. For these people, the integrated pattern (the elimination

of official invidious distinctions beween Negroes and whites) may be considered, in itself, an
important moral end. Others, guided by our
hypothetical research results in the South, may
still favor an integrated pattern but will, at the
same time, try to create the conditions which
will make it result in a reduction of prejudice
and in the creation of friendly, equal-status
interracial relations. It may well be that striving
to create such a policy is one of the most
effective means for creating the conditions necessary to its successful execution.

Though we have indicated the possibility that
the integrated pattern at this moment of history is not feasible in the Deep South, we must
confess to a lack of verified knowledge about
this point. Our research has not contributed to
an understanding of the socio-political conditions which favor the adoption and the successful execution of an integrated policy. We would
however, hazard the guess that, in most circumstances, if sufficient political power can be
obtained by its proponents to result in the
adoption of this policy, then sufficient political
power exists for its successful execution; the
reverse is also probably true – that is, if there is
not enough political power for its successful
execution, there is not likely to be enough
power for its adoption. Possibly the major exception to this statement occurs when the political
power resulting in the adoption of a policy has
no relevance to its execution (e.g., if the federal
government were to ban segregation but the
responsibility for its execution were in the
hands of local officials in the South) – that is,
when there is no firm resolve, backed by enforcement provisions, to execute policy.

We are, in effect, rejecting the notion that
has characterized much of sociological thinking
in the field of racial relations: the notion,
originating with William S. Summer, that
" stateways cannot change folkways." The evidence of our study is that official policy, executed
without equivocation, can result in large changes
in beliefs and feelings despite initial resistance
to the policy. Thus, it is clear from our data
that although most of the white housewives in
the integrated projects we studied did not, upon
moving into the projects, like the idea of living
in the same buildings with Negro families (and

certainly the community as a whole did not
favor it), a considerable change in attitudes and
" folkways " has taken place as a consequence
of their experiences resulting from a " state-
way."

We believe (though additional research is obviously necessary to replace beliefs by verified
knowledge) that the socio-political conditions
throughout most of the North and in the West
are such as to make integrated interracial housing feasible; and in terms of democratic values,
if it is feasible, it is preferable, by far, to the
segregated bi-racial pattern. The free mixing of
Negroes and whites in buses and trolleys, in
downtown cinemas and in shopping centers,
and, to some extent, in schools and at work, the
lack of legal or moral pressures to segregate,
and the growing political significance of the
Negro vote – all suggest its feasibility in much
of the North and West. In contrast, the pervasive " Jim Crow " of the South, the legal and
extralegal supports for prejudice and discrimination, the almost complete lack of political rights
and of political power by Negroes, and the
organized and semilegalized violence to keep
Negroes in an inferior status suggest that considerable political-economic change (internally or
externally imposed) will be necessary before integration will be either a likely or a feasible
policy in much of the South.

*Implications for intergroup relations in
general.* In a sense, we are on considerably
firmer ground when we discuss the theoretical
implications of our research. Other related
studies have been made in rather different social
settings in which more or less similar socio-
psychological conditions were at work. These
studies, which we have previously cited, in the
army, in industry, in the merchant marine, in
universities, and in government agencies all provide results which are in essential agreement
with the results of the present study. They all
indicate that under certain types of conditions
equal-status contacts with Negroes will result in
a considerable change in the behavior and attitudes of the prejudiced person.

What are these conditions? In brief it seems
that prejudices are likely to be diminished when
prejudiced persons are brought into situations

which compel* contacts between them and the objects of prejudice, provided that:

1. The behavior of the objects of prejudice is such as to be at variance or not to conform, with the beliefs of the prejudiced. That is, the Negroes, with whom the prejudiced person has contact, are not " lazy," " ignorant," " delinquent," etc.

2. The intimacy and amount of contact with the objects of prejudice, not conforming to the stereotypes of the prejudiced, are such as to result in experiences which are sufficiently compelling to resist marked perceptual and memorial distortion.

3. The contact takes place under conditions which make the nonconforming behavior seem relevant to the basis on which the objects of prejudice are grouped together. Thus, even though a Negro attendant is seen to be clean and honest, there may be little effect on stereotypes if the perception of cleanliness and honesty is connected primarily with the requirements of the situation, with the classification of the individual as an attendant rather than as a Negro or Negro attendant.†

4. The prejudiced person has values or is exposed to social influences (e.g., democratic values or the social influences emanating from a policy of an official, public body) which would strongly conflict with the unabashed retention of unrationalized prejudices.

In addition, if the contact situation is such that it encourages the development of new sentiments to replace prejudiced sentiments either as a result of the experience of cooperative activity with the objects of prejudice or as a result of the internalization of the social norms of an unprejudiced group, the reduction of prejudiced sentiments will be much facilitated.

# The urbanization of the Negro

*ROBERT C. WEAVER*

By 1960 it was clear that although there had been shifts in the regional intensity of residential segregation, its incidence remained universally high throughout urban areas of the nation. There was a slight decrease in spatial segregation in Northeast and north central cities from 1950 to 1960. Residential segregation in the urban South, however, increased, so that by 1960 it was more pronounced in Southern cities than in those of any other region. Although the decline in spatial segregation in the North was small, it took place in the face of large in-

---

* " Compel " either because of ecological factors, such as in an interracial housing project, or because of compelling individual goals, such as a desire to use a swimming pool open to all groups.

† Just as there is likely to be little effect upon prejudiced beliefs if " good " behavior upon the part of the objects of prejudice is seen to result from the requirements of the situation rather than from the person or from the person's membership in a minority group, so, too, can one expect a reduction in prejudice if " bad " behavior upon their part comes to be seen as emanating from their circumstances rather than from their personality or minority group membership. This is why changes in theories of behavior (from a genetic to an environmental emphasis) may have a subtle influence even upon prejudice.

*Reprinted from* The Urban Complex, *Doubleday and Company, Inc., 1964, pp. 249–263, with permission of the publisher.*

creases in the non-white population. In the absence of future large-scale in-migration this could represent a trend, and there were institutional reasons for believing that it would. Clearly the impact of new federal open-occupancy policy, more effective enforcement of state and local fair housing laws (which existed in nineteen states and over fifty cities as of July, 1963), the existence of some three hundred citizens' fair housing committees working toward open occupancy in white neighborhoods, and the pressures of the Negro people will combine to accelerate the reduction of enforced residential segregation, primarily in the North and border cities.

The situation in the South seemed to reflect projection of a trend which had become apparent soon after the Supreme Court school decision of 1954, when residential segregation became a means of evading the court order. At the same time, as has been delineated, the spatial distribution of urban Negroes combined with the growth of the middle class in facilitating the development and expansion of new Negro suburbs in the South and border states. This trend toward increased residential segregation will probably be offset somewhat in the border states and upper South by the impact of President Kennedy's Executive Order for Equal Opportunity in Housing. It will also be reduced by *de facto* desegregation of school and other public facilities. Only time can tell how fast the process will occur.

As was suggested above, dislocation of non-white families incident to urban renewal, highway construction, various public works undertakings, and private decision in the market, as well as population growth, increased their demand for public housing. At the same time, the greater economic upward mobility of whites and their access to a much wider housing market reduced their demand for public housing. As a consequence, the proportion of non-whites in this housing increased during the decade from 1950 to 1960. In the former year, 35.6 percent of those in federally assisted public housing were non-whites; by 1960 the figure was 45.8 percent. Thus, although these public housing units were but 0.8 percent of all dwelling units, they were 3.9 percent of the housing stock

available to non-whites. Since 1960, the trend has continued. As of June, 1963, of the 494,000 units of federally assisted public housing in occupancy, 49 percent were occupied by non-whites.

Public housing continued to play a peculiar role in influencing racial occupancy patterns. It is still instrumental in occasionally introducing non-whites into neighborhoods where they had previously not lived. At the same time, an increasing number of formerly integrated public housing projects are becoming all, or practically all, non-white in occupancy. To complicate the picture further, in the first few months after issuance of President Kennedy's Executive Order, several housing authorities in the Midwest, long urged to integrate their programs, did so, and in the upper South one city in which there had been continuing vacancies in a "white" public housing project adopted an open occupancy policy.

As long, however, as there is a disproportionately intense demand for low-rent public housing on the part of non-whites, the limited supply will be increasingly occupied by this segment of the population. While open-occupancy policies and practices will make available some previously all-white projects, it will probably initially increase the number and proportion of completely non-white projects. On the basis of first-come first-served tenant selection, non-whites will often fill existing vacancies at a much more rapid rate than whites. Thus, some existing bi-racial projects will become exclusively or predominantly non-white. In newly constructed developments a similar situation will often obtain.

The experience in Washington, D.C., documents this analysis, although, due to the large proportion of Negroes in the total population, it exaggerates the typical speed of events. In June, 1953, the local housing authority initiated a general policy of open occupancy for all public low-rent housing in the District of Columbia. Prior to that time, it had decided in 1952 that three projects in the postwar program should be available on an open-occupancy basis. In 1952, the percentage of non-white occupancy had been some 84 percent. In 1962 it had risen to approximately 95 percent, and by the end of June,

1963, it had inched up almost 96 percent.

On the latter date, there was no project completely occupied by whites, two projects had completely non-white tenants, and only one project had 10 percent or more white occupants. An additional project had slightly over 5 percent white participation, and two others slightly less than 5 percent. The remainder of twelve projects had token white participation.

One thing is sure. Open occupancy in public housing will result in non-whites' becoming an even larger proportion of the programs' population. And since early experience under the Executive Order indicated no significant diminution in community acceptability of public housing (between November 20, 1962, and August 31, 1963, there were some 74,000 units of public housing in pre-construction which, when completed, will be subject to the covenant against discrimination), this will mean a larger number of low-rent units for non-whites. At the same time, as the Executive Order and other legislative and institutional forces extend patterns of open occupancy throughout urban areas, low-income non-whites will have wider choices, which should result in an upgrading of the supply of private shelter available to them and a decline in its cost. Ultimately, open occupancy in urban areas and an increasing volume of Section 221 housing will slowly tend to reduce the concentration of non-white applicants upon public housing, and thereby lessen the tendency of open occupancy in *public housing* to occasion greater racial concentrations in that program. The impact of this force may, of course, be more than offset by the pressure of increasing non-white populations in cities.

The situation in middle-income housing is even more complex and also more hopeful. There can be no doubt about the contribution that the federally supported moderate-income housing program can make, and is making, in improving the quality and augmenting the quantity of housing available to non-whites. Its price range is at levels where there is a large pent-up demand among non-whites as well as among whites. In the past this demand among non-whites has been concentrated upon older, existing structures, many of which were ill-adapted to the needs of moderate-income families. The

new program will supplement this supply, thereby easing the pressures in the market, providing greater choices, and reducing the price of the existing supply.

These results will be reinforced by any successes we achieve in accelerating rehabilitation and upgrading of housing in the gray areas. By the fall of 1963, it seemed that there were real potentialities in these fields. As methods of increasing rapidly the supply of reasonably priced housing, they should contribute significantly to improving the quality of shelter occupied by non-whites.

The impact of the Section 221(d) (3) housing program is already evident in Southern cities. In a growing number of localities in the region, this program was supplying a new type of housing available to Negroes. A typical case, from the point of view of sponsorship, upgrading of amenities, and cost, occurred in Dallas, Texas. A new residential community was developing around the campus of Bishop College in South Dallas, where the St. John Missionary Baptist Church of the city sponsored Highland Village, a 300-unit Section 221(d) (3) rental apartment development.

The new living facility will have central heating and air-conditioning; pile carpeting and draperies; completely equipped kitchens with electric ranges, refrigerators, and garbage disposal units; tiled baths; and a child care and day nursery center. Renters will range from $75 a month, including utilities, for a one-bedroom unit to $90 a month for a three-bedroom, one-and-a-half-bath apartment. It is expected that there will be a tax abatement resulting in a $5-a-month reduction in rentals. The forthcoming accommodations will set a new standard of comfort for those moderate-income families which qualify for occupancy in the garden apartments.

Early results were no less striking in urban renewal areas. Philander Smith College is sponsoring a three-million-dollar, 240-unit apartment development in the Dunbar Redevelopment area of Little Rock. Rents begin at $55 for a one-bedroom unit, will be as high as $88 for three bedrooms. The Wheat Street Baptist Church is sponsoring a 520-apartment development in Atlanta's Butler Street Urban Renewal; there rents will start at $70. In Cumberland Urban Renewal in Greensboro, North Carolina, a non-profit group is undertaking a similar development; rents will range from $60 for a one-bedroom unit to $77.50 for three bedrooms.

In contrast to the situation in the low-income groups, non-whites are far from being a principal source of effective demand for moderate-income housing, even in cities with large non-white populations. Thus, if favorably located (from the point of view of attractiveness to white families) moderate-income housing is well designed, it will be bi-racial in many sections of the nation. This already exists in urban renewal areas in San Francisco; New York; Paterson, New Jersey; Madison, Wisconsin; Cincinnati; and Minneapolis. It is suggested by token non-white participation in moderate-income redevelopment projects in Brookline, Massachusetts, and the beginnings of white participation in Marine City, California. Existing allocations and commitments for Section 221(d) (3) housing suggest that additional bi-racial areas may be developed in Los Angeles, New Haven, Chicago, Boston, Detroit, Kansas City (Missouri), St. Louis, Madison, Denver, Hartford, Binghamton (New York), Bridgeport, and a score of other cities.

In addition, of course, a larger amount of Section 221(d) (3) housing is planned or under construction on sites outside of urban renewal areas, primarily in cities with sizable non-white populations. The resulting housing, too, will upgrade the quality of shelter available to non-whites in many instances. Much of this new construction will be in developments where whites and non-whites will reside as neighbors.

There are several major forces working to extend the housing choices available to non-whites of higher incomes. First, the increasing number of state and local open-occupancy laws and their constantly broadening coverage is important. Secondly, the Executive Order on Equal Opportunity in Housing banned racial discrimination in housing financed with FHA- and VA-underwritten mortgages, and these two agencies had title to over 90,000 dwelling units which were immediately available to non-whites. Concurrently, between November 20, 1962, and October 15, 1963, some 55,000 completed FHA-aided units were subject to the non-discrimination order. Thirdly, applications for 169,000 FHA-aided new homes and 78,000 units of new multi-family housing, as well as about 100,000 VA-aided units, were pending; those in this group completed and financed with FHA- and VA-underwritten mortgages would be similarly affected. Fourthly, Negro pressure for equality included housing on its agenda, and results were apparent as early as mid-summer. Finally, and perhaps in part as a consequence of the first four developments, hundreds of fair-housing groups were actively encouraging Negroes to find homes in the suburbs.

The situation in the New York City metropolitan area has been summarized:

> Two developments are expected to accelerate the movement to break the color line in New York suburban housing. One is the national surge to obtain equal rights for Negroes and the other is the adoption of legislation this year by New York and Connecticut.
>
> The legislation, effective September 1 in New York and October 1 in Connecticut, bars discrimination on account of color in the sale or rental of virtually all housing. A similar measure is pending in the New Jersey Legislature.*

As the article quoted above reports, there are more than fifty fair-housing groups in the New York City area. These groups had been effective in extending help to, and securing acceptance of, non-whites in new areas of living. The significant social factors incident to their work were: (1) the number of non-white families which elected to move into the new areas was small; (2) although there had been great apprehension on the part of white owners to the

---

* Clarence Dean, "Drive for Homes for Negroes in Suburbs Will Be Intensified," New York Times, (August 14, 1963), p. 19. In a Maryland suburb of Washington, D. C., a fair-housing group had similar successes as those set forth in the text for New York City. The income groups involved, neighborhood reactions, and techniques were substantially the same as those reported for New York. See Robert E. Baker, "Suburbs Opening Up for Negro Housing," Washington Post, (October 17, 1963), pp. 1, 8.

prospect of a Negro neighbor, once the individual, as contrasted to the concept, became a reality, there was little opposition; (3) the non-whites involved (and they were relatively high-income professionals) found warm acceptance on the part of their new neighbors.

All of this suggests that the American people are capable of adjustment to new racial patterns when and if they realize these are inevitable. This was true in employment during World War II, and it will be true of housing in the decade ahead,* although in shelter the initial opposition will probably be greater, as it has been in school desegregation.

A significant development during the decade from 1950 to 1960 was the increasing utilization of government-underwritten mortgages by non-whites. This was one of the few areas in which minorities had improved their relative status during the period. Thus, in 1960, some 43 percent of white and 29 percent of non-white owners of mortgages had availed themselves of FHA-insured and VA-guaranteed mortgages, compared to 32 percent and 18 percent, respectively, in 1950. Involved in this development was an increase of 145,000 non-white homeowners with government-underwritten mortgages, for the most part under the VA program. Over the decade, there had also been an increase of 254,000 in the number of non-white homeowners with conventional mortgage loans.

These developments were encouraging because prior to 1950, non-white participation in governmental programs designed to encourage and financially ease home ownership had been minimal. In 1950, for example, 22,322 non-whites had VA-guaranteed first mortgages, and non-whites represented 2.2 percent of those having such mortgages. By 1960 some 124,000, or 3.7 percent of the total, were non-whites. For the FHA, comparable figures were 24,407 or 2.3 percent, in 1950; and 68,000, or 2.5 percent, in 1960. No doubt the 1960 figures reflected the availability of a sizable amount of older urban housing to non-whites in all parts of the nation, the rise of Negro suburban developments in the South and border states, access to increasing but still greatly limited suburban areas in the North (as a consequence of fair-housing laws), and rising incomes among middle-class Negroes in all parts of the country. They also indicated that non-whites still benefited much less from FHA and VA mortgage programs than did whites.

It is revealing that the median incomes of whites and non-whites having FHA-insured first mortgages were substantially the same in 1960 – for whites, $6,900; and for non-whites, $6,800. For homeowners with VA-guaranteed first mortgages the figure for whites was also $6,900, but for non-whites it was $5,000. For conventional loans, there was the greatest discrepancy: $6,500 for all, and $4,200 for non-whites. These relationships occurred in a situation where median incomes for those with all types of mortgages were as follows: for whites, $6,800; and for non-whites, $4,500. The consequences are what would be expected. In the FHA and VA programs whites and non-whites paid the same median interest rates. On conventional loans, where 70 percent of the non-white financing was concentrated, the median for non-whites was .5 percent higher than for the total. Since

---

* As 1963 came to its close, there were evidences of realization that the homebuilding industry would have to adjust to open occupancy. The editor of *Practical Builder*, addressing himself to home builders, observed: ". . . Limited experience in 1963 indicates that open occupancy need not be an important handicap for builders. Most problems have been settled according to law and local opinion. We believe that most of the few incidents that have occurred have been the result of hasty or ill-considered reaction on the part of the builder or his employees.

"Builders have learned that this problem cannot be evaded or solved by avoiding the prospect. It has also become apparent that complacent local authorities do not have the final answer to a national problem. The builder's decision may vary according to the community where he builds, but the need for full information, tact and decisive action applies everywhere.

"Every builder should know the laws under which he operates and the temper of his community. He knows what he should do and what he must do. Equally important is a well prepared advance plan of how he will do it.

"Until you have planned what you will say and do as you meet each problem of open occupancy—and until each of your representatives to the buying public is thoroughly trained according to your plan—you are not ready for 1964" (Larry Drake, "Open Occupancy in 1964," *Practical Builder*, December, 1963, p. 6).

the non-whites were such a small proportion of the total number of mortgagors, it works out that, for all loans, non-whites paid a median rate almost 1 percent higher.

The relative extent and proportion of non-white participation in government-underwritten first mortgages is set forth in detail in the following table. With the exception of the $3,000 to $4,000 income bracket, only non-whites with incomes of $10,000 or more had as large a proportion of government-underwritten

figures set forth in the table, it must be realized that the downpayment required for VA-guaranteed loans has consistently been lower than that required for FHA-insured loans. As a matter of fact, downpayments have been required for VA loans only during two limited periods since 1950 – July, 1950, to September, 1952; and April, 1955, to April, 1958.

These data suggest certain conclusions. It is obvious that as non-whites had access to a wider segment of the housing market and achieved

*Nonfarm Homeowner Properties with Government-Underwritten First Mortgages, by Color and Income of Mortgagor, United States, 1960[a] (Number of Properties in Thousands)*

| Household income[b] | White[c] Properties with | | | | Non–white Properties with | | | |
|---|---|---|---|---|---|---|---|---|
| | All mortgaged properties | Government-underwritten first mortgage | FHA first mortgage | VA first mortgage | All mortgaged properties | Government-underwritten first mortgage | FHA first mortgage | VA first mortgage |
| Number total[d] | *13,805* | *5,857* | *2,600* | *3,257* | *648* | *192* | *68* | *124* |
| Less than $2,000 | 524 | 110 | 64 | 46 | 89 | 10 | 3 | 7 |
| 2,000 to 2,999 | 425 | 129 | 70 | 59 | 85 | 14 | 7 | 7 |
| 3,000 to 3,999 | 774 | 235 | 96 | 139 | 92 | 29 | 8 | 21 |
| 4,000 to 4,999 | 1,457 | 577 | 255 | 322 | 113 | 33 | 6 | 27 |
| 5,000 to 6,999 | 4,245 | 1,985 | 838 | 1,147 | 133 | 47 | 13 | 34 |
| 7,000 to 9,999 | 3,897 | 1,933 | 849 | 1,084 | 89 | 42 | 22 | 20 |
| 10,000 or more | 2,483 | 888 | 427 | 461 | 47 | 18 | 10 | 8 |
| Median | $6,800 | — | $6,900 | $6,900 | $4,500 | — | $6,800 | $5,000 |
| Percent total | 100 | 43 | 19 | 24 | 100 | 29 | 10 | 19 |
| Less than $2,000 | 100 | 21 | 12 | 9 | 100 | 11 | 3 | 8 |
| 2,000 to 2,999 | 100 | 30 | 16 | 14 | 100 | 16 | 8 | 8 |
| 3,000 to 3,999 | 100 | 30 | 12 | 18 | 100 | 32 | 9 | 23 |
| 4,000 to 4,999 | 100 | 40 | 18 | 22 | 100 | 29 | 5 | 24 |
| 5,000 to 6,999 | 100 | 47 | 20 | 27 | 100 | 36 | 10 | 26 |
| 7,000 to 9,999 | 100 | 50 | 22 | 28 | 100 | 47 | 25 | 22 |
| 10,000 or more | 100 | 36 | 17 | 19 | 100 | 38 | 21 | 17 |

[a] One-unit owner-occupied nonfarm properties. [b] Income of owner and relatives living with him. [c] Derived by the Housing and Home Finance Agency. [d] Totals may not add to sum of components due to "rounding."

Source : Department of Commerce, Bureau of the Census, *1960 Census of Housing*, Volume V, Part 1, Table 2 and Part 1, Supplement, Table 2.

mortgages among the total held by the group as did whites. Interestingly, at the $10,000-and-over income level, this non-white rate of participation exceeded that of whites. Here, too, there was another peculiarity : the rate of this participation of non-whites at this income level and at the $7,000 to $10,000 level was greater than for whites in FHA and lesser in VA. It was at the $3,000 to $4,000 and the $4,000 to $5,000 income levels that the rate of non-white participation in VA-guaranteed loans exceeded that for whites. In order to understand the

higher incomes, they secured better mortgage terms. This was accomplished, primarily, by their qualifying for a larger volume of government-insured and guaranteed mortgages. The new Executive Order should accelerate this development. Of equal immediate impact will be the continuing expansion of the new FHA-insured low- and moderate-income housing programs, provided for under the expanded Section 221 in the Housing Act of 1961. These new programs are already providing mortgage insurance for scores of thousands of new dwelling units that will be occupied by non-whites. The utilization of Section 221(d) (3) for rehabilitation in the gray areas, will, if successful, also accelerate non-white participation in the benefits of FHA mortgage insurance activities.

Ironically, the least affluent among non-white home purchasers have traditionally benefited least from lower-cost government-underwritten mortgages. This was typical of the programs, and applied to whites as well as non-whites. However, the degree of lack of participation was almost twice as intense for low-income non-whites in 1960. Clearly this reflected the latter's concentration in the older areas of core cities, their consequent restriction to a limited and generally less desirable section of the market, and the long-established expensive forms of credit available to them. Here, too, recent developments should provide some relief.

In this situation, we shall probably see in the next decade, a continuing upgrading in the amount and quality of shelter available to low-income non-whites. This occurred during the decade 1950–1960, although during that period the average upgrading of housing at all price ranges for whites outstripped that among non-whites.[1] Whether or not this qualitative gap will close in the current decade depends primarily upon the relative income structure among non-whites (as compared to whites) and the degree of access non-whites have to the total housing market.

Higher-income non-white families will probably make the most significant gains in terms of better facilities and wider choices in the housing market. This will reflect their ability to pay for good accommodations and their desire for racially integrated neighborhoods, no less than the wider receptivity on the part of whites to a limited number of middle-class colored neighbors as contrasted to the fear of inundation by a large number of low-income non-whites. It is also in the American tradition, which has afforded the descendants of the newcomers greater access to better housing in the total market as they have effected significant economic, social, and cultural improvement.

Insofar as wider opportunities for housing available to non-whites are concentrated in the suburbs, they will provide an additional divi-dend benefiting the whole urban complex. An important impediment to metropolitan approaches to area-wide problems of community development and housing has been the residential racial distribution of our population. Any modification in these patterns will facilitate greater cooperation between the core areas and the suburbs that surround them.

The most stable interracial neighborhoods will be those of relatively high-cost and the well-located moderate-cost, new developments. It has been indicated that the income distribution and the effective demand for high-cost shelter among non-whites is such as to limit the volume of colored residents in this price range, while in the moderate-income sector, the effective demand is bi-racial. Ironically, in light of its image and early history, urban renewal, in all probability, will facilitate the greatest advances. Already it has introduced a new phenomenon: a growing number of whites living next door to non-whites of comparable income by choice.

At the same time, the recent Executive Order and the work of the fair-housing groups and others are gradually opening the suburbs to non-whites. In this segment of the housing market, progress will be somewhat slower initially. In proportion as desirable high- and moderate-cost new housing in the core cities is available to minorities, their demand for suburban facilities will be lessened. While in moderate-cost housing the pressure of numbers may result, in some instances, in non-white occupancy of most of the available units in a development, such a situation is highly improbable in the higher-cost counterparts. And, as indicated above, many of the moderate-income developments in the central city will remain bi-racial.

Low-income non-whites will get a larger supply of housing, too, but it will probably be in a market that is either now, or will soon become, racially homogeneous. Some of the forthcoming low-income public housing will initially be racially mixed. Much will be predominantly or exclusively non-white in occupancy. Simultaneously, many of those displaced will gravitate to existing areas of non-white concentration or to contiguous areas. For class as well as color reasons bi-racial areas with large numbers and proportions of low-income non-whites will tend to lose their racially hetero-geneous character. But for most low-income non-white individuals and households involved, the latter circumstance will be of secondary importance. In time two factors will serve to accentuate low-income non-whites' desire for residential integration: the qualitative and quan-titative limitations inherent in ghetto residential patterns and the paucity of public facilities (especially schools) characteristic of racially seg-regated low-income neighborhoods.

Of course, a large part of non-whites' housing problems stems from their low incomes and resulting restricted purchasing power. There is, however, another recent development which has great pertinence to the housing, no less than the general status, of non-whites. It is the pioneer-ing efforts to deal with the human problems of urban living. Success in dealing with these needs can, in the long run, be the most significant single force in upgrading housing and living conditions of all low-income families in our society. Clearly, neglect of these human needs will not only prevent success in meeting the housing requirements of low-income families but will also delay, complicate, and, perhaps, ulti-mately destroy urban renewal.

# The housing industry

V

## The organization of the construction industry

*MILES COLEAN and ROBINSON NEWCOMB*

The special characteristics of structures, the enormous variety and variability of construction activity, the dependence upon external decisions which determine the type and volume of demand, and the extent of governmental influence combine to produce organizational patterns that are as unique as the environmental circumstances described in the previous chapters.

### Requirements imposed on the construction industry

To demonstrate this, we may imagine that no organizations for doing construction work existed and, consequently, that it was necessary to create them. We would find that such newly created organizations, in order to perform the manifold tasks to be assigned them, would call for the following characteristics:

1. *Specialization to meet the variety of*

*demand.* The first requirement is an industry that can provide the diverse expertness essential to produce the multiplicity of structures and facilities that make up construction activity. Two possible methods of organization could be used to accomplish this:

a. The establishment of a number of specialized types of organizations corresponding to the distinct types of demand.

b. The formulation of a more general type of organization having sufficient internal adjustability to permit it to provide different combinations of special skills to suit the different demands as they appear.

The choice is actually less simple than this because the general types of construction – residential, commercial, institutional, military, and so forth – display an almost infinite variety of differentiation. In the industrial area alone,

*Reprinted from* Stabilizing Construction, *McGraw-Hill Book Company, 1952, pp. 90–105, with permission of the publisher.*

there are no less than 20 fairly distinct sub-types, each with many special features.

Specialization by type of structure offers no general solution to the problem of industrial organization. The number of specialist organizations would be legion and the task of keeping occupied, even though they were foot-loose as the medieval Freemasons, would be insuperable. This type of organization is possible only for the few classes of work which combine uniqueness with a fairly uniform composition – so as to make specialization possible – and a sufficiently steady demand to make specialization practicable. This is possible for the engineering and contracting firms that erect oil refineries, steel plants, and certain classes of chemical plants, and, to a lesser extent, those that build roads and bridges. Even with such highly integrated and specialized firms, an exclusive concentration on a single type of work would probably not be feasible over a long period of time. And their shiftability in times of stress, like that of less specialized firms, has often been demonstrated.

A considerable degree of concentrated specialization is common among operative builders; and when housebuilding is brisk, specialization may become largely exclusive of anything but commercial work incidental to residential projects. This situation, however, is likely to be limited to a few large places. For the industry as a whole, the ability to handle a wide range of activity is essential to economic self-preservation.

Organization characterized by great internal flexibility – in other words, permitting a continued reshuffling of its elements – is therefore a necessity. Such an organizational pattern implies the existence of a variety of organizations specialized in the major kinds of operations that are common to a wide range of construction activity and which may be grouped under a managing or general contracting establishment (which may itself perform a number of specialties) as a particular operation may dictate. Such specialty organizations would be skilled in the installation of parts of the total structure, such as masonry, carpentry, plastering, sheet-metal work, structural-steel work, electric wiring, elevators, plumbing, heating, and so on.

2. *Flexibility to meet variability in demand.* The *variety* of construction demand requires an industry sufficiently flexible in organization to allow a constant regrouping of specialists to meet a succession of differing assignments. The *variability* of construction demand from season to season and from one year to another requires a flexibility of a different sort – the ability to expand rapidly to meet an increase in the volume of demand. Conversely, the industry has the problem of finding means of contracting its organizations with a minimum of financial disruption when demand is satisfied or withdrawn.

In terms of industrial organization, these requirements would imply the following characteristics:

a. Looseness of managerial combinations, to permit rapid regrouping, expansion, and contraction.
b. A minimum of fixed capital investment, to keep down fixed charges in times of low activity.
c. A floating labor force that is not tied to the fortunes of any specific employer and for whose welfare no specific employer is responsible.

3. *Flexibility to meet local demand.* Amid these needs for great organizational flexibility stands one inescapable rigidity – the fact that the final products of construction are immobile in any true sense and must be produced where they are to be used. In construction, the producer must go where the product is used and there conduct his work. He cannot, like other producers, manufacture at a central point and send his product to the market.*

The total construction demand is the sum of

---

* The prefabricated house manufacturer is to a certain extent an exception to this, but up to the present time neither a complete nor an important one. Not only is the relative volume of work classed as prefabrication still small, but the product is never complete to the extent of eliminating all site work. Moreover, the market area which may be served by a central plant is limited by the cost of transporting a heavy, bulky, and relatively fragile product.

a number of local demands, and each locality must be provided with the means of satisfying its own separate activity. This activity will vary greatly in volume and character from year to year; yet some demand will exist at all times, and the means for taking care of it must also exist. In large metropolitan centers, which provide at least an average diversity and continuity of opportunity, this problem is less serious than in smaller places. In the latter, a single hotel, apartment building, warehouse, or factory may satisfy all such demand for a number of years. The more highly specialized the work, the larger the locality must be to offer continuity of demand.

These circumstances impose two further requirements upon the construction industry:

a. Sufficient mobility to follow demand where it is active and to withdraw capacity from areas where demand is slack.

b. At the same time, sufficient stability and continuity to maintain stand-by facilities in every community to meet at least the day-to-day and month-to-month demands for alterations and repairs.

Just as the producer of construction must go to the site of its use to do his work, so must his plant and equipment. Only to a limited degree can a builder operate from a fixed plant as does the manufacturer; and, by comparison with the latter, his scope for centrally controlled, highly mechanized operations is limited. Every tool and piece of equipment that the building mechanic uses must be portable; and, for the most part, they must not only be transportable to and from the job but must also be easily taken from place to place within the job. This fact is seldom sufficiently recognized when the technological problems of the construction industry are under discussion.

## From requirement to reality

Around the several requirements described above, the construction industry has taken form; and, all in all, it must be recognized that these requirements have been substantially fulfilled. The industry has been able to produce the full range of facilities demanded of it; and it has demonstrated its capacity to shift rapidly both as to the kinds and volume of work.

The means by which this has been done are several:

1. *The general contracting system.* General contractors, and also builders operating on their own account, represent top management in the construction industry. It is for the most part they who are in contact with the market, seek the work, and form the associations and combinations necessary to a particular job. In size they range from the small builder, who will undertake one or a few alterations or new structures at a time, to large firms capable of constructing a huge reclamation project or erecting simultaneously a number of large buildings. Although in numbers the small firms predominate, the greater part of the total contract construction is done by a relatively few large organizations. Thus, about half the work reported in the 1939 Census was done by the less than 4 percent of total contractors (general and special-trade, and also the builder group) who did $100,000 or more of work in the year for which the reports were made, and about 27 percent of the work was done by the 0.5 percent of the contractors who did $500,000 or more of work in that year.*

Roughly classed by the Bureau of the Census as building, highway, and heavy (dam, bridge, etc.) contractors, according to the main emphasis of their operations, the general contracting group as a whole is less bound by locality than either the operative builders or the special contractors. This is particularly true of highway- and heavy-construction contractors, the nature of whose work necessitates a considerable operational range, and who do about one-fifth and one-third of their work, respectively, outside of their home states. It is less true of building contractors, who perform only about 12 percent of their work out of state, or under half

---

* The 1939 Census of Construction does not permit a classification of general contractors according to the total size of their jobs, including work subcontracted.

The quoted figures, however, probably give at least a fair idea of the actual situation.

the proportion of out-of-state work done by the other two groups combined. Operative builders, and then the special-trade contractors, perform the smallest proportions of out-of-state work.

Because of the relatively large investments in equipment, highway- and heavy-construction contractors tend to confine themselves to their specialties, although this is by no means universally the case. Building contractors, however, show great variations in the type of work undertaken and provide the basis of the great adaptability which is characteristic of the industry. Their flexibility is increased by their usually small investment in operating equipment. Through rental or subcontracting, they may obtain the equipment specially suitable for the work in hand, while their nuclear organizations can be expanded or supplemented as the occasion requires. The same freedom from fixed investment and organization aids them in weathering periods of little or no activity.

Evidence of the flexibility of the industry is found in the high rate of turnover of construction firms. During the years 1944–1950, for instance, the records show that the rate of entrance into contract construction (including general and special contracting and operative building)* was greater than in any other of eight main categories of enterprise, not only for the period as a whole, but also for every year in the period except one in which it had next to the greatest number of entrants. The rate of discontinuance, like the rate of entry, is high. From 1944 to 1950, it exceeded that of all other enterprise groups for the period as a whole and ranked among the top three for each of the years during the period.

2. *The subcontracting system.* Without the large and almost infinitely diverse aggregation of special-trade contractors, the construction industry could not function under its existing requirements. This group provides the specialization within flexibility that permits the industry to accommodate itself to any assignment. The subcontractors, moreover, make possible the

rapid mobilization and dismissal of job organizations necessitated by the changes both in the kind and volume of demand.

With the increasing intricacy of structures, the number of special trades has grown. At present nearly 20 specialty operations may be required on a detached house of moderate size, while on a larger and more complex structure more than 50 will be required. Usually a general contractor will himself perform only a few of these specialties – ordinarily those of a structural character, mainly such as bricklaying, carpentry, and concrete work – and will handle the remainder through subcontracts. In some cases practically the entire work will be sublet, the general contractor providing only coordination and supervisory services.

On their own part, special-trade contractors may act as subcontractors under a general contract or may contract directly with the owner (especially common in the mechanical and painting trades), or, where a job is predominantly but not wholly in their own field, may act as general contractors. The latter is frequent in maintenance and alteration work.

Special-trade contractors are much more numerous than general contractors, and while again there is great variation in size among them, the average size of firms is smaller than the average general contracting firm. With some notable exceptions, the special-trade group as a whole is, as noted previously, more localized in its operations than is commonly true of general contractors.

3. *The differentiated labor force.* The subdivision of construction into a number of diverse specialties requires that labor capable of performing each specialty be available. The result is the craft system of labor organization. Today more than 75 distinct specialties can be differentiated. Some artisans will be skilled in and will alternately work in more than one of these, such as painting and paperhanging, or carpentry and floor laying; and since all of the specialties are distributed among only 19 sepa-

---

* Again it is not possible statistically to separate general contractors, builders, and special-trade contractors. In all probability the rate of turnover for the former groups

is as great as, or even greater than, the rate for the latter because the lesser amount of capital investment increases the ease of entry and exit.

rate building-trade unions, a considerable movement from one closely related specialty to another is evident.* Crafts are likely to be more distinctly differentiated in large than in small places and on large than on small operations.

The construction labor force obviously must have greater mobility than is required of most other occupations. The places where work may be found will often vary from month to month and may vary from day to day. Highway- and heavy-construction workers particularly must be prepared to go long distances to obtain employment, and, except in the larger places, any job of more than average size is likely to require recruitment from outside communities. Nevertheless, the workers as a group are likely to range less far than special-trade contractors and less still than general contractors.

The construction labor force must not only be highly specialized and relatively mobile but also for the most part must be a floating force in terms of its employer relationships. Workers, like special-trade contractors, are assembled for the job in hand, and when the job is finished, so also is the employment, unless by chance the employer has another job of the same character. A tenure of employment lasting more than one year, except for key men, is unusual on all but very large jobs, while a workman who serves three or even more employers during a year is not uncommon even in active periods.

4. *The complex system of materials distribution.* The servicing of an activity as widespread, diverse, and irregular as construction requires a materials-distributing system of extraordinary range and flexibility. The materials and equipment that go into construction come from more than 15,000 producers,† and they are installed by as many as 215,000 building, general contracting, and special contracting firms of one sort or another,[1] without estimating the countless householders, farmers, and maintenance men who are also purchasers of these items. Between these groups stand more than 40,000 wholesalers, jobbers, and dealers, whose func-

tion it is to see that all types of users are able at all times to obtain what they require.[2]

There is no single fixed pattern of distribution in the construction industry. Fairly well fixed systems of distribution exist for certain classes of materials or equipment, but the variations among products are numerous. Brick, structural tile, and structural steel are generally distributed directly by the manufacturers or fabricators; ceramic tile, composition tile, and linoleum are ordinarily installed by the distributer; for numerous materials, such as lumber, hardware, paint, wallboard, etc., the distributing function is generally wholly distinct from either manufacturing or installation. Moreover, there will be some departures from even these regular methods of distribution according to the size of the operation and the resources of the builder.

The distribution function is manifold as well as varied. Assembly, storage, and delivery of materials are the primary and most important functions of the distributer. He must buy from numerous sources – in quantities appropriate to his estimate of local demand and to efficient methods of transportation – those items that he assumes will be required by his customers. To allow adequate selection, he must in ordinary times maintain well-assorted inventories and be prepared to make deliveries to meet builders' schedules. For small builders, the make-up of delivery loads may even have to be arranged so as to provide the particular items needed at the time with a minimum of rehandling at the site.

In small communities and for small builders generally, the distributer frequently provides some sort of architectural service, from stock plans to special designs, specifications, material lists, and cutting diagrams. Another service often provided is the processing of materials, particularly lumber. Precut framing members, prefabricated roof trusses, and panels for floors, walls, and ceilings are the items most commonly available. Distributers also serve as centers of information and for the exchange of experience about different types of products. With the ever-

---

* It is by no means always the case, however, that a member of a union can or is allowed to perform all the specialities organized in a particular union.
† *Census of Manufacturers: 1947*, Vol. I, Chap. I, Table

2. Producers of basic raw materials, including the major part of the lumber industry, are not included in this figure.

increasing range of specialty products, alternate products for the same use, and multipurpose products (such as a single material providing both thermal insulation and sheathing), this function is of more than minor importance.

Distributors are often the main source of temporary financing for the builder. For small building operations in particular, it is common for the dealer to grant or arrange for credit on all materials that he supplies until payment is received by the builder, or, in the case of houses built for sale, even until the sale is made and the permanent financing arranged. Dealers may also help to obtain the long-term financing for the builder or his customer; and they are a main source of local promotion and market stimulation through their advertising, their displays and plan services, consultations with prospective buyers, and recommendations to contractors.

5. *Specialized design services.* The range of type and uniqueness of individual structures due to site conditions, and the vast possibilities for variety in appearance, layout, and specifications create a demand for skilled designers, who often operate on an independent, professional basis. Most prominent among these are architects and engineers.

The architect, in addition to preparing the general drawings and specifications for a structure, frequently selects the other specialists and directs and coordinates their activities. He acts as agent for the owner in soliciting bids for the work, selecting contractors, preparing contracts, supervising construction, and arbitrating disputes. For many types of structures, the line of function between architects and engineers is not clearly denoted. For some types, such as bridges, chemical plants, refineries, and the like, the engineer may displace the architect altogether and perform all the functions ascribed above to the architect.

Besides acting in a professional capacity, architects may serve in the employ of builders, contractors, materials dealers, and industrial organizations, doing force-account work. It is probably even more common for engineer designers to be part of contracting and manufacturing organizations. There appears to be a trend away from the predominance of the strictly independent practitioner in favor of the designer who is either part of a construction organization or who serves such an organization on a retainer or other basis.

In this connection may be mentioned the appearance of a new group vaguely described as consultants, who offer to owners, builders, and others specialized advice on design, selection of materials and equipment, financing, and government relations, but who neither perform the complete function nor assume the responsibility of the professional architect or engineer. This group has been called into being by the increasing complexity of structures, the broadening range of materials and methods, and the expanding area of contact of government with construction activity.

6. *Technological progress.* Another means of achieving flexibility within the construction industry has been through the very considerable technological progress that has taken place throughout our construction history, especially great during the recent past. We are not concerned here with the many changes and additions in materials and equipment that have increased the quality, intricacy, or costliness of structures – plumbing equipment, heating equipment, electric wiring, insulation, glass, and so forth – but solely with changes that have given the industry greater adaptability and efficiency in meeting its requirements. Such changes have occurred in method, materials, and operating equipment.

Many of these have resulted in notable savings in labor and materials; but to a very large degree they have been designed to save time rather than cost. The main source of pride in erecting the Empire State Building, for instance, was not the lowness of its cost but the fact that, from land clearance to completion, the job was done in one year. This attitude is a natural reflection of a sporadic rather than a constant demand. The miracle of war construction, again, was not in its economy but in the vast amount of work done in a critically short period of time.

Time and cost saving went together, however, in the "balloon" frame, introduced into wood-frame residential construction during the first half of the nineteenth century, which provided a great advance in saving of lumber and rapidity of erection over earlier methods.* At the other end of the scale, the development of skeleton steel framing after 1885 not only resulted in savings in the amount of mason work for a given enclosure and in an unmeasurable flexibility in the design of structures but, again, greatly speeded the construction operation. There has been a gradual but steady shift from site to shop assembly of parts of buildings – doors and doorframes, window sash and frames, cabinets, trim, office partitions, and so forth – while the more recent development of prefabricated wall, floor, and roof panels for residential construction is a continuation of the same trend.

Numerous materials – such as ready-mixed concrete, plywood, laminated wood, wallboard, plaster base, prefinished flooring, plastic sheets, light steel shapes, light metals in sheet, tubular, and extruded forms, bituminous roofing – have added greatly to the ability of the construction industry to meet its diverse demands. At the same time, progress has been under way toward simplifying and standardizing the number and sizes of individual products and, lately, through an interproduct movement, toward coordinating dimensions to reduce cutting, fitting, and waste at the site.

Notable also has been the steady increase in the mechanization of site operations, a movement stimulated by war and postwar labor shortages. Beginning about the end of the Civil War with the introduction, in large construction operations, of excavating machinery, pneumatic drills, and riveters, and followed later by power-driven hoists and concrete and mortar mixers, the use of power equipment has steadily expanded until now, even on small jobs, the list of power tools includes automatic saws, sanders, drills, light mixers, power shovels, pipe threaders and paint sprayers. For larger work, the list is much longer.

The increased availability of power tools has had its reflection in job organization, permitting a more efficient use of labor and creating possibilities for precutting and preassembly of materials either at the site – in a temporary shop at the site if the job is extensive – or in an off-site shop.

## The construction industry today

The organization of the construction industry as we find it today is a response to its environment. It has operated under conditions of rapid and often unpredictable shifts in demand. It has encountered periods when additional capacity always seemed to be needed, later to face times when all possible reductions seemed still to leave excess capacity.

To these circumstances, intensified as they have been by the effects of two major wars within three decades, the construction industry has manifested considerable adaptability. It has devised organizations that coalesce and dissolve readily. It has developed a variety of organizational patterns, designing methods, and operating techniques to meet the diverse and shifting character of its demand. It has endeavored to improve its technology to give it greater speed and flexibility.

Placed in less tempestuous surroundings, construction would have responded differently. For instance, it is likely that mechanization would have proceeded more rapidly and have been more definitely directed to cost reduction than to increasing the speed of operation. As things now stand, a heavy capital investment in equipment offers a hazard which is recognized by sound management, as witness the fact that some of the largest contractors – in terms of size of contract handled – maintain no permanent investment in equipment at all but acquire and charge off what they need for each job. The ideal situation in the industry is maneuverability – freedom both to move in and to withdraw quickly as the prospects indicate.

---

* The first balloon-framed structure appears to have been a small Catholic church built in Chicago in 1833. See Walker Field, "A Re-examination into the Invention of the Balloon Frame," *Journal of the American Society of Architectural Historians,* (October, 1942), p. 22.

# Classifications of the construction industry

*JAMES GILLIES and FRANK MITTLEBACH*

There are two basic ways in which an industry may be defined: in terms of the product produced, or in terms of some central characteristic which is common to a group of firms. Difficulties are encountered in defining the construction industry, regardless of which of these two methods of definition is chosen.

When definitions are attempted in terms of construction activity, the great variety of activity makes such definitions so broad that they are hardly useful. For example, Lowell J. Chawner defines construction activity as including " the design, production, and maintenance of fixed works and structures, such as inclosed space for residential, commercial, governmental, manufacturing and similar purposes; fixed works for transportation and for the storage and transmission of commodities such as water, oil, gas and electrical energy; and substantial changes in the earth's topography."[1] But as Colean and Newcomb point out,[2] this broad definition omits many activities which should not be excluded and includes some nonconstruction activities. The U.S. Departments of Labor and Commerce have used the same type of approach and state that " ... construction covers the erection, maintenance, and repair (including replacement of integral parts) of immobile structures and utilities, together with service facilities which become integral parts of structures and are essential to their use for any general purpose...."[3] Obviously, definitions in terms of what the industry does are subject to qualification.

The other approach to a definition, through some central characteristic feature, leads to a conclusion similar to that developed by Colean and Newcomb, i.e., the construction industry includes " only those professional designing organizations, general contractors, builders, special-trade contractors, and workmen whose principal business is construction."[4] This definition implies that there is a difference between construction activity and the construction industry on the grounds that a great deal of construction activity is performed by organizations and individuals whose principal business or occupation is not construction. Similarly, firms whose principal business is construction may engage in other activities.

While such a definition appears most appropriate when examining management activities, it may be argued that a delineation of an industry which groups general contractors, builders, and special-trade contractors together is too broad for effective analysis. For example, it is argued, primarily by Maisel, that there is a separate, identifiable housebuilding industry. He contends that " the housebuilding industry does exist as an entity, separable from general contracting at one extreme and from owner-builders at the other."[5] He argues " ... that in discussing housebuilding it is possible to deal with the producing organizations rather than merely with processes ... that producer initiative is a dominating characteristic of postwar housebuilding ... and ... the overlap between housebuilders and others in the building industry is not great."[6] From this, the conclusion is developed that " although yesterday belonged to the con-

Reprinted from Management in the Light Construction Industry, *Real Estate Research Program, University of California at Los Angeles, 1962, pp. 6–9 and 24–25, with permission of the publisher.*

tractor, this study shows that the contractor is not growing; that the merchant builder, taking advantage of to-day's (1949) techniques in mass production and mass merchandising, is moving in on tomorrow."[7]

There are other indications that it is appropriate to consider housebuilding as an identifiable industry with characteristics so unique that it should be studied independently of the construction industry as a whole. For example, the growth and success in the post-World War II period of the National Association of Home Builders, a most influential trade association in the construction industry, and of journals such as *House and Home* and the *Journal of Homebuilding* devoted almost entirely to housebuilding activity are cited as support for the belief that there is a large group of firms which are housebuilders and housebuilders only. It is usually suggested that these firms have problems essentially different from those of contractors in general.

A detailed appraisal of the construction industry in southern California during the period 1955–1959, however, does not support the proposition that there is a housebuilding industry basically separate from general construction. A questionnaire submitted to builders in 1956 indicated that 50 percent were exclusively in homebuilding in 1955. However, in 1957 and 1958, when the same group was again studied, it was clear that as a result of a decline in the demand for single-family housing, builders had switched over to public, commercial and industrial construction as well as the building of apartments. More persuasive evidence comes from 50 firms studied in detail. While 58 percent reported that their operations were diversified among different types of construction, only 42 percent reported that they concentrated their construction activity on one type of construction. In addition, of the 42 percent who were not diversified, more than half reported that sometime in the past they had engaged in a variety of other types of construction activity.

It is true that a number of the very large builders studied had undertaken nothing except homebuilding prior to 1955. However, as housebuilding declined from a peak in 1955, many of these firms began operating in other markets, whereas few merely reduced their output of homes. In a short period of time a large proportion of builders found opportunities in apartment or other building on a speculative basis. Others began to bid on commercial and industrial jobs. Clearly, firms have a much greater degree of flexibility than has been commonly attributed to them, primarily because the differences between homebuilding and the construction of apartments, small commercial buildings, or other types of structures are not great. Firms did not switch from speculative home construction to bidding on dams or public utilities, but they did seek activity where members of the firm had previous experience or where the technical problems occasioned by a change created no particular difficulties.

The situation in the period 1955–1959 in southern California may, of course, be unique. But there is little reason to suppose that it is less typical of national patterns than the situation in the San Francisco Bay area in 1949. Indeed, it may be more so since in 1956, 1957, and 1958, 6.5 percent, 5.2 percent, and 4.1 percent respectively of all the homes started in the United States were in the Los Angeles metropolitan area; whereas, in the period upon which Maisel's conclusions are based, only 1.9 percent of all homes started in the nation were in the San Francisco area.*

A more logical explanation for the distinct differences between Maisel's results and those of the present study is that in 1949 Maisel confined his examination to a one-year period – a recession year to be true, but still one in which profits in housebuilding were such that many entrepreneurs with little or no experience in construction were attracted to this type of work. Forty-seven percent of the firms that built 100 or more houses in 1949 in the San Francisco area

---

* The comparison is confined to the Los Angeles metropolitan area and the San Francisco area. No exact data on the number of single-family homes constructed in either the San Francisco Bay area or the southern California area as a whole are available. The San Francisco data reflect estimates by Maisel, see *Housebuilding in Transition, op. cit.*, p. 342. For the Los Angeles metropolitan area data, the source is the Security-First National Bank of Los Angeles.

had been in existence less than 10 years.[8] In southern California the mass housebuilders of 1949 may or may not have been the tract builders in 1959. If they were still in home-building, it is probable that they were also the commercial developers, industrial contractors, and apartment builders. With experience, firms have shifted their operations to meet new and different demands. At least in southern California, the precise distinction between house-builder and general contractor, in terms of the type of work in which the firm engages, is not valid. This is particularly true when the opera-tions of the various firms are examined over time rather than at a particular moment. It might be argued that the term "housebuilding industry" has validity for a group of firms at a particular moment, but one of the fundamental characteristics of an industry is some continuity in the operations of firms that are part of it.

For the purpose of this study, therefore, the construction industry is defined as including all general contractors, builders, special-trade con-tractors, and workmen whose principal business is construction, excluding those firms whose major activity is in the area of heavy construc-tion, road, and public utility building.

It is probable that more types of firms are associated with the final production and sale of the product in the construction industry than in any other industry. It is not unusual for a fairly uncomplicated construction project to in-volve a land owner, an architect, a lawyer, a market analyst, a realtor, an investor, a mort-gage lender, a general contractor, various sub-contractors, an advertising firm and materials dealers. Yet, few of these individual firms are solely in the construction industry. In fact, al-though some of the enterprises listed above may work only in the general real estate area, the construction industry is essentially limited to general contractors, subcontractors, operative builders and civil engineers. Even this classifica-tion is not mutually exclusive since in many cases operative builders are also general con-tractors.

Theoretically, a *general contracting firm* bids

on construction jobs and supervises the con-struction process; a *subcontracting firm* bids on jobs held by general contractors and supervises the construction process of that portion of the job covered by its contract; an *operative builder* integrates the entire construction process by buying land, building structures and selling them; and finally a *civil engineering firm* pro-vides the engineering services for major con-struction operations. In fact, however, few firms within the construction industry operate solely as defined. In the process of construction they take on additional functions. For example, it is not unusual for an operative builder to design houses or for a general contractor to design structures without using an architect. This illu-stration can be multiplied almost *ad infinitum*. Only rarely does one find what might be called a "pure" general contractor, subcontractor or engineer, in terms of the above definitions. As a result, analysis of the operations of the firms within the industry on the basis of such classi-fication is difficult.

It is equally unsatisfactory to analyze opera-tions of firms in terms of individual firm sizes.* A major problem in using any standard firm size is the lack of historical continuity among firms. In one year a firm may produce 150 houses and in the next only 5. Yet, in both years, it may be the same firm in terms of ownership and probably in terms of manage-ment. In addition, size is a very unreliable guide to the type of functions performed within a firm. For example, two firms may each produce 50 houses within the same year. Both would normally be classified as medium-sized firms. However, in one case production may be a com-pletely integrated operation – the builder buys land, subdivides it, designs and builds houses and sells them. In the other, the builder may construct 50 units of different designs on dif-ferent lots for 50 different customers under a variety of contracts. In the first case, the builder is an entrepreneur with probably a substantial amount of his own capital in the project; in the second, the builder has relatively little or no capital in the operation, and if the houses are

---

* For certain purposes, of course, such a classification is useful. See Sherman Maisel, *Housebuilding in Transi-* tion (Berkeley and Los Angeles: University of California Press, 1953).

built under a construction service system* he may not even see any of the funds involved. He is operating on the basis of a fee for services rendered.

From a management point of view, the problems of the two firms are different. Indeed, there is practically nothing in common between the two operations except that at completion 100 housing units have been added to the housing stock. To classify these firms together for analytical purposes obscures their actual operations and unique characteristics.

For these reasons the *management* of firms within the construction industry cannot be analyzed either on the basis of their classification as "general contractors," "operative builders" etc. or by size of operations. Rather analysis must recognize that the operations of firms vary in nature. For want of a better term, "integration" is utilized to denote the fact that construction firms are organized in a variety of ways.† Integration is of two types – vertical and horizontal. *Vertical integration* refers to changes in the operation of the firm from the "pure" form of general contracting into related areas (designing, selling, etc.). *Horizontal integration* applies to movement of contractors from housebuilding into other types of construction operations, or vice versa.

# Structural changes in the housebuilding industry

*JOHN P. HERZOG*

Having tentatively established that housebuilding does constitute an industrial entity which is separable from construction in general, the next problem is to describe the structure of the housebuilding industry and to determine what, if any, changes have taken place in that structure in recent years. That the competitive structure of an industry determines, to a great extent, its responsiveness to the changing tastes of consumers is well recognized. The curious thing is that housebuilding, in contrast to many other industries, has been a source of concern because competition has been thought to be too free. Ease of entry and exit has frequently been blamed for many of the industry's problems – inept management, capital shortages, lagging technology, poor design, inability to control costs, and bad labor relations, among others. Consequently, there has been considerable emphasis placed on developing a more workable competitive structure for the industry. What seems to be implied by the term "workable competition" for housebuilding is that a little monopoly may be a good thing. More precisely,

---

* The most widely known form of construction service system is builders' control. Under this system the contractor never handles the money involved in the operation, but merely receives a fee at the completion of the project. Under the voucher payment system utilized by many mortgage lending firms, the results are essentially the same.

† The word "integration" is not used in the formal manner in which it is used in economic theory.

*Reprinted from* The Dynamics of Large-Scale Housebuilding, *Research Report 22, Real Estate Research Program, University of California, Berkeley, 1963, pp. 19–32, with the permission of the publisher.*

the goal appears to be an industry which has oligopolistic tendencies but with a fairly large competitive fringe.

## Evidences of structural changes

The existence of the kinds of internal forces which could bring about the desired change in the industry's structure was detected by Maisel as early as 1949. In the course of assessing the strength of these forces he noted that:

> ... a more rapid polarization of the industry into large merchant firms, at one extreme, and small contractors, at the other, may be expected. The industry is still highly heterogeneous in sizes and types of builders, all in sundry stages of development. More vigorous competition should speed concentration at the two poles. If the housebuilder's evolution follows a survival-of-the-fittest pattern, many medium-sized firms, unable to stand the test of a stabilized or decreased demand, may become extinct.[1]

What Maisel, or any other researcher looking into the future, could not have known was just how strong these forces were. In fact, changes in the relative market shares of large- and small-scale firms between 1950 and 1960 were no less than the revolutionary.* In the short span of 11 years large-scale firms in the 45 northern California counties increased their share of new house production from 32 to 74 percent of the total (see Table 1). To put this another way, in 1950 one out of every three houses in northern California was built by a large-scale firm. By 1960 large-scale producers were accounting for three out of every four houses being put up in the area. The one house in four not being built by the large-scale firm represented the combined production of medium-scale firms (25–99 houses), small-scale firms (1–24 houses), and owner-builders. Although the year-to-year data on which this study is based are from northern California, the structural shift in output does not appear to be confined to that area. For example, Maisel estimated that in 1949 large-scale builders accounted for about 24 percent of

the total volume of housing starts in the United States but, according to recent estimates of the National Association of Home Builders, that figure had climbed to 64 percent by 1959.[2] The NAHB estimate, significantly, is very close to the 62 percent share registered by northern California large-scale builders in that same year, indicating that developments in northern California were probably typical of what happened nationally.

Quite apart from the fact that a significant shift in relative market shares came about, the way in which the change occurred appears to be of some importance. The most outstanding feature in the observed pattern of development is the fact that during the years in which housebuilding in general was declining large-scale builders increased their share of total starts. Conversely, with the exception of 1954, the proportion produced by large-scale builders declined whenever total starts turned up. This pattern certainly lends strong support to Maisel's thesis that the growth of the large-scale sector should be accelerated in periods when demand slackens and competition becomes keener. Also noteworthy is the fact that as the great pent-up

### TABLE 1

*Production of One-Family Houses in Northern California*

| Year | Total for northern California | Total large-scale northern California | Large-scale output as percent of total |
|------|------|------|------|
| 1950 | 49,800 | 16,096 | 32 |
| 1951 | 35,700 | 17,459 | 49 |
| 1952 | 35,800 | 15,397 | 43 |
| 1953 | 33,800 | 16,827 | 50 |
| 1954 | 50,300 | 30,904 | 61 |
| 1955 | 57,800 | 32,812 | 57 |
| 1956 | 38,600 | 27,393 | 71 |
| 1957 | 31,500 | 23,500 | 75 |
| 1958 | 36,227 | 25,970 | 72 |
| 1959 | 46,663 | 28,933 | 62 |
| 1960 | 35,766 | 26,365 | 74 |

Source: Total for northern California was derived from *Housing Statistics*, published by the U.S. Housing and Home Finance Agency; *Survey of Building Permits Issued in the Fourteen Southernmost Counties in California, 1954–60*, Research Department, Security-First National Bank, Los Angeles; *Bay Area Real Estate Report, 1952–57*, San Francisco Bay Area Council; *Fresno Area Real Estate and Housing Report*, January 1961, Fresno Area Residential Research Council; Sherman J. Maisel, *op. cit.*, p. 342; *Dwelling Units Authorized by Local Building Permits*, U.S. Department of Labor, Bureau of Labor Statistics.

---

* A firm was considered to be large-scale if its output reached 100 or more houses in the indicated years.

demand which existed at the beginning of the decade was gradually reduced, through increases in the housing stock, smaller-scale builders were just not able to regain lost ground. Thus, even though the proportion of the market going to large-scale builders has, from time to time declined, these declines were never sufficiently large to completely offset the gains registered during the contractionary phases of the cycle. The result was that even though the big builders' market share fluctuated, each successive valley (see Chart 1) was higher than the immediately preceding one.

thought to lie in a firm's ability to shift rapidly into other types of building, or even to get out of construction altogether. Neither alternative appeared to be open to the large operator because of the complexity of his organization and the degree to which his work force is specialized. Thus, it was thought, his very size would be his undoing.

While this argument has logical persuasiveness, it ignores the possibility that large-scale firms could move against the cycle. In practice, the big builders have exhibited remarkable abilities in this direction. It is true that the big

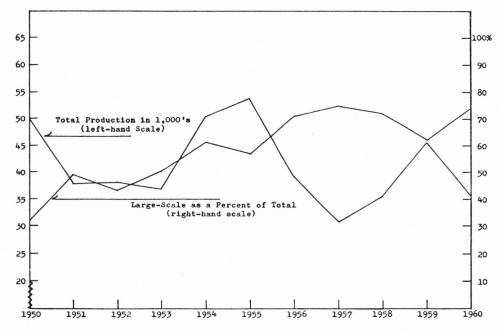

Chart 1. Northern California production of houses and large-scale production as a percentage of total.

Source: Table 1.

## Some probable causes

These developments can be at least partially attributed to the successful manner in which large-scale builders have overcome some of the disadvantages of volume production. Because of the inherent instability in the demand for new houses and the big firms' cumbersome overhead structures it has long been thought that they would experience serious difficulties during the contractionary phases of the housebuilding cycle. The key to success during such periods was

builders' volume showed some tendency to follow upward or downward movements in the cycle, yet at the same time builders evidenced an exceptional ability to resist severe cutbacks. The brunt of the cyclical declines has been borne by builders outside the large-scale sector.

The fact that the large-scale operators have been able to shift the burdens to the smaller firms is probably a reflection of the advantages which arise from volume production. To begin with, the big builder's bargaining position vis-à-vis materials suppliers, subcontractors, and in some cases lending institutions is strengthened by the sheer volume of his purchases. In addition, his large volume almost certainly makes bona fide costs savings possible for these same groups and they, in turn, are able to pass some of the savings on to him in lower prices or better service. Besides this, the big builder is able to use his labor and materials more efficiently through greater specialization, reduction of waste by moving leftover materials to the next job, and elimination of some intermediate production processes. Finally, there is the added effort a large-scale firm is able to put into marketing, design, financing, and research in that the considerable expenditures involved in these activities can be spread over large numbers of houses, making the cost per unit small indeed. While these benefits are not directly measurable, they almost certainly give a competitive edge to the large-scale builder in a thin or sluggish market.

Another factor which would mitigate against drastic or rapid changes in the large-scale builder's output levels is his longer-than-average planning horizon. Whereas the small builder specializes in spot developments and has practically no commitments beyond the few houses he may currently have under construction, the volume operator is a creator of communities – or at the very least, sizeable subdivisions. Even when, as is common practice among large-scale firms, very large tracts are broken up into smaller parcels (called units) and only a unit at a time is built, commitments for such things as financing, development, staff, and subcontracts frequently extend several months into the future. While failure to live up to his commitments can be costly to the builder, these commitments permit him to escape some of the short-run uncertainties of business. The smaller builder may find his sources of supply (particularly of credit) suddenly dry up in response to changes in business activity, but large-scale firms are able to rely on contractual commitments to carry them over for several months.

## Concentration among large-scale producers

In spite of the drastic changes which have taken place in market shares of large- and smaller-scale firms, the degree of concentration within the large-scale sector itself has changed only slightly. In 1950 each large-scale producer turned out, on the average, 273 houses. By 1960 this figure has climbed only to 297 houses – an increase of less than 10 percent (see Table 2). What these averages tend to show is that

### TABLE 2
*Annual Output of Large-Scale Housebuilders, 1950–60*

| Year | Total output | Number of firms | Average output per firm |
|------|--------------|-----------------|-------------------------|
| 1950 | 16,096 | 59 | 273 |
| 1951 | 17,459 | 70 | 249 |
| 1952 | 15,397 | 62 | 248 |
| 1953 | 16,827 | 70 | 242 |
| 1954 | 30,904 | 100 | 309 |
| 1955 | 32,812 | 102 | 322 |
| 1956 | 27,393 | 90 | 304 |
| 1957 | 23,500 | 74 | 317 |
| 1958 | 25,970 | 83 | 313 |
| 1959 | 28,933 | 83 | 340 |
| 1960 | 26,365 | 89 | 297 |

Source: See Herzog, *The Dynamics of Large Scale Housebuilding*, Appendix.

most of the increase in large-scale output came about through the influx of new firms, rather than through continued growth of just a few giants.

Further confirmation of this fact can be found in Chart 2, which portrays, graphically, the distribution of large-scale output for selected years between 1950 and 1960. While the change in concentration within the large-scale sector was not great, two aspects of it deserve brief comment. First, there is the relentless way in which the move to greater concentration has come about. Even though some of the annual shifts (all are not shown) were so slight as to be almost imperceptible, there was not one year between 1950 and 1960 when the trend toward greater concentration was reversed. Secondly, there appears to have been an acceleration in the move toward concentration in the latter part of the period. It is still too early to tell whether this acceleration will continue or not. However, there is good reason to believe that the speed-up is largely a reflection of the fact that by the latter half of the 1950's the steam had gone out of the postwar housing boom, thereby permitting the forces of competition to take their toll. If this is the case, it is almost certain that there will be some slowing up in the movement toward greater concentration as the market stabilizes. There may even be some movement back toward a more equal distribution of output among the firms producing 100 or more houses annually.

In any case, the tendency of the industry to move toward a more oligopolistic structure remains no more than a tendency. Even the changes which took place between 1950 and 1960 were not sufficient to remove the industry from the competitive (as opposed to oligopolistic) class. In 1960, for example, the four largest

tor? Maisel probably established the reason in his *Housebuilding in Transition* study referred to earlier. There he notes that:

> There is no indication that further important decreases in costs would occur if large firms continue to increase in size, unless further growth brought a complete change in the housebuilding process. Most of the direct costs approach their minimum point within the size of existing firms ... [and] the costs curve levels off, with only a slight [further] decline as size increases. Meanwhile, in opposition to the [slight] down curve in pro-

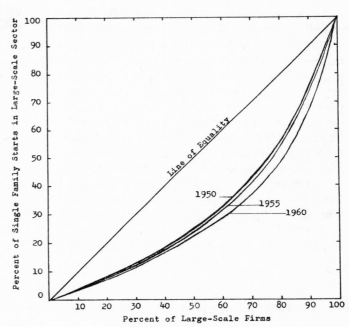

Chart 2. Lorenz curve showing distribution of large-scale production.

Source: Mail Questionnaire.

northern California firms accounted for only about 11 percent of the total housebuilding in that area. The eight largest built only 22 percent, and even the twenty largest could garner no more than 35 percent of the market. These percentages (concentration ratios) are well below those found in most other industrial sectors of the economy. Only in the service and distribution trades, and in about 15 percent of the manufacturing industries (representing about 20 percent of manufacturing output) can one find lower ratios.

Why hasn't there been a greater move toward concentration within the large-scale sec-

duction costs, a point is reached where indirect costs turn up.[3]

Just where the point of diminishing returns for any given firm is reached is not certain. However, Maisel goes on to point out that by the time a firm is turning out two or three houses a day it has pretty well exploited its opportunity for reducing on-site production costs.[4] It would thus appear, at least from the production standpoint, that the optimal scale lies somewhere between 500 and 800 units per year. Few firms in northern California ever exceeded this range, and those that did seldom pushed beyond a scale of 1,000–1,200 units annually.

### Freedom of entry and exit

The lack of scale economies beyond the 500–800 house range has probably prevented established volume builders from gaining sufficient advantages to keep potential entrants out of the market. This situation, in turn, may help account for the fact that the industry has not come under the domination of a few giant firms. That there has been considerable shifting into and out of the large-scale sector is evident, not only in the averages referred to above, but in the measures of industry population (Table 3) as well. Comparison of changes in business population reveals that the number of firms engaged in large-scale housebuilding fluctuated cyclically, paralleling housing market activity. In this respect, the housebuilders displayed considerably more flexibility than either the average of all industries or firms engaged in contract construction. This flexibility is reflected in both entry and discontinuance rates, but perhaps the most encouraging sign is in the former. Entry rates for large-scale builders (expressed as the number of new firms per 1,000 firms in operation at the beginning of the year) were, in 1958 and 1960, higher than the 1951–57 average. In addition, these far exceeded the average

rates for firms engaged in contract construction, and contract construction entry rates were well in excess of the average for all industries. The same general observations hold with respect to rates of discontinuance except that, as one might expect, discontinuance rates among housebuilders tended to move counter-cyclically, whereas entry rates more or less paralleled movements in the housebuilding cycle. It appears then, that while some additional concentration has taken place in the large-scale sector, this cannot be attributed to restricted entry.

### Influence of mobility

While the absence of barriers to entry was, no doubt, an important factor limiting concentration, additional competitive forces may well have come from firms expanding or shifting their operations into new locations. There is little question that the product of construction is immobile, but it does not necessarily follow that the producing organizations themselves must be. There are certainly limits to builder mobility, but discussions with the big producers leave one with the impression that many of them are quick to seize upon opportunities to produce for any new market – whether within a given metropolitan area or outside. Just how this mobility can be measured statistically, however,

## TABLE 3

*Index of Firms in Operation, Rates of Entry and Discontinuance, Selected Industries, 1951–60*

| Year | Index of firms in operation (1951-100) | | | Entry rate (Per 1,000 firms on January 1) | | | Exit (discontinuance) rate (per 1,000 firms on January 1) | | |
|------|------------------|-----------------------|-------------------------------------------------|------------------|-----------------------|-------------------------------------------------|------------------|-----------------------|-------------------------------------------------|
| | All industries | Contract construction | Large-scale house-building northern California | All industries | Contract construction | Large-scale house-building northern California | All industries | Contract construction | Large-scale house-building northern California |
| 1951 | 100 | 100 | 100 | 80 | 142 | 271 | 68 | 116 | 85  |
| 1952 | 101 | 103 | 89  | 84 | 159 | 71  | 67 | 112 | 186 |
| 1953 | 103 | 107 | 100 | 84 | 148 | 306 | 72 | 120 | 177 |
| 1954 | 104 | 110 | 143 | 86 | 148 | 471 | 75 | 116 | 43  |
| 1955 | 105 | 114 | 146 | 95 | 160 | 150 | 73 | 104 | 140 |
| 1956 | 108 | 120 | 129 | 98 | 151 | 147 | 80 | 117 | 265 |
| 1957 | 110 | 123 | 106 | 91 | 121 | 89  | 76 | 116 | 267 |
| 1958 | 112 | 124 | 119 | 91 | 129 | 189 | 79 | 112 | 68  |
| 1959 | 113 | 123 | 119 | 92 | 144 | 133 | 76 | 123 | 133 |
| 1960 | 115 | 126 | 127 | 95 | 143 | 169 | 83 | 133 | 96  |

Source: Data on large-scale builders from mail questionnaire. Data on other industries adapted from U.S. Department of Commerce, *Survey of Current Business* (various issues) 1950–60.

presents a perplexing problem. Builders are notorious for their failure to keep more than very crude records of their operations. If pressed for too much detail on periods too distant in the past, they simply cannot supply useful information. When general information is needed, however, builders' memories and sketchy records are frequently reliable enough to be quite useful. In view of recall limitations and the nature of the builders' records, it was decided to collect mobility information on a county line basis. Admittedly, using county lines to declineate markets has serious limitations. However, the simplicity of the system, together with the fact that markets do not, in many areas, extend beyond the county in which they are located, more than compensates for its drawbacks. The drawbacks stem largely from the fact that a metropolitan area may cover more than one county. While overlapping exists, many builders indicated that they were more reluctant to cross county lines within, say, the Bay Area than they were to move around within a given county. This reluctance, due primarily to lack of familiarity with such things as differences in building codes from one county to another, is difficult to measure. It did, however, appear to influence the builders' decisions to a significant degree.

Whatever its limitations, the county line basis of analyzing builders' markets brought two interesting points to light. In the first place, it appears that while the majority of firms did not attempt to build in more than one market at a time, a fairly substantial number did, at some time or other, operate over larger areas (see Table 4). The bulk of these confined their activities to two or three markets during the early 1950's, but more recently the urge to spread out resulted in some firms being operational in five or six markets at once. Many builders expressed a belief that geographical diversification was becoming more of a necessity as local markets were apparently becoming thinner. Some indicated that they had two or more tracts under construction within a single county, which would indicate that the figures shown in Table 4 may actually understate the extent to which firms have spread out.

The second point brought out by the analysis

is that the firms demonstrated a marked tendency to move from one market area to another over time. Less than half the firms which reached large-scale proportions during the period confined their activities to a single market. Presumably, the ones who were able to avoid moving from one area to another were either firms headquartered in the larger metropolitan areas or firms which were in the industry for just a short time.

## TABLE 4

*Number of Firms by Number of Markets in Which They Operated, by Year*

| Years | 1 | 2 | 3 | 4 | 5 | 6 | 7 | 8 | 9 | Total active firms |
|---|---|---|---|---|---|---|---|---|---|---|
| 1950 | 45 | 11 | 3 | | | | | | | 59 |
| 1951 | 54 | 13 | 2 | | 1 | | | | | 70 |
| 1952 | 46 | 9 | 6 | 1 | | | | | | 62 |
| 1953 | 56 | 9 | 5 | | | | | | | 70 |
| 1954 | 78 | 11 | 11 | | | | | | | 100 |
| 1955 | 70 | 21 | 5 | 4 | 2 | | | | | 102 |
| 1956 | 50 | 28 | 12 | | | | | | | 90 |
| 1957 | 37 | 25 | 10 | 2 | | | | | | 74 |
| 1958 | 52 | 22 | 8 | | | 1 | | | | 83 |
| 1959 | 47 | 21 | 14 | | 1 | | | | | 83 |
| 1960 | 48 | 30 | 6 | 1 | 3 | 1 | | | | 89 |
| 1950–60 | 68 | 36 | 19 | 14 | 2 | 7 | 4 | | 1 | 152 |

Source: See Herzog, *op. cit.*, Appendix.

How widely separated were the markets for any one firm? Unfortunately, there was not sufficient regularity in the practices of individual firms to permit generalization. For example, it was not at all uncommon for a firm to operate in the San Francisco-Oakland and Fresno areas, or in Santa Clara and Sacramento. Other markets may have been as close together as San Francisco and San Mateo. A less common practice, but certainly one which was in evidence in every year studied, was for some of the northern California builders to have tracts under way in southern California, or other western states. Some firms even conducted large-scale operations in areas as far away as Alaska and Hawaii. These firms were, of course, the exception rather than the rule, but the mere fact that they were able to hold such far-flung operations together is itself significant.

The successful manner in which the big builder has been able to move outside his small, local market is beneficial in at least two respects. In the first place, firms are able to achieve a scale large enough to take advantage of many of the attendant economies without fear of over-building in the process. The problem of thin markets has long been recognized as one of the critical factors in limiting the size of firms. It is, no doubt, true that it costs a firm something to maintain this kind of flexibility and that the cost places an upper limit on the degree to which it can be practiced. The fact remains, however, that it has been successfully used by a number of firms and is likely to continue.

The second important advantage of being able to move from one market to another is that it promotes competition among the large-scale firms. In the absence of such ability smaller markets, away from the larger metropolitan areas, might become dominated by one or two large firms making excessive profits, or might entirely lack large-scale producers. In neither case would the resident population receive the benefits of volume production.

In summary, the fact that a drastic structural shift has taken place within the housebuilding industry since 1950 seems beyond dispute. Whether one looks at northern California or at national figures, there has clearly been a complete reversal in the relative market shares of large- and smaller-scale firms. What the nor-thern California figures seem to reveal, however, is that most of this shift can be attributed to more firms entering the large-scale category rather than to a continued growth of firms which were already large-scale in the early 1950's. Actually, additional concentration within the large-scale sector was negligible through 1955, and even the perceptible movement to-ward unequal market shares which character-ized the latter part of the period was more a shakeout of inefficient producers than a con-tinued expansion of the leading firms. That more concentration did not take place can prob-ably be attributed to (1) a lack of economies of very large scale, and (2) a relatively high degree of mobility among large-scale builders. The fact that diminishing returns to scale show up in the 500–1,000 house per year range has prevented existing firms from gaining sufficient competiti-tive advantage over potential entrants to keep them out of the high volume market. The builders' mobility has prevented older firms from monopolizing local markets and, at the same time, has opened up broader markets to the big firms. The net result of all these forces has ap-parently been a movement toward a more work-able competitive structure in housebuilding, and it is hoped, a change for the better.

# New directions for the housing industry

*THE EDITORS OF* HOUSE & HOME

Sometimes the big news is in the ads. Amid the plethora of recent economic pronouncements were two that appeared as advertising:

Sunset International Petroleum Corp. took four pages in the *Wall Street Journal* to present its 1962 annual report. The major message: Sunset has converted itself to a real estate development company with 20,000 acres of planned communities in the path of California suburban expansion.

Del E. Webb Corp. took a two-color page in *Business Week* to plug its Clear Lake City, a totally-planned community of 15,000

*Reprinted from* House & Home, *vol. 23, No. 1 (January, 1963), pp. 67–68, vol. 24, No. 5 (November, 1963), pp. 112–116, with permission of the journal.*

acres (homes, apartments, golf course, mobile home park, shopping center, industrial area) next to the Manned Spacecraft Center in Houston. (The project, far from incidentally, is a joint venture with Humble Oil.)

In many ways, these casual bits of intelligence illustrate the deceptively mild manner of new trends in housing that seem likely to shake the traditional organization of the industry to its roots in the years just ahead.

For one thing, both Sunset International and Del Webb are publicly-held corporations, both bright examples of a trend only three years old in housing. Both are operating in several cities at once. Both are diversified – Sunset in oil and land, Webb in housing and heavy construction.

Up to now, not many people in the traditional housing or home finance field – or anywhere else – have paid much attention to the portent of a slow build-up of change in the tradition-bound housing industry. There hasn't been much fanfare. Yet change – mostly managerial change – is now the outstanding characteristic of the housing industry. Taken individually, the changes may look unimportant. Taken together, they loom large – so large that Industrial Economist Richard Trestrail of Stanford Research Institute calls housing " an industry in transition involving basic structural change." And he predicts: "This change will have a very substantial impact, not only upon the number and economic environment of its participants, but also upon the urban and suburban environment in which we live." In other words, first a revolution in housing's ways of doing business, then perhaps a revolution in the product itself.

This sequence is one that such discerning analysts at Dean Burnham Kelly of Cornell's school of architecture have been predicting for decades. This conviction is coming to be shared by some thoughtful builders, too. Says Robert Fox of Plymouth Meeting, Pa.: " Just as General Motors, Ford, and Chrysler have emerged from a large number of small auto manufacturers, I think large building corporations will be doing a large percentage of the homebuilding in this country ten years from now." Builder Andy Place of South Bend, Ind., has ventured the

opinion that builders are "destined to become nothing more than connectors of utilities and developers of land."

Most vivid of the changes is the virtual disappearance of the giant builder of, say 2,000 homes a year on a single site and the emergence of new kinds of housing giants – chiefly in land development. The big difference among today's developers is better planning. It is their chief sales weapon. And it builds much more true value into today's new communities than the slap-dash subdivisions of a decade ago.

A few builders are still starting 2,000 or more dwelling units in a year. But (excepting some New York City apartment tycoons) they aren't all in one area as was often the case in the mid-fifties for such builders as Levitt, Aldon, Diller-Kalsman, Aetna, and Grandview. The surviving old giants have adapted to new ways. Bill Zeckendorf's Webb & Knapp, the nation's urban renewal giant, started 3,812 units last year – on two New York City sites plus one each in Philadelphia and Pittsburgh. Bill Levitt, who in 1953 began 7,000 units at Levittown, Pa., at best estimate began only 1,500 units last year – at three places, Belair, Md., Levittown and Matawan, N.J.

Land development is the commonest, but not the only, business formula for housing's new crop of big companies. At least four different patterns are emerging.

1. Housing markets are being invaded by more and more giant corporations whose historical central interest is not housing – companies like Alcoa, Reynolds, and Koppers. And the housing business is being invaded by some concerns wholly outside construction – like Sunset International, Humble, and Christiana Oil Corp.

2. Some have solved builders' chronic problem of undercapitalization by turning to the stock market for equity money. The stocks of no less than forty-four building and land development companies are widely enough traded today to merit inclusion in HOUSE & HOME's monthly listing of publicly-held housing companies. Five years ago only three of these concerns were publicly held *and* in housing (Webb Knapp, All-State Properties, and General Development).

3. Some builders solved the problem by a

variety of joint ventures with or financial aids from capital-rich materials makers.

4. A few all-purpose combines are developing from inside the industry – like the Berens Companies of Washington, D.C., a mortgage company with $200 million servicing, which is also an insurance agency, home-improvement loan company, small-business investment company, real estate investment company (land development and several joint ventures in urban renewal construction as far afield as Huntsville, Ala.), and a real estate company that manages 4,000 apartments, shopping centers, office buildings (but stopped selling homes in 1961). Says President George DeFranceaux: "We find diversification feeds everything backwards and forwards very nicely." Or like Realtor Jack Havens' Equitable Investment Corp., which owns a savings and loan association, develops subdivisions for builders, builds shopping centers, and builds and manages apartments and office buildings.

## Ten government research programs —and how they affect homebuilding

### Housing & Home Finance Agency: experiments in housing the poor

HHFA has made twenty-three grants to public and private agencies totaling $3.8 million (out of its $5 million kitty) to demonstrate new or improved ways of housing low income families. They key word is *demonstrate* since HHFA will make a grant only if the results are to be tested (by an independent third party) in actual field experiments.

Among the ideas being tested: (1) a new look at mortgage risk criteria for low-income minority group buyers of single-family houses in Gainesville, Fla; (2) housing for Detroit's Skid Row population of low-income men; and (3) use of rent certificates as a substitute for public housing in St. Louis. The first grant was made in 1962. None of the twenty-three projects has reported final results.

The grants may, but do not have to, involve the construction of new housing; and can deal with design, land planning, land acquisition and use, financing tenure, or rehabilitation.

### FHA's technical studies: expert guidance for its building rules

FHA'S technical studies program, started in 1956 and operated on about $300,000 a year, has outside experts currently analyzing no less than twenty-one ideas involving possible changes in FHA'S construction bible, the Minimum Property Standards.

Results have ranged all the way from a simple device for measuring the thickness of glass to a $10,000 study of impact noise in apartments that tested and then rated forty-seven different floor and ceiling systems (only fourteen of which exceeded FHA'S minimum rating) (see H&H, May, 1963). Another important revision based on a study is the agency's new requirement of safety glass in exterior doors with large glass areas, as well as in shower doors and tub enclosures.

Most of the work has been carried out by the Building Research Advisory Board (BRAB), which calls together panels of experts to make the studies.

Among the current studies: durability of vapor barrier materials under slabs; national and local failure rates of septic tank systems; storage space requirements; and the creation and maintenance of common properties in residential developments.

### Defense Project 12: unrestricted testing ground

Unhampered by zoning, building codes, or local restrictions, the armed services have offered their facilities to builders and manufacturers to test new materials and methods. Under a directive setting up Project 12 in May of last year, Secretary McNamara charged the Defense Department "to experiment with techniques which may bring new productivity to the construction industry."

The Department sets up no research facilities of its own, but offers its huge housing program (16,000 units under construction, another 7,500 going up this fiscal year) and its maintenance program (370,000 housing units must be kept in repair) as a field laboratory. Among the most promising avenues being explored: (1) the relocatable house (H&H, March, 1963), of which 1,300 are on order for both stateside and overseas use; (2) combined subspace and finish-floor-ing in full house-width panels; (3) plumbing systems using plastic pipe and fittings, with various venting arrangements. Under considera-tion is a full scale test of the critical path method (H&H, April, 1963) and its applicability to homebuilding.

Project 12 is not budgeted separately, but promising ideas are incorporated into Defense's $300 million housing construction, repair, and maintenance budget.

### National Bureau of Standards: framer of basic rules

Nothing affects the housing industry more basically than the National Plumbing Code, the National Electric Safety Code, and the fire safety provisions of building codes. Much of the technology in these codes came out of NBS' building research division.

NBS has been the government's most effective – and perhaps its least controversial – research arm in housing since the early twenties when Herbert Hoover, as assistant Commerce Secre-tary, started it writing a national building code. This job was amputated by the depression, but in the 'thirties NBS turned out some 150 studies of materials and standards that remain standard reference works. Much of this was financed by $100,000-a-year grants from FHA, PHA, and HOC.

It takes a 92-page booklet to describe the bureau's current building research projects. NBS cooperates with both public and private agencies in developing the technical facts and means of measurement on which codes and standards for the safe and effective use of materials and equipment may be based. It also conducts re-search in chemistry, engineering, and physics on the properties of specific building materials, structures, and equipment.

Currently, 12 projects are underway for other government agencies. Among them: ways and means of testing and appraising venting systems in house plumbing in an effort to determine the necessity for venting; a study of thin-shell, pre-cast and pre-stressed concrete structures; a study of insulation and the effects of moisture on its performance. Also underway: studies of water-vapor permeance of building materials and of

means of measuring the coefficient of perform-ance of several methods of air-conditioning. The 175 scientists and engineers of the bureau spend almost $2 million a year in building research, about half of which is paid for by other govern-ment bodies.

### Building Research Advisory Board: where experts advise the experts

This division of the private non-profit Con-gressionally-chartered (1863) National Academy of Sciences-National Research Council was set up in 1949 to study and advise on building science and technology. It grew out of the in-dustry's contention that the government itself should stay out of technical housing research.

BRAB's thirty-man body of appointed building experts tries to " bring the best brains to bear on the problems that government agencies need help on." For several years, its biggest client has been FHA, whose own technical staff is chronically too shorthanded to cope with the welter of new ideas sprouting from the industry. BRAB studies for FHA include: criteria for warm-air ducts, slab-on-grade standards, vapor barriers, ground cover in crawl spaces, and soil studies to determine foundation requirements.

BRAB's services may be contracted for by pri-vate industry as well as government agencies. It does no actual laboratory or field research itself, but compiles the findings of engineers, scientists, universities and research facilities throughout the country. It correlates unrelated research in building technology, stimulates in-vestigations where a need is demonstrated, and advises and monitors research bodies and funds where impartial guidance is desired.

BRAB has two contracts to serve FHA. It pro-vides interim opinion on specific problems like the ones above, and it has set up an advisory committee to help FHA pick out what research is most essential.

### Forest Products Lab: incubator of tomorrow's wood technology

One of the oldest government research pro-grams, Forest Products Laboratory was set up (under the Department of Agriculture) as an adjunct of the University of Wisconsin in 1910, moved to its own ten-acre facility in Madison in 1932. Its explorations into better ways to use wood have produced a long list of technological advances – though some of them have been taken up by industry with agonizing slowness. Case in point is the stressed skin sandwich panel, a principle used today in almost all factory-built wall, roof and floor panels. FPL developed it more than thirty years ago, and for twenty years almost nobody put the idea to use. FPL has also done research on laminated floorings, paint failures, and stress grading of lumber by machine (H&H, June, 1963).

FPL's current studies add up to a strong effort to keep wood competitive in tomorrow's building methods. They include investigations of: the potential of water jets and lasers for cutting wood (to reduce the waste of timber inherent in all sawing methods); a method of pre-stressing glue-laminated beams for improved load capacity; the use of polyethelene glycol to improve the dimensional stability of wood (one of the biggest drawbacks to the material); and a framing and wall-coverage system for houses based on a 3 ft. or 4 ft. spacing of framing members, instead of the usual 16 in. module.

### Agricultural Research Service: from rural problems come housing answers

At Beltsville, Md., two divisions of the Department of Agriculture are digging into problems affecting the farm family and its housing. Their work is tailored to rural needs and problems, but much of it applies as well to general housing construction. *Agriculture Engineering Research* has developed a series of plans for farmhouses and offers working drawings through the agricultural extension service at most state agricultural colleges. Currently, the division is testing wood floors laid directly on the ground over gravel fill and a vapor barrier in hopes of getting a warm, resilient wood floor with the economy of the slab-on-grade.

*Clothing and Housing Research* has developed standards for the planning of labor-saving kitchens based on studies of housewives' work patterns. The division has also published guides for planning storage and activity areas in housing for low and middle-income families.

Much rural housing is free from zoning, codes, and/or restrictive labor practices, so agriculture feels free to experiment with materials or methods that could not be used in urban markets. For example: no building code would presently accept wood floors on grade, or the experimental panels.

### Agency for International Development: technical help for overseas

One concern of this affiliate of the State Department is the use of American research and technological know-how to help underdeveloped countries find quicker solutions to their housing shortages. Housing an expanding population with limited natural resources and primitive building methods and labor is one of the biggest problems in many countries. So AID commissions studies into methods for minimum housing.

Sample project: a study of stabilized earth (a mixture of dirt and cement) housing, carried out by Texas A&M. It produced the negative, but still important, finding that such construction would save money only in areas where low cost and/or abundant aggregates were scarce or nonexistent. Reason: just as much cement would be needed to stabilize soil as in conventional concrete masonry construction.

### NASA: down-to-earth dividends from space

An orbiting space capsule, carrying a man around the earth in ninety minues, appears pretty remote from a single-family house that will never leave its site. But, like much other government research, NASA's efforts to solve space problems constantly turn up findings useful to earthbound industries. The ten NASA field centers report all successful technical innovations to the recently established (May, 1962) Office of Technology Utilization, which attempts to publicize them to the U.S. scientific and industrial community. Many industrial firms have adopted – or adapted – NASA processes to solve problems that their own research had never licked. Among them: metals forming methods, welding techniques, and nonstick coatings for molds and plywood presses. Ahead lie possibilities of more dramatic technical advances. For instance, better ways to fireproof steel structures than our present bulky wrappings of concrete could come from processes, designs and materials used to dissipate the heat from the re-entry of a capsule into the atmosphere.

### Public Health Service:
### prober of housing's effect on health

Since 1958, PHS's Bureau of State Services has been giving research grants for studies of environmental health problems – about $226,000 per year in twelve projects.

At least two bear directly on housing: (1) a study of shortcomings in occupied space – room sizes, noise, vibration, lighting, ventilation, plumbing, and accident prevention and (2) an inquiry into problems of urban and recreation areas – air and water pollution, building-lot areas, sewage and waste disposal, water supply, and population and density standards. Results have not yet been divulged.

### Technology's roadblocks—and how they can be broken

There is just no doubt that the housing industry cannot take full advantage of the technology available.

There are many new systems, developed and field tested, available right now – as you have seen on the previous pages. We know how to fuse brick together with lasers – souped-up light rays; we know how to build fuel cells that can supply electricity for years without refueling; we know how to build single-material panels with strong solid skins and insulating foamed cores. We have the knowledge to build anything from paper houses for underdeveloped countries to steel houses that can be fired into space.

Why hasn't more of this know-how been fed into the everyday – but all-important – problem of building better houses cheaper? Why are so many good ideas lying unused?

### Up to now there have been no criteria for choosing the best of the new ideas, and getting them to market

The problems of introducing a new idea, material, or system into the housing industry are unique. First, the merits of a given idea are hard to evaluate because, most often, they depend on a complex interaction with other parts of the house. (For example, when trusses first came along twenty years ago, they could not be sold purely as a substitute for roof rafters. They were, and are, more expensive to buy. They became popular only when the industry became aware of the indirect savings in construction time and plan flexibility that trusses make possible.)

Second, in the housing industry the decision to adopt a new system must be made thousands of times by thousands of individual architects and builders. And, typically, an innovation must perform well for a long period of time before it is widely accepted. By contrast, in the auto industry the decision of a handful of men can introduce a new idea to the nation.

Third, a new idea acceptable in one part of the country may not be acceptable in another – for technical reasons of climate, or soil conditions, or the availability of materials; or because of the personal prejudices of the market in various parts of the country.

"We have to be prepared for a lead time of three to five years to bring a major innovation to market," says Edward Riley, marketing director of Simpson Timber Co. "After research and development get through with a new idea, marketing men take it over and test it with sometimes as many as a hundred dealers and builders. Then when we know it will work more executive decisions must be made, distribution established, code bodies and building officials thoroughly acquainted with the innovation [for more on codes, see below]."

### . . . but criteria are being developed for picking the most important innovations

"First and foremost we must be guided by the market," says Martin Bartling, vice president for research of U.S. Gypsum and past president

(1960) of NAHB. " We're in a buyers' market and are likely to remain in one. We can only bring to market an innovation that gives a builder's house added sales appeal – either by boosting quality or cutting costs."

Builder Don Huber of Dayton lists a second practical guide: in-place cost. "Many ideas" says Huber, "get lost because their costs are not known. The costs of producing something the first time don't mean much. And even if these costs can be projected for volume production, most builders want to know what it will cost installed in the field. TAMAP studies [H&H, August and October, 1961, and January, 1962] have shown clearly that many innovations costing more to buy result in a lower in-place cost. And don't underestimate the effect of cutting in-place costs. Suppose you could save 5 percent of the sales price of a house with new technology. With other costs and operations remaining as they were, that 5 percent could push your gross profit up more than 50 percent."

Housing Consultant Carl Boester suggests an unusual – but knowledgeable – guide: "One of the best ways to tell whether a new system is sound is to weigh it. This criteria is admittedly empirical, but most innovations in housing do weigh less than the thing they replace. One exception is the asphalt shingle, which weighs more than wood shingles. I don't believe anyone ever bothered to weigh the Lustron house."

Says NAHB's Ralph Johnson: "The Research Institute has worked out a list of goals for any new system. It must reduce on-site labor and number of skills needed; reduce the total weight of the house for transportation; improve the structure; minimize the effects of weather; improve handling and use of tools on the site; and increase the use of multiple-function parts."

And, adds Housing Consultant Leonard Haeger, "No major innovation can get to market unless the innovator has a pipeline to the local level. You have to do more than invent a better mousetrap. You have to have a marketing plan and the ability to carry it out right to the ultimate consumer."

## The biggest roadblock of all is the chaotic plethora of local building codes in the U.S.

An NAHB survey of 900 cities with more than 10,000 population shows that 71 percent base their codes on one of the four proprietary regional codes.* But this kind of code unity is illusory. NAHB also finds that almost all of the 900 cities have modified the model code to their local liking. Over 90 percent of the cities have adopted the National Electrical Code – but 73 percent of them have amended it to suit their tastes. About half the cities adopted the National Plumbing Code – but most of them had changed parts of it to suit local conditions. Over half of the cities prohibit the use of prefabricated wall components. Over half prohibit the use of 3 in. waste lines in one-bath houses – even though National Bureau of Standards' tests show that this size provides a more dependable flow because the pipe force-cleans itself.

Summing up wasteful code chaos in official language, the White House Science Advisory Subcommittee on Housing points out that code requirements vary so much from place to place that "housing is denied the full advantages of mass production which have contributed so significantly to other sections of the economy."

## A real solution to the code problem may have to come from the government— in form of performance standards

Housing experts of all persuasion – including code officials themselves – have long agreed that code unification would be a good thing. Abortive efforts to this end date from the twenties, and the major code groups themselves had a go at it in the early fifties (and got nowhere). This year, the three major groups of building officials (SBCC, ICBO, and BOCA) again made a tentative move toward unification by establishing a national coordinating council "to collaborate in matters of mutual interest." All three of these proprietary regional groups have done much to improve codes, but they have

---

* International Conference of Building Officials (ICBO) code, Building Officials Conference of America (BOCA)       code, Southern Building Code Congress (SBCC) code, and National Board of Fire Underwriters (NBFU) code.

always been subject to pulling and hauling by materials makers, insurance companies, and other interests – and none of them – as HOUSE & HOME pointed out (November, 1962) – has a big enough budget to do the job properly (the biggest of them has only $309,000 a year to spend).

The only quick solution, many experts believe, is to let the federal government take a hand in code unification. Few people in housing want the government to assume any larger role in the industry; yet codes are one area in which only the government seems likely to supply anything like an impartial forum with enough muscle to get the job done. There is a ground swell of interest in a White House conference on this sticky problem. The goal: to write national performance standards – not codes – for new housing, and to create a set of tests to be used to determine whether or not a new product or system meets the standards.

(Performance standards differ from codes in that they govern only the *function* that must be performed by any part of a house. For example, under a performance standard, a wall could be made of pressed corn flakes as long as it met the requirements of strength, durability, heat loss, and so on. In contrast, a performance *code* would read that " the frame walls must support ..." tying you into an established system by implication. And a specification code, the commonest form, simply dictates " walls must be 2x4 studs 16 in. oc.")

*National performance standards could open*

*the way to sweeping changes in houses and the way they are built.* Under a realistic performance standard, for example, mechanical cores would stand a real chance of broad acceptance – and a real chance of sharply reducing building costs. The industry would be in a position for the first time to reap the benefits of true industrialization – innovations that would not only lower housing costs (and this grows more important with every passing year) but provide a better product. With such basic changes made possible. . . .

*Housing's major problem would then be adapting industrialization to a product buyers will want.* There is no doubt that if all other problems now blocking the industrial revolution in housing were magically swept away, the industry would still be faced with the problem of facing up to its disciplines, and selling the public on the result. Some architects complain about the design discipline imposed by industrialization – but architects have always had to subscribe to one discipline or another, and surely today's lack of discipline in housing design is a bad thing. Would buyers accept unfamilar materials and forms? They would if the price was right. Efficiency in production, economy in building, and beauty in the end product are not mutually exclusive ideas. Housing technology – the existing ideas waiting to be used and the fresh ideas yet to be developed – can indeed produce a better house for less. What we need to do now is clear away the roadblocks, and start taking giant steps ahead.

# VI

# Housing finance

## The environment of real estate finance

*MILES COLEAN*

Although the existing influence of government on real estate finance in the United States is for the most part the product of a few decades, the encompassing measures of the 1930's and 1940's were not strictly the inventions of that short period. Instead, as it has been the purpose of this study to point out, they were the outgrowth of a long period of mounting tensions, which, in turn, were largely the product of earlier attitudes toward government and earlier expressions of governmental power.

Although the initial course of real estate development in this country was marked by resistance to all forms of social and economic control, the force of government, as a means for advancing popular objectives, was not neglected. The wilderness was a great absorber of capital, and continuous public and private efforts were pursued to make the capital available. State credit was used lavishly for public improvements, and large sections of the federal domain were donated for the same purpose. The desire to attract private capital was reflected in the first era of settlement and expansion by simplifying foreclosure, strengthening the lender's remedies, and regularizing transfer procedures as compared with English precedents. It continued to be reflected in numerous early land bank schemes and, later, in the immersion, directly and indirectly, of state-chartered commercial banks in real estate finance. In this period demands for easy mortgage credit were initiated that have persisted to the present day.*

### Growth of conflict

The combination of diffused, small owner-

---

* Charles J. Bullock (*Essays on the Monetary History of the United States*, New York, 1900, p. 1) states: " . . . a strong movement for cheap money has existed continuously in this country from the earliest period of colonization."

*Reprinted from Miles L. Colean.* The Impact of Government on Real Estate Finance in the United States, *National Bureau of Economic Research, 1950, pp. 134–160, with permission of the publisher.*

ship, overexpansion, excessive speculation, and heavy borrowing gave inherent weaknesses to both urban and rural real estate investment. At times the risks accepted by borrowers became intolerable. The favored methods of amelioration were the granting of temporary relief from debt payment and the modification of the mortgage laws to give increased protection to borrowers – as, for example, successive moratoria from the panic of 1820 onward, as well as the tendency to increase redemption periods, which appeared at about that time.[1]

The risks were hardly less painful to savers than to lenders, as the repeated waves of bank failures testify, and an assurance of future safety was sought by limiting the freedom of lending institutions to make real estate loans. To the extent that these limitations were effective – and, for the most part, they tended to be so immediately after a severe liquidation – they served to lessen the availability of mortgage funds. At the same time the easing of the mortgage contract in favor of the borrower increased the risk to the lender and hence tended to raise interest rates. The net result of the paliatives was to make mortgage money scarce or dear, or both; in other words, to run squarely in face of the demand for easy credit. The situation was, of course, complicated by the cumbersomeness of legal structure and the apparent unwillingness of the states to maintain the flexibility and adaptability that often characterized early legislation.

The conflict in policy thus engendered found no resolution; and indeed it was incapable of satisfactory resolution so long as borrowers insisted on maintaining their hard-won protections and lending institutions were subjected to rigid limitations on their lending activities. The stage was set for some special intercession that would promise both cheap and plentiful credit and that would still protect the participants from catastrophe. The federal government alone could produce such a prodigy.

And further, as good farm lands were taken up and cities became congested and far-flung, new problems impinging on real estate investment developed. In order to bring an end to, or at least to moderate, the overexploitation of land to the detriment of physical and human resources, state and national governments sought to strengthen their means of control. Conservation became a rallying cry; building codes were amplified, and zoning codes and other means of regulating urban land improvement, buildings, and occupancy were widely adopted. Under broadened interpretations, economic as well as physical considerations were included within the purview of the police power, and zoning was expanded to cover rural as well as urban areas. Land planning gradually became a governmental function, claiming broad power over methods of land use and hence over the environment and substance of real estate investment.

Because of the dependence of most of these new forms of intervention on the police power, they first appeared, for the most part, through state and municipal action. Except for the federal government's diminishing land transactions, its flood control activity, and a tentative approach to conservation and reclamation, the power of intervention was not sought. Nevertheless, it became gradually evident that the problems of settling arid lands, of protecting national resources, of bolstering the farm economy, and of restoring rural and urban districts would not, or could not, be solved by the types of measures already devised. And, to a steadily increasing number of people, the federal government alone appeared to have the power necessary to achieve these large objectives. It was not, however, until after World War I, and, more particularly, until the 1930's that the pressure for federal action appeared in any large measure and that the constitutional means for effectuating it were discovered.

## Shift to federal dominance

The first resort to federal authority directly affecting real estate finance grew out of mounting demands for specialized farm credit facilities and resulted in the creation of the Federal Land Bank System in 1916. When this system met the test of constitutionality, the pattern for much future federal intervention was set. Devices of one sort or another to extend or facilitate real estate credit became the principal means of satisfying the demands for federal aid following the mortgage crisis of the 1930's.

The credit authority, however, was not the only means of federal intervention. The power over inland waterways was expanded to permit comprehensive planning schemes such as the Tennessee Valley Authority; the power of eminent domain was invoked in the advancement of public housing; and under World War II emergency powers the scope of the government's influence on realty investment was again greatly expanded through limitations on construction, rents, the sale of new residential properties, and lending activity.

In the resurgence of intervention there was a marked emphasis on the concept of control for the sake of protecting the welfare of the individual, a point of view in marked contrast to that which characterized governmental action in the nineteenth century. Broadly speaking, the main aim of government land policy during the period of national expansion was to encourage enterprise rather than to provide it with physical or economic protection. An individual's welfare, from this viewpoint, rested mainly on the vigor of his own initiative rather than on state aid or support.

In the past, stays of foreclosure were exceptions, and these were always temporary and aimed at restoring the functioning of enterprise and initiative. Another exception was the development of governmental supervision of financial institutions. In this case both the consideration of welfare (that of depositors, shareholders, and the like) and the substitution of governmental restraint and direction (over the investment policies of the institutions) were present. Despite these exceptions, it is still broadly true that until the 1930's the main and continuous objective of government (both federal and state) was to encourage real estate as a form of enterprise. Secondary efforts (left almost wholly to the states) were concerned with the temporary support or restoration of enterprise when it was in danger.

With the establishment of the Federal Land Bank System, however, a modification in the government approach became evident. This agency was designed to make credit available under terms and conditions which did not then exist in the private financial market. There was the same point of view in creating the Federal Home Loan Bank System, and it was pursued further in establishing the Federal Housing Administration for the purpose of influencing the specialized use of credit to finance certain classes of housing. As this last-named agency developed, specialization became more definite: certain classes of housing received greater aid than others (single family houses below a set value, cooperatives, nonprofit corporations, etc.); certain classes of borrowers (first, war workers, then veterans, then families of "moderate" or "lower" income) received benefits not available to others. The device, moreover, was used to accomplish ends not strictly germane to the credit transaction, such as the improvement of housing standards, the influencing of land planning, and the regulation of wages paid to construction workers.

During this evolution, the government has become a guardian of individual welfare, exercising an enlarged influence on private decisions and taking greater responsibility for results. The movement is even more clearly evident in the resettlement and tenant-purchase activities of the Farm Security Administration (later the Farmers' Home Administration) and in the subsidized housing activities of the Public Housing Administration and its ancillary local authorities. It was evident also in the continued regulation of rents, in enforcing priorities for veterans in newly built houses, and in the special provisions for maintaining a fixed interest rate for loans to veterans following World War II.

## Extent of control

Out of this development, in which practically every source of governmental power has been invoked, real estate activity and its financing emerge more fully subject to governmental influence, regulation, and control than any part of the economy not distinctly of a public or public utility character. A review of the controls now existing and of the means by which they were brought about will illustrate this conclusion.

The power of the state as the original owner of the land has been asserted in the planning and use of land still in its ownership or reacquired through tax delinquency and purchase.

In the reacquisition of land, the power of eminent domain, employed under new and broadened definitions of public purpose, has been a powerful instrument in both local and federal hands. It has permitted local governments not only to provide land for thoroughfares, parks, public buildings, and public utilities, but to remove land for public housing and redevelopment purposes from private ownership, and by so doing to bring about major alterations in the structure of cities. Thus the government goes beyond the mere reassembly of land to support numerous projects in social and economic planning.

In the federal jurisdiction, the power of eminent domain is becoming steadily more important as a means of exercising control over forest and grazing lands, certain mineral deposits, and for carrying through such comprehensive undertakings as the Tennessee Valley Authority. When constitutional limitations impeded the use of the condemnation power, jurisdiction has frequently been obtained (as with TVA) through an interpretation of the federal power to regulate interstate commerce, and, on some occasions (as in the divesting of huge acreages of private farm land for permanent or temporary military purposes), by invoking the emergency power.

The police power has developed to a degree surpassing even that of the power of eminent domain. It now appears in a vast body of state, county, and municipal laws affecting such aspect of real estate investment as the construction of buildings (building codes, sanitary codes, electrical codes, fire regulations), the occupancy and use of buildings (housing codes, sanitary codes, smoke control ordinances, closing and demolition ordinances), and the use of urban and rural land (zoning codes, subdivision regulations, planning restrictions, etc.).

The original ideas about nuisance abatement and the protection of public health and safety have been enlarged to cover matters relating to the general moral and economic welfare of the community. As they are now applied, particularly in cities, but also to a steadily increasing extent in rural areas, nearly all improvement and use of real property are subject to regulation – and there is no evidence that this development has stopped. Greater limitations on the occu-

pancy of housing and more drastic requirements for modernization and demolition, for instance, are possible; less regard may be given in the future to the rights of nonconforming uses under zoning regulations; and planning regulations may go beyond social and economic to esthetic considerations.

The police power, combined with the chartering power, has provided the means for establishing and regulating financial institutions. Through the banking and insurance laws, the types of loans and other investments, as well as the volume of funds that can be made available for real estate investment, are regulated. The decisions of financial institutions are limited not only by the stipulations of the law but also by the attitudes and instructions of examining officials. Moreover, the law of real property, with its complex ritual of transfer and mortgage, adds another strong influence on the flow of institutional funds.

The indirect and passive effects of the taxing power on real estate investment are, of course, manifold. In addition, the taxing power has been directly used as a means of influencing investment. Inducements for investment in industrial property have been offered for many years through a decrease or elimination of the real estate tax for a period of years. The extension of the homestead exemption principle to limit property taxation, and the use of tax exemption and tax limitations, have been employed to encourage home ownership, to induce investment in rental housing property, and to stimulate slum clearance and rebuilding by private investors.

During World War II, special depreciation allowances were permitted under the federal corporate income tax in order to induce private investment for war production. Since the war, suggestions have been made for using a similar method for real estate corporations in order to encourage investment in rental housing. Another form of tax exemption has appeared in the financing of public housing projects by the issuance of the bonds of local housing authorities. Because these are authorities emanating from local government, the interest on their obligations is exempt from federal taxation. This fact, combined with a virtual guarantee of principal and interest, has resulted in a much lower interest rate than is available for other real estate financing.

The power to act in the general welfare and the power to spend in support of welfare measures have been the sources of numerous impacts, both direct and indirect, on the real estate market. Subsidies for public housing and slum clearance, for instance, have been defended on these grounds, as have the extensive measures to support the prices of farm products and hence the value of farm land.

The powers discussed above have been long recognized. Out of World War I, the depression, and World War II, however, has come a new assertion of power, departing from both the legal heritage and the former definition of constitutional limitations of the federal government. The new source of power is that created by Congress, or assumed by the President, on the grounds of "national emergency." During World War I, emergency powers (as regards real estate activity) were invoked to curtail construction, to grant priorities in the use of building materials, and to engage directly in industrial and residential building. The declaration of a national emergency during the 1930's gave support to the innovations of that period. For instance, the ease with which such measures as the National Housing Act and the United States Housing Act escaped serious constitutional challenge, as compared with the much less novel Land Bank Act of a few years before, indicated the new force which that crisis brought to the interventionary trend.

With the sweeping assertion of emergency power occasioned by World War II, real estate investment was again affected. The control of construction operations through priorities and limitation orders; the control of rents, sales prices on newly built houses, prices of building materials, wages of construction workers, and the price of certain building operations; the financing of industrial construction and the direct building of emergency housing; the creation of the National Housing Agency and the temporary abolition of the Home Loan Bank Board, all resulted from extraordinary wartime powers. The same powers, in force after hostilities ceased, permitted the continuance of rent control, the limitation of construction, the issuance of priorities, and the range of activity authorized by the Veterans' Emergency Housing Act of 1946.

Although the specific measures enacted under emergency conditions have usually been of limited duration,* the right to invoke emergency power to meet new crises may now be considered a settled interventionary principle.

To the powers thus far discussed must be added the right to exert control directly over real estate credit. This stems mainly from broad interpretations of the monetary power delegated to the federal government by the Constitution. In nearly every respect, particularly in the federal sphere, the power to influence credit has in the long run surpassed the importance of other powers. Constitutional limitations prevent the federal government from using the police power except where interstate commerce is involved (a rare occurrence in real estate activity); the power of eminent domain has been restricted to taking land essential for public buildings, control of navigation, and the national defense.† The federal government is no longer important as a landholder, except in a few states; and the federal taxing power has limited application as a means of influencing realty investment. Credit, therefore, is the main avenue of federal influence and with the shift of emphasis from state to federal jurisdiction it has come to be the most direct means of governmental impact on the realty market.

### Credit as an all-purpose instrument

The federal government has used its power

---

* This has not been true in every case; for instance, the Trading with the Enemy Act of October 6, 1917 (50 App. U.S.C., § 5 (b) [1946]), which was never repealed, provided the basis for the emergency power assumed by the President in closing the banks in 1933, and for many of the executive orders prior to, and during, World War II.

† The control over navigation (under the interstate commerce clause), as previously noted, has been sufficient to permit an extensive use of the power to effectuate general planning schemes. The right to exercise the power of eminent domain in the interests of national defense seems likely to expand further with the development of atomic energy. In the general field of real estate activity, however, the federal use of eminent domain is still negligible.

to influence lending activity and to accomplish a number of objectives not all directly related to credit conditions. A number of examples may be given. First, the credit instrument has been used to grant privileges to special groups. Initially, privileges were extended only to borrowers in distress* but now, under the Bankhead-Jones Act and the Cooley Act (Farmers' Home Administration), they include loans for farm purchase and improvement by tenant farmers, sharecroppers, and owners of submarginal farms, as well as loans for the benefit of low-income urban families under the United States Housing Act. The same principle was used to provide for war workers and later for veterans, under amendments to the National Housing Act and through the Servicemen's Readjustment Act.

In extending credit to special groups two important principles are apparent: (1) credit is made available in accordance with a measure of need rather than a measure of risk; and (2) the terms of credit are such as to meet the need. The objective of protecting certain groups from the risks they have incurred has always been present in times of distress, but there is a tendency now to embody protective measures in the original credit instrument. For example, there is the ease with which debt obligations may, on the occasion of distress, be modified under the Bankhead-Jones procedure and under the Servicemen's Readjustment Act for loans to veterans.[2]

Second, mortgage credit has been used to influence the type of tenure. Thus, special credit devices have been aimed at the encouragement of the family-operated farm. In cities they have been directed at the expansion of individual home ownership, and under some circumstances at the erection of rental housing.

Third, not only tenure but the character of the property has been subject to influence through the credit mechanism. Under Bankhead-Jones loans, the government maintains a measure of control over farm size and management, while under Federal Housing Administration procedure the mortgaged property is required to meet prescribed standards of location, planning, and construction. In many respects,

FHA standards have provided a means of overcoming the inability of the federal government to exercise the police power directly. Land selection, land planning, building design, and construction of public housing projects are, of course, subject to almost complete control by the federal government through its loans and subsidies to public housing authorities, and a strong measure of such control will follow the loans and grants to cities for redevelopment purposes.

Fourth, the federal government influences real estate prices through FHA and Veterans' Administration appraisals and limitations on loan amount. It also controls the prices veteran borrowers are permitted to pay for their houses and the rents at which apartment properties subject to FHA-insured financing and public housing properties can be offered and assumes considerable jurisdiction over operating policies in respect to these properties. Through loans to cities for redevelopment purposes it has the final voice in setting the price at which the assembled lands are offered for re-use.

Fifth, credit devices have been used to influence many aspects of construction, such as the encouragement given to large merchant builders by the FHA system, the special appeal offered to the large contract builder by public housing, and the aid extended to manufacturers of prefabricated housing by direct loans from the Reconstruction Finance Corporation. Federal Housing Administration standards influence the whole technology of the construction industry, while the greater means of control exercised over public housing contracts and other direct loan operations, such as loans to farmers, have a similar but even more far-reaching effect.

Finally, the extension of mortgage credit has been used as an instrument for increasing employment. Closely allied was the objective of establishing a " fair " wage. Thus, where public credit was used directly, as in public works and public housing, construction wages have been set at what the Secretary of Labor found to be the " prevailing wage " in the area. Where government operates more indirectly, as in FHA-insured financing of rental housing construction,

---

* Through the Home Owners' Loan Corporation and the Federal Farm Mortgage Corporation.

the same procedure has been applied, and a recurring effort has been made to apply it to all FHA insurance activity.

These new objectives in the use of the credit power have carried it far from its original status. The increase in availability of mortgage funds is no longer the single end; indeed, it may be overshadowed by numerous other objectives. In its new function, credit plays an integral part in a general welfare program under which government assumes responsibility for better standards of income, health, and shelter.

### Persistence of conflict

The relationship between government and real estate finance has not developed in the direction of greater simplicity or uniformity. Starting with a legal system of great complexity and a multitude of jurisdictions (from the forty-eight states to the thousands of counties, municipalities, and taxing authorities), the number of agencies with which investors must deal, and the number of matters about which they must be concerned, have grown with the years. Amid the increasing diversity of governmental powers many old conflicts have persisted and new ones have appeared. Conflicts, of course, are inevitable as long as interests differ; and the making of working compromises between interests is the basis of all law. The conflicts, however, do not arise merely from differences among the interests in an otherwise private transaction but also in different sets of governmental jurisdictions, among contrary attitudes of the function of government, and among the very objectives that government undertakes to achieve. No resolution of these conflicts has yet been accomplished.

So far, the conflict between state and local law, on the one hand, and federal initiative, on the other, has found no solution except by the federal government's reaching over state jurisdiction by insuring and guaranteeing mortgage loans, chartering specialized lending institutions, and making direct loans and subsidies. These means have served not only to draw under federal influence a large part of farm and residential finance but also to give the federal government influence on matters of land development and building that otherwise would be subject only to the police power of the states.

The second realm of conflict – that between the concept of government as an arbiter in an economic system where activity springs mainly from private decisions and the concept of government as a prime mover and director of economic activity – has so far come even less near to a working compromise. Perhaps one reason for this failure is the fact that the character of the conflict itself has not even now been clearly defined.

In its relationships with mortgage credit, government has not been guided by any consciously stated principle; intervention has been largely a matter of expediency rather than principle. As often shown in the course of this study, it has come in response to a crisis; and the nature of the crisis, rather than some basic concept of the function of government, has determined the nature of the action taken.

In most early instances of intervention, the government's role was that of a salvaging or corrective agent, and not of a permanent directive force; and it tended to withdraw soon after the immediate danger was past. This was true, for instance, of state action in staying foreclosure proceedings during financial panics. In the federal sphere, it was true of the Home Owners' Loan Corporation and the Federal Farm Mortgage Corporation. However, many crisis-bred measures, such as the extension of redemption periods, the limiting of the deficiency judgment, and restrictions on the lending power of financial institutions, have continued to exemplify governmental policy after the immediate occasion for them had passed. Except where the original enactment has carried a definite expiration date, positive action to eliminate it has rarely been taken. Successive crises, therefore, have produced an accumulation of interventionary measures; and the attitude has generally been to continue a measure, once it has become familiar or in respect to which special interests have developed.

Beginning with the crisis in farm credit about the time of World War I, and continuing through the 1930's and 1940's, crises became the occasion not only for temporary supporting and protective measures but for a number of designedly permanent new governmental operations (from the Farm Loan Board to the Farmers'

Home Administration and from the Federal Housing Administration to the Public Housing Administration). Even here, the ultimate scope of these new activities was rarely contemplated at their inception. In nearly every case, however, there has been a drift that has placed steadily more responsibility and directive power in the hands of government. Despite the extensive advances resulting from the state and federal legislation of 1949, there is still no indication of the extent to which governmental control will finally impinge upon or supersede the operation of market forces.

The final source of unresolved conflict lies in the diversity of the objectives that government attempts to pursue. Thus, during the period immediately after World War II, the immediate demand was for an increased number of new houses and for the easy credit, subsidies, or grants that might be helpful in getting them built quickly and in enabling families to acquire them when built. Yet longer range considerations required that demand be held back as much as possible while the risk of inflation was present, an objective that called for measures contrary to those invoked for the first purpose. Where long-range objectives conflict with shorter-run demands, political pressures are almost certain to tip the balance to the latter.

But even among concurrent purposes, conflicts in governmental policies are frequent. The purposes of the housing agencies, for example, have often been at variance with those of the supervisory agencies. The desire to encourage equity investment in income-producing property has been countered by the tax policy.

The problems raised by these unresolved conflicts in public policy are of immediate and inescapable concern to all participants in realty finance whether as lenders or borrowers, or as private persons, institutions, or government agencies. So far, there has been little reason to believe that a means for bringing consistency into the vast range of governmental impacts on real estate finance is likely to be brought about in the near future.

## The indirect impacts of government

Direct governmental influence, vast as it has become, does not include all phases of the state's impact on real estate financing. Numerous other means of influence exist, and, although these exert their force indirectly, they are nonetheless real and important. The area of indirect impact is, indeed, almost as broad as the whole range of legislation dealing with economic conditions. A tariff law, immigration, labor, or transport policies, a revenue measure, or any act affecting farm or urban prosperity will ultimately have some influence on real property. It is not practicable here to identify all these manifestations of government nor even to examine thoroughly the major indirect forces. But even a limited discussion of a few of them will suffice to show how the real estate market is dependent upon political action.

### The property tax

The property tax is one of the most important secondary influences. From a time when wealth was largely in land and chattels, and manufacture and trade were incidental, the property tax remains the main support of local government and, with a number of exceptions, a contributor to the financing of state government. Since, as the tax is administered, property has come mainly to mean real property, its incidence has a definite influence on real estate investment. In an area with high property taxes, the property tax may well amount to one-fifth or more of the gross income on an income-producing property such as rental housing. If conditions in the market do not permit the shifting of the property tax to the tenant, net income may be reduced relative to other investments, the value of the property reduced relative to other investment goods of similar cost, and hence the volume of new investment retarded. On the other hand, if the tax can be shifted the effect is to direct new investment to properties that will appeal to tenants financially able to carry the load. The property tax also has an influence on the location of residential and other structures, a drift to relatively low tax areas being inevitable where the choice of location is optional. As between comparable properties within a locality, but in different taxing jurisdictions, a difference in the current property tax tends to become capitalized into a difference in property value, so the effect of the tax is to create artificial differences in real estate investment opportunities. Even compensating differences in services rendered in high tax areas are likely to offset only to a limited degree the attraction of lower property tax rates.

Because real estate is necessarily a long-term investment offering a slow return of total capital and because, at the same time, the income from real property is highly variable, the property tax creates special hazards. The tax is relatively inflexible and, over long periods, its tendency has been to rise. Thus in bad times a property may suddenly be thrown into a deficit, while, on older properties, taxes may be borne only at the neglect of maintenance. The total influence of the property tax is not only to limit the amount and type of real estate investment but also to increase its speculative character, and to induce "milking" of property in its early years and neglect thereafter.[3]

The search for new sources of local and state revenues has been proceeding rapidly. New York City with its telephone and sales taxes and Philadelphia with its payroll tax are but two examples. Additional franchise taxes, tobacco, gasoline, and liquor taxes, and special charges for city services are other methods pursued.[4] These efforts, however, amid the constantly increasing costs of municipal government, have at best served to retard or prevent increases in the property tax. Through income taxes, general or specific sales taxes, license fees, and other means, many of the states and some municipalities have reduced their dependence for revenues on direct levies on real estate. So far, however, the basic difficulty with respect to financing local governments has hardly been met, and the uneven load on realty investment remains. The remedy offered by the limitations on the property tax, which are a feature of some state constitutions, are only a partial remedy. They set bounds to the amount of the load but do not solve the problem of inequality.

## The income tax

The income tax creates additional problems

for corporate-owned real estate. Applied to an investment that already is carrying a large share of the total cost of local government, the corporate income tax further reduces a relatively thin margin of net income.* For real-estate-owning corporations, the only escape is through the creation and maintenance of a high proportion of debt, since interest payments are deductible in the tax calculation. In this case the result is to induce dependence on mortgage rather than on equity financing and even to encourage disguising, as some form of fixed debt, that which would normally be equity financing.

Another hazard is created by the incompatibility of the tax system with the repayment of mortgage debt, since amortization payments are made from net income and are not deductible for tax purposes. The situation creates an incentive either to maintain a high fixed debt or to substitute for it an arrangement involving a sale of property and taking back under a long-term lease with fixed rental payments (which are deductible). The latter device, applied mainly to industrial and store properties, has been a feature of insurance company investment since the war. The difficulty created by the corporate income tax system is especially sharp in connection with loans having a fixed regular payment compounded of decreasing interest and increasing amortization shares, such as is characteristic of most insured mortgage loans on rental property. The interest portion is deductible from income in calculating taxable net income; the amortization portion, on the other hand, is not deductible. The depreciation allowance is deductible and this may exceed amortization, but, whereas amortization requirements increase under the level payment plan, depreciation allowances are fixed, and when the former equal the latter (usually at an early point in the life of an individual investment) the mortgagor is required to pay an increased income tax and to continue to disburse cash to meet amortization and interest requirements. This may be a very heavy burden on the cash resources of the owner, and, under some circum-

---

* According to U.S. Treasury, *Statistics of Income*, Part 2, 1938–42, the net return to urban real estate corporations, figured on its relation either to total invested capital or to equity capital, was lower than for any

other form of corporate enterprise. It is probable that this unfavorable dividend status for real estate corporations is at least partly offset by heavier salary payments to owner-officers of these corporations.

stances, might be serious enough to cause a default. The net effect is to induce the equity holder to be more concerned with the quick recoupment of a minimum equity than with considerations of long-term investment. The tax system thus aggravates the speculative character of the equity investment and, in doing so, adds to the risk of the mortgagee.*

In respect to owner-occupied housing, the interest payment deduction allowed under the personal income tax is often looked upon as a special benefit to the homeowner. But it is a benefit only as long as he remains in debt. Consequently, there is a lessened incentive to repayment of debt in order to maintain a maximum income tax benefit. Another income tax advantage to the homeowner, which indirectly influences housing investments, is the exclusion from gross income of any amount for the rental value of owner-occupied homes.

### Tax exemption

Both the property and income tax systems contain exemptions or abatements that give special advantages to certain types of investment or investing institutions. Thus, public housing developments are generally relieved of any substantial contribution to the maintenance of the municipalities in which they are located. New York and Massachusetts, for instance, provide for less-than-normal taxes for property developed and operated under their urban redevelopment statutes. Tax concessions on industrial property are widespread,[5] and a number of the states have laws exempting homesteads from all or part of the property tax. Federally-owned property is not subject to state or local taxation. And religious and eleemosynary institutions receive substantial tax concessions in many states. Designed as incentives to certain types of

investment and as a special protection to others, all such concessions add to the inequalities already existing in property tax assessments; and, even more important, they inevitably increase the burden on the remainder of real property excluded from the benefits. While by no means a general rule, the tendency is to favor industrial property, owner-occupied dwellings, and "social purpose" housing to the corresponding disadvantage of investment in income-producing property of commercial and conventional residential types.

Income tax exemptions are also significant in the realty investment picture, since certain types of mortgage lending institutions obtain a competitive advantage both as to the interest rates that may be charged and the income that may be returned. Thus, national farm loan associations, federal savings and loan associations, state-chartered savings and loan associations, and mutual savings banks enjoy immunities under the federal income tax laws and in general are also given favored treatment under state and local tax laws. National banks and state commercial banks are not thus privileged. Life insurance companies, by special arrangement, are taxed only for the amount of income in excess of that allocable to legal reserves, with the result that the incidence of the tax on total income is minor.† Government corporations and agencies (federal, state, and local) engaged in realty financing pay no income taxes, a circumstance which, combined with the low interest at which they can obtain their funds, gives them a strong advantage if their activities become competitive with unprivileged private institutions.

### The problem of municipal organization

Adding to the difficulties created by the pro-

---

* For a fuller treatment of the investment problems raised by the corporate income tax, with particular reference to the "constant payment" plan of mortgage financing, see Randoph E. Paul and Miles I. Colean, *Effect of the Corporate Income Tax on Investment in Rental Housing* (National Committee on Housing, Inc. New York, 1946). Also to be noted is the fact that the capital gains feature of our income tax is biased in favor of investment in securities as against investment in real estate. A man who buys and sells real estate

is more readily regarded as a dealer than is a securities trader and his gains are taxed as ordinary income rather than as capital gains (H. M. Groves, *op. cit.*).
† The minor burden of income taxes on insurance companies makes it advantageous for these institutions to invest in income producing properties suitable for long-term lease to substantial tenants. In such cases, the tenants avoid income taxes on the rental paid and the investing insurance company also has the advantage of comparative tax immunity.

perty tax is the problem created by the organization of our municipalities and metropolitan districts. As the demand for additional services from government has grown, the tendency has often been to set up independent taxing authorities to provide the services. Thus, we have not only an overlapping of state, county, and municipal levies on property, but often a congeries of levies from school, park, and sanitary districts, special assessment areas, and others, all independently computed, but all placed against the same property. Rarely is there a single authority to correlate the claims of all agencies in terms of their relative importance and with due regard for the ability of property owners to pay.

Even more far reaching in its effect on urban realty investment is the independent jurisdiction of satellite communities. In most metropolitan areas the central city is prevented from extending its limits by the suburban communities that surround it. The satellites depend on the central city for their existence and profit from the services it provides; yet they are free from the burden of its support. At the same time the movement of industry and population to outlying sections deprives the central city of revenue. The result is an increasing burden of taxes on centrally located properties, a decrease in their ability to pay (and consequently in their value), and discouragement of new investment in core areas. On the other hand, lower taxes and frequently more lenient building regulations tend to cause new real estate investment to follow population to the suburban regions.

Various attempts have been made to compensate for this situation. New York led the way with its Redevelopment Companies Acts of 1942 and 1943, which provided that taxes on housing properties built in reclaimed areas might be frozen for twenty-five years at the level existing before redevelopment.[6] This measure has an effect on the financial structure of a housing investment more than equivalent to the complete writing off of land value during the period of the abatement. Massachusetts offered a more complex but less beneficial plan of the same nature.[7] Legislation with a similar purpose had, by September 1, 1949, been passed in twenty-seven states and the District of Colum-

bia.[8] Indiana, for instance, authorized Indianapolis to levy a special realty tax to furnish funds for the purchase of blighted urban areas, and empowered the redevelopment authority to resell the land at prices compatible with its earning power when redeveloped.[9] Illinois provided for outright state and municipal grants to support these functions.[10] The federal Housing Act of 1949 supplements state and local funds for redevelopment activity.[11]

Such efforts to induce private investment in central areas are usually accompanied by some extension of governmental control over management. Generally, a requirement is made that the re-use be in keeping with approved redevelopment plans or general city plans. Among the more common controls established are those that regulate the capital structure and restrict rental charges and return on the investment. The regulation may, directly or indirectly, affect the physical character of the development, methods of operation, and selection of tenants.

### Influence of fiscal policies

Because of the direct bearing of municipal, and often of state, expenditures on the tax load carried by real property, the fiscal policies of these authorities obviously have a very considerable effect upon the returns from realty investment. The fiscal and monetary policies of the federal government, while perhaps less direct, may be more profound in their influence. For example, the need for intervention to save mortgagors from economic catastrophe in the panic of 1837 can be traced closely to the loose credit and monetary practices of the 1830's followed by the suddenly instituted hard money policy of the federal government.[12] Other periods of strain on the mortgage credit system need thorough study to determine the extent of their relationships to the general monetary situation. The present time is a case in point.

The increase in the public debt following fifteen years of depression and war (1930–45) naturally caused the federal government to be much concerned not only with the sale of its bonds but also with the bond interest rate. The heavy dependence placed by the Treasury on the banking system for absorption of successive issues (resulting in an increase in the money supply) and the low interest rate policy maintained throughout this period had two effects on real estate investment. One was to contribute to the inflation of capital values, already stimulated by a short supply of residential and commercial structures during and after the war; the other was to create a downward pressure on the mortgage interest rate.

During 1947 and 1948, fear of further inflation caused some modification in Treasury policy, which tended both to reduce the amount of debt held by the banks and to relieve some of the pressure on interest rates. Demands for new industrial loans added to the upward movement of rates. These influences were reflected in some tightening in mortgage credit. Although the new trend was welcomed in some quarters for its presumed counterinflationary effect, it faced opposition in other directions as endangering the expansion of residential construction and as increasing the federal burden of debt financing.

Up to this time, the policy of direct pressure on the mortgage interest rate (through the Federal Housing Administration and the Veterans' Administration) as a means for increasing the housing supply had harmonized with, and benefited from, the general fiscal policy. The modification of fiscal policy thus created a new realm of conflict and gave impetus to proposals to fix mortgage interest rates independently of fluctuations of rates in the financial markets and indeed of the broader governmental attitude on credit expansion. However, by mid-1949 general fiscal policy of the government, as well as housing policy, again favored low interest rates.

It should be noted that the stress on the maintenance of low interest rates on mortgage loans threatens to remove one means of effecting market readjustments. If rates are kept at low levels during an inflationary period, further reductions to provide a stimulus in any subsequent period of deflation become difficult or impossible except in combination with a government subsidy. A settled policy of low mortgage interest rates would thus point to an expansion of governmental controls to compensate for the weakening of automatic market adjustments.

## Public works

Public works affect real estate investment by their cost, location, and timing. The majority of community projects are financed either from special assessments or from general property tax funds; in either case the cost is carried by the owners of real estate. A community which, in spite of high tax charges, carries out well-devised programs of public improvement is likely, within limits, to have an investment advantage over a community where a low tax rate is combined with inadequate services. However, the possibility of excessive burdens from such expenditures is one of the hazards of realty investment.

The building of a bridge, tunnel, or rapid transit extension may open a dormant urban area to investment. Such improvements may also drain value from older areas. In Chicago, for instance, the subdivision boom of the 1920's resulted mainly from a series of actual or projected transit extensions. Streets, schools, and parks all play a vital part in determining the point and profitability of investment. The power of public works to contribute to, or detract from, the investment potentials of an area is thus exceedingly great.[13]

Real estate investment is also affected by the timing of public works in so far as the coincidence of high public and private activity aggravates a construction boom. Traditional methods of financing and public demand both for necessary extensions of community services, such as water and sewer facilities, and for additional improvements in times of prosperity and high building activity tend to concentrate locally financed public works in periods of prosperity. Public construction under such circumstances becomes directly competitive with private investment for short supplies of labor and materials and so contributes to higher costs and nonmaintainable levels of property values. On the other hand, state and local public works, which ordinarily constitute the bulk of the total, tend to be sharply reduced during the early stages of a contraction. Thus, customary public works policies not only tend to increase costs during expansions but also tend to add to deflationary pressures during contractions.[14] Actually, therefore, they must be looked upon as important contributors to the instability of realty values and to the hazards of real estate investment.

## Security legislation

A new type of impact on real estate investment is developing from a wide range of state and federal social security measures, such as old age and health benefits, unemployment insurance, minimum wage laws, parity prices, subsidies for production or nonproduction, crop insurance, and so forth. This source of impact on realty investment is too complex for analysis in this study, yet it warrants brief consideration.

All of these measures affect the level and continuity of private income. Those affecting agriculture directly influence farm income and hence will tend to be reflected in farm real estate prices, while security benefits for urban workers may help to determine the rents and prices that may be afforded for urban houses, modifying in some degree the trend of investment. To the extent that such benefits are constant, or increasing in value, they may tend to give an element of stability to real estate finance, and to improve the opportunity for investment. To the extent, however, that the payments are of limited or of limitable duration, the results may be to the contrary.

## Government research activities

The technical and economic research carried on by governmental agencies has had, and promises increasingly to have, profound influences on realty investment. Early in the 1930's, following the leadership of Cleveland the first "real property inventories" appeared. Prior to that time, land-use maps had been prepared in a number of places, but the inventories disclosed, for the first time, organized facts regarding the type, size, condition, age, and rental of urban dwellings. Financed with relief funds and carried out under the direction first of the Department of Commerce and later of the Works Progress Administration, these surveys were conducted in a large number of cities. Some of the inventories were supplemented by the "Financial Survey of Urban Housing" (also financed as a

relief project) which provided information not hitherto available on values, rents, debt and debt delinquency, type of tenure, and similar data for sixty-one cities or metropolitan areas.

The Home Loan Bank Board and the FHA undertook a considerable amount of research useful to investors and mortgage lenders. All this led up to the general Housing Census of 1940, in which comprehensive data on the nation's housing supply were brought together. Related to these data are the building permit figures of the Bureau of Labor Statistics (Department of Labor), the construction estimates of the Construction Division (Office of Domestic Commerce, Department of Commerce), the population and business data of the Bureau of the Census (Department of Commerce), and other material collected by a number of federal agencies. There remain, however, many serious gaps in the economic data needed by realty investors to formulate sound judgments.[15]

In 1935, the Division of Economics and Statistics of the FHA listed the following series as essential in the field of housing : rents, occupancy and vacancy, building operating expenses, real estate values, real estate transfers, subdividing activity, new construction, construction costs, mortgage recordings, foreclosures, real estate taxes and delinquencies and population data (growth, shifts, marriages, etc.). At that time, current information on only a few of these subjects was available and most of that was inadequate. Yet the inadequacies of the data on housing were as nothing compared to those on other types of real estate. During World War II, the Census, by the use of sampling techniques, contributed greatly to current knowledge, particularly of congested centers. But the effort was scattered and sporadic and no means have been provided for its continuance. Fourteen years after the FHA report referred to above, the situation was much the same. The Housing Act of 1948, passed during the special session of the Eightieth Congress, authorized the Housing and Home Finance Agency to conduct technical research to promote standardized building codes and standardized dimensions for building materials. In the Housing Act of 1949, this authorization to the Housing and Home Finance Agency was extended to permit a broad range of technical and economic research in the field of housing.

In the past, construction (much the same sort of small local business as agriculture) has received little from the government for technological research compared with the scientific and developmental work done for agriculture. During the 1920's the Department of Commerce made a beginning in this field. Programs were instituted for simplifying the variety of manufactured products and processes, for model building codes, planning laws, zoning ordinances, mechanic's lien laws, and for making tests necessary to substantiate code requirements.

Modest as this endeavor was, and fruitful as it promised to be, nearly all the activities mentioned were drastically curtailed in 1933, just at the time when the government was assuming a major part of the risk and direction of farm and residential mortgage activity. Since that time, in spite of meager appropriations, the Forest Products Laboratory of the Department of Agriculture has done notable original research beneficial to construction, particularly in the development and use of plywood,* while the National Bureau of Standards of the Department of Commerce has carried on simplification and construction standards programs and a much limited testing program.

War and postwar pressures disclosed the desirability of a more advanced technology of construction, particularly housing construction. Emergency funds were allocated to the War Production Board and the National Housing Agency for specific research projects. After the end of hostilities the technical research functions of the War Production Board were transferred to an Office of Technical Services in the Department of Commerce, where, during 1945 and 1946, a relatively small allocation was made for research in construction methods.

This chapter has tried to suggest, without attempting to be inclusive, the ramifications of indirect governmental influences on realty finance. It is clear that the impacts are numerous and that their effects are substantial; certainly remoteness is no criterion of their consequence. For example, there are many influences on real estate finance resulting from the numerous impacts of government upon the construction industry through such matters as local licensing laws for contractors, engineers, architects, and artisans (which in some cases serve to enforce local restrictive practices and hence to raise costs), the federal antitrust laws (which are designed to maintain competition and hence to keep costs down), the relatively weak state anti-monopoly legislation (which fails to prevent local restraints beyond federal reach), and the broad immunity of labor organizations from federal antitrust action. While it is clear that these conditions are significant elements of the essentially political environment in which real estate financing operations are carried on, their ramifications are too complex to be described satisfactorily in a study of this scope.

---

* The main impetus to prefabricated house construction in the prewar period came from this activity.

# Background of Federal housing credit

*CHARLES M. HAAR*

During the past twenty-five years the Federal government has played a vital and impressive role in stimulating and directing the home-building industry to meet the needs of a wide section of the population. Although housing is a commodity which is traded in local markets, and is traditionally subject to municipal regulation, increasingly since 1934 it has been to Washington rather than to state and local government that the consumer, the builder, and the lender have turned for a solution to their different problems.

In exerting its considerable influence, the Federal government has leaned heavily on one particular piece of machinery: the provision and insurance of credit. And despite the almost annual reframing of housing policy, this chosen instrument for wielding Federal power has remained substantially unchanged. Thus, Congress has initiated and maintained, with common approval, Federally insured and guaranteed mortgages with easy monthly carrying charges and national negotiability, and it has underpinned the scheme with provisions for secondary mortgage operations to help assure liquidity of

investment and to provide a primary supply of funds in times of credit shortage.

Any study of the current housing scene in the United States soon brings the inquirer to an awareness of the wide-ranging impact of Federal credit policy. The availability or dearth of credit influences the way financial institutions invest, the volume and standards of house construction, the nature of the building industry – and even the pattern of land tenure. By extending the availability of credit, Congress has caused houses to rise on vacant subdivisions; it has encouraged one form of tenure – home-ownership – at the expense of another – tenancy; and it may now ensure to certain classes of society, the Negro, the elderly, those of low incomes, a greater or different type of participation in the nation's wealth. If the power to tax involves the power to destroy, as John Marshall phrased it, then conversely the power to grant credit involves the power to create and divert.

It was an economic crisis which first* spurred Congress to take a direct interest in housing. By sanctioning the Home Loan Bank Act,†

---

* There were precedents for Federal action. In 1918, urgent need of housing for war workers led to direct loans to building companies by the United States Shipping Board Emergency Fleet Corporation. 40 Stat. c. 19 (1918). Projects in 24 localities were developed, providing some 9,000 houses, 1,100 apartments, and 8 hotels. Committee on Banking and Currency, *Federal Housing Programs: Chronology and Description*, 80th Cong., 2d Sess., 1948. It also led to the U.S. Housing Corporation —40 Stat. c. 74 (1918)—which built and operated about 6,000 homes in 26 states. See Dept. of Labor, *Report of the U.S. Housing Corporation*, 1920, p. 23. The corporation was liquidated in 1947, with a fiscal deficit to the

government of nearly $29 million or 37.3 percent of the total investment. See Housing and Home Finance Agency, *1st Annual Report*, (1947), p. 11. It should be added that incurrence of a large deficit was owing in part to a decision, after the Armistice was signed, to abandon all projects not in an advanced construction stage.

† 47 Stat. 725 (1932), 124 U.S.C.A. §1421. As far back as 1919, Senator Calder had introduced a " Bill to Create a Federal Home Loan Board and Home Loan Banks for the Purpose of Aiding and Financing the Construction of Homes " but it never became law.

*Reprinted from* Federal Credit and Private Housing, *McGraw-Hill Book Company, 1960, pp. 1–18, with permission of the publisher.*

which provided credit reserve funds for institutions specializing in home financing, the Federal government made its first move toward stopping the downward drift in home building in the Depression days.* With the passage of the National Housing Act of 1934,† a revolutionary program of home finance insurance was introduced, and to this were soon added provisions for secondary mortgage operations and a new institution for the purchase of insured mortgages.

After World War II, machinery which had been designed to meet Depression needs became, in the words of the 1949 Housing Act, the instrument for providing " a decent home and suitable living environment for every American family." This congressional mandate, based on the apparent conclusion that housing " need " cannot be satisfied by the undirected operations of a private housing market, is an undertaking by the Federal government – by way of either control or inducement – to foster the production of good houses in adequate numbers at prices or rents that are within the reach of different income groups.

Although this basic ideal would claim the support of a majority of both parties, the Republican victory of 1952 brought a reconsideration of home-credit policy. The Housing Act of 1954 represented the fruits of this rethinking. Embracing much of the earlier legislation, it gave a stamp of approval to FHA and VA insurance and guarantee; but stressed urban renewal (in fact, it created two new insurance programs especially aimed at this area) and recast the Federal National Mortgage Association.

Since 1956 general economic events have introduced new factors into the consideration of intricate apparatus for increasing the volume of housing investment and construction in

Federal policy, but these have not yet taken legislative form. In the first place, the decision by the Federal Reserve Board to tighten its monetary controls, as a reaction to postwar inflation, put the relationship of housing and fiscal policies into a new perspective. And more recently, the rather different question has arisen of whether the decline in housing activity, attributed by many to the actions of the Federal Reserve Board, should by some means be arrested and reversed in order to strengthen general economic activity. It remains to be seen whether the great social invention of government mortgage insurance and the elaborate structure of credit incentives built up over the past twenty-five years will prove appropriate and adequate to the economic conditions and housing requirements of the next decade.

## The impact of credit policies

The Federal government has not attained its present strategic role in the private housing market by creating with one stroke a large and intricate apparatus for increasing the volume of housing investment and construction in America. Rather, it developed its program details through trial and error. As an evolutionary process – largely one of selection of method and refinement of technique – it never veered too far, however, from the initial outer limits set in the 1930's. This basic cast of character was dictated by the fundamental choice of power made by the Congress to meet an emergency of national proportions. The point of decision was the Depression starting in the early 1930's, a point when the separation of powers under the Federal and state constitutions began to come under a series of new tests, and the chief instru-

---

* And, of course, the formation in June, 1933, of the Home Owners' Loan Corporation by P.L. 43, 73d Cong. During the three-year period ending June 12, 1936, it refinanced home indebtedness in the amount of $3.093 billion on over a million individual homes. It was essentially a successful salvage operation. When HOLC was liquidated on December 31, 1951, it showed net earnings of over $14 million.
† P.L. 479, 73d Cong. (1934), 48 Stat. 1246. During the hearings before the House Banking Committee on May 18, 1934, concerning the bill to create the FHA, Relief Administrator Harry Hopkins, speaking on behalf of

the administration, stated that he favored the bill on four grounds: " One, on the present unemployment situation as it relates to the building trades, and our relief organization and relief work as it relates to the building trades; second, on the social value of housing; third, on the importance of moving heavy industry; and fourth, on the great importance of our getting private credit into this picture rather than government bonds." In one of the basic housing finance bills, the prime objective of the legislation was to " put substantial numbers of workers in the building trades back on payrolls."

mentality selected to transmit Federal housing policy was the money power.*

It is largely an accidental combination of an historical and an economic factor that lies behind the peculiarly powerful influence which the Federal government is able, today, to exert in the field of housing. The first is the constitutional and historical dictates which impelled the government to make its impact on housing development through the device of credit manipulation; the second is the exceptionally strategic position of credit in the housebuilding process.

## Congress finds a means of intervention

The American Constitution, with its firmly entrenched Federal structure, reserves to the states (and to their local subdivisions) the power to make decisions over the use, misuse, and re-use of land. Even under a system where land uses are determined through the market mechanism and by private agreements, disputes are bound to arise; these conflicts, such as common-law nuisance cases or those arising under doctrines like the Rule Against Perpetuities or restraints on alienation, are settled in the state courts. Even what classes of contracts and leases relating to real property will be specifically enforced by a court of equity are questions for each state to decide for itself. With the increase in direct-planning guidance and in control over land use, these matters are similarly funneled through state administrative, legislative, and judicial branches. State constitutions (true, subject always to the restraint of the Fourteenth amendment to the Federal Constitution) determine the extent of permissible regulation; state enabling legislation sets the boundaries for controls over land and housing. Thus, zoning, subdivision regulations, official maps, and street controls – to isolate a few prominent examples – are all state creations. The taking of land for housing and other public purposes is a state determination. Again, property taxation, of vast influence on home and rental property development, is in the main exclusively a local prerogative.

There is, in the strict sense, no Federal police power.[1] Although the Federal government, in dealing with a subject within its enumerated powers, may enact police regulations in connection with that matter,† this would prove of limited applicability to land and housing.‡ There does exist an independent Federal eminent domain power, but it is narrowly confined to the status of handmaiden to other powers. The Federal Constitution contains no express grant of eminent domain, and as a government of delegated powers, it was not really settled until 1875 that the United States could condemn in its own name in its own courts.[2] Before that date, the state would condemn the property and turn it over to the Federal government.[3] Thereafter, the courts found eminent domain to be an implied power, "necessary and appropriate" for the execution of powers expressly conferred.§

---

* This is not to gainsay the importance of the competing philosophy of direct Federal intervention, expressed in such activities as WPA, PWA, and greenbelt developments. The United States Housing Authority Act of 1937 is a prime example of direct Federal construction adopted as an anti-Depression measure.

† Thus, under the commerce power, the Federal government may exercise power analogous to the state police power. *United States* v. *Carolene Products Co.*, 304 U.S. 144 (1938). Of course there is no problem with respect to District of Columbia matters, where Congress acts like a state legislature. *Berman* v. *Parker*, 358 U.S. 34 (1954). Under the war power, see *Hirabayoshi* v. *United States*, 320 U.S. 81 (1943) and under the taxing power, see *Speeyt* v. *Morgenthau*, 116 F. 2d 301 (App. D.C., 1940).

‡ There are intimations that although the police power was reserved to the states by the Tenth Amendment, a corresponding power in appropriate cases in the Federal government is traceable to the general welfare clause (Art. 1, sec. 8, par. 1) of the Federal Constitution.

See *Oklahoma City* v. *Sanders*, 94 F. 2d 323 (CCA 10, 1938); *Bowles* v. *Willingham*, 321 U.S. 503 (1944).

§ *U.S.* v. *Gettysburg Electric Co.*, 160 U.S. 668 (1896); cf. *United States* v. *2771.29 Acres of Land*, 31 F. 2d 617 (E.D. Wis., 1928). The Fifth Amendment is now contructed as a recognition of a preexisting power, rather than a grant of power. *U.S.* v. *Carmack*, 329 U.S. 210, 241 – 242 (1946). How restrictions on legal power may shape housing policy is interestingly illustrated in the case of public housing. When the court decided in *U.S.* v. *City of Louisville*, 78 F. 2d 684 (6th Cir., 1935) that the Federal government had no power to take land by eminent domain for its own low-rent housing projects, great impetus was lent to shift the public housing program in this country from Federal to local construction and operation through state enabling legislation and local housing authorities. Instead of direct Federal action, the U.S. Housing Act of 1937 provided for this new form of Federal aid on a decentralized basis for low-income families. 50 Stat. c. 896 (1937); 42 U.S.C. 1401 (1943).

In the past, also, legislation relating to the flow of capital and investment was dominantly a matter of state concern. Regulation of savings banks and insurance companies – the repositories of the people's savings – is still controlled by the state legislature, and the minute controls with respect to mortgages, such as permitted area for investment and the loan-to-value ratio, are supervised by state administrative agencies.* Even the very methods of proof of titles and rules of foreclosure, so crucial to determining the relative merits of mortgage investments, are jealously guarded provinces of the state. A striking example here is the wrecking of the hopes of the Uniform Commissioners on State Laws of passing a uniform foreclosure law; local interests and customs proved too strong.† It is a fact of vital importance in the shaping of a national housing policy that in the control of credit institutions dealing with housing, as in land control, the role of the states is constitutionally dominant.

With the onset of the great Depression, however, the weakness of the real estate market seemed beyond the ability of the states to correct. In the homebuilding field, eyes turned quickly toward the only source, at that time, of funds and initiative, the Federal government; and the Federal government exploited this invitation to launch its own policy for housing and land, mainly through the use of credit.‡ The new Federal agencies dealing with housing credit encountered no special difficulties with the courts. "The preservation of homeowners and the promotion of a sound system for home mortgage," stated the court in *First Federal Savings and Loan Assn. v. Loomis*,[4] " is none the less national in scope than the provisions for the unemployed and the aged." When considering, in connection with Federal insurance of mortgage loans, the extent of the fiscal powers

granted the Federal government under the Constitution, the Attorney General stated:[5]

It is one of the latest of a series of enactments, extending over more than a century, through which the Federal government has recognized and fulfilled its obligation to provide a national system of financial institutions for handling the credit and exchange requirements of industry, commerce and agriculture, supplying a national currency and promoting the fiscal affairs of the government.... It further seems to me incontrovertible that the purposes of the National Housing Act are for the welfare of the nation as a whole. Not only does the Act provide protection for our national financial structure, but it will also result in encouragement of better housing conditions throughout the country, in the provision of cheap and safe credit for the homeowners of the United States, and in the stimulation of the building industry, and indirectly of the durable goods industry, with consequent improvement in general conditions, including the furnishing of employment to many of the nation's unemployed.

The die was cast. Credit policy was to provide the main instrument for forging a national housing program.

## The central role of credit in housing

It is the extreme sensitivity of the house purchaser to the terms of mortgage credit which gives such significance to the actual form that Federal intervention took. A house, to the average American owner-occupant, represents the largest capital investment of his lifetime; its cost may average two or three times his annual income. Few American families have sufficient personal savings to acquire a single-family house

---

* The limited nature of this control should be noted: it sets the rules of the game, but the lender then operates as business judgment dictates—primarily by appraisal of the money-market returns.
† The federal system of government throws up some sizable problems. Obstacles to investment in housing may exist in individual states because of state-imposed antiquated procedures of mortgage lending and the protection of security investments. Other consequences involve the relative merits (from the perspective of

providing an adequate supply of housing) of lien versus title theory, of judicial or private power of sale, the variation in notice requirements, the length of redemption period, and the various fees and processes throughout the forty-eight states.
‡ The Federal government also undertook salvage operations, such as the HOLC and the RFC Mortgage Company. But these were emergency measures and unsupportable on this basis.

without resort to mortgage capital; 85 out of every 100 homes are bought with mortgage credit. In spite of the ceremonial transfer of ownership at the time of " closing of title," the homeowner may have a relatively slight interest, economically speaking, in his housing. The real claim may be the security interest held by the lender. Also, as the most durable of " durable " consumer goods, a house can stand a great capitalization of income in the form of mortgage debt. Moreover, the consumer is encouraged to look beyond his own accumulated assets by the government-favored pattern of a small down payment for the desired accommodation, with the remaining debt paid off over time.

Whereas renting involves no initial capital outlay for the consumer (except where a security deposit or advance rent is bargained for by the landlord) and involves no long-term commitment, it requires a substantial outlay, with slow repayment, from the investor's standpoint. In theory, capital funds for rental investments could be (and occasionally have been) entirely in the form of equity; in practice, little rental housing is built without extensive use of borrowed money.

The sensitivity of house purchasers to the ruling terms of credit results from the long period over which most houses are bought.* Considerably more than for most other consumer goods, the acquisition of residential real estate depends on the costs, contract terms, and availability of debt capital. Decisions about the size and quality of the dwelling purchased, about whether to buy or to rent, thus largely hinge upon the amount of down payment and

monthly debt service required. This being the case, control over the supply of mortgage funds, the length of time allowed for repayment, and the rate of interest charged become powerful tools for deciding how much housing will be made available and to whom.

The rate of interest is of prime importance in determining the activities of the real estate market. First, it is an important determinant of the final cost of housing to the consumer, since funds are typically borrowed for periods of fifteen to forty years. Given such long maturities, small changes in interest rates have sizable effects on monthly carrying costs and therefore on the consumer's ability to acquire a home. For example, on a twenty-five-year mortgage an increase in the interest rate from 4 to 5 percent raises monthly debt service by over 10 percent. According to the testimony of many builders, a change in debt service of this amount is sufficient to cause a consumer to shift to a lower-priced house or to withdraw from the market entirely.

Clearly, the more the real estate market can extend its operations into progressively lower-income groups, the smaller the down payment must be and the longer the term of the loan. In this field credit terms are crucial in determining whether the type of accommodation – purchased or rented – sought can fit within the budgets of lower-income people.

Not only from the consumer's perspective, but also from that of the producer does credit play a central role. Unlike many industries, where expansion since World War II has come in large part from internal capital financing,

---

* Is housing " abnormally " sensitive to the impact of credit compared, say, with automobiles? A car, we will assume, is bought for $2,400. It is to be paid for in twenty-four monthly installments over a two-year period, and the rate of interest is 12 percent on the unpaid balance. The total interest cost will be $144 (12 percent of the average unpaid balance of $1,200), or $6 per installment. With the addition of the $100 repayment of principal every month, each installment will total $106. Now, if the rate of interest goes up by one-half, to 18 percent, the monthly charge will be $109 instead of $106–an increase of less than 3 percent.

By comparison, consider a house bought on a thirty-six-year mortgage for $24,000, bearing an interest rate of 5 percent on the unpaid balance. Amortization of principle will require $666.67 each year and the annual interest charge will be $600 (5 percent of $12,000). The

total annual charge will therefore be $1,266.67, or $105 a month. If, again, the interest rate goes up by one-half, to 7½ percent, the annual interest charge on the house will rise to $900, and the total cost of buying the house per year will increase from $1,266.67 to $1,566.67. The increase on a monthly basis will be from about $105 to $130, or nearly 24 percent. Thus a 50 percent rise in interest rates increases the cost of purchasing an automobile (on the basis of the figures given) by 3 percent and a house by 24 percent. Moreover, not only do changes in interest rates bring a disproportionate percentage change in the size of the repayment installment, but since the amount of money involved is so large compared with the total income of the house purchaser, these changes effectively shift particular houses from one income-group market to another.

the home builder has relatively little equity investment – in fact in his dependence upon credit he resembles more closely the retailer than the ordinary producer. Hence even modest shifts in central monetary and fiscal policies evoke sharp reactions in the housing industry.

Moreover, the rate of interest largely determines how much mortgage money will be made available by lenders. Most mortgage loans are made by financial institutions which are alert to relatively small differences in the yields to be obtained from mortgages compared to alternative types of loans and investments.

The buyers, sellers, and brokers engaged in the real estate business are predominantly made up of individuals or small business units. Most houses are bought and sold by persons with little or no experience of real estate marketing, although the exceptional mobility of American families since the war has brought increased know-how to those on the move. Similarly, the typical builder is a small man with limited capital; recently a new type of large-scale builder, with considerable market experience, has emerged, but as yet his impact is relatively small.* Thus, in this largely amateur market, the role of the lender is dominant. For this reason the actual form that Federal intervention has taken – credit control – has assured it a powerful position in the manipulation of the housing market. Lenders being the primary source of power in the production and marketing of housing, government action affecting them is most likely to have direct and widespread influence.

There has been a notable change on the supply side of the mortgage market. The proportion of urban mortgage debt held by institutional lenders increased from 50 percent of the total outstanding in 1920 to nearly 80 percent in 1953. Institutional lenders accounted for 86 percent of the net increase in the mortgage market from 1939 to 1954, and this trend has accelerated.† In addition to affecting the organization and operation of the mortgage market, this emphasizes the point already made – the importance of the instrument chosen for Federal intervention. Federal loan insurance and guarantee programs have clearly made residential mortgages a more attractive investment for financial institutions.‡ It also means that, as Morton has suggested[6] from the point of view of the lender the major consideration is not the quality of the individual loan but rather the ability to anticipate correctly Federal policy changes.

The particular characteristics of the different groups of lenders are important in the more detailed formulation of Federal policy. For instance, resources of savings and loan associations are almost exclusively extended to single-family dwellings, whereas life insurance companies§ (and to a far lesser degree mutual savings banks and commercial banks) invest also in mortgages outside this field. A policy which fosters saving in savings and loan associations or permits activities for which they are functionally designed would presumably increase the share of single-family house building in the construction market.** Again, a policy which favors deposits of

---

* See Housing and Home Finance Agency, *Housing in the United States: A Graphic Presentation*, 1956, pp. 54 – 55. Of course, his importance varies from region to region. Stressing the significance of large-scale builders is Sherman J. Maisel's study, *The Structure and Problems of the House Building Industry*, University of California Press, 1953.

† From 1953 to 1956, savings and loan mortgages alone went up from some $20 billion to $34 billion, life insurance companies from $13 billion to $20.3 billion, mutual savings banks from $7.3 billion to $12.8 billion, commercial banks from $12 billion to $16.2 billion; whereas individual holdings of mortgages went up from $10.1 to only $12.7 billion in this period. At the end of 1957, savings and loan associations, with holdings of more than $38 billion in home mortgages, were clearly the largest institutional holder of the nation's mortgage debt. They held more than one-third of the total; life

insurance companies, with $21.5 billion, and commercial banks, with $16.4 billion, accounted for one-fifth and one-sixth of the total debt.

‡ Life assurance companies provide a striking example. Of all state-chartered lending institutions, they have the greatest freedom in crossing state lines with their investments. And, to a marked extent, these companies judge any loan sound which has VA and FHA approval and insurance.

§ This is truer of the larger companies. Smaller life insurance companies tend to concentrate the mortgage portion of their portfolio in FHA and VA mortgages.

** However, there may be many unintended consequences. Other lenders may withdraw from this market; or only transactions in old homes may be encouraged. By and large, savings and loan associations make minor use of government-insured and guaranteed loans, concentrating their investments in the so-called " conven-

*Figure 1. Mortgage recordings of $20,000 or less for nonfarm residences, showing types of lenders.*

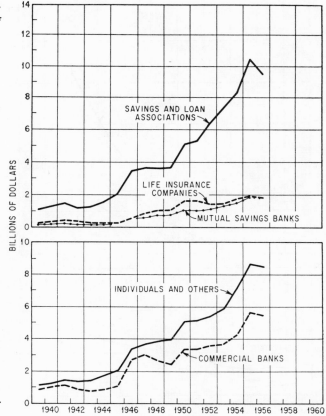

Source: Board of Governors of the Federal Reserve System.

savings in commercial banks* may work against the availability of home mortgages since these institutions require a high degree of liquidity in their investments.† However, government-insured mortgages, unlike the conventional type of mortgage, more nearly meet these liquidity requirements (especially in the days of FNMA support), and commercial banks have in fact invested heavily in this type of mortgage.‡ The important point is that the incentive must be

tionals." The reasons are varied: they are essentially local in saving and investment; they are not as interested as others in liquidity demands; and the yield on their deposits being traditionally high, operation on FHA's and VA's is deemed economically undesirable by many of them.

The role of state legislation and of fitting it into national credit programs is exemplified, again, by the experience of the mutual savings banks, which shifted from a concentration in United States government to FHA (and later VA) mortgages as a result of the post-1949 revisions to permit out-of-state investments.

* Such as the action of December 3, 1956, authorizing commercial banks to raise their interest on savings accounts to 3 percent.

† This also follows from the requirement of the National Bank Act, which prescribes a limit to the duration of the mortgages in which commercial banks may invest. The Housing Amendments of 1955 broadened the participation of national banks by permitting them to commit themselves to twenty-year

mortgages under prescribed circumstances. Again, ready availability to FNMA, as a government policy, enhances the attractiveness to commercial banks of government-backed loans, owing to the increased liquidity.

‡ See a study of twenty-five major cities in 1950 in James Gillies and Clayton Curtis, "Structure of Local Mortgage Markets and Government Housing Finance Programs," *Journal of Finance*, vol. 10, (September, 1955), pp. 363 – 375. The authors' findings indicate the following:

Cities where commercial banks held more than

| | |
|---|---|
| 20% of mortgage holdings in FHA | 18 |
| 30% of mortgage holdings in FHA | 12 |
| 20% of mortgage holdings in VA | 13 |
| 30% of mortgage holdings in VA | 7 |
| 40% of mortgage holdings in FHA-VA combined | 20 |

These are overall figures: the policies followed in different cities varied widely. This underlines a major difficulty of exerting national policy to affect local market situations.

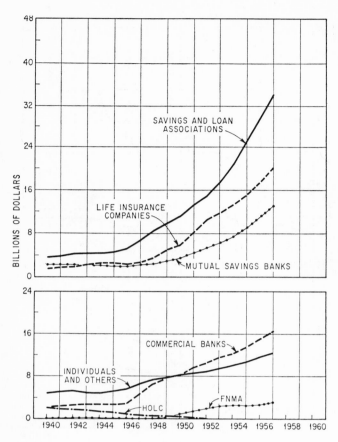

Source : Board of Governors of the Federal Reserve System.

*Figure 2. Mortgage holdings on one- to four-family nonfarm residential properties (end-of-year figures).*

geared to the nature of the lender's requirements.

The armory of the Federal government is extensive. But the primary tool it will probably employ in meeting the nation's housing needs is that of credit. In view of the direct and affirmative impact of credit in inducing private action in urban real estate, the lender's dominant position in the housing industry, and the historical and constitutional grounds for the use of the fiscal power, it seems safe to conclude that the Federal government will continue to channel through credit mechanisms whatever housing influence it decides to exert.*

This conclusion highlights the importance of exploring and evaluating the activities of Federal housing credit agencies, their impact on the conduct of private institutions, and the full implications of the Federal government's reliance on credit devices. The formulation of new legislation to improve this mechanism requires careful examination of the consequences of alternative policies. Certain courses of action seem foreclosed for the immediate future by the currently accepted philosophies of government, history, and the on-going institution of credit. The chief point to remember, however, is the range of open choice, the richness of possible gradations and shadings. Housing credit policy is not

---

* However, other alternatives must always be reckoned with. Federal income taxation constitutes an important source of social control. Land banks and land value controls may be desirable. Newer techniques of mass production and home marketing may only be awaiting further publication and dissemination among the building trades. Examination of obstructions due to building codes may lead to more effective reductions in the cost of housing. Thus, there must be kept in mind the poten-

tiality of a conclusion that Federal activity in the home mortgage insurance field should be terminated as a misallocation of Federal resources. Although the lesson of history and the presence of strong pressure groups make such a possibility remote, to say the least, a rescrutiny of credit policies may at least underline the need for combining such social weapons with other types of controls and incentives in order to reach most effective results.

## TABLE 1

*Nonfarm Mortgage Recordings of $20,000 or Less by Type of Holder*[a]

| | June | | | First 6 months | | |
|---|---|---|---|---|---|---|
| | 1959 | 1958 | Percentage change | 1959 | 1958 | Percentage change |
| | $ | $ | % | $ | $ | % |
| Savings and loan associations | 1,261 | 910 | +38.6 | 6,353 | 4,511 | +40.8 |
| Insurance companies | 120 | 110 | + 9.3 | 690 | 648 | + 6.4 |
| Commercial banks | 543 | 429 | +26.4 | 3,003 | 2.204 | +36.2 |
| Mutual savings banks | 168 | 140 | +20.5 | 781 | 642 | +21.7 |
| Individuals | 338 | 279 | +21.0 | 1,913 | 1,643 | +16.4 |
| Miscellaneous | 544 | 407 | +33.6 | 2,961 | 2,149 | +37.8 |
| Total amount | $2,974 | $2,275 | +30.7 | $15,701 | $11,797 | +33.1 |
| Total number | 342 | 287 | +19.1 | 1,849 | 1,549 | +19.4 |

[a] Number in thousands; amounts in millions of dollars.

## TABLE 2

*Sources of Residential Mortgage Funds, 1947 to 1957 (billions of dollars)*

| Year | Life insurance companies | Savings and loan associations | Mutual savings banks | Commercia banks | United States government | Corporate pension funds | All others | Total |
|---|---|---|---|---|---|---|---|---|
| 1947 | 1.1 | 1.7 | 0.4 | 1.8 | c | a | 0.8 | 5.7 |
| 1948 | 1.7 | 1.4 | 0.8 | 1.1 | 0.1 | a | 0.7 | 5.9 |
| 1949 | 1.6 | 1.3 | 0.8 | 0.6 | 0.5 | a | 0.5 | 5.3 |
| 1950 | 2.7 | 2.0 | 1.5 | 1.8 | 0.3 | a | 0.5 | 8.7 |
| 1951 | 2.6 | 1.9 | 1.5 | 0.8 | 0.6 | a | 0.4 | 7.8 |
| 1952 | 1.4 | 2.8 | 1.3 | 0.9 | 0.5 | c | 0.6 | 7.5 |
| 1953 | 1.5 | 3.5 | 1.5 | 0.7 | 0.4 | c | 0.6 | 8.2 |
| 1954 | 2.0 | 4.2 | 1.9 | 1.2 | c | c | 0.9 | 10.2 |
| 1955 | 2.6 | 5.2 | 2.4 | 1.7 | 0.3 | c | 1.1 | 13.3 |
| 1956 | 2.7 | 4.2 | 2.2 | 1.1 | 0.5 | 0.2 | 1.1 | 12.0 |
| 1957[b] | 1.5 | 4.3 | 1.3 | 0.2 | 0.9 | 0.1 | 1.1 | 9.5 |

[a] Included with "All others" prior to 1952.
[b] Preliminary.
[c] Under $50 million.
Components may not add to totals because of rounding.

a simple case of free market function on the one hand, or total government direction of credit, on the other; it is a matter of isolating issues, testing hypotheses, and finding, amidst the diversity of available means, that combination which can realize the housing goals selected at any one time and thereby most effectively serve the general welfare.

*Figure 3. Holdings of FHA-insured mortgages by type of institution, December 31, 1956.*

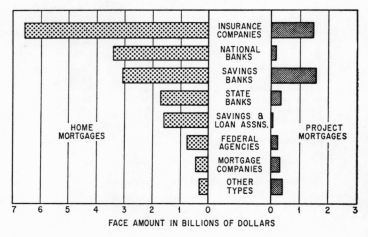

*Figure 4. Sources of residential mortgage funds, 1947–1957.*

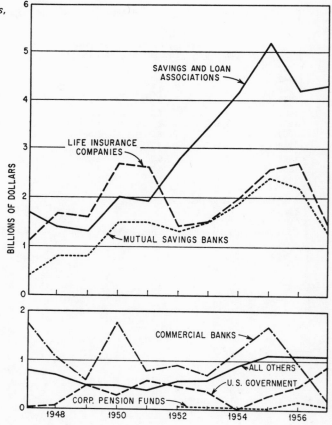

# The growth of the residential mortgage debt

*LEO GREBLER, DAVID M. BLANK, and LOUIS WINNICK*

Investment in residential real estate, like most forms of investment, has been financed by a combination of internal and external funds. However, the capital funds which enter the residential sector differ substantially in character from the funds which finance other capital sectors. In the first place, the bulk of housing investment represents the purchase of a consumer durable, with the closest approximation to internal funds represented by down payments and external funds for the most part supplied by borrowing on mortgages. Decisions as to the type of funds or, more likely, as to the relative proportions of both types of funds that are to be used, are not based on the same determinants as are business decisions. In the acquisition of new residential real estate, the choice is largely determined by the liquid assets of home purchasers or other holdings convertible to liquid assets and by the maximum amount obtainable from mortgage lenders. The relative costs of different types of funds compared with anticipated net yields, which are important in business financing, are of less importance in the choice between internal and external financing for purchase of new housing facilities. Income tax considerations, which enter significantly into business decisions on the type of funds used, have only recently begun to influence the proportion of borrowed funds in the financing of additions to residential capital.

More important, the internal funds used for the acquisition of new residential real estate are almost entirely derived from the personal savings of individuals or groups of investors and almost never, even in the case of large properties, from depreciation reserves accumulated in the operation of existing property. While all residential structures are depreciable assets and while depreciation is an important tax consideration for the owners of income property, from an investment point of view depreciation funds are not intentionally accumulated by the owners of residential real estate with the object of providing for the replacement of worn-out or obsolete assets. Consequently, there is virtually no direct connection between the use of such depreciation reserves as may be established by owners of residential real estate and the financing of new residential facilities. Demolished or deteriorated structures are replaced, in the main, not by current owners but by other investors.

Any analysis of internal sources of capital funds in housing investment would require an analysis of the use of personal savings and personal holdings of liquid assets, a subject outside the scope of this study. The sources of external funds, on the other hands, are limited chiefly to the mortgage market. Unlike customary practice in many other industries, external funds for residential real estate are obtained only in the rarest instances through public stock issues and only somewhat less rarely through nonmortgage borrowing.* An historical study of sources of

---

* Little is known about the extent of personal nonmortgage borrowing for the purchase of a home. The purchase price less the mortgage indebtedness is cus-tomarily considered equity, with the understanding, however, that equity does not always involve actual cash flows. The proportion of down payment that repre-

*Reprinted from* Capital Formation in Residential Real Estate, *Princeton University Press, 1956, pp. 159–171, with permission of the publisher.*

funds for the acquisition of new residential construction must therefore concern itself with the size and distribution of the residential mortgage debt, the gross flow of mortgage funds, and the change in these measures of external financing over time. This analysis necessarily pertains to both existing and new residential real estate. Available data provide no segregation of lending activity or of net change in debt in terms of new and existing construction.

## Factors influencing changes in the residential mortgage debt

In general terms, changes over time in the total nonfarm residential mortgage debt are the net resultants of a host of gross additions to, and gross reductions from, the debt. Broadly, the mortgage debt increases because of (1) new residential construction, (2) increases in the rate of turnover of existing dwellings, since new owners tend to raise the amount of outstanding debt, (3) rising prices for both new and existing property, and (4) loosening of credit terms as evidenced in loan-to-value ratios. Debt increases may also be influenced, on the demand side, by long-run modifications in social attitudes toward mortgage indebtedness and, on the supply side, by the relative attractiveness of mortgage loans as investment outlets. The operation of all these factors is reflected in long-term increases in the proportion of mortgaged homes and in larger amounts of debt relative to the value of mortgaged homes.

The mortgage debt is reduced by (1) repayment – i.e. the substitution of internal for external funds – the volume of which appears to be related to levels of personal income as well as to contractual mortgage terms, and (2) the cancellation of indebtedness because of foreclosures and voluntary surrenders of title in lieu of foreclosure, which results primarily from general declines in business activity.

Thus new construction is only one of many elements affecting the level and change of the residential mortgage debt. The relationship between changes in the mortgage debt and the flow of funds into new construction appears even more indirect when the questions of land and the transfer of residential mortgage funds to other uses are considered. Real estate mortgages are based, with few exceptions, on the security of both land and improvements. While the separation of land value from structure value is a necessary step in the measurement of capital formation, no satisfactory analytic procedure exists for the separation as far as mortgage debt is concerned. The mortgage debt, therefore, inescapably reflects changes in the use and value of residential land. Available data also show that a substantial fraction of the proceeds of mortgage loans are channeled into ordinary consumption or into business investment.[*]

## Relation of debt changes to cash flows

Changes in the outstanding mortgage debt cannot be considered to measure even the net flow of funds between mortgagees and mortgagors if a flow of funds is interpreted to mean a debit or credit to the cash accounts of the parties to the transaction. There are many transactions which affect the size of mortgage debt without any accompanying change in the cash account.[†] Foreclosures and voluntary surrenders of title to mortgagees are the most important examples of noncash transactions which reduce the outstanding mortgage debt. During severely depressed phases in the real estate market, foreclosures may actually exceed repayments as a factor reducing the mortgage debt. Thus during the years 1932–1936 mortgage portfolios of Massachusetts savings banks were reduced nearly $300 million by foreclosures and only $173 mil-

---

sents personal borrowing has always been low in comparison with the proportion of nonmortgage funds that represents personal savings derived from liquid assets and the sale of other assets, including currently owned homes.

*Over 40 percent of first mortgages on owner-occupied properties taken out at some time after the property was acquired were originated for reasons other than real estate investment. Census of Housing 1950, Bureau of the Census, Vol. IV, Residential Financing, Part 1, p. 50.
† Some of the equity investment in new construction does not involve a cash flow but is rather the direct contribution of labor or services on the part of an individual building his own house of a sponsor of an apartment project.

lion by repayments.* Write-downs and the transfer of unpaid interest to outstanding debt, although of unknown magnitude, are other examples of noncash transactions.

Of the noncash transactions which increase the mortgage debt, the purchase money mortgage is undoubtedly of greatest importance. A purchase money mortgage is a lien taken back by the seller from the buyer of a parcel of real estate. Unfortunately, few data are available on this type of financing. A large but unknown share of purchase money mortgage transactions result from the resale by mortgagees of foreclosed property. Nearly all purchase money mortgages in institutional portfolios arise in this manner. Such foreclosures and purchase money mortgages are thus noncash mortgage debt changes which largely offset each other over a period of years.† For long-run analysis, only those purchase money mortgages held by non-institutional investors, and not originating in a prior foreclosure, can be considered noncash increments to the mortgage debt.‡ There are virtually no data on the purchase money mortgage holdings of noninstitutional investors, or on the proportions which arise from transactions involving new construction compared with existing dwellings, or on the average period of holding of such mortgages. It is believed that the

bulk of purchase money mortgages arising from the purchase of *new* homes are relatively small second, rather than relatively large first, mortgages. Conceptually, purchase money mortgages have importance insofar as they are "cash economizing"; the use of these instruments facilities the transfer of real estate by reducing the downpayment requirements of the purchaser and by eliminating the frictions involved in third-party financing.

Because debt change does not necessarily result in a cash flow and because of the complexity of factors influencing net changes in debt, these changes must be interpreted with caution.

## The residential mortgage debt 1890—1952 §

From 1890 to 1952 the residential mortgage debt (excluding real estate bonds) increased about thirty times, rising from $2.3 to 69.1 billion. Furthermore, the growth in the mortgage debt has been almost continuous, with brief interruptions only during the early 1930's and during World War II; the continuity of growth for much of the early period, however, may be largely a spurious product of the series' derivation.**

---

* John Lintner, *Mutual Savings Banks in the Savings and Mortgage Markets*, Harvard University Press, 1948, pp. 228 – 229. The data refer to nonresidential as well as residential mortgages. During the year 1933 mortgage reductions through foreclosures were more than three times as large as reductions through repayment.
† The experience of Massachusetts saving banks indicates that purchase money mortgages made during the period 1932 – 1945 offset more than 75 percent of the mortgage reductions through foreclosures. *Ibid.*, pp. 227 – 228.
‡ Even this statement requires qualification. A purchase money mortgage sold by the mortgagee to a second party results in a cash flow, although with an indeterminate lag after the original real estate transfer.
§ The quality of the mortgage data for the period before 1925 leaves much to be desired. There is a distinct impression that the debt estimates for the beginning of the period, though lower than those of other investigators, are still too high and that, as a consequence, the growth in the debt between 1896 and 1924 is understated. While a good case for reduction of the early debt figures could be made, the extent of the required reduction would depend upon arbitrary assumptions. Furthermore, any sizable lowering of the initial residential mortgage debt figures would make quite implausible the movement of the nonresidential mortgage debt

derived as a residual. The truth of the matter is that mortgage debt estimates for the first three decades are badly in need of the thorough revision that only a new and major research effort could yield.

Though the mortgage series since 1925 are much superior, the results of the 1950 mortgage census indicate a possible overstatement both in the Home Loan Bank Board estimates of debt on one- to four-family houses and in the total residential debt estimates made in this study. On August 1, 1950, the HLBB estimated the one- to four-family debt at $41.5 billion and the Census Bureau estimated it at $37.1 billion. Differences in coverage and definition account for part but not all of the $4.4 billion discrepancy. For the same date Census estimated the debt on multi-family properties at $7.4 billion. The multi-family debt estimate for August 1, used in this study (taken at seven-twelfths of the difference between the December 31, 1949, and the December 31, 1950, totals), is about $8.9 billion. For a discussion of the nature of these differences see *Census of Housing 1950*, Vol. IV, *Residential Financing*, Part 1, pp. XXX – XXXIII.
** For the period before 1925, the annual movements in the debt are partially the result of linear interpolation between bench-mark dates and hence are useless for cyclical analysis.

The residential mortgage debt has shown net gains in every decade except 1930–1940 (Table 1). The debt rose at an increasing rate during

### TABLE 1

*Growth in Nonfarm Residential Mortgage Debt, by Decades, 1890-1950* (dollars in millions)

| End of Year | Mortgage debt | | Percent change over preceding decade | |
|---|---|---|---|---|
| | Excluding bonds | Including bonds | Excluding bonds | Including bonds |
| | $ | $ | % | % |
| 1890[a] | 2,292 | 2,292 | — | — |
| 1900 | 2,917 | 2,917 | 27.3 | 27.3 |
| 1910 | 4,426 | 4,466 | 51.7 | 53.1 |
| 1920 | 9,120 | 9.354 | 106.1 | 109.4 |
| 1930 | 27,649 | 30,176 | 203.2 | 222.6 |
| 1940 | 23,810 | 24,930 | −13.9 | −17.4 |
| 1950 | 54,362 | 54,882 | 128.3 | 120.1 |

[a] June 1.
Source: Tables L–1 and L–3, *Capital Formation in Residential Real Estate*.

the first four decades, declined absolutely during the depression decade, and resumed a rapid rate of growth during the 1940's. The average annual gain from 1920 to 1930 of 20.3 percent net of real estate bonds, and 22.3 percent inclusive of real estate bonds, remains a historical peak barely approached in the 1940–1952 period. An increase in the aggregate debt of this size, taken together with the extremely steep increase in the per household mortgage debt (Table 2) and the ratio of debt to residential wealth, offers indirect evidence of a fundamental revision in homeowners' and probably lenders' attitudes concerning mortgage indebtedness during the 1920's. While the proportion of mortgaged owner-occupied dwellings had been rising since 1890,* a marked acceleration in this trend probably occurred from 1920 to 1930 (although no data on this ratio exist for 1930). The reluctance of home owners to incur mortgage debt, a characteristic of earlier decades, was undoubtedly reduced in keeping with the change in general attitudes toward all forms of consumer debt.

The failure of the 1940–1952 percentage gain

to reach the proportions of 1920–1930, a surprising result in view of the postwar residential building boom and of the great liberality in mortgage credit terms, is explainable by the war-induced construction controls during the first half of the decade. Practically the entire increase in the residential mortgage debt occurred during the period 1945-1952, with a rise in the debt of 180 percent (excluding bonds). In fact, the increase from 1945 to 1950 is higher than that for any other five-year period during the past six decades.† The 1920–1925 rise was 89 percent (over 96 percent including bonds), and the 1925–1930 rise was 60 percent (64 percent including bonds). In absolute terms, the 1945–1950 increase in the mortgage debt of $30 billion is substantially greater than the rise during the entire period from 1890 to 1945 and even greater than the rise between 1890 and the peak of 1930.

### TABLE 2

*Per Capita and Per Household Nonfarm Residential Mortgage Debt, by Decade, 1890-1950* (dollars)

| End of year | Per capita | | Per household | |
|---|---|---|---|---|
| | Excluding bonds | Including bonds | Excluding bonds | Including bonds |
| 1890[a] | 68.4 | 68.4 | 289.3 | 289.3 |
| 1900 | 65.1 | 65.1 | 283.9 | 283.9 |
| 1910 | 73.9 | 74.6 | 313.2 | 316.0 |
| 1920 | 123.1 | 126.2 | 518.2 | 531.5 |
| 1930 | 298.5 | 325.8 | 1,186.7 | 1,295.1 |
| 1940 | 234.7 | 245.7 | 854.2 | 894.4 |
| 1950 | 425.9 | 429.9 | 1,465.7 | 1,479.7 |

[a] June 1.
Source: Tables 23, L-1, and L-3, *Capital Formation in Residential Real Estate*.

The residential mortgage debt for the period as a whole has grown at a more rapid rate than either nonfarm population or nonfarm households. The debt per nonfarm capita increased from $68 in 1890 to $426 in 1950; per nonfarm household, the respective figures are $289 and $1,466 exclusive of real estate bonds (Table 2).

The rising trend in per capita and per house-

---

* Table 5 below.
† Over 80 percent of all first mortgages in existence on August 1, 1950, were made or assumed after the begin-

ning of 1946. *Census of Housing 1950*, Vol. IV, *Residential Financing*, Part 1, Table 2, p. 6.

hold debt cannot, however, be interpreted as a secularly increasing "burden of indebtedness." The burden of the mortgage debt can be measured only in connection with other variables such as amortization schedules and interest rates and with levels of income. When measured against the growth in personal or disposable income since 1900 (Table 3) the trend of residential mortgage debt was downward until the

## TABLE 3

*Ratio of Nonfarm Residential Mortgage Debt to Personal and Disposable Income, Various Years, 1900–1952 (percent)*

| End of Year | Ratio to personal income | | Ratio to disposable income | |
| | Excluding bonds | Including bonds | Excluding bonds | Including bonds |
|---|---|---|---|---|
| 1900 | 19.4 | 19.4 | 19.7 | 19.7 |
| 1910 | 15.8 | 16.0 | 16.0 | 16.1 |
| 1920 | 11.9 | 12.3 | 12.3 | 12.6 |
| 1930 | 36.3 | 39.6 | 37.5 | 41.0 |
| 1940 | 30.4 | 31.8 | 31.4 | 32.9 |
| 1945 | 14.3 | 15.0 | 16.3 | 17.1 |
| 1950 | 24.0 | 24.2 | 26.4 | 26.7 |
| 1952 | 25.6 | 25.8 | 29.4 | 29.6 |

Source: Residential mortgage debt from Tables L-1 and L-3, *Capital Formation in Residential Real Estate.* Income data from the Dept. of Commerce, and, for the earlier decades, from Raymond W. Goldsmith et al., *A Study of Saving in the United States,* Princeton University Press, 1955, Vol. III, Table N-3.

1920's, when a significant rise in the debt level occurred. This abrupt change was followed by a renewed decline over the following two decades. Between 1900 and 1920 the ratio of residential mortgage debt to disposable income dropped from 19.7 to 12.3 percent; by the end of 1930 the ratio stood at nearly 38 percent excluding residential real estate bonds and at about 41 percent including these bonds, a manifestation of the critical significance of the 1920–1930 decade in the historical growth of mortgage indebtedness. In 1952 the ratio stood at about 29 percent, substantially below the 1930 and even below the 1940 level.

## Growth in nonfarm mortgage debt relative to other types of debt

Nonfarm mortgage debt, residential and nonresidential, has accounted for an increasing share of total private long-term debt during the past half century. The gain in the relative importance of nonfarm mortgage debt has been almost entirely due to the residential component; the relative growth of nonresidential mortgage debt has been substantially equal to that of the total private long-term debt. Between 1900 and 1952 the share of total nonfarm mortgage debt in total private long-term debt increased from 26 to 55 percent (Table 4), while the share of the residential mortgage debt rose from about 16 to 46 percent. The ratio of the residential mortgage debt to the total nonfarm mortgage debt increased from about 60 percent in 1890 to over 80 percent in 1952, regardless of whether real estate bonds are included or excluded.

By the end of the period the residential mortgage debt had emerged as the most important component of net private long-term debt. At the close of 1952 the residential mortgage debt surpassed the net long-term corporate debt, $69 billion (excluding real estate bonds) compared with $62 billion.* The historical significance of this relative shift is seen more clearly when it is realized that in 1916, according to a rough comparison of the two forms of debt, corporate debt was about three times as great as the residential mortgage debt and in 1929, after the boom of the twenties, half again as large. An explanation of these changes in the private debt structure would involve an analysis of changes in corporate financial policy beyond the scope of this study; nevertheless, the fact remains that nonfarm mortgages, particularly residential mortgages, have become a primary debt investment medium in the capital market. When measured against the total long-term debt including public, the share of the mortgage debt is, of course, greatly reduced by the growth in the federal debt; the residential mortgage debt has, how-

---

* The Department of Commerce estimate for outstanding corporate long-term debt in 1950 is $69.9 billion. This total includes, however, some $7.9 billion of mortgage debt owned by corporate borrowers. See *Survey of Current Business,* Dept. of Commerce, September,

1953, pp. 17–19. Since mortgage indebtedness is measured in this study without regard to the debtor's form of business organization, the Commerce corporate total has been accordingly reduced.

ever, historically been larger than state and local debt.* In 1916 the residential mortgage debt was about 50 percent larger than the net state and local debt, and by 1952 it was nearly three times as large.[1]

## TABLE 4

*Ratios of Total Nonfarm, Nonfarm Residential, and Nonfarm Nonresidential Mortgage Debt to Total Net Private Long-Term Debt, Various Years, 1900–1952* (percent)

| End of year | Total nonfarm mortgage debt | Total nonfarm residential mortgage debt | Total nonfarm nonresidential mortgage debt |
|---|---|---|---|
| 1900 | 26.1 | 16.1 | 10.0 |
| 1916 | 22.2 | 14.8 | 7.4 |
| 1925 | 34.9 | 24.3 | 10.6 |
| 1929 | 41.9 | 30.6 | 11.2 |
| 1934 | 38.0 | 29.3 | 8.6 |
| 1939 | 38.0 | 29.9 | 8.2 |
| 1950 | 53.1 | 43.3 | 9.8 |
| 1952 | 55.1 | 45.5 | 9.6 |

Source: Table L-5, *Capital Formation in Residential Real Estate.* The mortgage debt data are exclusive of real estate bonds.

## The ratio of mortgage debt to residential wealth

The residential wealth series† and the residential mortgage debt series can be used for the derivation of an aggregate debt-to-value ratio, that is, the ratio of mortgage debt to total residential wealth. This aggregate debt-to-value ratio lies substantially below the debt-to-value ratio of mortgaged residential real estate because the value of unmortgaged real estate is included in the wealth total. The movements of the ratio reflect changes in the equity position of the owners of residential real estate, resulting from changes in the incidence of indebtedness and in real estate prices.

The aggregate debt-to-value ratio at each of the three peaks in residential construction has shown an unmistakable upward trend, rising from 11.5 percent in 1909 to 22.4 percent in 1926 and to 23.5 percent in 1950 (Chart 1). The increased indebtedness of residential real estate can also be inferred from census data on owner-occupied homes, which reveal a sharp rise in the proportion of mortgaged houses and

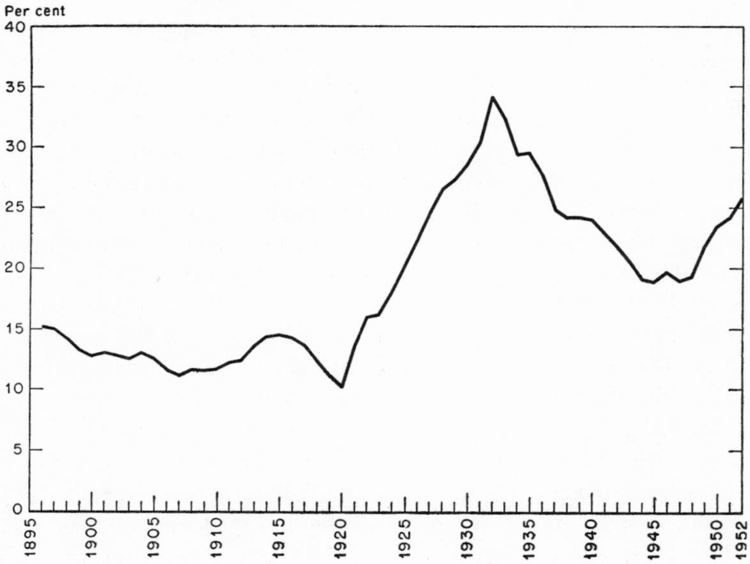

Chart 1. Ratio of nonfarm residential mortgage debt to nonfarm residential wealth, 1896—1952.

---

* Part of the relative gain can be explained by changes in residential construction financing practices. There has been a tendency to shift the financing of street utilities in new subdivisions from the municipality to the private builder. That is, certain construction costs are financed by residential mortgage debt rather than

by local bonds. On the other hand, the construction of publicly financed housing increases the municipal debt rather than the residential mortgage debt.
† See Appendix D of *Capital Formation in Residential Real Estate.*

a small rise in the average debt-to-value ratio since 1890.

The annual aggregate debt-to-value series does not, however, show the same pattern of persistent growth as is suggested by the census data for owner-occupied houses. Apparently, the most striking rise in the debt ratio took place after 1920, continuing until 1932, when a peak ratio of 34 percent* was reached. Between 1932 and the end of World War II the ratio declined to 18.8 percent. The postwar real estate boom was accompanied by a rise in the ratio, which by the end of 1952 stood at 25.7 percent.

In the period before World War I the movements of the aggregate ratio are puzzling. The aggregate debt-to-value ratio registered a decline between 1890 and the end of 1919 in the face of an increase in the percentage of owner-occupied houses mortgaged, which is revealed by census data. It seems likely that an exaggerated 1890 mortgage estimate has overstated the initial debt ratio and that valuation by means of a construction cost index understated the ratio for 1920.† A discussion of the 1890 mortgage estimate points to a demonstrable weakness in one of the estimating assumptions, capable of producing a significant overstatement in the aggregate debt of that year.‡

Some timing relationships between the debt ratio and construction expenditures are of interest. The two minor upswings in construction expenditures, during 1900–1909 (for which period, however, the data underlying the debt ratio are far from trustworthy) and 1932-1941, were accompanied by declining debt ratios; the two major upswings following both wars were accompanied by rising debt ratios. Second, the debt ratio continued to rise for a considerable period after construction expenditures turned down. This phenomenon occurred in the years following 1909, 1926, and 1950, though not after 1941. The exception may be attributable to the intervention of the war. Both World Wars were associated with sharp declines in the debt ratio. War periods are exceptionally conducive to reductions in the debt ratio, being times of an unusual combination : rising incomes (which lead to debt repayments), rising real estate price and drastic curtailment of new construction.

The debt ratio by the end of 1952 barely surpassed the 1939 level in spite of a tripling in aggregate mortgage debt. An increase in the debt ratio was held in check by rising real estate prices and a heavy volume of repayments, which was evidenced in both a decline in the incidence of indebtedness among owner-occupants and a decline in the debt-to-value ratio of mortgaged houses between 1940 and 1950 (Table 5).§

## Residential construction expenditures and changes in mortgage debt

In every decade except the 1930's the gain in the residential mortgage debt increased relative to residential construction expenditures (Table 6).** In the 1890–1899 decade, for

---

* The derivation of residential wealth estimates by the use of a construction cost index probably leads to a higher-than-market valuation in periods like the 1930's. The aggregate equity ratio for 1932 would presumably be lower than 64 percent if it were based on actual sales prices in market transactions, to the extent that a market existed in 1932.
† Construction costs rose precipitously in 1920, accounting for the sharp troughs in the ratio for that year. The 1920 mortgage census was based on market values, which were less volatile than construction costs in the years immediately following World War I.
‡ The Census Bureau reported an aggregate debt-to-value ratio of 13.96 percent in 1890 for all nonfarm real estate (*Eleventh Census of the United States*, Part III, " Real Estate Mortgages," p. 116), compared with the 15.3 percent ratio for residential real estate derived in this study.

§ The rise in real estate values is probably the primary explanation of the paradoxical decrease in the debt-to-value ratio of mortgaged houses during a decade when the loan-to-value ratio on new construction (Chapter XII) moved substantially upward. Owner-occupied mortgaged homes with a debt-to-value ratio of 42 percent in 1950 were originally purchased with a debt-to-value ratio of 77 percent (*Census of Housing 1950*, Vol. IV, *Residential Financing*, Part 1, Table 6, p. 51).
** The comparison of increases in the residential mortgage debt with residential construction expenditures is instructive but not exact. The debt is based on both structures and land and on new as well as existing construction, while construction expenditures relate to new structures only.

## TABLE 5

*Percentage of Houses Mortgaged and Debt-to-Value Ratios, Owner-Occupied Nonfarm Homes, Census Dates, 1890–1950*

| Census year | Mortgaged houses as a percent of total owner-occupied houses | Debt-to-value ratio of mortgaged houses |
|---|---|---|
| June 1, 1890 | 27.7[a] | 39.8[b] |
| June 1, 1900 | 31.7[a] | — |
| June 1, 1910 | 33.1[a] | — |
| Jan. 1, 1920 | 39.7[a] | 42.6[b] |
| Apr. 1, 1940 | 45.3[a] | 52.3[c] |
| Apr. 1, 1950 | 43.6[d] | 42.0[e] |

[a] *Census of Housing 1940,* Bureau of the Census, Vol. IV, *Mortgages on Owner-Occupied Nonfarm Houses,* Part 1, Table III, p. 3.
[b] *Mortgages on Homes in the United States, 1920,* Bureau of the Census, p. 45.
[c] *Census of Housing 1940,* Vol. IV, *Mortgages on Owner-Occupied Nonfarm Houses,* Part 1, Table VII, p. 4.
[d] *Census of Housing 1950,* Preliminary Reports, Series HC-5, No. 1, p. 18.
[e] *Census of Housing 1950,* Vol. IV, *Residential Financing,* Part 1, Table 6, p. 50. This figure refers to the median debt-to-value ratio of owner-occupied houses, whereas the ratios for earlier years are based on the aggregate debt and the aggregate value of mortgaged houses. A slight understatement may, therefore, be involved (cf., however, *Survey of Current Business,* Dept. of Commerce, April 1953).
Note: The 1940 and 1950 data are limited to owner-occupied, one-to four-family houses without business use. The earlier data refer to all types of structures occupied by the owner. The debt-to-value ratio for 1950 is as of August 1.

example, an aggregate outlay on housekeeping facilities of $6,452 million (current prices) was accompanied by a $543 million increment in the mortgage debt, the ratio of the latter to the former being 8.4 percent. In the 1920–1929 decade the ratio of mortgage debt increment to expenditures for housekeeping residential construction was nearly 60 percent, while in the last full decade, 1940–1949, the corresponding ratio was 69 percent. In the half decade 1946–1950 the increase in the mortgage debt reached a peak of 83 percent of the outlay on housekeeping units, compared with 62 percent in 1925–1929, 52 percent in 1920–1924, and 74 percent in 1948–1952. The inclusion of expenditures on additions and alterations does not significantly modify these results.

The rise in the ratio of mortgage debt increment to construction expenditures in part expresses the increasing tendency to finance the acquisition of new residential real estate facilities by external funds. But the upward drift of the ratio is also the result of changes in mortgage financing of the existing housing inventory.

## TABLE 6

*Ratio of Increase in Residential Mortgage Debt to Residential Construction Expenditures, Selected Periods, 1890–1952 (dollars in millions)*

|  | Total housekeeping expenditures (1) | Housekeeping plus addition and alteration expenditures (2) | Change in mortgage debt (3) | Column 3 as percent of column 1 (4) | Column 3 as percent of column 2 (5) |
|---|---|---|---|---|---|
|  | $ | $ | $ | % | % |
| 1890–1899 | 6,452 | 7,229 | 543 | 8.4 | 7.5 |
| 1900–1909 | 8,579 | 9.544 | 1,333 | 15.5 | 14.0 |
| 1910–1919 | 10,195 | 11,300 | 3,830 | 37.6 | 33.9 |
| 1920–1929 | 35,962 | 38,392 | 21,442 | 59.6 | 55.9 |
| 1930–1939 | 11,330 | 13,740 | −5,500 | — | — |
| 1940–1949 | 32,547 | 37,257 | 22,516 | 69.2 | 60.4 |
| 1920–1924 | 14,357 | 15,322 | 7,516 | 52.4 | 49.1 |
| 1925–1929 | 21,605 | 23,070 | 13,296 | 61.5 | 57.6 |
| 1946–1950 | 35,752 | 38,987 | 29,499 | 82.5 | 75.7 |
| 1948–1952 | 46,001 | 50,630 | 33,860 | 73.6 | 66.9 |

Column   Source:
1     Table B-3, *Capital Formation in Residential Real Estate.*
2     Table B-6, *Ibid.*
3     Table L-3, *Ibid.*

# The subsidy and housing

CHARLES ABRAMS

The subsidy is only a single aspect of housing policy; yet the form it ultimately takes will influence more than the housing program alone. In all its long history, both here and abroad, the subsidy has never been more significant than it is currently. It involves more than monetary outlay. The kind of economy in which we are to live may be influenced by the policy we devise for its dispensation.

The developments around the housing subsidy have taken place without benefit of maxim or definition. Each innovation creates its own precedent, forging another outward link to its further extension. Formulation of principles on the subsidy was never more crucial than it is today.

## The subsidy defined

In the broad sense, a subsidy is any kind of grant or aid extended to an undertaking to which the public interest is imputed. The term has latterly been broken down into classifications embracing those subsidies which promote private operations in trade, industry, commerce, and agriculture and "grants in aid" made to assist other governmental units in their fulfillment of public purposes. A large number of government subsidies were prompted by economic or military considerations, such as the need to stimulate infant industries or to promote self-sufficiency in war. Today, however, a growing proportion of subsidies is used to advance infant social services. The government in recent years has committed itself to strengthening the nation's health and welfare, to encouraging employment, to reducing the hazards of insecurity. All of these social subsidies rest upon the proposition that government should intercede when private enterprise or private philanthropy proves unable or unwilling to meet the need.

## Criteria for subsidies

The principles governing use of subsidies have never been explored with the thoroughness devoted to some aspects of public finance such as taxation. Recent uses and abuses of the subsidy mechanism call for fresh examination of principles and their practical application to the changed American scene. As a background for discussion of the subsidy in relation to housing, five general criteria for subsidies are put forth here. Exceptions may be found but they should not affect their validity as general criteria.

A. *The subsidy should serve a public purpose.* Opening the public purse and public privilege to private companies offers unlimited opportunity for abuse and even corruption. From the Yazoo land frauds of 1789–1795 down to the Elk Hills oil leases, the evils have been recurrent and obvious. The history of the United States is spotted with infamy rooted in the dispensation of public property to private interests on the pretext of public benefit.

Enlargement of the federal welfare power has opened almost boundless opportunities for misuse. To prevent perversion of public funds, the states that always had the welfare power sur-

*Reprinted from "The Subsidy of Housing," Journal of Land and Public Utility Economics, vol. 22 (May, 1946), pp. 131–139, with permission of the journal.*

rounded themselves with many checks – constitutional inhibitions, limitations upon their cities' expenditures, taxpayers' remedies, and supervision by courts. Many of these self-imposed limitations followed in the wake of local scandals. These limitations are absent on the federal plane. The problem is made doubly difficult by ambiguity and variability in the definition of public benefit at the national level.

In the housing field particularly, a public benefit can be attributed to almost every appropriation. It is to the general good that more people buy homes, that these homes not be foreclosed, that home-building be more active. Therefore, an ample supply of building funds seems beneficial to the public welfare. Government insurance of lending institutions as well as the small creditors who deposit the funds with them would tend to increase the supply of building funds. Housing shortages spell inflation and public inconvenience. Therefore, subventions to the builder seem authorized as well as yield insurance to lending institutions, and liberal credit aid to enable building of more homes. Slums are a menace to health. Therefore, authorization is claimed for urban redevelopment by private enterprise. The list can be drawn out endlessly and in each case an argument made that the public welfare is served.

More than ever, a greater responsibility for determining whether a subsidy is in the public interest now rests upon the electorate. Public vigilance and ability to distinguish public service from opportunism are more important than ever.

Subsidies to improve health and safety should occupy a prime place in the definition of public welfare. Here profit to private agencies should not be the primary end of the subsidy but should exist only as a by-product in the performance of the main aim, in the same way as contractors would benefit from the building of a school.

*B. The administration of the subsidized operation should be public or be publicly controlled.* Usually no private agency should get a subsidy for any public purpose if it can be administered by a public agency. It cannot, of course, be said summarily that subsidies should go only to public agencies, for there are fields in which private companies, given some public aid, might function more beneficially. The subsidies to encourage the aviation industry are a current example. A condition in most cases should be continuing regulation by the government. Sometimes rigid regulation may be dispensed with, as where a slum site is bought by public enterprise, cleared, and then resold through public bidding to private enterprise for private development. Here, use zoning or covenants running with the land might properly be used to protect the future public interest.

Sometimes rigid regulation is not practical, as when industries are induced to settle in a community – a subsidy of dubious wisdom – or when homesteads or eleemosynary activities are encouraged by tax exemption. Here, if the subsidy be granted, the aim should be to make the opportunity available by general law and to a broad general group rather than by special arrangement, or to a specially selected few, or worse still, to a single company.

*C. The subsidy should be defined and certain.* Hidden or devious subsidies are often preferred to minimize complaints from taxpayers. Examples are loans at low interest or none, favorable tax policies, free city services or facilities, and insurance predicated upon presumably sound but untested actuarial schemes. The word " insurance " has a soft tonal quality since it presupposes no cost at all to the taxpayers – until the actuarial formula breaks down.

It seems obvious, too, that the terms of subsidies should be fully known to both the taxpayer and the recipient, so that the public may weigh the benefits or the subsidy against the costs, and the recipient may base his commitments on the sum-certain subsidy payment.

*D. The subsidy should burden the taxpayer as little as possible.* No argument against excessive subsidies is needed. But there is often confusion over the question of when a subsidy is excessive. The capital grant for housing is an example. The issue over the capital grant became heated when the Wagner-Steagall Bill, which subsequently became the United States Housing Act, was being formulated. Instead of annual subsidies for a period of sixty years, an outright capital grant was advocated by the then Secretary of the Treasury, Henry Morgenthau. Great Britain, Holland and Norway had abandoned lump-sum payments. There is no reason why sixty years of deficits should be fused into one and paid off in a single year. We do not do this for education or other governmental commitments. The annual grant is more practical from the budgetary standpoint, too, since the subsidy can be adjusted upward in hard times when tenants pay less, downward in good times when tenants pay higher rents, as during the Second World War. On the other hand, the capital grant tempts the recipient to build more expensively and affords no opportunity for adjustment to the variations of the economic curve.

Another example of excessive subsidies is the exemption of building funds from income tax proposed by the National Association of Real Estate Boards. This would exempt wealthy investors from taxes on the income placed in bonds for land acquisition and housing construction. A housing unit costing $2,000 for land and $40,000 for building and receiving $131.00 in annual federal contributions under the United States Housing Act, would entail, under the tax-abatement plan, a capital grant equivalent to $4,800, if the investor were in the 80 percent tax bracket.[1]

Sometimes the subsidy and the method of paying for it create more nuisance than is justified by the benefit. An instance is the local housing subsidy of New York City, raised through an occupancy tax of $1 per $1,000 of rent paid on all gainfully occupied premises (minimum of $1, maximum $6). In 1943–1944, the tax yielded $456,000 and had to be paid by 350,000 people, though it could rehouse less than 3500 families. To make that microscopic nick in the housing problem, every business in New York has to fill out an elaborate form each year and remit an average of $1.30. Taxes like this make subsidies unpopular without accomplishing anything substantial.

E. *The subsidy should be one that can be practically administered.* Excessive supervision is one factor that may increase the costs of the improvement or service and neutralize the value of the subsidy. Here, a distinction must be drawn between public and private recipient agencies. Local public agencies administering a subsidized program should have the greatest measure of administrative freedom consistent with carrying out the purpose practically. They should not be looked upon as dependents on the federal bounty but as auspicious instrumentalities for carrying out state and national purposes effectively.

On the other hand, private companies carrying out public purposes require rigid regulation. For such regulation the public too often pays an excessive price. Either few honorable companies agree to the restraints imposed or there is evasion and reaping of secret benefits. For this reason, the performance of public functions by public agencies is indicated.

Examples of subsidies not practically administered are the FHA limited-dividend formula, which in the effort to limit return on speculative building operations produced few bona fide applicants, and the PWA subsidy for public housing where much of the subsidy was cancelled out by over-rigid federal overseeing.

## The subsidy and state governments

Only one state, New York, has joined with the federal and local governments in a subsidy for public housing; yet, as a long-range welfare program, housing should have state support. Either the current, federal-city formula should be revised to provide tripartite participation, or the states should launch independent programs. More favorable federal treatment of localities aided by states would be an effective inducement.

Some governors have voiced demands for restoration of states' rights which they feel have been injured by the federal government's social programs. Though New York State's limited contribution could not possibly solve the slum problem without federal aid, Thomas E. Dewey of New York, in his first gubernatorial campaign of 1938, said the federal slum clearance program was an "invasion of the business of the states" and that it meant "increasing concentration of power in Washington." The general emphasis on states' rights was again in evidence when Republican governors of states that contributed no state aid to housing opposed federal aid.*

Rights cannot be separated from responsibilities. The state officials who suggest that federal welfare programs be scuttled because they encroach upon the state's domain have a first duty, it would seem, to prove their readiness to take up the burdens carried by the federal government. The legislatures of forty states made it possible for local housing authorities to exist and to receive federal aid. Having approved the federal program and set up the agencies, the states must either continue to let federal money cross their borders, substitute state cash, or repeal the laws. In any case, federal participation in housing does not usurp any of the powers reserved to the states.

### The cash subsidies

The cash subsidy, as noted earlier, is the most honest and respectable type but is apt to be the least popular politically. In times of stress, welfare activities supported by such a subsidy make an easy target for economy marksmen who specialize in canceling out welfare appropriations. Too often, the taxpayer's feeling for his fellowmen is lost in the seams of his purse. Hence, we find that municipal governments eschew any cash grants to their local housing authorities, taking the alternative of tax exemption which, on the surface, seems less costly because nothing is paid out.

### Lending of superior credit

Lending of superior public credit is a variety of subsidy despite a prevalent illusion that a government loses nothing in the transaction. The element of risk is generally present and often undeterminable. There is no certainty, for example, that FHA insurance reserves will be enough to cover the losses, particularly since its whole experience so far is based upon a rising real estate market and a shortage in homes. A

substantial increase in the public debt, or extensive use of the federal credit, may ultimately affect the marketability and interest rate of federal bonds. In any event, monetary loss should not be the true test of subsidy. Responsible endorsement of a note can create substantial income for the maker from the funds borrowed. The endorser may never be called upon to make good but he still makes a contribution of substance. One's credit is as much an asset as one's cash and the use of either for another's benefit brings it within the subsidy classification whether or not anything is lost in the transaction.

Use of superior credit is effected through guarantee or insurance by the government of mortgages or yields, or by federal borrowing and re-lending of the borrowed funds at its costs to the government. This form of subsidy has stirred the imagination of private real estate groups, particularly since it costs the government nothing on paper. They are urging that speculative builders be given government loans and subsidies under the same terms as extended to local housing authorities, on the claim that private enterprise could then build for the low-income group. The cases where social motivations and private profit will go hand in hand are rare, the dangers of abuse too patent to be ventured. The rigid regulation that would be necessary to guard against such abuse would reduce the quantity of honorable applicants to a trickle.

### Interest subsidies

An *interest subsidy* may take several forms. It may be represented by a subsidy payment equivalent to the interest or by a loan of principal with the interest waived.

Interest subsidies when made to public agencies for public purposes are in a different category from those made to private companies, particularly where the public borrower is carrying out a common public purpose. Under the United States Housing Act, the government lends to local housing authorities at $\frac{1}{2}$ of 1 per-

---

* But in his later addresses Governor Dewey seemed to veer toward a greater federal recognition of its welfare responsibilities including slum clearance.

cent above the going federal rate when it should be made at the cost of the money. RFC refused to lend to authorities at less than the rate it charged private borrowers, then over 4 percent. The federal government should not profit here, though it might properly pass on part of the administrative cost of borrowing. There is a marked difference between loans of money to private individuals at higher than government cost, as in RFC private loans, and loans to public agencies for performance of common public purposes. In the latter, the recipient is as much in the category of an agent or co-operator in the public welfare as it is a borrower, and the superior government should not seek to effect a profit.

### Land as a subsidy

Land grants are a common and useful form of subsidy. The federal government still owns 24 percent of the continental United States, but little of this land is suitable for housing projects. State-owned lands are likewise of little use.

Cities own both unusable and usable land. Property acquired for nonpayment of taxes usually consists of undesirable land on the outskirts, or of isolated plots in the central areas. Lands used for municipal purposes, such as parks and playgrounds are well located but such areas should not be diminished in the planning of housing projects though the projects can often be advantageously laid out around a park; playgrounds have been relocated and expanded as a result of soundly planned housing developments.

City streets represent the principal type of land that can be used, especially in congested areas where streets were laid out on the gridiron plan. Considerable land has been wasted in the laying out of these streets and less street area may be needed today in a properly designed project. A substantial part of street land can be used for buildings and open spaces, at the same time effecting a smaller land coverage and a more livably-designed undertaking. In many metropolitan projects, for example, 30 percent or more of the project site consists of old streets,

a great deal of which can be better utilized by relocation.

While the conveyance of streets for public housing is a desirable subsidy, where the streets remain in public hands, donation to private interests (as in the Stuyvesant Town project in New York City) should be discouraged.

Instead of giving tax exemption as a subsidy to private interests, cities might undertake to assemble privately-owned land and sell it at or below acquisition cost to private developers for higher rent developments. The distinction between these two kinds of aid is important because of recent agitation for large-scale assemblage in blighted areas for postwar private building. The key to understanding is that in spite of the high cost of slum areas, the land cost is not the dominant investment. It should be clearly understood that, generally, the high land cost in slum areas bears a small ratio to the tax revenues that the city would gain through the construction of private projects. The new buildings might be worth two or four times as much as the land, depending upon the coverage deemed desirable. Taxed on that basis, they would frequently provide handsome repayment for the city's " loss " in the land sale.

To illustrate, suppose that a city buys land in a slum area at market price and resells, through public bidding, for private development at a price near its use value. The city would suffer a temporary loss in the difference between the buying and selling price, but it would count continuing dollar gains out of new taxes after the project was built. There would be no subsidy at all. Here the city acts as a frugal proprietor while carrying out its public functions. It would be good business judgment to encourage as much new taxpaying private construction as possible.

### Leasing or sale of projects to public agencies

This type of subsidy has been used by federal agencies in the past and may be employed again. Both PWA and the Farm Security Administration built and leased dwellings on terms that constituted a subsidy. PWA projects were government-built, then leased to local housing authorities for a rental that would enable the authorities to accommodate low-income families. Homes built by the Farm Security Administration were rented at prices the tenants could afford.

The principal objection to the leasing plan in public housing is that it may check local initiative and eliminate the possibility of local private financing which is more feasible when the property is owned in fee.

A good subsidy by sale of public property might be made if the government's war housing projects were sold to local housing authorities. It would be a useful and worthy subsidy and a justifiable shift in the use of public property from the public-wartime-federal to a public-peacetime-local-federal use.

### Subsidies based on project cost

The great bulk of public housing in the United States was built under the United States Housing Act, which prescribes a serial subsidy equal to the going federal interest rate plus one percent of the development cost of the project.

The advantage of this plan is the flexibility which permits adjustment to varying local costs and conditions and changing national conditions. Since the subsidy is based upon development cost rather than upon the number of persons rehoused or the number of dwellings built, slum clearance with its higher costs is not discouraged.

The central government does not automatically pay out the maximum subsidy to the local housing authorities. It pays only the sum required to bridge the gap between rental income and total carrying costs. The maximum annual contributions have never been reached. For project fiscal years ending in 1941 the contributions actually paid averaged 88.2 percent of the maximum permitted for these projects. Because of rent increases due to increasing income of tenants, the percentage of maximum paid each

year has declined steadily until for project fiscal years ending 1945 only 51.2 percent of the maximum was actually paid. As families whose incomes have increased above the limit for continued occupancy are moved out of projects and as lower-income families move in, it is expected that annual contributions will again increase.

The subsidy based on development cost may sometimes encourage purchase of expensive land, since local political considerations favor the demolition of slums and construction by the housing authorities on slum sites. Another objection to this subsidy is that the public finds it hard to understand, a condition which has been capitalized upon by the opponents of public housing. An innovation in American fiscal practices, the workings of the formula are still muddled in many Congressional minds.[*] Laymen can more easily grasp the fact that a federal subsidy amounts to $100 annually for each family rehoused, but a subsidy based solely upon so much per family rehoused has objections to it too, as the English learned after the Chamberlain formula of 1923.[†]

There are few formulae which are objection-free. Most depend for their successful operation upon sound administration. While the subsidy based on project cost may not be all-perfect, it has functioned reasonably well and despite these few objections ought to be continued for the present. Wider publication of the cost per family of the subsidy and the more liberal dissemination of information generally on the program would help keep the public apprized of the cost.

### Rent-certificate subsidies

Subsidies paid directly to the tenant are advocated by real estate groups. Among the many objections to this plan, one is that it would make the tenant a permanent recipient of public charity. There is a vast spiritual difference between paying the required rent on a government-owned building and being on a per-

---

[*] The subsidy is often exaggerated by multiplying the annual contribution by the number of years it is to be given, a calculation which assumes that given conditions will persist unchanged for sixty years. See *Congressional Record*, No. 84:3452.

[†] Rise in costs, differential costs in various communities, and changes in the interest rates would complicate the working of the formula.

manent dole. In any case, this so-called rent-certificate plan or slum dole (advocated in November, 1943 by the National Association of Real Estate Boards) would operate to perpetuate the slums, not remove them. Since every landlord would seek to benefit from as much of the payment as possible, he would make little if any expenditure. Administration would be difficult if not impossible for each building would require separate and continuing inspection. During the depression in the 1930's, New York City's emergency relief bureau spent $30,000,000 annually for rent – a sum which, if paid annually, would have been sufficient to subsidize modern, low-rent housing for more than half of the city's slum dwellers. Yet, not a single family got a decent home. If standards were raised adequately, the landlords would not have complied and the tenants would not have gotten homes. The dumb-bell flats that were 30 percent empty simply filled up with the undoubling of families encouraged by rent relief and slum values zoomed. The plan would produce no new housing for slum dwellers and would extend the life of the old ones.

## Tax exemption as a subsidy

There is a distinction between tax exemption granted for private housing and that granted for public low-rent housing. This must be grasped, particularly because of the indiscriminate tendency to extend huge tax exemption grants to urban redevelopment companies and other private operations.

The realty tax revenues on which a city depends for its support are not constant. As some real property depreciates and its valuation shrinks, other revenues from new construction take their place. If the city depended solely upon existing properties, declining values resulting from their physical depreciation would soon wipe out a major part of its revenues. Its future solvency is therefore hinged to the existing, as well as to the potential revenues resulting from replacements or other new construction.

When, therefore, exemption is extended to private development for a higher income tenantry, the city is deprived of the potential revenues which would have accrued to it when private enterprise in the normal course of events got around to providing dwellings for that group. Exemption of a project housing those whom private enterprise could provide for, either through new or acceptable used housing, is a gift of public moneys for a private purpose.

When, however, the city exempts low-rent public housing projects from tax on the improvements (charging only the old levy existing prior to the building of the new project), it loses no potential revenues since the low-income families are not prospective customers for the potential private enterprise market. Therefore, such exemptions on public housing, while technically they may be subsidies, represent no out-of-pocket loss. The tax exemption on such projects represents a dollar loss only to the extent that payments in lieu of taxes run less than the taxes paid on the site prior to its reconstruction and here it must be matched against the social and economic gains resulting from rehousing.

# VII

# Housing standards and controls

## Building and land use controls

*BURNHAM KELLY, in association with CASTLE N. DAY, ALBERT G. H. DIETZ, JOHN T. DUNLOP, CARL KOCH, JAMES A. MURRAY, HIDEO SASAKI, BERNARD P. SPRING*

A major consideration in the production of houses, particularly for those who seek to introduce new materials or methods of construction, is the network of controls that has grown up over the years to assure public health and safety, fire protection, structural strength, investment security, and balanced community relationships in housing. No one doubts that these are appropriate subjects for regulation, or that the public benefits to be expected from such regulation amply justify a reasonable degree of added complication and cost for producers. Despite obvious flaws in the actual operation of controls over so vast an area of enterprise, the general situation in the housing field is perhaps not worse than that in many other areas of public regulation.

Yet certain current aspects of building and land use control need review and consideration if design and production potentials are to be realized. This chapter will seek to identify problem areas and to suggest possible solutions. For convenience in discussion, the controls are divided into four groups. Most of the chapter is devoted to the direct municipal regulations dealing with land and building development (building codes, houing codes, zoning ordinances, subdivision regulations, and various engineering specifications). Second are the indirect public controls, such as the imposition of taxes, the location of major roads and extension of municipal services, the power to take land by eminent domain, and the power to add land to a municipal corporation by annexation. Third are the private controls such as deed restrictions and the lending regulations of financial institutions. Last are the Federal regulations that affect the lending process, in particular those of the Federal Housing Administration.

The effects of many broader forces, parti-

*Reprinted from* Design and Production of Houses, *McGraw-Hill Book Company, 1959, pp. 303–338, with permission of the publisher.*

cularly those of overall government fiscal policy and of the manipulation of money and credit to combat inflation or depression, are beyond the scope of this study; they are covered elsewhere in the ACTION series.[1] It is worth noting, however, that although these may have greater overall effect than any of the more specific controls discussed in this chapter, since they can determine the total housing industry volume, they have little direct effect on housing design and technology. The controls which are the subject of this chapter, on the other hand, have an often crucial effect on the use of new methods, even though, in many cases, those who establish and administer the controls do not understand this.

## Building codes

Direct public regulation of land and of the construction of buildings is carried on under the so-called police power, through which a government exercises its function of assuring the health, safety, and general welfare of its citizens. Generally speaking, the courts have determined that such regulation is a matter of state rather than Federal police power under our Constitution, and in the states this power has been delegated within specified statutory limits to local municipal governments. Local building codes are the most direct and obvious example of local police power regulation in the housing field.

Building codes have been generating heat for years. The building industry regularly claims that prevailing codes are obsolete or arbitrary. Typically a magazine speaking for the industry asks the editorial question, *does code Babel add* $1,000 *to small-house building cost?* and gives this answer:

The most expensive thing about today's house is the local building code under which it has to be erected, with its countless unpredictable and often senseless variances from sound national standards. The variances cost the home-buyer (and the homebuilder) a lot more than it would cost to make all the living rooms and all the bedrooms 20% larger – more than wall-to-wall carpeting, more than com-

plete insulation and double glazing, more than an extra bathroom.[2]

The article calls upon the strengthened and organized home builders to fight these cost increases rather than have them offset by special fiscal arrangements or passed on directly to the public.

Undoubtedly many building codes call for exaggerated standards of public safety; such standards are far easier to put into effect than they are to remove from the books. In part this difficulty stems from the natural tendency of many local building officials to favor the most conservative practices of the conventional system under which they have developed their experience; in part, it stems from the very real difficulty of defining public safety in such a way as to assure protection without penalizing innovation and advance. A major factor is the autonomy of local government, which tends to encourage a wide divergence of local standards and to put many difficulties in the way of broad definition of national or state standards. It is in our tradition to leave it to local communities to determine for themselves the level of standards they will require. A magazine speaking for the building officials put the argument in its purest form:

It is about time the critics of the codes recalled a fundamental of government. Building regulations are a legislative problem subject to local legislative choice. City councils are free to choose a building code consistent with their ideas of local needs. If they wish, they are free to provide protection ranging from no code at all to one that is highly restrictive and which would provide complete protection. Most cities select a reasonable building code which will provide a reasonable degree of protection.[3]

Cities decide for themselves the level of water and sewer service they wish to provide, so long as they exceed minimum state regulations. They provide wide variation in quality of streets, of protection services, and of public education. Why should they not set their own levels of fire and structural safety?

The answer is that new elements of public policy must enter the picture when the question is one of encouraging the rational development of a top national industry supplying the most expensive product purchased by the average family. Clearly building regulation requires a broader view, but as clearly this is hard to obtain. The average voter is no more aware of the potential benefits to him of a modernized building industry than the average builder is aware of the long-range effect on the community of the subdivision and construction decisions he makes on the basis of small points of convenience and profit.

Students of building codes generally agree that local excesses and variations are usually the result of honest intentions but inadequate knowledge and that difficulties would be sharply reduced if codes were based on performance standards, that is, if the objective were stated, but not the specific means of complying with it. Legislation which spells out the specifications of technical details and requirements quickly becomes antiquated and restrictive, for the tremendous scope of progress in the building field makes it impossible to encompass all acceptable variations. Since it is humanly impossible for enforcement officers to be acquainted with all the variations, they hesitate to use discretion and tend to enforce the law to the letter.

One method of keeping up to date employed by many local communities is the adoption of the national model code provisions of some public or private code-drafting organization. The situation with respect to code restrictions and inspections in one group of such communities (in the San Francisco Bay area) has been described by Maisel in these terms:

> In houses built in the localities where the uniform codes applied without changes – some 33 per cent of the total number built in the area – no inefficiency could be charged to the restriction of codes. Fifty per cent had their costs raised less than 1 per cent for the typical house through code alterations.

Even in the case of the final 15 to 20 per cent, where greater code restrictions were in force, the increased costs did not run more than 3 per cent above the uniform code areas. . . .

Although some instances of delays and arbitrary rulings were reported, most builders in the area stated that neither was of any consequence in the total cost of the building. Between 5 and 10 per cent of the builders reported that they had occasional difficulties in obtaining inspections on time or in having their plans approved, but the remainder said any delays or problems were unusual.[4]

If the difficulties are small, why do building industry spokesmen complain about codes? First, because adoption of the national model codes is not common. A recent report indicated that fewer than 10 percent of the 37,400 municipalities in the country have taken this step.* Second, the national codes are not uniform, even in their relatively simple residential construction provisions, and there are many of them. Even within the government, the Army, Navy, and public building agencies all have their own separate codes. Furthermore, the national model codes can hardly be accused of throwing off all restraint. They tend to be the guardians of good standard practice.

Maisel suggests that the observed lack of builder complaints in San Francisco stems from the fact that the average builder is not an innovator, but is content to build a house in a traditional manner, familiar both to him and to the building inspector. Many of the ablest producers, on the other hand, are deeply aware of the importance of innovation, both technological and entrepreneurial, if significant progress is to be made in the provision of housing and if real values is to be offered to the public. The codes may be criticized for unnecessarily delaying or even prohibiting significant progress in building, yet there are difficulties with most of the suggested approaches to this problem.

---

* *House & Home*, vol. 13, no. 6, (June, 1958), p. 61, gives the following claimed figures for adoptions of the four largest, noting that there is probably overlap:

| | |
|---|---|
| Building Officials Conference of America | 300 |
| International Conference of Building Officials | 1,167 |
| National Board of Fire Underwriters | 1,100 |
| Southern Building Code Congress | 712 |

The national electric code may be adopted by as many as 70 percent of United States communities, at least in part, but only about three hundred have adopted the national plumbing code.

*Performance standards.* To have only objectives in engineering terms stated, rather than detailed specifications of materials and methods of construction, is not in itself the complete answer, for such standards require a level of administration higher than the average community can afford. Systems that aim to take full design advantage of the potentialities of new approaches are not subject to easy calculation. It may take a man with skill equal to that of the innovator and the testing facilities of an industrial laboratory to decide whether a reinforced plastic panel can handle the required loads. For the large-scale builder, the expense and delay of submitting a full portfolio of test results to every local board of appeals constitutes a severe penalty whatever the final decisions.

Furthermore, local inspectors may insist that inspections be locally made. A panel assembly may have to be torn apart, inspected, and then reassembled at the site, even though many identical assemblies have previously been given the same treatment and all have passed. In this way a principal advantage of producing such assemblies is lost. Often the men concerned with the regulation of local building tend to work together to preserve conventional methods. The local builder, laborer, materials supplier, and inspector have all gone through the same background of experience. They have long relied on the same techniques, and to some extent, individuals have exchanged roles from builder to inspector on the local scene. In the case of a complex innovation, their firm and outspoken doubts and fears can give pause to the most enlightened banker, government appraiser, or prospective purchaser. Needless to say their practical judgment has often averted trouble. But the reassurance offered by local inspection may be too high a price to pay if it destroys the opportunity for significant production advances. Furthermore, localism may be motivated primarily by the desire to block further housing development by any means easily available. Such an environment is obviously not one in which the new is encouraged and the efficient is praised.

*Model codes.* Even when they make use of such national model codes as those developed by the Building Officials Conference of America, the International Conference of Building Officials, the National Board of Fire Underwriters, or the Southern Building Code Congress, local communities can and frequently do add extra and purely local requirements to the carefully standardized provisions. True, education on the value to community and to builder of genuine uniformity is spreading; progress may be illustrated by the New York State Building Code, adopted by 33 of 62 cities and by 250 of 1,500 communities through mid-1958, and with a high degree of uniformity among these communities. This code itself is short. A separate booklet lists the standards of national organizations, like the American Concrete Institute, that may be used. A code manual indicates in specification form the materials and methods that represent acceptable versions of the code provisions. Most important of all, perhaps, a central testing and approval body is staffed and supplied with state funds* to keep the code up to date and to issue certificates of acceptability for new ideas and combinations. Although these certificates are passed along to the adopting communities for information only, and have no legally binding local effect, they have had good local acceptance, and many of the nation's largest prefabricators have taken advantage of the system to speed approvals in the large and lucrative New York market. Like all state-wide uniform codes, however, this has one important defect: concentration is on state-wide minimum requirements and no ceiling is placed over locally enacted variants.

*Broad area controls and maximum requirements.* Sound engineering principles do not change at community boundaries, and the public has much to gain by the administrative recognition of this simple fact in the form of a

---

* Other model code organizations depend on memberships, fees, and contributions for their expenses, and operations are considerably less expeditious as a result.

single code setting maximum as well as minimum provisions over a wide area. Public attention tends, perhaps naturally enough, to dwell on negative arguments such as the threat of invasion by millions of cheap, look-alike houses that will clutter the land and inflate the cost of education. For the most part, these negative arguments have little or nothing to do with the public health, safety, and welfare considerations which form the basis for police power controls over building, but they are very clear and real to the public. The positive arguments are more abstract because they deal mostly with potentials – with estimates and projections of what the building industry might be able to provide if it were free to innovate and to recoup the necessary development costs by sales over broad market areas.

It would seem to be highly desirable to assure the prospective manufacturer of a new product or process that, if his research men work out a good idea and his development men get it into production, he can pass a single series of extensive tests and then distribute without further local approvals throughout an area at least as large as a metropolis, preferably as large as a state, and potentially even throughout the whole nation. There are climatic variations and other differences from region to region, but these need offer no serious obstacle. FHA's proposed new Minimum Property Standards use simplified maps to reflect regional differences affecting factors like earthquake resistance, wind loading, and insulation. In view of the long legal tradition putting controls over local property in state hands, however, it is probably advisable to attempt national uniformity not through direct regulation, but rather through the device of uniform state laws.

If building approval agencies were set up to cover very large areas, it would be administratively justifiable to bring into play extensive testing facilities and expert officials, whose contributions could even include significant improvements in the original design ideas. Under these circumstances, performance standards could actually be made to perform for the bene-

fit of innovator and public alike. Even if margins of safety were made conservatively high, many producers would be glad to comply in return for the assurance that they could then concentrate on sales over a broad area.

*Revision procedure.* It will be generally conceded that many building codes are sadly out of date, remaining operative only because able inspecting staffs are making extensive use of the discretion granted to them. Even the best need frequent revision to reflect advances in building technology, but this can be a costly, complex, and frustrating experience; hence many small communities give up and make do with adaptations of the codes of other communities thought to be suited to their purposes.

The typical revision procedure starts with a conference of technical experts seeking to set the character of technical requirements. Since there is no sharp line dividing reasonable from unreasonable, and since only judgment can set levels for fire safety and public health or mediate between low initial cost and low maintenance, the process becomes one of broad-front negotiation wherein a small but determined group insisting upon a single vested interest generally can force a compromise in its favor. In the next stage, the operational and administrative form for the execution of these technical requirements is under consideration, and the same process occurs. It is worth noting that loosely phrased technical requirements call for extra specification in administrative requirements, and vice versa. Finally, the code draft goes to the legislative body, and the process of logrolling starts in earnest. In the end, despite expert help and extensive effort, the community may have a code that holds little practical advantage over the outdated one that provoked the drive for revision.*

In short, any procedure by which code revision may be simplified and new ideas introduced without arousing all the forces of traditional resistance must be welcomed. One solution would be to bypass the usual process entirely, perhaps through a procedure for revision by

---

\* Even the adoption of a standard code may be a major effort. Many committees, several years, and thousands of dollars were required in St. Louis for the local adoption of the national electrical code.

the accumulation of a series of individual decisions on specific new methods and materials over a period of time. A key element here would be the creation at metropolitan or state level of a review board like that of New York, with a budget sufficient to provide well-qualified personnel and full testing resources. To this board would come designers, builders, or fabricators for decisions on new materials and methods. Implementation of the decisions would take the form of certificates of approval, supplemented by detailed description of the new material and by a careful analysis of the conditions of its use. Such certificates would by statute be legally established as acceptable alternatives to local code provisions. They would be sent to all code jurisdictions which would then be obliged to give a local permit to any application embodying the approved system. It is on this last vital point only that the procedure differs significantly from that of New York.

A procedure of this sort would guarantee each innovator a full and fair hearing directed at the merits of his proposal and a chance at a large market if he obtains approval. From the community's point of view there would be a gradual modernization of building regulations by a procedure that tends to bring up most-needed changes first and never involves the expense and frustrations of a full-scale code revision. Meanwhile local regulations and code officials could continue to handle traditional problems in the time-honored manner, supplying the detailed specifications of conventional construction which often serve as a sort of construction manual for local small builders. Local authority in building matters would not be rudely uprooted, and since most of the proposals seeking the advantage of the new procedure would involve structures regarding which the local inspector would have little opportunity for effective judgment because of his limited experience and resources, his objections would tend to be reduced. Furthermore, the principal underlying this system – that of

referring new and complex technical decisions to a specially qualified central review board – should not prove politically unpalatable in the state legislature. Such a procedure warrants further consideration.

*Incorporation by reference.* A simpler proposal to the same end is the extension among the states of the grant of power to local communities to incorporate by reference the provisions of codes worked out by independent experts. If all states would grant this power, any community could accept for local building-control purposes the appropriate code of a major code-drafting group, in its latest amended form. Currently in many states, such a model code must be adopted word for word in the local ordinance; if it is later amended, the community must also amend its ordinance.* This becomes too complex to warrant the trouble.

If the power to incorporate by reference were granted for this purpose, the model code might well be that of a central state agency, like the one in New York, which could also serve as an appeal board for matters of interpretation, analysis, and testing. It is important to repeat, however, that the significant gain for the innovator is not mere uniformity among communities of similar requirements, nor uniformity plus minimum state-wide standards. More important for the stimulation of new production ideas and of overall advance in the housing industry is the insistence that there be a maximum level of building-code requirements throughout the state, above which individual communities will not be permitted to establish their own special regulations.

*Action on codes.* Experience indicates that the public is not likely to take the initiative in improving the building-code situation, and in any case progress is likely to be greatest when those who understand the complex problems involved are brought together.† An important

---

* A possible way around this roadblock, at least in some states, would be the incorporation of a provision that conformance to provisions of nationally accepted standards shall constitute adequate performance under the local code.

† In 1958, Henry Luce of Time, Inc., ACTION, and fourteen trade and professional associations asked the

American Standards Association to consolidate the residential provisions of the major national codes into a single set of construction requirements for one- and two-family dwellings, and then to set up a procedure for annual review. Because a number of other code interests objected, ASA declined.

resource would be the participation of producers who see and can explain the general benefits that will result when localized conventions have been removed from the control system. Equally important (and often overlooked) would be the active participation of those who understand the emerging patterns of housing design and construction and will insist that advances be made in the procedural and administrative as well as the technical provisions. Only when all aspects move forward together may major innovations be fairly reviewed, tested, and put into practice. Only a broad approach can set the groundwork for advances in the whole pattern of living, as opposed to making a few detailed corrections in provisions regarding materials and systems of construction.

In many ways the building-code situation has already improved during the 1950's. Large builders operating across community and even state lines have tended to break down extremes of localism. The increasing mobility of the people is tending to reduce regional differences in design and in the regulations that go with them. And the increasingly national approach to financing is a powerful standardizing influence. Nevertheless the vast majority of communities retain individual local codes, most of which pay little attention to the future of housing.

*Coordination of regulatory measures.* The discussion of building codes would not be complete without calling attention to the need for coordination among the various police power control measures used by a community to regulate building development. To require high standards of fire resistance in panel-wall structures, when the major part – if not all – of the wall may be simple sheets of glass, is clearly illogical. Panelized and component approaches that offer considerable design and production innovations may be blocked by minor points in the plumbing or electrical codes. Many such conflicts and cross-purposes may be weeded out by the use of performance standards in the legislative language adopted by the community,

leaving interpretation and application to the innovator and the administrator. But constant attention must be focused on the final result to be obtained by the interplay of all the various police power tools. Although the application of such tools as zoning and subdivision control must remain essentially local because of the need for detailed familiarity with local conditions, this is not true of building codes, and the combined effect upon the larger community over the long haul increasingly calls for review at a higher level than the local one.

*Housing and health codes* are focused on maintaining minimum standards of fitness for human occupancy in old as well as new structures, and in units that may have been remodeled and subdivided many times in their long history.* The major concern of such controls is the up-grading of the existing stock of housing or, where this proves to be out of the question, its elimination.

Similar tools are found in laws providing for the compulsory vacation of deficient structures, in compulsory repair and lien laws, and in laws assessing fines for a variety of health and safety offenses. Although this sort of local provision is aimed essentially at the opposite end of the housing-supply picture from that with which this book is concerned and serves to stimulate mostly the repair and rehabilitation organizations, it is still important to builders because aggressive use of such provisions enlarges the market for new housing. Currently, new housing costs are relatively so high and the need for inexpensive housing is so great that communities hesitate to eliminate existing units or – by requiring extensive repairs – to put them out of reach of families now able to afford them. Major innovations could alter this situation considerably, by bringing down the costs of remodeling or of new units so that the enforcement of reasonable housing standards would not work a social hardship. Clearly, therefore, all aspects of public control are related parts of a single picture, with which builders should be more familiar than they are.

---

* This is a subject to which ACTION has devoted a good deal of attention, as may be seen from *Reports from ACTION*, nos. 2, 11, 15 (1956), dealing respectively with the Housing Court in Baltimore, the court decisions on municipal housing codes, and a reference guide to housing-code provisions for citizens organizations.

## Zoning

In 1916, zoning was first applied in the United States to assure light and air in city streets and to avoid incompatible land use mixtures. Soon zoning was embraced by development interests as a means of avoiding the worst effects of hit-and-run speculative building and of protecting sound neighborhoods, maintaining real estate values, and guiding extensions of existing urban patterns. City growth had become so chaotic that almost any orderly control system would be an improvement, and the choice naturally fell upon a system which was relatively simple to define, understand, follow, and enforce.* Potential land uses were listed, graded according to intensity and unpleasantness, and allocated to carefully mapped zones ranging from high-priced and well-protected residential areas at one extreme to nuisance industry at the other. Building permits were granted only for uses permitted within the zone affected.

Urban growth has accelerated in recent years, and it has become clear that the simple hierarchy of zones which was the model during the 1920's is not suited to the kind of metropolitan and suburban pattern being created today. Thus a great outcry has developed in design and building circles against zoning as a crystallization of outmoded needs, desires, and patterns. Because the old ordinances were inelastic, many would like to do away with zoning itself; others, including the city planners, argue rather for adaptation of the tool to modern needs, pointing out that potentially this extension of the basic police power is a control of very great importance† and one capable of a much higher degree of subtlety in reflecting the interests of both community and building industry than is usually provided.

A principal difficulty in zoning has been the familiar one of poor education. Those most eager for land controls had little knowledge of the future potentials in building and land development and tended to establish control patterns based on the assumption of conventional practices. Those most interested in new design, building, and land-development ideas, on the other hand, tended to dismiss zoning as dull administrative routine until they ran afoul of its provisions. It is a rare designer who has taken the trouble to suggest how zoning provisions might be effectively modified to handle his new ideas.‡ Especially in dealing with multifamily construction have the provisions and principles of zoning tended to be behind the designers, though perhaps this reflects a general backwardness in this country regarding the design potentials of multifamily construction.

The typical builder's attack on zoning in recent years, however, is probably focused elsewhere. He suspects that the community is indirectly trying to run up his costs or keep him out of town, and he has little patience with the city planners' talk of elastic guidance for new types of urban growth.

Housing developments are far more extensive than in the past, however; they tend to take the form of entire neighborhoods and even communities designed and built at one time for which an overall plan is needed from the start. The community is suddenly confronted with the need for miles of streets, water mains, and sewers and – dominating all other considerations – a skyrocketing demand for new schools. The typical voter, thoroughly frightened, supports the use of any tactic that will stem the flood of houses.

*The builder's view.* Community design opportunities are of little concern to the typical

---

* No doubt the simplicity and orderliness of the concept was of great importance (together with its thoroughly demonstrated acceptance by communities throughout the land) in convincing the Supreme Court in the case of *Euclid v. Ambler* 272 U.S. 365 (1926) that the Constitution was not violated when similar parcels of land were governed by the same regulations within a carefully defined zone, usually large in size and homogeneous in character, but smaller than the legal boundaries of the community.
† The British were considered radical when they con-

demned private development rights, though the original act provided for a token payment in compensation. The zoning concept allows control of development under the police power, without compensation of any sort, if private rights are not unreasonably restricted and if a suitable background in public benefit and development policy has been created.
‡ There are exceptions. See Charles K. Agle, "A New Kind of Zoning," *Architectural Forum*, vol. 95, no. 1 (July, 1951), p. 175.

builder. His main interest is to find buildable land and get construction under way. In many cases, however, he finds himself faced with a zoning plan devised to delay or even prohibit growth. There has been a trend toward requiring ever-larger house lots, up to several acres in the most restrictive zones,* on the assumption that larger lots require more expensive houses and thus create a better tax base for the community, tend to slow down development, or (preferably) both.† The fear motive is made perfectly clear when a Westchester town attempts to ration building permits according to average numbers granted over previous years, or when one on Long Island defines the speculative building of houses as a business use, not permitted in residential areas except by special permit from the town. When communities go too far, the courts intervene,‡ but recently the courts have extended the benefit of doubt when a provision shows evidence of careful study and seems to be in the broad interests of the community.

The advantage to the community of new building designs and methods tends to be little understood and sought at the local level. Indeed, far more study is needed on the effects on home building of zoning and other land-development controls. The relations and linkages, the accessibility requirements of different types of activities, and many other aspects of these controls should be the subject of research studies.§ More than study is needed, however. Builders must find a way to make clear to the voters that tangible benefits can be gained by permitting the use of new methods and designs. Demon-strations and illustrations and sound examples will help to stir interest, but something must be done at the same time to counter fear. The National Association of Home Builders could provide few more useful services to its members than the stimulation of a full-dress reconsideration of the allocation of school costs among forms of taxation and levels of government.

*Project development provisions.* In view of the increasing trend toward rapid, planned construction of large-scale developments, interest has been growing in special zoning provisions that allow builder and community to sidestep the conventional lot-by-lot approach and consider the plan of the project as a whole. Under many of these provisions, which represent one type of " special exception " in zoning, it is possible to vary bulk and density of individual units within a project in order to achieve design improvements and land use economies, so long as the average over the project as a whole is up to requirements and the general aims of the ordinance are observed. Under others, dwelling type as well as bulk and density may vary. Under a few, it is even possible to introduce different land uses – a shopping center or possibly a small light industrial enterprise – where they will appropriately serve the project. Provisions authorizing these special projects are typically spelled out in the initial zoning ordinance, but the area so to be zoned is actually shown on the map only when the owner of a specified minimum acreage in a specified general area comes in and requests planning-board permission to undertake such a development, sub-

---

* A zoning requirement of five acres was upheld in the case of *Fischer v. Bedminster Township*, 11 New Jersey 194, 93 A.2d 378 (1952).
† A study based on communities in the Boston area found no evidence of a correlation between increased lot size and deferred development. See *The Effects of Large Lot Size on Residential Development*, Urban Land Institute, Technical Bulletin no. 32, Washington, D. C., (July, 1958). Indeed, if the community sets high general standards of development, it may make itself only more attractive to builders and purchasers. Of course, if lots are large, fewer total families can be placed on available building land, and the expected urban growth must take over proportionately more land and extend proportionately farther out. On the other hand, evidence from all sources is clear that average lot size is going up as much from consumer demand as from zoning requirement.

If the consumer had his way, there is little doubt that outlying raw land would be turned into larger lots, and the study suggests that, with appropriately reduced subdivision standards, this could be done at relatively little added cost to builder and community.
‡ In New York, both the devices cited have been ruled unconstitutional.
§ An example of such a study is Shirley Adelson Siegel, " Relation of Planning and Zoning to Housing Policy and Law," *Law and Contemporary Problems*, vol. 20, no. 3, (Summer, 1955), in which zoning was found inadequate in many respects in its handling of public housing projects. Articles like Charles M. Haar. " The Wayne Township Case," *Harvard Law Review*, vol. 66, no. 6 (April, 1953), raise basic issues regarding the aims and objectives of local zoning control.

ject to a review of details of design and planning before the board gives its approval.[5]

Such special-exception procedures are of considerable importance today, and likely to be even more so in the future. They also represent a considerable extension of the original theory of zoning control, including as they do many of the characteristics of subdivision regulation. This is a development that offers hope of providing the environment in which innovation in housing and site-planning design may flourish, and designer and builders should find it very much in their interests to encourage its extension.

*Flexible controls.* Experimentation in all aspects of zoning is needed in order to develop means of assuring community objectives without needlessly restricting design and construction innovation. Those who draft and enact zoning ordinances are often unfamiliar with new ideas in design and building and therefore tend to devise regulations which perpetuate conventional practices and requirements. Furthermore, administrative officers have a natural and reasonable tendency to prefer provisions that are simple to understand and express as well as to enforce. Unfortunately, such provisions, although working well for conventional builders, may constitute a block against the inventive designer or builder who is willing to deal with a complex formula or a subtle series of checks and balances so long as he gains thereby the chance to innovate. Every encouragement should be offered to the development of elastic controls which will permit both the conventional and the creative approaches without lowering the standards of public benefit and protection. Builders must find ways of identifying the major paths of innovation developed by designers and producers, getting this information into the hands of administrative officers, and helping to make sure that control systems will provide the needed elasticity.

Much progress has been made along these lines in recent years. To an increasing degree

the method of regulating bulk and density in zoning has moved away from the requirement of specific yards and heights and toward the setting of ratios of floor area to lot area. Provision for light and air in dense development areas may be made through formulas dealing with the amount of sky area that must be visible from each window, rather than through the conventional routines of setting buildings back from the street at various distances according to height. Such provisions require more explanation and consequently appear more complex to the average person, but they offer the prospective designer little difficulty and a tremendously broadened range of freedom. Other examples of elasticity are the zoning of industry by the use of performance standards* instead of by oversimplified listings according to nuisance level and the use of special-exception provisions to permit certain unusual but necessary land uses in specified zones – for example the construction of hospitals in the most restrictive residential areas.

At the present time, the general public is alarmed at growth problems and local officials are sharply aware of the need for development planning. Trained planners are much in demand, have good local support, and generally receive the benefit of every doubt in case of judicial review. In some cases, these factors have induced a tendency to plunge into bold experiments and to authorize a great deal of discretionary power in watching over the public interests. This growing civic zeal has to be balanced with a sharper recognition of the needs of private development. One decided advantage of the observed increase in builder size is the resulting builder ability to make certain that zoning regulations reflect his interests adequately. The large builder can afford the time to clear away improper restrictions, and he has the resources to do so, both in money and in practical experience and test results.

*Other zoning problems.* Brief mention may be made of several other items in the zoning

---

* This idea has been given wide attention by city planners; it is far more difficult to apply the idea to the zoning of residential development.

field which are of general concern to the builder. One of these is the common complaint of poor and occasionally high-handed administration in the processing of variances, special exceptions, and appeals. To this, the best solution is to encourage the builder to stand upon his rights, in court if necessary, and through the medium of his association if he dares not risk local retaliation following individual action.

In general, zoning controls are too often treated as isolated matters and not adequately related to the other means of local building control: building codes, subdivision regulations, and general planning provisions. In some states, Massachusetts, for example, zoning and subdivision control must be absolutely separate, although they deal with different aspects of a single problem. True, zoning generally was introduced into most communities years in advance of subdivision control, and often in advance of planning regulations having any aspect of effective local control.* This does not prohibit the designer and builder from insisting that the various regulations be reasonably related to each other and to a master plan.

From the designer's point of view as well as the community's, there is reason for concern that measures of local regulation may tend to put an unnecessary strait jacket on innovation. Careful attention should be paid to the recent expansion of municipal regulation of aesthetic qualities in building development. In upholding the District of Columbia in its redevelopment activities, Mr. Justice Douglas of the Supreme Court recently commented that nothing in the Constitution stands in the way if the District seeks to make areas of Washington beautiful, as well as efficient.[6] From this and from other developments in the states (historical districts, for example, and measures to preserve breathing spaces and skylines), planners have been given a boost in what may prove to be a dangerous direction. For there are significant difficulties in regulating aesthetics; average public tastes are

not sophisticated, and over time they change. To be required to adhere in the future to a current common denominator of design taste is not only to face frighteningly dreary prospects in terms of visual pleasure (as anyone may observe for himself if he will but check back through magazine illustrations of buildings of a generation ago), but also to put a tremendous barrier in the path of innovation in design and construction. Yet just such a trend appears to be in the air at the present time. A specific zoning illustration may be found in an ordinance adopted in 1951 by Rye, New York, which set up a five-member Board of Review instructed to disapprove projected house plans of excessive similarity or dissimilarity. One can sympathize with the emotions behind such a regulation, but it is only too clear that in ordinary administration, the device was expected to keep out unconventional houses, and very likely also to keep out any large-scale merchant builder.

So long as the general public regards such a provision as nothing more than a convenient way to avoid the shocking modern and the crass speculative, there is little chance of arousing opinion against it. Yet the chances are substantial that it will also bar sensible and cost-saving innovations of all sorts and generally present just such a block to the advance of the housing industry as we seek to identify and remove.

The general experience of this country has been that the public welfare is advanced, rather than injured, by encouraging experimentation of all sorts, even though the initial form may seem strange and may be very different from the one finally accepted by the mass market. The "picture window" is a commonplace variation by conventional builders on a theme developed by a small number of very advanced designs in exploring the free use of glass areas. The ranch house with its outdoor sitting areas and cooking facilities is a popular adaptation of free-flowing housing designs once considered

---

* Consequently, requirements in state enabling acts that local zoning shall be "in accordance with a comprehensive plan" have in the past been assumed to mean only that the zoning shall not be trivial, arbitrary, or partial, but shall represent a considered scheme for the entire community. Recent years have seen a significant advance in other local controls, however, and the courts are beginning to see to it that there is in fact a relationship between these tools. See Charles M. Haar, "In Accordance with a Comprehensive Plan," *Harvard Law Review*, vol. 68, no. 7 (May, 1955).

dangerously radical, and the carport and breeze-
way would have caused serious problems under
the zoning yard requirements of a very few
years ago. The public likes and benefits from
these developments; it should not let itself be
persuaded to cut off the sources from which
they spring.

### Subdivision control

It was early recognized as an important
function of local government to review the proposals of land developers for the creation of new
streets. The importance of guiding the street
pattern became evident in the nineteenth century when the outskirts of many cities were
becoming a patchwork of subdivisions, patterned
by the accident of landholdings and the speculative interests of the developer more than by
any concern for the resulting effect on public
circulation throughout subsequent decades of
service. Boards of survey and comparable official
community bodies undertook to designate the
location and design as well as the character
and quality of street pavement.

In the building boom following World War I,
however, new problems made their appearance.
Speculative land developers subdivided hundreds
of square miles of outlying land, had streets and
services put in at municipal expense, and then
found themselves unable to sell their lots. As a
result of this experience, municipal governments sought a way of checking more closely
the developer's plans, and requiring him to put
enough capital into land development so that
his calculation of market possibilities would be

sharpened by the concrete dimensions of his
own potential loss. It came to be generally
understood that the level and expense of normal municipal services are such that the government can no longer provide them without cost
to new development lots; municipal tax returns
from residential development are not enough to
warrant such an outlay, and long-range cost to
the community of poor design is far too great
to encourage it by municipal assumption of risk.
Hence today the developer, who plans to make
a profit from converting undeveloped local land
into lots and houses, is generally required to
pay most or all of the costs associated with
streets, drains, and other required municipal
services, and his plans are typically made to conform to overall community development plans
and standards.

As a result, normal development costs can be
high; in some rapidly growing areas of the
country additional charges are made: a pro rata
contribution to school construction cost in California communities,* for instance, or a fee in
lieu of dedication of land for public purposes
within the development. Although in some cases
the corrective action may have gone too far, the
public objective has been to find the level of
regulation that will assure high-grade development and at the same time equitably allocate
its overall costs among purchaser, developer,
and community.†

*The builder's view.* Subdivision control is
under heavy fire from builders all over the
country; they call it extreme and arbitrary and
say it is being used in many communities to
raise costs artificially in order to stop or hinder

---

* Attacked in recent court tests.
† See J. Ross McKeever, " Utilities and Facilities for New
Residential Construction," Urban Land Institute, Technical Bulletin no. 27, Washington, D. C. (December,
1955), which notes that progress is being made in the
equitable sharing of costs. For example, there is increasing agreement that developers should not be charged the
full price of utility installations designed for extra
capacity in order to serve areas beyond the current
development. There remains, however, the likelihood
that adjoining communities will have different specifications governing land development within the same
region. Summarizing the regulations of 114 cities:
  1. One hundred and two had subdivision regulations.
  2. Fifty-three extended subdivision controls beyond

the city limits. (On this, and subsequent, questions,
some did not answer.)
  3. Developers must pay for improvements as follows:
    *a.* Street grading: all 95, part 3
    *b.* Street paving: all 80, part 9
    *c.* Curbs and gutters: all 79, part 7
    *d.* Sidewalks: all 75, part 4
    *e.* Water mains: all 61, part 13
    *f.* Sanitary sewers: all 81, part 9
    *g.* Storm sewers: all 71, part 7
  4. Completion guaranteed by bond or otherwise: 81
  5. Developer reimbursed for one or more items: 36.
  6. City pays additional cost of larger installations
needed to serve areas outside subdivision: all 43, part
40.

development.* On the other side, planners claim that in too many cases effective controls become politically acceptable only after major damage has been done. These claims and counter-claims have brought the matter to a head, particularly in view of the proclaimed shortage of prime development land in the outskirts of many of our metropolitan areas.

It is significant that in their general objections to subdivision regulations, builders frequently confuse the issue with complaints about lot size, yards, and other requirements established by the zoning ordinance rather than the subdivision regulations, and occasionally an argument is raised that stems in fact from the building code. This underlines the point that for the builder a control is a control. Even though he is currently required to make separate visits to different people at City Hall to handle each of these requirements, in his mind these are all part of a single municipal control system.

*Administration.*   For both builder and community, increased time and expense are required as a result of recent refinements in subdivision control. As the procedure has grown in effectiveness, title companies and conveyances have been shocked to discover the possibility of hidden title defects stemming from the subdivider's failure to get the required approvals before filing a subdivision plat with the recorder of deeds;† they have promoted laws requiring the municipalities to put on record at the recorders' offices all the details of the local regulatory structure and, for each subdivision plat, a full certification of acceptability or nonacceptability by the approving agency.‡

In addition, builders have called for the holding of open meetings and the maintenance of complex records. As a result of all these demands, many a suburban planning commission finds itself swamped by the administrative aspects of subdivision control and unable to keep up with its other work. Many have been forced to charge filing and examination fees, thus to reimburse the costs of trained review personnel and so both speed and strengthen the approved process.

*Relationship to zoning.*   In the discussion of zoning we noted a trend in the direction of flexible controls, designed more to guide rapid new development than to preserve the *status quo* in settled communities. Subdivision control has the same objective and tends to rely on the same principles. The time has come to undertake a combined approach to these two control measures. If our level of skill warrants the use of performance standards and of community guidance on specific aspects of large-project design, then it is only causing confusion to call part of this activity "zoning" and the rest of it "subdivision control." No administrative realist lightly throws away an established body of legislation and decision as well tested as that on zoning, but up-to-date lawyers, planners, and builders can quickly agree that the time has come for simplification and improvement. It is not necessary to know the exact steps a new joint approach might take in order to underline the importance of starting discussion on the subject.

An illustration is the common failure to adjust subdivision improvement standards to zoning lot size. Since improvement standards are a reflection of the contemplated character and intensity of land use, it is only reasonable to expect them to bear some relationship to the permitted intensities. It is patently foolish for a community to require, in an area that is zoned to permit only one family to the acre, a level of improvement and development engineering designed to serve a density of one hundred families to the acre. Yet upper-income suburbs sometimes do just this. The resulting develop-

---

* A typical extra cost per lot of $1,500 might include $600 for concrete streets, $400 for lots an extra 10 feet in width, and $500 for curbs, sidewalks, and storm sewers.

† In several states the sensible provision has been adopted that the innocent purchaser of a lot in an unapproved subdivision may, if he wishes, void the purchase and sue his seller.

‡ This illustrates the effectiveness of private enforce-

ment methods as contrasted with reliance on reviews and inspections by public officials. Since every banker will insist on clear title, the public may be sure that every subdivision approval formality is observed without spending a cent for enforcement. If failure to comply with other community controls should result in a prior lien or a title defect on the property, compliance with controls might become all but automatic.

ment costs may be such that no one can afford to develop his land at the permitted density, and in the end the community is compelled to permit development at a density better suited to the required standards. On the other hand, it can be expected* that if, as lot size increases, the standards of improvement are reduced to reflect the reduction in requirements for drainage, traffic, and other service loads that is inherent in such an increase, the land-development costs may be reduced enough so that the larger, less-engineered lot will cost the developer and community little if any more than the smaller, more highly-engineered lot. Under such circumstances, the builder can afford to give the homeowner the larger lot which he seems to prefer. Thus large-lot zoning requirements need not necessarily raise land-development costs and so reduce the output of lower-priced houses, as is sometimes alleged by builders. Adjustment of subdivision improvement standards to suit permitted development density is nowhere near common enough, however, and when it is found it typically is granted at local official discretion and not as a matter of right. This is one aspect of the relationship between zoning and subdivision control on which builders could call for immediate action.

Yet in the few cases where such adjustments in standards have been put into effect, builders tend to misunderstand the purpose and enter loud complaints. They feel it is unreasonable that in the large-lot areas, which they regard as suited to high-priced houses, few improvements are required, while in the congested small-lot areas, "the bus driver, who is trying to buy a $10,000 house, must pay for all the excessive requirements." In fact, of course, the smaller lots mean more families; hence they require full streets, sidewalks, curbs, sewerage, and other engineering services, and as a result, far higher development cost per acre. The low-cost builder uses small lots because they spread these costs and thus offer the best per-lot price

within the area of high accessibility that has been considered essential for low-income families.†

*Other subdivision control problems.* What is the fair method of getting from the builder the land areas required for schools, parks, and other community purposes? In some states he may simply be required to convey such areas, on the assumption that his abutting land gets the benefit from the subsequent community development of the public areas and so he suffers no real loss. This is particularly true where the facility provided is required to serve his development. In others he may be required to hold the land available for the community when it wants it, and increasingly a time limit is being placed on the period within which the community must act. Some developers still argue that the community should pay for such land areas at the start if it wants to reserve rights over them. This issue calls for more detailed information concerning real costs and benefits accruing to both sides than is now available.

From time to time communities explore procedures by which a subdivision may be prevented on the grounds, not that it is poorly designed or below development standards, but only that it is premature. Experts often note a need for such procedures, and there persists in many areas of the country a sharp memory of the waste, cost, and subsequent legal tangles attending the flood of premature subdivision during the boom of the 1920's. A continued rise in the basic knowledge and understanding of overall planning agencies may one day make it possible to determine without a doubt the full extent of needed development, but for the present it seems clear that the best defense against premature subdivision is the general requirement that the subdivider invest substantial amounts of development money, so that he does not dare move too far ahead of market demand. Since development land tends to be sold today

---

* Borne out in a study of selected Boston area communities by the Massachusetts Department of Commerce, *The Effects of Large-Lot Size on Residential Development*, Urban Land Institute, Technical Bulletin no. 32, Washington, D. C. (July, 1958).
† High accessibility to jobs and urban facilities may no

longer be essential for such families. Inexpensive houses often go up on good-sized lots that are far out in the suburbs, with low prices reflecting freedom from codes (and so construction-cost savings) as much as reduction in improvement standards.

in the form not of building lots but of completed speculative houses, the required investment is very high indeed, and the developer moves with caution unless special programs and policies of the FHA or VA allow him in effect to speculate without personal risk.

But development may still be premature in terms of community facilities: schools, major utilities, etc. City planners are sympathetic to attempts to control the *pace* of development on the theory that smoother social, technical, and economic adjustments to new needs can be made when rates of growth are moderate than in periods of violent changes. Recognition of this fact has led large builders like Levitt to take the sting out of rapid community growth by building the required schools and turning them over to the community.

### The larger view

Many difficulties arise for both builder and community from the failure to see the system of building and land use controls as a comprehensive whole, rather than a collection of independent pieces, and to consider the operation of this system of controls as one having definite objectives and applying over a broad geographical area. The building-code discussion brought out the importance to a would-be innovator of obtaining uniform treatment from many communities. The interdependence of zoning and subdivision control measures has just been demonstrated. Needed as the indispensable foundation upon which all the applications of individual police power tools must rest is a continuing program of comprehensive community analysis and planning. For the essence of the problem is to find out what really needs to be controlled, and to control only that, by as simple and as direct means as possible, while allowing a maximum degree of freedom elsewhere.

*Community planning.* At the present time most communities have established programs of community planning, and some have made a

considerable effort in this direction, with a trained staff, a system of referring proposed public improvements for report, a capital budget procedure, and a series of published and approved reports on elements of the general plan for the community.

Programs of Federal assistance have placed a growing importance on local planning. Highway programs give recognition to local plans if they can. Public housing requires consideration of local plans. And the urban renewal program not only calls for specific reference to local plans but also, in specifying the preparation of a municipal "workable program" for long-range planning development on the part of any community seeking Federal assistance, requires that there be an effective planning agency with a full range of basic planning tools and controls. Federal funds are granted specifically for the advance planning of public works. And for smaller communities, Federal grants-in-aid share the cost of initiating planning studies beyond the resources of the community.

From the point of view of the average builder, these planning tools and controls are often exercised in an arbitrary manner because the planners either do not understand the facts of life in building development or are content to take a narrowly local view of the matter. Yet he typically does little about it, other than become intimate with key local officials in order to be in line for the benefit of a friendly doubt. He rarely seeks direct legal recourse for alleged injustices. In the first place, this procedure takes time, which he cannot afford.* In the second place, he suspects that the local officials will all support one another, and that if he should succeed in upsetting one ruling, he would find himself subjected to constant harrassing technicalities that would make it almost impossible for him to go about his normal business. In any case, the average builder is not an innovator. He is usually concerned not with removing blocks to new methods, but only with getting red tape cleared away so that he may move ahead with his building operations. And he readily adjusts details of his designs to local pre-

---

* Priority on the docket, or other means of expediting court review, can be important to the builder. In some states this has been specifically granted by statute. It is a measure that deserves broader consideration.

ferences, in order to eliminate a major source of trouble.

If his building volume grows, his point of view changes, as does his relative ability to do something about it. The medium-sized builder may be perfectly willing to follow local regulations so far as materials and methods of construction are concerned, but he must have development land ready in advance of need in order to operate efficiently. On a few structural points he may argue with the local building inspector. But typically he is much more concerned with the restrictions covering available land, the cost involved in providing the lot frontages and yards required under the zoning ordinance, and the general engineering layout and site design called for under the subdivision regulations. In recent years his complaints about land-planning controls have become louder and clearer whenever the mortgage-money pinch is not the overriding concern. These problems are still regarded by the National Association of Home Builders as major fighting issues for the industry.

The medium-sized builder tends to feel, and with some justification, that local control devices are being exercised for the purpose of excluding him from the community, or failing that, of forcing up his costs and prices until local tax assessments will balance rising municipal costs. Even so, he prefers not to take a case to court, for he, too, must keep going at full steam during the building season in order to make profits.

The large builder frequently solves the problem of land-planning controls by staying clear of the regulatory structure. He buys outlying land, where community controls are either nonexistent or weak, or else he operates in a community where his size, power, and experience give him a great deal of local influence. He is able to invest time and effort in clearing away local difficulties, because he will have a large and continuing operation in one place after the way has been cleared.

Thus one way for the builder to deal with the problems of local control is to grow large. Not all builders can achieve such a solution,

however; many would prefer in any case not to become so large as to alter their basic pattern of operations. All are glad to benefit from such liberalization of building and planning controls as may be brought about by the efforts of some of their larger brothers, but relatively few are inclined to band together and present a united front on this problem or to use local associations as negotiating or fighting instruments. The independent builder is simply too independent a personality, on the one hand and, on the other, too thoroughly imbued with the short-range view that all profit lies in expedition and compromise. Still, the benefits of size are rapidly becoming clear and the undoubted trend of local building in this direction may be credited in part to the growing complexity and breadth of planning controls.

*Larger geographic areas.* It is increasingly clear that urban growth problems cannot be understood or solved if they are cut up and treated within the boundaries of individual small communities. As metropolitan area population pours into the outlying suburbs and as residential, industrial, and commercial developments extend along new highway systems, it becomes increasingly evident that reasonableness of development regulations and characteristics of the public interest must be considered in terms of larger development areas, probably the entire metropolitan area.

In most communities, for example, the purposes of zoning are formulated on a local basis, and it is the traditional view that the citizens of an independent municipality should guard jealously the power to determine their own goals and standards.

The courts have made it clear from the very start in the Euclid[7] case that extreme local zoning disregard of the needs of the larger community would be corrected, and in several recent cases they have specifically taken account of developments outside of the municipal jurisdiction in judging the reasonableness of local provisions.* The courts are not intended, qualified, or staffed to work out metropolitan development plans, however; they cannot supply an

---

* See, for example, *Cresskill v. Dumont*, 15 New Jersey 238, 104 A.2d 441, 1954.

efficient building program for a multitude of independent local governments or see that maximum public benefit is gained from the use of productive resources. Indeed, as a matter of policy, they will uphold a local determination unless it is invalid beyond a reasonable doubt.

In general, therefore, there is merit to the claim that the broad public interest is not adequately identified and protected in current zoning. A sound builder may be prevented by the concerted action of a whole ring of suburbs from providing housing that offers hope of advanced standards at reduced cost. Or on the other hand, an outlying piece of raw land may be purchased, incorporated as a municipality, and ruined by a speculative developer before any effective representation of the future public interest can be brought to bear. Such factors are increasingly recognized by planners, and metropolitan groups frequently offer guidance and advice to local communities regarding their development problems and the implications of their control proposals. It will soon be necessary to go further, however, and to formalize the means by which local zoning controls may be checked against the basic interests of the larger community.

An additional point should be made regarding enforcement of zoning. The courts called on to settle disputes in this field are less concerned with creating a structure of principles and precedents than with identifying the nature and extent of the conflicting interests of the general public and of the individual landowner or developer. They need some frame of reference in policies and facts within which to compare costs and benefits. Local control systems often fail to provide a suitable frame of reference, and in defending local provisions, individual communities often fail to supply the background of information and evidence required by the court. Similarly, builders tend to limit their presentations to the narrowest details, with no united effort to show the broad public benefits to be gained from a healthy industry. Under the cir-

cumstances, zoning decisions may be expected to be unpredictable.

As in the case of zoning, it is important under subdivision control to recognize the needs of an entire metropolitan area as well as those of the immediate community. These two types of control differ in this respect from building codes, where the concern is for the design and construction of a building rather than the use of local land, and where such regional variations as may be required – for example, by temperature and precipitation – can be reflected as factors to be read from generalized maps so that uniform regulations may be applied over very extensive areas. In zoning and subdivision control, it is important not only that detailed recognition be given to the characteristics of the local community and the land on which it lies, but also that underlying the regulations there be a basic understanding of the structure, functioning, and growth potentials of the broader area of which the community is a part. Thus, for subdivision control as for zoning, consideration should be given to setting up a review and analysis function on at least a metropolitan scale.

Such a review function might be exercised by a variety of agencies, from an unofficial committee to a formal department at a higher level of government, with a variety of areas of concern, from the metropolitan area to the county, state, or region. An unofficial metropolitan planning agency with power only to advise would perform this function better than no agency at all. The exact form and authority are less important than the fact of such an agency, provided that it has an adequate budget and a skilled staff. Such an agency could serve this purpose far better than the courts and indeed would soon find itself swamped with local requests for background analysis and professional guidance. Should matters finally require formal adjudication, the courts would be considerably aided by having before them a clear record and a well-considered frame of reference within which to judge it.*

---

* See Charles M. Haar, "The Master Plan, an Impermanent Constitution," in *Law and Contemporary Problems*, vol. 20, no. 3 (Summer, 1955), p. 353.

Although a check on the operational practices and procedures of local communities would weed out many problems, the important element in the review procedure would be the creation of a framework of policy and planning assumptions against which the reasonableness of local programs could be checked. Population forecasts, economic base determinations, and the locations of major transportation lines are typical elements of such a framework, and they are elements essentially beyond the determination of a single local community. In the final analysis, many of these elements may have to be determined at the state level, and since they are questions of policy, they should be considered by a body politic that is directly responsive to an electorate.

From the builder's point of view, there is much to recommend the creation of some sort of higher review function or trained appeals board. If the mechanism were easy to use and could reach rapid decisions in an emergency, the builder might more often challenge the local regulations, and the overall result might be beneficial to all concerned.

Such an appeal mechanism could also be used by local citizens or bodies to protect the public against inadequate local administration or against the pressures that can be brought to bear on small communities by large and aggressive developers.*

This is not the place to discuss the formal governmental alternatives for dealing with metropolitan problems,† but it may be urged that a review mechanism be considered, and a few extreme possibilities may be noted to illustrate the implications of the proposal. The higher policy body might spell out overall development goals and determinants, leaving the entire structure of local controls to be freely established by local communities within these limits. Or it might work out the general nature and extent of certain uses (housing, industry, etc.) that each local community must provide, and let the community arrange these uses much as it pleased, so long as adjacent communities harmonize at mutual boundaries. Or it might spell out standardized zone descriptions and provisions, with the decision left to the local community whether and where to use them but with the benefits of standardization assured to builders. Eventually, there might be a large-scale, highly flexible "design plan" with a schedule of related provisions regarding zoning, subdivision control, and other development regulations.

However far along this line the builder and the public may be prepared to go, it is to their interests to recognize that the different kinds of municipal regulation and the different individual communities within a metropolitan area are all parts of a whole and that improved operation of the parts can come only from a closer study of the whole.

---

* An appeals proposal of this sort in Massachusetts in 1955 was resoundingly opposed by towns as an invasion of local liberty. There are many problems to be solved, for example, the pressures by vested interests who can afford to concentrate efforts on a board with such great potential influence.

† See Edward C. Banfield and Morton Grodzins, *Government and Housing in Metropolitan Areas*, McGraw-Hill Book Company, Inc., New York, 1958.

# Housing standards

*RICHARD U. RATCLIFF*

The subject of housing standards is interwoven into the whole fabric of the housing problem; in fact, in the absence of the concept of standards, there is no housing problem. Minimum housing standards are incorporated by law and regulation in local police power controls. The whole public housing controversy stems from differences in the levels of housing quality which are assumed to be socially tolerable. Standards appear in the concerns of builders and bankers who must interpret design features in terms of market demand or mortgage risk. The architects, the legatees of centuries of professional effort to relate design features to human requirements, are crying for a more realistic scale of values.

The term "standards" has acquired many connotations but most frequently implying minimum situations, with the situations expressed in physical terms. It is the purpose of this discussion to give emphasis to the point that the only standards which have relevance in housing programs are those which have their basic expression in human values, and that the concept of standards has meaning at all levels of housing quality.

As a starting point for the discussion of housing standards, let us look at the essence of housing. Housing is both a situation and a process. As a situation, housing is a current set of relationships between a person or group of persons of given biological and cultural attributes and a certain immediate physical environment – the structure and artifacts – together with the associated parcel of land and the land uses, individuals, groups and activities which comprise the community. Viewed dynamically, housing is a process. It is a process of investment, a process of the production of usable space by land developer, building products processor and manufacturer and home builder. It is the workings of the market which bring together buyer and seller, landlord and tenant. It is a process of utilization and consumption by the occupants of housing space. It is the evolutionary development of the community environment as a physical and cultural complex. It is the continuing change in social institutions which regulate land use and condition the way of life.

The problems of housing lie in the unsatisfactory living situations of individuals and families; the cures can come about by evolutionary or socially-induced modifications of the housing situations and housing processes.

To appreciate the role of standards in housing, consider the steps in the provision of housing space. All but a small proportion of housing is provided as a business proposition by investors and merchant-builders. The builder is interested in the immediate sale and thus attempts to interpret the design preferences of current purchasers. He picks that segment of the market which promises the liveliest sales and attempts to anticipate the combinations of space allocation, design features and equipment items which will be preferred by his customers within the limits of their financial capacities. Because few home buyers can afford all they would like to have in a house, the builder tries to foresee what the typical pattern of compromises will be.

*Reprinted from " Housing Standards and Housing Research," Land Economics, vol. 28 (Nov. 1952), pp. 328–331, with permission of the journal.*

The builder will be inclined to interpret the prompt sale of his houses as verification of his choice of planning standards. Such a conclusion may not be justified; it proves only that the houses could be sold. It might well be that, as in recent years, the sales simply reflect the housing shortage. In other cases, locational advantages may have been great enough to offset planning deficiencies. Finally, the experience and observation of the buyers may have been so limited that they were not aware of the range of alternative design features which could be available to them without increased cost.

In practice, the builder is restricted in setting the planning standards of the homes which he builds. He is limited by the attitudes of the banker from whom long-term credit must be secured. Because the banker takes the long-view of mortgage risk considerations, his scale of values is somewhat different than that of the builder, who tries only to interpret the present market; the banker is inclined to be more conservative. In addition, when the mortgage is to be insured or guaranteed, FHA or VA standards are applied.

Building codes, zoning ordinances and other local regulations constitute another set of limitations within which the builder must make his decisions on design standards. Here, in these regulatory codes, we find the product of what is technically a democratic determination of standards. But it is well known that these standards typically are determined without benefit of adequate objective measurements.

A primary objective of housing legislation and housing programs is to raise housing standards, to modify or create housing situations so that they are acceptable. Housing standards which are incorporated in police power controls or which are implicit in the assumption that the public housing device is necessary, are standards of minimum social acceptability. In the case of police power regulations, few economic considerations are involved; there is little weighing of the cost of attaining the minimum standard. Where public housing is to be provided as the alternative to unacceptable housing conditions, society undertakes a financial burden in order to free certain of its members from intolerable living conditions. Where private

choices are made by families above the subsistence level but below that level of wealth which requires no abstinence, housing standards are established by a complex balancing of values over the whole range of alternative allocations of available funds. The housing situation which results from this process of private decision does not necessarily, nor even typically, reflect the minimum levels acceptable to the family nor the maximum levels of full satisfaction.

Enough has been said up to this point to demonstrate the inadequacy of that popular connotation of the term " standards " which is limited to the notion of " minimum " standards. Minimum standards are not effective absolutes. True, we might agree that a line could be drawn around those housing situations which will inevitably kill off the occupants or assure an epidemic, but this is a practical absurdity. Housing situations involve degrees of probability that some undesirable results will ensue – fire, accident, ill health, insanity; or on the other hand, that favorable results will develop – contentment, comfort, health, aesthetic satisfaction. To set a standard, or to make a choice in respect of some housing attribute we should have a measure of the human reactions to varying degrees of the attribute, such as the incidence of TB under varying levels of ventilation and sunlight. Having a measure of these relationships, the minimum acceptable window area would be automatically established by the minimum acceptable TB rate. But note that the minimum TB rate is not a scientifically determined absolute, but a human choice based on considerations which go far beyond housing. Nor are the FHA or PHA minimum standards on room sizes more than a consensus of experts who combine their judgments on how people prefer to live and how they ought to live.

It is clear that the basis of standards determination is found in human values. We all know that houses are built for people and that the basic test of housing quality lies in the effects upon people. It should follow, therefore, that the judgments of housing situations, of space and space arrangements, of design features and equipment items, of neighborhoods and environments are only valid when related to the people and families who are exposed to them. It is shocking, therefore, to contemplate the continued setting of standards by legislative act, by judicial decision, by administrative determination, by the business judgments of builders and bankers, by the pencils of architects and land planners, by the unenlightened or forced choices of consumers, standards which irretrievably determine the housing destinies of our people for decades to come, standards which may perpetuate socially-dangerous living conditions for millions of families, all without benefit of a valid measurement or real understanding of the true impact of housing attributes on physical and mental well-being. How can we hope to evaluate the housing problems of this nation, let alone solve them without such understanding?

The measurement of the impact of housing attributes on human beings is a complex and imposing task. Yet, because it is central to the objective of raising the level of housing conditions and reducing housing costs, it must be undertaken by those who have faith in the instrumentality of research in accelerating social progress. Somehow the available studies which purport to demonstrate the relationships of housing and health are not very convincing. The association of slum conditions and abnormal morbidity rates, of housing blight and high indices of social disorganization can be established wthout throwing much light on direct causal relationships. Medical science must devise better techniques for isolating the relationships between specific housing features and specific physical ills. Psychological and social science must find methods for dealing with the even more complex problem of the measurement of mental health and attitudes.

There appear to be two categories of standards involved in the multiform problems of housing – which we might label "minimum" and "volitional." An important distinction lies in whether they are matters of the social conscience.

*Minimum* housing standards are those levels of living, directly determined by housing situations, which are no more than just socially acceptable. Whether these standards be codified in local housing regulations or administratively determined under broad definitions as in the public housing program, the process is one of democratic decision. Presumably the decision is based upon knowledge of how certain housing situations affect human beings. Actually this knowledge exists in only the crudest of forms, if it exists at all, and the standards which are established are expressed as physical specifications and not as levels of living.

*Volitional* housing standards reflect living situations which are generally in excess of levels of minimum social acceptability and which apply in the housing situations of families above the subsistence level, where choice exists over the whole range of expenditure. Here the standard is not one set by formal democratic devices to forestall deplorable living conditions; these are standards which represent the choices of consumers to whom a range of choice is open. A volitional housing standard is a design or equipment feature which, for the consumer, yields the optimum satisfaction, all other alternative expenditures considered, within a given total of available income.

The major criteria in determining volitional standards are related not alone to the functions of housekeeping and family life but also to the culturally-determined value systems against which design features are judged.

We have already considered some of the ways in which volitional standards are determined in practice, and we recognize that for the most part such housing standards are voluntary but not necessarily enlightened. The practical problem for the researcher is how to develop design criteria, based on human reaction to housing features and combinations of housing features, which will guide householders to wise choices and which will thus ultimately influence the banker and the builder and the various governmental regulatory agencies.

Lest there be confusion over the term "design criteria," we might consider an example or two, oversimplified to make the point. The prospective home owner is sometimes presented with the choice of designs involving a front door entering directly into the living room with a vestibule or one with no vestibule. He must judge the advantages of a vestibule against the cost. He should be provided with objective measures of the advantages of a vestibule if he is to make a wise choice. How many times will the front door be opened under situations when there is a temperature differential between outside and inside? How much temperature change is involved with and without a vestibule; how significant is this change in terms of comfort and health, and the utility of parts of the room near the door? What is the effect in extra cleaning effort and in damage from wet and snowy feet, from rain and snow blowing in when the door is open? All of these factors can be subjected to analysis and some of them measured with fair accuracy.

Another choice often encountered is between a separate dining room and a living-dining combination room. Here cultural and practical considerations are combined. There can be measurement of the extra steps required in the case of a separate dining room, of the reduction in sizes of other rooms which would be required;

the extra furniture requirements and added maintenance in effort and money cost. But these disadvantages may be outweighed by a cultural background and a way of life in which formal dining ranks high in subjective value. There can be no direct measurement of those values, but other measureable considerations can be presented in such a way as to be useful to those who must make the choice.

Perhaps we could classify design criteria which are relevant to volitional housing standards as: cost criteria, functional criteria and personal-cultural criteria. The cost is the dollar cost of providing the feature, sometimes in terms of alternative costs or cost differentials. Functional criteria relate to the utilization of the feature and the complementary effects on other features, measured in terms of effort, comfort, health, safety. Personal-cultural criteria are subjective, and largely culturally derived.

# An appraisal method for measuring the quality of housing

ALLAN A. TWICHELL, *American Public Health Association*

Few if any domestic problems facing America are more urgent or complex than that of providing a decent home for every family. A major part of the population is affected; emergency and long-range programs are required; many types of public and private agencies must cooperate in working out sound policies and specific programs. The importance of a broad-front attack by all agencies concerned is increasingly evident, and is recognized on a

national scale in the Taft-Ellender-Wagner Housing Bill, which would lay the basis for a program aimed to meet the need within a generation.

The basic factors which make housing adequate or inadequate for human living are widely recognized as elements of healthfulness, health being broadly interpreted to include physical safety and emotional well-being. If the elements of housing can be appraised from a progressive

*Reprinted from* The American Sociological Review, *vol. 13 (June, 1948), pp. 278–287, with permission of the journal. Prepared for the journal from a paper read before the annual meeting of the American Sociological Society December 28–30, 1947.*

public health viewpoint, by sound investigative methods, a valid and broadly useful measurement of housing adequacy will have been achieved. This is the purpose of the procedures to be described.

Emergency housing may be catch-as-catch-can, but long-term programs for any community depend on systematic inventory of present housing, and on thoughtful appraisal of conditions under which families live. This calls for information of at least the following kinds:

Facts which will classify the physical quality of housing as to conformance with contemporary standards of healthfulness, safety and amenity. Such classification should furnish a guide to judgment on remedial measures needed: clearance and replacement of extreme slums, law enforcement and conservative measures in somewhat better areas, and prevention or control of blight in obsolescent but not yet substandard neighborhoods. Not only dwelling conditions but physical neighborhood environment must be taken into account in such classification.

Facts which will describe the relation between households and the dwellings they occupy, or in order to judge whether present facilities are appropriate as to type, size and cost; and to guide the planning of needed new facilities. Under this heading come such data as household size, composition, race and income; and dwelling type, size and rental value.

Facts which will guide corrective measures short of new construction, including enforcement of legal regulations and voluntary rehabilitation. Needed here are workable data on the areas and types of dwellings and families among which substandardness is concentrated; the relative importance of poor dwelling facilities, of insanitary maintenance and disrepair, and of crowded occupancy; with distribution of specific defects under each of these headings.

## Why is a new
## appraisal method needed?

Systems of housing classification in general use are too limited to meet the needs outlined above. Data from the customary legal inspections of building and health departments should be a mine of basic data, but as a rule they show only the violations of archaic codes that fail to give a balanced appraisal according to contemporary standards. American cities devote thousands of man-days every year to housing inspection service in their slums, but there are few communities in which this effort answers the questions on which housing and city planning programs must be built. Such questions, for example, as: Just what is the size and nature of the extreme slum areas? Who are the overcrowded families? Are any groups, as groups, subject to special hazard or discrimination? How much worse is district A than district B, and in what respects? How many dwellings should be designated unfit for habitation, and either demolished or rehabilitated? Aside from the condition of dwellings, are the problem areas, as neighborhoods, fit to live in? May structural improvements be nullified in the long run by adverse environmental factors?

The two most widely used systems of housing classification are the U.S. Housing Census and Real Property Inventory technique. These have been invaluable in showing the approximate size and nature of the housing problem and in mobilizing support for constructive programs, both nationally and locally. They have been found, however, of very limited value in dealing with the complex, highly localized problems that confront operating agencies like city planning commissions, housing and redevelopment authorities, and law enforcement bodies. The chief limitations can be briefly stated.

These systems largely or altogether omit consideration of neighborhood environment; and they cover too few qualitative items on the dwelling and its occupancy to measure compliance with contemporary standards. They lean heavily on gross indices of quality such as lack of toilet and bath, omitting lesser but significant defects which must be shown if an appraisal is to measure conditions above the slum level.

These systems report individual deficiencies without a means for measuring their cumulative effect. Tabulation by discrete characteristics makes difficult an overall comparison of housing quality. Limited tabulations of the data make it difficult to study many of the conditions on which local policy must be based. Finally, these systems do not distinguish clearly between family dwellings (with cooking facilities) and rooming houses. Fundamental problems associated with the latter type of housing, highly important in many cities, tend to be obscured in the statistics.

Techniques of market analysis recently developed by federal housing agencies deal most valuably with broad economic factors which may determine a city's growth and future housing demand, but insofar as they depend on Census or similar data for the measurement of present housing conditions, they are subject to the limitations previously noted.

In an era of precision chronometers, we in housing have been telling the time of day with an hourglass. We need something at least as good as the dollar watch.

## Purpose and content of
## the APHA appraisal method

In developing a new appraisal method, the Committee on the Hygiene of Housing has attempted to overcome the limitations and to consolidate the merits of earlier systems of evaluation. The object of its technique is to measure the housing needs of a community in such fashion as to serve the policy-making purposes of all agencies concerned with housing and planning; and, by providing information of wide value, to stimulate a joint attack on fundamental housing problems. The procedures are intended primarily for use in selected areas known to contain poor or mediocre housing, not for city-wide application. In obvious nonproblem areas, classification by less refined methods may be quite accurate enough. With some modifications the method can be applied to rural dwellings.

The technique reports and evaluates housing deficiencies which may adversely affect health, safety or essential livability. The principal features of the system can be summarized as follows:

Factors covered for dwellings include the usual survey items such as toilet and bathing facilities and overcrowding. New indices have been developed for condition of repair, safety of egress, adequacy of heating and lighting, sani-

tary condition of the premises, and other items significant for health and safety. Criteria of overcrowding have been greatly sharpened as compared with the usual single index of persons per room.

Descriptive characteristics such as family size, income, rent paid and type of structure are also reported, as a basis for classification and analysis of the deficiency findings. In presenting the dwelling results, distinction is made between the relatively fixed physical facilities and the changeable factors of occupancy and maintenance, since remedial action must recognize the difference between these two types of defects.

The physical neighborhood environment is recognized as an essential part of housing. Environmental factors appraised include crowding of the land by buildings, intermixture of business and industrial uses with residence, proximity to major traffic streets and railroads, adequacy of sanitary services, and availability of essential community facilities: schools, public transportation, parks and playgrounds.

The quality of housing is measured by a system of numerical scores. Schedule items calling for subjective judgment by the inspector have been largely replaced by objective items which give consistent results from different enumerators. This permits assignment of standard scores to deficiencies reported. Total scores for dwelling conditions, for environment, or for these two combined permit instant comparison between individual dwellings, blocks or larger areas; or between racial groups, housing by rental classes or other wanted categories. The scoring system will be more fully explained later.

Dwelling data are collected by inspection in the field, using separate schedules for structures and for dwelling units. Sampling is used where this is appropriate to the purposes of a given study. Field work of the dwelling appraisal may be combined with the legal inspection of enforcement agencies or may be done separately. Completed schedules from the field are processed and rated in the office, using a scoring template which greatly speeds and simplifies the work. Scores and descriptive information for each dwelling unit are transcribed to a Unit Appraisal Form, which summarizes the field data for ready understanding. The results are punched on cards for tabulation.

The environmental survey is conducted both by field observation and through maps or other office sources. An abridged series of environmental indices is often used to match the economy of sampling in the dwelling survey.

Either the dwelling or environmental appraisal can be made alone, but only the combined surveys give a full picture of the problem. For both parts of the appraisal, complete manuals of instruction are provided for the local staff.

The method can be carried out by personnel available among the regular staffs of city government departments. Costs of the appraisal have been of the order of two dollars per dwelling unit schedule.

The Committee on the Hygiene of Housing supplies consulting service of a member of its staff to advise on local adjustments in the technique, to help plan a study suitable for the purposes of the local sponsors, and to train the local staff in all the operations.

Results of the appraisal can be applied to a wide variety of housing and related problems. The method provides the technical basis for a broad attack by public and private agencies working in cooperation. In official surveys with the method, local health departments, housing authorities and city planning commissions have worked together most effectively – each contributing stipulated personnel or funds and each sharing in interpretation and use of the results.

This joint approach is believed by our Committee to offer the pattern for a new and fruitful type of cooperation in framing basic policies – cooperation not only among city government departments but broadened to include such private bodies as the real estate board, the council of social agencies, and the chamber of commerce.

## The rating system

Scores are a distinctive feature of the method. They consist of penalty points assigned to conditions that fail to meet accepted housing standards. The standards used have been adapted from our Committee's " Basic Principles

of Healthful Housing." Penalties rather than credit scores are used because the method measures departures downward from a level of acceptability.

It should be stressed that field enumerators do no rating. Their only duty is to observe and record the facts. Scoring is done later in the office, using templates which carry the rating scale for each qualitative item.

The penalty value assigned to each deficiency has been determined by a panel of consultants on scale-construction, including members of our Committee and others experienced in housing, public health and related fields. Each deficiency is graded according to the seriousness of that condition as a threat to health. or safety or as an impairment of comfort or general livability, in the judgment of these specialists. Each member of the panel on scale-construction evaluated separately every condition reportable on the field schedules.

In assigning scores to a schedule item, members of the panel used specially designed scale-construction forms which assured systematic reviews of essential factors. They considered, for instance, whether the field information is of a type tending to give reliable and objective data; whether the item can be expected to have constant significance as between the several types of dwellings, different localities, various economic levels and the like; and whether the item is a true reflector of the detriment it seeks to measure.

The provisional scale constructed by reconciling the panel's recommendations was first tested in 1943 by a pilot study at New Haven, co-sponsored by city and state agencies in cooperation with the Committee. Thirty-five blocks containing 2,500 dwelling units were selected to cover the range from high income neighborhoods to the worst slums of the city. A 50 percent sample of these dwellings was surveyed, and the complete environmental appraisal was made. The resulting classification of housing conditions was found by the reviewing group to correspond so closely to the manifest total character of the neighborhoods as to prove the essential validity of the scale.

Particularly noted by reviewers of this test were the accuracy with which the scale measured breaks in quality from block to block (or even within blocks) and the fact that the ranking of blocks by scores was heartily endorsed by officials with intimate knowledge of these areas. Minor revisions in the scoring values have been made as the result of subsequent experience in other cities.

Under the rating scale, factors of the dwelling or its environment which show no deficiency receive a zero score. Penalties for individual deficiencies range from one point to a maximum of thirty points. For example, scores of twenty to thirty points are assigned to conditions which offer extreme and ever-present threats to health or safety, such as overcrowding at the ratio of four persons per room or a single means of egress from a third floor dwelling unit. A penalty of ten points is charged for a toilet shared with another dwelling unit. Lesser deficiencies such as minor obstruction of daylight by neighboring structures, or closets lacking in part of the rooms of a dwelling unit, may be scored from one point upwards. Similar gradations occur in the environmental scores.

Under this scheme a total score of zero penalty points for a dwelling unit and its environment will indicate housing conditions which are excellent from the viewpoint of official agencies and are presumably free from defects of public concern. For broad comparative purposes, housing is classified into quality grades, depending on median total penalty scores. Class intervals of thirty points are normally applied to dwelling conditions and environment separately. Thus an area will fall in grade A if its median score is less than thirty points for dwelling or environmental conditions, which will normally mean a combination of minor defects not basically impairing the livability of houses or neighborhood. Scores of ninety points or over, which cannot be incurred except by combinations of basically substandard conditions that violate fundamentals of decent living, will put the housing in grade D. Thoroughgoing slum conditions are indicated by grade E, with median scores of 120 points or more for dwellings or environment.

Scores for certain items are modified to fit local or regional conditions. For example, the penalties used in New England for inadequate heating facilities are moderated for southern climates. Once the penalty scale has been adjusted and ratified for a given community, the scoring of field schedules becomes a rapid mechanical process, requiring no further judgment on the part of the survey staff. A clerk can score a dwelling unit in three to four minutes, or at the rate of one hundred units or more per day.

An auxiliary score is provided by designating basic deficiencies in dwellings when certain of the items incur penalties of ten points or more. In general, a basic deficiency is a lack of dwelling facilities, a state of disrepair, or a degree of overcrowding so serious that it has been widely recognized by public health and housing agencies either as calling for a correction order by a local enforcement agency or as justifying the removal of the affected family to other quarters if the condition is not or cannot be remedied in their present home.

In other words, a basic deficiency is a major substandard condition in the sense that progressive housing regulations acknowledge it as warranting drastic corrective action by an official body. Examples of basic deficiencies are lack of dual egress, a toilet outside the structure, and sleeping area of less than forty square feet per person. Dwellings with one or more basic deficiencies are designated as substandard, and this term takes on a definite official meaning. The number of basic deficiencies gives a measure of this gross substandardness.

A dual criterion of adequacy is thus provided: first, the penalty score which measures major and minor deficiences together, and second, the designation of individual basic defects that make a house substandard, regardless of the total score. The latter is an essential safeguard in this type of scale.

## Analysis and interpretation

A common weakness of housing surveys has been that when the results are presented it is difficult to tell what they mean and what should be done about them. A system of nonadditive, unscored items is likely to result in a bewildering array of maps, tables and graphs which fail to give a summary picture that will be understood by the busy public official or the layman. Under the present method, a small number of maps and charts will show both the relative quality and the specific problems of the housing studied. The procedures for analysis and presentation of results take full advantage of the fact that a scoring system expresses complex relationships in a single index figure, making it possible to consider broad policy before proceeding to details.

Total scores distinguish a good house and environment from a poor one. Subtotal scores show the broad nature of deficiencies, including the occupancy relation of a household to its dwelling. Item scores reveal the incidence of individual defects.

Analysis proceeds from total scores as a broad measure of quality to item scores as description of specific problems. For instance, the first map in the usual analytic series will classify geographic areas into quality grades according to median total scores for dwelling and environment combined.* This map summarizes the entire appraisal on one sheet, and tells how good or poor overall an area is for families to live in. It does not, of course, show what remedies are needed. The answers to this question begin to appear with the first two breakdown maps, one based on dwelling total scores, the other on total scores for environment. The first of these reveals the areas in which need for slum clearance or other extreme measures with respect to dwellings can be expected. The second map indicates, among other things, those areas where poor environment may be expected to preclude redevelopment with housing. Thus a broad understanding of basic problems begins to emerge from the first three steps of an orderly analysis. Further study in terms of subtotal and item scores will indicate the need for specific programs. Areas warranting slum clearance, for instance, are commonly delimited by study of subtotal scores for dwelling facilities, or of these scores in combination with the maintenance subtotal. Occupancy scores are excluded from such interpretation, as use-crowding of dwell-

ings has no causal relation to their physical fitness.

Enforcement programs and numerous other activities are framed from study of individual deficiencies, in terms of their percentage incidence and item scores. For instance, high penalties for inadequate means of egress will call the attention of the fire or building department to problems in its domain. A wide spread of infestation by rats has been taken in several cities as an equally clear mandate to the health department.

Quite as important for housing and planning policy as the study of geographic areas is the study of conditions which run with population groupings, types of dwellings or economic status. The housing and families surveyed can be readily grouped according to such classifications, and here too the analysis proceeds in an orderly way from general to particular. For example, in a community with a concentration of nonwhite families, a single tabulation will indicate whether they are the victims of discriminatory rents and whether there is need for more careful study of this problem. The tabulation needed is one which crosses total scores with rent paid, separately for white and nonwhite households. If results are similar for the two groups, it is evident that the minority group is not disfavored in terms of general quality of housing per dollar paid. If this is not the answer, and it seldom is, further breakdowns will quickly show the nature and extent of the discrimination. Armed with such measurements, a community is in a position for the first time to prove these inequities and to act upon them. Equally sharp understanding is readily gained of problems associated with tenement structures, with families living in light housekeeping suites, or with rents below any given level.

Because the technique provides enough information to register the difference between extremely poor, moderately poor and genuinely good housing, the results are quite sensitive to conditions far above the slum clearance level, as where obsolescence or incipient blight is of concern to residents but not to law enforcement

---

* Sixty-point class intervals are used for this combination.

agencies. Surveys depending on gross measures of quality such as absence of toilets or baths give little discrimination in this middle part of the quality range.*

It is hardly possible to overstress the importance of the fact that this new rating scale is sensitive to conditions in mild problem areas as well as in extreme slums. Heretofore we have had such crude instruments of measurement as to disclose the blacks and imply the whites of a quality scale, the middle grays being largely lost. Is it not partly for this reason that the idea of housing surveys has become associated in the minds of realtors and other conservative groups with the notion of slum clearance, and with public housing as the chief object of an official housing program? Who can wonder that these groups have lacked enthusiasm for housing studies?

With an instrument available which will measure conditions in the mild problem areas where law enforcement is not concerned, but where pocketbooks of owners are becoming sensitive, there is a basis for expecting private business and realty groups to support broad housing studies.

In short, the availability of an adequate measuring instrument makes it possible for the first time to put all the housing cards on the table in objective fashion, free from name-calling, and let every group concerned with housing and city planning – from whatever angle – work out its own part in a balanced program that starts with the extreme slums and goes as far up the quality scale as anyone may find it desirable to measure.

The content and procedures of the method have been described only so far as may give a general understanding of the machinery and results to be expected, for it seems equally desirable to sketch also the practical consequences that are following where the technique has gone to work. With this audience in particular, however, it is a matter of regret not to consider more fully such things as schedule design, scale construction, devices evolved to

expedite the work, theory and practice in tabulation and various other matters of methodology which have occupied a major part of our Committee's staff efforts for the past seven years. In several of these matters we believe that contributions have been made of general utility to investigators in the social sciences. However, many of these things can be read in the published manuals of the technique, and at least one of today's discussants should be qualified by previous study of the manuals to give a methodological critique of the procedures.

One item of mechanics, however, seems worthy of special mention to this group. From the outset, our Committee was determined that all users of the method should enjoy the speedy and flexible analysis which comes from use of statistical punch cards rather than manual tabulation. At the same time we recognized that many surveys, at least in small communities, might not have access to machine tabulation. We therefore experimented with alternative use of the marginally punched card, a cheap and simple instrument not seriously esteemed by many investigators. The fact that recorded data can be read in the mass from the edges of these cards conveys an important advantage which has been surprisingly overlooked. This characteristic makes it possible to apply a geometric principle of diagonal division – familiar to every engineering draftsman – to produce from the sorted cards an instantaneous scale reading of percentage distributions. This eliminates many counts and the calculation of percentages. With this characteristic of the marginal punch card recognized and exploited by a simple scaling device, our staff and local users of the technique have in some instances chosen the marginal punch card, not as a makeshift substitute for machine tabulation, but as a preferable method of analysis.

## Application to administrative policy

There are some rather simple tests of a use-

---

* For instance, the general map produced by local study of Housing Census data for Los Angeles as an implied measurement of housing quality suggests the vast majority of that city to be of the best grade of quality, with one unbroken area of this grade almost fifteen square miles. Who can believe that there is even any five-mile square section of any American city without internal differences that are significant for public policy?

ful housing survey. First, does it answer the questions on which housing policy must be based – the questions that decide where money and manpower will be spent? Second, do the answers make sense? Are the statistics produced satisfactory to those who know the community? If these two things are not true, no appraisal is worth making, nor is it cheap no matter how little it may have cost. Third, is the cost commensurate with the information produced? Fourth, is the resulting information of a kind which tends to stimulate action? It is one purpose of this paper to indicate that affirmative answers to these questions are characteristic of studies by the system under discussion.

One reviewer of the method has well said, "It would be a pity if the years of time and effort put into the development of this appraisal scale resulted merely in an intricate tool to show how bad the slums are." Were this the only result, the work would indeed have been ivory tower. The effects, however, are quite otherwise.

For example, in Milwaukee not only have areas of slum clearance and rehabilitation been delimited in cooperative studies initiated by the health department, but problems of policy were so clearly brought out in relation to many other agencies that an interdepartmental coordinating body has been created to frame a concrete ten-year program of reconstruction, rehabilitation and control for the areas affected.

In the currently important field of urban redevelopment by private capital, major cities are using the method for the basic task of selecting reconstruction areas for certification to redevelopment authorities. This is among the uses in Milwaukee. Philadelphia is engaged in a large study for this purpose, co-sponsored by the city planning commission and redevelopment authority. Plans have been laid for a similar study in Washington, D. C.

In Los Angeles, the method has been used by the housing authority and health department to select families most in need of rehousing and to qualify them for admission to public housing projects. A systematic plan for rehabilitating houses thus vacated, when these are salvageable, has restored hundreds of dwelling units to the usable supply. In the same city, it has been demonstrated that overcrowding among Negroes and Mexicans, while prevalent to roughly the same degree, is due to wholly different causes. Negro households are crowded because families of normal size are crammed into one or two-room units. Mexican families, on the other hand, generally have dwellings of normal size, but 70 percent of the families contain six persons or more. These factors, combined with income and other characteristics revealed by the study have profound implications for public policy, ranging from questions of dwelling design to possible methods of finance.

In Los Angeles also, the findings have been used by the health department to demonstrate to the city council that specific sanitary problems extend into areas and types of accommodations not previously recognized as deficient. As a result, inspection personnel and the enforcement program have been substantially enlarged, and housing regulations are being restudied to plug their loopholes.

In New Haven, not only was the obvious fact shown that three-fourths of the families in slum and substandard areas pay less than $25 a month for rent, but also that these families have less than one chance in five of getting a house not substandard in the official sense described in an earlier paragraph. This is a potent argument against those glib folk who would consider the housing problem to be solved with $60 rents. Occupancy scores disclosed that 54 percent of large households in these areas are so crowded as to warrant their admission to public housing projects on that basis alone. Such evidence has led the housing authority to include an unusually high proportion of large dwelling units in its plans for projects that are ready to build when a national housing program comes out of mothballs.

The list of impacts on local behavior could be extended to describe the St. Louis scheme for basing the enforcement of a new housing ordinance on findings of this survey method; and Battle Creek's community council of over forty agencies joining with the health department to determine a practicable housing program for that city and its county; and the plans of state groups in Colorado and New Jersey to measure the housing need among small town and rural populations, including migrant farm laborers, to the end that regulations and constructive measures may be shaped to meet these long-neglected needs. It is flesh-and-blood reactions such as these which have led the U.S. Public Health Service to offer instruction in this appraisal technique at its national in-service training center for professional personnel of public health departments – a move which should materially speed the general adoption of these procedures.

The method has been used thus far primarily by official municipal agencies for programs of the types described. Limited studies, however, have been made by other groups, including university research departments. Further experimental studies by such groups appear to offer promise. For example, it would seem that this technique might supply all or part of the housing component of studies measuring the relation between housing and specific diseases, or the contribution of inadequate housing to emotional stress and family maladjustment.

## Summary:
## significance for local programs

Systematic information is a key to results. It becomes possible for the first time to map with accuracy the housing assets and liabilities of a city, to show clearly what the gross housing problems are and where they are concentrated. Manpower of enforcement agencies now largely wasted in nuisance inspection can produce basic information for shaping policy; a current inventory can be kept as a normal part of municipal administration, using locally available resources. Problem areas of the city can be classified according to the basic treatment they require: clearance – with or without rehousing – law enforcement, voluntary rehabilitation, protection against blight. Such classification is being made the basis of official programs. This has cash value. Costly improvements may not be enforced, for instance, in areas scheduled to be bought for early clearance.

Regulations and enforcement are directed to a purpose. Results of the appraisal can be used as a check on inadequate building and housing codes. The appraisal facilitates intelligent selec-

tion by the health, building and fire departments and other law enforcement agencies of houses subject to orders for condemnation or rehabilitation; and it supports such orders by objective evidence that should stand up in court. Enforcement can be tapered off in slum clearance areas and concentrated in substandard neighborhoods above the clearance level. A means is provided by which progressive health departments are resuming their proper responsibilities in housing.

Under a joint attack, each program reinforces the others. The appraisal puts housing standards to work on a broad front, providing the technical basis for a joint attack by all agencies concerned with housing and planning. It becomes possible for regulatory and constructive agencies to buttress one another. Where the worst slums of a city are beyond redemption through law enforcement by health and building authorities, and are so declared by agreement of these agencies, powerful leverage is brought to bear in support of needed slum clearance and rehousing. Agencies with a secondary or incidental housing responsibility – such as welfare and social work bodies – will benefit by adoption of improved official standards developed from the appraisal. Data on punch cards can be used for special purposes by welfare bodies, housing management, tax officials, and others. New housing surveys need often not be made for special purposes. The system is flexible enough to carry special information for secondary users if they share in planning the appraisal.

The method helps to put in the local community, where it belongs, both the ability to evaluate its housing problem and the responsibility for framing a program suited to its own needs. State or federal help can be based on the demonstrated need, but imported schemes can be intelligently criticized on the basis of joint thinking by local groups.

These things are happening in progressive cities. In communities where the method has been put to use, local agencies concerned with health, housing, and planning have found that they begin to think together when they work together around this new tool for measuring the condition of present housing. The existence of a sound technical instrument is carrying interagency cooperation beyond the realm of speeches at professional conventions and into the daily work of the health officer and building commissioner, the city planner, the housing authority executive and the director of social welfare programs.

The system is offered as one of the technical tools in that larger kit – including legislative, financial and administrative tools – which must be boldly put to work if we of America do actually intend to solve our housing problem within a generation.

# The quality of housing "before" and "after" rehabilitation

RALPH J. JOHNSON, HUNTINGTON WILLIAMS, M.D., and ROY O. McCALDIN

Health regulations governing existing housing began in this country some three hundred years ago and were well developed as long as a half century ago.[1] However, programs for the improvement of substandard housing by the enforcement of health and safety regulations governing existing housing have developed in this country only within the past decade.

The period since the end of World War II has seen the development of widespread recognition of the need to rehabilitate existing substandard housing, as well as to build new housing and carry out extensive slum clearance programs. Although housing rehabilitation is an accepted program for increasing the supply of satisfactory housing, relatively little basic information about that program is at hand. Questions such as the following are continually being raised: Is the quality of substandard dwellings significantly improved as the result of the rehabilitation effort? What quality of dwelling is it feasible to rehabilitate? Is the rent and quality of the dwelling so interrelated that the improvement merely results in forcing low-income families to seek other substandard quarters?

It was questions such as these that led the Public Health Service and the Baltimore City Health Department to investigate the change in housing quality in a pilot area in East Baltimore before and after rehabilitation. The primary purpose of the study was to determine the change in housing quality in a selected area before and after the enforcement of the Baltimore Housing Code and related ordinances and regulations. Second, an attempt was made to determine the direct effect of the enforcement on whatever change in housing quality occurred. And third an attempt was made to analyze the results to determine if questions such as those mentioned above could be answered at least for the Pilot Area.

The Public Health Service provided general direction for the study, supervision of the field work, and prepared the analysis of the data. The Baltimore City Health Department pro-

*Reprinted from* The American Journal of Public Health, *vol. 45 (February, 1955), pp. 189–196, with permission of the journal.*

vided the enumerators and related data and
assistance. The scale of the study was such that
conclusions as a result thereof cannot be assumed
to be representative of housing rehabilitation in
other cities or perhaps even in other parts of the
City of Baltimore. However, it does supply
some basic information which, if carefully considered, may well provide an indication of the
trend of results that may be expected in other
communities.

Only a brief summary of some of the findings
and procedures are presented in this paper. A
later publication will cover such items as validity testing, control procedures and findings,
rent and quality studies, and much more detailed and extensive information on the results
of the study.

## Method

The basic concept of the study is simple.
The quality of housing in the Pilot Area in East
Baltimore before and after rehabilitation was
measured by the use of the American Public
Health Association's Appraisal Method for Mea-
suring the Quality of Housing.[2]

*Appraisal Method* – The principal objective of
the Appraisal Method is to measure and evaluate the quality of the dwelling as it relates to
health, safety, and satisfaction in living. A
numerical score is obtained which consists of
penalty points assigned to conditions that fail
to meet reasonable contemporary standards related to the promotion and protection of the
health and safety of the occupants. Penalty
scores are used because the Method measures
departures downward from a base of acceptability. Improvement of housing quality is indicated by a decrease in score. Conditions of the
dwelling which meet the standard contained in
the Method receive a zero score and each reportable deficiency is assigned from one to thirty
points, according to its seriousness as a threat to
health or safety.

The Appraisal Method consists of the dwelling survey and the environmental survey. The
dwelling survey is subdivided into nineteen
items related to facilities, such as plumbing,
lighting, and heating; five items related to main-

tenance, such as deterioration, sanitation, and
cleanliness; and five items related to occupancy,
such as room and area crowding. The abridged
environmental survey was used in this study,
but it was not repeated at the time of the after
survey because no major plan or land use
changes occurred in the area during the interval
between the before and after surveys.

All told more than one-quarter million dwelling unit schedules in approximately sixty-five
cities have been completed using this Appraisal
Method. Nonetheless, the validity of the Method
was tested under the conditions obtaining in
Baltimore during the survey periods. A 10 percent randomly selected sample of both the before and after universes was resurveyed within
two weeks following the dates of the before and
after surveys. The total and subtotal scores
were compared on identically matched units.
The validity of the Appraisal Method as used
in Baltimore was substantiated, since the small
differences between the means of the before
and after total and subtotal scores and the
sample resurvey check of these scores was found
not to be statistically significant.

*Study area.* The area for study was named
the Pilot Area and was selected to be representative of a cross-section of substandard housing which for the most part it would be feasible to rehabilitate. The median dwelling score
by blocks varied from a high of approximately
155 to a low of about 45. Therefore, it can be
seen that the Pilot Area contained a wide range
of generally low quality housing.

*Normal deterioration and improvement.*
The before survey was made in May, 1951, and
the after survey was made in October, 1952.
During the eighteen month interval some
change in the quality of dwellings occurred as a
result of normal deteriorating forces. Likewise,
some improvement would have been made without the enforcement effort. Detailed consideration of these phenomena was beyond the scope
of this study.

*Control.* A control method was used to
determine the direct effect of the enforcement
effort on the change in housing quality and to
estimate the effect of normal improvement

actions. The control showed that the enforcement effort did have a direct effect on the improvement in housing quality and that normal or usual improvements were of some significance.

## Scope

The Pilot Area at the time of the before survey contained 1,042 dwelling units in 25 adjacent blocks on which the score was completed on 989 dwelling units. The after survey was made in the same area which then contained 1,017 dwelling units on which the score was completed on 976 dwelling units. About 90 percent of the dwelling units on which the score was not completed were vacant.

Accordingly, the scores of 989 units in the before universe were compared to the scores of 976 units in the after universe. The differences in these two numbers may be accounted for by conversions, change in basement occupancy, use or abandonment of third-floor dwellings, and different vacancies and percent of vacancies at the time of each survey. Although these two universes are not precisely identical, average and median scores may be compared without incurring significant error.

*Enforcement.* Originally it was planned to make the after survey only when all enforcement work had been completed. As the study progressed it became evident that it would be practical to make it at the end of eighteen months of enforcement effort. At that time, approximately 56 percent of the cases requiring enforcement were closed. We were informed by the staff of the Housing Bureau of the Baltimore City Health Department that most of the items in most of the remaining 44 percent of the cases were completed. The after survey was done then at a time which essentially represents the point at which considerable diminution of results are obtained as a result of effort expended. The effect of resurveying before all enforcement was completed was lessened by deliberately giving credit for improvement work which was in progress at the time of the after survey and upon which considerable progress had been achieved.

While it is not possible to determine the exact extent of these facts upon the results of the after survey, it is our opinion that if a similar survey had been made after all cases were closed, the median dwelling score would have been improved (i.e., decreased) by about 10 percent.

*Housing code.* The Ordinance on the Hygiene of Housing, the Rules and Regulations Governing the Hygiene of Housing adopted March 11, 1942, and to a lesser extent the Rooming House Ordinance and related rules, regulations, and ordinances, such as the Building Code, Fire Prevention Ordinance, and General Nuisance Abatement Ordinance of Baltimore comprise the legal bases for the enforcement effort in the Pilot Area. Special attention should be called to the fact that the Baltimore Housing Code and related ordinances and regulations do not establish the same standards or even cover the same items that are used as the base for fixing the penalty scores in the Appraisal Method.

Major differences between the Housing Code and the Appraisal Method relate to private bath, toilet, sink and wash basin facilities; and sleeping space, total area, and crowding provisions. For the most part the Appraisal Method is based on higher standards than those contained in the Housing Code, although the standards contained in the regulations authorized by the Housing Code were significantly raised on March 11, 1954.

## Results

Ordinarily, results of housing surveys obtained by using the APHA Appraisal Method are reported in terms of median scores. However, in this case presentation of median scores does not provide a sufficiently refined and understandable method of comparing the quality of housing in the Pilot Area before and after enforcement. Accordingly, an average penalty score was calculated for each item in the before and after survey. The average score for each item was obtained by multiplying each penalty by the number of times it occurred and dividing that figure by the number of dwelling units in the universe.

The average penalty scores before and after are listed in Table 1.

## TABLE 1
### Average Scores*

|                | Before | After |
| -------------- | ------ | ----- |
| Dwelling total | 93.75  | 60.51 |
| Facilities     | 51.47  | 44.56 |
| Maintenance    | 34.76  | 8.97  |
| Occupancy      | 7.52   | 6.98  |

*Improved conditions are indicated by a numerically lower score.

The mean subtotal scores for facilities, maintenance, and occupancy in the before and after surveys were tested to determine whether the differences between the before and after mean subtotal scores are statistically significant. As a result, it appears that there is less than one chance in a hundred that the observed differences between the before and after mean subtotal scores for facilities and maintenance are not significantly different from zero. In other words, the differences between the before and after average scores for facilities and maintenance are statistically significant. It also appears that there is less than one chance in a hundred that the observed difference between the before and after mean subtotal scores for occupancy is significantly different from zero. In other words, the observed difference between the before and after average scores for occupancy is not statistically significant.

Table 2 contains a detailed breakdown of the average score before and after for each of the twenty-nine items in the dwelling score. A detailed explanation of each item may be found in the APHA publications describing the Appraisal Method.[3]

As can be noted from Table 2, the average total dwelling penalty score decreased (i.e., improved) from 93.75 to 60.51 or 35.5 percent. The average penalty score for facilities decreased from 51.47 to 41.56 or 13.4 percent. The average penalty score for maintenance items decreased from 34.76 to 8.97 or 74.2 percent. Although the decrease in occupancy score from 7.52 to 6.98 was not statistically significant, at least it shows that the enforcement effort did not result in an increase in overcrowding.

For ease of consideration the nineteen items under facilities are separated into four groups as follows: Sanitation, Heat and Light, Design, and Fire Safety. Table 3 contains the breakdown of these items.

While the average subtotal score for facilities decreased only 13 percent, there was approximately a 36 percent reduction in the average penalty score for "Sanitation" items and approximately a 29 percent reduction in the average penalty score for "Heat and Light" items. On the other hand, there was virtually no change in the facilities scores due to "Fire Safety" and "Design" items. In other words, the change in facilities score in this case essen-

## TABLE 2
### Average Scores

| Item | Before | After |
| ---- | ------ | ----- |
| **Facilities** | | |
| 1. Structure, main access | 0.18 | 0.18 |
| 2. Water supply (source for structure) | 0.01 | 0.00 |
| 3. Sewer connection | 0.01 | 0.00 |
| 4. Daylight obstruction | 0.01 | 0.01 |
| 5. Stairs and fire escapes | 8.11 | 8.83 |
| 6. Public hall lighting | 0.74 | 0.45 |
| 7. Unit: location in structure | 0.05 | 0.08 |
| 8. Kitchen facilities | 0.59 | 0.31 |
| 9. Toilet (location, type, sharing) | 4.55 | 1.84 |
| 10. Bath (location, type, sharing) | 3.89 | 2.39 |
| 11. Water supply (location and type) | 1.60 | 0.89 |
| 12. Washing facilities | 5.04 | 4.63 |
| 13. Dual egress | 11.61 | 10.78 |
| 14. Electric lighting | 0.06 | 0.03 |
| 15. Central heating | 0.94 | 0.82 |
| 16. Rooms lacking installed heater | 2.79 | 1.90 |
| 17. Rooms lacking window | 2.86 | 3.13 |
| 18. Rooms lacking closet | 4.53 | 4.28 |
| 19. Rooms of substandard area | 3.90 | 4.01 |
| 20. Combined room facilities | — | — |
| Subtotal facilities | 51.47 | 44.56 |
| **Maintenance** | | |
| 21. Toilet condition index | 0.91 | 0.21 |
| 22. Deterioration index | 23.20 | 5.22 |
| 23. Infestation index | 2.16 | 0.39 |
| 24. Sanitary index | 4.56 | 1.60 |
| 25. Basement condition index | 3.93 | 1.55 |
| Subtotal maintenance | 34.76 | 8.97 |
| **Occupancy** | | |
| 26. Room crowding persons per room | 1.71 | 1.55 |
| 27. Room crowding: persons per sleeping room | 2.59 | 2.23 |
| 28. Area crowding: sleeping area per person | 1.63 | 1.37 |
| 29. Area crowding: nonsleeping area per person | 0.90 | 1.01 |
| 30. Doubling of basic families | 0.69 | 0.82 |
| Subtotal occupancy | 7.52 | 6.98 |
| Dwelling total | 93.75 | 60.51 |

tially represents improvement in plumbing, heating, and lighting conditions.

## TABLE 3
*Facility Scores by Special Groups*

| | Before | After |
|---|---|---|
| **Sanitation** | | |
| Washing facilities | 5.04 | 4.63 |
| Toilet (location, type, sharing) | 4.55 | 1.84 |
| Bath (location, type, sharing) | 3.89 | 2.39 |
| Water supply (location and type) | 1.60 | 0.89 |
| Kitchen facilities | 0.59 | 0.31 |
| Water supply quality | 0.01 | 0.00 |
| Sewer connection | 0.01 | 0.00 |
| | 15.69 | 10.06 |
| **Heat and Light** | | |
| Rooms lacking installed heater | 2.79 | 1.90 |
| Central heating | 0.94 | 0.82 |
| Public hall lighting | 0.74 | 0.45 |
| Electric lighting | 0.06 | 0.03 |
| | 4.53 | 3.20 |
| **Design** | | |
| Rooms lacking closet | 4.53 | 4.28 |
| Rooms of substandard area | 3.90 | 4.01 |
| Rooms lacking window | 2.86 | 3.13 |
| Structure, main access | 0.18 | 0.18 |
| Unit location in structure | 0.05 | 0.08 |
| Daylight obstruction | 0.01 | 0.01 |
| | 11.53 | 11.69 |
| **Fire Safety** | | |
| Dual egress | 11.61 | 10.78 |
| Stairs and fire escapes | 8.11 | 8.83 |
| | 19.72 | 19.61 |
| Total | 51.47 | 44.56 |

By far the largest percent improvement (74 percent) was represented by the decline in score due to " Maintenance " items. The five maintenance items in the appraisal schedule represent conditions indicative of the state of repair and cleanliness of the dwelling. The deterioration score, item number 22, refers to the physical condition of walls, ceilings, floors, steps, and windows. In a sense these maintenance items may be considered to measure the degree to which the dwelling is restored to its original condition.

## Comments

*Certain score interpretations.* The after score for six items was higher than the before score. Although the score of some of these items could not have been expected to have decreased because there were no ordinances or regulations pertaining thereto, these scores actually increased slightly. An analyses of these unexpected changes revealed that the changes are not statistically significant in any case.

*Rent and quality.* Gross and shelter rents were reported on about two-thirds of the dwellings in the before and after universes. The average shelter rent for the before universe increased $6.40 per dwelling unit per month from $36.40 before, to $42.80 after. The average gross rent increased $5.70 per dwelling unit per month from $48.20 before, to $53.90 after.

The residential rent index in Baltimore increased 6.5 percent during the enforcement period. When the recorded average rent increases are adjusted for the general rent increase, only a little more than half the actual rent increase may be attributable directly to the enforcement effort. In the consideration of rent change, however, it must be borne in mind that rent control existed in Baltimore during the time of the enforcement effort.

Extensive studies were made in order to determine whether there was a relationship between housing quality and rent. Briefly, it may be reported here that no reasonable relationship between rent and housing quality existed in the Pilot Area either before or after enforcement. This is true even when identically matched dwelling units are compared. It is also true when the number of rooms in the dwellings are held constant and the subtotal occupancy scores are excluded from the total penalty score. This would appear to indicate that there is opportunity for the improvement of at least some substandard dwellings without the rent being raised in direct proportion thereto.

*Owner-renter relationship.* Both the before and after universes showed 41.5 percent owner occupancy. Therefore, it may be logically assumed that the net effect of the enforcement effort was such as to not result in the forced sale of a significant number of dwelling units.

*Family income.* The median income of those families reporting income and living in the dwellings in the before universe in May, 1951, was $239 per month and $259 per month in October, 1952, for the after universe. This represents an increase of 8.4 percent. Since the general income level was rising during the enforcement period, it is apparent that either the majority of people living in the area remained there or if they moved they were replaced by families with substantially the same income.

Furthermore, comparison of the distribution of income for the before and after universes reveals virtually no change in the number of families with incomes below $150.00 per month and above $400.00 per month. These incomes account for approximately 14 percent and 10 percent, respectively, of the total number of families. This tends to show that the enforcement effort did not cause a displacement of even the lowest income families living in the area.

*General neighborhood appearance.* It was quite apparent that the enforcement effort not only improved the general appearance of the Pilot Area, but also brought about a changed attitude on the part of the residents toward their place of living. Unsightly sheds, fences, and debris were removed; litter was hauled away; flowers and grass seed were planted; paint was applied; and the whole complexion of the area improved. Several groups of residents bought vacant lots and turned them into flower gardens or play areas.

In short, while a substandard area was not changed into a beautiful residential neighborhood, the residents developed a new pride of occupancy. Surely this is an important intangible benefit of housing rehabilitation.

## Summary

The quality of approximately 1,000 dwelling units in 25 adjacent blocks in a Pilot Area in East Baltimore was measured by the APHA Appraisal Method, before and after the enforcement of the Baltimore Housing Code and related ordinances and regulations. The before and after scores and other related data were compared. As a result of this comparison, the following items are apparent:

The average total dwelling score improved about 36 percent. The average subtotal score for facilities improved about 13 percent. Most of this was accounted for by improvement in the scores of items related to the provision of heat, light, and plumbing fixtures. The average subtotal score for maintenance improved about 74 percent.

The average subtotal score for occupancy improved about 7 percent, but this change was not statistically significant. However, at least it did show that the enforcement effort did not result in increasing overcrowding. On the average, owner-occupants were not forced to move because owner occupancy remained the same at 41 percent.

Modest increases in rent occurred, but rent control was in effect during the enforcement period. The average shelter rent increased $6.40 from $36.40 to $42.80 per month. The average gross rent increased $5.70 from $48.20 to $53.90 per month.

Low-income families were not displaced by the enforcement effort. The median income of families in the pilot area increased about 8 percent from $239 to $259 per month during an eighteen-month period of generally rising incomes.

The examination of rent and housing quality revealed that they had no reasonable relationship to each other either before or after rehabilitation. This tends to indicate that there is opportunity to obtain compliance with minimum health and safety standards for at least some substandard housing without the rent being raised in direct proportion thereto.

The data indicate that the rehabilitation effort resulted in significant improvement of the quality of housing in the Pilot Area. As a matter of fact, the improved dwellings are healthier and safer places in which to live. Furthermore the improvement in maintenance scores alone should insure that the useful life of these dwellings as a decent place in which to live will be significantly extended.

# VIII

# Residential renewal

## The slum: its nature, use, and users

*JOHN R. SEELEY*

To cling to a dream or a vision may be heroic – or merely pathetic. Slum-clearance, slum renewal, or, more grandiosely, the extirpation of the slum, is for many planners just such a dream: brightly imagined, cherished, fought for, often seeming – but for stupidity here or cupidity or malice there – at very finger-tip's reach. To ask how realistic this orientation is, what is possible at what costs and to whose benefit, is almost as idle-seeming an enterprise to many as it would be to raise doubts about the sanctity of American motherhood or the sound-ness of the American home. If a direct chal-lenge to the orthodox view seems too bold, let us tease at the fabric of the dream only a little, to see how it appears – and perhaps still shim-mers – in the cooler light of moderately dis-interested curiosity as against the warm glow of programmatic commitment.

**I**

The very notion of a " slum " depends on a number of more primitive notions. We must invoke at least – (and I believe only) – the notions of

*Space*
*Population*
A *value-position* defining " goods " and " ills "
*Dispersion* in the distribution of any good (or ill) among the population so that, in that respect, all men are not equal
*Correlation** among goods (or ills) so that one good tends to be attended by another, rather than offset by an ill
*Concentration* (in space) of those who have the most (and also those who have the least) of what there is to get

---

* " Positive correlation," of course.

*Reprinted from* Journal of the American Institute of Planners, *vol. 25, No. 1 (February, 1959), pp. 7–14, with per-mission of the journal.*

Any alteration in any of the realities that lie behind these six terms changes what "the slum problem" is; the elimination of any corresponding reality eliminates slums; and anything short of that guarantees the slum's survival. It cannot be overemphasized that no change in the plane of living – as for example, the doubling of all real incomes – would remove the problem. It is not a matter of absolutes. In a society where nearly everyone walks, the man with a horse is a rich man, and the man without is a poor man; in a society where nearly everyone has (or could have) a car, the man who can only afford a bicycle is *by that much* disadvantaged, and, potentially, a slum-dweller. The criteria for what is a slum – as a social *fact* – are subjective and relative: for one brand of mystic this world is a slum (relative to the next) and for another there *is* no slum, because the proper objects of desire are as available in one area as another.

Since, for the planner, space is an eternal datum and population is also given, at least in the moderately long run, any attempt to "deal with" the slum must turn on affecting in some way one of the other factors. Since, commonly, the value-position from which goods or ills are to be defined is uncritically received from the culture or projected by the individual planner, this too appears as something given – although this unexamined acceptance undoubtedly leads to much of the defeat and frustration which the planner encounters and manufactures. We shall have to return to this question of values later, but for the moment we may ask, what is possible if indeed a single value-scheme – the value-scheme of middle-class materialism – is applicable? The answer, if the analysis is correct so far, is obvious: we can attempt an attack on any one or on all of the remaining factors: dispersion, correlation, and concentration. These are discussed in decreasing order of difficulty.

To attempt to diminish the dispersion in the distribution of any one good – say, money – is actually a matter of high politics rather than "planning" in the customary sense. Two courses are classically open politically: the periodic redistribution of goods gained; and the blocking of opportunities to gain them. An example of the first is the combination of income

taxation or succession-duties with "equalizing" distribution of the proceeds – as, for instance, by differential "social security benefits." An example of the second – insofar as it is effective at all – lies in antitrust or antimonopoly proceedings, more particularly in the form which they have taken in recent years, that is, the prevention of particularly blatant potential concentrations before they actually occur. Not only is this whole route attended by vexing ethical and political problems, but also limits are set for it by the culture and, in the ultimate analysis, by economics itself. We may or may not be anywhere near those limits in North America, but it is obvious that dispersion-reduction beyond a certain point may, in fact, reduce the total of what there is to distribute – may, in fact, reduce it to the point where the least advantaged are in absolute, though not relative, terms more disadvantaged than before. We may discover limits and optimum points by trial-and-error or experiment in the course of history, but this clearly falls outside the planning procedure. This leaves us with correlation and concentration to examine.

An attack upon the correlation of goods with goods and ills with ills, in the life of any person or group, is notoriously difficult. Nothing multiplies like misfortune or succeeds like success. As the work of Bradley Buell[1] so unequivocally demonstrated for the whole range of problems with which social work deals, disaster is so wedded to further disaster in the lives of families that the combined case-load of innumerable separate agencies in a city is very largely represented by only a small core of "multi-problem families," families in which economic dependency may be the child of poor nutrition and poor physical health and the father of overcrowding and desperate family relations and poor mental health – and so, in a new and horrible incest, in turn the father of its own father, more economic dependency . . . and so on. And what Buell finds for social work problems is not restricted to that field. Within single problem-fields themselves, diseases tend to follow diseases in the field of medicine, just as one bungled social relation generally follows another, as students of society observe, and one psychological catastrophe is the ancestor of the next in the case history of almost any psychiatric patient. Every social agency, every "caretaker institution,"* is concerned to break up or diminish these correlations or to palliate their effects; but the whole apparatus can deal with only the few, worst cases; and nothing short of a society quite different from any yet seriously contemplated is likely to make sensible inroads upon the fact of correlation itself. In any case, this too falls outside the domain of local, or even regional, planning. So we are left with geographic concentration as our last point, seemingly, of promising attack. And it is at this point, if I am not mistaken, that the weight of the planners' planning has so far largely fallen.

The problem of "deconcentration" may be seen as the problem of moving from the present state of a heterogeneity of neighborhoods each homogeneous within itself to a homogeneity of neighborhoods each heterogeneous within itself. Upon succeeding, we should no longer be able to write of *The Gold Coast and the Slum*[2] but only, perhaps, of the gold coast within the slum and the slum within the gold coast. It is hard to doubt that – if we are willing to pay the price – here we *can* be successful. And it is equally hard to doubt that some increases in positive goods and some diminutions in positive evils would follow upon such a geographic transfer of the "variance" in fortune from the "between communities" label to the "within communities" one.

No one, perhaps, has put the case for the positive benefits so well as Catherine Bauer who brings knowledge, experience, vision, and passion to her task.[3] She argues, in reality, from the full depth of her feelings, but, in form at least, from primitive democratic principles against the one-class, one-occupation, one-economic-level community and for the broad-spectrum neighborhood where a child may at least encounter the aged, the ethnically strange, the poorer, the richer, the better, the worse, the different, and, therefore, the educative and exciting. The essence of her argument, I think, is that since the efficacy of our type of democracy depends on the achievement of con-

sensus even in a highly differentiated society, whatever militates against "understanding" diminishes the national welfare. This is a telling point, especially if lack of direct exposure does militate against "understanding," and if increased exposure promotes it.

Another argument for "deconcentration" can be made, I believe, on negative grounds; and for some it may have considerable force. The argument is that the very concentration of evils or ills is itself an additional ill or evil – quite separate from the mere sum of the evils concentrated. I think this is a valid point. Anyone who has watched a child checking quite equably his separate bruises and scratches before bedtime, only to be suddenly overborne emotionally as their totality dawns upon him, will know what is meant at an individual level.[4] The pervasive air of squalor of a Tobacco Road or any of its innumerable counterparts is, I think, differentiable from the separately existent miseries that otherwise go to make it up.

However, even at this level of analysis, things are not so simple as they seem. If it is true that the concentration of the defeated and despairing casts a pall, a psychological smog, of defeatism and despair, it is also true that "misery loves company" and that support to bear the hurt comes chiefly from the hurt. Beyond this, awareness of one's disabilities and disasters is heightened if they must be borne in the presence of the able and successful; and this awareness – unless it can lead to a remedy – is itself an additional, and perhaps disabling, disaster. It is also to be noted that to the extent that compresent misery adds to misery at one end of the scale, the "slum," compresent abundance adds to the sense of abundance and security at the other end, the elite community or "gold coast." Thus, at the very least, "deconcentration" is not likely to be an unmixed good to anyone or even a mixed good to everyone.

Things are much less simple again if we are willing to be realistic and to recall for re-examination one of the premises accepted for the sake of argument earlier: that the question may properly be examined at all in the light of the planner's value-system, or the one he as-

---

* To use the phrase of Eric Lindemann.

sumes to represent the society at large. The first possibility we shall not even examine; few would argue seriously that an urban plan should rest ultimately purely on the private preferences of the urban planner who plans to please himself. The second is worth some study.

It is a persistent illusion characterizing, I believe, only the middle-class meliorist, and only the middle-class meliorist in America – where it is least true! – that there is some particular case-applicable value-system that may be ascribed to the society at large. I do not doubt that *at a very high level of abstraction* consensus around value-statements can be obtained: America believes in justice; it simply divides on segregation. America believes in due process; it divides, however, on the propriety of what happens at many a Congressional investigation. What is at issue regarding the slum is a case and not an abstraction, and around it Americans divide, not simply in terms of slum-dwellers versus non-slum-dwellers, but within as well as between both groups.

It must be recognized at the outset, I believe, that the slum is almost as much a " social necessity " for some sizable segment of the elite as is, say, an adequate, centralized, and appropriately located medical center. I do not mean this only in the relatively trivial sense, referred to earlier, in which those who enjoy the greater proportion of social goods also desire protection against the debris entailed in their production. I mean it in the quite literal sense that, like the supermarket in its locus, or the central business district in its locus, the slum provides on an appropriate site a set of services called out by, produced for, delivered to, and paid for by the selfsame elite whose wives are likely to adorn with their names the letterheads of committees to wipe out or " clean up " the slum. Many of the services provided by the slum are not within the monetary reach of slum people: the bulk of the bootlegging, the call-girl services, a great part of what some feel able to call " vice," the greater part of the gambling, and the whole set

of connections that connect the underworld with the overworld serve the latter rather than the former, and are as much a response to effective (that is, money-backed) demand as is the price of a share of A. T. & T. or General Motors.

Given this " effective demand," taking it for granted that such demand will indeed call out " supply " somewhere, the question for the planner – at least in the moderately long run – must not be *whether?* but *where?* To the degree that the services are highly specialized, as many of them are,* there seems no economically appropriate locus for them too far from the core of the central city proper. To the degree that the services are not so specialized, they will generally have already found their way – by a combination of economic logic with police pressure – to the ring of satellite municipalities immediately outside the city itself.

If these services, and a whole chain of other " opportunities " that the slum presents, were solely of interest and profit to an elite group who already had most of what there was to get, a case might be made out for the abolition of the slum (if possible) as being in the public interest. (There is a sense in which this is true just as, no doubt, sinlessness or prohibition are in the public interest.) But this view of a one-sided exploitative interest in the maintenance of the slum by *outside* landlords or " service " users simply will not fit the facts. The facts are that the slum-dwellers also have sizable investments, of interest, of sentiment, and of opportunity, both in the site of these services and its appurtenances and in the way of life that goes on there.

Slums differ, of course, and I have lived intensively only in one, Back-of-the-Yards, Chicago, in the early forties, and, together with others,[5] have studied another, " Relocation Area A " in Indianapolis. I do not intend to give in detail any account of the former, especially as the main features of a somewhat similar area were sketched in William Foote Whyte's *Street Cor-*

---

* Compare, for instance, the (twelve at least) institutionalized sets of provisions for sex satisfaction demanded and supplied in a large mid-Western metropolis simply out of the changes to be rung on gender, race, and activity as against passivity. Omitting further

variations and refinements, and using an obvious code, we have: (MNA–MNP), (MNA–MWP), (MNP–MWA), (MWA–MWP), (FNA–FNP), (FNA–FWP), (FNP–FWA), (FWA–FWP), (MN–FN), (MN–FW), (MW–FN) and (MW–FW).

*ner Society.*[6] Something of the intensity, excitement, rewardingness, and color of the slum that I experienced is missing from his account of his slum, either because his *was* different or because sociological reporting militates against vibrancy of description (or, perhaps, because we cut into the material of our participant-observer experience in different ways). In any case, I would have to say, for what it is worth, that no society I have lived in before or since, seemed to me to present to so many of its members so many possibilities and actualities of fulfillment of a number at least of basic human demands: for an outlet for aggressiveness, for adventure, for a sense of effectiveness, for deep feelings of belonging without undue sacrifice of uniqueness or identity, for sex satisfaction, for strong if not fierce loyalties, for a sense of independence from the pervasive, omnicompetent, omniscient authority-in-general, which at that time still overwhelmed the middle-class child to a greater degree than it now does. These things had their prices, of course – not all values can be simultaneously maximized. But few of the inhabitants whom I reciprocally took "slumming" into middle-class life understood it, or, where they did, were at all envious of it. And, be it asserted, this was not a matter of "ignorance" or incapacity to "appreciate finer things." It was merely an inability to see one moderately coherent and sense-making satisfaction-system which they didn't know, as preferable to the quite coherent and sense-making satisfaction-system they did know. This is not analogous to Beethoven versus boogie-woogie, but more nearly to the choice between English and French as a vehicle of expression. (I will not even say which is which.)

Possibly I can give a clearer impression of the variety of dwellers in one slum and the variety of uses they make of it by quoting at length from the published report of the Indianapolis area that we studied. Section II of this paper is accordingly taken from that report.[7]

## II
## Types of slum-dwellers

There are always, of course, innumerable ways of classifying a population so immensely various as that of the slum, or, perhaps, of any urban area. We were struck again and again (both when we examined the way in which these people thought about themselves and when we examined behavior objectively) by two major differences: the difference between necessity and opportunity, and the difference between permanence and change.

Quite obviously, for many the slum constitutes a set of opportunities for behavior which they want (at least at the conscious level) to indulge in or to be permitted. For others, equally obviously, the slum constitutes a set of necessities to which, despite their wants, they have been reduced.

Similarly – though changes are *possible* – some are in the slum and feel they are in the slum on a temporary basis only, and others are there and feel they are there to stay. These distinctions establish four major types:

1. The " permanent necessitarians "
2. The " temporary necessitarians "
3. The " permanent opportunists "
4. The " temporary opportunists "

The meaning of these terms* will become clear as we proceed. Schematically, these might be represented as follows:

### TABLE 1
*Principal Slum Types: Area " A "*

| Time | Relation | |
|---|---|---|
| | *Necessity* | *Opportunity* |
| Permanent | 1 | 3 |
| Temporary | 2 | 4 |

Within each of these primary types, the data cast up a dozen or more fairly obvious subtypes whose characteristics are worth recording. The chart below (Table 2), which locates some twelve of these, fills in some details for the chart above

---

* The distinction—like other human distinctions—must not be "overworked." The difference between necessity and opportunity is largely subjective—a necessity welcomed with joy is often regarded as an opportunity; an opportunity accepted only with regret may be construed as a necessity. Even "permanent" and "temporary" refer largely subjectively to expectations and intentions, though they also partly (on that account) refer objectively to probabilities of later behavior.

(Table 1) and gives an orderly way of arranging what is to follow in this section.

## TABLE 2

*Types and Subtypes of Slum-Dwellers: Area " A "*

| Likeliest term of involvement | Primary reason for slum involvement | |
|---|---|---|
| | *Necessity* | *Opportunity* |
| *Permanent* | 1. | 3. |
| | a. The indolent | a. Fugitives |
| | b. The "adjusted" poor | b. Unfindables |
| | c. Social outcasts | c. "Models" |
| | | d. "Sporting Crowd" |
| *Temporary* | 2. | 4. |
| | a. The respectable poor | a. Beginners |
| | b. The "trapped" | b. "Climbers" |
| | | c. "Entrepreneurs" |

## 1.  The permanent necessitarians

Those in the slum permanently and by necessity evidently include at least three subtypes: the "indolent," the "adjusted poor," and the "social outcasts." In Area " A," these three subtypes seem to constitute the greater part of that "hard and unmovable core," which in turn constitutes about half of the population still living in Redevelopment Commission property. These are the people who feel they "cannot" leave the area, and who will or can do nothing to find alternative housing.

The "indolent" are those whose most striking characteristic* is a general apathy or immobility. Whether from inherited characteristics, disease, maleducation, malnutrition, the experience of perennial defeat, religiously founded "resignation," or mere valuation of other things – these are the do-nothings, those who "have no get up and go," those whose immobility is grounded now in their very physique or character.

Whatever the cause for the "indolence," and no matter what miracles feeding, better care, or therapy (physical or psychological) could accomplish for such people in the very long run, at least in the short run no plan looking to them for even moderate effort or initiative is a feasible one. "Care" and "custody" are the only public-policy alternatives to neglect;† rehabilitation, if possible at all, would be a long, hard, slow process of uncertain outcome or economy.

The *"adjusted poor"* represent similarly, though likely less immovably, a population living in the slum by necessity but adapted by deep-seated habit (and now almost by preference) to its ways. This group represents the concentration in the area of the destitute, or nearly destitute, whose adaptation consists in "acceptance" of the nearly unfit-for-human-habitation shacks and shanties, holes and cellars of the area – provided only they be available at "that low rent." Among them are many of those who value independence fiercely enough that they would rather cling to this most marginal physical existence in independence than accept relative comfort in dependency – even supposing they could have the latter. (At least this is their first and habitual reaction. Some few who were persuaded later to move into Lockefield Gardens are now glad they made the exchange of relative independence for relative comfort.) In this group are many of the very old, the "single" women with many dependents, and other persons prevented in one way or another from working continuously enough or at pay high enough to qualify for a more respectable poverty. Many, if not most of these, are still in the area in Redevelopment Commission property, "unable to move" and unlikely, in the absence of harder necessity than they yet know, to do so.

The last subgroup among the "permanent necessitarians" are the "social outcasts."‡

---

* It should not be overlooked that we have classified only by the most obvious characteristic. Many people have several characteristics, e.g., one could find examples of the "indolent-adjusted poor" or the "adjusted poor and trapped."

† "Neglect," as used here, means "leaving them alone" or "not interfering" with the "natural" process by which these people are able to get along and to subsist.

‡ They are so classified although some of them belong no doubt among the permanent opportunists (those who feel they *chose* the slum as a place of operation rather than that they were excluded from better areas) and some (those few who find their way to "respectable" roles) among the "temporary necessitarians." The peculiar arrow in Table 2 symbolizes this difficulty of classification.

Police evidence, tradition, and common gossip have it that these people were relatively prominent in Area "A" at one time, but left when redevelopment became imminent or even earlier. These people included the "winoes," the drug addicts, peddlers and pushers, the "hustlers," prostitutes and pimps, and others whose marginal, counter-legal, or "shady" activities both excluded them from better-organized neighborhoods and made the slum a more receptive or less rejecting habitat.

In any case, by 1955 these had largely disappeared from the area. By that date, all that was left of this group seemed to be those living in common-law relationships, a handful of "winoes," and a few others living habitually in unconventional ways, for whom the slum provided escape, refuge, sympathy, tolerance, and even some stimulation by the very fact of their being together.

## 2. The temporary necessitarians

The "*respectable poor*," who are in the slum by necessity but whose residence there is or may be more temporary, usually spend a good part of their lives in it – now in and now out, although mostly in. Though slum-dwellers, and often as poor financially as the "adjusted poor," these people are unadjusted or unreconciled to the slum in the sense that all their values and identifications and most of their associations are outside it. They pay their bills, mind their own business, remain well inside the law, hold the aspirations and, within their means, practice the lifeways of a socially higher class, most of whose members far outrank them economically.

Some of these wind up in public housing, but more often than not they resist such a solution, hoping that "things will take a turn for the better," a turn that will permit them to live more nearly where they feel they belong and how they feel they should. For many of these, redevelopment provided either the money (if they owned their homes) or the incentive or both that made that "turn for the better" reality rather than wish.

The "*trapped*" are people who, having bought a home (or had one left to them by a parent or relative) at a time when the area was not so run down, one day find themselves living right in the middle of a slum. Blight filters insensibly in and around them, destroying the value of their property. Though many remain, through a program such as redevelopment many more are induced finally to get out.

## 3. The permanent opportunists

Those who are in the slum to stay, primarily because of the opportunities it affords, are the fugitives, the unfindables, the "models" and the "sporting crowd."

The *fugitives* are really of two types: those whose encounters with the law or the credit agency have led them into a life of subterfuge and flight, more or less permanent; and those whose nature or experience has decided them to flee the exigencies of rigorous competition in a better area in their own business or profession.

The former, probably not numerous, are really using the possibility of anonymity which the slum offers. To them it offers literal sanctuary or asylum, a cover or protection from the too-pressing inquiries of the more respectable world. These people, poorly circumstanced for the most part, had also left Area "A" in large numbers before our study began.

The latter, seeking escape from the status struggles of the world outside, or looking for a more easily maintained economic niche, occupied some of the best property within the area, and when catapulted out by redevelopment, found successful ways to maintain themselves and even to enhance their position outside the area. Many of them were merchants, doctors, lawyers, or other professionals who had served that part of the population that was later to migrate to the "better neighborhoods" with them. (They resembled the "climbers" discussed below, except that they did not want or expect to escape from their refuge in the slums.)

Somewhat like the first group of fugitives are the "*unfindables*." By definition, we had no contact with them, although we did have contact with those who had had contact. From their descriptions, there is suggested the presence in the population (before the advent of redevelopment) of sizable "floating population," who could not readily be located, rarely got counted in any census, and lived a shadowy kind of existence both in terms of location and social identity. These were not so much people in flight as people whose individualism of outlook and whose detachment from urban ways led them to seek no clear social identity (or to operate under many). Some could be found by laboriously following a chain of vague touch-and-go relationships, some only by sorting out and tracing down a variety of "names" and nicknames under which each had serially or simultaneously lived. Most could not be found at all – with our resources or the census-taker's. These, too, had mostly disappeared from the area by the time we came, although some were left, and the memory of others was still green.

The "*models*" constitute a rare but interesting type. These are people who have somehow become, or conceived of themselves as, social or religious missionaries. They are people who stay in the slum (actually, or as they interpret their own behavior) primarily in order to "furnish an example" or "bring a message" to "the others," the "less cultured," or the "unsaved." Some of them are people who were first among "the trapped," but who have adapted further by finding a satisfying permanent life in the slum; the satisfaction consists in bring culture or religious light to "those still less fortunate." Some of them patently find some martyr-like satisfaction in such "service," but others more soberly find genuine relatedness and utility in this adaptation.

Some of these remained in Area "A"; some went early. Those who went seemed shortly to find themselves cast in the same role in their new neighborhoods.

Finally among the (relatively) permanent opportunists are the members of the "*sporting crowd*." This term, in local use, evidently connotes a range of characters noted primarily for their jollity and informality – perhaps a certain breezy offhandedness is their distinguishing characteristic – rather than for any necessary preference for illegal or marginal activities as such. They live in the slum for a complex of reasons. First, living in the slum leaves them more money to spend on "other things"; second, having spent a large share of their incomes on those "other things," what is left is

only enough for slum rents; third, the slum is the place to meet others similarly situated; fourth, the slum itself provides (or, rather, in the case of Area "A," did provide once) facilities for their pursuits, such as taverns, book-making and other betting facilities, and so on. Marginal to this type are those who have been described to us as ranging from "the rough-necks who make it unsafe for others to be in the area" to the less violent types who just create nuisances, which, as one woman explains, "... cause you to be afraid to have a friend visit, because you never know whether someone is going to walk in on you without any clothes on." The informality, rather than roughness or nudity as such, is the hallmark of this group.

These, too, by now have mostly fled the area.

## 4.  The temporary opportunists

It remains to describe the temporary opportunists, a most important group both because of their numbers and because the slum of these people is a way – perhaps the only way – to the pursuit of those things that American culture has taught them are worth pursuing: "self-improvement," independence, property, a savings account, and so on. It may be only for this group that the general reader will feel fully sympathetic, and it may be only here that he will ask himself, "How are these people to get where we want them to get, if we systematically destroy the slums which are the traditional, if unspoken-of, way of getting there?" The question is a good one, and the study leaves its answering to the wisdom of the agencies, public and private, charged or self-charged with such responsibility.

We find that in this group are three sub-types: the "beginners," the "climbers," and the "entrepreneurs."

The "*beginners*" are mostly the unattached immigrants to the city who have neither helpful kin nor access to powerful agencies of assimilation, such as churches and ethnic associations. The slum is simply their "area of first settlement" where they rest on arrival in the city not for "the pause that refreshes" so much as for the pause that instructs, the pause that permits them a precarious period in which to "get oriented," find a first job, and learn the elements of urban living. Many of these are young married couples, some with first children, trying to learn simultaneously to be citizens, husbands and wives, and parents in the urban manner. Their slim resources, financial, educational, and psychological, necessitate a place to stay that will not strain these resources much further; the slum furnishes an opportunity to rest, to gather fresh forces, and to prepare for moving on as soon as may be – if disease, misfortune, or the fortune of more children does not exert more "drag" than can be overcome. From this source the city replenishes its labor force at the lower economic levels, and its "respectable poor" and other types at the lower social rungs.

The "*climbers*" are somewhat similar to the beginners except that they may have been in the city for some time and that their plans are somewhat more long-term and ambitious. These are the ones who live in the slum in what amounts to a period of apprenticeship, self-denial and self-sacrifice with a view to accumulating enough goods, money, and know-how to leap later into a much "better" area, a considerably higher standard of living, and a much more "respectable" way of life. They are "saving" – out of the very stuff of their own lives – the material and nonmaterial means of achieving better housing, greater status, "success," and homeownership.

For many of these, the period of stay becomes protracted because the dream tends to become embellished even as savings accumulate, and the time to move seems always "a little later, when we have a little more." Redevelopment, for many of these, helped toward a settlement with reality by putting period to an unduly prolonged stay in the slums or overextended plans; for a few, it cut off the possibility of any great "improvement" at all, insofar as it caught them in the initial phases of their plans. Some of those thus "caught" simply moved into neighboring slums to begin again. Some abandoned plans for ownership and became renters outside the area.

Last are the "*entrepreneurs*," a special class of climbers, oriented similarly to the climbers, mostly more ambitious, but saving out of businesslike enterprises – rather than their own miseries – the wherewithal to escape misery in due time. Beginning usually as people of small financial means, they establish a small business or, more frequently, make the slum itself their business. They somehow (frequently by a kind of financial skin-of-your-teeth operation) get hold of a duplex or house that can be "subdivided." That part of it in which they do not themselves reside must, if possible, pay the costs of the whole, and moreover, yield "a little something" so that more property can be bought as time goes by. Often they purchase property, first, in the slum and, later, in better neighborhoods. In the case of at least one person in the area, a drug store was eventually purchased out of the money thus saved by living in the slums.

This kind of person lives a large part of his life in the slum, but usually leaves about the time he reaches fifty. He may by then own enough slum property to live very comfortably in a better neighborhood; or he may, out of his small-scale slum business operation, develop a larger business in a different area, becoming thus an undifferentiable element of the respectable business community.

### III

If the earlier part of this paper made – or even labored – the point that in no way within reach of local planning could the slum be "wiped out," and if the second part drew attention via a particular case to the general situation of a vast variety of people coexisting in the slum's complex fastnesses, what, it may be asked, happens when planned steps are nevertheless taken to "do something" about an area, in this case to "redevelop" it. No general answer can be given – it depends on the steps and the people – except that the greater part of what happens is a redistribution of phenomena in space. We say "the greater part of what happens" because, as is evident from the original report,[8] this is not all that happens: in the very act of relocation *some* "positive" potentialities that were formerly only latent are released or actualized. As far as the redistribution in space is concerned, it is hard to say whether it should be viewed as "deconcentration": it is rather like a reshifting and resorting, a speeding up of the city's "natural" ecological processes, with results both "good" and "bad," certainly unintended as well as intended. In this process, opportunities are created for some and destroyed for others, or very often for the same person; certainly, lifelong adjustments or habituations, comfortable and uncomfortable, productive and nonproductive, are overset, disturbed, interrupted, or destroyed. Moreover, in most cases one population is advantaged and another further disadvantaged, and it is not at all clear that the balance is tipped in favor of those who initially had least – perhaps, rather, the contrary.

# Economic aspects of urban renewal

*A. H. SCHAAF*

As of 1956, roughly 11 million nonfarm dwelling units in the United States were within the Census Bureau's definition of substandard.[1] These units and the blighted urban areas that contain them constitute a major domestic problem. Precise quantitative estimates of the causal effects and resultant economic costs of slums and blight are not easy to make. However, there can be little doubt that antisocial housing and environmental conditions sap an individual's economic productivity. They may also constitute a net drain on the community in terms of both the costs of direct public services and the efficiency with which the urban economy operates. Additionally, of course, important humanitarian and aesthetic considerations are involved.

The term "urban renewal" is used to denote various efforts and programs designed to alleviate these problems. In its broadest sense, renewal may be defined as any change in the characteristics of a given residential structure.* Such change may be accomplished through work done to the existing structure, i.e., rehabilitation, or through clearance of the existing structure and new construction, i.e., replacement. Thus renewal is used as a general term encompassing both rehabilitation and replacement.

## The role of public policy

It is of the utmost importance to recognize at the outset that the renewal of residential structures occurs constantly as a normal private market operation. Every time a homeowner modernizes his kitchen or a landlord paints his apartment house, some rehabilitation has taken place. Every time an existing house or apartment building is torn down and a new structure erected in its place, some replacement has oc-

---

* Urban renewal may refer to both residential and nonresidential land uses. The present study is concerned only with residential renewal.

*Reprinted from* Economic Aspects of Urban Renewal: Theory, Policy and Area Analysis, *Research Report 14, Center for Research in Real Estate and Urban Economics, University of California, Berkeley, 1960, pp. 1–9, with permission of the Center.*

cured. Such actions are taken voluntarily by the owners of the properties in the expectation that the cost of the work done will be more than justified by a resulting increase in the property's value or – essentially the same thing – by an increase in the amenities that the property provides its owner-occupant. If such were not expected, the action would not be taken.

The widespread existence of slums and blight in American cities is evidence that voluntary, privately initiated renewal has not been – and presumably will not be – sufficient to eliminate or perhaps even reduce appreciably the number of dwelling units that lie below generally accepted norms of minimum health and safety. Anticipated profits are the requisite for private market renewal, and the very existence of substandard housing and blight attests to the absence of profitability. This is not to argue that the real estate market is perfect or that there are no unexploited opportunities for profitable renewal. Many such opportunities undoubtedly exist.[2] However, the general quality range of the product that stems from the workings of the housing market is the result of the interaction of supply and demand forces. In any aggregative sense, it is absurd to argue that the existence of slums and blight is due to the failure of either current property owners or new investors to realize hitherto untapped profits through renewal.

The role of public policy is to bring about renewal in situations where it would not otherwise occur. Belief in the motivating power of the profit incentive leads us to presume as a general rule that privately initiated renewal will be forthcoming whenever profitable circumstances exist and that such circumstances are not present if public implementation is necessary. If renewal is to be accomplished in situations where it would not otherwise occur, changes in the variables affecting the private investment decision are required. Such changes are the function of the various public policies that have been devised in the urban renewal field.

Two main approaches have been employed in these policies. The *first approach* is that contained in the Housing Act of 1949. An agency of the local government, using eminent domain powers and subsidized by direct federal grants equal to two-thirds of total project costs, establishes an Urban Renewal Area with the advice and consent of the federal government, acquires all of the properties in the area, clears the existing structures, and resells the land to private developers at whatever price is necessary to insure that the profitability requirement of the private investment decision is met. In this approach direct public initiative is relied upon at the outset and direct subsidies in the form of writedowns in land values are used to stimulate the private initiative that enters the picture in the later stages of the development. The need for and use of such subsidies is simply the manifestation of the fact noted above that those situations in which public intervention is necessary are those where private market action would not otherwise be forthcoming due to the absence of profitability.

The *second approach* to the implementation of urban renewal through public policy is that contained in the Housing Act of 1954. In this legislation, certain areas may be designated as Urban Renewal Areas by a local government again with the advice and consent of the federal government. Two main types of federal assistance are then available. One consists of absorption of two-thirds of the cost of public environmental improvements in the area – landscaping, expanded recreational and educational facilities, increased maintenance and protective services, limited replanning of streets and spot clearance of nonconforming structures to enhance the seclusion and residential character of the area, and the like. The other is represented by the insurance of mortgages secured by either rehabilitated or newly constructed properties in the area by the Federal Housing Administration (FHA) as authorized by Section 220 of the National Housing Act. These two forms of public assistance – area improvements and liberal financing – are relied upon together with code enforcement as stimulants of renewal in the second approach. The owners of the properties in the area are to supply the initiative and supervise the renewal of their properties from the start. The public intervention that again is the indispensable stimulant for any action takes two forms – coercion through code enforcement and assistance through liberal financing and area improvements.

### The objectives of the present inquiry

The present study is divided into two parts. The first consists of an analysis of certain aspects of public policy in urban renewal. Based on the concepts and conclusions developed in this analysis, a framework is developed in the second part of the study designed to predict various quantitative effects that the implementing policies contained in the second public policy approach might be expected to have in an Urban Renewal Area.

The analytical part of the study deals with two main issues. The first relates to the question of whether to rehabilitate or to replace a given structure. As we shall see, this question – the determination of the economic feasibility of rehabilitation – is in large measure, although not exclusively or necessarily so, also a question of which of the two public policy approaches to use.

The second aspect of policy treated here deals with the effects of the implementing policies contained in the second approach – code enforcement, liberal financing, and area improvements – on private renewal investment decisions. We have noted the reliance on private initiative from the outset in the second approach and yet we have also argued that the properties in question are ones that cannot in general be expected to be renewed solely on the basis of private market decisions. The three implementing policies must act so as to alter the private decision framework, and we will attempt to analyze the nature and effects of such alterations.

The analytical framework that stems from the consideration of the above aspects of public policy is employed in the second part of the study for the purpose of making quantitative estimates in an Urban Renewal Area. In an area selected for illustrative purposes we will attempt to answer the following eight questions:

1. To what extent will the private entrepreneurship of renewal be forthcoming fol-lowing the use of coercion (code enforcement) and assistance (area improvements and liberal financing) both separately and in combination?

2. To what standards will the properties be renewed?

3. What will be the initial losses faced by the current property owners as a result of code enforcement?

4. How may these losses be affected by the provision of area improvements and liberal financing?

5. What increases in the market demand for the shelter amenities provided by the properties following renewal would be necessary in order to generate the private renewal of every property without loss to the owner?

6. What direct public outlays would be required to insure that all of the area's properties are renewed to a uniform standard following the use of the three implementing policies studied here?

7. What direct public outlays would be required for renewal of the area's properties if either coercion (code enforcement) or assistance (liberal financing and area improvements) are not employed as implementing devices?

8. What will be the relative roles of rehabilitation and replacement as the two methods through which renewal is carried out?

### Summary

The present study is analytical rather than descriptive. Thus, with few exceptions, there are no empirical "findings" to report. Rather, a condensed preview of the results of study, stripped of the many details and qualifications discussed in the main body of the report, consists of a summary of analytical conclusions and the resulting methodology they suggest for quantitative area analysis.

1. In the absence of any change in conditioning circumstances, private entrepreneurship of renewal will be forthcoming only if the value of the property following renewal exceeds the sum of the cost required for its renewal and its value prior to renewal.

2. Renewal may affect the value of the property chiefly in two ways. It may alter the market demand for the shelter amenities provided by the property and thus alter the income stream that the property generates – rents in the case of income properties and shelter expenditures (cash outlays and imputed costs) in the case of owner-occupied, single-family properties. It may also, by increasing the longevity of the structure, increase the period of years over which a given income stream applies and thus increase the present value of the income stream.

3. The presence of substandard housing and blight in a Renewal Area indicates that the above two effects have not been sufficient in the past to generate renewal and that public implementation is therefore necessary. Three general forms of public implementation are studied here – code enforcement, environmental improvements, and liberal financing.

4. Code enforcement implements private renewal initially by presenting the property owner with the alternatives of either complying with the code or withdrawing the property from residential use. Thus the precode residential value of the property is no longer a relevant consideration in the private market renewal decision. Private renewal is feasible, not necessarily as long as it is profitable, but only if it represents the owner's least-loss course of action. Compliance may also increase the value of the property in either or both of the two ways noted above but presumably not by enough to eliminate every current owner's capital loss else enforcement would not have been necessary. Current mortgage lenders may also share in the total capital losses that may result from code enforcement.

5. Environmental improvements increase the total shelter amenities offered by the properties in the Renewal Area and may thereby increase the demand for them. In this event, private renewal has been implemented since the values of the properties following renewal have been increased without an immediate corresponding cost to the property owners.

6. The availability of liberal financing implements private renewal by permitting a given cost investment in renewal to be amortized by smaller periodic outlays and thus by a smaller income stream – either rents of tenants or shelter expenditures of owner-occupants of single-family properties. The effects of the availability of liberal financing may also be thought of as increasing the present value of a given income stream and thus the value of a property following its renewal to the standard required for the provision of liberal financing.

7. The decision as to whether renewal will take the form of rehabilitation or of replacement is primarily determined by public policy since renewal in a Renewal Area occurs only as a result of public implementation. Certain areas may have a potential value that can be realized only through complete clearance and replanning, in which case different public policies are involved than those of principal interest in this study. In the aggregate, such areas are apt to be few in number. In all other potential Renewal Areas, the increase in the market demand for the properties following renewal may be expected to be limited, and the primary consideration of the property owners would be to meet the renewal standard required by public policy at the least possible cost. Thus the renewal standards are determined by public policy and the question of whether to rehabilitate or to replace a given property is decided within the private market on the basis of the comparative costs of the two methods of achieving the given renewal standard. Different public policies will result in different renewal standards and thus a difference in the relative prevalence of the two methods, but in general rehabilitation can probably be expected to predominate. Such a result is desirable from the standpoint of public policy objectives. Understanding of the reasoning that underlies the result will also improve techniques of preliminary area planning by public agencies.

8. As a result of the analytical conclusions summarized above, the following methodology for quantitative area analysis is adopted in the study:

a. Two renewal standards are specified. One is that required for code compliance. The other is that required for the provision of environmental improvements and liberal financing.

b. The renewal cost and property value magnitudes associated with each standard are determined as well as the values of the properties prior to renewal.

c. The magnitude of private renewal that will be forthcoming and the renewal standard that will be achieved in the case of each property are then estimated by determining the course of action that will maximize profit or minimize loss, as the case may be. Three general results are possible – private renewal to either of the two standards or withdrawal of the property from residential use and thus no private renewal. The framework developed for projecting the private actions that will result from public implementation also illustrates the effects that renewal may have on asset and market positions and provides estimates of the direct public outlays required for renewal in various circumstances.

## Rehabilitation vs. replacement

Viewed as a private investment decision, the question of whether to rehabilitate a residential structure or to replace it is simply a special case of the private renewal decision framework. If we let $V_1$ equal the prerenewal value of the property, $V_2$ equal its postrenewal value, and $C$ equal the structural renewal cost, renewal will be forthcoming as long as $V_2 > (V_1 + C)$, i.e., $V_2$ is greater than the sum of $V_1$ and $C$. The amount and type of renewal, including the decision of whether to achieve it through rehabilitation or replacement, would be that which maximized the difference between $V_2$ and the sum of $V_1$ and $C$, i.e., that which maximized profits. The simplicity of this statement belies its complexity. Replacement theory, like the general investment theory of which it is a part, is a very complex subject involving many questions relating to the costs of various courses of action, the values of the existing assets, the expected but uncertain future asset values that will result from the alternative courses of action, and the optimum final decision among a range of possible choices.

In the case of renewal of the type with which we are concerned, the problem is somewhat different. There are no expected profits and no renewal at all will be forthcoming in the absence of public implementation. Thus the ques-

tion of rehabilitation versus replacement, which is really just a part of the broader question of the determination of renewal standards in an Urban Renewal Area, is primarily a function of public policy considerations. Such considerations are of two main types – those that relate to the area as a whole and those that relate to any given property in the area. By examining these considerations we will be able to arrive at a resolution of the rehabilitation versus replacement question that is simple enough to be useful for preliminary area planning and is at the same time defensible and realistic as a projection of the course that would actually be decided upon by the owners of Renewal Area properties following public implementation. It is also one that leads to the most desirable result from the standpoint of the reason for the use of public intervention in the first place – the promotion of the general welfare.

## Area considerations

As will be more fully discussed below, rehabilitation and replacement are simply two of many classifications that can be used to categorize the type and amount of renewal work done to a given property. The main reason for the distinction so often made between them stems largely from area-wide considerations. Rehabilitation precludes the complete replanning of the area that is possible in the case of replacement. In some instances, such replanning may be quite desirable on the basis of considerations relating to the private investment attractiveness of renewal as well as to the objectives of public policy.

In the first place, there may be certain areas with a location that is uniquely suited to attract higher-income occupants but only if the entire area is cleared and replanned. All surrounding blight must be eliminated, and a complete change in occupancy and environment is required. The massiveness of the task effectively blocks private entrepreneurship and necessitates the eminent domain powers and large amounts of at least temporary financing that only direct public action can supply.

A second consideration, closely related to the first, involves density. Although it may be possible in certain cases to alter the number of dwelling units that an existing structure contains, rehabilitation typically forestalls major increases in densities. This is particularly apt to be true in blighted areas. Typically, few unexploited possibilities remain for increasing the number of dwelling units in the structures in such areas. Indeed, any changes resulting from rehabilitation would probably be more apt to result in a reduction in the number of dwelling units or, more likely, a reduction in the number of persons currently housed in the area due to the enforcement of codes relating to maximum permissible unit occupancy. However, from the standpoint of city planning considerations and as a stimulant to private renewal investment, a substantial increase in density may be indicated. Again, complete clearance and replanning would probably be required in order to attract and efficiently accommodate the greater number of occupants that are desired.

Finally, it is possible that the desired place of the area as a part of the structural shell within which the metropolitan economy functions can be achieved only through complete clearance and replanning. The existing street and land use patterns may be hopelessly out of step with the city's master plan. In this event, rehabilitation would only compound the problem by increasing the sunk investment in an area that is already obsolete and inefficient from the standpoint of the long-range land use objectives of the city as a whole.

The presence of any of these three factors may be of sufficient importance to rule out rehabilitation. It may also constitute a qualification of our earlier statement that, in general, publicly implemented renewal is by definition unprofitable. It is possible that once the area has been completely cleared and replanned, its reuse value will be great enough to eliminate the need for a write-down of land values. The only reason for the previous absence of private market action was the massiveness of the job and the absence of the public's eminent domain

powers and greater risk-bearing ability. In this regard, however, it is well to note briefly certain differences between the three considerations discussed above.

The second and third considerations – relating to greater density and improved efficiency, respectively – pertain to renewal achievements that represent real, aggregative gains. Greater intensity of land use, where appropriate, and improvements in the efficiency of carrying on economic activity in the metropolitan area can be expected to reduce public service and private factor costs and increase the productivity of the urban economy. If renewal results in an aggregate improvement in housing conditions, long-run increases in human productivity and reductions in public service costs might also be realized. Only in these ways can urban renewal ever partially or completely " pay for itself " in any aggregative sense. Cost reductions and expanded productivity are the real benefits that may result from the expenditures for new construction and extinguished existing assets that are required for urban renewal.* To say these things, however, is not to measure them. Quantitative determination of the benefits of urban renewal is most complex and probably can at best represent only tenuous approximations.

The first consideration – the possibility of attracting higher-income occupants – is a different matter. Although a number of side effects are possible, the principal result of this occurrence is simply a transference of the residential location of upper-income groups and a similar shift in the residence of the low-income pre-renewal occupants of the area. Such a dual shift could result in a gain to a particular city if it occurred across city boundaries. But this gain and the resulting rise in land values in the Renewal Area is not an aggregative benefit; what one city gains another loses and vice versa.

Although such an occurrence has probably been the chief goal of the renewal efforts of most cities and is the usual way in which renewal is expected " to pay for itself," it is apt

---

* These gains would result in greater real income and thus an expanded tax base out of which the public expenditures for urban renewal could be repaid. In the case of the third consideration, however, other than property taxes might be required since traditional rent and land-value theory argues that improvements in efficiency will result in lower aggregate land values. Cf. Richard U. Ratcliff, *Urban Land Economics* (New York: McGraw-Hill, 1949), pp. 385f.

to occur in only a few unique cases, particularly if the city in question is very large. Retaliatory renewal projects by other cities, intensified competition for the housing dollars of upper-income groups by suburban developers, the continued preference by many of these groups to so spend their dollars, the difficulties involved in meeting the federal requirements to provide standard relocation housing for the prerenewal occupants of the area, the disruption of the city's labor supply that would result from any major success in " exporting the slums "; all are factors that impede and limit the possibilities for higher-income occupancy. Even without these factors there are simply not enough upper-income groups available to fill existing blighted areas. It should not be inferred from these comments that renewal will not involve any occupancy shifts within the housing market. Such effects will be discussed below. As the Urban Renewal Program expands in scope, however, the simple idea of " paying for renewal " through higher-income occupancy becomes increasingly unrealistic.

### Property considerations

The decision to use the second public policy approach to implement renewal in an Urban Renewal Area must be reached only after an initial determination that the three considerations discussed above are not sufficient to warrant complete clearance of the area. The second approach leaves the clearance decision up to each individual property owner. Neither the owners, acting individually or collectively, nor outside investors can be expected to undertake area-wide clearance. In these circumstances the question of rehabilitation versus replacement is decided on a property-by-property basis.

Considered from the standpoint of an individual property, the question of replacement versus rehabilitation is a function of renewal standards and alternative costs. Rehabilitation and replacement are simply two different ways of achieving a standard of renewal and, given

the standard, the choice between them is determined by their alternative costs. With a low enough standard, rehabilitation will almost certainly prove to be less expensive and thus the preferred choice, since replacement by definition results in a standard represented by a new building. On the other hand, there are undoubtedly standards so high that they can be achieved only, or at least most inexpensively, though new construction.

Some might argue that rehabilitation can never produce as sound a structure nor one of as high a value as can even the most minimum level of new construction. Rehabilitation can be quite extensive, however, and a structure may actually have architectural or historic features that considerably enhance its value and that cannot be reproduced.* Renewal standards may vary from those required for the barest code compliance to those producing housing of the very highest quality and, in general, all can be achieved through rehabilitation or through new construction although the costs involved in the two methods may vary considerably. Indeed, the distinction between rehabilitation and replacement is itself somewhat arbitrary since a wide range of standards may be achieved within each category. Regardless of whether it involves rehabilitation or replacement, the cheapest method of achieving the given standard would obviously be the expected course of action.

Thus the specifications of the renewal standard become the crucial determinants of the rehabilitation versus replacement question. We have already noted that in the analysis of the profitability of renewal as a private investment decision the standard of renewal would be tailored to fit the potential market. The work done would have to add an increment to the value of the property greater than the cost of work. In the case of the properties in an Urban Renewal Area, however, the situation is quite different. There is no " profitable " renewal standard and there will be no renewal at all in the absence of public intervention.

In these circumstances, the standard of re-

---

* Such features contributed to the strong market, for rehabilitated properties in the Georgetown section of Washington, D. C. For an account of this and similar instances of " prestige " rehabilitation see Nash, *op. cit.*, Chapter 2.

newal is initially a function of the public implementing policies. Two general types of policies may be employed in the second policy approach – (1) coercion through code enforcement, (2) assistance through the provision of liberal financing, environmental improvements, better public services, and the like. Each of these two types of policies presupposes a renewal standard – that which can be required for code compliance and that which would be sufficient to justify the various forms of public assistance. Henceforth we shall refer to these two standards as the *code compliance standard* and the *long-term renewal standard*, respectively.

The amount of renewal represented by code compliance depends on the specifications of the relevant code and the vigor with which they are enforced. It is probably safest to assume that only the more flagrant and immediate dangers to health and safety would be eliminated and that the code compliance standard would not call for any basic structural repairs, elimination of functional obsolescence, or significant extensions in the remaining life of the buildings.

As a written stipulation of specifications, the Minimum Property Requirements of the FHA would probably play a role in the determination of the long-term renewal standard similar to that played by housing codes in the determination of the code compliance standard. The FHA determines for each Urban Renewal Area the standard it requires for certification of a property as eligible to serve as security for a Section 220 loan. Loans so insured may then be made with the same maturity terms, interest rates, and loan-value ratios as are permitted on loans insured under Section 203, the original and chief authorizing section of the FHA's permanent home mortgage insurance program. Variations may be expected in different areas and for different types of structures but, in general, the resulting long-term standard could be expected to include two main components in addition to minimum code compliance. In the first place, each building's plumbing, wiring, and heating systems and the surfaces and structural members of its foundations, floors, exterior and interior walls, roof, and other shell elements would be in such condition as is required for the

provision of standard housing for a minimum of around forty more years. Second, some elimination could be expected of more important instances of functional obsolescence such as insufficient electrical outlets, outmoded electrical and plumbing fixtures, deficiencies in the use of space, inadequate kitchen facilities, and the like. The end result would be designed to approach the quality and approximate longevity of minimum-standard new construction and would thus be thorough and permanent enough to justify public environmental improvements and the provision of long-term financing.

Given the specifications of these two standards, the conclusion reached here is that the question of rehabilitation versus replacement is resolved solely on the basis of alternative costs. Apart from the area-wide considerations discussed earlier, rehabilitation is economically feasible as long as it is the cheapest method of achieving the publicly stipulated renewal standard. If replacement is the cheaper method, rehabilitation is not economically feasible and replacement is.

## Realism and usefulness of the least-cost criterion

The realism and usefulness of the least-cost criterion developed above for the purpose of judging the economic feasibility of rehabilitation may be appraised from three standpoints. The first concerns the realism of the criterion as a prediction of the results of private investment decisions in an Urban Renewal Area. The second concerns the usefulness and realism of the criterion as a tool for preliminary area planning by the local government in cooperation with the federal government. The third concerns the usefulness of the criterion in furthering the primary objectives of public policy in urban renewal.

*Private investment decisions.* As noted earlier, the private investment decision of whether to rehabilitate or replace a property is not decided on the basis of alternative costs alone but also on the relative values of the end products of rehabilitation and replacement. Any property owner would be expected to make his decision by comparing both costs and values and choosing the course of action that results in the greatest value increment per dollar of investment. The reliance on cost comparisons alone in the present analysis rests upon the assumption that the value of the property in question cannot be higher than it will be following long-term renewal and that its value following long-term renewal will be the same regardless of whether such renewal takes the form of rehabilitation or replacement.*

Two arguments may be raised to contest the validity of this assumption. First, it may correctly be argued that a new structure would almost certainly have a life expectancy greater than the forty-year life called for in the long-term renewal standard specified here and would probably have more such additional years of life than would a building that has been rehabilitated to meet the long-term renewal standard. However, the present worth of a residual value forty years hence is not of much significance in private investment decisions, particularly those made only in response to public implementation. Public considerations might place a greater premium on such long-range possible value differentials. Yet many of today's problems in urban renewal are due to the presence of structures that are obsolete for current needs and yet are still sound enough and hence valuable enough to make their removal a very expensive proposition. In such instances durability is a curse rather than a blessing and, from the standpoint of public policy, actually has a negative value.

Second, it might be argued that a new building would generate a higher level of market demand in the forms of both tenant rents and the shelter expenditures of owner-occupants than

would a rehabilitated one. We have seen, however, that rehabilitation can be very extensive and that the question is rather one of the characteristics of the long-term renewal standard. Given this standard, it makes little difference whether the structure providing it is a new building or a rehabilitated one. It is important to remember that the renewal of properties in a Renewal Area will be forthcoming only as a result of public implementation and, as will be discussed in the next chapter, any increases in rents or shelter expenditures that renewal might generate are more apt to represent involuntary cost absorption by the market than a simple increase in market demand. It is for this reason that the specifications of the given renewal standard must be publicly determined. In the "involuntary" renewal that follows, it is safest to postulate that the primary objective of any property owner would be to meet the required standard in the least expensive manner possible.

In short, it appears most realistic to argue that each property owner, once he has determined his least-loss course of action given the two renewal standards, will do what he has to do as cheaply as possible without concerning himself about whether doing more or doing it in a different way, e.g., replacement, might pay off in a sufficiently greater property value. The uncertainties surrounding the latter possibility are simply too great. If this proposition is accepted, however, it is tantamount to arguing that the expected private investment value that the owner of a given property places upon it is the same when the property is to be renewed to meet the long-term standard regardless of whether such renewal is achieved through rehabilitation or replacement.

---

* A qualification to this statement should be noted here although its relevance may perhaps be more apparent following the discussion of the economic effects of public renewal policies in the next chapter of *Economic Aspects of Urban Renewal, op. cit.* Given the value-equivalence assumption stated above, we are safe in predicting that any property for which rehabilitation is the cheapest method of achieving the long-term renewal standard will always be rehabilitated. The owner does, however, have two standards to choose from and, as discussed in the next chapter, the value of the property following long-term renewal can be expected to be higher than its value

following code compliance. Thus there may be some properties for which replacement is the cheapest method of achieving the long-term renewal standard but which will be rehabilitated to the code compliance standard instead because the difference between code compliance value and long-term renewal value is not great enough to justify the additional cost required for long-term renewal. In specifically projecting private investment decisions, the rule would more precisely be that rehabilitation or replacement would be selected depending upon which was the least costly method of achieving the least-loss one of the two renewal standards.

*Preliminary area planning.* The great virtue of the use of the least-cost criterion in preliminary area planning is that its adoption lays to rest the profitability criterion as a test for the economic feasibility of rehabilitation. Perhaps the most common misconception in urban renewal planning has been the belief that rehabilitation must be profitable in order to be feasible and that, in the absence of profitability, clearance is the only course open.

Undoubtedly this thinking stems from the fact that rehabilitation is most commonly associated with the second public policy approach. Since this approach relies on private initiative from the outset, it has seemed to many that if renewal is not profitable, direct subsidization through the first approach must be used. We have seen, however, that renewal in an Urban Renewal Area, whether in the form of rehabilitation or replacement, cannot be expected to be profitable and hence will only be forthcoming through public implementation. Each method of renewal should be viewed simply as a means of achieving a given renewal standard. To accomplish this through public implementation all policy weapons must be intermingled as necessary whether they be code enforcement, public rehabilitation, rent certificates, liberal financing, environmental improvements, public purchase, property value write-downs, or public housing. Just as in the case of clearance, it is quite in order to undertake public rehabilitation or otherwise directly subsidize it if the three implementing policies of code enforcement, liberal financing, and environmental improvements do not bring about the desired amount and standard of renewal.[3] Failure to recognize these concepts may result in costly delays and administrative inefficiences. It may also lead to the demolition of sound structures on the grounds that they cannot be " profitably " rehabilitated and the replacement of these structures with heavily subsidized new construction involving far greater expense but little better housing conditions than could be provided through the long-term rehabilitation of the existing buildings.

The least-cost criterion has the added planning advantage of simplicity. The delineation of standards and the costs of achieving the resulting specifications are questions of fact that are relatively simple to answer. With the cost estimates at hand, a direct measure is available of the cost savings, if any, that will accrue through the use of rehabilitation. These savings may in turn be compared with the possible gains from area-wide clearance discussed earlier, although the measurement of such gains is a far more difficult quantitative problem than is the determination of the comparative costs of rehabilitation and replacement.

If the second policy approach is selected, the cost estimates also allow projections of the extent of replacement and rehabilitation through private initiative.* Least-cost will determine the choice given the proposition that, apart from area considerations, replacement will not produce higher property values than will rehabilitation to the long-term standard. Projections based on least-cost will generally be more realistic than those that attempt to justify the economic feasibiliy of rehabilitation on its profitability, usually on the basis of predicted success in the ephemeral quest for a higher-income market.

*Public policy objectives.* The advantage of the least-cost criterion from the standpoint of public policy objectives is that it emphasizes the minimization of costs. It may be presumed that a major goal of public policy in urban renewal is to improve aggregate housing standards. When the substandard housing problem is considered in an aggregative sense, as it must be, the objective of securing a higher-income market is not relevant. The presence of substandard housing is fundamentally due to poverty, and its elimination will involve outlays for labor and materials in excess of those that result from voluntary private spending decisions. Such outlays are the real costs of housing improvement and these costs must be absorbed by someone.

The forms that this absorption may take will be discussed below. It may be noted here that the Urban Renewal Program as now established

---

* Such projections pertain only to those properties where some private renewal will be forthcoming.

is not necessarily the best vehicle through which equitable cost absorption (however equitable be defined) is achieved or, for that matter, through which aggregative housing conditions can be improved. The use of the least-cost criterion at least results in keeping the required cost absorption at the minimum amount necessary to a-

chieve the desired housing standard. Misguided use of the profitability criterion, however, may increase the total cost of producing a given amount of standard housing by causing the demolition of structures that can still provide such housing through comparatively inexpensive rehabilitation.

# Urban renewal

CARTER McFARLAND

Urban renewal is often thought of as a program to clear unhealthy slums, to provide better living accommodations for city dwellers and to replace cluttered, unsightly, and obsolescent downtown areas with wide avenues, attractive parks, handsome housing and monumental buildings. All of this it is. But to the central city it may well be much more than this. It may be the necessary and indispensable condition to economic survival and municipal solvency.

It is by now widely recognized that commercial, industrial and residential slums and blight mean economic disaster and strangulation to the central city. They mean inefficient land uses. Traffic congestion, inadequate loading and customer parking facilities lead to a deterioration of business. They mean low tax revenues and high municipal service costs. The situation creates a vicious cycle. For slums and blight drive prosperous business firms and prosperous residents to the suburbs, further accentuating the conditions which started the flight to the suburbs and, by reducing tax revenues, further impairing the city's capacity to repair the situation.

The President's Advisory Committee on Government Housing Policies and Programs noted the plight of the central city in these words: " The fact is that our cities are caught in a descending spiral which leads to widespread municipal insolvency. The accumulated and continuing spread of blight eats away at the assessable base of the cities. As the blight spreads it is inevitably followed by crime, fire, disease, and delinquency. Thus, does the need for city services increase. But the city's ability to meet the increased budget is automatically impaired by the very blight that creates the demand. More blight, more demand for services, less revenues to meet the demand – that is the downward spiral in American cities. Most often the cities with the greatest slum problem have the least capacity to deal with it."[1]

## The economic consequences of blight to the city

*Blight reduces tax collections, and increases municipal services costs.* It has long been a well-established fact that areas of slum and blight are inherently uneconomic from the

*Reprinted from* The Challenge of Urban Renewal, *Urban Land Institute. Technical Bulletin, No. 34 (1959), pp. 15–27,* *with permission of the publisher.*

standpoint of municipal finances. As early as 1934 a study in Boston highlighted the wide disparity between city costs and revenues for good and bad neighborhoods. The study found that high class rental districts produced a per capita tax income substantially above the per capita cost of municipal services for the same area while a low rental area resulted in a per capita loss to the city.

## TABLE 1

*Income and Cost for Various Types of Areas in Boston*

| Area | Per capita income | Per capita cost | Per capita net cost |
|------|------------------:|----------------:|--------------------:|
|  | $ | $ | $ |
| High rental district | 312.80 | 73.80 | — |
| Miscellaneous district | 114.40 | 65.10 | — |
| Total city | 74.40 | 77.80 | 3.40 |
| Suburban | 41.80 | 62.30 | 20.50 |
| Low rental district | 13.30 | 92.30 | 79.00 |

Source: Boston City Planning Board. Report on income and cost of six districts in the City of Boston, 1934.

Many studies since that time have shown the same trend. Newark, N.J. found that per capita revenues for a good housing area exceeded expenditures by $108 while in a slum area per capita expenditures exceeded revenues by $88.[2] Richmond, Virginia estimates that its worse slum areas cost from seven to ten times the amount of tax revenue derived from the same areas.[3] A good residential area in San Francisco yielded $556,000 in revenue per year and cost only $87,000 in city expenditures, while a slum area produced $368,000 in revenue and took back $741,000 in expenditures.[4] Hartford, Connecticut found that its slum areas required 5.54 percent of city expenditures to maintain and service and produced only 1.24 percent of city revenue.[5] Detroit, Michigan has estimated that its slums and blighted areas were costing the city $30 million a year.[6] Baltimore, Maryland estimated the loss to the city from all blighted areas to be $14,300,000 per year.[7]

Generally, the high ratio of municipal costs to revenues in slum areas can be traced to high population densities and to poor social conditions which produce a great demand for police and fire protection, health, welfare and other city services coupled with a low assessed tax base and high delinquency rates.

Denver, Colorado estimated that a blighted area received seven times its per capita share of general relief funds; six times its share of all aid to dependent children; three times its share of police calls; five times its share of hospital care load; and five times its share of workload for the city sanitation department.[8] In Los Angeles, California it was reported that the per capita costs for fire, police, health and park services were $7.11 for blighted areas and only $3.67 for areas which were not blighted.[9] Cleveland, Ohio reported that its slum areas, covering 0.73 percent of the total land area and containing 2.47 percent of the city population, required 6.47 percent of the city's police protection expenditures; 7.3 percent of health expenditures; 12.29 percent of social service expenditures; and 14.14 percent of fire protection expenditures.[10] Indianapolis, Indiana reported the 10.4 percent of its population living in slum areas absorbed 16.7 percent of the cost of extinguishing fires; 26 percent of expenditures for social services; almost 25 percent of the cost of arresting, trying and imprisoning those committing misdemeanors; and 36 percent of the costs involved in apprehending those committing felonies.[11]

A Canadian study, covering cities in all the provinces, showed that the percentage of unpaid property taxes bears a direct relationship to the proportion of substandard dwellings in each city.[12]

*Blight leads to inefficient land uses.* In past years it was not uncommon for land economists to hold that natural economic forces at work in a city tended to produce the highest and best use of land. Even the most casual inspection of the downtown area of an American city will raise serious questions about the validity of this pleasant theory. Indeed, as Miles Colean has pointed out in his book *Renewing Our Cities* it is the failure of natural processes to restore to their "highest and best use" vast numbers of structures and neighborhoods which constitutes the crux of the urban crisis.[13] As Colean shows, the modern city is dynamic, its various parts constantly in a state of change. In the course of this vast and complicated process of growth and adaptation many structures and entire neighborhoods become obsolete and ill-adapted to the uses for which they were first built. This is particularly true, he says, of the residential areas immediately surrounding the central business district. Once these areas become outmoded and obsolete, they start the vicious spiral downward which produces blight and slums. The problem of urban renewal, according to Colean, is essentially that of finding a way to assure that the dynamic urban organism gets rid of its waste products – deteriorated dwellings, obsolete commercial and industrial structures – and restores the land on which they rest to appropriate and productive uses. For such inefficient use of land, the city pays a high cost in both social and economic terms.

*Blight triggers the flight of industry, commerce and housing to the suburbs.* An important facet of the downward spiral of American cities is the flight of industry, commerce and housing to the suburbs. It is a fact for all to observe that a large proportion of the over 11 million homes produced in this country during the last decade have been placed in ever widening bands of suburban developments. Save for a small volume of apartment house construction, the number of new houses built in the downtown parts of our large cities during this period has been negligible. This has been due, of course, not only to population growth which forced residential development beyond the city's boundaries but also to the shortage of downtown land available for building. The peripheral explosion of residential construction has not only created the suburban sprawl, it has also left center city residential areas to rot and decay without a natural thrust to renew themselves.

To a somewhat lesser extent, the same thing is happening to commerce and industry. Downtown retail stores have followed the fleeing families to the suburbs. Other commercial establishments have sought outlying facilities better suited to their needs. Industry, too, goes out to find space with light, air, easy access and room for expansion. The city of Detroit found in its recent *Industrial Study* that 40.6 percent of the city's industrial firms were dissatisfied with their sites. In one downtown area of the

city, Detroit found that the number of manufacturing firms had decreased sharply in recent years and that those firms which remained were either operating on a reduced scale or had moved their manufacturing operations to other localities.[14]

A recent report of the Planning Council of The Greater Baltimore Committee asserted: "The most important single explanation why regional growth has not been reflected in downtown development is that there is, at present, little real opportunity for major private investment downtown. A disproportionately high percentage of the buildings are deteriorated, obsolete or unattractive. Many of these might have been replaced in the normal course of events if it had not been so much easier for investment to go elsewhere. They seriously inhibit investment downtown."[15] At another place the same report concluded: "In the face of such problems, Baltimore's new growth in downtown-type activities has been decentralized at a rapid rate. Unless the opportunity and proper conditions for downtown investment can be created – and soon – the Baltimore area might well end up without a recognizable downtown."[16]

In nearly every American city the experience is the same. As blight spreads and the middle- and higher-income families escape it by moving to the suburbs, the nature of the urban market changes and the economic base of urban income-producing properties is affected. Any business which is surrounded or bordered by blight will tend to adapt itself to its environment or attempt to move elsewhere, just as families do. In residential areas, good rental units are sensitive to neighborhood deterioration and are quickly affected by it. Stores, recreational establishments, and office buildings cannot maintain a healthy life in the midst of filth, disease, and crime. Thus, the enormous economic advantage of a central location in the metropolis becomes neutralized in time by decay.

## The economic effects of urban renewal for the city

By definition, present day formalized urban renewal programs are designed to eliminate central city blight and obsolescence which are primarily residential, to restore economic uses of land, to increase tax revenues and reduce the cost of city services, and to arrest the flight of housing and business to the suburbs. At least from an economic standpoint, the measure of the success of an urban renewal undertaking is the extent to which it does these things.

Because urban renewal as a national program is relatively new – many Federally assisted projects are underway but relatively few have been completed – and because urban renewal experience has been inadequately documented and analyzed, concrete before and after statistics are difficult to find. This is a question which deserves more study that it has received. However, even now it is possible to assemble striking evidence of the potential benefits of the urban renewal projects which are underway. It should be borne in mind that these figures are estimates and the actual results of urban renewal may or may not bear them out. More concrete evidence of the actual economic results of urban renewal will have to await the completion and analysis of projects now under way.

Four years ago Pittsburgh estimated that its Golden Triangle project – a privately financed redevelopment of the city's downtown area – had added $29 million to assessed valuations.[17] With full development of the Golden Triangle since that time Pittsburgh estimates that the tax base has continued to increase. In Tarrytown, New York it is reported that assessed values have risen from $18 million to $40 million in the last six years as a result of urban renewal activities.[18] San Francisco, in connection with one of its urban renewal projects, estimated an increase in value from $29 million to $170 million.[19] A study made for Washington, D. C. estimated that the Southwest Redevelopment Project would increase assessed values in the area from $20.5 million to $157 million.[20]

If urban renewal improves the assessed valuation of properties in urban renewal areas it follows that tax revenues will be correspondingly increased. The table opposite summarizes the annual taxes before redevelopment and the estimated annual taxes after redevelopment for projects in nine American cities of varying sizes:

In a survey of 123 cities having a total of 294 urban renewal projects, the American Municipal Association reported that, for all the projects, taxes before redevelopment were $26 million while taxes after redevelopment were estimated to total $93 million.[21]

In addition to the increase in tax base and property tax revenues, cities throughout the country expect their urban renewal programs to increase their revenues in other ways:

(1) Attraction of new industry and retention of present industry;

(2) Increased revenues from building permits, utility charges, licences and sales taxes;

(3) Increased labor force with consequent increase in payrolls. In a study of its Milwaukee Junction area, Detroit estimates urban renewal will add 3,000 new industrial jobs and that this will add $17,700,000 in personal income to the area;[22]

(4) Stimulation of actual construction work. In estimates prepared for the District of Columbia consultants James Rouse and Nathaniel Keith estimated that a ten-year renewal program could result in additional construction expenditures for labor and materials of more than $35 million a year;[23]

## TABLE 2

*Tax Revenues Before and After Redevelopment in 9 American Cities*

| City | Annual taxes before redevelopment | Estimated annual taxes after redevelopment |
|------|------------------------------------|---------------------------------------------|
|  | $ | $ |
| Sacramento | 2,800,000 | 7,000,000 |
| District of Columbia (S. W. Area) | 451,000 | 3,430,000 |
| Chicago, Illinois (Lake Meadows Project) | 140,000 | 575,000 |
| Baltimore, Maryland (Waverly Project) | 15,000 | 23,000 |
| New York City (Stuyvesant Town) | 412,000 | 2,837,000 |
| Perth Amboy, New Jersey | 35,000 | 178,000 |
| Murfreesboro, Tennessee (Rehabilitation) | 2,000 | 20,000 |
| Nashville, Tennessee | 23,000 | 178,000 |
| Detroit, Michigan (6 projects) | 757,000 | 8,318,000 |

Sources: Report of the President's Advisory Committee on Government Housing Policies and Programs; Detroit City Plan Commission Reports; and Urban Renewal Administration.

(5) Attraction of middle- and high-income families into the downtown area;

(6) Attraction of more suburban shoppers into downtown area stores.

We have seen that an important element in the uneconomic nature of blight is the high cost of the municipal services required by slum areas. The clearance or rehabilitation of residential slums through urban renewal can be expected to reduce substantially this drain on municipal finances. However, a caution needs to be expressed on this score. Experience with public housing in the United States suggests that the replacement of substandard slum housing with decent housing is not alone sufficient to reduce the high municipal service requirements of slum dwellers. Experience with public housing leads to the conclusion that municipal service costs in hitherto slum areas can be reduced only to the extent that the living habits of slum dwellers are rehabilitated through education and social work.

City officials, planners and a large number of business men also confidently expect successful urban renewal to reverse the flight of business and housing to the suburbs. The report of the Planning Council of the Greater Baltimore Committee found reasons for the belief that the central city or downtown area can be renewed and reborn. The Report concluded: " The Planning Council has uncovered conclusive evidence that if the opportunity for investment downtown is opened up, private investment will not only flood in, but many of the decentralizing trends can be reversed. A significant number of firms are now near the point of making decisions on new space or location. Some of these involve the needs for expansion; some involve the need for more suitable locations; some involve a change in taste or upgrading in the character of space or location. Of the firms that are facing a change, most expressed a desire to remain downtown if possible. Many expressed willingness and ability to pay the cost of new space. Several very important firms indicated a willingness to reverse decisions to decentralize if the opportunity to invest wisely downtown were present. There are equal evidences that investors will be forthcoming given the opportunity for sound invest-

ment and a good investment environment. These are the ingredients of a revitalized downtown."[24]

## Private residential redevelopment

A basic objective of the urban renewal program is to make possible a large volume of private housing construction and rehabilitation in blighted areas. As John H. Blandford, wartime head of the National Housing Agency, put it " . . . Government aid should be extended toward reducing the cost of acquiring and clearing our vast blighted areas, in order that the redevelopment of the surface . . . may be accompanied by a large volume of privately financed housing."[25]

From an economic standpoint, it can be assumed that private residential redevelopment in urban renewal areas will occur if there is a market for downtown residential housing at rents or sales prices which will cover costs (construction, land and services), including interest and amortization of debt plus a profit to the entrepreneur sufficient to induce him to risk his time, effort and money. Implicit also is the assumption that funds are available to finance the residential housing redevelopment. Indeed, it is self-evident that the terms on which financing is available will substantially affect the feasibility of residential redevelopment under any given set of costs and rents. Congress recognized this when it authorized FHA mortgage insurance on liberal terms to finance residential redevelopment in urban renewal areas.

### What goes into rent

In a rental housing project financed with a mortgage, rental income must be sufficient to pay a return on the equity, provide for vacancies, retire the debt and cover operating expenses. If the mortgage is insured by the FHA, an insurance premium of $\frac{1}{2}$ percent must also be paid. Under its special program for the insurance of mortgages for rental housing in redevelopment areas (Section 220), the FHA will permit a mortgage for a maximum term of almost forty years. (This is approximately the same term permitted for other FHA-assisted rental housing programs). For this special program, FHA requires a first year reduction of mortgage principal of 1½ percent. (This increases gradually as the loan is repaid.) This is somewhat more liberal than the 2 percent initial curtail of mortgage principal required by FHA on most other rental housing programs and is based on the expectation that the market attractiveness (and consequently, capacity to command rental income) will increase as urban renewal efforts improve the surrounding neighborhood. To this initial curtail of 1½ percent of mortgage principal, there is added the current interest rate of 5 percent* and the FHA mortgage insurance premium of ½ percent. Thus for rental projects to be insured in redevelopment areas, FHA arrives at a required total annual debt service payment of 7 percent. This 7 percent is applied to FHA's estimate of the entire replacement cost of the project, with 90 percent of the resultant amount being applied to debt service on the mortgage (the mortgage can be 90 percent of replacement cost). The remainder becomes the sponsor's return on his equity.

In calculating the total rental income required, FHA includes, in addition to the 7 percent debt service, an allowance of 7 percent for vacancies and collection losses and the amount necessary to cover annual operating expenses. While other factors in this calculation remain fairly constant, operating expenses vary widely by locality, type of project, level of services provided, and other circumstances. FHA has found that the expense ratio for a rental project consisting of row-house structures usually falls between 30 percent and 40 percent of gross rents; for garden-type or walk-up apartment projects, the expense ratio is usually between 40 percent and 50 percent; for elevator structures the expense ratio normally reaches between 50 percent and 60 percent of gross rents.

To see how these cost factors work in a concrete situation, let us assume a 100-unit garden-type project costing $1 million with an expense ratio of 45 percent. Based on the factors enumerated, such a project would require a gross monthly rental of $114 per unit to carry the forty-year mortgage, cover expenses and vacancy allowance and yield a reasonable return to the owners. If the same $1 million, 100-unit project were an elevator structure with an expense ratio of 55 percent, a monthly rental of $140 per unit would be required. However, if the same project were made up of row houses with an expense ratio of 35 percent, it would require a monthly rental per unit of only $95.

These cost factors can be looked at in another way. Let us assume that the market will pay an average gross monthly rental per unit of $114 in a given redevelopment project. Based on the factors and costs we have used, an average per unit rent of $114 would support construction costing $10,000 per unit if the project were of the garden type (expense ratio – 45 percent). However, the same $114 a month rent would support elevator apartments (expense ratio – 55 percent) costing an average of $8,200 per unit. A rent of $114 a month would support a cost of approximately $11,800 per unit in a row-house project with a 35 percent expense ratio.

## FHA experience under Section 220

Through July 1958, FHA has committed under Section 220 to insure 37 new rental housing projects in 21 urban renewal areas. Twenty-five of these projects are elevator structures; eight are garden-type or walk-up apartments; three consist of row houses; and another is a combination of row houses and walk-up apartments.

The lowest rents in completely private projects with FHA-insured financing are in the walk-up apartment structures, which have average monthly rents of $75 to $99 per unit and from $17 to $30 per room.

Average monthly rents in the elevator projects range from $107 to $184 per unit and from $33 to $45 per room.

The highest average rents range from $189 to $266 per unit per month for town-house type row-house projects. These downtown houses in

---

* This rate is, of course, subject to variation. FHA alters its maximum rate as money market conditions vary. A lender may also take a Section 220 mortgage at a rate below the maximum.

Detroit and Washington, D. C. have 5.6 to 6.0 rooms per unit and average $34 to $44 monthly rent per room.

A combination walk-up and row-house project in Philadelphia with an FHA-insured mortgage, has average monthly rents of only $66. (This is a " middle income " development with a substantial capital subsidy from the State of Pennsylvania).

The following table gives a summary of the characteristics of the new rental housing projects insured so far by FHA under Section 220.

ment cost of housing. He said " ... a write-down in the cost of land, while essential, will not go far enough to induce private redevelopment on a scale to recall armies of families from the suburbs."[26]

In a 1953 article in *Land Economics*, Leo Grebler analyzed the effects of land write-down on rents. He observed " ... while actual figures will vary from case to case, a 50 percent write-down of land costs will rarely produce a rent reduction by more than 10 percent as compared to rentals for the same kind of housing without

## TABLE 3

*Summary Characteristics of New Rental Housing Projects Committed or Insured by FHA Under Section 220 (Through July 1958)*

|  | Walk-up | Elevator | Row | Walk-up & row |
|---|---|---|---|---|
| Number of developments | 6 | 12 | 2 | 1 |
| Units per development | 10 to 292 | 208 to 1,271 | 81 to 94 | 229 |
| Average rooms per unit | 3.1 to 4.83 | 3.05 to 4.1 | 5.6 to 6.0 | 4.8 |
| Average monthly rents per unit | $75 to $99 | $107 to $177 | $189 to $266 | $66 |
| Average monthly rents per room | $17 to $30 | $33 to $45 | $34 to $44 | $14 |
| Mortgage amount per unit | $7,200 to $10,800 | $8,400 to $15,000 | $16,900 to $19,500 | $6,524 |

Source: Federal Housing Administration.

### Effects of land write-down on cost

Under the present urban renewal program land is sold for redevelopment at its appraised value for uses specified in the urban renewal plan. While this is substantially below the price the slum properties would have brought before clearance and write-down, it is by definition not a lower price than that for other open land available for housing construction. Indeed, because of the central location, it can be assumed that the appraised value of land sold for residential redevelopment will be somewhat higher than the price of land available to builders in outlying sections of the metropolitan area. Thus, the effect of the land write-down is, at best, only to put central city land in a reasonably competitive relationship to outlying land.

In fact, it is worth noting that a land write-down of whatever magnitude will only make a limited contribution toward reducing the cost of redevelopment housing built upon the land. In 1950, Ferd Kramer, then President of the Metropolitan Housing and Planning Council of Chicago, pointed out that the cost of land is only a small percentage of the total develop-

benefit of the write-down of land costs through government aid. Rent reduction of this magnitude will tend to widen the market for new construction in only moderate degree, since elasticity of demand for rent is probably low. The write-down of land costs of itself does not produce rentals which would make occupancy of new housing possible for large numbers of households which otherwise would be unable to do so."[27]

Thus, even a complete write off of the cost of land for redevelopment and its donation to the redeveloper (a proposal which is sometimes made), would have limited significance as a means of broadening the market for redevelopment housing.

### The market for residential redevelopment

FHA has obviously concluded that a rental market exists for the units in those redevelopment projects on which it has so far insured mortgages. Of course, relatively few projects, among the many which are being planned, have yet reached the stage of mortgage insurance.

Whether there is a rental market for a large volume of residential redevelopment at the rents which must be charged, given current construction costs and financing terms, is a question which only the future will answer.

Some are pessimistic. *Fortune Magazine*, in a recent article on redevelopment, says the city is not for the average family now. It cites the $5,000 median income of families in urban areas and concludes that they could afford rents of about $25 per room. *Fortune* goes on to point out that, with the exception of public housing, the redevelopment housing now being produced is out of reach of the family making $5,000. The *Fortune* article concludes that some kind of subsidy program will be necessary to reach the great bulk of the middle-income market.[28] The figures cited earlier on redevelopment projects already insured by FHA do not fully confirm this pessimistic view. Four projects insured in Cleveland will rent for $17–$23 per room per month. However, FHA's experience to date does suggest that the elevator structures which are planned in many urban renewal projects will be beyond the reach of *Fortune's* $5,000 a year " middle-income " family.

Of course, *Fortune's* use of median incomes does not tell the whole story. By definition, one-half of the urban families have incomes above the $5,000 a year median. There are certainly many in the top half of the income scale who can afford the $33 to $45 a room rents to be charged for the elevator apartments so far insured by FHA.

Nevertheless, the relatively high cost of redevelopment housing has given pause to many of those concerned with urban renewal. Redevelopment housing at lower rents would not only assure a broader market, it would also make it possible to serve with downtown housing both the lower as well as the upper income brackets. The need for lower cost redevelopment housing is, in the minds of many, underlined by the simple fact that most of those who are displaced by urban renewal are in the lower income brackets. This has caused some to suggest Federal, State or local subsidies to reduce the cost of redevelopment housing. The $14 per room rents achieved in the FHA-insured redevelopment project in Philadelphia with the

assistance of a State subsidy, show what can be done. Others have suggested even longer amortization terms to make it possible for private enterprise to reach a larger segment of the market with redevelopment housing. There are others who hold that residential redevelopment should be separated from the housing needs of middle-income families and that previous land uses and incomes of displacees should in no way determine the future use or economic level of a redevelopment project.

While *Fortune* is pessimistic about the income-cost relationship for redevelopment housing, it is decidedly optimistic about the number of families who would be willing to rent or buy housing in downtown areas if it were available at prices they could afford. In reporting on a survey recently conducted by ACTION, *Fortune* concluded that changes in ages of the United States population between now and 1975 will involve a substantial increase in those age groups who generally prefer renting (20–29) and among those past child-rearing age (50 and up) who are likely to return to the city. The same study also reported that projections of household formation between now and 1975 suggest that the kinds of families who usually want to live in central cities will rise much faster than those who usually want a detached house in the suburbs. Among the types of householders who would want to live downtown, the ACTION study listed : Young married persons, widows, bachelors, divorcees, childless couples of any age, and elderly couples whose children have grown. The *Fortune*-ACTION survey made another finding which bears on the willingness of suburbanites to return to the central city if suitable housing is available. Of the city dwellers interviewed in the survey, 41 percent had lived in the suburbs sometime in the past.[29]

### The residential redevelopers

The urban renewal program's objective of making possible and stimulating a large volume of privately sponsored residential redevelopment will be realized, of course, only if a sufficient number of entrepreneurs appear who find the construction of redevelopment housing profitable. While the redevelopment phase of urban renewal is still in its infancy, the interest shown in the program by private redevelopers has been substantial. Few cities with cleared land available for sale have had difficulty finding private redevelopers ready and willing to bid In many instances interested redevelopers have sought out the cities long before existing slum dwellings had been cleared from project areas.

A recent survey of 75 urban renewal projects in 44 communities conducted by the *Journal of Housing* provides an interesting insight into the types of redevelopers who have emerged. The *Journal of Housing* reported that what it referred to as the *big professional redevelopers* were involved in 15 cities. The big redevelopers – Zeckendorff, Sheuer-Stevens, Greenwald, Pierre Bonan – appear to be interested mostly in urban renewal projects involving both residential and commercial redevelopment and like to be brought into the project in the early planning stages.

Another group of redevelopers were characterized by the *Journal of Housing* as *big business*. This group is involved in 22 cities. Represented by Mellon and Alcoa in Pittsburgh, David Rockefeller in New York and the Downtown Business Group in Philadelphia, these redevelopers appear to be primarily interested in projects designed to improve the downtown business area, to provide improved locations for industry, or simply to improve housing conditions.

In 18 cities surveyed by the *Journal of Housing* the redevelopers were *smaller business men.* This group was represented by homebuilders who operate mostly in one town as well as by small scale merchants and industrialists. In general, this group appears to be interested in projects involving residential redevelopment. In 21 cities surveyed the redeveloper was an *institutional investor* – universities, hospitals and the like. This group was, of course, interested primarily in projects which provided sites and improved surroundings for medical centers, university centers including classrooms, dormitories and faculty residences.[30]

### Motivation of residential redevelopers

Save during the immediate postwar period under the stimulation of the very liberal and much discussed Section 608, the volume of rental housing constructed with FHA mortgage insurance has never been great. The American homebuilding industry has generally displayed a preference for the construction of housing for sale and during the postwar period it has produced an unprecedented volume of sales units. This has certainly been, in part, a reaction to the widespread desire on the part of American families for a home of their own. The high percentage of homebuilding activity which has gone into the construction of sales housing is also related to the very liberal mortgage financing terms which have been available under the FHA and VA programs. Why build or rent an apartment when a house can be purchased with little or nothing down and paid for on easy monthly installments like rent? The reluctance of homebuilders to go into rental housing is also, many observers believe, a reflection of the character of the homebuilding industry. The average homebuilder is a small operator who works with limited capital. Such capital as he has, in addition to his skill and know-how, he seeks to turn over rapidly. The less capital he has to tie up and the more quickly he can turn it over, the greater are his profits.

It is not surprising that rental housing offers limited incentive to this type of operator. Under normal FHA programs rental housing requires the builder to put up some equity and to leave it in the project for an indefinite period of time. Rental housing also requires the builder to accept continuing responsibilities for management and upkeep.

Writing in *The Architectural Forum*, Economist Miles Colean has observed that the motivation of rental housing sponsors is essentially speculative, in that they have no desire to leave capital in a rental housing project but, rather, seek to get it out as quickly as possible for use in other ventures. Even for a short time, Mr. Colean concludes that the average rental-housing sponsor is prepared to supply only a small amount of equity.[31]

While FHA's Section 220 rental-housing program for redevelopment has been made more liberal by Congress than FHA's normal program for rental housing, it contains cost certication and other requirements which presumably make it less attractive to sponsors than the earlier Section 608 program was. It remains to be seen whether private redevelopers will find in the present program sufficient inducements and profit opportunities to cause them to build the volume of redevelopment housing which is planned in the urban renewal projects now under way.

A further possible impediment to widespread participation of private builders in redevelopment housing is the element of time. A redevelopment project involves a much longer time period than the typical rental-housing project. The redeveloper frequently has to wait while project planning and land acquisition occur, then he has to negotiate with the local redevelopment agency for the purchase of the land. The redevelopment plan itself also puts restrictions on the type of structures he can build. As one redeveloper has put it, " to a businessman, time is money." Thus, the time lags and delays which, despite serious efforts to reduce them, appear to be inherent in redevelopment can be both costly and discouraging to the private redeveloper.

## Residential rehabilitation

As we have seen, one of the basic contributions of the Housing Act of 1954 was to broaden the concept of slum clearance to include slum prevention and treatment through neighborhood conservation and rehabilitation. Thus, neighborhood conservation and rehabilitation are to be used to supplement and, perhaps, ultimately to eliminate clearance and redevelopment. This represents a very significant national act of faith in the process of upgrading existing neighborhoods through voluntary repair and rehabilitation to individual properties, code enforcement and the provision, where needed, of streets, parks and other public facilities. This process, however, has never been rigorously defined and it is, as yet, largely untested and certainly unproven. In a very important sense, then, the challenge of the Housing Act of 1954 is to make neighborhood conservation and rehabilitation work on a large scale.

There is, of course, some experience from

which to draw. A number of American cities have carried out programs of voluntary rehabilitation, most of them before the passage of the Housing Act of 1954. Baltimore was one of the first cities to undertake a mass assault on blight through rehabilitation. It is reported that this city has restored 16,000 slum homes to decency through its program.[32] It has been estimated that Charlotte, N. C. has rehabilitated 8,800 blighted dwelling units.[33] New Orleans, where a very vigorous rehabilitation program was carried out, reported in 1956 that 4,000 badly blighted housing units in controlled areas and an estimated 10,000 units outside these areas had been brought up to minimum housing law requirements.[34] A substantial program of voluntary rehabilitation has been carried out in Chicago in the so-called " Back of the Yards " area. The successful and entirely spontaneous transformation of Georgetown in Washington, D. C. by rehabilitation is often cited as the classic example of what can be accomplished if the conditions are favorable.

Since the passage of the Housing Act of 1954, communities throughout the country have recognized the wisdom of a more comprehensive approach to the slum problem and have, in overwhelming numbers, accepted the challenge to rehabilitate and conserve their declining neighborhoods. In 1957, under the Federally-aided Urban Renewal Program, the conservation and rehabilitation of existing housing as opposed to straight slum clearance had been stepped up almost eleven times over the rate two years earlier. One hundred and six communities throughout the country were in 1957 planning rehabilitation programs in areas containing more than 213,000 run-down dwellings. By the end of 1957, 96 of these projects had been approved and 30 more were in the application stage. Ninety of these projects at the end of 1957 were in the preliminary stage and 6 were in execution.[35] While little neighborhood rehabilitation has actually been completed under the 1954 program, it is clear that much is underway.

## Basic cost-price relationships

From a purely economic standpoint it can

be presumed that, assuming cities can motivate property owners through code enforcement or some other means, residential rehabilitation will occur if nonresident property owners can be shown that money spent on property rehabilitation will add sufficient value and income to their properties to pay for the improvements, service the debt and provide at least as high a profit rate as the property did before rehabilitation. The resident property owner will probably not analyze rehabilitation in the same profit and income terms as the nonresident owner can be expected to do. Basic considerations for the resident property owner are probably his evaluation of the increased amenities which will be created by the rehabilitation of his home and the general improvement of the neighborhood through the urban renewal plan in relation to his own income and the terms of the financing which are available to pay for the rehabilitation.

The basic cost factors applying to rehabilitation are essentially the same as those discussed earlier in connection with the construction of new redevelopment housing. However, there is one important difference. The remaining economic life of a rehabilitated dwelling is quite likely to be, for mortgage lending purposes, shorter than that of a new unit. FHA, for example, finds it prudent to permit a mortgage on a rehabilitated dwelling for a term no longer than three-fourths of its estimate of the remaining economic life of the dwelling. The reduction of the amortization term below the forty-year maximum allowed by FHA for new rental construction will, of course, correspondingly increase the debt service charge, or in the case of a rental property, the rents which will be required to carry any given investment. This does not, of course, mean that rents on rehabilitated structures will be higher than those on new structures. It does mean that the cost of carrying each thousand dollars of debt will be higher to the extent that the amortization term is lower than that allowed on new construction.

## The market

Insofar as the market for rehabilitation consists of present property owners in the area it depends, of course, on their willingness and ability to increase their housing expenses to cover the added costs. Insofar as rehabilitation is carried out by nonresident owners the market will depend upon the willingness and ability of existing tenants or tenants who may move into the areas as a result of the rehabilitation to pay the rents required to cover costs. In general, rehabilitation programs attempt to retain present tenants and owners, thus reducing the relocation problem. However, if the level of rehabilitation is high and the neighborhood is characterized by rental units, a substantial turnover of tenants can be expected. The willingness of families to move into the rehabilitation area will depend on the desirability of the neighborhood and of the particular dwelling unit in comparison with housing values available elsewhere. The same will be true with regard to families who may move in and buy houses in the rehabilitation area. One fact should be recognized. Many factors bearing on the value of a rehabilitated property depend on circumstances beyond the control of the individual property owner. These are the decisions of other property owners to rehabilitate surrounding properties and actions of the city in providing neighborhood improvements such as streets, parks and the like. This is the basic reason why the Housing Act of 1954 requires the development of a comprehensive urban renewal plan for rehabilitation areas and authorizes Federal financial assistance for neighborhood improvements in rehabilitation areas.

## Feasibility of rehabilitation

The rehabilitation of individual structures, as of entire neighborhoods, presents difficult technical and economic problems. Technically, any structure can be rehabilitated. But rehabilitation usually ceases to have meaning when the cost of rehabilitation plus the original purchase price approaches that of constructing a new dwelling on the site. (Exceptions to this can be found in the rehabilitation of the White House a few years ago and in many homes in Georgetown, D. C. and Alexandria, Virginia, where unique historical associations give old structures more value than any new structures could have). The principal technical problem presented by rehabilitation is that of determining in advance the extent of structural and other work which will be necessary and feasible to bring about a given improvement in a particular dwelling. Not only does estimating the cost of rehabilitation, particularly with regard to foundation and other hidden structural components, present difficult technical problems, but because of the limited experience of contractors with this type of work the art is not very highly developed.

Another problem presented by rehabilitation is that of estimating the added value which will be brought about by virtue of a given amount of rehabilitation. Far too little is known, as yet, about the general relationships between the costs of rehabilitation and the values deriving from it. Equally difficult is the job of estimating the increased property values which will result from public improvements to the neighborhood.

Perhaps these are the reasons why there is still considerable uncertainty even among experts on the economic feasibility of a widespread program of neighborhood rehabilitation, as well as upon the extent and the permanence of property and neighborhood improvement which can be economically accomplished by the methods usually employed.

Several varying opinions will emphasize the point. Based on his experience, Francis Lammer, Director of Redevelopment in Philadelphia, has called voluntary rehabilitation a myth. He says Philadelphia has found that it can acquire a typical downtown dwelling for $5,500. Rehabilitation of the unit, he says, will cost $3,500. However, the rehabilitated dwelling will have a value of $7,000. Thus, he concludes, a subsidy of $2,000 per dwelling is needed plus a substantial city investment in neighborhood improvements.[36]

A contrasting view was taken by the Zisook Construction Company of Chicago which made a study of the feasibility of rehabilitation in an area in that city. Zisook found, after a careful building-by-building study of rehabilitation requirements and costs, that the vast majority of structures in the area could be feasibly and economically rehabilitated privately provided long-term financing was available.[37] The current value of the units covered by the Chicago study was approximately double that mentioned by Mr. Lammer. In contrast to the Philadelphia case, the houses covered by the Chicago study were largely rental units.

Another study of the feasibility of rehabilitation was recently completed in an area in New York City consisting largely of "brownstone" row houses. The study concluded that this type of dwelling, if structurally sound, could be economically rehabilitated providing

### TABLE 4
*Estimated Capital Costs, Operating Expenses and Returns, Three Types of Brownstone Rehabilitation (Pilot Area)*

| | Minimum (1 structure) 8 d. units or 15 Rms. | Intermediate (1 structure) 7 d. units or 13½ Rms. | Extensive (2 structures) 15 d. units or 27½ Rms. |
|---|---|---|---|
| | $ | $ | $ |
| Cost of land and old building | 24,000 | 24,000 | 48,000 |
| Cost of alteration | 30,000 | 48,300 | 104,500 |
| Total cost | 54,000 | 72,300 | 152,500 |
| Total cost per dwelling unit | 6,750 | 10,328 | 10,167 |
| Total cost per room | 3,375 | 5,356 | 5,545 |
| Average monthly rent per dwelling unit | 119.25 | 135.40 | 138.40 |
| Range of monthly rent per dwelling unit | 80–125 | 90–175 | 97.50–175 |
| Annual gross rent | 9,540 | 9,480 | 20,760 |
| Annual operating expense | 5,350 | 5,925 | 11,358 |
| Net return—free and clear | 4,190 | 3,555 | 9,402 |
| Free and clear return as a percent of cost | 7.8% | 4.9% | 6.2% |

Source: New York, N. Y. City Plan Commission. Urban Renewal 1958. P. 51. (A Report on The West Side Urban Renewal Study undertaken by The New York City Planning Commission as a Demonstration Project under Section 314 of the Housing Act of 1954).

long-term financing were available. It is perhaps significant to note that the study concluded that rehabilitation to a relatively low
standard had more economic advantages than
rehabilitation to a higher standard.[38]

It is evident that rehabilitation presents complex and difficult questions, clear answers to
many of which must wait more concrete experience. It also seems clear that the costs, the
nature and even the feasibility of rehabilitation
will vary widely from neighborhood to neighborhood and from structure to structure.

In 1953 Jack M. Siegel and C. William
Brooks, consultants to the President's Advisory
Committee on Government Housing Policies and
Programs, studied the rehabilitation experience
of some nine cities. Their conclusions furnish
an excellent summary of the complexities and
limitations of neighborhood conservation and
rehabilitation. Here are the conclusions:

" (1) The feasibility of structural rehabilitation varies with the type of architecture
and construction involved. Many buildings
have hidden defects not ascertainable on cursory inspection.

(2) Minimal rehabilitation of individual
structures as a result of law enforcement cannot fundamentally change the character of a
slum neighborhood.

(3) The cost of rehabilitation which has
produced structures that compete with new
construction, is beyond the means of slum
dwellers.

(4) The cost of unsubsidized thorough rehabilitation ('reconstruction') is often equal
to that of new construction.

(5) Rehabilitation work requires unusually
close supervision, and a wide variety of skills.

(6) Rehabilitation must be carried out over
a wide enough area to produce its own en-   ·
vironment.

(7) Rehabilitation of high density dwellings
in slum areas is usually not feasible.

(8) Financing of rehabilitation is difficult
because of the problems of estimating the
mortgageable life of the structure and the
uncertainty surrounding the future of the
area.

(9) Even buildings outlive their usefulness.
Large slum areas have deteriorated to the
point where clearance and redevelopment are
the only answer.

(10) Minimum rehabilitation in blighted
areas may tend to perpetuate rather than
eliminate slums."[39]

### Rehabilitation standards

Before the passage of the Housing Act of
1954 most of the rehabilitation programs undertaken had sought, through systematic enforcement of housing codes and ordinances, to require residents of the rehabilitation area to bring
their properties up to city's minimum housing
requirements. This usually amounted to elimination of illegal over-occupancy, painting and
repair of leaky roofs and siding, elimination of
basic structural defects, and installation or improvement of basic sanitary facilities. While the
enforcement of such requirements certainly improves housing conditions in the affected area,
they are not standards calculated to accomplish
a basic upgrading of a neighborhood. As the
consultants to the President's Advisory Committee observed in 1953, such minimal rehabilitation does not basically change the character
of a slum neighborhood and there is a real
question whether it is sufficient to reverse permanently the decay cycle.[40] This is perhaps
why opinion has been so divided on the true
success of past programs of this type.

The many rehabilitation programs being
planned under the provisions of the Housing
Act of 1954 typically aim to achieve a higher
standard than that required by local housing
codes and ordinances. Indeed, the benefits of
FHA's liberal Section 220 mortgage insurance
are not available to finance the rehabilitation
of a property in an urban renewal area unless
it is to be brought up to the FHA minimum
property standards for rehabilitated properties.
FHA's standards for rehabilitation, while often
substantially above those required by city codes,
are not so high as those required by FHA for
new construction. The FHA property standard
for rehabilitation is the level to which FHA
believes the properties must be brought to make
them marketable and thus to provide reasonable
security for the mortgage loan. It is, therefore,
presumably FHA's judgment of the physical
level to which the properties must be brought
(taking into account also the general neighborhood improvements which are a part of the

plan) to reverse the decay cycle and to restore the neighborhood to economic life. To restore the area to the minimum FHA standards, which are normally worked out with the local urban renewal agency during project planning, thus becomes the objective of the rehabilitation program.

Most cities are planning to reach this objective through a two-stage operation. First, the city will, through use of the police power, enforce upon property owners rehabilitation up to the level of the municipal codes and ordinances. Lacking the authority to enforce a level of rehabilitation beyond this, the city will, as a second step, seek to persuade property owners voluntarily to bring their properties up to the higher project standards. Since the liberal Section 220 FHA financing is available only to properties which are brought up to the higher project standard, cities are putting heavy reliance on the incentive of FHA's more liberal financing terms to induce property owners to raise their properties to the higher standard.

### Enforcement

The authority of a city to enforce its minimum housing codes and ordinances and to deny further use of a structure which does not conform seems well established. More obscure, however, are the means by which a city can assure that rehabilitation is carried out to project standards which are higher, as most of them are, than the minimum code. Not many cities have yet faced up to what they would do if a large proportion of property owners refuse to rehabilitate their properties voluntarily to the above-the-code standards of the rehabilitation project. Not many, either, are clear on what they would or could do in the event that it develops, as it might in some cases, that the rehabilitation of a given property to project standards is uneconomic. What is to be done when the value added by rehabilitation does not equal the cost of rehabilitation? Some cities believe that under these conditions they would have the authority to condemn the property and carry out the rehabilitation themselves or sell it to someone who will agree to do so. To make this feasible, however, it would be necessary for the city to write off the difference between the value of the property and the cost of acquisition plus rehabilitation.

# Facts and fictions in urban renewal

*LOUIS WINNICK*

The accomplishments to date of publicly-sponsored urban renewal are unimpressive, largely because the interval between plan and execution is so awesomely long.

There are many obvious reasons why performance has lagged so badly: insufficient financing; a scarcity of trained personnel; the tooling-up time needed for state and local enabling legislation; the difficulties encountered in establishing operating agencies and administrative procedures. But the most important cause of delay has been the absence of clear-cut urban renewal objectives.

Legislators and administrators understandably become dilatory as they discover that we are not altogether sure what we want to do with our

*Reprinted from* Ends and Means of Urban Renewal, *Philadelphia Housing Association, 1961, pp. 23–45, with permission of the publisher.*

urban renewal programs and that our petitions to Washington seem to be framed more in terms of money than ideas.

The public has not yet given the policy-maker any clear mandates on urban renewal goals or priorities. Virtually every renewal plan is greeted with sharply mixed reactions by the community and, no matter what its content, strong and vocal groups will find fault with the particular location chosen, the type of replacement facilities, the relative proportions of clearance and rehabilitation and, most of all, with the accompanying burden of tenant displacement.

We will debate for many years to come what urban renewal is supposed to do for the city. Is the urban need really a physical improvement program to replace old bricks with new and rehabilitated buildings? Or should our resources go for social programs to correct deficiencies in family behavior? To what extent should urban redevelopment become a device for resettling population – i.e., for exchanging one population group for another at various points in the city in order to achieve a better "mix" of race, income or social desirability? Is urban renewal mainly a housing program or should it freely encompass all types of real estate? Should redevelopment be conceived as slum-eradication or as a broader program for land assembly and clearance to overcome the city's greatest lacks – vacant sites and the planned arrangement of buildings? To what degree should renewal be used as a device for strengthening the city's fiscal base by increasing tax revenues and reducing expenditures? Finally, if there can be a "finally" in this catalogue of questions, should the prime mover in renewal be the federal or the local government?

These questions will be settled only by time and public discussion. I would like to intrude on this discussion in the immodest hope of clarifying some of the issues. I suspect, though, that I shall succeed only in provoking still more debate. But, after all, this is the purpose of a forum.

## Urban renewal versus urban redesign

No matter how broadly the concept of urban renewal is drawn, it will still fall short of a true program for urban redesign. By its very nature, urban renewal is confined to neighborhoods of present or impending slum and blight. Which is to say that public intervention in reshaping private land use is largely reserved for the city's weak areas where there can be little or no unaided private investment and is absent in the strong areas where a considerable volume of private construction is taking place.

It would be going too far to say that such an arrangement is topsy-turvy. Yet in many ways it is ironical that the *planned* reconstruction of our cities will take place only where there have been slums; everywhere else the private developer is left virtually to his own devices, subject only to the limited and negative controls of building and zoning ordinances.

The unaided private investor – no matter how enlightened – cannot give us a city in the image we desire. For private redevelopers can seldom assemble sites of optimal size or location. They make do with what they can. Frustrated by multiple titles, by existing leases and stubborn holdouts, by the existing street system and unpurchasable public buildings, they forego their best opportunities for the next best; they design their structures according to the size and shape of the site they are able to get and without much reference to adjacent structures. Private land assembly in the core of the metropolis will always be fortuitous and haphazard and likewise will be its results.

Consider the case in New York City. Since World War II some 40 million square feet of office space and more than 250,000 private dwelling units have been built or started. The buildings vary in design from very good to very bad, density varies from a floor area ratio of 30 to 6, and the structures are spotted about in no clear-cut relation to each other and with none of the "external economies" that could accrue from a large-scale joint planned effort.

Were we to conceive the need of urban areas to be the planned placement of real estate facilities rather than renewal alone, and make much wider use of public assistance in land assembly, whole new possibilities of form and arrangement would be opened up, exemplified by our

Rockefeller and Penn Centers. If the municipality were able to offer private redevelopers cleared land at full cost anywhere in the city, most of New York's 40 million square feet of new office space could have been built around six or seven large plazas or landscaped green areas having common underground parking facilities, a more serviceable street pattern, and harmony of form and placement. Similarly, the hundreds of apartment structures built in and around the central ring could have been grouped in more efficient and esthetically satisfying arrangements.

The grouping of buildings is land and cost economizing. It permits the pooling of the small bits of open space required by zoning into truly usable open areas. Grouped buildings also require much less street and parking space per unit of building space. And predetermining the location of structures allows better advance planning – and more efficient utilization – of complementary facilities such as schools, restaurants, stores and transportation.

All of this may seem wild-eyed, particularly coming from one with a healthy respect for free enterprise and a deep skepticism of visionary plans. For what is suggested is massive intervention in the private real estate market, going far beyond our present timorous approach. But genuine city planning on a master scale is not likely to be achieved under the existing rules of private property. The private real estate market works quite inefficiently in altering the physical structure of highly developed cities. The invisible hand cannot lead to correct solutions from the standpoint of the economist or the planner, only to very visible compromises if not downright errors.

Publicly-sponsored urban redevelopment may be more, not less, necessary in the non-slum growth areas. For it is in those places where effective demand for new real estate is strongest that the greatest opportunities exist for shaping the city to a preconceived design.

## Limitations on urban redevelopment

Having just expanded the horizons of urban redevelopment let me now hastily shorten the perspective.

There is a prevailing tendency to define the scale of the country's urban redevelopment and renewal programs by criteria of need rather than of economic feasibility. As a result, the estimated costs of such programs become astronomical, with some figures ranging as high as $1 trillion. Whether the American economy is capable of supporting such a vast urban investment program, given so many competing claims for the use of resources, I confess I do not know. But I would venture that the future scale of urban redevelopment will be determined much less by needs or available resources than by what we can sell to private occupants. Apart from reuse with public or quasi-public facilities, urban redevelopment cannot proceed any further or faster than markets can be found for the replacement real estate.

How large a market exists in the older cities for large amounts of new building space remains to be seen. The economic disabilities of present cities – as was most recently and forcefully brought out in the Vernon studies of the New York Region[1] – are too great to take for granted a large, not to speak of a limitless, market for new or rehabilitated real estate at rents required by current and future building and operating costs. True, the market can be widened by public aids to reduce rents. But, even with such aids, rents can be lowered only so far; and rent cuts are effective only in the degree to which demand is responsive to price.

Regional and suburban shifts in population and economic activity have been highly unfavorable to the market for real estate in the typical older city. The demand for office space, for example, has become exceedingly selective. In the 1920's and earlier, office construction was quite diffused, reaching into nearly all cities of 50,000 and over. Today, largely as a result of improvements in transportation and communication, a sizable amount of administrative office space is being built in only a handful of cities.

The potential market for new downtown retail facilities is even poorer; disinvestment is more common than new investment.

While industrial reuse has many possibilities in the outer rings of the city, the average industrial plant requires so much land per unit of building space that formidable economic barriers would have to be overcome.

Residential investment, given the favorable demographic trends of the next two decades and the greater ability of housing to command support for public aids, is likely to have a more promising market but only in the larger and more urban cities. We must also remember that as more and more places within a metropolitan region get on the renewal bandwagon they will find themselves competing for the same set of occupants. Estimates of potential demand become inflated because each of a number of communities in a housing market area tends to measure its anticipated housing demand from the same total.

The most reasonable picture one can draw is that the future market for renewal real estate is likely to be quite spotty: very strong in some cities, very weak in others, stronger for certain types of real estate than for others and, in some sections of even the strongest cities, no market at all for any kind of private real estate.

We must continually remind ourselves that the dramatic renewal plans now being drawn in so many cities have yet to meet the stern test of the market. We should not be deluded by the initial rush of private sponsors into renewal. The individual sponsor is concerned with the success of his own venture. He may well fill his new office building, hotel or apartment house, but the real test of long-run economic feasibility is: will the space vacated by his new tenants be filled? Or will there be an overhang of vacancies in existing buildings which can offer powerful competition with respect to rents? Because the capital costs of existing buildings are sunk, rents in such structures can drop to levels just sufficient to meet operating costs. The trend in vacancies and rents of existing buildings, other than those which are woefully obsolete or poorly located, will measure the potential for redevelopment.

In short, large-scale redevelopment must lead to more than a mere redistribution of present occupants. There must be a sizable net expansion in the demand for urban real estate facilities. Only in the latter event can renewal efforts be sustained and continuous. In some cities one can already observe that new facilities have resulted in redistribution rather than expansion. The new buildings have been tenanted at the expense of vacancies in existing buildings. In other cities the demand for new space depends heavily on civic-minded financial institutions and businessmen who, eager to further local renewal efforts, may sponsor new facilities even when the added cost for space exceeds the gain in convenience or utility. A measure of philanthropy is involved, and no market can long survive on philanthropy.

The scale of redevelopment will be largest in those cities where the underlying demand for space is genuine but cannot be filled because the private market is unable to assemble sites of the right size or location or on a scale sufficient to change neighborhood environment. That is, redevelopment will succeed in urban areas where the impediments to capital investment lie more on the supply side than on the demand side of the market. Redevelopment, therefore, is likely to be most successful in urban centers where real estate markets are already comparatively strong and where the rate of private construction in the inner rings is high. To mention names, redevelopment is likely to fare better in New York than in Newark, in Washington compared to Baltimore, in Chicago rather than Detroit.

One never knows where to draw the line between realism and gloom. But future prospects do not point to the replacement of all or most existing slums by private real estate facilities. In a very large number of cities, particularly smaller cities near major urban centers, the choice will be between limited rehabilitation plus stricter occupancy controls on existing structures or reuse with nonmarket facilities such as public and institutional buildings or even parks. It is in such places that federal Title I aids will be most necessary.

## Title I versus urban redevelopment

I would like to challenge a prevailing notion that publicly-sponsored urban redevelopment is either synonymous with Title I or economically possible only with federal aids.* As a result of such a view, local redevelopment programs have become almost completely dependent on federal initiative and control. The size and scheduling of our redevelopment programs are left to the vagaries of each session of Congress, to the political coloration of the national administration, and to the rules set forth by the Urban Renewal Administration.

But let us consider the economic realities of urban redevelopment and ask ourselves whether local programs cannot succeed without massive help from Washington. As presently conceived, planned redevelopment seeks to bring about the reuse of slum or blighted areas in two ways: first, by encouraging the exercise of eminent domain for assembly of privately-held real estate; second, by making reuse economically feasible through government help to bridge the gap between the acquisition cost of land and its market value in reuse. (For reasons I do not wish to get into here, I will refrain from using that abused word, subsidy.)

Eminent domain is clearly a state and local power to which Title I adds nothing. The real contribution of Title I is financial aid to balance part of the difference between the cost and reuse value of sites, an aid commonly referred to as land writedown. Our redevelopment concepts all seem to be centered on the importance of reducing the selling price of land to private sponsors.

In my judgment, the emphasis on land writedown is unwarranted and has resulted in mistaken policies.

The success of private redevelopment hinges not on land writedown as such but on the rent (or price) per unit of space in the new improvement. Rent must be low enough to attract occupants, so that sufficient income will be generated to meet capital and operating costs, including an adequate return to the investor. Obviously, the final rent (or price) on new or rehabilitated facilities is determined by a large number of costs besides the price paid for the site: architect's fees, building materials,

bricklayers, taxes, mortgage funds, janitors, elevator operators and doormen. There is no special quality about the cost of sites that makes it essential for this single component of total costs to become the be-all and end-all of financial aid.

We shall remain confused on the economics of urban redevelopment until we understand that the real objective of government aid is to *bring down the rent (or price) of new private real estate to its market level.* Land writedown is a misnomer for what should be more accurately termed *rent (or price) writedown.*

Clearly, no financial help would be required if the earning power of the new real estate facility (in its re-created environment) were deemed sufficient to pay full capital and operating costs. This is by no means an impossible case; indeed, most urban redevelopment in America has required no public grants-in-aid. Moreover, there are instances in the present Title I program where land costs have been unnecessarily or excessively written down, i.e., the reuse real estate could have commanded a rent sufficient to pay all costs, including the full cost of the site. But in most urban neighborhoods which are deteriorated enough to justify redevelopment, market rent on the reuse real estate is likely to be insufficient to defray full capital and operating costs so that government aid becomes obligatory.

Writedown of land, however, is by no means the most effective, and certainly not the only, way of achieving economic feasibility. The cost of land plays usually but a minor role in rent determination, accounting for 15 percent or less of the monthly rent per unit of space in elevator apartments or office buildings. For example, in New York City an apartment house built on cleared land costing $25 a square foot and financed with an FHA mortgage would, at typical density, require a monthly rent of approximately $50 per room. Of this, less than $6 is attributable to the cost (purchase price and subsequent taxes) of land. Each $5 per square foot in writedown would therefore re-

*Title I of the Housing Act of 1949 is the basic federal legislation under which slum clearance or redevelopment programs are carried out.

duce rent by little more than $1 per room per month. Thus with a $25 (100 percent) write-down, monthly rent would remain at $44 (actually more since the site would carry more than a zero assessment). Where land can be assembled and cleared for $10 or less per square foot the effect of land writedown on the rent of high-rise structures at urban densities would be quite negligible.

By contrast, the rent-reducing power of easier credit terms or real estate tax concessions, or a combination of both, is far greater. For example, under a New York City program of low ($3\frac{1}{2}$ percent) interest rates plus 50 percent tax abatement, the monthly rent on the above hypothetical project could be reduced to $32.25 per room *without* land writedown. In other words, credit and tax aids would, in this illustration, reduce rents by three times as much as a full land writedown.

The significance of this financial arithmetic cannot be overstated. For it tells us that not only is redevelopment possible by local action but, more important, that tax and credit aids can result in the redevelopment of areas *which are now beyond the reach of Title I.* There are many neighborhoods in every large city, the so-called gray areas outside the core, where land and clearance costs are not excessive, perhaps $8 or less per foot, and where it would be difficult to find a market for apartments renting for more than $18–25 per room. In such cases, something more powerful than land write-downs may be needed.

When we recognize that the real purpose of government financial aid is to reduce the rent (or price) of the redevelopment facility rather than the cost of land, and that large rent reductions can be brought about by extending local credit and tax aids to renewal areas, it becomes clear that Title I assistance is neither a necessary nor a sufficient condition for redevelopment. However, none of the foregoing means that the search for federal assistance should be relaxed. For one, not all communities are in a position, politically, to evolve tax-exemption and mortgage loan programs. For another, every city contains neighborhoods where the spread between cost and market rent is so great that there will be a necessity for some form of direct financial grants which, if it so pleases us, can be applied as land writedown.

By adding tax and credit aids to land write-down, the city is provided with a much fuller set of redevelopment tools, three aids instead of one. Each aid could then be used singly or in a wide variety of combinations, depending on the cost-rent factors of every reuse plan. The scope of urban redevelopment programs could thus be expanded well beyond the limits of Title I and local redevelopment authorities would be enabled to conduct independent programs without the delays and uncertainties that stem from federal controls.

## The " disappearing " middle-income family

Social concern over the middle-income housing problem equals or exceeds the concern over the housing of the poor a generation ago. Everywhere, the exodus of middle-income families from the city is decried. Yet no one is quite sure why the loss of middle-income families has more serious consequences than the loss of high-income families who build and support the city's cultural facilities, or, for that matter, the loss of low-income families who not only perform the menial tasks that need doing but give a city its highly-prized economic balance.

Nevertheless, the middle-income family has lately become enshrined, endowed with a nobility apparently lacking in other income groups. Perhaps such enshrinement, as was the case with the American Indian, is a natural sequel to the vanishment of any group. Or perhaps the community has been disappointed by the low-income family of the 1950's and is seeking a more deserving recipient of love and aid somewhere higher up the income ladder.

Obviously, there is a danger in thinking that social virtue is the property of some income group or even that virtue is related to income. As we are well aware – though do not often say – our eagerness to attract or retain middle-income families in public housing, for example, has really little to do with income as such but with anticipated behavior as residents. Similarly, low-income families as such do not create an urban problem (think of all the decent elderly individuals and couples with $3,000 or less living in quiet and independent respectability); the problem stems, rather, from families with undesirable traits whose incomes tend to be low, but who are also found with surprising frequency in middle or higher income brackets. The mistake we may be making is to use income as a symbol or proxy for other valuable attributes to which it may or may not be linked. As in the case of the rent-income ratio (discussed below), a very uncertain relationship is being converted into an instrument of policy.

I would prefer to leave such musings to better qualified social thinkers and turn to the examination of another widely-held notion: the disappearance of middle-income families from the central city. Let me start by offering a quotation:

> "Every man of moderate income saw that ... he could house his family more decently and at less cost in any one of the suburban towns of New Jersey ... even if twenty miles away.... Therefore, an exodus began to these towns which has continued for several years, to the detriment of the city that is hardly yet realized ... its middle classes in large part self-exiled and its laboring population being brutalized in the tenements...."

This observation on the disappearance of middle-income families from New York City was made in 1872, nearly a century ago. Similar statements can be found in the literature of succeeding decades. Surely, by now there must be hardly any middle-income families left at all! That planners' nightmare, *The City of the Rich and the Poor*, should by now be a very evident reality.

Considering the importance of the subject, it is surprising to find no systematic studies of historical shifts in the income pattern of the city. I realize, in turning to the few statistics which are available, that it would be hard to get agreement on how to define middle-income families. But if we accept a range of, say, $4,000 to $10,000, as descriptive of what we regard to be the middle-income class, we find that, in 1956, households in this income range were 51 percent of all households in the central

cities of major metropolitan areas. The corresponding proportion in the suburbs of these central cities was 60 percent, not strikingly higher. Indeed, the relative size of the gap between city and suburb was greater for high-income households ($10,000 or more) than for the middle-income class, so perhaps our concern over disappearance should rightfully extend still higher up the income scale.

Not only are middle-income residents still a large part of the city, but the group appears to be growing in relative importance. According to a Census survey, between 1950 and 1956, the proportion of families in New York City with $5,000–$10,000 income (in constant 1956 dollars) increased by approximately 50 percent. A comparable increase occurred in Chicago as well as in urban areas as a whole.

Obviously, no one will deny that middle-income families have been leaving the city in large number, though we badly need a full analysis of this trend. But it is equally obvious that we are dealing with a complicated phenomenon, having many cross-currents, and one which cannot be adequately described as the "disappearance" of an income group.

For the proportion of middle-income residents in any urban center is determined not merely by migration to and from the central core. It is determined also by "vertical" shifts, i.e., the rise to middle-income status of formerly low-income families, the rise to high-income status of middle-income families and the descent of higher-income families to lower-income status because of retirement or misfortune. These migratory and status shifts are continuous and would be best described in terms of rates of change over time, concerning which, unhappily, little is known. But the present high proportion of middle-income families in urban centers, after generations of exodus, and the increase in their number between 1950 and 1956, indicates the presence of a replacement process whereby losses from the middle-income group are compensated from other sources.

It may well be that decentralization, which in the postwar period carried beyond the political boundary lines of the city and was reinforced by a growing propensity for homeownership, has produced an increase in the rate of outflow and a decrease in the rate of replacement of the city's middle-income class, so that the proportion of middle-income residents is lower than economic circumstances warrant. But all this remains to be proved.

What fragmentary data seem to show is that city-suburban migration patterns have been more selective with respect to family type than income. The white family with children in virtually all income classes has tended to suburbanize most readily. At the same time, central cities, or at least the larger ones, have retained much of their hold on the childless adult, again in all income classes.

Simultaneously, too, there has been a considerable economic advance of minority and other low-income groups. Negroes and Puerto Ricans, particularly families with multiple wage-earners, have entered the middle-income range in great number. To be sure, many minority families, though statistically in the middle-income group, do not display the middle-class behavior patterns we are prone to admire. But this again merely points up the error of referring to income when we are thinking of something else.

## Economically balanced neighborhoods

One renewal objective currently in favor among planners is the economically-balanced neighborhood, i.e., housing inhabited by a wide variety of income groups.

It is not clear why economically heterogeneous neighborhoods are innately superior to the homogeneous. We do not really know whether economically diverse groups truly mix or merely live side by side. And casual observation indicates that many exclusively high-income or middle-income neighborhoods seem to have withstood neighborhood decline extremely well while many economically-mixed neighborhoods have proved quite vulnerable. The social gains of mixture and social losses from economic homogeneity have yet to be demonstrated.

But a demonstration of the validity of our most cherished beliefs is seldom possible or wanted. The superior virtues of economically-

mixed neighborhoods will have to be taken as self-evident.

Even so, many questions remain on how economic balance can or should be attained. Most commonly, planners seek to achieve a balance of income groups by providing housing at different rent (price) levels: high-rent housing will bring high-income families; moderate-rent housing, middle-income families; low-rent (public) housing, low-income families. The optimal proportions of each class of housing are not specified – and, indeed, cannot be – since no one can say what "mix" of income groups is required to bring about socially desirable interaction.

The use of rent (or price) as a device for controlling the income mix of a neighborhood rests on a major premise: that a high, if not perfect, correlation exists between income and housing expenditures. The facts, however, are otherwise, i.e., the actual correlation is quite weak. As numerous types of data show, the income range of families which occupy housing at any given rent level is quite wide. According to the 1956 National Housing Inventory, for example, rental units with gross rent of between $80 and $100 per month were occupied by households at all income levels, from less than $2,000 to more than $10,000: one-fourth had incomes of $4,000 or less and 15 percent had incomes of more than $8,000. Comparable results will be found throughout most of the rent scale. In other words, a given rent (or price) is associated not with economic homogeneity but with economic variety.

Lest these figures be considered a freak of Census aggregates let us look at the income distribution in two Title I apartment developments in New York City. In a so-called luxury apartment project with rent averaging close to $50 per room, household incomes ranged from under $4,000 to more than $20,000, the median being about $8,800. In a nearby Title I co-operative with monthly charges of $25 per room, household income also ranged from under $4,000 to more than $20,000, with a median of $6,900. In both cases, the tenants were drawn from widely diverse income groups, with the bulk in the middle-income range. The proportion of households with incomes of $6,000 to

$10,000 was virtually identical in both projects, 42 percent. Note, too, that median income in the high-rent project was only 27 percent higher than in the cooperative despite a 100 percent difference in monthly housing costs – an indication that the relation between income and rent is far from simple. True, the high-rent project had a higher proportion of high-income tenants ($14,000 or more) and a lower proportion of low-income tenants (under $4,000). There is, after all, *some* relation between income and rent. But we are forced to conclude from these survey data that (a) both redevelopment projects achieved a considerable degree of economic balance; (b) rent is an inefficient mechanism for controlling the income composition of a neighborhood (a desired income mix can be obtained with certainty only by direct selection of tenants, provided there is sufficient demand to permit choices to be made); and (c) the term "middle-income housing" does not seem to be a very meaningful one.

Other data could be brought to bear but all would show the same thing: families with the same income vary greatly in monthly outlays for housing with the result that housing at every given cost level will have occupants of differing economic status.

To be sure, in virtually all new private housing there is likely to be a deficit of very low-income families. Such a deficit could be corrected by inclusion of public housing in a redevelopment plan. But, here, two caveats must be offered.

First, there will be few if any renewal neighborhoods that will not continue to have a high proportion of low-income families in surviving structures in or adjacent to the redevelopment site. In such cases, the goal of economic balance would reqire that new housing *be restricted* to middle- and upper-income groups.

Second, public housing, unless sharply limited in quantity, may lessen considerably the market for adjacent new private housing and endanger the success of the redevelopment scheme. While this is not the place to review the developing faults of our public housing programs, it has become increasingly clear that, unless carefully planned with respect to scale and tenancy, public housing is unwanted in most communities.

These adverse attitudes would quickly be reflected in the renting or sales experience of new private housing, particularly since many of the prospective tenants or owners have sufficient income to choose from among alternative housing opportunities.

We could afford to be generous or indiscriminate in determining the mix of rents (or prices) for redevelopment housing were there not a real economic loss whenever cleared sites (a very scarce resource in the center of most cities) are not developed for their highest use. As I have written elsewhere, a city is like a theatre, with a relatively fixed number of locations each having different utility to prospective occupants. Generally, the close-in, center seats can bear higher price tags than the distant and peripheral because they offer more convenience, enjoyment and status. It would be irrational, if not disastrous, for a theater manager to ignore the gains from differential pricing and give everyone entry at the same terms, i.e., to offer all his seats at the same price. The likely result would be excess demand (a waiting list) for the desirable orchestra seats and vacant seats (wasted idle capacity) in the balcony.

Likewise, giving equal entry to all types of redevelopment housing in the desirable core of the central city will usually result in a higher burden on government – a lower resale price, lower taxes, and excessive use of public aids for rent writedown. Public resources which could be used for slum clearance elsewhere are correspondingly lessened. Worse yet, and a factor not yet clearly perceived by renewal planners, is that public financial aids to reduce costs can serve as a powerful incentive for resettling the less preferred outlying gray areas as well as areas undergoing racial transition. If families are offered housing at equal costs, regardless of the relative desirability of the location, there will be little reason for them to seek out the "balcony seats" of the city and consequently little hope for their renewal. We must begin to think of public aids to reduce consumer housing costs not merely as a welfare benefit to be given to some lucky recipients, but as the single most effective means at our disposal for guiding the locational distribution of new construction.

Recognizably, the doctrine that renewal housing should charge what the traffic will bear – particularly since the goal of economic balance would not be seriously compromised – is not likely to be popular. One reason is that all of us are on occasion guilty of weighing policy decisions as if they were isolated and independent rather than viewing every decision as one of a family of alternatives, each yielding a different balance of gain and loss.

As Paul Ylvisaker has said, we want representation without taxation, seek a benefit without consideration to cost or to the value of a superior benefit foregone. The answer to the question, " why shouldn't the poor as well as the rich have a prime or central location? " is this : as a matter of social equity, perhaps they should, but is a prime location worth more than the extra housing that could be built or extra slum acreage cleared on lower-priced sites elsewhere?

What the lessons of the foregoing little essays are, I'm not altogether sure.

One is clearly the need for stronger factual underpinnings for urban renewal policies, even if at times we grow impatient with the plea for more and larger research projects which will only infrequently fulfill their promise. For research can contribute to policy only where the requisite information is observable and measurable and where the facts uncovered can lead to unambiguous conclusions concerning the rationality of some course of action. Such is rarely the case.

More important than research, perhaps, is the need to sort out our beliefs, to avoid confusing those which we truly hold with those acquired from slogan and soothsaying. For the most difficult decisions in urban renewal policy must inevitably collide with those ancient totems, the ponderous Value Judgement and the teetering Balance of Social Costs. On these matters we must seek the guidance of our convictions and not the charts of the researcher. One may demonstrate through research the effect on rents or municipal costs of alternative controls on building size, but not whether a high- or low-density city is best for urban life. Likewise, research may (hopefully) be able to demonstrate the greater economy and efficiency of metropolitan government. But research cannot tell us if such gains outweigh the advantages that accrue to a free society where millions of consumers are able to choose from a wide range of autonomous residential communities, each with its own social and political structure, and each self-determining the quality of its schools, the permissiveness of its zoning, and whether garbage should be collected at the front or back door.

Urban renewal policies, like all policy, will be shaped much more by public opinion than by the factfinder. And the public is not always swayed by even well-established facts on least cost or maximum efficiency, else the automobile would have never triumphed over mass transit. The area of irrationality in policy decisions will always remain wide because we are, in varying degree, ourselves irrational. The least we can do is to exchange and assess our thoughts – rational or otherwise.

# The lessons learned

*MARTIN MILLSPAUGH and GURNEY BRECKENFELD*

Does rehabilitation change the attitudes, values and behavior of the residents of blighted neighborhoods?

The record in Baltimore, in Chicago, in New Orleans and Miami shows that there can be a dramatic change in attitudes accompanying properly organized and well-managed neighborhood rehabilitation programs. The change appears to be more striking among residents of the neighborhood than among the people who have a hand in the program but live elsewhere.

*Inside the neighborhood*, these things can (and have) happened:

Residents of one-time slum buildings, which have been renovated and repaired along with the general clean-up of alleys and junk-heaped back yards, almost invariably register appreciation at the physical improvement, at the increased comfort and cleanliness. In Baltimore's Pilot Area, mothers note gratefully that the possibility of rats biting their children is no longer a major worry. In Miami's Coconut Grove, a Negro gardener remarks on how good it feels to come home at night and be able to get all the dirt off in the bathtub he never before had. In Chicago's Back-of-the-Yards, juvenile problem-cases tell the neighborhood council's staff counselor: "This used to be a crummy neighborhood, but now it's all fixed up."

Such attitude changes are elementary – the least common denominator of cultural progress. In rehabilitated neighborhoods there are also more sophisticated indications of attitude change. Fewer people are affected. Even so, the upper levels of change may well be the more significant. These bear promise that rehabilitation can contribute more broadly and fully than is commonly supposed to raising the goals and cultural standards of the nation – in the places where they are lowest.

Some upper-level changes in attitude:

More neighborly visiting back and forth developed between residents of a block; there were more neighborhood social gatherings. In Baltimore's Mount Royal area, as the president of the neighborhood association put it, the neighborhood was no longer split into homeowners and tenants – that is, "good guys and bad guys."

Awareness grew of the need for housing and sanitation laws. In Baltimore's Pilot Area, for example, housing inspectors came to be commonly regarded as friends and protectors of the residents, instead of authoritarian symbols to be feared instinctively.

For a few families, horizons of living were raised so much that they moved out of their old homes into new subdivisions or better old neighborhoods. In Negro neighborhoods like the Pilot Area and Miami's Coconut Grove, the families who learned most from rehabilitation were likely to move out to better areas elsewhere. In white neighborhoods like Back-of-the-Yards, Hyde Park and the Mount Royal area, the proudest families were those who had been persuaded not to move by the effects of rehabilitation.

Statistics (such as are kept) do not prove that rehabilitation has cut crime or juvenile

Reprinted from The Human Side of Urban Renewal, *Fight Blight, Inc., Baltimore, 1958, pp. 223–233, with permission of the publisher.*

delinquency. But there is some testimony to the effect that rehabilitation works a change in the teenage attitudes that may underlie such antisocial behavior. The probation officer in the Pilot Area, for instance, reported that hoodlum gangs were no longer heroes to younger children. Vandalism at the area's new school was far below the level that teachers had come to expect in a low-income neighborhood in Baltimore. As for adult crime, the Baltimore policeman who saw a 50 percent decrease may be too optimistic. But certainly the elimination of board fences, broken-down shacks and open, vacant houses removes the hiding places of crime, and drives at least some of it elsewhere.

A few individuals and families – once frustrated and overwhelmed by worries too big for them to cope with – have learned to deal with their own problems much more adequately. This was a result not so much of the physical rehabilitation as of careful educational case work, such as that done by the Fight Blight Fund in Baltimore, or the Loan Fund in Coconut Grove, or Back-of-the-Yards' Credit Union. The Credit Union appears to have been particularly effective in changing attitudes on how families should spend their money. (And mismanagement of family income exacts a fearful price from many a slum family.) Indeed, the remarkable success of these activities shows there is a great unmet need where they do not exist. People in blighted neighborhoods need advice far more often than they need cash.

Some of this new self-reliance extended to the neighborhood level. As residents worked out their own problems in rehabilitation, they found they could handle not only housing problems, but many others besides. In Miami's Coconut Grove, for instance, the educated white residents fought the first battles for the Negro residents – battles with city hall over zoning and rehabilitation inspections. They organized all the supporting activities inside the Grove's Colored Town, like the summer training program and the nursery. Now, Negro leaders are beginning to carry on for themselves.

In all types of neighborhoods, perhaps the most gratifying development of all was the change in the children. Where children were drawn into the rehabilitation program and made to feel that they could contribute to the improvement of their own homes, they responded with enthusiasm and energy. In the Pilot Area, where the schools made a diligent effort to teach good housing principles, the youngsters proved to be the best possible instruments to educate their parents. In families where parents were deaf to the urging of rehabilitation workers, the children sometimes shamed their elders into activity. In Miami, it was through the Carver School that some parents learned not to flush garbage down their new toilets. Whenever children learned about sanitation, cleanliness, neatness and home decoration, there seemed to be a good chance that these new standards would remain with them wherever they live.

One area of attitudes that did not change in the neighborhoods studied was the religious life of the people. Religion was already a strong influence. It remained so after rehabilitation. In several of the neighborhoods, this established orientation toward the church was the key to reaching the residents. Churches became focal points for neighborhood action. Priests or ministers were among the most effective spokesmen and leaders of the rehabilitation programs. These, of course, were the churchmen who were not too aloof to fight for better zoning, to circulate petitions against taverns, or to promote neighborhood fairs.

*Outside the neighborhood*, these are some of the things that can and have happened – though not equally everywhere:

In some cities (but not all), politicians have learned they must treat once-blighted neighborhoods with new respect. The extent of this change in attitude seems to vary in direct ratio with the power of the neighborhood organization. Some key questions are: Has it bested city hall in some battles? Has its militant existence persuaded city officials that cooperation will win more votes at election time than hostility or indifference?

Outsiders whose interest or work took them into close contact with residents of rehabilitation neighborhoods have had their eyes opened wide. Many of them have been amazed, for instance, at the welcome given social workers of any stripe who have nothing to offer but guidance. For some professional social workers, exposure to rehabilitation has changed their view toward their own work. Some now feel for the first time that many a social agency is too far out of contact with those it seeks to serve. Sample: a supervisor in Baltimore's Family & Children's Society discovered: "We were weak on letting people know what services were available."

In any case, the effect of a rehabilitation program on outsiders was directly proportional to their amount of actual contact with the neighborhood. Those who met the residents face-to-face, and learned their problems firsthand, learned to have a great deal of respect and sympathy for the average blighted-area family. Those who administered, analyzed, or advised from afar, however good their intentions, seldom completely understood the problems. As their distance from the neighborhood increased, so did their chance of misunderstanding it – and so did the chance that their attitude toward it would remain frozen.

## The effects of homeownership

In each neighborhood studied, it became apparent that changes in a family's attitudes usually hinge on whether the family owns or rents. Homeowners are more susceptible to higher standards than renters. There are tenants, to be sure, who become permanent additions to their neighborhoods, and who participate in rehabilitation work as much as homeowners. Such tenants change in the same way as homeowners. But most tenants have less incentive to boost their neighborhood – partly because all physical improvements become the property of the landlord, partly because improvements are likely to mean higher rent, and partly because the very fact of renting indicates transiency – no deep roots in the neighborhood.

Most homeowners, on the other hand, seem to have a built-in incentive to better their surroundings, once given the opportunity and the know-how. Neighborhoods with a high percentage of homeownership – even if this is overhung with oppressive mortgage loans or unenforceable contracts of sale – seem far more fertile fields for rehabilitation than neighborhoods with

a high percentage of tenancy. Homeowning seems to provide the ground in which the attitudes of rehabilitation can grow. Still, there are some families classed as homeowners who have neither the money nor the competence to deal with the responsibilities of homeowning. Such families, already in fear of losing their homes through default or misunderstanding, tend to fear and evade a rehabilitation program as an additional burden that threatens to topple a shaky financial structure.

Landlords are the other side of the coin. Where homeowners have a built-in incentive to improve their neighborhoods, most landlords have a built-in incentive to perpetuate the slum. This seems to be due to the effect of property tax laws and assessing practices. Undertaxation of overcrowded property (whether or not the crowding is illegal) is the rule, not the exception. Hence the more crowding, the more profit. So far – at least in the cities studied in this survey – efforts to take the profit out of slums have proved unequal to the huge task. As a result, landlords usually did as little as possible in the way of rehabilitation, and the landlord who "got religion" in this field was so unique as to be newsworthy.

There is one class of landlord to whom this applies much less. This is the landlord-in-residence – the man who lives in the same building with his tenants, or nearby in the same neighborhood. Such landlords share the conditions of the block and the neighborhood with their tenants. Their relationship with their tenants is often a close one. As a result, such landlords often react like other homeowners. This is also true of the shopkeeper who lives above his store. Such businesses are often nonconforming uses, and, as such, are generally considered to be an influence working toward blight. But in old neighborhoods like the Pilot Area, the storekeeper who lived upstairs sometimes turned out to be at least as strong a supporter of rehabilitation, and all its goals, as the man whose only investment was a home.

## The problem of population change

In some neighborhoods, the success of rehabilitation – and the chance that it would produce changes in attitude – was undermined by rapid change in population. Rapid change in a neighborhood – whether it is a change from white to Negro or from middle- to lower-class families or some other rapid change – produces a basic instability that makes it almost impossible for the attitudes of rehabilitation to gather momentum. Chicago's Hyde Park and Baltimore's Mount Royal neighborhood are examples – similar in many facets, different in others. On the surface, the statistics would indicate that both areas were good prospects for salvage. Not only were most of the structures sound, but a large proportion of the residents were already well educated and attuned to middle-class standards and attitudes. The problem was that the influx of uneducated or low-income families – both white and Negro – was so swift that it threatened to destroy neighborhood morale. In both places, city ordinances against overcrowding proved impotent to stem the tide toward blight. Slum profiteers outpaced and outmaneuvered the enforcement agencies, fattening on the Negroes' need and push for living space, and the poor whites' ready acceptance of tenement conditions. In the Mount Royal area, a unique alliance between white neighborhood leaders and officials of the Urban League raised hope that the racial competition, at least, would be stabilized, and the desire for rehabilitation reinforced by middle-class families of both races. In Chicago's Hyde Park, the population continued to change so fast that middle-class stabilization remained only a goal.

The converse of this situation appeared in two neighborhoods with relatively stable populations: the Back-of-the Yards and the Pilot Area. In the latter, where racial patterns were changing slowly, rehabilitation produced similar attitude changes in families of both races. In the Back-of-the-Yards, the unspoken hope of preserving a way of life built around Catholic nationality churches was a powerful stimulant to the rehabilitation effort – and to the attitude changes that resulted.

### The question of race

Race tensions are still little mentioned in the millions of words now being spoken and written on rehabilitation and urban renewal. This silence is presumably well intentioned. Officials, planners and assorted volunteers grappling with blighted areas wish to avoid any ground for accusations of race prejudice. Yet the racial situation has a great deal to do with the outcome of a rehabilitation program, and the resulting attitude changes.

Throughout the nation, dwellers in slums are preponderantly Negroes (or, more recently in some places, Puerto Ricans). The slum rehabilitation problem, therefore, happens to be in large part a nonwhite problem, and as such, it cannot be separated from all other problems facing the nonwhite population. In the Southern neighborhoods studied (Miami and New Orleans), most Negroes seemed so far sunk in poverty, illiteracy, ignorance and dependency – the product of generations of scanty education and lack of economic opportunity – that neighborhood rehabilitation programs did not reach them with the uplifting, rejuvenating effect that was found elsewhere. There was, nevertheless, a thin veneer of Negro craftsmen, professionals and other leaders living in the same slum with the lowest economic group. To these leaders, rehabilitation has given a hope for better standards in the future. For this alone, the effort is surely worth its cost, anywhere. For the lower levels of Negro society, rehabilitation shows evidence of improving health, infant mortality and physical living conditions, but a general upgrading in educational level seems necessary before any but the most elementary attitude changes can be expected.

The problem of rehabilitating the southern Negro is not faced by the South alone. Every month, more and more migrating families pour into northern cities like Chicago, or border cities like Baltimore. These cities, which have made great strides in uplifting ther most ignorant and depressed citizens, have found that every family rehabilitated out of the slum is replaced by a family of newcomers, whose education in urban living must be started from scratch. The problem of where to put the new migrants, or how to treat them so that they do not drag down the values of the neighborhoods into which they move, had not been solved in either the Mount Royal area or in Hyde Park.

In the Pilot Area, transients moved into the landlords' tenements, destroying much of the confidence that the rehabilitation program had built up in homeowning families. Their other attitudes – nurtured by the program – suffered proportionately.

### Perils of publicity

Publicity is one of the important tools of creating attitude change within a neighborhood that undertakes rehabilitation. Indeed, some experts have suggested that repetitive pronouncements of success have helped create that success by persuading people to believe it. Still, publicity has its pitfalls.

It is easy to overstate the accomplishments of rehabilitation. This study has focused deliberately on rehabilitation efforts which could be classified either as (1) particularly successful or (2) so well-known they were becoming (rightly or wrongly) noted as pace-setting examples of how it ought to be done.

Close study has shown, unfortunately, that many a celebrated rehabilitation effort was really bungled, or that a vital part was botched, or that it succeeded despite mistakes that could have been fatal.

This does not mean that because rehabilitation does not cure every social ill, business sin, political shenanigan and ordinary cussedness, it is more or less a failure. The gratefulness of slum dwellers for simple results like good plumbing and the absence of rats, the friendliness of neighbors who have struggled together, the aspirations of children and the raised horizons of parents – these things alone make rehabilitation worth while.

But it is important that promoters of neighborhood fix-up, no less than its detractors, realize its limitations. Many enthusiasts have performed a disservice to a worthy objective by understating the amount of effort that is needed to turn a slum or near-slum into a good neighborhood. They trumpet as successes efforts which, on closer examination, look questionable. And they seem to ignore almost completely the efforts that must be made in fields outside the areas of building, planning and zoning if whole-

some environments are to rise from the rot of U.S. slums.

This narrow vision, indeed, plays into the hands of some political reformers who believe that government – not the citizens affected – should do most of the planning and thinking. Narrow vision and overblown huzzahs create false hopes of easy success by the mere physical renovation of blighted areas. When success does not follow token or inadequate efforts, disillusion over failure makes it harder than ever to mount the broad attack that is required to cope with the problem.

### Other unsolved problems

In none of the cities studied (nor anywhere else we know of) has the complete solution to the rehabilitation of neighborhoods (without a substantial change in occupants) been found. As a result, the potential of rehabilitation for molding attitudes has not yet been fully tested. The urban renewal program is making it possible to attack blight on an ever-widening front. Yet the heart of urban renewal must still be rehabilitation – unless the nation is prepared not only to give up its gigantic investment in existing structures, but also to step up its outlays for demolition and redevelopment to a level that staggers the imagination (and, amid heavy defense expenditures, is clearly impossible). But the long-run success or failure of rehabilitation is inextricably tied up with the attitudes of the people living in the neighborhoods to be renewed. Moreover, the most important effects of rehabilitation may be psychological and spiritual, rather than strictly physical. The problems faced by rehabilitation programs, therefore, are worthy of the attention of the nation's best minds in politics, economics and sociology. Two unsolved problems found in neighborhoods covered by this study are these:

1. Nowhere did a city or a neighborhood actually remove the causes of blight. Once the neighborhood has been rehabilitated – whether it is the Pilot Area in Baltimore or the Back-of-the-Yards in Chicago – it is faced with a continuing battle against the forces that would drag it downhill again before its time. In most neighborhoods, new blight still springs up faster

than old blight is removed. The big reason is
that slums are still very profitable, despite building inspectors, neighborhood groups, housing
codes and housing courts. Instead of preventing
the bootleg profit from overcrowding of aged
tenements by some such easily-enforced or self-
enforcing mechanism as property taxation, city
governments rely on police action to cope with
overcrowding after it occurs. This is like bailing
out a rowboat without plugging up the leak.
What is needed is an approach that makes the
creation of slums unprofitable and the maintenance of them financially disastrous to their
owners. To do this without an army of housing
policemen apparently will require far-reaching
changes in our national attitudes toward property ownership, taxation and land use.

2. Organizing neighborhood groups to fight
blight – a necessary first step toward rehabilitation – takes a discouragingly long time. Progress is being made, it is true. In Chicago, the
organization effort was ably sparkplugged by
the Office of the Housing and Redevelopment
Coordinator. In Baltimore, Negro neighborhoods
have made big strides under the leadership of
the interracial Citizens Planning and Housing
Association. But the prime success story in this
area is Back-of-the-Yards. Its organization long
antedated city efforts to help; indeed, it took
Alinsky, Meegan and their aides sixteen years
to achieve such local strength that rehabilitation
came quickly and smoothly. Few neighborhoods
can afford to wait that long.

## Political attitudes

Rehabilitation can change a citizen's attitude toward his local government, or, to state
it another way, change political and civic attitudes. Such changes appear to develop in step
with the residents' responsibility for their own
rehabilitation efforts. In the Pilot Area, where
the rehabilitation program was primarily something done to the residents, instead of done by
them, there was little sign of more civic responsibility or interest in city affairs. When inspectors were no longer making daily trips
through the area, residents lost even the habit
of making complaints about nuisances.

On the other hand, the individuals who did
participate in the leadership of the Pilot program – who entered into the decision-making
process affecting their own environment – had
to learn what their problems really were, and
to decide what they wanted their environment
to be. The families who fought their own zoning and liquor-license fights were the nucleus
who sustained . the neighborhood committee.
When the city planned to take over a square of
trees and grass for a paved playground, the committee decided an oasis of green was more valuable than an asphalt athletic field. It made this
decision stick.

In Back-of-the-Yards, too, participation helped
produce more self-reliant attitudes in its residents. As James Downs, then Chicago's housing
and redevelopment coordinator, has put it : " Rehabilitation forces people who live in the
affected areas to get to understand government
and how it works. The process is a great seminar
in political knowledge." Saul Alinsky has dwelt
on this in words that deserve re-emphasis : " In
today's world of the fix and the angle, everybody assumes he can't do anything without
influence. But the truth is that 98 percent of the
things people want done they can accomplish
without any special pull at all. Every time an
individual citizen gets a service done for him
by someone else, he becomes indebted to the
man who helped him. This is how political
machines are built."

As the Back-of-the-Yards Council battled for
its life against a city political machine intent
on perpetuating the dependency of Back-of-the-
Yards residents, it built itself into such a power
center that the Council itself, to some observers,
now bears earmarks of a political machine. But
powerful neighborhood councils, if they are
political machines, are machines with a crucial
difference. They are not absentee-controlled.
They cover territories small enough so they
remain responsive to the needs and wishes of
their residents. In a sense, they become a big-
city counterpart of the New England town
meeting.

One trouble with representative government
today is that it often works poorly in large
cities. Individual citizens come to feel their
voices can have no effect on the course of
events; so they withdraw from participation

in government altogether. The neighborhood urban renewal or rehabilitation organization gives promise of restoring grassroots vitality to the democratic process.

## Some broader implications

Wherever the spark comes from – within a neighborhood or outside it – one common thread runs through the stories of all six rehabilitation movements included in this study : housing cannot be vacuum-sealed and separated from other needs and problems of city families.

To create any lasting change in attitudes (beyond an elementary appreciation of clean yards and new plumbing) a rehabilitation program must attack a host of nonhousing problems, from loan sharks to juvenile delinquency. In the Mount Royal area, this attack involved only the most depressed of the residents. But in Coconut Grove and the Pilot Area, what started as housing improvement broadened into a whole rainbow of uplift efforts.

One of the best things about rehabilitation is that hopes are established, and a frame of mind created in people that makes the field more fertile for useful work by others – social workers, schools, churches, probation officers. Rehabilitation, if successful, creates a new climate – which is a changed attitude in itself.

A characteristic of blighted neighborhoods before rehabilitation is a hopelessness, a lostness. Rehabilitation makes the residents feel more important, lets them feel they have acquired friends. Given attention by officials, lenders or do-gooders, they come to feel their wishes mean something.

So rehabilitation produces a climate favorable to changes in attitude. But if neighborhood identity is not also established (or maintained), the climate usually proves transitory. This seemed true in New Orleans (although the rehabilitation efforts there fell short of matching the city's problem in many other ways, too). A clearer example is the Pilot Area. There was no natural neighborhood with which residents could identify themselves. Nothing was done to distinguish the Pilot Area from the surrounding sea of monotonous, blighted blocks. When the program was over it was still a collection of unplanned blocks, with too much traffic, too many taverns, too few play areas and practically no open space. Even the mailman did not know where the Pilot Area began and ended. Soon after, the neighborhood began to be overwhelmed by the same forces that had pulled it down into blight in the first place. The vigilance required to prevent this was more than an amorphous, boundary-less neighborhood could sustain.

In Back-of-the-Yards, on the other hand, and to some extent in the Mount Royal Area and Coconut Grove, there was a strong feeling of community – and it was intensified by rehabilitation. Uniting to fight blight, residents remained together to achieve other gains they had not thought possible.

This sort of neighborhood solidarity – of small-town unity inside a great metropolis – may prove to be a key to the rebirth of cities. It seems to have great promise not only for saving the nation's biggest investment, urban real estate, but also for fostering human aspirations. People who have mastered their physical environment can turn their attention to the fulfilment of their cultural and spiritual needs. And in mastering their environment through neighborhood morale and rehabilitation, they may discover for themselves a new pattern of democracy – a pattern for tomorrow's urban age.

# An evaluation of the redevelopment plan and process

*HERBERT J. GANS*

## Author's note

This paper is based on the conclusions of an eight-month sociological community study which I made in the West End of Boston. During this period, I lived in the neighborhood as a participant-observer, and conducted formal and informal interviews with many West Enders, as well as with redevelopment officials. The study was conducted under the auspices of the Center for Community Studies, affiliated with the Department of Psychiatry, Harvard Medical School, and Massachusetts General Hospital. The Center is conducting a five-year research project, " Relocation and Mental Health : Adaptation Under Stress," under a grant from the National Institute of Mental Health. Drs. Erich Lindermann and Gerald Caplan are coprincipal investigators; Dr. March Fried is coordinator of research.

The field work for this article was carried out independently of the longer study, and the conclusions discussed here are therefore strictly the author's, and not necessarily those of the rest of the research staff. From a scientific standpoint, these conclusions are hypotheses and preliminary findings based on observational and interview evidence. Although the author talked with many West Enders, he probably had less contact with the poorest, least educated residents, who lived in the worst buildings in the area, than would be desirable from a research point of view. However, they are the least likely to talk to a middle-class researcher.

The five-year research project is measuring the effects of clearance and relocation on the people of the West End in a systematic manner, and should provide scientifically tested data on many of the observations provided here. It will also show to what extent these effects are beneficial or detrimental. When I first began my research, I had not intended to evaluate the fate of the West End from a planning and more general social welfare perspective. In fact, my point of view developed as a result of the field work. Consequently, it is relevant to preface the evaluation by describing briefly how I reached my conclusions.

At the start of the study, I had not thought systematically about the pros and cons of redevelopment, or taken a position on any of its policies.* As my field work in the West End progressed, however, I began to develop that identification with the people, and sympathy for their problems which is experienced by many participant-observers. Contact with planners in the Boston area acquainted me with the problems of the city, and encouraged me to look at the West End from a planning perspective.

---

* Some years before, I had worked in a renewal agency, but my functions were such that I did not give much thought to the overall program. The conclusions which I eventually reached about the West End, however, were influenced by many conversations about planning and redevelopment in earlier years with two old friends and colleagues, planners both : John Dyckman and Martin Meyerson.

*Author's note is taken from "The Human Implications of Current Redevelopment and Relocation Planning,"* Journal of the American Institute of Planners, *vol. 25 (February, 1954), pp. 15–25. The body of the text is reprinted from a revised version of the article, which appeared as part of Herbert J. Gans,* The Urban Villagers, *The Free Press of Glencoe, 1962, pp. 305–335, with permission of the journal and publisher.*

Inevitably, then, I began to feel not only that the redevelopment decision itself was not entirely justifiable, but also that the planning being done for the West End did not take into account the needs of the residents who, among others, were supposed to benefit from slum clearance. My thinking on the issue was stimulated further by discussions among the research staff of the Center for Community Studies. Several of my colleagues believed the area to be a slum in need of redevelopment; some – especially those of us doing field work in the West End itself – took the opposite position, and I defended this point of view in a number of staff meetings.

My feelings regarding the redevelopment came to a head about three months after the beginning of field work. One day, I had attended, as an observer, a monthly meeting of West End settlement house staff members and other caretakers at which redevelopment agency officials explained the redevelopment process and the planning that had taken place for it. Appalled by the lack of planning for the West Enders, I felt, more than ever, that something ought to be done about it. Since the research project had been originally designed also to include service functions in the area of mental health, I thus circulated a memorandum on the topic. In it, I took the position that were the West Enders' mental health to be served, the project's service function might best be accomplished by action to correct the redevelopment planning. My proposal was not feasible, however, since the Center staff was too small to undertake any kind of service activity.

In the weeks that followed, I found it difficult to keep my ideas to myself, and, in the course of my field work, talked about them to West Enders.* I had come to know the leaders of the Save the West End Committee, and they urged me to publish a critique of the redevelopment process. For a month or so, I was torn

between my research role and my desire to correct what I felt to be a prime example of social injustice as well as poor planning. At one point, I even considered resigning from the research project, and joining the Committee. Eventually, I decided to forego any attempt at individual action, feeling that since I was not myself a West Ender, I really had no right to take what would probably have been a leading position in the fight. More important, I believed that it was too late to halt the redevelopment process in the West End, and that my activities might endanger the Center's research project. For while the results of this study could not help the West Enders, they could later contribute more to correcting the abuses of redevelopment on a nation-wide scale than would my desire to act have helped the West Enders. Consequently, I stuck to my research role until the end of my field work, when, through the help of a Harvard colleague, I obtained an interview with one of the Redevelopment Authority commissioners. He listened to my critique of the redevelopment process, and then asked that I write a memorandum detailing my proposals for changing it. This I wrote at once, drawing on the earlier paper I had circulated among the Center staff, but disassociating it from my opinions. The paper listed a number of policies which could still be instituted to improve the relocation process and to reduce the injustice which would soon be meted out to the West Enders. The proposals contradicted much of the then existing program, but they were feasible. They could have been implemented, however, only by someone passionately concerned with the West Enders, and ready to spend a considerable amount of time, energy, and political influence to change the scheduled procedures.

The memorandum was never acknowledged. The rest of this chapter is an expanded revision of this memorandum. Since it was written, a number of the more advanced cities have stressed

---

* Under some conditions, such talk might bias the results of participant-observation research. Since almost all West Enders were opposed to the renewal project long before I came on the scene, the research results were not affected. Indeed, once I had made my position clear, a number of people who previously refused to talk to me changed their minds, and made my research task easier. I should explain that at the start of the Center for Community Studies' work, the Center was regarded by some as a front for the Housing Authority. For a while, the research project thus served as a scapegoat for the redevelopment, and a substitute target for the West Enders' hostility to it. As a participant-observer, I was spared from this scapegoating, and the practice subsided before the Center began its interviewing program.

rehabilitation rather than clearance in their urban renewal programs, Boston included. At this writing (January, 1962), the new emphasis is still to be tested in practice, but I have taken account of it in this revision.

The planning analysis considers three questions: whether or not the West End was in fact a slum; the benefits and costs of the redevelopment for the individuals and institutions affected by it; and the quality of the redevelopment and relocation planning. Some recommendations for urban renewal generally are appended.

### The West End:
### slum or low-rent district

The term "slum" is an evaluative, not an analytic, concept. Consequently, any definition of the term must be related, explicitly or implicitly, to the standards of the age, and more important, to the renewal policy in which it is used. Current definitions of the term include two criteria – the social image of the area, and its physical condition. Federal standards for determining whether an area is eligible for renewal funds are based almost entirely on the latter. It is the local agency, however, that selects the area to be proposed for action; and, in most communities, the area's physical condition is a necessary but not sufficient criterion. What seems to happen is that neighborhoods come to be described as slums if they are inhabited by residents who, for a variety of reasons, indulge in overt and visible behavior considered undesirable by the majority of the community. The community image of the area then gives rise to feelings that something should be done, and subsequently the area is proposed for renewal. Consequently, the planning reports that are written to justify renewal dwell as much on social as on physical criteria, and are filled with data intended to show the prevalence of antisocial or pathological behavior in the area. The implication is that the area itself causes such behavior, and should therefore be redeveloped.

Usually, the physical condition of the area is such that it is eligible for renewal. Conversely, there are areas, such as Boston's North End, which meet physical criteria, but which are socially and politically strong enough to dis-

courage any official or politician from suggesting them for clearance or large-scale rehabilitation.

The federal and local housing standards which are applied to slum areas reflect the value pattern of upper-middle-class professionals. These professionals, like the rest of the middle class, allot a higher value to housing (as measured by percentage of income to be spent for shelter), and place greater emphasis on the status functions of housing than does the working class. Also, the signs of housing status used by the two classes differ. In addition, the professionals' evaluation of the behavior of slum residents is based on class-based standards that often confuse behavior which is only culturally different with pathological or antisocial acts.

Generally speaking, these standards are desirable bases for public policy, despite their class bias; and many of them should be applied to the poorer areas of the city – *were they followed by a program which provided the residents of these areas with better housing*. Presently, however, these standards are used to tear down poor neighborhoods, while better housing for the residents is not made available.

Consequently, unless urban renewal policy is drastically altered, other definitions of the slum should be developed. Existing physical standards so far have failed to make a distinction between *low-rent* and *slum* housing, or low-rent and slum districts, community facilities, street patterns, and the like. This distinction, however, is an important one. Residential structures – and districts – should be defined as slums only if they have been proven to be physically, socially, or emotionally *harmful* to their residents or to the larger community. Low-rent structures and districts may be distinguished from slums by the fact that they provide shelter that may be *inconvenient* but that is not harmful. Slums should be eliminated, but low-rent structures must be maintained – at least in the absence of better housing – for people who want, or for economic reasons must maintain, low rental payments and who are willing to accept high density, lack of modernity, and other inconveniences as alternative costs.

Buildings that are structurally unsound, for example, are clearly harmful to their residents.

So are dwelling units infested by rats. Five-story tenements, however, cannot be considered harmful – except for old people who cannot climb stairs. Nevertheless, such structures are usually described as obsolescent by planners and housing officials, and obsolescence in turn is a major criterion for defining a building as a slum. But obsolescence per se is not harmful; the judgment is merely a reflection of middle-class standards – and middle-class incomes. Indeed, there is no talk of obsolescence when alley dwellings of an earlier vintage than tenement buildings are rehabilitated for high rentals, as in Washington's Georgetown district.

A set of parallel social standards is even more difficult to define, because most of the social problems found in slums cannot be traced to the area itself. Undoubtedly, some people live in slums because they have problems or unacceptable behavior patterns. But economic and social conditions, rather than the slum itself, have caused these. While the neighborhood environment may "infect" a few people previously without problems, this happens much less frequently than is commonly believed.[1] For purposes of definition, then, it is necessary to distinguish between undesirable behavior patterns which are related causally to the neighborhood and those which are not. Thus, for renewal purposes, a slum may also be defined as an area that, because of the nature of its social environment, can be proved to create problems and pathologies, either for the residents or for the larger community.

Should children be drawn into illegal activities, for example, and it can be *proved* that the neighborhood, rather than conditions of lower-class life, is responsible, that neighborhood might be called a slum. The same would apply if residential overcrowding inhibited privacy and led to intra- or interfamilial conflict. Overcrowding, however, is caused by soco-economic deprivations that force people to live under such conditions, rather than by the neighborhood or the dwellings themselves. Urban renewal policies that require such people to move without giving them the wherewithal or the housing to live under less crowded conditions thus do not solve the problem. It should be clear that absolute standards for determining whether a building or an area is harmful to its residents cannot be easily formulated. Some conditions are harmful to some types of occupants and not to others. Consequently, each area must be studied and evaluated individually. More important, while some conditions that are harmful can be eliminated by urban renewal, others cannot.

This critique of the conventional definition of slum can be applied to the West End. The planning study used to certify that the area was a slum concluded that:

> ... the West End is in dire need of redevelopment because (1) the land is overcrowded with buildings served by narrow streets where housing is mixed in with marginal commercial uses; (2) the majority of the dwellings in the area are dilapidated and substandard: (3) the steadily declining population of the area suffers from high rates of such indices of bad environment as juvenile delinquency and tuberculosis; (4) the standard of school, community services, and play spaces is far below a desirable level.[2]

Each of these criteria deserves brief comment. There is no doubt that the area was overcrowded with buildings, and that some, though not all, of the streets were narrow. According to the report, buildings covered 72 percent of the land. Overcrowding of buildings on the land must be distinguished, however, from overcrowding of people within buildings or apartments. Whereas the latter is harmful, the former is not, except that it may deprive some people of inadequate supplies of air and sunlight, and prevent fire engines and sanitation equipment from proper access. Although the first and second floors of many of the West End buildings did receive less air and sunlight than is desirable, there is as yet no proof that this was harmful to West Enders, for they spent much time outside. These apartments may have been harmful, however, to older people who could not get outside. I do not defend them as desirable, but I can understand why low-income West Enders preferred them at rentals of $30 or less to lighter and airier apartments elsewhere that would have cost $75 or more. While the area's high land coverage was inconvenient for parking, it could not be considered harmful, except on those streets too narrow for fire engines and sanitation trucks.*

Partially because of the high land coverage, the West End had little playground space. Even so, the children made little use of a playground located in the center of the area, and preferred to play on the streets – where the excitement and action they valued was available – or on the paved yards surrounding one of the schools. Additional open space for baseball and one or two modern playgrounds would have been desirable, but these could have been supplied without tearing down the entire neighborhood.

Nor can the fact that housing was mixed with marginal commercial uses be considered harmful. As far as I could ascertain, none of the industrial firms created undesirable noise or smoke. More important from the West Enders' standpoint, they did provide employment to people in the area. Many of the small stores were economically marginal when compared to modern chain stores, but they served the West Enders, and were able to compete with a supermarket located on the edge of the neighborhood.

While the report is correct in noting that the population of the area had been declining steadily, this is no indication that the neighborhood was harmful to its residents. Much of the decline can be attributed to reduction in family size, which in turn increased the amount of space available for each family. Five- and six-room apartments that once had housed families with eight or ten children now provided comfortable living quarters for families with three or four children. Moreover, until the announcement that the area would be redeveloped, there were few vacant apartments. The decline in population and family size did leave the area with more school facilities than it needed, but this problem could have been solved by tearing down the oldest school buildings and creating play space instead.

The Authority's statement that the area was saddled with high rates of tuberculosis and juvenile delinquency has been questioned by a study conducted by the Save the West End

Committee. This study showed that of the twenty-one existing cases of tuberculosis in the district in 1955, all but three were located in the skid row area adjoining the West End, rather than in the area proposed for clearance.[3] A similar critique was made of the delinquency statistics provided by the Authority.[4] Although I did not make an independent study of these statistics, my observations did not suggest any undue incidence of either of these pathologies.

The Authority's report also indicated that the West End had a high rate of payments for Aid to Dependent Children and old-age assistance; that West Enders had a median income 23 percent below the city median and a low level of education.[5] These facts, however, prove only that the area was inhabited by poor people, many of them old or in need of help; they do no prove one way or the other that the area was a slum.

The Authority's main argument for describing the area as a slum rested on the fact that 63.5 percent of the dwelling units were judged substandard in 1953 by an appraisal based on criteria developed by the American Public Health Association.[6] The APHA appraisal, which has been used widely in urban renewal, consists of thirty differentially weighted items for judging buildings and individual dwelling units. Although the appraisal items are generally sound, the weighting does reflect middle-class values, and the items themselves do not distinguish sufficiently between harmful conditions, such as rodent infestation, and inconvenient ones, such as rooms lacking closets.[7] Further, the Authority's survey of the West End reported only total appraisal scores, but did not indicate to what extent these scores measured harmful, as compare to inconvenient, conditions. Nor did it distinguish between items requiring demolition and those that could be taken care of by rehabilitation or minor repairs.[8]

The findings of this survey were questioned by other evaluations. On the basis of my own observations, I wrote in 1958:

I would estimate that at the time of the land taking, probably from 25 to 35 percent

---

* For a more detailed—and even more favorable— defense of these and other characteristics of neighborhoods like the West End, see Jane Jacobs, *The Death and*

*Life of Great American Cities*, New York: Random House, 1961, especially Part I, and Chap. 15.

of the buildings in the project area were structurally unsound, uninhabitable because they had been vacant for some time, or located on alleys too narrow for proper sanitation and fire prevention.[9]

This judgment has since been supported by the more systematic study conducted by the Center for Community Studies. Its interviewers found that of the *buildings*, 23 percent were excellent or good, 41 percent fair, and 36 percent poor or very bad. Hartman, who analyzed these judgments, also found that of the *dwelling units*, 40 percent were in excellent or good contion, 34 percent were fair, and only 25 percent were in poor or very bad condition.[*] He noted that these characterizations " implicitly refer to the context of West End standards – an excellent West End apartment is not likely to be of the same quality as an excellent apartment on Beacon Hill."[10]

These figures also include an increase in dilapidation between 1953 and 1958, some of which can be attributed to the fact that when the plans for redevelopment were announced in 1951, landlords were advised not to make extensive repairs on their properties. Many West Enders claimed – with some justification – that parts of the area deteriorated rapidly as a result, especially where apartments or entire buildings became and remained vacant in the years that followed. The worst buildings were those owned by absentee landlords; many of the resident owners maintained their buildings more adequately.

I do not mean to claim that the West End was free of slum buildings prior to 1951. Such structures did exist. They were most numerous in the lower end of the area, and, ironically, in the blocks just outside the area slated for redevelopment. Even so, the 1950 United States Census – the sole source of information about West End housing conditions prior to the announcement of redevelopment – showed that only about 20 percent of all dwelling units were dilapidated, or lacked a private bath.[†] Since most West End apartments had private baths, this figure represents an index of dilapidation.

It would be fair to conclude that the majority of the structures in the West End provided low-rent rather than slum housing. Moreover, tenants kept their apartments in good order, and during the postwar prosperity, many West Enders had been able to modernize the interiors. As Hartman's figures document, poor buildings frequently contained well-kept apartments. Indeed, visitors to the area were often surprised at the discrepancy between the outside of the buildings and the apartments themselves, and had some difficulty maintaining their belief that the West End was a slum.

Rents were extremely low – a fact that enabled the many people in the area who never escaped the threat of job loss and layoff to keep their fixed housing costs low enough to survive. Low rents also made it possible for the many elderly people in the area to maintain independent households even while remaining near married children.

The West Enders themselves took the poor maintenance of the building exteriors, halls, and cellars in stride, and paid little attention to them. The low rents more than made up for these deficiencies, and for the generally run-down appearance of the area. Moreover, they did not consider these conditions a reflection on their status. Having no interest in the opinions of the outside world, they were not overly concerned about the image which the West End had in the eyes of outsiders. They did not like to be called slum dwellers, of course, and resented the exaggerated descriptions of West End deterioration that appeared regularly in the Boston press. Nor were they happy about the rooming houses that bordered the West End, or the skid row occupants who sometimes wandered into it. Unlike the middle class, however, they did not care about " the

---

* Chester Hartman, " Housing in the West End," Boston: Center for Community Studies Research Memorandum C1, October, 1961, mimeographed, p. 2. These figures are based on observations made while interviewing women aged twenty to sixty-five, and thus exclude rooming houses and units occupied by older males, and all unoccupied buildings. There were, however, fewer vacant units in 1953 than at the time of the interviewing in 1958.

† Hartman, *op. cit.*, p. 2n Census figures are based on the judgment of hastily trained enumerators, and are thus less reliable than other appraisals.

address." Consequently, the cultural differences between working- and middle-class residential choice suggest that the prevailing professional housing standards – which reflect only the latter – could not be rigidly applied to the West End.[11]

Nor did the West End satisfy the social criteria that would have made it a slum. Residents with social and emotional problems, with behavior difficulties, and with criminal records could be found in the area, partially because of the spillover from the adjacent skid row, and because of the low rents. This was especially true after 1950, when increasing vacancies attracted single transients, Gypsies, and "multi-problem" families. Such people obtained apartments in the West End because landlords could no longer afford to reject what they defined as "undesirable" tenants. The presence of such tenants helped to convince the community at large that the West End was a slum. Yet all this time the West End was also a major area of first settlement for newcomers without problems or criminal records: especially immigrants from Italy, from Displaced Persons camps in Europe, from rural New England, and from French Canada. Thus, the area had an important but unrecognized function in the city. Even so, the majority of West Enders were people who had lived there since before 1950. Many of them also had problems, especially those associated with low income and acculturation. But the problems of old residents and newcomers alike had not been created by the neighborhood. If anything, the stability of a large part of the population created a more desirable social climate for newcomers than existed in the other major area of first settlement in Boston, the South End.

In summary, the West End was a low-rent district – both physically and socially – rather than a slum. Total clearance might have been justified if the end result had been better living conditions for the West Enders, that is, if the

area could have been rebuilt for them with modern structures and in such a way that the existing social structure could have been preserved there for the people who wanted to remain in it. But none of this would have been possible under the urban renewal policies of the 1950's, which required the relocation of site residents and rebuilding for a new set of occupants by private enterprise.* This scheme was no solution for the West Enders, however, for it did not improve their living conditions and relocation only added new problems.

A wiser scheme would have been to rehabilitate drastically the harmful structures and tear down those that were structurally unsound or otherwise beyond salvage. The majority of buildings could have been given less intensive treatment or left alone. Spot clearance could have created additional open space for small parks, playgrounds, and parking areas. This solution would have maximized the benefits of renewal for the West Enders. But renewal is supposed to consider the public interest as well. Therefore, it is necessary to discuss the benefits and costs of redevelopment for the larger community.

## The benefits and cost of redevelopment

The certification of the West End for redevelopment was not entirely the result of its alleged or actual status as a slum. Because of its central location, realtors and civic leaders had long felt that the area should be devoted to economically more profitable uses. The Charles River frontage, for example, was thought to be desirable for high-rent apartments. As noted earlier, the desire of the Massachusetts General Hospital for higher income neighbors and the belief that the shrinkage of the central retail area could and should be halted by settling "quality shoppers" nearby contributed to the clearance decision. So did the city's desperate

---

* It should be noted that the Housing Authority study which described the area as a slum did not propose total clearance. About 12 percent of the existing dwelling units were to be retained or rehabilitated. Moreover, in the reuse plan, only 58 percent of the residential acreage was alloted to high-rent housing; 27 percent was devoted to public or middle-income private housing, and 15 percent to retained and rehabilitated structures. Boston Housing Authority, op. cit., p. 32. Even so, such a plan would not have allowed more than a handful of West Enders to remain in the area. As noted earlier, fears that investment capital would not be attracted by this plan caused it to be changed to one totally devoted to high-rent housing.

need for a higher tax base, and its equally urgent search for some signs of economic revival. Throughout the 1950's, politicians, business leaders, and the press described the West End redevelopment scheme as a major factor in – and symbol of – the city's emergence from its economic doldrums.

Even so, the plans were implemented only because developers were interested in buying the cleared land for high-income housing. Meanwhile, other Boston neighborhoods in which the housing was more deteriorated and even dangerous received a much lower priority for renewal,* because they were not attractive for high-rent housing, or because of area political opposition.†

The rebuilding of the West End should be profitable for the builders. They are obtaining the cleared land in sections and can cease building – with only the loss of a $100,000 bond – if the demand for luxury apartments is satiated before all the sections are developed.‡ No one knows as yet whether there will be enough tenants for 2400 high-rent units. The ongoing redevelopment of the Scollay Square area for an office building complex, however, probably will aid the West End project. A successful West End project should also add to Boston's declining tax base, and could give a psychological lift to the business community. Several questions can be raised, however, as to its overall benefit to the larger community:

1. The project has been planned on the assumption that high-income residents benefit the city, while low-income ones are only a burden and a source of public expense. This assumption ignores the vital economic and social functions played in the city economy by low-income people. Indeed, the reduction of the

city's low-rent housing supply by close to 3000 units will undoubtedly make it more difficult for the present and future industrial force of a low-wage city to find centrally located and suitably priced housing.

2. The tax and other economic benefits of the redevelopment may be counteracted by the loss of property values and tax yields in the areas from which tenants will be drawn. Although no one can predict who will rent the new West End apartments, the majority will come most likely from older high-rent areas of the city, rather than from the suburbs or from newcomers to the metropolitan area.

3. The central business district may benefit less than expected: the new tenants probably already do much of their shopping downtown, and many of the West Enders who did all but their food buying downtown have left the city.

Moreover, the benefits that will accrue to the city must be weighed against the economic and social costs paid by the West Enders in being forced out of their neighborhood with nothing more than a moving allowance of $75 to $100. Tenants had to bear the financial burdens of higher rentals for new apartments – not necessarily better in quality than the old ones. For many West Enders, this required drastic budgetary changes with consequent cutbacks in other sectors. Because of the shortage of suitable apartments, a number of them had to buy suburban houses at prices which were beyond their ability to pay.

Most of the small businessmen in the area lost their stores, and thus their source of livelihood. Although federal relocation regulations did allot $2500 for moving expenses to those who re-established their businesses elsewhere, few were able to do so since the city is already

---

* In 1960, the city reorganized its redevelopment agency, and brought in a new director. He is embarking on a city-wide renewal program based on different criteria, and stressing rehabilitation more than clearance.

† As noted earlier, this was especially true of the North End, where apartments were in poorer condition than in the West End. According to the 1950 Census, 78 percent of its dwelling units were either dilapidated or lacked a private bath. Hartman, *op. cit.*, p. 3.

‡ A number of questions could also be raised about the developer; the fact that the corporation was formed only a few days before the contract was awarded it,

that it had only $1000 in equity at that time, that it was only the second highest bidder for the land, and that it may have received the contract through political influence. I could not make an independent study to answer these questions. For a detailed description of these charges, see Robert Hanron, " West End Project Could Be Spark to Revitalize Boston," *Boston Sunday Globe*, (December 20, 1959). Conversely, it should be noted that the developer chose an architect-planner of national repute to design the new West End, and has attempted to make it an attractive—albeit very expensive—place to live.

oversupplied with small stores. Ironically, the businessmen who were prosperous enough to relocate, and who therefore needed less help, were given funds for moving. But those who lost their stores, and were most in need of aid, were given nothing.

Many resident owners of tenement buildings who were able to live modestly from rentals also lost their source of livelihood, for they did not receive enough for their buildings to allow them to purchase others. Conversely, the absentee landlords, who had not maintained their buildings, and who had been losing money from vacancies during the years preceding redevelopment, were benefited by the clearance.*

For tenants, owners, and businessmen alike, the destruction of the neighborhood exacted social and psychological losses. The clearance destroyed not only buildings, but also a functioning social system. The scattering of family units and friends was especially harmful to the many older people. Whereas the younger West Enders felt that they could adjust to a new neighborhood, the older ones will probably be less adept at making the change. Even while I was still in the West End, a number of deaths were attributed to the impact of the redevelopment decision.† People with serious social, economic, and emotional problems were faced with yet further problems by the need to move from a familiar and inexpensive neighborhood. Also, since the redevelopment had publicly identified West Enders as slum dwellers, some were met by discrimination and rejection in their new neighborhoods.

Some West Enders did benefit from the redevelopment, especially those among the most poorly-housed who were able to find better apartments. Others gained by being given a push toward a move to middle-class neighborhoods and the suburbs which they had wanted to make but had delayed because of inertia.‡ Some will be benefited by new experiences and unexpected opportunities resulting from the move.

More detailed analyses – some of them over a long period of years – will be necessary to determine the final benefits and costs of the redevelopment for the larger community, as well as for the builders, the central district, and the West Enders themselves.§ Even so, the variety of costs which West Enders have already paid are heavy. They represent hidden subsidies to the redevelopment program. In effect, a low-income population has subsidized the clearance of its neighborhood and the apartments of its high-income successors both by its own losses and by its share of the federal and local tax monies used to clear the site. It is doubtful whether the moving allowance that West Enders received can even begin to balance these costs.

### The relocation plan and process**

The city's planning for redevelopment concerned itself primarily with the land of the West End once it had been cleared. It paid little attention to the West Enders and their needs before or after clearance. To make matters worse, very little planning was done for the relocation of the 2700 households in the area – and that was done poorly. The process by which redevelopment and relocation actually

---

* At the time of my study, it was commonly thought that since they had the funds for legal fees, and the political know-how for choosing the right lawyers, they would be able to go to court, and obtain higher prices for their buildings than would the resident owners.
† I was not able to discover whether these attributions were at all justified.
‡ Actually, many of the families in this position had already left the West End between 1950 and 1958.
§ My statements about the economic, social, and emotional costs of clearance and relocation are hypotheses based on my observations at the time the area was facing clearance, and on subsequent observations of a handful of relocated families. These costs will be described in more detail by the Center for Community Studies' ongoing research program among relocated West Enders. Corroboration of my hypotheses has already appeared, however, in the Center's initial findings. Thus, Fried reports that 54 percent of the women and 46 percent of the men interviewed expressed severely depressed or disturbed reactions to the tearing down of the buildings in which they lived. This rose to 64 percent among the women who had lived in the West End for a very long time, and to 73 percent among those who had felt very positive about the area before they had to move. Marc Fried, "Grieving for a Lost Home," in *The Urban Condition: people and policy in the metropolis,* Leonard Duhl, ed. New York: Basic Books, 1963.
** The contents made in the previous footnote apply to this section also.

proceeded also ignored the West Enders' needs, thus placing yet further burdens on their shoulders.

The city's relocation plan assumed that 60 percent of the people were eligible for public housing, that all of them would move into such units, and that the private housing market would provide enough apartments and houses for the remainder. Although the plan was approved by federal officials, none of these assumptions were preceded by adequate study, and all of them were open to serious question at the time of the land taking in 1958.

Many eligible West Enders, for example, were unwilling to go into public housing. They rejected this alternative partly because they accepted the negative image given public housing by the Boston press; because they knew they would be unable to live with relatives, friends, and neighbors of their own ethnic group; because they considered public housing tenants to be inferior in status; and because they did not wish to be subjected to administrative restrictions on their activities, especially those limiting family income.

As a result, anyone even slightly familiar with the West Enders could have predicted that the vast majority would have to find housing in the private market. The Authority's relocation plan, however, did not consider this possibility. Even the assumption that enough private housing would be available for the 40 percent ineligible for public housing was based on inadequate study. The Authority made an analysis of apartments listed in the classified sections of the newspapers, without any attempt to discover whether these units would satisfy the federal requirements that they be " decent, safe, and sanitary," or whether they would meet the needs of the West Enders. Many of these advertised vacancies, in fact, were of such low quality that they could not be rented to anyone. Landlords listed them with the West End

relocation office because they knew that the West Enders had little choice in the housing market.

As it turned out, only about 10 percent of the West Enders moved into public housing.* The rest obtained housing in the private market and did so by their own efforts. That they were successful was probably due in large part to the aid of relatives and friends in other parts of the metropolitan area who looked for vacancies in their own neighborhoods. What proportion of the West Enders did find satisfactory and suitably priced housing and how many have adjusted to new neighborhoods and new neighbors is not yet known. My own limited observations suggest that many moved into old, low-rent neighborhoods in the cities surrounding Boston, some of which were already being considered for future urban renewal. Moreover, the arrival of the West Enders – publicly branded as slum dwellers – seems to have fortified the conviction of some of these cities that these areas too should be renewed. Thus it is possible that some West Enders will have to go through the entire process all over again.†

The failure of the official relocation procedures to help the West Enders can be traced to several deficiencies. First, these procedures were developed by middle-class professionals, who thus assumed that the West Enders' housing requirements and preferences were similar to their own. Although the West Enders were asked into which neighborhoods they wished to move, the relocation procedures gave first priority to the requirement that the new unit be decent, safe, and sanitary. This in turn was usually interpreted to mean fitting middle-class standards.‡ West Enders, however, were equally if not more concerned about social considerations. They wanted to move into neighborhoods in which they could find relatives, friends, and neighbors of their own ethnic group. They also

---

* This figure is based on the number of West Enders in the Center for Community Studies interview sample who moved into public housing. I am indebted to Chester Hartman for this tabulation.

† Thus, a Boston reporter wrote in 1960 that " certain cities are ' squawking to the skies ' about the influx of West Enders," and noted also that " it is appalling the

number of moves some people have had to make because . . . Boston failed to know the relocation plans of Cambridge." Virginia Bright, " Officials Have Learned a Lesson from West End," *Boston Sunday Globe* (May 15, 1960).
‡ I have no quarrel with the requirement, which is written into federal housing law, but only with narrow interpretations of it.

wanted physically satisfactory housing; but, as already indicated, their own criteria for such housing differ from middle-class ones. The relocation staff's lack of interest in social criteria for housing choice was based partly on a desire – implicit in much of planning and housing ideology – to break up ethnic ghettos, in the belief that this would encourage people like the West Enders to adopt middle-class standards and behavior patterns. Moreover, the middle-class values embedded in the relocation procedures assumed that nuclear families were self-sufficient and independent. Consequently relocation officials failed to see the ties that existed between such families. They did not know of the existence of family circles, and could not comprehend the desire of West Enders to be near relatives.

Finally, while relocation was geared to move households, it failed to consider the need for moving institutions and social systems in which people live.* Admittedly, no one knows at this point how such institutions and social systems can be moved, but the procedures used in the West End precluded any experimentation in " social relocation."

The processes by which relocation and clearance were implemented were as negligent of residents' needs as had been the prior planning. During the five years in which the Housing Authority and its successor were obtaining the proper local and federal approvals, communication from the two Authorities to the West End kept the people in a state of constant uncertainty. True, the agencies did follow the letter of the law – and of bureaucratic procedure – but they failed to consider the West Enders' attitudes. For example, during the period when the plan was awaiting approval by the various participating agencies, the local Authority was extremely careful to give out no information about which it was not absolutely certain, or which was not required by the rule books. The informational vacuum thus created in the West End was filled with rumors. Moreover, the officials assumed that the West Enders were as expert as they in understanding the complex administrative process of redevelopment, and that they could thus interpret properly the cryptic news releases which were issued periodically.

The officials neither attempted to discover the effects of their announcements, nor the way in which these were actually interpreted. Thus, the long years of delay between the announcement of redevelopment and the final taking were generally assumed by the West Enders to stem from the city's desire to confuse them, scare them out of the West End, and thus reduce the acquisition costs of property and the scope of the relocation problem. Since the West Enders did not organize in middle-class ways to protest the redevelopment, the officials failed to realize either the amount of hostility toward the project, or the reasons for this hostility. This in turn helped to stifle any incentive to plan for the West Enders' needs.

The pattern of poor communication on the part of the redevelopment officials and the negative interpretation of their plans and procedures by the West Enders continued after the Authority had set up a project area relocation office and had announced the taking of the properties by eminent domain. The agency continued to be vague on those topics of most importance to the residents, for example, on the relocation and clearance schedules. As a result, some West Enders understood admonitions to move as soon as possible to mean that the relocation office had been set up to scare people out of the area. Suggestions as to the availability of vacant housing in areas of lower socio-economic status than the West End were interpreted to mean that the city wanted to push West Enders into the worst slums of Boston. Moreover, the redevelopment agency's official notification to the landlords that their structures had been purchased for $1 under eminent domain procedures – plus its failure to include this token payment or to explain why it was not included – convinced many people that the city was not keeping its promises to treat them fairly and was going to cheat them out of their payments.

Likewise, the way in which the redevelop-

---

* Peabody House's move to Somerville was dictated in part by the assumption that many West Enders would move into this community, and by the House's desire to help them adjust to their new neighborhoods. Settlement houses however, played only a minor role in the West Enders' social system.

ment agency took the land caused considerable hurt among the older immigrants. They could not understand how the buildings they had worked so hard to own could suddenly be taken away from them, with no assurance as to when or what they would be paid. Moreover, they were told at the same time to pay rents for their own apartments in these buildings or face eviction. Thus, many of the landlords who earned their livelihoods from rents were simultaneously deprived of both a source of income and the funds with which to pay the rent demanded from them.

Although the residents and redevelopment officials attributed the communication failure to each other's negative motivations, the actual difficulties originated elsewhere. The redevelopment agency was concerned mainly with following local and federal regulations governing relocation. These regulations said nothing about understanding the consequences to the residents of its official acts. Thus, the agency had no real opportunity for learning how the West End received its letters and announcements, or interpreted its actions.

Indeed, it is questionable that such an opportunity would have been exploited. The officials concerned were not policy-makers; they were hired to carry out their prescribed duties. They did feel sorry for some of the West Enders, especially those with serious problems, and these they tried to help in various ways not required by their job. But since they believed that relocation would improve the living conditions for most of the residents and that the redevelopment was for the good of the city, they could not really understand why the West Enders were hostile and often unwilling to cooperate. As a result, when redevelopment officials took action affecting project area residents, they were not likely to deliberate either on the residents' attitudes or on their predicament.

Finally, the scheduling of relocation and of clearance did not take into consideration the fact that the developer was acquiring the land in sections, or the possibility that he might not find enough tenants to justify his purchase of the remaining sections. Indeed, should it turn out that those portions of the West End farthest away from the Charles River and from Beacon Hill cannot be rebuilt for high-income tenants, other plans will have to be made for the vacant land. Meanwhile, people may have been relocated and buildings demolished needlessly.

## Some causes of the defects in urban renewal

In summary, redevelopment proceeded from beginning to end on the assumption that the needs of the site residents were of far less importance than the clearing and rebuilding of the site itself. Great pains were taken with planning for buildings, but planning for the West Enders was done on an *ad hoc* basis, almost as an afterthought. To give just one example, although the local and federal agencies had detailed maps of the West End's sewer system, they did not seem to know the simple fact that a number of owners living in the area depended on the rents they collected for their income.

Perhaps the clearest indication of the relatively low priority of the West Enders in the redevelopment process is the fact that the funds allocated to relocation were less than 5 percent of the total cost of taking and clearing the land. This represented only about 1 percent of the cost of clearance and rebuilding. The real cost of relocation, however, was very much higher, and was paid in various ways by the people who had to move. In short, the redevelopment of the West End was economically feasible only because of the hidden subsidies which the residents provided – involuntarily, of course.

This critique is directed neither at renewal nor relocation per se, but at the specific policies which use public funds to subsidize the erection of high-rent housing, and which penalize the low-income population, without any proof that these inequities are in the public interest.*

---

* In addition, the critique applies to the redevelopment agency as it was constituted in 1958. The reorganization of this agency, noted earlier, should result in an improvement of the renewal process. Many of its less desirable features are built into the federal regulations, however, and these had not been altered significantly by the Kennedy Administration as of January 1962.

Moreover, the specific criticisms made of Boston procedures are not intended to blame any individuals within the local or federal agencies. It is important to emphasize that what happened cannot be attributed to evil motives. No laws were broken, and many officials acted with only the best intentions toward the West Enders. Needless to say, more empathy and research on the part of the officials involved, and more criticism of the program by planners, and those who make Boston's public policy, might have ameliorated the process to some extent. Even so, the officials who carried out the program in Boston were no better or worse than their colleagues in other cities.

Good intentions, empathy, and criticism are of little help, however, if the basic procedures are at fault. Thus, the responsibility for what happened in the West End rests to a considerable extent on the system of procedures that has emerged from years of legislative and administrative decision-making beginning with the 1949 Housing Act. It also rests on the unintended or unrecognized consequences of these procedures when they are actually implemented. This system, however, is intrinsically related to the country's economic and political structure, especially to the long-standing public policy of giving private enterprise a free hand in the profitable sectors of the housing market. This policy then, and the powerful realtor, builder, and banker lobbies which have insisted on its inclusion in all urban renewal legislation, must also be implicated in the process that took place in the West End. For example, since the Boston redevelopment agency, like all others the country over, had to provide sufficient incentives to attract a private redeveloper, its decisions – beginning with the selection of the West End as a renewal site – were shaped by the demands or the anticipated demands of the developer and the sources of investment capital.

Once more it must be stressed that the observations presented here about the effects of relocation were made before the advent of relocation. The study now being conducted by the Center for Community Studies is measuring the effects of clearance and relocation in a systematic manner, and will provide scientifically validated data on many of the observations reported here. The Center's study will thus answer the most important question raised: to what extent are the effects of relocation beneficial or detrimental for those who have to move? The answer should supply renewal and planning agencies with the kind of information they need, to decide whether the benefits of rebuilding the city are worth the costs that renewal area residents must bear under present policies. Whatever the conclusions of the Center's studies, however, my thesis – that current renewal policies benefit the developer most, the area residents least, and the public interest in as yet unmeasured quantity – will remain valid. For even if all of the effects of relocation were positive, the unequal and unjust distribution of costs and benefits built into current procedures still would not be justified.

## Some recommendations for urban renewal

Urban renewal and the rehousing of slum dwellers are necessary and desirable objectives. The means of achieving them, however, ought to be chosen in relation to these objectives, rather than to such extraneous ones as attracting middle- and upper-income citizens back from the suburbs, contributing potential shoppers to a declining downtown business district, creating symbols of "community revival," or providing more statusful surroundings for powerful community institutions. Redevelopment should be pursued primarily for the benefit of the community as a whole and of the people who live in the slum area; not for the redeveloper or his eventual tenants. The recommendations that follow are based largely on this principle:

1. Renewal projects should be located first in those areas which are slums as defined above, that is, in which it can be proven that the housing and facilities present social and physical dangers to the residents and to the larger community. The availability of a redeveloper ought to be a consideration, but one of lesser priority.

2. Before areas for renewal are finally chosen, independent studies should be made which not only provide proof that the area is a slum, but which also take into account the values and living patterns of the residents. These studies

should be made by persons who have no connection either with the project area or the redevelopment agency.

3. Renewal proposals that call for the relocation of an entire neighborhood should be studied closely to determine whether the existing social system satisfies more positive than negative functions for the residents. Should this be the case, planners must decide whether the destruction of this social system is justified by the benefits to be derived from renewal.

4. Projects that require large-scale relocation – especially any project that requires the rehousing of more people than is possible, given the existing low-rent housing supply in the community – should be studied in a similar manner. Such projects should not be initiated until the community has built sufficient relocation units to assure the proper rehousing of the residents. *Proper* should be defined by the standards of these residents as well as by those of housing and planning officials. If private enterprise is unable to provide these units, city, state, and federal funds will have to be used. Moreover, if relocation housing is built prior to the renewal project, and in sufficient quantity, and if it is attractive, it is likely to draw enough people out of the slum areas to reduce the market value of slum structures. Consequently, some of the costs of providing such relocation housing will be offset by lower acquisition costs at the time of renewal.

5. Should a community be unwilling or unable to provide the required relocation housing, it should not be permitted to engage in renewal operations.

6. Urban policy makers ought to recognize the functions performed in the city by the low-income population. Moreover, they should make sure that sufficient housing is available for them and in the proper locations (including some near the central business district) for their needs. The federal government should encourage the supply of such housing by increasing its subsidies when the renewal plan calls for the rehabilitation or construction of low-income dwellings.

7. Greater emphasis should be placed on the rehabilitation of low-rent housing, and less on

its clearance. Such rehabilitation should be based on standards that provide decent, safe, and sanitary – but economically-priced – dwelling units. In order to make this possible, existing standards should be restudied, to distinguish between those requirements which bring housing up to a standard but low-rent level from those which are "fringe benefits" and cause rehabilitated units to be priced out of the low-rent market. Frequently, current rehabilitation takes low-rent apartments and transforms them into dwelling units that fit the demands, tastes, and pocketbooks of middle- and upper-class people, rather than those of their present residents.

8. Experiments should be made with:

    a. Flexible subsidies, so that federal contributions are increased if the reuse is low- or middle-income housing; and reduced if it is luxury housing.

    b. Requirements that the redeveloper construct or finance some relocation housing, especially if he proposes to redevelop the site with housing out of the price range of the present site residents.

If the purpose of urban renewal is to improve the living conditions of the present slum dwellers, relocation thus should become one of the most important, if not the most important, phases of the renewal process. This principle suggests a number of proposals for procedural change:

9. As a general policy, relocation should be minimized unless adequate relocation housing is available in the proper locations, and unless the relocation procedures can be shown to improve the living conditions of the people who are moved. When the plan calls for rehabilitation, it should be implemented without relocation as much as possible.

10. The relocation plan should take priority over the renewal phases of the total plan, and no renewal plan should be approved by federal or local agencies until a proper relocation scheme has been developed.

11. This relocation plan should be based on a thorough knowledge of the project area residents, so that the plan fits their demands and needs and so that officials will have some understanding of the consequences of their actions

before they put the plan into effect. The federal agency ought to re-evaluate its relation to the local agencies, raising its requirements for approval of the local relocation plan and relaxing its requirements for such phases as rent collection. This would make it possible for the local agency to be more sensitive to the needs of the project area residents, and more flexible in ways of dealing with them.

12. Local and federal agencies should provide interest-free or low-interest loans to relocatees who wish to buy new homes.

13. These agencies should provide similar loans to project area landlords whose present buildings provide decent, safe, and sanitary housing; thus allowing them either to purchase new buildings in other areas, or to rehabilitate old buildings and make them available to project area residents.

14. Landlords with units eligible for relocation housing anywhere in the community should be encouraged to rent to relocatees through such incentives as rehabilitation loans, subsidies for redecorating, and the like.

15. When project area rents have been low, so that residents' housing costs are raised sharply as a result of relocation, the federal and local agencies should set up a rent moratorium to allow relocatees to save for future rentals before moving. The length of this moratorium should be based on the gap between project area and relocation area rentals.

16. Liquidation funds in lieu of moving allowances should be provided to small store owners and other businessmen who will not be able to reopen their firms elsewhere. Other federal and local programs should be made available to provide occupational retraining and similar vocational aids to those who want them.

17. Communication between the redevelopment agency and the residents, and other agency-resident relationships should assure that:

a. The amount of information given to site residents is maximized, and the development of rumors due to information vacuums is prevented.

b. Officials are trained to understand the inevitably deprivatory nature of relocation for the residents, so that they have more insight into what relocation means to the residents, and can develop a more tolerant attitude toward their reactions of shock and protest.

18. The relocation staff should be strengthened by the addition of:

a. Social workers who can provide aid to residents faced with additional problems resulting from relocation, and who can make referrals to other city agencies that deal with such problems.* The relocation staff should also call on resource persons in those areas to which site residents are moving, and employ them to facilitate the adjustment of the relocatees in their new neighborhoods.

b. Real estate technicians who can develop a thorough inventory of the city's housing supply, and who can also weed out unscrupulous landlords who are likely to exploit the relocatees.

19. In relocation projects that involve the destruction of a positive social system, experiments should be conducted to:

a. Find ways of relocating together extended families living in separate but adjacent households – provided they want to be moved en masse.

b. Make it possible for important project area institutions and organizations to re-establish themselves in those neighborhoods which have received the majority of relocatees, or in central locations where they are accessible to scattered relocatees.

c. Develop group relocation methods to allow members of an ethnic group who want to stay together to move into an area as a group. This is especially important in neighborhoods with available relocation housing in which there are presently no members of that ethnic – or racial – group.

20. The experience in most renewal projects

---

* The West End relocation office has done some pioneering work in this respect, partially as a result of the efforts of area caretakers.

indicates that the large majority of people relocate themselves, and that only a small proportion are relocated by the agency. In the future, procedures should be revised with this in mind. Then, the major functions of the relocation agency should be:

a. To make sure that the supply of relocation housing is sufficient to give relocatees a maximal choice of decent, safe, and sanitary dwelling units at rents they are willing to pay and in neighborhoods in which they want to live.

b. To provide information and other aids that will enable relocatees to evaluate these dwelling units, and to make the best housing choice in relation to their needs and wants.

c. To offer relocation service to the minority that chooses to be moved by the agency.

Many of the proposals will increase the cost of relocation, which in turn will raise the cost of renewal.* This is only equitable. Project area residents should not be required to subsidize the process, as they do presently. In time, the higher cost of renewal will become the accepted rate. Moreover, since redevelopers often stand to make considerable profit from their renewal operation, they should eventually be asked to bear part of this increased cost. The redeveloper, for example, could be asked to include some proportion of relocation expenses in his costs and pass them on to his tenants as their share of the renewal charges. Alternatively, the city could bear the initial relocation costs, and require the redeveloper to repay part of them should his project show more than an agreed upon reasonable profit. In either case, the higher the rentals of the new housing, the higher

should be the share of relocation costs to be paid by the redeveloper.

Current renewal and relocation procedures have been discussed mainly in terms of the inequities being born by the project area residents. These procedures, however, can also be shown to have undesirable consequences for renewal itself. For example, projects based on inadequate relocation plans simply push site residents into the next adjacent low-income area, and create overcrowding that leads to the formation of new slums. Thus, the city is saddled with additional problems and new costs, which eventually overwhelm the apparent short-run benefits of the renewal project. Moreover, poorly handled relocation frequently results in political repercussions which can endanger the community's long-range renewal plans. Consequently, my proposals have beneficial implications not only for the site residents, but for the future of urban renewal itself.

The conclusions and recommendations presented here are based on observations in a single redevelopment project. Even so, most of them are applicable to renewal projects in other cities. Similar ones, in fact, have been developed in studies of the process in such cities.[12]

In a number of ways, however, the West End project was atypical. First, the plan called for total clearance, a method that has been proposed less frequently of late. Many of the projects currently being planned emphasize rehabilitation. This method is as yet untested, however, and frequently requires almost as much relocation as a clearance project.

Second, the West End differed from most other urban renewal projects in that it was a neighborhood of European ethnic groups. Whereas over 95 percent of its population was

---

* In commenting on these proposals, Martin Meyerson has suggested the possibility of substituting instead a sizable "relocation bonus" to tenants, land-lords, and businessmen, to compensate them for the discomforts and other costs of relocation. Such a bonus, which might be $2500 or more, would relieve the renewal agency of all further obligations and thus simplify its operations. Moreover, since the size of the bonus would be such as to provide a real incentive for relocation, slum dwellers would welcome renewal rather than resent it. The size of the bonus would decrease the likelihood of their being identified as slum dwellers. The cost of the premium would probably be no higher than that of the

measures I have proposed, while at the same time reducing the possibility of undesirable forms of government interference. Moreover, the recipients would be free to spend the money on alternatives that are more important to them than housing. There is, of course, always the danger that lower-class recipients would spend their bonus unwisely or lose it to unscrupulous entrepreneurs. This could be counteracted, at least in part, by raising the bonus if the money is spent on housing and by postponing payment until the relocatee has moved to nonslum housing. Such a qualification would also encourage relocatees to spend at least part of their premium on housing.

white, most other renewal projects have been in predominantly nonwhite areas: 8o percent of them according to one estimate.[13] In such areas, the housing is usually of a poorer quality. Moreover, there is probably less community life, fewer long-standing relationships between residents, and less attachment to the neighborhood than in the West End. Therefore, my argument against clearance would often be less justified in these areas.

Conversely, nonwhite slum dwellers have far lower incomes, poorer jobs, less job security, as well as more social and emotional problems than do West Enders. Also, they have considerably more difficulty in finding other housing. Consequently, the negative effects of relocation are probably much greater, and the lack of proper planning for redevelopment and relocation much more serious than it was in the West End. The recommendations proposed above are therefore more urgent for typical renewal areas than for those resembling the West End.

# Notes

## | Background

### A century of the housing problem / *Wood*

[1] N.Y. Laws 1867, c. 908.
[2] N.Y. Laws 1901, c. 334, 555.
[3] Mass. Acts 1917, c. 309.
[4] 40 *Stat.* 595 (1918).
[5] Wis. Laws 1921, § 1771b, *Wis. Stat.* 1929, § 180.04.
[6] *Cal. Stat.* 1921, c. 519.
[7] N.Y. Laws 1926, c. 823, N.Y. Cons. Laws (Cahill, 1930) p. 2781.
[8] 47 *Stat.* 725 (1932), 12 USCA (Supp.) c. 1421.
[9] 47 *Stat.* 5 (1932), 15 USCA (Supp.) c. 14, § 605 b (a) (2).
[10] 48 *Stat.* 195 (1933), 15 USCA (Supp.) § 701.
[11] Wood, *The Housing of the Unskilled Wage Earner* (1919).
[12] Barnes, *The Slum, Its Story and Solution* (1931).
[13] 11 and 12 Vict. c. 63 (1848).
[14] 214 and 15 Vict. c. 34 (1851).
[15] 53 and 54 Vict. c. 70 (1890).
[16] 31 and 32 Vict. c. 130 (1868); 42 and 43 Vict. c. 64 (1879); 43 Vict. c. 8 (1879); 45 and 46 Vict. c. 54 (1882).
[17] 38 and 39 Vict. c. 49 (1875); 42 and 43 Vict. c. 63 (1879); 43 Vict. c. 2 (1880); 45 and 46 Vict. c. 54 (1882).
[18] 20 and 21 Geo. V. c. 39 (1930).
[19] 9 and 10 Geo. V, c. 35 (1919).
[20] 13 and 14 Geo. V, c. 24 (1923).
[21] 15 Geo. V. c. 14 (1925).
[22] *Supra*, note 17.
[23] *Supra*, note 21.
[24] Simon, *The Anti-Slum Campaign* (1933).
[25] Ohio Laws 1933, H.B. 19.
[26] Mich. Pub. Acts 1933, no. 94, at 118.
[27] Md. Laws 1933, c. 32, at 152.
[28] N.J. Laws 1933, c. 444.
[29] Wis. Laws 1921, § 1771b, *Wis.Stat.* (1929) § 180.04 (8).
[30] N.Y. Laws 1934, c. 4, p. 185.

### The social psychology of housing / *Merton*

[1] John P. Dean, *Problems in Social Aspects of Housing*, Interim Report to the Social Science Research Council (in manuscript), 1948. (For a critical review of studies on social effects of bad housing.)
[2] A. Goldfield, *Substandard Housing as a Potential Factor in Juvenile Delinquency*. Unpublished Ph.D. dissertation, New York University, 1937.
[3] American Public Health Association. *An Appraisal Method for Measuring the Quality of Housing: A Yardstick for Health Officers, Housing Officials, and Planners*, Part 1, *Nature and Uses of the Method*. New Haven, Connecticut, 1945.
[4] Jay and S. Shuman Rumney, *Cost of Slums*. Housing Authority of the City of Newark, 1946. (One of the few studies in this field which detects the complexity of the problem.)
[5] John P. Dean, *Home Ownership: Is It Sound?* New York: Harper and Brothers 1945.
[6] John P. Dean, "The Orientation of Housing Research: A Commentary on the Program of the Conference on Research in Housing," *Journal of Land and Public Utility Economics*, February 1947, XXIII: 76–80.
[7] G. E. Howard and R. U. Ratcliff (reporters), Proceedings of the University of Wisconsin Conference on Social and Economic Research in Housing, December 1945, *Journal of Land and Utility Economics* (supplement) February 1946, XXII: 93–116.
[8] R. K. Merton, *The Expert and Research in Applied Social Science*, Unpublished manuscript, 1947.
[9] John Dewey, *Logic: The Theory of Inquiry*. New York: Henry Holt & Co. 1938.

[10] R. K. Merton, "Sociological Theory," *American Journal of Sociology*, May 1945, L: 462–473.

[11] R. K. Merton and Patricia J. Salter, *Studies in the Sociology and Social Psychology of Housing*. (Under a grant from the Lavanburg Foundation.) Unpublished manuscript, 1945–48.

[12] F. S. Chapin, "An Experiment on the Social Effects of Good Housing," *American Sociological Review*, December, 1940, V: 868–879.

[13] F. S. Chapin, "New Methods of Sociological Research on Housing Problems," *American Sociological Review*, April 1947, XII: 143–149.

[14] F. S. Chapin, "The Effects of Slum Clearance and Rehousing on Family and Community Relationships in Minneapolis," *American Journal of Sociology*, March 1938, XLIII: 744–763.

[15] R. K. Merton, "The Bearing of Empirical Research Upon the Development of Social Theory," *American Sociological Review*, October 1948.

[16] Louis Wirth, "Housing as a Field of Sociological Research," *American Sociological Review*, April 1947, XII: 137–143.

[17] R. K. Merton and Patricia Salter, op. cit.

[18] R. K. Merton, *The Expert and Research in Applied Social Science*, Unpublished manuscript, 1947.

[19] James S. Plant, *Personality and the Cultural Pattern*. New York: The Commonwealth Fund, 1938.

[20] Svend Riemer, "Sociological Theory of Home Adjustment," *American Sociological Review*, June 1943, VIII: 272–278.

[21] Svend Riemer, "Sociological Perspective in Home Planning," *American Sociological Review*, April 1947, XII: 155–159.

[22] Svend Riemer, "The Adjustment of Family Life to its Physical Shelter," *Research Studies, State College of Washington*, 1941, IX: 49–55.

[23] Ruth Durant, *Watling: A Survey of Social Life on a New Housing Estate*. London: P. S. King, 1939.

[24] Terence Young, *Becontree and Dagenham*. London: Pilgrim Trust, 1934.

[25] Charles P. Loomis, *Studies of Rural Social Organization*, East Lansing, Michigan, 1945, Chapter 2.

[26] Berelson P. Lazarfield, and H. Gaudet, *The People's Choice*. New York: Columbia University Press, 1948.

[27] R. K. Merton, "Patterns of Interpersonal Influence and of Communications Behavior in a Local Community." In P. F. Lazarsfield and Frank Stanton (editors), *Communications Research*, 1948–49. New York: Harper and Brothers, 1948.

[28] R. E. Park, E. W. Burgess, and R. D. McKenzie, *The City*. Chicago: University of Chigago Press, 1925.

[29] R. M. Williams, *The Reduction of Intergroup Tensions: A Survey of Research on Problems of Ethnic, Racial and Religious Group Relations*, New York: Social Science Research Council, Bulletin 57, 1947.

[30] Howard R. Cottam, *Housing and Attitudes Toward Housing in Rural Pennsylvania*, Pennsylvania State College Architectural Experiment Station, Bulletin 436, December 1942.

[31] Institut National d'Etudes Démographiques *Desirs des Francais en Matiere d'habitation urbaine*. Travaux et Documents, Cahier No. 3. Paris: Presses Universitaires de France, 1947.

[32] Mass Observation, *An Enquiry Into People's Homes*. London: John Murray, 1943.

[33] Svend Riemer, "A Research Note on Sociological Home-Planning, *American Journal of Sociology*, May 1941, XLVI: 865–872.

[34] L. Festinger et al. *A Study of the Sources of Satisfaction and Dissatisfaction in a Housing Project*. Unpublished manuscript, Research Center for Group Dynamics. Massachusetts Institute of Technology, 1947.

[35] National Housing Agency, *The Livability Problems of 1,000 Families*, FPHA Bulletin No. 28, October, 1945.

[36] R. K. Merton, and Patricia Salter, op. cit.

[37] W. H. Form, "Status Stratification in a Planned Community," *American Sociological Review*, October 1945, X: 605–613.

[38] Ruth Durant, op. cit.

[39] A. Goldfield, *What Happened to 386 Families Who Were Compelled to Vacate Their Slum Dwellings to Make Way for a Large Housing Project?* New York: Lavanburg Foundation, 1933.

[40] R. K. Merton and Patricia J. Salter, *The First Year's Work, 1945–46: An Interim Report*. Unpublished manuscript, June 1946.

[41] Dennis Chapman, *Sound in Dwellings*. Buildings Research Station of the Department of Scientific and Industrial Research, Wartime Social Survey. New Series Region S. 6, November 1943.

[42] C. Kilbourn and M. Lantis, "Elements of Tenant Instability in a War Housing Project," *American Sociological Review*, February 1946, XI: 57–66.

[43] R. K. Merton and Patricia J. Salter, op. cit.

[44] Lillian Kessler, *The Social Structure of a War Housing Community: East Vanport City*, Unpublished thesis, Reed College, Portland, 1945.

[45] Douglas Marshall, *Greendale: A Study of a Resettlement Community*, Unpublished Ph.D. dissertation, University of Wisconsin, 1943.

[46] S. C. Couch, *A Study of the Atlanta University Homes: A Negro Housing Project*, Unpublished M. A. thesis, Mercer University, 1936.

[47] R. K. Merton, and Patricia J. Salter, op. cit.

[48] H. G. Brunsman, "Current Sources of Sociological Data in Housing," *American Sociological Review*, April 1947, XII: 150–155.

[49] R. K. Merton, "Selected Problems of Field Work in the Planned Community," *American Sociological Review*, June 1947, XII: 304–312.

[50] F. S. Chapin, "Some Problems in Field Interviews When Using the Control Group Technique in Studies in the Community," *American Sociological Review*, February 1943, VIII: 63–68.

[51] F. S. Chapin, *Experimental Designs in Sociological Research*. New York: Harper and Brothers, 1947.

# II **Housing in the neighborhood**

The structure and growth of residential neighborhoods in American cities / *Hoyt*

[1] Hurd, R. M., *Principles of City Land Values*, Record and Guide, New York, (1924), p. 59.

[2] U.S. Department of Commerce. *Statistical Abstract of the United States, 1937* (Washington, D.C., 1938), pp. 394, 399.

[3] Automobile Manufacturers Association. *Automobile Facts and Figures 1938* (New York City), p. 16.
[4] Ratcliff, Richard U. *An Examination Into Some*

*Characteristics of Outlying Retail Nucleations in the City of Detroit.* A doctoral dissertation—University of Michigan, 1935.

## The theory of residential growth and structure / *Rodwin*

[1] H. Hoyt, *The Structure and Growth of Residential Neighborhoods in American Cities*, Government Printing Office, Washington, D. C., 1939, p. 114.
[2] *Ibid.*
[3] *Ibid.*
[4] W. Firey, *op. cit.*, pp. 44, 50, 55 and 62.
[5] *Ibid.*, p. 44.
[6] W. Firey, *op. cit.*, p. 50 and Figure 2 on p. 56.
[7] *Ibid.*, pp. 62–63.
[8] *Ibid.*, pp. 77–78.
[9] H. Hoyt, *op. cit.*, p. 117.
[10] W. Firey, *op. cit.*, p. 326.
[11] W. Firey, *op. cit.*, p. 340.
[12] *Ibid.*, p. 23.
[13] H. Hoyt, *op. cit.*, p. 117.
[14] H. Hoyt, *op. cit.*, p. 117.
[15] *Ibid.*

[16] H. Hoyt, *op. cit.*, p. 117.
[17] *Ibid.*
[18] *Ibid.*, p. 118.
[19] A. B. Wolfe, *The Lodging House Problem in Boston*, Houghton Mifflin Co., Boston, 1906, p. 17.
[20] H. Hoyt, *op. cit.*
[21] *Ibid.*
[22] *Ibid.*, pp. 118–119.
[23] *Ibid.*, p. 114.
[24] *Ibid.*, p. 116.
[25] *Ibid.*, p. 75.
[26] W. Firey, *op. cit.*, pp. 78–80.
[27] H. Hoyt, *op. cit.*, p. 75.
[28] See, for example, Lloyd Rodwin, *Middle Income Housing Problems in Boston*, (Unpublished Ph.D. Thesis, Widener Library), Cambridge, 1949, Chapter 4.

## The neighborhood unit formula / *Perry*

[1] Perry, Clarence Arthur, The Neighborhood Unit, Monograph 1 in vol. 7, Neighborhood and Community Planning, of the Regional Survey of New York and Its Environs. Published by Committee on Regional Plan of New York and Its Environs, New York, 1929. (To be found in most public libraries).

Since discussion in the present study will involve frequent references to the original presentation, the following condensed form will hereafter be used: New York Regional Plan, vol. 7.

[2] Strayer, George D., and Engelhardt, N. L., New York Regional Plan, vol. 7, p. 45.
[3] *Ibid.*
[4] New York Regional Plan, vol. 7, p. 52.
[5] Urban Land Policy, 1936.
[6] Zoning: The Laws, Administration, and Court Decisions during the First Twenty Years. Russell Sage Foundation, New York, 1936, p. 83.

## Attack on the neighborhood unit formula / *Isaacs*

[1] The Twentieth Century Fund, "Background and Aims," *Annual Report, 1947*, New York, 1948.
[2] James Dahir, *The Neighborhood Unit Plan*, New York: Russell Sage Foundation, 1947, p. 5.
[3] Tracy B. Augur, "Objectives of Neighborhood Planning," *The Architectural Forum*, April 1944, pp. 79, 80, 184.
[4] Louis Wirth, "Human Ecology," *American Journal of Sociology*, May, 1945, p. 485.
[5] Ruth Glass, "Social Aspects of Town Planning," *Architectural Review*, London, England, March, 1945, pp. 67–72.
[6] Thomas E. McCormick, now Executive Director, City Planning Board, Boston, in a letter to the author, May 24, 1943.

[7] Chicago Plan Commission, 1948, *Building New Neighborhoods*, p. 6.
[8] The City Club of Chicago, *City Residential Land Development*, University of Chicago Press, December, 1916.
[9] From a confidential federal agency report on the conservation of neighborhoods, 1944.
[10] Federal Agency Report, *op. cit.*
[11] Federal Agency Report, *op. cit.*
[12] Richard Dewey, "Peripheral Expansion in Milwaukee County," *American Journal of Sociology*, September, 1948, pp. 118–125.
[13] Federal Agency Report, *op. cit.*
[14] *Land Economies*, vol. 25, February 1949, pp. 69–72.

## In defense of the neighborhood / *Mumford*

[1] De Lauwe, Pierre Chombart, *Paris et l'Agglomération Parisienne.* 2 vols. Paris: 1952.

[2] Yeomans, Alfred (Editor). *City Residential Land Development*, Chicago, 1916.

# III **The housing market**

## Housing design and family values / *Dean*

[1] Svend Riemer, "A Sociologist's View," paper presented at the 17th Annual Conference, National Association of Housing Officials, October 1950: Publication N 298, *Livability of Housing: What Is It?*

[2] Blanche Halbert, "P.H.A.'s View," paper presented by the 17th Annual Conference, National Association of Housing Officials, October 1950, Publication N 298, *Livability of Housing: What Is It?*

3 See, for example, Heiner & McCullough, " Analysis of Kitchen Space," *Architectural Forum*, (February, 1946), p 155.
4 Discussion with Robert K. Merton.
5 Leon Festinger, Stanley Schachter, Kurt Black, *Social Pressures in Informal Groups—a Study of Human Factors in Housing*. (New York: Harper & Row, 1950).
6 Mary Evans Collins and Merton Deutsch, " Interracial Housing," three articles in the *Journal of Housing*, (January, March, and April, 1950).
7 Robert K. Merton, " The Social Psychology of Housing," *Current Trends in Social Psychology*, (University of Pittsburgh Press, 1948).

8 For more extended discussion see: F. Lundberg and M. F. Farnham, *Modern Women: The Lost Sex* (New York: Harper & Row 1947), especially chapters V and IX: M. Komarovsky, " Cultural Contradictions and Sex Roles," *American Journal of Sociology*, (November, 1946), pp. 184 – 189; and three articles on age and sex roles in the *American Sociology Review*, (December, 1942), by Ralph Linton, Talcott Parsons and Leonard S. Cottrell, Jr.
9 Financed by a Social Science Research Council post-doctoral research fellowship (unpublished).

## Family housing expenditures: elusive laws and intrusive variances / *Maisel, Winnick*

1 *Family Housing Expenditures*, pp. 411 – 433.

## Housing: has there been a downward shift in consumers' preferences? / *Winnick*

1 Simon Kuznets, *National Product Since 1869*, p. 106, Table II – 8 and p. 107, Table II – 9, col. 1.
2 1950 Census of Housing, Vol. IV, *Residential Financing*, Part I, p. 272.
3 1929 – 100. Simon Kuznets, " Nine Year Moving Averages of National Product and Components by Types of Use, 1873 – 1945," Capital Requirements Study, Memorandum No. 19, (New York: National Bureau of Economic Research), July, 1951, pp. 4 – 6.

4 James S. Duesenberry and Helen Kistin, " The Role of Demand in the Economic Structure," *Studies in the Structure of the American Economy*, Wassily Leontief, et al. (New York: Oxford University Press, 1953).
5 *The Volume of Residential Construction 1889 – 1950* (New York: National Bureau of Economic Research, 1954), Technical Paper No. 9.

## Reply / *Winnick*

1 J. Frederick Dewhurst, *America's Needs and Resources* (New York: Twentieth Century Fund, 1954).
2 Department of Commerce, *National Income Supplement 1954.*
3 *Ibid.*

## The consumer votes by moving / *Abu-Lughod, Foley*

1 Branch, *op. cit.*
2 U.S. Bureau of the Census, *Current Population Reports*, April, 1954 – April, 1955.
3 1940 Census on Family Mobility as cited in Glick, " The Family Cycle," *American Sociological Review*, vol. XII, (April, 1947), pp. 164 – 174.
4 Katona and Mueller, *op. cit.*
5 Rossi, *op. cit.*, p. 72.
6 Katona and Mueller, *op. cit.*, table 39, p. 87. Data are for June 1954.
7 U.S. Bureau of the Census, " Mobility of the Population of the United States: April, 1954 to April, 1955," *Current Population Reports, Population Characteristics*, ser. P-20, no. 61, Oct. 28, 1955. Based on computations from data appearing in table 5, p. 12.
8 Glenn Beyer, *Housing: A Factual Analysis*, The Macmillan Company, New York, 1958, pp. 6, 8; citing U.S. Bureau of the Census, " Family Income in the United States: 1954 and 1953," *Current Population Reports*, ser. P-60, no. 20, December 1955, p. 17.
9 William H. Whyte, Jr., *The Organization Man*, Doubleday, New York, 1957, p. 298.
10 E. Haveman and P. S. West, *They Went to College*, Harcourt, Brace, New York, 1952. (Survey by *Time*, analysis by Columbia University Bureau of Applied Social Research.)

11 U.S. Bureau of the Census, *op. cit.*
12 Betty Tableman, *Intracommunity Migration in the Flint Metropolitan District*, University of Michigan Institute for Human Adjustment, 1948; and Peter Rossi, *Why Families Move*, New York: The Free Press, 1955, table 8 – 1, p. 135.
13 U.S. Bureau of the Census, *Statistical Abstract of the United States, 1956*, tables 27, 28, 33, 34, pp. 33 – 39; see also *Historical Statistics*, 1945, and Supplement, ser. B. 205 – 230, p. 31.
14 U.S. Bureau of the Census, *Special Census: New York City, 1957.*
15 Eunice Grier and George Grier, *Race Relations in Syracuse*, New York State Commission Against Discrimination, January, 1958, Summary, iii; " The People: Numbers and Distribution," pp. 1, 2.
16 *Population Growth in the Chicago Standard Metropolitan Area*, Chicago Community Inventory, University of Chicago, 1958.
17 Indianapolis City Planning Commission.
18 Theodore Caplow, " Incidence and Direction of Residential Mobility in a Minneapolis Sample," *Social Forces*, vol. 27, May, 1949, pp. 431 – 417.
19 Richard Dewey, " Peripheral Expansion in Milwaukee County," *American Journal of Sociology*, (September, 1948), pp. 118 – 125.

### The filtering process / *Grigsby*

1 See Ernest M. Fisher and Louis B. Winnick, "A Reformulation of the Filtering Concept," *Journal of Social Issues*, VII, (1951), 47 – 85.
2 Richard U. Ratcliff, *Urban Law and Economics* (New York: McGraw-Hill, 1949), pp. 321, 322.
3 Fisher and Winnick, *op. cit.*
4 *Ibid.*, p. 50.
5 *Ibid.*, p. 54.
6 *Ibid.*, p. 52.
7 *Ibid.*, p. 55.
8 Ira S. Lowry, "Filtering and Housing Standards,"
*Land Economics*, XXXVI (November, 1960), 362 – 370.
9 Ratcliff, *op. cit.*, p. 324.
10 Louis Winnick, "Housing: Has There Been a Downward Shift in Consumers' Preferences?" *Quarterly Journal of Economics*, LXIX (February, 1955), 85-98.
11 Leo Grebler, "The Housing Inventory: Analytic Concept and Quantitative Change," *American Economic Review*, XLI (May, 1951), 555 – 568.
12 Lowry, *op. cit.*, pp. 364 – 365.
13 Fisher and Winnick, *op. cit.* p. 56.

### Components of change in the nation's housing inventory in relation to the 1960 census / *Kristof*

1 U.S. Bureau of the Census, *Intercensal Housing Surveys*, (1957).
2 Glenn H. Beyer, *Housing: A Factual Analysis*, Macmillan, New York, 1958, p. 281.
3 *Ibid.*, p. 285.
4 William C. Wheaton, "American Housing Needs, 1956 – 1970," *The Housing Yearbook*, 1954, Washington National Housing Conference, p. 11.
5 Rapkin, Winnick, and Blank, *Housing Market Analysis*, U.S. Housing and Home Finance Agency, 1953, p. 60.
6 *Wall Street, Journal*, (November 2, 1959), p. 1, col. 1.
7 U.S. Bureau of the Census, Current Population Reports, P-20, No. 76, Table 1.
8 Louis Winnick, *Rental Housing: Opportunities for Private Investment*, McGraw-Hill Book Co., New York, 1958.

# IV Requirements of special groups

### Living arrangements of unattached persons / *Rose*

1 John N. Webb, *The Transient Unemployed* (Washington, D. C.: Works Progress Administration, 1935), pp. 1 – 3, 12, 88 – 93.
2 Howard B. Myers, "Defense Migration and Labor Supply," *Journal of the American Statistical Association*, 37 (March, 1942), 75.
3 John H. Clapham, *An Economic History of Modern Britain* (Cambridge, England: University Press, 1926), esp. Chapters 2 and 14. Adna F. Weber, *The Growth of Cities in the Nineteenth Century* (New York: Columbia University, 1899), esp. Chapters III – VI.
4 U.S. Bureau of the Census, *Sixteenth Census of the United States: 1940. Population*, Vol. IV, Part I (Washington, D. C.: Government Office, 1943), p. 17.
5 Marcus L. Hansen, *The Immigrant in American History* (Cambridge: Harvard University Press, 1940), p. 150. Caroline F. Ware, "Immigration," *Encyclopaedia of the Social Sciences*, VII (New York: The Macmillan Co., 1932), pp. 587 – 594.
6 Karl Pribram, "Unemployment," *Encyclopaedia of the Social Sciences*, XV (New York: The Macmillan Co., 1935), 147 – 162, (esp. pp. 147 – 148, 152).
7 Samuel A. Stouffer and Paul F. Lazarsfeld, *Research Memorandum on the Family in the Depression* (New York: Social Science Research Council, 1937), pp. 139 – 186. Robert C. Angell, *The Family Encounters the Depression* (New York: Charles Scribners' Sons, 1936). Ruth S. Cavan and Katherine H. Ranck, *The Family and the Depression* (Chicago: University of Chicago Press, 1938).
8 Unpublished manuscript by the author, "Interest in the Living Arrangements of the Unattached."
9 National Resources Committee, *Consumer Incomes in the United States, Their Distribution in 1935 – 36* (Washington, D. C.: Government Printing Office, 1038), pp. 4, 18. U.S. Bureau of the Census, *Sixteenth Census of the United States: 1940. Population and Housing, Families, Income and Rent* (Washington, D. C.: Government Printing Office, 1943), p. 9.
10 National Resources Committee, *op. cit.*, pp. 4, 18.
11 *Ibid.*, p. 30.
12 U.S. Bureau of the Census, *Sixteenth Census, Population and Housing, op. cit.*, p. 9.
13 See, for example: (1) Community Service Society, "Life in One Room," mimeographed report by the Committee on Housing, Community Service Society (New York, 1940). (2) Information Bureau on Women's Works, Toledo, *Rooms, Inquire Within* (Toledo, Ohio: 1927). (3) James Ford, *Slums and Housing* (Cambridge: Harvard University Press, 1936). (4) Edith Abbott, *The Tenements of Chicago: 1908-1935* (Chicago: University of Chicago Press, 1936). Many other sources, most of them written before World War I, are available on the characteristics of rooming houses.
14 Chicago Plan Commission and Work Projects Administration, *Residential Chicago*, Vol. I of the *Chicago Land Use Survey* (Chicago Plan Commission, 1942), pp. 232-234. Although these data were not published until 1942, they were collected in 1938—before the war housing shortage.
15 Lyonel C. Florant, "The Impact of the War on the Norfolk Negro Community," (Unpublished manuscript, Richmond: Population Study, Virginia State Planning Board, May 26, 1942). Mary Skinner and Alice S. Nutt, "Adolescents Away from Home," *Annals of the American Academy of Political and Social Science*, 236 (November, 1944), pp. 51 – 59.
16 The Defense Housing Act of October 14, 1940, as amended January 21, 1942.
17 Unpublished statistics made available through the courtesy of Miss Corienne K. Robinson, National Housing Agency, Federal Public Housing Authority (Letter, August 28, 1942).

### Housing for the elderly / *The Subcommittee on Housing for the Elderly, U.S. Senate*

1 Henry D. Sheldon, "The Older Population of the United States," John Wiley & Sons, Inc., 1958, p. 112.
2 See "Sources and Size of Money Income of the Aged," by Lenore A. Epstein in the January 1962 Social Security Bulletin.

3 Hearings before the Subcommittee on Housing for the Elderly, pt. 1, Washington, D. C., Aug. 22, 1961.


### Guiding policies / *The Committee on the Hygiene of Housing, American Public Health Association*

1 *Journal of Housing*, (December, 1952).
2 Eugene C. Gardner. *Illustrated Homes. Describing Real Houses and Real People*. Boston, 1875.

3 Gladston. *Social and Biological Challenge of Our Aging Population.*


### How the poor are housed / *Schorr*

1 Warren Jay Vinton, "Working Paper," in *Interim Report on Housing the Economically and Socially Disadvantaged Groups in the Population*. Proceedings and working papers of Conference sponsored by the Metropolitan Housing and Planning Council of Chicago in cooperation with Action, Inc., New York, February 26 – 27, 1960.
2 Joseph P. McMurray, *Ways and Means of Providing Housing for Families Unable to Afford Rentals or Mortgage Payments Necessary for Adequate Private Housing*, National Association of Home Builders, Washington, D. C., December 30, 1960.
3 Helen H. Lamale, and Margaret S. Stotz, "The Interim City Worker's Family Budget," *Monthly Labor Review* (August, 1960), LXXXIII: No. 8, 785 – 808.
4 U.S. Department of Commerce, Bureau of the Census, *1956 National Housing Inventory—Characteristics of the 1956 Inventory*. Washington, D. C., 1959, III: part 1.
5 Beverley Duncan and Philip M. Hauser, *Housing a Metropolis—Chicago*, New York: The Free Press, p. 147.
6 U.S. Department of Commerce, Bureau of the Census, *op. cit.*
7 U.S. Department of Labor, Bureau of Labor Statistics, *Study of Consumer Expenditures, Incomes and Savings*, Statistical Tables, Urban U.S.—1950, XVIII, University of Pennsylvania, Philadelphia, 1957, Table 1 – 2.
8 Louis Winnick, "Economic Constraints," Chapter 1 and 2 of *Housing Choices and Housing Constraints*, ed. by Nelson N. Foote, Janet Abu-Lughod, Mary Mix Foley, and Louis Winnick, New York: McGraw-Hill, 1960, p. 34.
9 U.S. Department of Labor, Bureau of Labor Statistics, *op. cit.*, Table 2 – 2.
10 U. S. Department of Commerce, Bureau of the Census, *op. cit.*
11 Louis Winnick, *op. cit.*
12 Alvin L. Schorr, *Filial Responsibility in the Modern American Family*, U.S. Government Printing Office, Washington, D. C., 1960, pp. 9 – 10.
13 U.S. Housing Authority in cooperation with the Social Security Board, *Housing and Welfare*, Federal Works Agency, Washington, D. C., May 1940.
14 Kurt W. Back, *Slums, Projects and People: Social Psychological Problems of Relocation in Puerto Rico*, Durham, N. C.: Duke University Press, 1962.
15 Social Planning Council of St. Louis and St. Louis County, Research Bureau, *Public Housing Residents and Welfare Services*, Missouri, August, 1955.

16 Daniel M. Wilner, et al., *The Housing Environment and Family Life*, Chapter 17, "Summary and Conclusions," July, 1960, processed.
17 Kurt W. Back, *op cit.*, p. 102.
18 Lawrence N. Bloomberg, *Mobility and Motivations*, Housing and Home Finance Agency, Public Housing Administration, Washington, D. C., April, 1958.
19 Joint Committee on Housing and Welfare, *Community Services and Public Housing: Seven Recommendations for Local Housing Authority Action*, National Association of Housing and Redevelopment Officials and the National Social Welfare Assembly, October, 1961.
20 Department of Public Welfare, Public Assistance Division, "Five Years of Cooperative Effort by the National Capital Housing Authority and the Public Assistance Division, 1956 – 1961," Washington, D. C., mimeographed, p. 6.
21 Murray E. Ortof, "Public Housing: New Neighbors in Old Communities," *Social Work* (April, 1959), IV: No. 2, pp. 55 – 63.
22 United South End Settlements and the Boston Housing Authority, *First Evaluation Report of the Community Services Center*, Massachusetts, November, 1961.
23 Janet E. Weinandy, *Families Under Stress*, New York: Syracuse University Press, February, 1962.
24 Housing and Home Finance Agency, Public Housing Administration, *Families in Low-Rent Projects—Families Re-examined During Calendar Year 1960 for Continued Occupancy*, Washington, D. C., August, 1961.
25 Data were provided by a study of Aid to Families with Needy Children by the Institute for Research in Social Science, University of North Carolina, for the American Public Welfare Association.
26 *Ibid.*
27 Florida Department of Public Welfare, *Suitable Home Law*, Preliminary Report, September, 1960, p. 16.
28 John M. Romanyshyn, *Aid to Dependent Children in Maine*, State of Maine, Department of Health and Welfare, June, 1960, p. 10.
29 Greenleigh Associates, Inc., *Facts, Fallacies and Future*, and *Addenda to Facts, Fallacies and Future*, New York, 1960.
30 Charles T. O'Reilly, and Margaret M. Pembroke, *Chicago's ADC Families . . . Their Characteristics and Problems*, Chicago: Loyola University Press, 1960.
31 Charles T. O'Reilly, and Margaret M. Pembroke, *OAA Profile*, Chicago: Loyola University Press, 1961.

[32] Fulton County Department of Public Welfare, *Slow But Sure*, Annual Report 1960, Atlanta, Georgia.
[33] Daniel M. Wilner, and Rosabelle Price Walkley, "Housing Environment and Mental Health," *Epidemiology of Mental Disorder*, ed. by Benjamin Pasamanick, Publication No. 60 of the American Association for the Advancement of Science, Washington, D. C., 1959.
[34] *Washington Post*, "Winter Evictions Pose Welfare Agency Problems," (November 25, 1961).
[35] Philadelphia Housing Association, "Relocation— The Human Side of Urban Renewal," *Issues*, Philadelphia (November, 1958).
[36] Westchester County Council of Social Agencies, Inc., Committee on Housing, White Plains, New York, July, 1957.
[37] Henry Coe Lanpher, *Welfare Aspects of Housing*, Alexandria Community Welfare Council, Virginia, March, 1962, processed.
[38] Cuyahoga County Welfare Department, "Ill-Starred Children," *Annual Report*, Ohio, 1959, p. 5.
[39] Dr. Jean Pakter, Dr. Harold Jacobziner, Henry J. Rosner, and Frieda Greenstein, "A Study of Out-of-Wedlock Births in New York City," Paper delivered to the American Public Health Association, Annual Meeting, November 1, 1960, pp. 15 – 16, (for a brief summary, see *Public Health Reports*, February, 1961, LXXVI, No. 2 : 107 — 153).
[40] Cuyahoga County Welfare Department, "Special Report," *Annual Report*, Ohio, 1960.
[41] Housing and Home Finance Agency, Public Housing Administration, *op. cit.*

[42] Joint Committee on Housing and Welfare, "Statement of Fundamental Principles for Establishment of Rentals for Public Assistance Families in Federally Aided Public Housing," National Association of Housing and Redevelopment Officials and the National Social Welfare Assembly, 1959.
[43] *Ibid.*, p. 1.
[44] "Housing Codes Are Subject of Two Major Studies," *Journal of Housing* (June, 1957), XIV: No. 6, 200 – 201.
[45] Maurice B. Hexter, *Report of the Mayer's Committee of Inquiry on the New York City Department of Welfare*, September 30, 1959, mimeographed, p. 19.
[46] Mary F. Bogue, *Administration of Mothers' Aid in Ten Localities*, U.S. Department of Labor, Children's Bureau, publication No. 184, 1928, p. 15.
[47] U.S. Housing Authority in cooperation with the Social Security Board, *op. cit.*, pp. 6 – 7.
[48] Joseph P. McMurray, *op. cit.*
[49] Ernest M. Fisher, "A Study of Housing Programs and Policies." Prepared for the U.S. Housing Administrator, January 1960. Included as a working paper in *Interim Report on Housing the Economically and Socially Disadvantaged Groups in the Population*, *op. cit.*
[50] Metropolitan Housing and Planning Council, *Housing the Economically and Socially Disadvantaged Groups in the Population, Recommendations*, Chicago, January, 1961.
[51] Housing Act of 1949, Act of July 15, 1949, Chapter 388, 63 Stat. 413.

## Housing and slum clearance : elusive goals / *Grigsby*

[1] For example, see Robert C. Weaver, "Address to a Joint Housing Industry Dinner, Sponsored by the Milwaukee Builders Association, Wisconsin Mortgage Bankers Association, Milwaukee Council of Savings and Loan Association, Milwaukee Board of Realtors, and Wisconsin Bankers Association," Milwaukee, Wisconsin, November 19, 1963, mimeographed by Housing and Home Finance Agency.

[2] "Factual Data for Sales-Type Middle-Income Housing" and "Factual Data on Rental-Type Middle-Income Housing," prepared by the Housing and Home Finance Agency for Senator Joseph S. Clark and printed in *Congressional Record* (March 21, 1963).

## The myths of housing reform / *Dean*

[1] Frank, L. K., "Social Problems," *American Journal of Sociology*, January, 1925, p. 467.
[2] A good summary of these studies appears in Part III of the *Cost of Slums*, a pamphlet prepared for the Housing Authority of the City of Newark by Dr. Jay Rumney and Sara Shuman, Newark, 1946, pp. 32 ff. Also see: Mowrer, E. R., *Disorganization: Personal and Social*, Phila., 1942; Faris, R. E. L. and Dunham, H. W. *Mental Disorders in Urban Areas*, Chicago, 1939; Shaw, C. L. and McKay, *Juvenile Delinquency and Urban Areas*, Chicago, 1942; Ford, James, *Slums-Housing*, Cambridge, 1936, 2 vol.
[3] Goldfeld, Abraham, "Substandard Housing as a Potential Factor in Juvenile Delinquency in a Local Area in New York City," abstract of Ph.D. Thesis, N.Y. University, 1937 (reprint).
[4] Myer, Dillon S., Commissioner of the Federal Public Housing Authority, at the *Hearings* before the Committee on Banking and Currency, U.S. Senate, 80th Congress, on S. 866, Gov't. Printing Office, Washington, 1947, p. 118.
[5] Housing Authority of the City of Gary (Indiana), *A Report*, Gary, 1945 : Housing Authority of the City of

Newark (N.J.) *The Social Effects of Public Housing*, Newark, 1944; Phila. Housing Authority, *Homes for War Workers and Families of Low Income*, Phila., 1943, and Bureau of Social Research, Federation of Social Agencies of Pittsburgh and Allegheny Counties. *Juvenile Delinquency in Public Housing*, 1944, and *Vital Statistics of Public Housing Residents*, 1945.
[6] Barer, Naomi, "A Note on Tuberculosis Among Residents of a Housing Project," *Public Housing*, August, 1945, p. 133.
[7] Barer, Naomi, "Delinquency Before, After Admission to New Haven Housing Development," *Journal of Housing*, December 1945 – January 1946, p. 17.
[8] Chapin, F. Stuart, "An Experiment on the Social Effects of Good Housing," *American Sociological Review*, December, 1949, pp. 868 – 79.
[9] See "The Social Psychology of Housing," in *Current Trends in Social Psychology*, Wayne Dennis (ed.) University of Pittsburgh Press, Pittsburgh, 1948, pp. 188 ff.
[10] See Leon Festinger, Stanley Schacter, and Kurt Bach, *Social Pressures in Informal Groups: A Study of Human Factors in Housing*, Harper & Row, New York, 1950.

## Where shall we live? / *The Commission on Race and Housing*

[1] A detailed analysis of the economic status of non-whites and characteristics of their demand for housing is presented in Davis McEntire, *Residence and Race,* Part II: "Minorities in the Housing Market," University of California Press, 1960.

[2] Herbert H. Hyman and Paul B. Sheatsley, "Attitudes Towards Desegregation," *Scientific American,* Vol. 195, No. 6 (December, 1956), pp. 35 – 39.

[3] Luigi Laurenti, *Property Values and Race: Studies in Seven Cities,* University of California Press, 1960.

[4] *Ibid.*

[5] This discussion is based on interviews with some 200 builders in various sections of the country, reported more fully in *Residence and Race,* Chapter 11: "The House Building Industry," and in the special study by N. J. Demerath and Associates, *Private Enterprise Housing for Negroes in Seven Metropolitan Areas.*

[6] Eunice and George Grier, *Privately Developed Interracial Housing: An Analysis of Experience,* University of California Press, 1960.

[7] Federal Housing Administration, "Message from FHA Commissioner to be Read by Insuring Office Directors at NAHB Local Meetings Relating to Providing Homes Available to Minorities," July 16, 1954.

[8] Birmingham's recent efforts to control the residence of Negroes by zoning and other legal devices are described in Thompson, Lewis, and McEntire, *Southern Approaches to Housing for Negroes.* A brief history of municipal legal measures to establish residential segregation is given in *Residence and Race,* Chapter 15: "Race Discrimination and the Law."

[9] Forrest E. LaViolette, with the assistance of Joseph T. Taylor and Giles Hubert, *Negro Housing in the New Orleans Community.*

[10] Further discussion and instances are given in *Residence and Race,* Chapter 15: "Race Discrimination and the Law"; Thompson, Lewis, and McEntire, *Southern Approaches to Housing for Negroes;* and Eunice and George Grier, *op. cit.*

[11] A more detailed analysis is presented in *Residence and Race,* Chapter 9: "Housing Quality and Cost."

[12] See *Residence and Race,* Chapter 13: "Mortgage Financing."

[13] Albert M. Cole, "What Is the Federal Government's Role in Housing?" Address to the Economic Club of Detroit, February 8, 1954.

[14] Relevant studies are examined in the research reports by Claire Selltiz and Stuart W. Cook, and by Helen E. Amerman. An important study demonstrating the effects on racial attitudes of shared experiences and community of interest is Robert K. Merton, Patricia S. West, and Marie Jahoda, *Social Facts and Social Fictions: The Dynamics of Race Relations in Hilltown* (New York: Columbia University, Bureau of Applied Social Research, 1949, hectographed); part of a larger work by the same authors to be published under the title, *Patterns of Social Life: Explorations in the Social Psychology and Sociology of Housing.*

## Property values and race / *Laurenti*

[1] Davis McEntire, "A Study of Racial Attitudes in Neighborhoods Infiltrated by Nonwhites," *Bay Area Real Estate Report, Second Quarter,* 1955, p. 127.

[2] Paul F. Cressey, "The Succession of Cultural Groups in the City of Chicago" (unpublished Ph. D. thesis, University of Chicago, 1930).

[3] E. F. Schietinger, "Real Estate Transfers During Negro Invasion, A Case Study" (unpublished Master's thesis, Department of Sociology, University of Chicago, 1948); "Racial Succession and Changing Property Values in Residential Chicago" (unpublished Ph.D. thesis, Department of Sociology, University of Chicago, 1953); "Racial Succession and the Value of Small Residential Properties," *American Sociological Review,* XVI, no. 6 (December, 1951); "Race and Residential Market Values in Chicago," *Land Economics,* XXX, no. 4 (November, 1954).

[4] Thomas L. Gillette, "Santa Fe: A Study of the Effects of Negro Invasion on Property Values" (unpublished Master's thesis, Department of Sociology, University of Kansas City, 1954).

[5] Richard Stewart Wander, "The Influence of Negro Infiltration Upon Real Estate Values" (unpublished Master's thesis, Department of Sociology and Anthropology, Wayne State University, 1953).

[6] Richard Marks, "The Impact of Negro Population Movement on Property Values in a Selected Area in Detroit," City of Detroit, Mayor's Interracial Committee, January 16, 1950 (mimeo.).

[7] The Urban League of Portland, *Nonwhite Neighbors and Property Price in Portland, Oregon* (1956).

[8] Chester Rapkin and William G. Grigsby, *The Demand for Housing in Racially Mixed Areas: A Study of the Nature of Neighborhood Change,* Special Research Report to the Commission on Race and Housing (Berkeley: University of California Press, 1960); Eunice and George Grier, *Privately Developed Interracial Housing: An Analysis of Experience,* Special Research Report to the Commission on Race and Housing (Berkeley: University of California Press, 1960); McEntire, *Bay Area Real Estate Report,* Second Quarter, 1955, p. 127.

## Concerning studies of price trends in mixed areas / *Rapkin, Grigsby*

[1] Principally in situations of isolated Negro entry see Luigi Laurenti, *Property Values and Race: Studies in Seven Cities* (Berkeley: University of California Press, 1960), chaps. vi, vii, and xi. See also Arnold M. Rose, Frank P. Atelsek, and Lawrence R. McDonald, "Neighborhood Reactions to Isolated Negro Residents: An Alternative to Invasion and Succession," *American Sociological Review,* vol. 18, no. 5 (October, 1953), 497 – 507. Also Henry G. Stetler, *Racial Integration in Private Residential Neighborhoods in Connecticut* (Hartford: State of Connecticut Commission on Civil Rights, 1957), pp. 6 – 7.

[2] Morgan, *The Review of the Society of Residential Appraisers,* XVIII, no. 3 (March, 1952).

[3] Laurenti, *op. cit.,* chap. i.i.

### Interracial housing / *Deutsch, Collins*

1 See G. W. Allport and B. M. Kramer, "Some Roots of Prejudice," *Journal of Psychology* Vol. 22, pp. 9–39; I. N. Brophy, "The Luxury of Anti-Negro Prejudice," *Public Opinion Quarterly*, Vol. 9, (1946), pp. 456–66; J. A. Davis, A *Management Can Integrate Negroes in War Industries*, Albany, N. Y., State War Council, Committee on Discrimination in Employment, 1942; B. K. MacKenzie, "The Importance of Contact in Determining Attitudes Towards Negroes," *Journal of Abnormal and Social Psychology*, Vol. 43 (1948), pp. 417–41; A. Rose, *Race Relations in a Chicago Industry*, unpublished study, University of Chicago, 1946; F. T. Smith, *An Experiment in Modifying Attitudes Toward the Negro*, Teachers College, 1943.

### The urbanization of the Negro / *Weaver*

1 For an analysis of the changes and relative status of housing among whites and non-whites from 1950 to 1960, see Marion P. Yankauer and Milo B. Sunderhauf, "Housing: Equal Opportunity to Choose Where One Shall Live," *Journal of Negro Education*, (Fall, 1963), pp. 402–414.

# V The housing industry

### The organization of the construction industry / *Colean, Newcomb*

1 *Census of Business: 1939*, Table I, p. 12.
2 *Ibid.*, Vol I, *Retail Trade: 1939*, Part 1, Table 2A, and Vol. II, *Wholesale Trade: 1939*, Table 1.

### Classifications of the construction industry / *Gillies, Mittlebach*

1 Lowell J. Chawner, *Construction Activity in the United States, 1915–37*, U.S. Department of Commerce, Domestic Commerce Series, No. 99, 1938, p. 3.
2 Miles L. Colean and Robinson Newcomb, *Stabilizing Construction: The Record and Potential* (New York: The McGraw-Hill Book Co., 1952), p. 4.
3 "Construction Volume and Costs, 1915–1956," a statistical supplement to *Construction Review*, U.S. Departments of Commerce and Labor, 1958.
4 Colean and Newcomb, *op. cit.*, p. 7.
5 Sherman Maisel, *Housebuilding in Transition*, (Berkeley and Los Angeles: University of California Press, 1953), p. 16.
6 *Ibid.*, pp. 16–17.
7 *Ibid.*, p. 20.
8 Maisel, *op cit.*, Table 26, p. 354.

### Structural changes in the housebuilding industry / *Herzog*

1 Maisel, *Housebuilding in Transition* (Berkeley and Los Angeles: University of California Press, 1953), p. 292.
2 *Ibid.*, p. 26; National Association of Homebuilders, "The Home Builder—What Does He Build?" *Journal of Homebuilding* (March, 1960), p. 17.
3 Maisel, *op. cit.*, p. 221.
4 *Loc. cit.*

# VI Housing finance

### The environment of real estate finance / *Colean*

1 Robert H. Skilton, *Government and the Mortgage Debtor* (Philadelphia, 1944) pp. 28–34, shows the dates in which the redemption statutes were enacted in the several states.
2 The provision for veterans' loans referred to is in § 506 of the Servicemen's Readjustment Act, 59 Stat. 626 (1944). This permits the Administrator of Veterans' Affairs, on notification of default, to pay the holder of the obligation the unpaid balance of the loan plus accrued interest and to take an assignment of the loan and security, thus allowing the Administrator to make any modified arrangement for payment that he may deem advisable.
3 For more detail on the impact of the property tax on realty investment, see Miles L. Colean, *American Housing* (The Twentieth Century Fund, New York, 1944) pp. 236 ff. See also, Carl Shoup, Roy Blough, and Mabel Newcomer, *Facing the Tax Problem* (The Twentieth Century Fund, New York, 1937) pp. 10 ff.; Harold M. Groves, *Postwar Taxation and Economic Progress* (New York, 1946) pp. 344 ff.
4 Urban Land Institute, *News and Trends in City Development*, Vol. 5, No. 4 (April, 1946).
5 H. M. Groves, *op. cit.*, pp. 341–43.
6 New York Laws c. 845 (1942): New York Laws c. 234 (1943).
7 Acts and Resolves of Massachusetts c. 654 (1945).
8 Data from Urban Land Institute, Washington, D. C.
9 Indiana Laws c. 276 (1945).
10 Illinois Senate Bills 39 and 201, Session of 1945.
11 Public Law 171, 81st Congress; Chapter 8.
12 See Ray Allen Billington, *Westward Expansion* (New York, 1949) pp. 364–68.
13 See Herbert D. Simpson, "The Influence of Public

Improvements on Real Estate Values," *Annals of the American Academy of Political and Social Science*, Vol. 148, (March, 1930), for a review of a case in which the supposed benefits to specific property owners from a public works program were badly miscalculated.
[14] For a discussion of the difficulties involved in expanding public works during depression periods, see

Miles L. Colean, *Stabilizing the Construction Industry* (National Planning Association, Washington, D. C. 1945).
[15] Many of the existing series are subject to grave shortcomings. See *Report of the Conference on Housing Statistics*, Housing and Home Finance Agency, January – March, 1947.

### Background of Federal housing credit / *Haar*

[1] *A.F. of L. v. Watson*, 60 F. Supp. 1010 (D.C. Fla., 1945); *reversed on other grounds*, 327 U.S. 582 (1945).
[2] *Kohl v. U.S.*, 91 U.S. 367 (1875).
[3] Philip Nichols, *The Law of Eminent Domain*, 2d ed., Bender, 1917, vol. 1, p. 34; John Lewis, *Treastise on the Law of Eminent Domain in the U.S.*, 3d ed., Callaghan, 1909, vol. 1, p. 309.

[4] 97 F. 2d 831, 340 (7th Cir., 1938).
[5] 38 Ops. Atty. Gen. 258 (1935). And see *U.S. v. Brooks*, 28 F. Supp. 712. (W.D. Wash., 1939).
[6] J. E. Morton, *Urban Mortgage Lending*, Princeton University Press, 1956.

### The growth of the residential mortgage debt / *Grebler, Blank, Winnick*

[1] *Survey of Current Business*, September, 1946, p. 13, and September, 1953, p. 16.

### The subsidy and housing / *Abrams*

[1] See Address by Sen. Allen J. Ellender before the National Public Housing Conference, published in *Public Housing* (April, 1944).

# VII **Housing standards and controls**

### Building and land use controls / *Kelly, Day, Dietz, Dunlop, Koch, Murray, Sasaki, Spring*

[1] Charles M. Haar, *Federal Credit and Private Housing: The Mass Financing Dilemma*, McGraw-Hill Book Company, Inc., New York, 1959.
[2] *House & Home*, vol. 2, no. 3 (September, 1952), p. 108.
[3] *Building Standards Monthly* (March, 1957).
[4] Sherman J. Maisel, *Housebuilding in Transition*, University of California Press, Berkeley, Calif., 1953, p. 249.

[5] See Fred W. Tuemmler, "Zoning for the Planned Community," *Urban Land*, vol. 13, no. 4 (April, 1954), for a discussion of a number of the recent provisions of this kind. Also, William C. Vladeck, " Large-scale Developments and One-house Zoning Controls," *Law and Contemporary Problems*, vol. 20, no. 2 (Spring, 1955).
[6] *Berman v. Parker*, 348 U.S. 26 (1954).
[7] *Op. cit.*, p. 316n.

### The quality of housing "before" and "after" rehabilitation / *Johnson, Williams, McCaldin*

[1] Johnson, Ralph J. Housing Law Enforcement. Pub. Health Rep. 66 : 1451 – 1460, 1951.
[2] American Public Health Association : An Appraisal Method for Measuring the Quality of Housing, Parts I, II, and III. New York : American Public Health Association, 1946.

[3] American Public Health Association : An Appraisal Method for Measuring the Quality of Housing. Part II, Vol. A. Survey Directors Manual. New York : American Public Health Association, 1946.

# VIII **Residential renewal**

### The slum : its nature, use, and users / *Seeley*

[1] See Bradley Buell, *Community Planning for Human Services* (New York : Columbia University Press, 1952).
[2] See Harvey Zorbaugh, *The Gold Coast and the Slum* (Chicago : University of Chicago Press, 1937).
[3] See, e.g., Catherine Bauer, " Good Neighborhoods," *The Annals of the American Academy of Political and Social Science*, Vol. 242 (1945), pp. 104 – 115.
[4] Cf. Bruno Bettelheim, *Love is Not Enough* (New York : The Free Press, 1950).

[5] Mr. Ronald A. Saltzman and Dr. B. H. Junker.
[6] Second edition (Chicago : University of Chicago Press, 1958).
[7] *Redevelopment: Some Human Gains and Losses* (Indianapolis : Community Surveys, 1956), pp. 48 – 59. Field work by Mr. Donald A. Saltzman and others : report by Mr. Saltszman, Dr. B. H. Junker and the author in collaboration.
[8] *Ibid*, pp. 67 – 143.

## Economic aspects of urban renewal / *Schaaf*

1 Detailed estimates of the number of substandard dwelling units based on data from the 1956 National Housing Inventory are contained in papers by Sherman J. Maisel and Reinhold P. Wolff appearing in *Study of Mortgage Credit*, U.S. Senate Committee on Banking and Currency, Subcommittee on Housing, 85th Congress, 2d session (Washington, D. C.: 1958), pp. 32 – 58.
2 Cf. William W. Nash, *Residential Rehabilitation: Private Profits and Public Purposes* (New York: McGraw-Hill, 1959). As a good example of the many books and pamphlets that have been written extolling the profits that await the astute investor in residential renewal, see William Nickerson, *How I Turned $1,000 into a Million in Real Estate—In My Spare Time* (New York: Simon and Schuster, 1959).
3 For a recent expression of this view by a local urban renewal official, see Arthur Hoff, " Rehabilitation Means Subsidy," *Journal of Housing*, 17 (March, 1960), pp. 103 – 104.

## Urban renewal / *McFarland*

1 U.S. President's Advisory Committee on Government Housing Policies and Programs. Recommendations on government housing policies and programs; a report. [Washington, D. C.: Gov't. Print. Off.] December 1953, p. 109.
2 Newark, N. J. Housing Authority. The cost of slums in Newark, 1946.
3 Fay, Frederic A. Urban renewal—curing a municipal disease. Virginia Municipal Review. (July, 1956), p. 113.
4 San Francisco. Planning and Housing Association. Blight and taxes, 1947.
5 Hartford. Mayor's Housing Committee. An economic analysis of a substandard area in Hartford, 1935.
6 Sweinhart, James. What Detroit's slums cost its taxpayers. Detroit News Reprints. (1946), p. 12. Reprinted from Detroit News (November 26 – December 1, 1945).
7 Baltimore. Citizens Planning and Housing Association. Study quoted in United States Conference of Mayors. Newsletter. (November 15, 1948).
8 Denver Post. [Series of articles on Denver's blighted areas.] 1950.
9 Los Angeles. Department of City Planning. Conditions of blight, central area, City of Los Angeles, 1947.
10 Navin, R. B. An analysis of a slum area in Cleveland. Regional Association of Cleveland, Publication No. 3. (November, 1939), p. 8.
11 Wood, Edith Elmer. Slums and blighted areas in the United States. Federal Emergency Administration of Public Works, Housing Division Bulletin No. 1. Gov't. Print. Off., (1935), p. 72.
12 Gertler, Leonard. Economic problems of urban redevelopment. Community Planning Association of Canada. Community Planning Review. Ottawa, Canada (February, 1951), pp. 30 – 36.
13 Colean, Miles L. Renewing our cities. New York, Twentieth Century Fund, 1953.
14 Detroit City Plan Commission. Industrial study— A survey of existing conditions and attitudes of Detroit's industry. Master Plan Technical Report, Second Series. (July, 1956), p. 19.
15 Greater Baltimore Committee. The Planning Council. Progress Report No. 2 (Baltimore) August/November, 1957, p. 36.
16 Ibid.
17 Grove, John J. Pittsburgh's renaissance; industry's role in the rebirth of a city. USA Tomorrow. October, 1954, p. 20.
18 New York Times (January 31, 1958).
19 San Jose (California) Mercury (April 5, 1957).
20 Rouse, James W. and Nathaniel S. Keith. No slums in ten years; a report to the Commissioners of the District of Columbia. (Washington, D. C.) January, 1955, p. 8.
21 National Association of Housing and Redevelopment Officials. Newsletter, (December 30, 1957). (Data in text based upon analysis of questionnaires used in the American Municipal Association survey).
22 Preserving the industrial base of Detroit. Urban Land Institute. Urban Land News and Trends in City Development. Washington, D. C. July – August, 1957, p. 5.
23 Rouse, James W. and Nathaniel S. Keith. No slums in ten years; a report to the Commissioners of the District of Columbia. (Washington, D.C.) January, 1955, p. 9.
24 Greater Baltimore Committee. The Planning Council. Progress Report No. 2 (Baltimore) August/November, 1957. p. 36.
25 U.S. Congress. Senate. Subcommittee on Housing and Urban Redevelopment. Post-war economic policy and planning. Hearings. Washington, D.C.: Gov't. Print. Off., 1945 (79th Congress, 1st session). p. 1305.
26 Kramer, Ferd. The role of private enterprise. American Society of Planning Officials. Proceedings 1950, Chicago, 1951, pp. 32 – 33.
27 Grebler, Leo. Urban redevelopment as an outlet for capital investment. Land Economics (November, 1953), p. 359.
28 Whyte, William H., Jr. Are cities un-American? Fortune. (September, 1957), pp. 125 – 126.
29 Ibid., pp. 127 — 213.
30 Redevelopment. Part 1. Financing—where does the money come from? National Association of Housing and Redevelopment Officials. Journal of Housing. Chicago (October, 1957), p. 316.
31 Colean, Miles L. Realities of today's real estate investment. Architectural Record. (April, 1955), p. 125.
32 Lockett, Edward B. Slum towns are going. Nation's Business. May, 1953, pp. 52, 54, 56.
33 Ibid.
34 New Orleans. Office of the Mayor. Annual report, 1955/56, p. 41.
35 Data obtained from the Urban Renewal Administration, Housing and Home Finance Agency.
36 Lammer, Francis J. As quoted in National Association of Housing and Redevelopment Officials. Renewal Information Service Newsletter. Washington, D. C. (August 31, 1955), p. 2.
37 Zisook, David. Zisook Construction Company, Inc., and City of Chicago Community Conservation Board. Report on the feasibility of rehabilitation. [1958] 43 pp.
38 New York, N. Y. City Planning Commission. Urban renewal. 1958. (A report on the West Side urban renewal study undertaken by the New York City Planning Commission as a demonstration project under Section 314 of the Housing Act of 1954).

[39] Siegel, Jack M. and C. William Brooks. Slum prevention through conservation and rehabilitation. Report to the Subcommittee on Urban Redevelopment, Rehabilitation and Conservation of the Advisory Committee on Government Housing Policies and Programs. (Washington, D. C., Housing and Home Finance Agency, November, 1953), pp 2 – 3.
[40] *Ibid.* p. 3.

### Facts and fictions in urban renewal / *Winnick*

[1] Hoover, Edgar M. and Vernon, Raymond, *Anatomy of a Metropolis*. Cambridge, 1959.

### An evaluation of the redevelopment plan and process / *Gans*

[1] Irving Rosow, "The Social Effects of the Physical Environment," *Journal of the American Institute of Planners*, vol. 27 (1961), pp. 127 – 133.
[2] Boston Housing Authority, "The West End Project Report," Boston: The Authority, 1953, p. 1.
[3] Save the West End Committee, "A Plea against Smashing the Houses of the West End . . . ," Boston: no date indicated, mimeographed, pp. 12 – 15.
[4] *Op cit.*, pp. 15 – 17.
[5] Boston Housing Authority, *op. cit.*, p. 19.
[6] *Ibid.*, p. 14.
[7] American Public Health Association, "An Appraisal Method for Measuring the Quality of Housing," New York: The Association, 1946, Part II, Chap. 2.
[8] Boston Housing Authority, *op. cit.*, p. 14.
[9] Gans, "The Human Implications of Current Redevelopment and Relocation Planning," *op. cit.*, p. 17.
[10] Chester Hartman. "Housing in the West End," Boston: Center for Community Studies Research Memorandum C1, October, 1961, mimeographed, p. 2.
[11] For a more detailed analysis of these differences, see Marc Fried and Peggy Gleicher, "Some Sources of Residential Satisfaction in an Urban 'Slum,'" *Journal of the American Institute of Planners*, vol. 27 (1961), pp. 305 – 315, and Hartman, *op. cit.*
[12] Among the best of these studies are: Community Surveys, Inc., "Redevelopment: Some Human Gains and Losses," Indianapolis: Community Surveys, Inc., 1956 (by John R. Seeley and associates); and Philadelphia Housing Association, "Relocation in Philadelphia," Philadelphia: The Association, 1958. For a study of the impact on urban renewal on small businesses, see William N. Kinnard, Jr., and Zenon S. Malinowski, "The Impact of Dislocation from Urban Renewal Areas on Small Business," Storrs: University of Connecticut July, 1960. For an excellent analysis and evaluation of renewal in a number of American cities by a British sociologist, see Peter Marris, "A Report on Urban Renewal," London: Institute of Community Studies, 1962, mimeographed, and in Duhl, *op. cit.*
[13] Charles E. Silberman, "The City and the Negro," *Fortune*, vol. 65 (March, 1962), pp. 89 – 91, 139 – 140, 144 – 146, 152 – 154, at p. 90.

# Bibliography

## 1. Background

Abrams, Charles. *The Future of Housing*. New York: Harper & Row, 1946.

American Public Health Association. *Basic Principles of Healthful Housing*, 2nd edition. New York, 1939.

*American Sociological Review*. "The American Family and Its Housing," vol. XII (April, 1947).

Bauer, Catherine, *see* Wurster.

Beyer, Glenn H., et al. *Houses Are For People*. Ithaca: Cornell University Research Center, 1955.

Beyer, Glenn H. *Housing: A Factual Analysis*. New York: Macmillan, 1958.

Colean, Miles L. *American Housing: Problems and Prospects*. New York: Twentieth Century Fund, 1944.

Conant, James Bryant. *Slums and Suburbs*. New York: McGraw-Hill, 1961.

Cooney, Timothy, J. "How to Build a Slum," *The Nation*, vol. CLXXXVIII, No. 7 (February 14, 1959), pp. 140–141.

Cowles, May L. "Changes in Family, Personnel, Occupational Status, and Housing Occurring over the Farm Family's Life Cycle," *Rural Sociology*, vol. XVIII, No. 1 (March, 1953), pp. 35–44.

Crane, Jacob L. and Edward T. Paxton. "The World-Wide Housing Problem," *Town Planning Review*, vol. XXII, No. 1 (April, 1951), pp. 18–43.

Dewhirst, J. Frederick, and Associates. *American Needs and Resources, A New Survey*. New York: Twentieth Century Fund, 1954.

Dobriner, William M. (ed.). *The Suburban Community*. New York: Putnam, 1958.

Duncan, Beverly, and Philip M. Hauser. *Housing a Metropolis – Chicago*. New York: The Free Press, 1960.

Fergusson, Donald A. "Housing in a Growth Economy," *Land Economics*, vol. XXXVIII, No. 1 (February, 1962), pp. 9–19.

Ford, James. *Slums and Housing*. Cambridge: Harvard University Press, 1936.

Editors of Fortune Magazine. *The Exploding Metropolis*. Garden City: Doubleday, 1958.

Futterman, Robert A. *The Future of our Cities*. New York: Doubleday, 1961.

Gans, Herbert. *The Urban Villagers*. New York: The Free Press, 1962.

Grebler, Leo. "The Housing Inventory: Analytic Concept and Quantitative Change," *American Economic Review*, vol. XLI (May, 1951), pp. 555–568.

Hoover, Edgar M., Jr., and Raymond Vernon. *Anatomy of a Metropolis*. Cambridge: Harvard University Press, 1959.

Hoyt, Homer. *Economic Survey of Land Uses in Evanston*. New York: Homer Hoyt Associates, 1949.

Hoyt, Homer. "Recent Distortions of the Classical Models of Urban Structure," *Land Economics*, vol. XL, No. 2 (May, 1964), pp. 199–212.

Jacobs, Jane. *The Death and Life of Great American Cities*. New York: Random House, 1961.

Meyerson, Martin, (ed.) "Metropolis in Ferment," *Annals of the American Academy of Political and Social Science*, vol. CCCXIV (November, 1957).

Mitchell, Robert B. "National Objectives for Housing and Urban Renewal," *Recommendations on Government Housing Problems and Programs*, President's Advisory Committee on Government Housing Policies and Programs. Washington, D. C., 1953, pp. 129–139.

Natural Resources Planning Board. *Housing, the Continuing Problem*. Washington, D.C., 1940.

Pearson, John E. "The Significance of Urban Housing in Rural – Urban Migration," *Land Economics*, vol. XXXIX, No. 3 (August, 1963), pp. 231–239.

Perloff, Harvey S. "A National Program of Research in Housing and Urban Development," Resources for the Future staff study, September, 1961.

Rapkin, Chester. "Can the American Family Afford an Adequate Home," *Marriage and Family Living* (May, 1955), pp. 138–142.

"Social Policy and Social Research in Housing." *Journal of Social Issues*, vol. VII, Nos. 1 and 2 (1951).

Stein, Clarence. *Toward New Towns for America*. Liverpool: Liverpool University Press, 1951.

Straus, Nathan. *The Seven Myths of Housing*. New York: Alfred A. Knopf, 1944.

Temporary National Economic Commission. *Toward More Housing*. Washington, D.C., 1948

UAW-CIO. *Memorandum on Postwar Housing*. Detroit, 1944.

U.S. Housing and Home Finance Agency. *Annual Report*. Washington, D.C., 1949–1956.

U.S. Housing and Home Finance Agency. *How Big is the Housing Job*. Washington, D.C., 1951.

U.S. Housing and Home Finance Agency. *Its Organization and Functions*. Washington, D.C., 1952.

U.S. Senate, 79th Congress. *Hearings Before the Subcommittee on Housing and Redevelopment of the Special Committee on Postwar Policy and Planning*. Parts 6 through 15, Washngton, D.C., 1954. (Taft Committee).

Urban Land Institute. *Community Builders Handbook*. Washington, D. C., 1950.

Urban Land Institute. *New Approaches to Residential Land Development*. Technical Bulletin 40. Washington, D.C., 1961.

Wallace, Anthony F. C. *Housing and Social Structure*. Philadelphia: Philadelphia Housing Association, 1952.

Weaver, Robert C. *The Urban Complex*. New York: Doubleday, 1964.

Westchester County Council of Social Agencies, Inc., Committee on Housing. *Report of the Committee on Housing*. White Plains, New York, July, 1957.

Wheaton, William L. C. "American Housing Needs, 1955–1970," *Housing Yearbook*, Washington, D.C.: National Housing Conference, 1954.

Wingo, Lowdon, Jr. *Cities and Space: The Future Use of Urban Land*. Resources for the Future, Inc., Baltimore: John Hopkins Press, 1964.

Winnick, Louis. *American Housing and its Use*. New York: John Wiley & Sons, 1957.

Wirth, Louis. "Housing as a Field of Sociological Research," *American Sociological Review*, vol. XII, No. 2 (April, 1947), pp. 137-143.

Whyte, W. H., Jr. *The Organization Man*. New York: Simon and Schuster, 1957. Part VII.

Wood, Elizabeth. "Knowledge Needed for Adequate Programs of Public and Private Housing," *Needed Urban and Metropolitan Research*, Donald J. Bogue, ed. Oxford, Ohio: Scripps Foundation and Miami University Press, 1953, pp. 51–55.

Wood, E. E. *Slums and Blighted Areas in the United States*. Washington, D.C., 1935

Wood, Robert. *Suburbia, Its People and Their Politics*. Boston: Houghton Mifflin, 1959.

Wood, Robert. *Metropolis Against Itself*. New York: Committee for Economic Development, 1959.

Wright, Henry. *Rehousing Urban America*. New York: Columbia University Press, 1935.

Wurster, Catherine Bauer. *Modern Housing*. Boston: Houghton Mifflin, 1934.

## 2. Housing in the Neighborhood

Abrahamson, Julia. *A Neighborhood Finds Itself*. New York: Harper & Row, 1959.

Adams, Thomas. *The Design of Residential Areas*. Cambridge: Harvard University Press, 1935.

American Public Health Association. "Planning the Neighborhood," Public Administration Service, Chicago, 1948.

Bartholomew, Harland. *Land Uses in American Cities*. Cambridge: Harvard University Press, 1955.

Berkman, Herman G. "The Delineation and Structure of Rental Housing Areas," *Wisconsin Commerce Reports*, vol. IV, No. 5 (August, 1956), Madison: Univ. of Wisconsin, School of Commerce, Bureau of Business Research and Service.

Boston City Planning Commission. *Report of the Income and Cost Survey of the City of Boston*, Boston, 1935.

Chapin, F. Stuart. "The Effects of Slum Clearance and Rehousing on Family and Community Relationships in Minneapolis," *American Journal of Sociology*, vol. XLIII, No. 5 (March, 1938), pp. 744–763.

Dahir, James. *The Neighborhood Unit Plan. Its Spread and Acceptance.* New York: Russell Sage Foundation, 1947.

Form, William H. "Stratification in Low and Middle Income Housing Areas," *Journal of Social Issues*, vol. VII, Nos. 1 and 2 (1951), pp. 109–131.

Gans, Herbert J. "The Balanced Community: Homogeneity or Heterogenity in Residential Areas," *Journal of the American Institute of Planners*, vol. XXVII, No. 3 (August, 1961), pp. 176–184.

Hallman, Howard W. "Citizens and Professionals Reconsider the Neighborhood," *Journal of the American Institute of Planners*, vol. XXV, No. 3 (August, 1959), pp. 121–127.

Manheim, Uriel. "Residential Growth Patterns in Metropolitan Areas," (originally in) *Urban Land*, Washington, D.C.: Urban Land Institute (March, 1957), pp. 3–7. [Reprint in *The Appraisal Journal*, July, 1957.]

Miller, J. Marshall. "Layout of Residential Communities," *Forms and Functions of 20th Century Architecture*, ed. by Talbot Hamlin. 1952, pp. 193–219.

Mumford, Lewis. "Planning for the Phases of Life," *Town Planning Review*, vol. XX, No. 1 (April, 1949), pp. 5–16.

Rubin, Morton, Louis H. Orzack, and Ralph Tomlinson. "Resident Responses to Planned Neighborhood Redevelopment, *Community Structure and Analysis*, ed. by Marvin Sussman. New York: Thomas Y. Crowell, 1959, pp. 208–234.

Sarchet, Bettie B., and Eugene D. Wheeler. "Behind Neighborhood Plans: Citizens at Work," *Journal of the American Institute of Planners*, vol. XXIV, No. 3 (August, 1958), pp. 187–195.

Stonorov, Oscar and Louis I. Kahn. *You and Your Neighborhood.* New York: Revere Copper and Brass, 1944.

Wallace, Anthony F. C. "Planned Privacy: What's Its Importance for the Neighborhood?", *Journal of Housing*, vol. XIII, No. 1 (January, 1956), pp. 13–14.

Wheaton, William L. C., and Morton Schussheim. *The Cost of Municipal Services in Residential Areas.* Washington, D.C.: Housing and Home Finance Agency, 1955.

## 3. The Housing Market

American Institute of Real Estate Appraisers. *The Appraisal of Real Estate.* Chicago, 1951.

Blank, David M. "Relationship between an Index of House Prices and Building Costs," *The Journal of the American Statistical Association*, vol. IL (March, 1954), pp. 67–78.

Blank, David M. "The Structure of the Housing Market," *The Quarterly Journal of Economics* (February, 1953), pp. 181–208.

Brewster, Maurice R., William A. Finn, and Ernest Jurkat. *How to Make and Interpret Locational Studies of the Housing Market*, Housing and Home Finance Agency. Washington, D.C.: U.S. Dept. of Commerce, 1955.

Colean, Miles L. *Future Housing Demand.* Washington, D.C.: The Producer's Council, 1948.

Coons, Alvin, and Bert Glaze. *Housing Market Analysis and the Growth of Non-Farm Home Ownership.* Bureau of Business Research, College of Commerce and Administration, Ohio State University, 1963.

Dean, John P. "The Ghosts of Home Ownership," *Journal of Social Issues*, vol. VII, Nos. 1 and 2 (1951), pp. 59–68.

Dean, John P. *Home Ownership. Is It Sound?* New York: Harper & Row, 1945.

Federal Reserve Bulletin. "Survey of Consumer Finances," (Annual from 1949).

Fisher, Ernest M., and Louis Winnick. "A

Reformulation of the Filtering Concept," *Journal of Social Issues*, vol. VII, Nos. 1 and 2 (1951), pp. 47–48.

Fisher, Ernest M. *Urban Real Estate Markets: Characteristics and Financing.* New York: National Bureau of Economic Research, Inc., 1951.

Foote, Nelson N., et al. *Housing Choices and Housing Constraints.* New York: McGraw-Hill, 1960.

Freiden, Bernard J. "Some Local Preferences in the Urban Housing Market," *Journal of the American Institute of Planners*, vol. XXVII, No. 4 (November, 1961), pp. 316–324.

Grebler, Leo. *Experience in Urban Real Estate Investment.* New York: Columbia University Press, 1955.

Grebler, Leo. *Housing Market Behavior in a Declining Area.* New York: Columbia University Press, 1952.

Haar, Charles M. "Middle-Income Housing: The Cooperative Share? ", *Land Economics*, vol. XXIX, No. 4 (November, 1953), pp. 295–301.

Hauser, Philip, and A. J. Jaffe. "Extent of the Housing Shortage," *Law and Contemporary Problems*, vol. II, No. 1 (Winter, 1947).

Herbert, John D., and Benjamin H. Stevens. "A Model for the Distribution of Residential Activity in Urban Areas," *Journal of Regional Science*, vol. II (Fall, 1960), pp. 21–36.

Hoffman, Morton. "The Outlook for Downtown Housing," *Journal of the American Institute of Planners*, vol. XXVII, No. 1 (February, 1961), pp. 43–55.

Johnson, George G. "Trends in Residential Rents, 1950-55," *Construction Review*, U.S. Dept. of Labor – U.S. Dept. of Commerce (May, 1956).

Katona, George. *Relevant Considerations in Recent Home Purchases.* Housing and Home Finance Agency, Washington, D.C.

Keats, John. *The Crack in the Picture Window.* Boston: Houghton Mifflin, 1956.

Kish, Leslie, and John B. Lansing. "Response Errors in Estimating the Value of Homes," *Journal of the American Statistical Association* (September, 1954).

Leslie, Gerald R., and Arthur H. Richardson.

"Life-Cycle, Career Pattern, and the Decision to Move," *American Sociological Review*, vol. XXVI, No. 6 (December, 1961), pp. 894-902.

Lowry, Ira S. "Filtering and Housing Standards: A Conceptual Analysis," *Land Economics*, vol. XXXVI (November, 1960), pp. 362–370.

Maisel, Sherman J. "Policy Problems in Expanding the Private Housing Market," *American Economic Review*, vol. XLI, No. 2 (1951), pp. 599–611.

Maisel, Sherman J. "Variables Commonly Ignored in Housing Demand Analysis," *Land Economics*, vol. XXV, No. 2 (August, 1949), pp. 260–274.

Meredith, L. Douglas. *How to Buy a House.* New York: Harper & Row, 1947.

Muth, Richard. "The Demand for Non-Farm Housing," *The Demand for Durable Goods*, edited by Arnold C. Harberger. Chicago: University of Chicago Press, 1960, pp. 29–96.

Michigan Research Center. "Relevant Considerations in Recent Home Purchases," *Journal of the American Institute of Planners*, vol. XXI, No. 1 (February, 1955), pp. 9–16.

Rapkin, Chester. *The Real Estate Market in an Urban Renewal Area.* New York: City Planning Commission, 1959.

Rapkin, Chester, and William Grigsby. *The Demand for Housing in Eastwick.* Philadelphia: Institute for Urban Studies, 1960.

Rapkin, Chester, and William G. Grigsby. *Residential Renewal in the Urban Core.* Philadelphia: University of Pennsylvania Press, 1960.

Rapkin, Chester, Louis Winnick, and David M. Blank. *Housing Market Analysis.* Washington, D.C.: Housing and Home Finance Agency, 1953.

Ratcliff, Richard U. "Filtering Down and the Elimination of Substandard Housing," *Journal of Land and Public Utility Economics*, vol. XXI, No. 4 (November, 1945), pp. 322–330.

Ratcliff, Richard U. *Real Estate Analysis.* New York: McGraw-Hill, 1961.

Ratcliff, Richard U. *Urban Land Economics.* New York: McGraw-Hill, 1949.

Reid, Margaret G. "Capital Formation in Residential Real Estate," *The Journal of Political*

*Economy*, vol. LXVI, No. 2 (April, 1958), pp. 131–153.

Reid, Margaret G. *Housing and Income.* Chicago: University of Chicago Press, 1962.

Reid, Margaret G. "Increase in Rent of Dwelling Units from 1940 to 1950," *American Statistical Association Journal*, vol. LIV (June, 1959), pp. 358–376.

*Report of the President's Conference on Home Building and Home Ownership*, 11 volumes. Washington, D.C., 1932.

Riemer, Svend. "Architecture for Family Living," *Journal of Social Issues*, vol. VII, Nos. 1–2 (1951), pp. 140–151.

Riemer, Svend, and Nicholas J. Demerath. "The Role of Social Research in Housing Design," *Land Economics*, vol. XXVIII, No. 3 (August, 1952), pp. 230–243.

Rodwin, Lloyd. *Housing and Economic Progress.* Cambridge: MIT and Harvard University Press, 1961.

Rosow, Irving. "Home Ownership Motives," *American Sociological Review*, vol. XIII, No. 6 (December, 1948), pp. 751–756.

Ross, Thurston H. "Market Significance of Declining Neighborhoods," *The Appraisal Journal*, vol. XXIII, No. 2 (April, 1955).

Rossi, Peter H. *Why Families Move, a Study in the Social Psychology of Urban Residential Mobility.* New York: The Free Press, 1955.

Silberman, Charles E., and Todd May. "The Coming Changes in Housing," *Markets of the Sixties*, by eds., of *Fortune*. New York: Harper & Row, 1960, pp. 133–154; 234–238.

Smith, Wallace. *Filtering and Neighborhood Change.* Center for Real Estate and Urban Economics. Berkeley: University of California Press, 1964.

Sporn, Arthur D. "Empirical Studies in the Economics of Slum Ownership," *Land Economics*, vol. XXXVI, No. 4 (November, 1960), pp. 333–340.

Tomkinson, Donald. "The Marseilles Experiment," *The Town Planning Review*, vol. XXIV, No. 3 (October, 1953), pp. 192–214.

U.S. Housing and Home Finance Agency. "Determining What Kind of a Survey to Conduct," *How to Make and Use Local Housing Surveys.* Washington, D.C., April, 1954.

U.S. Housing and Home Finance Agency. *How To Test the Soundness of Rental Housing Properties.* Washington, D.C., 1951.

U.S. Housing and Home Finance Agency. *What People Want When They Buy a House.* Washington, D.C., 1955.

"The Urge to Own," *Architectural Forum*, vol. LXVII, No. 5 (November, 1937), pp. 370–378.

Weimer, Arthur M., and Homer Hoyt. *Principles of Urban Real Estate.* New York: Ronald, 1948.

Wickens, David L. *Residential Real Estate.* New York: National Bureau of Economic Research, 1941.

Willcox, Roger. "Cooperative Techniques and Effective Reduction in Housing Costs," *Land Economics*, vol. XXIX, No. 4 (November, 1953), pp. 295–301.

Winter, Alan R. "An Approach to Measuring Potential Upgrading in the Housing Market," *Review of Economics and Statistics* (August, 1963), pp. 239–244.

Wood, Ramsey. "Housing Needs and the Housing Market," *Housing, Social Security and Public Works* (by R. Wood, E. J. Swam, and W. R. Strottner), Board of Governors of the Federal Reserve System (June, 1946), pp. 1–39.

## 4. Requirements of Special Groups

### A. Single and Aged Persons

Armstrong, Florence. *Non-Cash Needs of Aged Persons Affecting Their Individual and Social Security.* An annotated bibliography. Washington, D.C.: Federal Security Agency, 1948.

Donahue, Wilma, ed. *Housing the Aging.* Ann Arbor: University of Michigan Press, 1954.

*Essays on the Problems Faced in the Relocation of Elderly Persons.* Philadelphia: Institute for Urban Studies, 1964.

Frieden, Elaine. "Social Differences and Their Consequences for Housing the Aged," *Journal of the American Institute of Planners*, vol. XXVI, No. 2 (May, 1960), pp. 119–124.

Grier, George W., ed. *Housing the Aging: Research Needs.* Washington, D.C.: The Brookings Institution, 1962, mimeographed.

Niebanck, Paul L. *The Elderly in Older Urban*

*Areas.* Philadelphia: Institute for Environmental Studies, 1965.

Smith, Wallace. "The Housing Preferences of Elderly People," *The Appraisal Journal.* vol. XXX, No. 4 (October, 1962), pp. 515–522.

U.S. Bureau of Labor Statistics. *Homes for Aged in the U.S.* Washington, D.C., 1941.

U.S. Housing and Home Finance Agency. *Housing the Elderly: A Review of Significant Developments.* Washington, D.C., 1959.

U.S. Housing and Home Finance Agency. *Senior Citizens and How They Live, Part 1 The National Scene.* Washington, D.C., 1962.

## B. Low-Income and Ill-Housed

Bemis, A. F. *The Evolving House,* Cambridge: Massachusetts Institute of Technology Press, 1934.

Boysaw, Harold E. "Meeting Tenants' Unmet Needs," *Public Welfare,* vol. XX, No. 2 (April, 1962), pp. 93–95 and 138.

Caplovitz, David. *The Poor Pay More: Consumer Practices of Low Income Families.* New York: The Free Press, 1963.

Carlson, David B. "The New Look in Public Housing – Too Little and Too Late?", *Architectural Forum,* vol. CXIX (July, 1963), pp. 116–119.

Chapin, F. Stuart. "Some Housing Factors Related to Mental Hygiene," *American Journal of Public Health,* vol. XLI, No. 7 (July, 1951), pp. 839–845.

Chapin, F. Stuart. "The Relationship of Housing to Mental Health," working paper for the Expert Committee on the Public Health Aspects of Housing of the World Health Organization (June, 1961), mimeographed.

Community Services Society of New York, Committee on Housing. *Not Without Hope,* a Report and Recommendations on Family Relocation (March, 1958).

Dahlstrom, Edmund. *Effects of High Buildings on Families with Small Children.* Stockholm: Swedish State Committee for Building Research, Report No. 38 (1957), pp. 1–11.

Dunham, Warren and Nathan D. Grundstein. "The Impact of a Confusion of Social Objectives on Public Housing: A Preliminary Analysis," *Marriage and Family Living,* vol. XVII, No. 2 (May, 1955), pp. 103–112.

Ferguson, Thomas and Mary Pettigrew. "A Study of 718 Slum Families Rehoused for Upwards of Ten Years," *Glasgow Medical Journal,* vol. XXXV (1954), pp. 183–201.

Festinger, Leon, Stanley Schacter, and Kurt Back. *Social Pressures in Informal Groups: A Study of Human Factors in Housing.* New York: Harper & Row, 1950.

Fisher, Ernest M. *A Study of Housing Programs and Policies.* Washington, D.C., 1960.

Fisher, Robert M. *Twenty Years of Public Housing.* New York: Harper & Row, 1959.

Fried, Marc. "Some Implications of Housing Variables for Mental Health, A Reply to Professor F. Stuart Chapin," Memorandum A4 of the West End Research Project of the Center for Community Studies, Department of Psychiatry, Massachusetts General Hospital and the Harvard Medical School, January 5, 1961.

Gutheim, Frederick. *Houses for Family Living.* New York: The Women's Foundation, 1948.

Gwinn, Ralph. *Public Housing: Disastrous Here and Abroad.* New York: Constitutional Educational League, undated.

Hartman, Chester. "The Limitations of Public Housing: Relocation Choices in a Working-Class Community," *Journal of the American Institute of Planners,* vol. XXIX, No. 4 (November, 1963), pp. 283–296.

Jackson, William S. "Housing and Pupil Growth and Development," *The Journal of Educational Sociology,* vol. XXVIII, No. 9 (May, 1955), pp. 370–380. Reports an unpublished Ph.D. thesis, "Housing as a Factor in Public Growth and Development," New York University, 1954.

Joint Committee on Housing and Welfare. *Community Services and Public Housing: Seven Recommendations for Local Housing Authority Action.* National Association of Housing and Redevelopment Officials and the National Social Welfare Assembly, October, 1961.

Joint Committee on Housing and Welfare. "Statement of Fundamental Principles for Establishment of Rentals for Public Assistance Families in Federally Aided Public Housing," National Association of Housing and

Redevelopment Officials and the National Social Welfare Assembly, 1959.

Kennedy, Robert Woods. " Sociopsychological Problems of Housing Design," *Social Pressures in Informal Groups*, ed. by Leon Festinger, Stanley Schachter, and Kurt Back. New York: Harper & Row, 1950, pp. 202–220.

Lanpher, Henry Coe. *Welfare Aspects of Housing*, Alexandria Community Welfare Council, Virginia, March, 1962, processed.

Lotwin, Gertrude. *A State Revises Its Assistance Standard*. Washington, D.C.: Department of Health, Education and Welfare, Bureau of Public Assistance, June, 1959.

McDougd, Myres S. and Addison A. Mueller. " Public Purpose in Public Housing: An Anachronism Reburied," *The Law Review*, vol. LII, No. 1 (December, 1942), pp. 2–33.

McMurray, Joseph P. *Ways and Means of Providing Housing for Families Unable to Afford Rentals or Mortgage Payments Necessary for Adequate Private Housing*, Washington, D.C.: National Association of Home Builders, December 30, 1960.

Metropolitan Housing and Planning Council of Chicago. *Interim Report on Housing the Economically Disadvantaged Groups in the Population*. Proceedings and working papers of a Conference sponsored in cooperation with ACTION, Inc., New York, February 26–27, 1960.

Meyerson, Martin and Edward C. Banfield. *Politics, Planning and the Public Interest*. New York: The Free Press, 1955.

" Minutes of the Quarterly Meeting of National Capital Housing Authority and the Department of Public Welfare," Thursday, January 26, 1961, Washington, D.C. Also " Report and Evaluation of Cooperative Program Between the National Capital Housing Authority and the D.C. Department of Public Welfare, Public Assistance Division," February 1, 1961, mimeographed.

Mogey, John M. " Changes in Family Life Experienced by English Workers Moving From Slums to Housing Estates," *Marriage and Family Living*, vol. XVII, No. 2 (May, 1955), pp. 123–128.

National Association of Home Builders. *What Public Housing Did to England*, Washington, D.C.: The Association, undated.

National Federation of Settlements and Neighborhood Centers. *A New Look at Public Housing*, New York, 1958.

National Housing Agency. *The Liveability Problems of 1,000 Families*. Washington, D.C., October, 1945.

National Public Housing Conference. *A Housing Program for Now or Later*. Washington, D.C., 1948.

Ortof, Murray E. " Public Housing: New Neighbors in Old Communities," *Social Work*, vol. IV, No. 2 (April, 1959), pp. 55–63.

Phalan, J. L. " The Private Business of Public Housing," *Harvard Business Review*, vol. XXXIII, No. 5 (September–October, 1955), pp. 112–120.

Philadelphia Housing Association. " A New Look at Public Housing," *Issues*, (November, 1957).

Plant, James S. " Family Living Space and Personality Development," in *A Modern Introduction to the Family*, ed. by Norman W. Bell and Ezra F. Vogel. New York: The Free Press, 1960, pp. 510–520.

Plant, James S. " Some Psychiatric Aspects of Crowded Living Conditions," *American Journal of Psychiatry*, vol. IX, No. 5 (March, 1930), pp. 849–860.

Pond, M. Allen. " The Influence of Housing on Health," *Marriage and Family Living*, vol. XIX, No. 2 (May, 1957), pp. 154–159.

Riemer, Svend. " Maladjustment to the Family Home," *American Sociological Review*, vol. X, No. 5 (October, 1945), pp. 642–648.

Riemer, Svend. " Sociological Theory of Home Adjustment," *American Sociological Review*, vol. VIII, No. 3 (June, 1943), pp. 272–278.

Riemer, Svend. " Sociological Perspective in Home Planning," *American Sociological Review*, vol. XII, No. 2 (April, 1947), pp. 155–159.

Rosow, Irving. " The Social Effects of the Physical Environment," *Journal of the American Institute of Planners*, vol. XXXII, No. 2 (May, 1961), pp. 127–133. (Originally published as " Specialists' Perspectives and Spurious Validation in Housing," *Marriage and Family*

*Living*, vol. XIX, No. 3 (August, 1957), pp. 270–278).

Rumney, Jay. "The Social Costs of Slums," *Journal of Social Issues*, vol. VII, Nos. 1 and 2 (1951), pp. 69–85.

Searles, Harold F. *The Nonhuman Environment in Normal Development and in Schizophrenia*. New York: International Universities Press, 1960.

"Single Family Houses in Public Housing," *Journal of Housing*, vol. XVIII, No. 10 (November, 1961), pp. 449–451 and 453.

Social Planning Council of St. Louis and St. Louis County, Research Bureau. "Public Housing Residents and Welfare Services." Missouri, August, 1955.

U.S. Public Housing Authority. "Check List for Development of Site Plans," *Design of Low Rent Housing Projects, Planning the Site*. Washington, D.C., 1939, pp. 79–84.

U.S. Public Housing Authority. *Public Housing Design: A Review of Experience in Low Rent Housing*. Washington, D.C., 1946.

U.S. Public Housing Administration. *The Low-Rent Public Housing Program – What It Is and How It Works*. Washington, D.C., 1952.

United States Public Housing Authority. "Site Selection," *Public Housing Design*. Washington, D.C. (June, 1946), pp. 5–35.

Washington Housing Association. "7,973 D.C. Families Waiting for Public Housing – Largest Number Since World War II," Letter to the Members, No. 47 (July, 1961).

Wood, Elizabeth. *Housing Design: A Social Theory*. New York: Citizens' Housing and Planning Council of New York, 1961. Cited and quoted at length as "Designing Human Housing Projects," *Current*, No. 17 (September, 1961), pp. 27–32.

Wood, Elizabeth. "Public Housing and Mrs. McGee," *Journal of Housing*, vol. XIII, No. 11 (October, 1956), pp. 424–427.

## C. Minority Groups

Abrams, Charles. *Forbidden Neighbors*. New York: Harper & Row, 1955.

Abrams, Charles. "The New Gresham's Law of Neighborhoods – Fact or Fiction," *The Appraisal Journal*, vol. XIX, No. 3 (July, 1951), pp. 324–337.

Becker, Gary S. "Discrimination and Segregation in Housing," *The Economics of Discrimination*. Chicago: University of Chicago Press, 1957, pp. 58–62.

Case, Fred E. *The Housing Status of Minority Families: Los Angeles, 1956*. Los Angeles: University of California Press, 1958.

Coe, Paul F. "The Non-White Population Surge to Our Cities," *Land Economics*, vol. XXXV, No. 3 (August, 1959), pp. 195–210.

Grier, Eunice and George. "The Impact of Race on Neighborhood in the Metropolitan Setting." Address to the Washington Center for Metropolitan Studies, April 27, 1961.

Grier, Eunice and George. *Privately Developed Interracial Housing*. Berkeley: University of California Press, 1960.

Handlin, Oscar. *The Newcomers: Negroes and Puerto Ricans in a Changing Metropolis*. Cambridge: Harvard University Press, 1959.

Hunt, Morton M. "The Battle of Abington Township." *Commentary*, vol. IX, No. 3 (March, 1950), pp. 234–243.

Leadership Conference on Civil Rights. *Federally Supported Discrimination*. New York: Futura Press, 1961.

Lee, Alfred McClung. "The Impact of Segregated Housing on Public Schools," in *The Countdown on Segregaged Education*, ed. by William W. Brickman and Stanley Lehrer, Society for the Advancement of Education, New York, 1960, pp. 77–83.

McEntire, Davis. *Residence and Race*. Berkeley: University of California Press, 1960.

Morgan, Belden. "Values in Transition Areas: Some New Concepts," *The Review of the Society of Residential Appraisers*, vol. XVIII, No. 3 (March, 1952).

Nesbitt, George B. "Dispersion of Non-White Residences in Washington, D.C.: Some of Its Implications," *Land Economics*, vol. XXXII, No. 3 (August, 1956), pp. 201–212.

Phillips, George. "Racial Infiltration," *The Review of the Society of Residential Appraisers*, vol. XVI, No. 2 (February, 1950).

Rose, Arnold M., et al. "Neighborhood Reactions to Isolated Negro Residents: An Alternative to Invasion and Succession," *American*

*Sociological Review*, vol. XVIII, No. 5 (October, 1953), pp. 497–507.

Schietinger, E. F. "Race and Residential Market Value in Chicago," *Land Economics*, vol. XXX, No. 4 (November, 1954), pp. 301–308.

Stetler, Henry G. *Racial Integration in Private Residential Neighborhoods in Connecticut.* Hartford: State of Connecticut Commission on Civil Rights, 1957.

Weaver, Robert C. "The Effect of Anti-Discrimination Legislation on the FHA and VA-Insured Housing Markets in New York State," *Land Economics*, vol. XXXI, No. 4 (November, 1955), pp. 303–313.

Weaver, Robert C. "Integration in Public and Private Housing," *Annals of the American Academy of Political and Social Science*, issue on "Racial Desegregation and Integration," vol. CCCIV (March, 1956), pp. 86–97.

Weaver, Robert C. *The Negro Ghetto.* New York: Harcourt, Brace and Co., 1948.

Weaver, Robert C. "Planning for More Flexible Land Use," *Journal of Land and Public Utility Economics*, vol. XXIII, No. 1 (February, 1947), pp. 29–41.

Weaver, Robert C. "Recent Developments in Urban Housing and Their Implications for Minorities," *Phylon Review of Race and Culture*, vol. XVI, 3d quarter, 1955, pp. 275–282.

Wilner, Daniel M., Rosabelle Price Walkley, and Stuart W. Cook. *Human Relations in Interracial Housing.* Minneapolis: University of Minnesota Press, 1955.

Wolf, Eleanor P. "The Tipping Point in Racially Changing Neighborhoods," *Journal of the American Institute of Planners*, vol. XXIX, No. 3 (August, 1963), pp. 217–222.

## 5. The Housing Industry

Editors of *Architectural Forum. Building U.S.A.* New York: McGraw-Hill, 1957.

Arnold, Thurman. *The Bottlenecks of Business.* New York: Reynal and Hitchcock, 1940.

Fisher, Ernest M., and Robert M. Fisher. *Urban Real Estate.* New York: Henry Holt, 1954.

Gibberd, Frederick. "Three Dimensional Aspects of Housing Layout," *Royal Institute of British Architects Journal*, vol. LV, No. 10 (August, 1948), pp. 433–440.

Grebler, Leo. *Production of New Housing: A Research Monograph on Efficiency in Production.* New York: Social Science Research Council, 1950.

Guttentag, Jack M. "The Short Cycle in Residential Construction," *American Economic Review* (June, 1961).

Haber, William. *Industrial Relations in the Building Industry.* Cambridge: Harvard University Press, 1950.

Haber, William, and Harold M. Levinson. *Labor Relations and Productivity in the Building Trades.* Ann Arbor: University of Michigan Press, 1956.

*House and Home.* Eight part series on the building industry commencing January, 1963. Reprinted as "The New Housing Industry," 1964.

*House and Home.* "The Industrial Revolution in Housing is Inevitable in the 1960's," (January, 1961), pp. 150–164.

Kelly, Burnham. *The Prefabrication of Houses.* Technology Press of MIT and John Wiley & Sons, 1951.

Kennedy, Robert W. *The House and the Art of its Design.* New York: Reinhold, 1953.

Lasch, Robert. *Breaking the Building Blockade.* Chicago: University of Chicago Press, 1946.

*Law and Contemporary Problems*, Housing Issue, vol. XII, No. 16 (1947). Articles by Robert L. Davison, "Technological Potentials in Home Construction," and Leo Loevinger, "Handicraft or Handcuffs – The Anatomy of an Industry."

Maisel, Sherman J. *Housebuilding in Transition.* Berkeley: University of California Press, 1953.

National Association of Home Builders. *Home Builders' Manual for Land Development*, Rev. Ed. 1958, pp. 28–58.

National Association of Home Builders. *Housing Almanac.* Washington, D.C., 1957.

National Association of Home Builders. "The NAHB Membership Survey: A Study of Builders and the Homes They Build," vol. I, Washington, D.C., 1959.

Smolkin, William R. *A Marketing Plan for Apartment Builders.* Barret Division of Allied Chemical and Marketing Department of

National Association of Home Builders, 1964.
"The Standard House," *Architectural Forum*
(January, 1938), pp. 189–9.

U.S. Senate, Special Committee to Study Problems of Small Business. *Anti-Trust Cases in the Construction Industry*, 79th Congress, 2nd Session, Washington, D.C., 1946.

Warren, George F., and Frank A. Pearson. *World Prices and the Building Industry*. New York, 1937, Chapter VI.

Wheaton, William L. C. "Private and Public Agents of Change in Urban Expansion," in *Explorations into Urban Structure*. Philadelphia: University of Pennsylvania Press, 1964, pp. 154–194.


## 6. Housing Finance

Banfield, Edward C., and Morton Grodzins. *Government and Housing in Metropolitan Areas*. ACTION Series. New York: McGraw-Hill, 1958.

Colean, Miles L. "The Impotency of FHA Policies on Apartment Finance," *Architectural Forum* (June, 1955), p. 110.

"Cooperative Housing in Selected Countries," *Housing Through Non-Profit Organizations*. New York: United Nations Department of Social Affairs, 1956, pp. 94–118.

Daly, Grover, and D. Robert Papera. "The Sale and Financing of On-the-Lot Housing," *Land Economics*, vol. XL, No. 4 (November, 1964), pp. 433–436.

"Federal Assistance in Financing Middle-Income Cooperative Apartments," *Yale Law Journal*, vol. LXVIII (1959), pp. 542–613.

*Financing Lower Middle Income Housing*. Bureau of Community Development, Department of Commerce, Commonwealth of Pennsylvania, 1964.

Gillies, James and Clayton Curtis. "The Structure of Local Mortgage Markets and Government Housing Finance Programs," *Journal of Finance*, vol. X (1955), p. 363.

Gordon, R. A. "Population Growth, Housing, and the Capital Coefficient," *American Economic Review*, vol. XLVI, No. 3 (June, 1965), pp. 307–322.

Grebler, Leo. "Flow of Funds Into New Residential Construction, 1911–1952," *Journal of Finance*, vol. IX (December, 1954), pp. 339–350.

Grebler, Leo. *Housing Issues in Economic Stabilization Policy*, National Bureau of Economic Research, Occasional Paper No. 72 (1960), pp. 1–15; 88–111.

Grebler, Leo. *The Role of Federal Credit Aids in Residential Construction*, National Bureau of Economic Research, Occasional Paper No. 39 (1953).

Guttentag, Jack M. *Some Studies of the Post-World War II Residential and Mortgage Markets* (unpublished Ph.D. dissertation, Columbia University, May, 1958).

Herrick, Allen. "What Borrowers Think of the FHA Plan," *Insured Mortgage Portfolio* (August, 1939), pp. 7, 24–25.

Home Loan Bank Board. *Outline of Functions*. Washington, D.C., 1952.

Howenstine, E. Jay. "Appraising the Role of Housing in Economic Development," *International Labour Review*, vol. LXXV, No. 1 (January, 1957), pp. 21–33.

Johnson, Ralph J., et al. "The Quality of Housing Before and After Rehabilitation," *American Journal of Public Health* (February, 1955), pp. 189–196.

Klaman, Saul B. *The Postwar Residential Mortgage Market*. National Bureau of Economic Research, Princeton: Princeton University Press, 1961.

Lintner, John. *Mutual Savings Banks in the Savings and Mortgage Markets*. Graduate School of Business Administration, Division of Research. Boston: Harvard University Press, 1948.

Long, Clarence D., Jr. *Building Cycles and the Theory of Investment*. Princeton: Princeton University Press, 1940.

McMichael, S. L., and P. T. O'Keefe. *How to Finance Real Estate*. New York: Prentice-Hall, 1953.

Morton, J. E. *Urban Mortgage Lending: Comparative Markets and Experience*. National Bureau of Economic Research, Princeton University Press, 1956, pp. 54–60.

Morton, W. A. *Housing Taxation*. Madison: University of Wisconsin Press, 1955.

National Housing Agency. *Housing Costs:*

*Where the Housing Dollar Goes.* Washington, D.C., 1944.

Osborn, F. T. "How Subsidies Distort Housing Development," *Lloyds Bank Review*, vol. XXXVI (April, 1955), pp. 25–38.

Paul, Randolph, and Miles Colean. *Effect of the Corporate Income Tax on Investment in Rental Housing.* National Committee on Housing, New York, 1946.

President's Advisory Committee on Government Housing Policies and Programs. *Recommendations on Government Housing Policies and Programs,* 1953.

Ratcliff, Richard, Daniel Rathburn, and Julie Homolka. "Residential Finance, 1890 to 1950," in *Residential Finance 1950,* New York: John Wiley & Sons, 1950, pp. 21–22.

Rawson, Mary. *Property Taxation and Urban Development,* Research Monograph 4, Urban Land Institute, Washington, D.C., 1961.

Reid, Margaret G. "Capital Formation in Residential Real Estate," *Journal of Political Economy*, vol. LXVI (1958), p. 131.

Rodwin, Lloyd. "Rent Control and Housing," *Social Research*, vol. XVII, No. 3 (September, 1950), pp. 302–319.

Rubloff, Arthur. "Let's Tax Our Slums to Death," *Look*, vol. XXIV, No. 26 (December, 1960), pp. 101–105.

Saulnier, Raymond J. *Urban Mortgage Lending by Life Insurance Companies.* National Bureau of Economic Research, New York, 1958.

Schaffer, Beldon M. *Growing Suburbs and Town Finance.* Institute of Public Service, University of Connecticut, November, 1954, pp. 1–13.

Sporn, Arthur D. "Some Contributions of the Income Tax Law to the Growth and Prevalence of Slums," *Columbia Law Review*, vol. LIX (November, 1959), pp. 1026–1064.

U.S. Housing and Home Finance Agency. *Cooperative Housing – United States, Denmark, Great Britain – etc.*, Washington, D.C., 1950, Supplement, 1951.

U.S. Housing and Home Finance Agency. *Cooperative Housing in the United States, 1949 and 1950.* Washington, D.C., 1952.

U.S. Housing and Home Finance Agency. *How FHA Mortgage Insurance Operates.* Washington, D.C., 1952.

U.S. Housing and Home Finance Agency. *A Summary of the Evolution of Housing Activities in the Federal Government,* Washington, D.C., 1950.

U.S. Senate, Committee on Banking and Currency, Subcommittee on Housing. *Study of Mortgage Credit.* Washington, D.C., 1958.

Wendt, Paul F. *The Role of the Federal Government in Housing.* Washington, D.C.: American Enterprise Association, Inc., 1956.

Winnick, Louis. "The Burden of the Residential Mortgage Debt," *Journal of Finance*, vol. XI (1956), pp. 166–179.

Winnick, Louis. *Rental Housing Opportunities for Private Investment.* ACTION Series, New York: McGraw-Hill, 1959.

Zimmer, B. G. and A. H. Hawley. "Home Owners and Attitude Toward Tax Increase: Flint Metropolitan Area," *Journal of the American Institute of Planners*, vol. XXII (1956), pp. 65–74.

## 7. Housing Standards and Controls

Allnuti, Robert F., and Gerald J. Mossinghoff. "Housing and Health Inspection: A Survey and Suggestions in Light of Recent Case Law," *George Washington Law Review*, vol. XXVIII; No. 2 (January, 1960), pp. 421–453.

American Public Health Association. *An Appraisal Method for Measuring the Quality of Housing,* Parts I–II–III, New York: 1945–50.

American Public Health Association. *Housing for Health.* New York, 1941.

American Public Health Association. *Planning the Home for Occupancy.* Chicago: Public Administration Service, 1950.

American Public Health Association. *Proposed Housing Ordinance Regulating Supplied Facilities, Maintenance, and Occupancy of Dwellings and Dwelling Units.* New York, 1952.

Barnhart, Dilbert R. *Local Development and Enforcement of Housing Codes,* U.S. Housing and Home Finance Agency, Washington, D.C., 1953.

Chapin, Stuart F. "An Experiment on the Social Effects of Good Housing," *American Sociological Review*, vol. V, No. 6 (December, 1940), pp. 868–879.

Coke, J. G., and C. S. Liebman. "Political Values and Population Density Control," *Land Economics*, vol. XXXVII, No. 4 (November, 1961), pp. 347–361.

Cornick, P. W. *Premature Subdivision and Its Consequences*. New York: Institute of Public Adminstration, 1938.

Florida Department of Public Welfare. *Suitable Home Law*, Preliminary Report, September, 1960.

International Union of Family Organizations. *Minimum Habitable Surfaces*. Cologne: Family Housing Commission, 1957.

McHarg, Ian. "The Court House Concept," *Architect's Yearbook*, Elek Books, London (1957), pp. 74–102.

New York Academy of Medicine. "Report of the Subcommittee on Housing of the Committee on Public Health Relations," *Bulletin of the New York Academy of Medicine* (June, 1954).

Nimlo, *Model Minimum Housing Standards Ordinance*. Washington, D.C.: National Institute of Municipal Law Offices, 1954.

Pacific Coast Building Officials Conference. *Uniform Building Code*. Los Angeles, 1952.

"Report of the Fairfax County Minimum Housing Standards Committee on a Proposed Housing Hygiene Ordinance," Fairfax, Va., November, 1960, mimeographed.

Siegel, Shirley A. "Relation of Planning and Zoning to Housing Policy and Law," *Law and Contemporary Problems*, School of Law, Duke University, vol. XX, No. 3 (Summer, 1955), pp. 419–435.

U.S. Bureau of Standards. *Building Code Requirements for New Dwelling Construction*. Washington, D.C., 1946.

Wehrly, Max. "Are Modern Subdivision Regulations Pricing Moderate Income Groups Out of the New Housing Market," *Proceedings: Local Government Conference on Subdivision Control*, vol. XIV (1957).

## 8. Residential Renewal

ACTION, Inc. *A Strategy for Improving Housing in Greater Cincinnati*. New York: Citizen's Development Committee, 1960, mimeographed.

Anderson, Martin. *The Federal Bulldozer, A Critical Analysis of Urban Renewal, 1949–1962*. Cambridge: MIT Press, 1964.

Bateman, Richard W., and Herbert J. Stern. "Baltimore's Housing Court Clinic," *Social Work*, vol. VI, No. 4 (October, 1961), pp. 43–49.

"Blight – Suburban Style," *Urban Land*, vol. 14, No. 5 (May, 1955), pp. 1–5.

Blum, Walter J., and Allison Dunham. "Income Tax Law and Slums: Some Further Reflections," *Columbia Law Review*, vol. LX (April, 1960), pp. 447–453.

Colean, Miles L. *Renewing Our Cities*. New York: Twentieth Century Fund, 1953.

Dyckman, John W., and Reginald R. Isaacs. *Capital Requirements for Urban Development and Renewal*. New York: McGraw-Hill, 1959. One in the ACTION Series on Housing and Community Development.

Federal Home Loan Bank Board. *Waverly, A Study in Neighborhood Conservation*. Washington, D.C., 1941.

Fried, Marc, and Peggy Gleicher. "Some Sources of Residential Satisfaction in an Urban Slum," *Journal of the American Institute of Planners*, vol. XXVII, No. 4 (November, 1961), pp. 305–315.

Frieden, Bernard J. *The Future of Old Neighborhoods*. Cambridge: MIT Press, 1964.

Hartman, Chester. "The Housing of Relocated Families," *Journal of the American Institute of Planners*, vol. XXX, No. 4 (November, 1964), pp. 266–286.

Herley, Mark K. "Rehabilitation." Speech to Potomac Chapter of the National Association of Housing and Redevelopment Officials. Washington, D.C., March 9, 1961.

Hoffman, Morton. "The Role of Government in Influencing Changes in Housing in Baltimore: 1940–1950," *Land Economics*, vol. XXX, No. 2 (May, 1954), pp. 125–140.

Hole, Vere. "Social Effects of Planned Rehousing," *The Town Planning Review*, vol. XXX, No. 2 (July, 1959), pp. 161–173.

"Home Builders' Slum Cures Failing," *Journal of Housing*, vol. XIII, No. 5 (May, 1956), pp. 165–166.

Hunter, David R. *The Slums: Challenge and Response*. New York: The Free Press, 1964.

Johnson, T. F., J. R. Morris, and J. G. Butts. *Renewing America's Cities*. Washington, D.C.: The Institute of Social Science Research, 1962.

Leach, Richard H. "The Federal Urban Renewal Program: A Ten-Year Critique," *Law and Contemporary Problems*, vol. XXV (Autumn, 1960), pp. 777–792.

Lewis, Charles Henry. "Redevelopment of Marshall Heights," M. A. thesis. Washington, D.C.: American University, 1954.

Lichfield, Nathaniel. "Relocation: The Impact on Housing Welfare," *Journal of the American Institute of Planners*, vol. XXVII, No. 3 (August, 1961), pp. 119–203.

Linn, Karl. "Neighborhood Rehabilitation," a lecture at the Washington, D.C., Center for Metropolitan Studies, April 18, 1962.

Loring, William C., Jr., Frank L. Sweetser, and Charles E. Ernst. *Community Organization for Citizen Participation in Urban Renewal*. Prepared by Housing Association of Metropolitan Boston for the Massachusetts Department of Commerce, Cambridge, 1957.

May, Ernst. "The One-Family House vs. Rebuilding the City," *Journal of the American Institute of Planners*, vol. XXII (1956), pp. 227–229.

Millspaugh, Martin. "Problems and Opportunities in Relocation," *Law and Contemporary Problems*, vol. XXVI (Winter, 1961), pp. 6–36.

Montgomery, Dorothy S. "Relocation and its Impact on Families," Paper before the National Conference on Social Welfare, Atlantic City, N.J., June 7, 1960.

Nash, William W. *Residential Rehabilitation, Private Profits and Public Purposes*. New York: McGraw-Hill, 1959. One in the ACTION Series on Housing and Community Development.

National Association of Housing and Redevelopment Officials. *Change for the Better*. NAHRO No. N468, Washington, D.C., May, 1962.

National Association of Housing and Redevelopment Officials, Joint Committee on Housing and Welfare. *Working Together for Urban Renewal*. NAHRO No. N407, Washington, D.C., September, 1958.

National Association of Real Estate Boards. A *Primer on Rehabilitation under Local Law Enforcement*. Washington, D.C., 1952.

Perkins, Maurice. *Neighborhood Conservation, A Pilot Study*. Detroit: City Planning Commission, 1958.

Philadelphia Housing Association. A *Citizen's Guide to Housing and Urban Renewal*. Philadelphia, 1960.

Philadelphia Housing Association. "Findings and Recommendations of the Philadelphia Housing Association on Relocation in Philadelphia," *Relocation in Philadelphia*, Philadelphia (November, 1958), pp. 2–9.

Philadelphia Housing Association. "Relocation – The Human Side of Urban Renewal," *Issues*, Philadelphia (November, 1958).

Philadelphia Redevelopment Authority. *Eastwick New House Study*. Philadelphia, 1957.

Ravitz, Mel J. "Effects of Urban Renewal on Community Racial Patterns," *Journal of Social Issues*, vol. XIII, No. 4 (1957), pp. 38–49.

Regional Association of Cleveland. *Neighborhood Conservation*, Cleveland, 1943.

*Report of the Urban Renewal Study Board*. Baltimore, 1956, Summary, pp. 1–19.

Reynolds, Harry W., Jr. "What Do We Know about Our Experiences with Relocation?" *Journal of Intergroup Relations*, vol. II, No. 4 (Autumn, 1961), pp. 342–354.

Rossi, Peter H., and Robert A. Dentler. *The Politics of Urban Renewal: The Chicago Findings*. New York: The Free Press, 1961.

Schaaf, A. H. "Public Policies in Urban Renewal: An Economic Analysis of Justifications and Effects," Reprint No. 36. Center for Real Estate and Urban Economics. Berkeley: Institute for Urban and Regional Development, University of California, 1964.

Siegal, Jack M., and C. Williams Brooks. *Slum Prevention Through Conservation and Rehabilitation*. Washington, D.C., 1953.

Slayton, William L. "Conservation of Existing Housing," *Law and Contemporary Problems*, vol. XX, No. 3 (Summer, 1955), pp. 436–462.

Slayton, William L. *Report on Urban Renewal*. Statement before Subcommittee on Housing, Committee on Banking and Currency, House of Representatives, Nov. 21, 1963, pp. 390–398; 402–406; 415–419.

Stokes, Charles J. "Theory of Slums," *Land Economics*, vol. XXXVIII, No. 3 (August, 1962), pp. 187–197.

U.S. Housing and Home Finance Agency. *Federal Laws Authorizing Assistance to Slum Clearance and Urban Renewal*. Washington, D.C., 1957.

U.S. Housing and Home Finance Agency. *Guide to Demonstrate Grants*. Washington, D.C., 1957.

U.S. Housing and Home Finance Agency. *A Guide to Slum Clearance and Urban Redevelopment under Title I of the Housing Act of 1949*. Washington, D.C., 1951.

U.S. Housing and Home Finance Agency. *How Localities Can Develop a Workable Program For Urban Renewal*. Washington, D.C., 1957.

U.S. Housing and Home Finance Agency. *State Enabling Legislation: Urban Redevelopment and Urban Renewal: List of Citation to Statutes, Constitutional Provisions, and Court Decisions*. Washington, D.C., 1958.

U.S. Housing and Home Finance Agency. *Workable Program for Community Improvement*. Washington, D.C., 1961.

U.S. Housing and Home Finance Agency. *Workable Program for Small Communities and Rural Non-farm Areas*. Washington, D.C., 1956.

Walker, Mabel. *Urban Blight and Slums*. Cambridge: Harvard University Press, 1939.

Weaver, Robert C. "Class, Race, and Urban Renewal," *Land Economics*, vol. XXXVI, No. 3 (August, 1960), pp. 235–251.

Wilson, James Q. "Planning and Politics: Citizen Participation in Urban Renewal," *Journal of the American Institute of Planners*, vol. XXIX, No. 4 (November, 1963), pp. 242–249.

Winnick, Louis. "Economic Questions in Urban Redevelopment," *American Economic Review*, vol. LI (May, 1961), pp. 290–297.

Wolf, Eleanor, P., and Mel J. Ravitz. "Lafayette Park: New Residents in the Core City," paper read at the Annual Meeting of the Ohio Valley Sociological Society, May 4, 1963, published in *Journal of American Institute of Planners*, vol. XXX, No. 3 (August, 1964), pp. 234–239.

Woodbury, Coleman (ed.). *The Future of Cities and Urban Redevelopment*. Chicago: University of Chicago Press, 1953.

Woodbury, Coleman. "Human Relations in Urban Redevelopment," in *The City in Mid-Century*, H. Warren Dunham (ed.). Detroit: Wayne State University Press, 1957, pp. 115–146.

Woodbury, Coleman (ed.). *Urban Redevelopment: Problems and Practices*. Chicago: University of Chicago Press, 1953.

## 9. Housing in the Economy

Alberts, William W. "Business Cycles, Residential Construction Cycles, and the Mortgage Market," *Journal of Political Economy*, vol. LXX, No. 3 (June, 1962), pp. 263–281.

Goldsmith, Raymond W., and Robert E. Lipsey. *Studies in the National Balance Sheet of the United States*. Princeton: Princeton University Press, 1963.

Grebler, Leo. "Urban Redevelopment as an Outlet for Capital Investment," *Land Economics*, vol. XXIX, No. 4 (November, 1963), pp. 358–361.

Grebler, Leo, David Blank, and Louis Winnick. *Capital Formation in Residential Real Estate*. Princeton: National Bureau of Economic Research, 1956.

Grebler, Leo and Sherman J. Maisel. "Determinants of Residential Construction: A Review of Present Knowledge," *Impacts of Monetary Policy*, prepared for the Commission of Money and Credit, Englewood Cliffs, 1963.

Maisel, Sherman. "Fluctuation in Residential Construction Starts," *The American Economic Review*, vol. LIII, No. 3 (June, 1963), pp. 359–384.

Maisel, Sherman J. "Varying Public Construction and Housing to Promote Economic Stability," Reprint No. 14, Real Estate Research Program, University of California, 1958, pp. 382–394.

Newman, W. H. *The Building Industry and Business Cycles*. Chicago: Chicago, 1935.

Thompson, Warren S. "The Effect of Housing on Population Growth," *The Milbank Memorial Fund Quarterly*, vol. XVI, No. 4 (October, 1938), pp. 359–368.

# Index

# Index

## A

Abrams, Charles, 284
  "The Subsidy and Housing,"
    356–71
Abu-Lughod, Janet, "The Consumer
  Votes by Moving," 175–91
ACTION, 13, 185, 211, 246
  building codes and, 378n, 379n
  rent study of, 435
Addison Acts (England, 1919), 7
"Adjusted" poor persons, 414
AFDC families, 236–37, 462
Africa, 286
Aged persons, see Elderly persons
Agency for International
  Development, 328
Agriculture, Department of, research
  programs, 327–28, 346
Aid, federal, see Federal aid
Aid to Families with Dependent
  Children (AFDC), 236–37,
  462
Alaska, construction industry in,
  323
Alcoa, 325, 436
Alexandria (Va.), 236, 438–39
Alinsky, Saul, 456
Aliquippa (Pa.), 257
All-State Properties, 325
Amana (Ia.), 124
Ambler Realty Co. v. Village of
  Euclid, 3n, 380n, 388
American Concrete Institute, 376
American Council To Improve Our
  Neighborhoods, see ACTION
American Dilemma, An (Myrdal),
  272n
American Hospital Association,
  227n
American Institute of Architects,
  Buildings for the
  Handicapped and/or Aged,
  228n
American Journal of Economics and
  Sociology, The, 9n
American Journal of Public Health,
  The, 403n
American Medical Association, 227n
American Municipal Association,
  431

American Public Health Association
  (APHA), 227n, 327
  Appraisal Method
    applied to Boston, 462
    average scores, 406t
    Baltimore study, 404–8
    facility scores, 407t
    outline of Method, 394–403
  Committee on the Hygiene of
    Housing, 37, 47, 396–400
    "Basic Principles of Healthful
      Housing," 397
    "Guiding Policies," 226–30
  standards set by, 39, 47, 392
American Public Welfare
  Association, 227n
American Sociological Review, The,
  217n, 255n, 394n
American Standards Association,
  378n
American Statistical Association,
  The, 202n
America's Needs and Resources,
  228n
Amerman, Helen E., 272n
  Studies of Attitudes Toward
    Housing and Race, 271n
Amsterdam (Holland), 114–15, 116
Anatomy of Wealth, The (Doane),
  160
Annals of the American Academy of
  Political and Social Science,
  The, 252n
Annual Report (FHA), 156
Apartment hotels, 220
Appraisal Journal, The, 75n
"Appraisal Method for Measuring
  the Quality of Housing, An"
  (Twitchell), 394–403
Architects
  Bauhaus school of, 250
  esthetic expression of, 43–44
  sociability sacrificed by, 124
  sociologists' conflicts with, 23, 26
  See also Design; specific architects
Architectural Forum, The (journal),
  245n, 436
Arizona, 225
Arlington Farms, 218
Ashley, 230
Asia, 286

Atlanta (Ga.), 236
  Butler Street Urban Renewal in,
    300–1
  in housing inventory, 214t
  rent-income ratio in, 171t
"Attack on the Neighborhood
  Unit Formula" (Isaacs),
  109–14
Automobiles, see Transportation
Axial urban growth, 54–55, 57–59,
  72–73, 83

## B

Bach, Kurt W., 234
Back-of-the-Yards' Credit Union
  (Chicago), 452
"Background of Federal Housing
  Credit" (Haar), 347–56
Bacon, Mrs. Albion Fellows, 10–11
Baltimore (Md.), 13, 54, 236, 444
  disappearing downtown area of,
    430, 432
  Family & Children's Society of,
    453
  growth of, 57, 59, 70, 71
  Housing Code, 405, 408
  Housing Court in, 379n
  planned suburbs of, 117–18
  schoolchildren in, 267
  slum costs in, 429
  urban renewal in
    changing attitude, 451–57
    rehabilitation study, 403–8
    taxes before and after
      redevelopment, 431t
Baltimore Plan, 13
Bankhead-Jones Act, 338
Barnes, Harry, 5
Barnett, Samuel Augustus, 117
Bartling, Martin, 329–30
Basement dwellings, illegal, 2
"Basic Principles of Healthful
  Housing" (APHA), 397
Bassett, Edward M., Zoning, 103
Battle Creek (Mich.), 401
Bauer, Catherine, see Wurster,
  Catherine Bauer
Bauhaus school of architecture, 250
Beaver Falls (Pa.), 257
"Beginners" (slum dwellers), 414t,
  416–17

Belair (Md.), 325
Belgium, 8
Beltsville (Md.), 328
Berens Company, 326
Berkeley (Calif.), interracial
   housing in, 295–96
*Berman v. Parker*, 349n
Beyer, Glenn, 204
Binghampton (N.Y.), 301
Bi-racial housing, *see* Interracial
   housing
Birmingham (Ala.), 256, 281
Birmingham (England), 2
Birth
   illegitimate, 20
   maternal morbidity and, 264–65
   rate of, 2
      Indianapolis, 189
      Newark's public housing, 259
      postwar, 18
      prediction, 37
Black, Robert B., 30n
Blandford, John H., 432
Blank, David M., 161
   *Capital Formation in Residential
      Real Estate*, 200n, 203n, 357n,
      360, 361, 362, 364
   "The Growth of the Residential
      Mortgage Debt," 357–64
Blight, urban, *see* Slums
BLS, *see* Labor, Department of—
   Bureau of Labor Statistics
Bluefield (W. Va.), 65
Boarding houses, 219–20
Boester, Carl, 330
Bonan, Pierre, 436
Bonds, 336, 360–61, 368
Boston (Mass.), 3, 54, 58, 254, 301
   city cost for areas of, 429t
   Housing Association, 230
   Housing Authority, 464, 468
   in housing inventory, 214t, 215
   rent-income ratio in, 171t
   studies of zoning in, 381n, 386n
   theories of growth and structure
      applied to, 75–79
      cultural ecology theory, 76–79,
         81
      sector theory, 76, 78, 81–88,
         91–94
   urban renewal in
      evaluation of renewal, 458–74
      rehabilitation, 437
*Bowles v. Willingham*, 349n
Branch, Melville C., Jr., 178
   *Urban Planning and Public
      Opinion*, 177n, 185n
Breckenfeld, Gurney, "The Lessons
   Learned," 451–57
Bridgeport (Conn.), 301
Bright, Virginia, "Officials Have
   Learned a Lesson from West
   End," 467n
Bronx, The (N.Y.C.), 57–58, 69,
   230
Brookline (Mass.), 301

Brooklyn (N.Y.C.), 57–58, 64
Brooks, C. William, 440
Bryce, Viscount (James Bryce), 9
Buell, Bradley, 410
Buffalo (N.Y.)
   home ownership in, 179n
   rent-income ratio in, 171t
   slums in, 256
Builders' control, 317n
"Building and Land Use Controls"
   (Kelly) 373–90
Building codes, 336, 347–49, 392
   check on inadequate, 402
   federal research on, 327, 330–31
   renewal and, 425
Building cycles, 15–16, 322
Building Officials Conference of
   America (BOCA), 303, 375n,
   376
Building Research Advisory Board,
   326–27
*Buildings for the Handicapped
   and/or Aged* (American
   Institute of Architects), 228n
Bullock, Charles J., *Essays on the
   Monetary History of the
   United States*, 333n
Bureau of Census, *see* Census—
   Bureau of
Business districts, 44
   Hoyt's theory of urban growth
      and, 60, 62–63, 70, 71, 82–84
   in neighborhood unit formula,
      96, 102, 103–4
   renewal affecting, 432, 436,
      464–66
   slums and, 1, 91, 430
   *See also* Shopping centers
Buttenheim, Harold S., 9, 13
   "Slum Improvement by Private
      Effort," 11

C

Calder, William M., 347n
California, 250, 301
   construction industry in, 315–16,
      318–19, 320–21, 323–24
   construction firms, 322t
   Northern California production,
      318t, 319t
   migration to, 187, 205
   "retirement communities" in,
      225
   Veterans Farm and Home
      Purchase Act (1921), 3, 10
   Veterans Welfare Board, 3
   *See also* Berkeley; Los Angeles;
      Oakland; Sacramento;
      San Francisco
California, University of, Real
   Estate Research Program,
   139n, 314n, 317n, 418n
Canada, 429, 464
Capehart housing, 241

*Capital Formation in Residential
   Real Estate* (Grebler, Blank,
   and Winnick), 200n, 203n,
   357n, 360, 361, 362, 364
Caplan, Dr. Gerald, 458
Cash flows, 358–59
Census, 184, 217n
   Bureau of, 160, 180, 202–4, 209,
      309
      Construction Office, 208n
      *Current Population Reports*,
         177n, 180
      *Current Population Survey*, 204,
         209
      Housing Division, 203, 205–6
      mobility statistics, 176n
      *Mortgages on Homes in the
         United States*, 364
      population estimate (1980), 18
      substandard units defined, 418
   of Construction (1939), 309
   1890, 161, 363n
   of Housing, 152, 283
      housing classification, 395–96
      Los Angeles, 400n
      Negro housing, 150
      1940, 345, 364
      1950, 141n, 144, 148–49, 154,
         155, 160, 169, 171, 202,
         269–70, 358n, 359n, 360n,
         363n, 364, 463, 465n
      1960, 202–16, 224, 243, 245,
         303
   of Manufactures (1947), 311n
   measures of quality in, 37
   of middle-income families, 447
   National Housing Inventory
      (1956), 148n; *see also*
      National Housing Inventory
   1930, 162
   "unfindables" uncounted by, 416
Central urban growth, 53, 55,
   57–59
"Century of the Housing Problem,
   A" (Wood), 1–8
Chadwick, Edwin, 5
Chamberlain Act (England, 1923),
   7, 370
Chapin, F. Stuart, 25
Charities and Corrections,
   Conference of, 9–10
Charleston (W. Va.), growth of,
   57–58, 63, 67, 70, 71
Charlotte (N.C.), 437
Chawner, Lowell J., 314
Chicago (Ill.), 13, 301
   Back-of-the-Yards area of, 412–13,
      437, 451–52, 454–57
   Department of Health, *Health
      Data Book*, 221n
   growth of, 54–57, 58, 59–60,
      62–63
   high-rent districts, 65, 67, 69,
      70–71, 72, 73
   in 1920's, 344
   population growth, 189

history of housing in, 4
in housing inventory, 213n, 214t
housing for poor of, 231–32, 236
immigrant housing in, 73, 74
middle-income groups in, 447
neighborhood unit formula
applied to, 112, 120
planned suburbs of, 118
in property value study, 289–91
rent-income ratio in, 171t
segregation issue in, 46
unattached persons in, 221
urban renewal in, 437, 444
changing attitude, 451–52,
454–57
rehabilitation study, 439
taxes before and after
redevelopment, 431t
Children's Bureau, U.S., 239
Chinese-Americans, 270–71, 294
Christiana Oil Corp., 325
Churches
European, 115
Negro, 270
in neighborhood unit formula,
102, 111, 120
rehabilitation affecting, 452, 454
Cincinnati (Ohio), 8–9, 13, 301
growth of, 69
Social Unit movement in, 118
Citizens' Housing and Planning
Council of New York, 13
Citizens Planning and Housing
Association (Baltimore), 456
City and Suburban Homes
Company, 9
City Housing Corporation (N.Y.),
229
City of the Rich and the Poor,
The, 447
City planning, 13, 41, 44
controls affecting, 387
zoning, 104, 380, 382n
ignores housing for unattached
persons, 219
land use and, 423
neighborhood units aligned with,
94–95
slums and, 410–12
Class segregation, 44–45
"Classifications of the Construction
Industry" (Gillies and
Mittlebach), 314–17
Clear Lake City (Tex.), 324–25
Cleveland (Ohio), 8, 345
AFDC families in, 236–37
growth of, 63, 67, 71
housing projects in, 435
slums in, 256, 429
"Climbers" (slum dwellers), 414t,
415, 417
Clubhouses, community, 102, 111
Coit, Elizabeth, 30n
Colean, Miles I., 314, 436
"The Environment of Real
Estate Finance," 333–46

"The Organization of the
Construction Industry,"
307–13
Renewing Our Cities, 429–30
Collins, Mary Evans, 129
"Interracial Housing," 294–98
Colorado, 401–2
See also Denver
Columbia-Lavanburg researches,
24–25
Commerce, Department of, 314,
345, 361
research programs sponsored by,
345–46
Survey of Current Business, 322,
361n, 364
See also Census—Bureau of;
National Bureau of Standards
Community, see Neighborhood
Community centers
British, 42
European, 115
as neighborhood core, 117–19
in neighborhood unit scheme,
101–3
social questions about, 23, 26–27
teen-age use of, 129
See also Settlement houses
Community facilities, 42–43, 130
in Boston's West End, 461–62
convenience of, 47–48, 396
critique of, 111, 112
influencing social adjustment,
265–66
moving and, 186
in subdivision planning, 386–87
use of, 50
See also Churches; Community
centers; Hospitals; Libraries;
Parks; Schools; Shopping
centers
Community planning (housing
projects)
controls affecting, 387–88
zoning, 380–82
for elderly persons, 225–26
FHA financing for, 432–34, 435
misapplied, 250–51
social questions about, 30–52
crescive communities and,
28–29
facilities, 42–43
segregation, 26
tenure, 38–39
See also Large-scale housing;
Neighborhood unit formula;
Public housing
Community services in public
housing, 235
Community Studies, Center for,
see Harvard Medical School
Center for Community Studies
Complementarity, 143–45
Components of Change survey
(1959), 203, 215–16

"Components of Change in the
Nation's Housing Inventory in
Relation to the 1960 Census"
(Kristof), 202–16
Concentration, problem of, 409,
411
"Concerning Studies of Price
Trends in Mixed Areas"
(Rapkin and Grigsby), 292–94
Condemnation, 74
orders for, 402
unfeasible, 62
Congress, U.S., 234, 251, 445
Banking Committee, 348n
comprehensive housing policy of,
32
federal finance and, 347–50
hearing in, on housing lobby, 35
reform discussed before, 256
subsidy decision of, 37
See also Senate
Connecticut, 189, 301
See also Hartford; New Haven
Constitutional limitations, 337, 349
Construction
affecting mortgage debt, 358,
362n, 363–64
analysis of, 32, 36
conflicts of interest over, 21
decline in, 154
decline in expenditures, 16–17,
156–57
fluctuations in, 14–16
of housing for unattached
persons, 222
inventory of, 203–6, 212–16
of low-cost housing, see Low-cost
housing—construction of
rising standards of, 13
of schools, 37, 96, 384
Construction industry, 195, 307–31
affected by renewal, 431, 435–37,
442–43, 465, 470–71, 473
annual output of large-scale, 322t
attempts to stimulate, 11–12,
159, 240, 338
booms in, 53, 75, 155
cavalier attitude of
attitude toward aged persons,
229
attitude toward middle-income
group, 253
attitude toward renewal, 420
attitude toward segregation,
276, 278–79, 281–89, 302n
change in
indicators of change, 324–25
pessimism about change, 93
structural change, 317–24
Cinderella-like quality of, 202
classification of, 314–17
conflict of interests and, 21
consumer influence on, 35
controls and standards affecting,
387–92

building codes, *see* Building
codes
control of planned communities,
387–88
subdivision control, 384–85
zoning, 380–83
credit for, 312, 320, 325–26
dependent on credit, 351–52,
392
economic importance of, 14
future of
new industrial directions,
324–31
predicted trends affecting,
18–20, 158–59
in neighborhood unit formula,
94, 108–9
number of firms in, 322*t*, 323*t*
organization of, 307–13
public housing and, 241–42, 246,
338
sales efforts of, 168, 391–92
technological advancement in,
165, 346
*See also* Design; Large-scale
construction firms
Consumer, *see* Market—consumer
Consumer durables, 14
depreciation of, 195
expenditures for, 143, 144*n*,
148*n*, 149, 156–57
*Consumer Expectations 1953–56*
(Katona and Mueller), 176*n*
"Consumer Votes by Moving, The"
(Abu-Lughod and Foley),
175–91
Contractors, function of, 309–10,
314–17
Controls
builders', 317*n*
over building and land use,
373–90
federal, of management, 343
federal financing and, 354*n*
increase in, 32
in national emergency, 337
quality
appraisal method, 394–403
minimum standards and
uniformity, 39–40
before and after rehabilitation,
403–8
*See also* Rent control; Standards
Conversion, housing, 283
design intended for, 229
ending filtration, 201
inventory of, 204, 206–7, 213*n*
to rooming houses, 221
Cook, Stuart W., 271*n*, 272*n*
Cooley, Charles Horton, 117
Cooley Act, 338
Cooperative housing, 37
financial aid for, 32
history of, 4, 10, 12
home tenure and, 38–39
need for, 13

Swedish, 42
Cooperative housing companies, 3
Copenhagen (Denmark), 225–26
Coral Gables (Fla.), 71
"Costs of Slums in Newark," 259
CPS, *see* Current Population
Survey
Craftown housing community,
129–30, 261
Credit, *see* Finance
Cressey, Paul F., 290
*Cresskill* v. *Dumont*, 388*n*
Crime related to slums, 20, 256,
416, 429, 464
*See also* Delinquency; Graft
Critical path method, 327
"Critique of Firey's Land Use in
Central Boston, A" (James),
81*n*
Cross Acts (England, 1875–82), 6
Crowding, 233, 283
history of, 5, 6, 10, 13
measurement of, 236, 396, 398,
401
census measurement, 149
before and after rehabilitation,
406*t*, 408
profit from, 453–54, 456
social research on, 25, 27, 136,
262, 284, 461
Cultural ecology theory, 76–81
Cummings, Homer I., 4*n*
*Current Population Reports*, 177*n*,
180
*Current Population Survey* (CPS),
204, 209
*Current Trends in Social
Psychology*, 20*n*
Czechoslovakian-Americans, 73

**D**

Dallas (Tex.)
in housing inventory, 213, 214*t*
Negro housing development in,
300
Day, Castle N.
"Building and Land Use
Controls," 373–90
*Design and Production of
Houses*, 373*n*
Dean, John P.
"Housing Design and Family
Values," 127–38
"The Myths of Housing
Reform," 255–61
Death rate
environmental influence on, 264
poor housing related to, 2, 20,
256
renewal decision raising, 466
Decentralization
by neighborhood units, 121
*See also* "New towns"; Suburban
housing
"Deconcentration," 411, 418

Defense Project, 12, 326–27
DeForest, Robert, 9
DeFranceaux, George, 326
Del E. Webb Corp., 324–25
De Lauwe, Pierre Chambart, 115
Delaware, 8*n*
Delinquency
rehabilitation affecting, 451–52
slums related to, 8*n*, 20–21, 34,
256–57, 461–62
studies of public housing and,
257–58
threat of, 275
Demand, *see* Market
Democratic Party, 11
Demolition, inventory of, 204,
207–8, 213*n*
*See also* Slums—clearance of
Denmark, 8, 225–26
Denver (Colo.), 256, 301
slum costs in, 429
Depreciation, 196–201, 357
federal allowances for, 336, 341
hypothetical curves of, 200*t*, 201*t*
of public housing, 371
*See also* Deterioration; Filtering
process
Depressions
construction fluctuations and,
14–16
1930's, 217
conversions, 204
federal finance, 348, 349*n*, 350
home tenure, 180
housing construction, 14–15,
243*t*
housing emergency, 32, 249,
337, 371
housing revolution, 11
migratory workers, 187
"shantytowns," 220
Design
controls from viewpoint of, 379,
380–83
dissatisfaction with, 186
European, 37
family values and, 41, 127–38
of farmhouses, 328
of housing for aged, 227–30
innovations in, 158
of schools, 118
social question of, 34, 40–44, 265
specialized services for, 312
standards of
overstandardized, 247, 250, 331
quick sales and, 391–92
survey scores, 407*t*
volitional standards, 393–94
urban redesign, 442–43
*See also* Architects; Construction
industry; Planning
*Design and Production of Houses*
(Kelly), 373*n*
Deterioration
causing filtering, 197–98
of housing quality, 157, 186

of neighborhood, 13, 74, 83, 91,
    177, 186, 285
of plumbing facilities, 208–9
after redevelopment
    announcement, 463
studies of, 257, 404, 407
See also Filtering process
Detroit (Mich.), 301, 444
    growth of, 60, 63–64
        high-rent districts, 67, 69, 70,
        74
    HHFA experiment in, 326
    housing authority in, 8
    in housing inventory, 214t
    Industrial Study of, 430
    in property value study, 289–91
    rent-income ratio in, 171t
    slums in, 256, 429
    taxes before and after
        redevelopment in, 431t
Deutsch, Martin, 129
    "Interracial Housing," 294–98
Dewey, Richard, 113
    "Urban Redevelopment and the
        Urbanite," 179n
Dewey, Thomas E., 367–68
Dickens, Charles, 5
Dietz, Albert G. H., "Building
    and Land Use Controls,"
    373–90
Discrimination, racial, see
    Interracial housing; Minority-
    group housing; Prejudice; Race
Displaced persons, 464
Distribution of Housing Space, The
    (Winnick), 170
Doane, Robert R., The Anatomy
    of Wealth, 160
Douglas, William O., 383
Downs, James, 456
Drake, Larry, "Open Occupancy in
    1964," 302n
"Dreary Deadlock of Public
    Housing, The" (Wurster),
    241–45
Duesenberry, James S., 156, 163,
    166
Dunlop, John T., "Building and
    Land Use Controls," 373–90
Duplex houses, 229
Durables, see Consumer durables
Dyckman, John, 458n
Dynamics of Large-Scale
    Housebuilding, The
    (University of California),
    317n

E

East
    lower rate of construction in, 15
    migration from, 36
Ecology
    social, 28–29
    theory of cultural, 76–81

"Economic Aspects of Urban
    Renewal" (Schaaf), 418–28
Economic segregation, 44, 116, 118
Economy
    balanced neighborhood, 448–50
    of elderly persons, 223–24
    Firey's theory of, 80
    national
        English, 7–8
        housing and, 14–20
        public housing and, 241, 243t
    of rehabilitation, 437–38
    of renewal, see Renewal—
        economic aspects of
    slums and, 410
        liability, 258–59, 428–30, 432
    social sciences and, 21–22, 30,
        37–38
    state of, 211–12
    See also Depressions;
        Employment; Expenditures;
        Finance; Income; Market;
        Poverty; Property values;
        Taxes; Wealth
"Economy Houses," 40
Edinburgh (Scotland), 2
Education, 262
    cost of, 259
    housing expenditures and, 142t,
        146t, 150–52
    of multiple movers, 183–85
    See also Illiteracy Schools;
        specific universities
Eisenhower, Dwight D., 286
Elasticity
    income, 146–47, 155–56, 163–66
    price, 164–67, 173
Elderly persons, housing for,
    223–30, 233, 347, 447
    in Boston's West End, 463
    expenditures for, 141, 149, 254n
    future trends in, 13, 18–19, 42
    health and, 225–30, 264
    mobility rate and, 180–81, 190
    in old neighborhoods, 74, 224
    special housing, 225–27
Eleanor Clubs, 218
Ellender, Allen, 12
Elmira (N.Y.), environmental
    influence study in, 129–30
Emergency Fleet Corporation, 3
Eminent domain, 336, 445
    court ruling on, 349
    renewal through, 419, 422, 423,
        468
Empire State Building (N.Y.C.),
    312
Empiricism
    hazard of, 24–25
    of Hoyt, 81
Employment (occupation), 338,
    462
    in construction industry, 14,
        310–11
    of elderly persons, 223
    future trends in, 19, 211–12

housing expenditures and,
    150–52
    average expenditures by
        employment, 146t, 151t
    employment of owners without
        mortgages, 142t
    moving and, 176, 183–85, 186,
        187, 188n, 189–90, 205
    travel to, 49, 64
    See also Income; Working-class
        housing
"End deprivation," 80
Ends and Means of Urban
    Renewal, 441n
Engineering, civil, 316
England, 42, 218, 230, 380n
    decentralization efforts in, see
        "New towns"
    discrimination in, 44
    history of housing in, 5–8
    rooming house inspection in, 222
    study of special housing in, 227
    subsidy in, 367, 370
    See also specific cities
"Entrepreneurs" (slum dwellers),
    414t, 417
Entry and exit (construction
    industry), 321–22
Environment, 29, 34–36
    adequacy of, 90–91
    basic social unit of, 27
    consumer-shaped, 31
    family life influenced by, 129–31,
        261–68
    housing expenditures for, 143
    moving to better, 185–86
    neighborhood, 12, 27–28, 186,
        265–66, 395–96
    of public housing, 234
    of real estate finance, 333–46
    renewal affecting, 421–22
    of slums, 257
    in studies of standards, 395–99,
        404
    See also Space
"Environment of Real Estate
    Finance, The" (Colean),
    333–46
Epidemics, 2, 9
Epstein, Jesse, 30n
Equitable Investment Corp., 326
Essays on the Monetary History
    of the United States
    (Bullock), 333n
Ethnic groups, see Minority-group
    housing; Race; specific ethnic
    groups
Euclid v. Ambler, 3n, 380n, 388
"Evaluation of the Redevelopment
    Plan and Process, An" (Gans),
    458–74
Expenditures
    housing, 139–55
        causing mobility, 186
        construction, 362n, 363–64
        decline, 16–17, 154–57

family, 14, 139–53, 219, 231–32, 449
future trends, 19
improvement, 15, 154–55
percentage of total expenditures, 18t
see also Rent; Rent-income ratio
of travel to work, 49

**F**

Face-to-face groups, see Primary groups
Factory Acts (England), 6
"Facts and Fictions in Urban Renewal" (Winnick), 441–50
Fair Lawn (N.J.), Radburn community of, 119–20, 123
Families in Low-Rent Housing (Public Housing Administration), 244
Family
aged members of, 224–25, 226–27
as basic social unit, 27–28, 134
disorganization of, 284
dwelling type for, 41–42
environmental influences on, 129–31, 261–68
housing expenditures of, 14, 139–53, 219, 449
low-income, 11, 32, 230–45, 252, 254n
controls affecting, 386
dissatisfied with housing, 186
economic segregation, 44
effect of rehabilitation, 408
filtering process and, 74–75, 195–96, 199
influx, 454
public housing, 228, 231, 233–39, 247, 250, 253, 257, 259
undesirable traits, 446–47
urban migration, 248
middle-income, disappearance of, 446–48
minimum standards for, 39–40
neighborhood based on needs of, 120
rehabilitated housing and income of, 407–8
reintegration of, 123–24
size of
federally aided public housing and, 244t
housing expenditures and, 142t, 146t, 148–49, 231
large, 13, 18–19, 134, 170, 232, 256, 401
mobility and, 179–82, 186–87
reduced size, 462
rent-income ratio and, 170
small, 228–29
unattached person contrasted to, 218, 220

values of
cluster of values, 134t
conflicting values, 136–38
housing design and, 41, 127–38
living near relatives, 467–68, 472
See also Households
"Family Housing Expenditures: Elusive Laws and Intrusive Variances" (Maisel and Winnick), 139–53
Farm Loan Board, 339
Farm Security Administration, 335, 369–70
Farmers' Home Administration, 339–40
Federal aid, 36–37, 159–60, 239
based on need, 237
community planning affected by, 387
emergency basis of, 249
low density afforded by, 41
nondiscriminatory, 45
to public housing, 173–74, 244t, 250–51
for urban renewal, 419, 445
aid for rehabilitation, 437–38
redevelopment aid, 12, 250
See also Subsidy
Federal Credit and Private Housing (Haar), 347n
Federal Emergency Housing Corporation, 4
Federal Farm Mortgage Corporation, 338n, 339
Federal Home Loan Bank Act (1932), 4, 347–48
Federal Home Loan Bank System, 335, 337, 345
Federal Housing Administration (FHA), 38, 46, 164, 234n, 248–49, 327, 340, 344, 387
Annual Report, 156
encourages "Economy Houses," 40
history of, 12, 335
Hoyt's study for, 92
insurance activities of, 339, 348, 352n, 368, 419, 425, 433–36
housing projects, 434t
liberal terms, 432
limited-dividend formula of, 367
mortgage holdings of, 353n, 436–37
holdings by institution, 355t
mortgaged rehabilitated units, 438
public housing mortgages, 432–34
production periods and, 241, 243t
research and, 345
reaction to social research, 22
technical studies program, 326
segregation policy of, 273, 279, 280–81, 283, 301–4

standards set by, 39, 338, 377, 392, 425, 440–41
Federal Land Bank System, 334–35
Federal National Mortgage Association (FNMA), 251, 280–81, 348, 353
Federal Reserve Board, 348, 353, 354
survey by, 223–24
Federal Reserve Bulletin, "Survey of Consumer Finances," 177, 180, 181
Federal Urban Renewal Administration, 239, 431, 445
Federally-Aided Urban Renewal Program, 437
Festinger, Leon, 131
FHA, see Federal Housing Administration
Field, Walker, "A Re-examination into the Invention of the Balloon Frame," 313n
Fight Blight Fund (Baltimore), 452
Filtering process, 191–201, 213, 248–49
defined, 191–97
special group housing vs., 37–38
urban growth and, 73, 74–75
"Filtering Process, The" (Grigsby), 191–201
Finance (credit), 333–71
for construction industry, 312, 320, 325–26, 351–52, 392
down payment size in, 163, 165
Dutch, 8
extended to poor families, 233
federal, 32, 333–71
background, 347–56
future trends, 13, 19
growth, 333–46
segregation policy, 280–82
see also Federal aid; Federal Housing Administration; Subsidy
history of, 3–6, 10–11
liberalization of, 160
racial issue and, 279–82
finance available to Negroes, 302–4
perpetuation of segregation, 269, 279, 281
racial change in community, 291–93
for relocation, 465–66, 469, 471–73
for renewal, 419–21, 432–38, 440–41, 445–46
See also Mortgages
"Financial Survey of Urban Housing," 345
Fire protection
narrow streets impeding, 461, 463
standards of, 5, 407t
Firey, Walter, 85, 86–87, 90–91, 92n, 93
cultural ecology theory of, 76–81

*Land Use in Central Boston,*
76n, 77, 78n
*First Federal Savings and Loan
Assn. v. Loomis,* 350
Fischer, Victor, 30n
*Fischer v. Bedminster Township,*
381n
Fisher, Carl, 71
Fisher, Ernest M.
Fisher-Winnick definition of
"filtering", 192–95, 197–98
"Speculation in Suburban
Lands," 54n
"Flexabilt" housing, 229
Flint (Mich.), 185
Flophouses, 220
Florence (Italy), 115
Florida, 71, 326
migration to, 187, 205
public aid in, 236
"retirement communities" in,
225
*See also* Miami
FNMA (Federal National
Mortgage Association), 251,
280–81, 348, 353
Foley, Mary Mix, "The Consumer
Votes by Moving," 175–91
Foote, Nelson, *Housing Choices
and Housing Constraints,* 175n
Forbes, Gerritt, 2
Foreign policy, U.S., 286
Forest Products Laboratory, 327–28
*Fortune* Magazine, 435
FOSDIC device, 205–6
Fox, Robert, 325
France, 8, 115, 123
Frank, L. K., 255
Fred F. French Company, 4
Freestanding housing vs. multiple
dwellings, 21, 27, 41–42, 179
Fresno (Calif.), 323
Fried, Dr. Marc, 458
"Grieving for a Lost Home,"
466n
"Fugitives" (slum dwellers), 414t,
415
Future trends
comprehensive approach to, 13
in consumer preferences, 158–59
in economy, 18–20, 211–12
housing industry affected by,
324–31
in property values, 291–92
in rehabilitation, 209
sociological trends, 29, 37, 42
in urban growth, 60

**G**

Gainesville (Fla.), 326
Gans, Herbert J., "An Evaluation
of the Redevelopment Plan
and Process," 458–74
Gardner, Eugene, 230
Gary (Ind.), 257

General Development Corporation,
325
Germany
functional zoning in, 120
working-class housing in, 7
Ghettos, 282
appearance of, 13
Negro, 271
*See also* Minority-group housing;
Slums; Tenements
Giddings, Franklin, 124
Gillette, Thomas, 290, 291
Gillies, James
"Classifications of the
Construction Industry,"
314–17
"Structure of Local Mortgage
Markets and Government
Housing Finance Programs,"
353n
Ginzberg, Eli, *The Negro Potential,*
284n
Glasgow (Scotland), 2
Glass, Ruth, 111
Glazer, Nathan, 275n
*Gold Coast and the Slum, The*
(Zorbaugh), 411
Goldfeld, Abraham, 256–57
Goldsmith, Raymond W.
"A Perpetual Inventory of
National Wealth," 156n
*A Study of Saving in the United
States,* 361
Goldstein, Sidney, *Patterns of
Internal Migration:
Norristown, Pennsylvania
1910–1950,* 185n
Graft, 365–66
in public housing, 260
Great Britain, *see* England;
Scotland; Wales
Great Depression, *see* Depressions—
1930's
Grebler, Leo, 434
*Capital Formation in Residential
Real Estate,* 200n, 203n, 357n,
360, 361, 362, 364
"The Growth of the Residential
Mortgage Debt," 357–64
Greeley, Roland, 30n
"Greenbelt" principle, 49, 51, 119
*See also* "New towns"
Greensboro (N.C.), 301
Greenwald (redeveloper), 436
Gridiron plan, 106, 107t, 116, 250,
369
Grier, Eunice, 275n
Grier, George, 275n
Grigsby, William G., 275n
"Concerning Studies of Price
Trends in Mixed Areas,"
292–94
"The Filtering Process," 191–201
"Housing and Slum Clearance:
Elusive Goals," 252–54
Griscom, Dr. (New York City
health inspector), 2

Gropius, Walter, 250
Gross National Product
(1909–1960) and new private
nonfarm housing units
(1889–1960), 16t
"Growth of the Residential
Mortgage Debt, The"
(Grebler *et al.*), 357–64
"Guiding Policies" (The
Committee on the Hygiene
of Housing), 226–30
Gutheim, Frederick, 30n
Guttentag, Jack
"Winnick's Case for a Changing
Attitude toward Housing:
Comment," 162–65
Winnick's rebuttal to, 166–68

**H**

Haar, Charles M.
"Background of Federal Housing
Credit," 347–56
"The Wayne Township Case,"
381n
Haeger, Leonard, 330
Hampstead, *see* London
Harkness, John, 30n
Hartford (Conn.), 256
interracial projects in, 25–96, 301
slum revenues in, 429
Hartman, Chester, 467n
"Housing in the West End," 463
Harvard Medical School Center for
Community Studies, 458–59,
463, 466n, 467n
"Relocation and Mental Health:
Adaptation Under Stress," 458
Hawaii, construction industry in,
323
Health, 20, 24, 235
design and, 34
in districts housing unattached
persons, 221
of elderly persons, 225–30
environmental influence on,
261–65, 268
housing reform aimed at, 255–59
research on
federal research, 329
social research, 458–62
slum clearance for reasons of, 8n
standards of, 392–93
health code, 379
inspection techniques, 394–408
restrictive standards, 32
subsidy to promote, 366
in tenements, 2
*See also* American Public Health
Administration; Birth; Death-
rate; Epidemics; Sanitation
Health, British Ministry of, 6
Health, Education and Welfare,
Department of, *Slums and
Social Insecurity,* 231n
Helper, Rose, 276n

Herzog, John P., "Structural
  Change in the Housebuilding
  Industry," 317–24
HHFA, see Housing and Home
  Finance Agency
High ground, urban movement to,
  69–70, 82, 85
High-rent districts, see Upper-class
  districts
Hilltown project, 261
Hirabayoshi v. United States, 349n
Hoad, William, "Real Estate
  Prices: A Study of Residential
  Real Estate in Lucas County,
  Ohio," 200n
HOLC (Home Owners Loan
  Corporation), 248, 338n, 339,
  348
Holland, 8, 114–16, 367
Home Loan Bank Board, 359n
Home Owners Loan Corporation
  (HOLC), 248, 338n, 339, 348
Home Owners Refinancing Act,
  248
Home ownership, see Cooperative
  housing; Ownership
Home tenure, see Tenure
"Homeless men" (hoboes), 218,
  219–20, 222
Hoover, Herbert, 327
Hopkins, Harry, 348n
Horizontal integration, 317
Hospitals
  in neighborhood units, 121–22
  in projects for aged persons,
    225–26
  in slums, 429
  zoning of, 382
Hotels, 218, 220, 221–22, 237
House and Home (journal), 375n
  growth of, 315
  "New Directions for the Housing
    Industry," 324–31
Housebuilding, see Construction;
  Construction industry
Housebuilding in Transition
  (Maisel), 315n, 316n, 318,
  321, 375
Households, 167–68
  AFDC, 236
  age of head of
  elderly head, 226
  housing expenditures and,
    141–42, 146t, 148, 149–50
  mobility and, 180–84, 188t
  public housing and, 243, 244t
  formation of, inventoried, 204,
    209–10, 211–15
  number and increase of
    households, 214t
  future trends in, 18–19
  housing space for, 167
  mobility of, 176, 180–83, 188t
  mortgage debt per, 360t
  size of, 37, 182, 224, 228–29, 395

as unit of demand, 16–17
  See also Family
Housekeeping dwelling units,
  132–34
"Housing Achievements"
  (Robbins), 9–13
Housing Acts, 228, 337–38, 350,
  366, 368–70, 467n
  1934, 348
  1937, 12, 172, 173, 246–47, 249,
    257, 349, 444–46
  1948, 345
  1949, 12, 36, 204, 234, 241,
    252, 343, 348, 419, 470
  1954, 202n, 348, 419, 437–38,
    440
  1961, 303–4
Housing and Aging Population,
  226n
Housing and Home Finance Agency
  (HHFA), 32–33, 202–3, 303
  Bauer proposal for, 251
  Housing Statistics, 242–43, 318
  low-cost housing financed by, 326
  research under, 345–46
"Housing and Slum Clearance:
  Elusive Goals" (Grigsby),
  252–54
"Housing and the National
  Economy" (Meyerson et al.),
  14–20
Housing Authority, U.S., 12, 239
Housing Choices and Housing
  Constraints (Foote et al.),
  175n
Housing controls, see Controls
Housing costs, see Economy;
  Expenditures—housing;
  Finance; Market; Mortgages;
  Rent
Housing demand, see Market
Housing design, see Design
"Housing Design and Family
  Values" (Dean), 127–38
"Housing Environment and Family
  Life" (Wilner et. al.), 261–68
Housing finance, see Finance;
  Mortgages
"Housing for the Elderly" (Senate
  Subcommittee on Housing for
  the Elderly), 223–26
Housing for the Machine Age
  (Perry), 94n
"Housing: Has There Been a
  Downward Shift in Consumers'
  Preferences?" (Winnick),
  154–62
"Housing in the West End"
  (Hartman), 463
Housing inventory, see Inventory
Housing market, see Market
Housing Markets and Public Policy
  (Grigsby), 191n
"Housing Needs and Housing
  Market" (Wood), 159n

"Housing of Low-Income Families"
  (The Journal of Housing),
  241–45
Housing of Special Groups (Scottish
  Housing Advisory Committee),
  227n
Housing of the Working Classes
  Act (England, 1890), 6
Housing, People, and Cities, 14n
Housing projects, see Community
  planning; Public housing
Housing reform, see Reform
Housing shortage, see Shortage—
  of housing
Housing standards, see Standards
"Housing Standards" (Ratcliff),
  391–94
Housing Statistics (Housing and
  Home Finance Agency),
  242–43, 318
Housing subsidy, see Subsidy
Housing supply, see Market
Housing surplus, see Surplus
Housing trends, see Future trends
Houston (Tex.), 231
"How the Poor Are Housed"
  (Schorr), 231–40
Howard, Sir Ebenezer, 2, 41
Hoyt, Homer
  sector theory of, see Sector theory
  "The Structure and Growth of
    Residential Neighborhoods in
    American Cities," 53–75
Huber, Don, 330
Huddersfield (England), 6
"Human Implications of Current
  Redevelopment and Relocation
  Planning, The" (Gans), 458n
Human Side of Urban Renewal,
  The (Millspaugh and
  Breckenfeld), 451n
Humble Oil and Refining
  Company, 325
Huntsville (Ala.), 326

I

Ihlder, John, 10–11
Illegitimacy, 20
Illinois, 8n, 343
  See also Chicago
Illiteracy related to poor housing,
  20, 256
Illness, see Epidemics; Health
Immigration, 1–2, 73–74, 270–71
  to Boston's West End, 464
  cultural imports by, 270
  of unattached persons, 218, 219,
    416
Impact of Government on Real
  Estate Finance in the United
  States, The (Colean), 333n
"Importance of Net Replacements
  in Housebuilding Demand"
  (Maisel), 208n

Improvement
  construction industry influenced
    by, 15
  expenditures for, 154–55
  filtering process and, 193–94,
    195–96, 199
  of low-income housing, 176
  See also Redevelopment;
    Rehabilitation; Renewal
Improving the Condition of the
  Poor, Association for (AICP),
  2
"In Defense of the Neighborhood"
  (Mumford), 114–28
Income, 37–38, 262
  in Boston, 429t
  distribution of, 1, 19, 174
  elasticity of, 146–47, 155–56,
    163–66
  of elderly persons, 223
  filtering process and, 195–96
  future trends affecting, 19–20
  market trends, 211–12
  housing deficiency and, 242t
  housing expenditures related to,
    144–47, 155
    age of household head and, 150t
    family size and, 149t
    geographic location and, 148t
    income elasticity, 146t
    income variables, 152–53
    occupation and, 151t
    percentage of income, 145t
    poor income, 231–32
    race and, 150t
  mortgage debt and, 361t
  of multiple movers, 183
  neighborhoods of mixed, 448–50
  of nonwhites, 269, 305
  property value and, 156t, 192,
    423n
  public housing and
    low income limits, 247–48,
      259–60
    public housing households, 243,
      244t, 245t
  ratio of rent to, see Rent-income
    ratio
  rehabilitation and, 407–8
  rental, 432–34
  rising, 15, 17
  sudden changes in, 14, 185
  tax on, 341–42, 354n, 357, 367
  of unattached persons, 219
  Veblen's analysis of, 28
  See also Family—low-income;
    Middle-income housing;
    Upper-class districts
India, 116
Indianapolis (Ind.), 189, 256
  realty tax in, 343
  slums of, 412–17, 429
Indians, American, 189, 446
Individualism
  laissez-faire, 259–60
  of "unfindables," 416

"Indolent" slum dwellers, 414
Industrial Revolution, 5, 218
Industrial Study (of Detroit), 430
Industry
  establishment of U.S., 2
  housing, see Construction
    industry
  in low-cost districts, 462
  small, in planned communities,
    381
  subsidized, 366
  suburban flight of, 430
  urban location of, 63–64
  zoning of, 64, 381, 382
Innovation, product, 158–59
  See also Technological progress
Interest subsidy, 368–69
Intermediate income groups, see
  Middle-income housing
International Conference of
  Building Officials (ICBO),
  330, 375n, 376
International Development, Agency
  for, 328
Interracial housing, 292–301
  controversy over, 21–23
  as democratic institution, 123
  history of, 12
  lack of enthusiasm for, 269,
    278–79
  in neighborhood unit formula,
    111–12, 116
  price trends of, 290–94
  public housing and, 234, 247,
    271, 280, 299–300
  social research into, 26–27, 29,
    44–47, 294–98
  New School's research, 261
"Interracial Housing" (Deutsch and
  Collins), 294–98
Inventory, 233, 241, 448
  average age in, 155
  change in national, related to
    1960 census, 202–16
  mortgage financing in, 364
  1956, 148n
  of nonfarm housing (1955), 16
  PHA, 394–403
  raising of, 193
  recommended, 472
Iowa, 225
Irish-Americans in Boston, 87, 91
Isaacs, Reginald R.
  "Attack on the Neighborhood
    Unit Formula," 109–14
  Mumford's critique of, 116, 120
Italian-Americans
  in Boston, 464
  in Chicago, 73
  social strata among, 87
Italy, 8, 115, 123


J

Jahoda-West-Merton study, 295

James, John, "A Critique of Firey's
  Land Use in Central Boston,"
  81n
Jews
  in Chicago, 73
  in Elmira, 130
  exclusion of, 46
  social strata among, 87
Johnson, Lee, 247
Johnson, Ralph J., 330
  "The Quality of Housing 'Before'
    and 'After' Rehabilitation,"
    403–8
Journal of Homebuilding, 315
Journal of Housing, The, 168n, 436
  "Housing of Low-Income
    Families," 241–45
Journal of Social Issues, 30n
Journal of the American Institute
  of Planners, 409n
Juvenile delinquency, see
  Delinquency


K

Kalamazoo (Mich.), 184–85
Kansas City (Mo.), 301
  growth of, 58, 63, 69–70, 71
  in property value study, 289–91
Katona, George, Consumer
  Expectations 1953–56, 176n
Keith, Nathaniel, 431
Kelly, Burnham, 30n, 325
  "Building and Land Use
    Controls," 373–90
Kennedy, John F., 469n
  Executive Order of, 299–301,
    303–4
Kennedy, Robert W., 30n, 131
Kistin, Helen, 156, 163, 166
Kleemeier, Robert W., 225
Koch, Carl, "Building and Land
  Use Controls," 373–90
Koppers Company, Inc., 325
Kramer, Fred, 434
Kristof, Frank S., "Components
  of Change in the Nation's
  Housing Inventory in Relation
  to the 1960 Census," 202–16
Kuznets, Simon, 154
  National Product Since 1869, 160


L

Labor, Department of, 314, 318
  Bureau of Labor Statistics (BLS),
    14, 203, 205–6
    building permit data, 345
    city worker's family budget, 231
    cost-of-living data, 254
  United States Housing
    Corporation, 3, 347n
Lammer, Francis, 439
Land Economics (journal), 109n,
    127n, 434
Land grants, 369

Land use, 81
    analysis of, 32, 36
    changes in, 60–64, 71, 84
    city planning and, 423
    control of, 373–90
    efficient, 89
    functional segregation of, 44–45
    inefficient, 429–30
    opposing theories of, 76–77
*Land Use in Central Boston*
    (Firey), 76n, 77, 78n
Land writedowns, 434, 445–46
Landlords, 200, 466, 467, 472
    advocating Baltimore Plan, 13
    confused by redevelopment
        practices, 468–69
    equipment supplied by, 144
    housing code and, 238–39
    public, 249, 260
    refuse to rent, 237
    rigidity of, 247
    slum, 417
        perpetuate slum, 453
        profit from slum dole, 371
    tenant difficulties with, 186
    tenants selected by, 38–39, 45,
        464
    undermaintenance by, 197, 463
Large-scale construction firms,
        318–24
    annual output of, 322t
    controls viewed by, 376, 382, 388
    curve of distribution of, 321
    disappearance of, 325
    emergence of, 352
    index of, 322t
    interested in renewal, 436
    Northern California production
        by, 318t
Large-scale housing, 42–44
    *See also* Community planning;
        Neighborhood unit formula
Large-Scale Operations, Committee
    on, 11
Lateral urban growth, 53–54, 58,
        62, 64
    of high-rent districts, 67
Laurenti, Luigi, 275n, 293
    "Property Values and Race,"
        286–92
Lavanburg Foundation, 48
Laveran, Alphonse, 24
Least-cost criterion, 425–28
Le Corbusier (Charles Jeanneret),
        41, 119
"Lessons Learned, The"
    (Millspaugh and Breckenfeld),
        451–57
Letchworth (England), 2, 117
Levitt, William, 325
Levittown (N.J.), 325
Levittown (Pa.), 325
Libraries in neighborhood units,
        101, 121–22
Life expectancy of housing,
        199–200, 426

Lindermann, Dr. Erich, 458
Lintner, John, *Mutual Savings
    Banks in the Savings and
    Mortgage Markets*, 359n
Little Rock (Ark.), 286, 300
Liverpool (England), 2, 6
"Living Arrangements of
    Unattached Persons" (Rose),
        217–22
Loan Fund (Coconut Grove), 452
Lodging houses, 218–21, 222
London (England), 2
    County Council, 6
    neighborhoods of
        distinction, 116, 123
        Hampstead Garden Suburb,
            102, 117, 119
        settlement houses in, 117
Los Angeles (Calif.)
    construction industry in, 315
    growth of, 58, 60
    Housing Census in, 400n
    in housing inventory, 213, 214t,
        215
    interracial projects in, 295–96,
        301
    PHA study in, 401
    rent-income ratio in, 171t
    slums in, 256, 429
Low-cost housing, 231–68, 304–5,
        470–71
    in Boston, 429t, 460–65
    construction of
        filtering process and, 193–94,
            198–99
        history, 3–7, 9–10
        increase, 17
        post-World War II, 7–8
    defined, 228n
    in economically balanced areas,
        448–49
    environment of, 90–91
        family life and, 261–68
        functional adequacy, 90
    expenditures for, 145t, 148t,
        149t, 150t, 151t
    financed by HHFA, 326
    housing reform and, 255–61
    improvement of, 176, 209
    for low-income families, 11, 32,
        241–45
    neglected on open market, 89,
        240
    poverty and, 231–40
    prestigious, 86n
    public housing as, *see* Public
        housing
    redevelopment housing as, 435
    rent-income ratio and, 173-74
    slum clearance and, 12, 51,
        252–54
    in theories of urban growth, 67,
        73, 84n, 85, 87
    types of, 41
    *See also* Slums

"Low Cost Housing and Slum
    Clearance," 1n
Lowell (Mass.), 3, 10
Low-income family, *see* Family—
    low-income
Lowry, Ira S., 194–98
Luce, Henry, 378n
Lunt, P. S., *The Social Life of a
    Modern Community*, 86n, 87n
Lynch, Kevin, 30n
Lynd, Robert S., and Helen M.,
    *Middletown in Transition*, 70n


**M**

McCaldin, Roy O., "The Quality
    of Housing 'Before' and 'After'
    Rehabilitation," 403–8
McFarland, Carter, "Urban
    Renewal," 428–41
McKeever, J. Ross, "Utilities and
    Facilities for New Residential
    Construction," 384n
McMurray, Joseph P., 231
McNamara, Robert S., 326
Madison (Wisc.), 301, 328
Maine, 236
Maintenance, 181
    depreciation and, 197–98, 200
    expenditures for, 15
    by landlords, 38, 197
    of large houses, 157
    in property value study, 291
    standards of
        raised standards, 13
        before and after rehabilitation,
            406t, 407, 408, 463
    by tenants, 23, 39
Maisel, Sherman J., 314–15
    "Family Housing Expenditures:
        Elusive Laws and Intrusive
        Variances," 139–53
    "Have We Underestimated
        Increases in Rents and Shelter
        Expenditures?," 194n
    *Housebuilding in Transition*,
        315n, 316n, 318, 321, 375
    "Importance of Net
        Replacements in Housebuilding
        Demands," 208n
    *The Structure and Problems of
        the House Building Industry*,
        352n
*Management in the Light
    Construction Industry*
    (UCLA), 314n
Manchester (England), 2
Manhattan, *see* New York City
Maps
    dynamic factor
        rental areas, 65–66, 86
        settled urban areas, 54–56, 58,
            60–61
    of health inspection, 398–99,
        400n
    of neighborhood unit streets, 106

official, 349
regional, 377
Marginal propensities, 146–47
Marine City (Calif.), 301
Market (supply and demand), 1,
  127–216
analysis of
  property values,
    287–88, 293
  federal techniques, 396
  geographical analysis, 253–54
  nonwhite market, 269–70
  sociological analysis, 37
changing inventory of, 202–16
consumer, 15, 17, 18*t*, 243
  consumer mobility, 175–91
  decline in consumer preferences,
    154–68, 172
  future trends, 20, 330–31
  importance of interest rate,
    351–52
  influence of standards, 391–92,
    393–94
  measuring consumer behavior,
    139–45
social questions, 31–35
of demand, 15
  construction industry serving
    demand, 307–9
  future demand, 18–20, 211–12
  minority group demand,
    269–71, 274–75
  mobility and, 204–5
  mortgage debt and, 358
  need vs. demand, 34
  renewal and, 420–21, 426,
    443–44, 449, 467, 470
  subdivision development and,
    386
  unit of demand, 16–17
"effective," 251, 257
eminent domain affecting,
  422–23
expansion of, 248
family and, 127–53
  family expenditures, 14, 139–53
  family values and housing
    design, 4, 127–38
filtering process in, 191–201;
  *see also* Filtering process
furnished rooms on, 221
large-scale building firms in,
  318–24, 352
  number of firms, 323*t*
low-cost housing alien to, 240–41
for rehabilitation, 438
rent-income ratio and, 168–75;
  *see also* Rent-income ratio
for residential redevelopment,
  434–35
segregation affecting, 282–83,
  299
theories of urban growth and,
  76–77, 78*n*, 88–89, 92–93
*See also* Low-cost housing;
  Property value

Marshall, John, 347
Maryland, 8, 57, 301*n*, 325, 328
  *See also* Baltimore
Massachusetts, 8*n*, 69, 301, 390*n*
  Homestead Commission, 3, 10
  mortgage debts in, 358, 359*n*
  tax exemptions in, 342
  zoning in, 383
  *See also* Boston
Massachusetts General Hospital,
  458, 464
Massachusetts Institute of
  Technology (M.I.T.), 129,
  261
Matawan (N.J.), 325
Materials-distributing system,
  311–12
Mathews Plan, 101
Meegan, 456
Mellon National Bank
  (Pittsburgh), 436
Mental health, *see* Health; Social
  research—psycho-social
  research
Mergers, housing, inventory of, 204,
  206–7, 213*n*
Merrick, George, 71
Merton, Robert K., 30*n*, 48, 295
  Craftown study by, 129, 261
  "The Social Psychology of
    Housing," 20–29
Mexican-Americans, 283, 285, 401
Meyerson, Martin, 458*n*, 473*n*
  "Housing and the National
    Economy," 14–20
Miami (Fla.)
  growth of, 60, 63
  high-rent districts, 65, 67, 69,
    71, 73
  urban renewal in, 451–52, 454,
    457
Michigan, 8, 184–85, 401
  *See also* Detroit
Michigan, Lake, 58, 73
Middle-income family, disappearance
  of, 446–48
Middle-income housing, 230, 249
  cooperatives as, 32
  decline of market for, 157
  desirable environment of, 90–91
  history of, 10, 12
  housing expenditures in, 145*t*,
    148*t*, 149*t*, 150*t*, 151*t*
  Hoyt's views on, 73, 74, 84–85,
    87, 88
  inadequate, 251–54
  mobility rate and, 183
  Negro, 271, 300–1
  predicted need for, 13
  renewal affecting, 466
  economically balanced
    neighborhoods, 448–49
  redeveloped areas, 432, 435
  types of, 41
*Middletown in Transition* (Lynd
  and Lynd), 70*n*

Migrant workers
  during Depression (1930's), 187
  housing for, 12, 402
Migration, *see* Moving; Urban
  migration
"Migration to a Medium-sized
  American City: Attitudes,
  Motives, and Personal
  Characteristics Revealed by
  Open-end Interview
  Methodology" (Turner), 184*n*
Milan (Italy), 115
Mills' Hotels, 218, 220, 222
Millspaugh, Martin, "The Lessons
  Learned," 451–57
Milwaukee (Wisc.), 3
  in APHA survey, 401
  municipal housing in, 8
  slums in, 256
Minimum Property Standards, 326
Minneapolis (Minn.), 301
  growth of, 67, 71
  mobility in, 190
Minority-group (segregated)
  housing, 29, 148, 248,
    269–305
  forces maintaining, 269–86
  history of, 10, 270
  mobility rate in, 189
  property values and, 274–75,
    286–94
  relocation and, 472, 473–74
  social effects of, 27, 282–86
  surveys of standards of, 399, 401
  urban growth and, 73, 87
  *See also* Ghettos; Interracial
    housing
Miscegenation, 273–74
Mission lodging, 220
Missouri, 225
  *See also* Kansas City; St. Louis
Mittlebach, Frank, "Classifications
  of the Construction Industry,"
  314–17
Mobility, *see* Moving
"Models" (slum dwellers), 414*t*,
  415–16
Moeschen, Katie, 2*n*
Morbidity, *see* Health
Morgenthau, Henry, 367
Mortgages, 21–22, 139, 248,
  350–64
  British, 7
  changes in credit on, 17
  debts on, 149, 153
    average housing expenditure by,
      142*t*
  construction and, 358, 363–64
  debt-to-value ratio, 362–63,
    364*t*
  federal policy and, 160, 339
  growth, 357–64
  income and, 361*t*
  income tax and, 341, 357
  refinanced, 248

tenure and, 141–43, 152
total debts and, 361–62
FHA, *see* Federal Housing
  Administration—mortgage
  holdings of
financial risks and, 334
foreclosures on, 339, 350,
  358–59
holdings of, 354t
interest rates on, 344, 351–52
sources of funds for, 355t
state jurisdiction over, 350
terms of, 157, 164–65, 252–53,
  358, 432, 436
by type of holder, 356t
types of lenders on, 353t
*Mortgages on Homes in the United
  States* (Census Bureau), 364
Morton, J. E., 352
Mother's Aid, 239
Moving, 40, 175–91
  average amount of, 153
  in construction industry, 322–24
  in environmental study, 262
  inventory of, 204–5, 209–11
  long-distance, 176, 184–85, 187,
    189, 210
  motivated by rehabilitation, 451
  in Paris, 115
  population change due to,
    453–54
  public housing and, 234, 258t
  social pattern and, 47–48
  in substandard areas, 255
  to suburbia (decentralization),
    36, 44, 49, 189–91, 205, 428,
    430, 448
  *See also* Relocation; Urban
    migration
Mueller, Eva, *Consumer
  Expectations 1953–56*, 176n
Multiple dwellings, 226
  freestanding housing vs., 21, 27,
    41–42, 179
  substandard, 256
Multiple movers, 177–84
  duration of occupancy of, 178t
Mumford, Lewis, 30n, 41
  "In Defense of the
    Neighborhood," 114–28
Murfreesboro (Tenn.), 431t
Murray, James A., "Building and
  Land Use Controls," 373–90
*Mutual Savings Banks in the
  Savings and Mortgage Markets*
  (Lintner), 359n
Myrdal, Gunnar, 281
  *An American Dilemma*, 272n
"Myths of Housing Reform, The"
  (Dean), 255–61


**N**

NAHB, *see* National Association
  of Home Builders
NASA, 328–29
Nashville (Tenn.), 431t

National Academy of Sciences
  National Research Council,
  327
National Association of Home
  Builders (NAHB), 246, 249,
  381, 388
  estimates construction by
    large-scale builders, 318
  growth of, 315
National Association of Housing and
  Redevelopment Officials, 13
National Association of Real Estate
  Boards, 246, 367
  advocates slum dole, 371
  Code of Ethics of, 276
National Bank Act, 353n
National Board of Fire Underwriters
  (NBFU), 303n, 375n, 376
National Bureau of Standards, 327,
  330
  research programs under, 346
National Conference on Family
  Life, 40
National Education Association
  Committee on School House
  Planning, 97
National Electric Safety Code, 327,
  330, 375n, 377n
National Housing Acts, *see* Housing
  Acts
National Housing Agency, 337, 346
National Housing Association, 9–11
National Housing Conference, 247
  1912, 9–10
  1932, 11, 13
National Housing Inventory
  (NHI), 202–16, 448
  results of, 205–15
  subjects of inquiry in, 203–4
National Industrial Recovery Act
  (NIRA), 4
National Opinion Research Center,
  272
National Plumbing Code, 327, 330,
  375n
*National Product Since 1869*
  (Kuznets), 154
National Public Health Act
  (England, 1848), 5
National Recovery Act, 3
Nebraska, 225
Necessitarians (slum dwellers),
  413–15
*Negro Potential, The* (Ginzberg),
  284n
Negroes, 237, 347
  crowding of, 401
  history of housing for, 4, 270
  housing expenditures of, 149–50,
    269–70
  in housing studies
    environmental study, 262
    interracial housing study,
      294–98
    property value studies, 290–94
  Hoyt's theory unfavorable to,
    92–93

income of, 243, 269–70, 448
oppose slum clearance, 46
as political force, 45, 297
rehabilitation affecting, 452, 454,
  456
segregation of, 269–74, 277–79,
  282–84, 296
  economic segregation, 44
  neighborhood unit segregation,
    113
  public housing segregation, 234,
    247
  self-segregation, 270–71
  social effects, 283, 284, 285–86
  social research on, 22, 26, 294–98
  social strata among, 87
  Southern, 72, 269, 271–74, 279,
    282, 296–97, 454
  urbanization of, 12, 73, 187, 189,
    219, 271, 273, 283, 298–305
  *See also* Interracial housing
Neighborhood, 40, 53–128
  defense of, 114–28
  deterioration of, 13, 74, 83, 91,
    177, 186, 285; *see also*
    Filtering process
  economically balanced, 448–50
  of elderly persons, 74, 224
  environment of, 12, 27–28, 186,
    265–66, 395–96
  moving within, 176, 177, 184–85,
    187–90
  planned, 46–49
  rehabilitation of, 408, 437–38,
    451–57
  segregation perpetuated by, 271,
    274–75, 277
  in study of property values,
    287–91
  theories of structure and growth
    of, 53–94
    Firey's theory, 76–81
    Rodwin's critique of theories,
      75–94
    statement of Hoyt's theory,
      53–75
  *See also* Community centers;
    Community facilities;
    Community planning
Neighborhood associations, 131
  critique of, 112–13
  function of, 285
  renewal associations, 456–57
  *See also* Tenant organizations
Neighborhood unit formula, 94–114
  applied to population, 96–98, 120
    200,000 population, 97t
  critical appraisal of
    Isaacs, 109–14
    Mumford, 114, 116, 117, 118,
      119–24
  principles of, 108t
"Neighborhood Unit Formula,
  The" (Perry), 94–109
Neighborliness, 113, 115–16, 131
  after rehabilitation, 451

studies of
  environmental study, 265–66
  interracial housing study, 294
Netherlands, 8, 114–16, 367
"New Directions for the Housing
  Industry" (*House and Home*),
  324–31
New Hampshire, 225
New Haven (Conn.), 9, 258, 301
  APHA pilot study in, 397–98, 401
New Jersey, 8, 58, 189, 301, 325,
  431*t*, 447
  coastal resorts in, 69–70, 73
  in housing inventory, 214*t*
  measurement of housing need in,
    401–2
  *See also* Fair Lawn; Newark
New Orleans (La.), 54
  growth of, 58
  rehabilitation in, 437, 451, 454,
    457
  segregated public housing in, 281
New School for Social Research
  (New York), 261
"New towns" ("greenbelt
  principle"), 2, 49, 51, 114,
  119
  isolation of, 123
  neighborhood absent from, 117
New York City, 205, 236–37, 325
  building code of, 378
  contact opportunities in, 131
  contemporary design in, 442–43
  Depression relief bureau in, 371
  distinctive neighborhoods in, 115,
    270–71
  fair-housing groups in, 301
  filtering process in, 193
  growth of, 57, 58, 59–60, 63
    high-rent districts, 67, 69–71,
    72, 83*n*
  history of housing in, 2–4, 9
  in housing inventory, 214*t*
  housing-movement leaders in, 13
  interracial housing in, 46, 292,
    294–96, 301
  lodging houses in, 218
  Mayor's Committee of Inquiry,
    238–39
  middle-class groups in, 447
  minority-group housing in, 73,
    189, 301
    Chinatown, 270–71
  mixed income areas of, 448–49
  planning of
    nineteenth-century planning,
    116
    Planning Commission, 439
    suburban planning, 118
  public housing in, 247, 259
  Rent Control Commission, 144*n*
  rent-income ratio in, 171*t*
  school construction in, 96
  study of slums in, 256–57
  Stuyvesant Town project in, 369,
    431*t*
  taxes in, 341, 367

urban renewal in
  land writedown, 445–46
  redevelopment, 444
  rehabilitation study, 439–40
  *See also* Bronx; Brooklyn; Queens
New York State, 8, 129, 189, 236,
  260
  Board of Housing, 3–4, 10
  Building Code, 376
  Commission on Housing and
    Regional Planning, 10
  Constitution, amended, 12
  financing in
    authorized loans, 12
    public housing subsidy, 367
  Housing Bank, 3
  housing code in, 238
  Housing Law (1926), 3–4
  League of Savings and Loan
    Associations, 10
  Redevelopment Companies Acts,
    343
  Republican Party in, 11
  tax exemptions in, 342–43
  Tenement House Law (1901),
    2–3, 5*n*, 9
  zoning in, 381
  *See also specific cities*
Newark (N.J.), 256, 257, 444
  Housing Authority, 259
  slum revenues in, 429
  study of interracial housing in,
    294–95
Newcomb, Robinson, 314
  "The Organization of the
    Construction Industry,"
    307–13
NHI, *see* National Housing
  Inventory
1950, 232
Nonfarm housing units started
  1889–1960
  average construction cost of, 17*t*
  Gross National Product
    (1909–1960) and, 16*t*
"Non-intrinsic" society-space
  relationship, 76
Norristown (Pa.), 185
North
  elderly population of, 225
  housing expenditures in, 146*t*,
    147–48, 150
  in housing inventory, 207*t*
  lower rate of construction in, 15
  migration to, 187, 189–90
  minority-group population of, 283
  public housing in, 247
  racial issue in, 280, 302
    anti-segregation laws, 272
    *de facto* school segregation, 282
    interracial housing, 297
    segregated housing, 45–46, 271,
    278, 298–99
    zoning, 281
Norway, 7–8, 367
Nursery schools, 133

**O**
Oakland (Calif.)
  construction industry in, 323
  in property value study, 288–89
Obsolescence, *see* Deterioration
Occupancy ratio, 173
Occupation, *see* Employment
Octavia Hill movement, 9
Ohio, county housing authorities in,
  8
  *See also* Cincinnati; Cleveland
"Okies," 187
*Oklahoma City v. Sanders*, 349*n*
Olmstead, Frederick Law, 11
One-story housing, 41, 247
  *See also* Freestanding housing
O.P.A. price ceiling, 221
"Open" design, 40–41, 118
Open occupancy, *see* Interracial
  housing
"Open Occupancy in 1964"
  (Drake), 302*n*
Open space, 247
  in neighborhood unit, 98–101
  new uses for, 123–24
  sociology of, 41, 49
  *See also* Parks; Recreational
    facilities
Opportunists (slum dwellers), 413,
  415–17
*Organization Man, The* (Whyte),
  183
"Organization of the Construction
  Industry, The" (Colean and
  Newcomb), 307–13
Oriental-Americans, 189, 270–71,
  294
Osborn, F. J., 114
Overcrowding, *see* Crowding
Ownership, 200
  federal stimulus to, 347
  higher income related to, 141
  by lower classes, 157
  maintenance and, 198
  mobility rate and, 176, 178–81,
    183, 186, 205, 209–11
  without mortgages, 142*t*
  percentage of, 13
  poverty and, 232–33
  preferred to public housing, 258*t*
  rehabilitation affecting, 407, 453
  rise in, 18
  sentiment attached to, 21–22, 38
  small proportion of, 256
  *See also* Cooperative housing;
    Landlords; Rent-ownership
    controversy

**P**
Paris (France), 115
Parker, Barry, 117
Parks, 369
  availability of, 396
  in civic structure, 49–50
  excessive space for, 80*n*

neglected on open market, 89
in neighborhood unit formula,
  98–101, 108, 120
  160-acre neighborhood, 99t,
    100t
  in subdivision planning, 386
  See also Recreational facilities
Paterson (N.J.), 301
Peabody House (Boston), 468n
Penn Center, 443
Pennsylvania, 185, 231, 257, 434
  See also Philadelphia; Pittsburgh
Perkins, G. Holmes, 30n
"Perpetual Inventory of National
  Wealth, A" (Goldsmith),
  156n
Perry, Clarence A., "The
  Neighborhood Unit Formula,"
  94–109
Perth Amboy (N.J.), 431t
Philadelphia (Pa.), 3, 13, 122, 236,
  325
  growth of, 57
  housing code in, 238
  in housing inventory, 213, 214t
  interracial housing in, 295–96
  mobility in, 182t, 185
  occupied rooms in, 167t
  payroll tax in, 341
  in property value studies, 288–89,
    293
  public housing in, 257
  rent-income ratio in, 171t
  rent index in, 194n
  urban renewal in
    Downtown Business Group
      renewal sponsors, 436
    redevelopment study, 401
    state-subsidized project, 434,
      435
Pilot program, Bauer proposal for,
  251
Pinkerton, Thomas, "Housing
  Environment and Family
  Life," 261–68
Pittsburgh (Pa.), 116, 122, 325
  bi-racial project in, 295
  Golden Triangle project in, 431
  public housing in, 257
Place, Andy, 325
Planning
  city, see City planning
  community, see Community
    planning
  democratic, 35
  government-controlled land,
    334–35, 338
  improved, in construction
    industry, 325
  mobility affecting, 36
  neighborhood
    problems, 122–24
    subdivision, 384–87
    suburban, 117–18

see also Neighborhood unit
  formula
of new towns, see "New towns"
redevelopment, see
  Redevelopment—planned
Playgrounds, see Parks; Recreational
  facilities
Plumbing, see Sanitary facilities
"Plus-Granny" flat, 229–30
Polish-Americans in Chicago, 73
Population
  decline in, 16–17, 154, 461–62
  of expanding neighborhoods, 53
  future trends in, 18–19, 230,
    390
  housing shortage and, 37
  neighborhood unit scheme
    applied to, 96–98, 120
    200,000 population, 97t
  shifts in, 189–90, 453–54
  slum, see Slums—population of
  stable, 2
  of unattached persons, 217
  urban European, 115
  on urban periphery, 63
  See also Census
Portland (Ore.) in property value
  study, 289–91
Poverty and housing, 20, 231–40
  1847 survey of, 2
  public housing, 231, 233–40,
    415
  residential stability due to, 269
  of slum dwellers, 414–15, 417
  substandard housing, 255, 427,
    462
  of unattached persons, 218, 222
  See also Family—low-income;
    Low-cost housing; Slums
Prefabricated housing, 308n, 346n
Prejudice, racial, 271–74, 276
  reduction of, 295, 297–98
  stimulated by segregation, 285–86
  See also Interracial housing;
    Minority-group housing; Race
President's Advisory Committee on
  Government Housing Policies
  and Programs, 428, 440
  Report of, 431
President's Conference on Home
  Building and Home Ownership
  (1931), 11
Price index, 194n, 196
Primary (face-to-face) groups,
  27–28, 48–49
  Cooley's views on, 117
  in neighborhood units, 120–21
Privacy, 29, 132–33
  diverse concepts of, 23, 26
  in public housing, 236
  in rooming houses, 220, 222
  space standards for, 40–41
  of upper classes, 72, 83
Production, housing
  in five economic periods, 243t
  public, 242t

Property values
  depreciation of, 74, 161–62
  devaluation of, 248
  in filtering process, 192–96,
    198–200
  impeding reconstruction, 49
  income and, 156t, 192, 423n
  inventory of, 210, 211t, 212t
  of old homes, 224
  race and, 277, 286–94
  ratio of mortgage debt to,
    362–63, 364t
  renewal affecting, 420–22, 423n,
    424–26, 431
  effect of rehabilitation, 437–39,
    441
  tax yields, 465
  taxes relative to, 195, 340–42,
    349, 423n
"Property Values and Race"
  (Laurenti), 286–92
Proportionalization of ends, 80
Proudfoot, Malcolm J., 63n
Providence (R.I.), 30n, 84n
Psycho-social research, see Social
  research—psycho-social
  research
Public Health Service, 329, 402
  rehabilitation study of, 403–4
Public housing, 21–22, 233–51
  for aged persons, 228–29
  city service requirements of, 432
  court ruling on, 349n
  deadlock over, 245–51
  environment of, 262, 263–64
  European, 7
  facilities provided by, 42
  Firey's theory applied to, 80
  financing of, 338
    bond issues, 336
    federal aid (1952–61), 244t
    government subsidy, 37–38,
      337, 367
    leasing to public agencies,
      369–70
    tax exemption, 371
  history of, 4–5, 10–12, 13
  inadequacy of, 253
  in Los Angeles, 401
  moving and, 234, 258t, 467
  necessitated by market economy,
    89
  pending legislation on, 24
  poverty and, 231, 233–40, 415
  production of, 242t
  racial issue concerning
    interracial housing and, 234,
      247, 271, 280, 299–300
    segregated housing, 44, 46, 234,
      247, 281
  as reform institution, 259–60
  rent-income ratio and, 168,
    172–75
  responsibility shown in, 32
  social research on, 25, 247–48,
    257–58, 262

standards of, 391–92
  minimum standards, 393
  space standards, 40
  tax-exempt status of, 342
  unwanted, 449
Public Housing Administration,
    235, 335, 340
  *Families in Low-Rent Housing*,
    244
  production periods and, 241, 243
Public Housing Conference, 11
Public utilities
  expenditures for, 143–44, 145,
    166, 171*t*
  installation of, 14
  restrictive standards of, 32
  water as, 2, 5, 208–9
  *See also* Sanitation
Public works, 344–45
Public Works Administration
    (PWA), 349, 367
  history of, 11–12
  projects leased by, 369–70
Publicity about renewal, 455, 468
Puerto Ricans, 273, 283, 285
  middle-income, 448
  in New York City, 189, 205
  as slum dwellers, 454
PWA, *see* Public Works
    Administration

## Q

Quality controls, *see* Controls—
    quality
"Quality of Housing 'Before' and
    'After' Rehabilitation"
    (Johnson *et al.*), 403–8
*Quarterly Journal of Economics,
    The*, 154*n*, 162, 166*n*
Queens (N.Y.C.), 99–100

## R

Race
  attitudes toward, 271–75
  government-financed mortgages
    and, 303*t*
  housing design and, 34
  housing expenditures by, 149–50
  invasion and withdrawal of, 26
  property values and, 286–92
  rehabilitation affecting, 454–55
  residential movement patterns
    and, 73–74
  *See also* Ghettos; Interracial
    housing; Minority-group
    housing; Negroes;
    Oriental-Americans
Race and Housing, Commission
    on, "Where Shall We Live?"
    269–82
Race Relation Service, 12
Radburn, *see* Fair Lawn
Rapkin, Chester, 275*n*
  "Concerning Studies of Price

Trends in Mixed Areas," 292–94
  "Rent-Income Ratio," 168–75
Ratcliff, Richard U., 63
  on filtering process, 192, 194,
    196, 198
  "Housing Standards," 391–94
Rating scales, APHA, 397–98, 400
Real estate boards
  advocating Baltimore Plan, 13
  segregation and, 273, 276–78
  *See also* National Association of
    Real Estate Boards
Real estate brokers perpetuating
    segregation, 274, 276–78,
    281–82
"Real Estate Prices: A Study of
    Residential Real Estate in
    Lucas County, Ohio" (Hoad),
    200*n*
Real estate promotion, 89
  of upper-class districts, 71, 84, 93
Real Property Inventory, 395
Recommendations on Planning for
    the Chronically Ill, Joint
    Statement of, 227
Reconstruction Finance
    Corporation (RFC), 338, 369
  history of, 4, 12
  Mortgage Company, 350*n*
Recreational facilities, 408
  in Boston's West End, 461–62
  European, 123
  in neighborhood unit formula,
    98–102, 108
    apartment house facilities, 101*t*
    community clubhouse, 102, 111
    160-acre unit, 99*t*, 100*t*
  in rehabilitation program, 456
  for unattached persons, 221
  *See also* Parks
Redevelopment, urban, 24
  demolition for, 160
  federal aid for, 12, 250
  limitations of, 443–44
  by neighborhood units, 121
  planned, 441–43
    evaluation, 458–74
    least-cost criterion, 425, 427
    social psychology, 22
  private residential, 432–37
  sociology of, 50–51
  survey determining need for, 401
  taxes before and after, 431*t*
  Title I vs., 444–46
  *See also* Renewal
Reed, William V., 30*n*
Reform, 21, 32, 41
  history of, 9, 11, 34
  myths of, 255–61
Regional Survey of New York and
    Its Environs, 95–96, 99*n*, 118
Regressions, 145–47
Rehabilitation, 246, 401–8, 471
  in Boston, 92, 458–74
  of brownstones, 439*t*

changes in attitude
    accompanying, 451–57
  future trends in, 19–20
  history of, 9–10
  housing code focused on, 379
  housing quality before and after,
    403–8
  lack of data on, 208–9
  replacement vs., 418–28
  residential, 437–41
  social, 235, 414
  *See also* Improvement;
    Redevelopment; Renewal
Relief related to poor housing, 20
Relocatable house, 326–27
Relocation, 25, 249
  of elderly persons, 224
  finance for, 465–66, 469, 471–73
  impeding slum clearance, 13
  social implications of, 257–59,
    261, 465–73
  tenant retention and, 438
  *See also* Moving
"Relocation and Mental Health:
    Adaptation Under Stress"
    (Center for Community
    Studies), 458
Renewal, 224, 246, 403–74
  affecting slum dwellers, 409–18
  changes in attitude
    accompanying, 451–57
  as comprehensive approach, 13
  defined, 418
  economic aspects of, 418–28,
    430–32
    benefits and cost of
      redevelopment, 464–66
    federal subsidy, 202*n*, 419, 435
    financing, 419–21, 432–38,
      440–41, 445–46
    rehabilitation, 437–38
    relocation, 465–66, 469, 471–73
  facts and fictions in, 441–50
  future trends affecting, 19
  housing quality before and after,
    403–8
  planned
    evaluation, 458–74
    performance and, 441–43
  recommendations for, 470–74
  segregation impeding, 284–85
  in South, 300–1
  *See also* Improvement;
    Redevelopment; Rehabilitation
*Renewing Our Cities* (Colean),
    429–30
Renovation, *see* Improvement;
    Redevelopment; Rehabilitation;
    Renewal
Rent, 23, 351
  capital value related to, 140–41
  1847 survey of tenement, 2
  expenditures for, 140–43, 152
    average expenditures, 142*t*
    dissatisfaction with costs, 186

geographic location and, 147,
231
racial factors, 399
rents of unattached persons, 219
utilities included, 144
see also Rent-income ratio
in filtering process, 192–96,
197–98, 200
history of British, 6–7
of low-cost housing, 4
mixed, 448–49
mobility rate and, 176, 178–81,
183, 186, 209–12
recent movers' rent, 211t, 212t
of poor families, 232–33, 238
proportionate to standards, 5
standardized levels of, 44;
see also Rent control
urban renewal affecting, 432–35,
443–44
Boston's West End, 461, 463,
465–66
changing attitude, 453
rehabilitation, 407, 408, 438,
439t
rent moratorium, 472
rent reduction, 443, 445–46
wartime, 367
Rent area maps, 65–66, 86
Rent certificates, 326, 370–71
Rent control, 144
effect of, on tenants, 158
history of, 10
moving and, 176
in North, 147
O.P.A., 221
Rent-income ratio, 157, 166–75
gross, 169t
of monthly contract rent, 170t,
171t
of nonwhites, 269–70
for public housing, 236, 260
subsidy covering, 370
theoretical, 254
total expenditures and, 171t
"Rent-Income Ratio" (Rapkin),
168–75
Rent-ownership controversy, 21–22
cooperatives and, 38–39
higher income and, 141
Repair, see Improvement;
Redevelopment; Rehabilitation;
Renewal
"Reply" (Winnick), 166–68
Republican Party, 11
Research
federal, 345–46
ten programs, described, 326–31
limits of, 109, 450
social, see Social research
Residence clubs, 220, 222
Residential Real Estate (Wickens),
160–61
"Respectable poor" (slum
dwellers), 414–15, 417
Retirement, 225–26

Reynolds Metals Company, 325
RFC, see Reconstruction Finance
Corporation
Richmond (Va.)
growth of, 65, 67, 72
slum revenues in, 429
Riemer, Svend, 114, 127
Riis, Jacob, 9–10
Riley, Edward, 329
Road construction, 14
contractors for, 309–10
houses moved for, 207
urban growth and, 60
See also Street systems
Robbins, Ira S., "Housing
Achievements," 9–13
Rochester (N.Y.), 117
Rockefeller, David, 436
Rockefeller Center, 443
Rodwin, Lloyd, 30n
"The Theory of Residential
Growth and Structure," 75–94
Rome (Italy), 123
Rooming houses, 218–19, 220–22,
237, 396
in Boston, 463
Rooms
average number of occupied,
167t
furnished, 220–21
spare, 218
standard size of, 392
Rose, Arnold M., "Living
Arrangements of Unattached
Persons," 217–22
Ross, Sir Ronald, 24
Rossi, Peter, 185n, 186
Why Families Move, 182, 188
Rouse, James, 431
Royal Commission on Housing
(England), 6
Ruskin, John, 5
Russell Sage Foundation Regional
Survey of New York and Its
Environs, 95–96, 99n, 118
Russian-Americans in Chicago, 73
Rye (N.Y.), 383

S

Sacramento (Calif.), 323, 431t
Safety
housing reform aimed at, 255,
257, 259
racial threat to, 275
research on
federal research, 329
social research, 263
in slums, 416
standards of
building codes, 374
effect of rehabilitation, 408
inspection, 396, 397–98
subsidy to promote, 366
St. Louis (Mo.), 234, 301, 377n
APHA study in, 401

City Plan Commission, 103
growth of, 69
rent-income ratio in, 171t
St. Paul (Minn.), 72
Salt Lake City (Utah), growth of,
58, 71
San Antonio (Tex.), 229
San Francisco (Calif.), 46, 301,
375
Chinatown district of, 270–71
construction industry in, 315,
323
growth of, 58, 69
property values in, 288–89, 431
slum revenues in, 429
San Mateo (Calif.), 323
Sanborn insurance atlases, 54
Sanitary facilities
availability of, 236t
in environmental study, 262
federal research into, 326–27
standards of
contemporary standards, 226
deficient, 242
inspection, 395–96, 398, 400,
401
before and after rehabilitation,
406t, 407t, 408, 463
substandard, 208–9, 210, 232,
236, 257
Sanitary Improvement Association,
9
Sanitation
controls affecting, 374, 384,
385n, 386
history of, 5–6, 10
narrow streets impeding, 461,
463
in slums, 429
See also Health; public utilities
Santa Clara (Calif.), 323
Sasaki, Hideo, "Building and Land
Use Controls," 373–90
Save the West End Committee
(Boston), 459, 462
SCE, see Study of Consumer
Expenditures
Schaaf, A. H., "Economic Aspects
of Urban Renewal," 218–28
Schietinger, E. F., 290
Schools
in Boston's West End, 461–62
child's performance in, 267–68
as community centers, 101–2,
118
construction of, 37, 96, 384
convenient access to, 90, 96–98,
396
defining neighborhoods, 47, 95,
110
in neighborhood unit formula,
120
access to schools, 96–98
school location, 101–2, 110–11
nursery, 133
parochial, 111, 143

racial issue and
  *de facto* segregation, 282
  integrated schools, 112–13, 272
  legislation, 299
  Little Rock crisis, 286
  shortage of, 37
  in subdivision planning, 386
  *See also* Education; Illiteracy;
    *specific universities*
Schorr, Alvin L., "How the Poor
  Are Housed," 231–40
Schwabe, 168–69
Scotland, 2, 7
Scottish Housing Advisory
  Committee, *Housing of
  Special Groups*, 227*n*
Scranton (Pa.), 231
Seattle (Wash.)
  growth of, 67, 71
  in housing inventory, 214*t*
  interracial housing in, 295–96
Sector theory, 65, 67
  Boston's housing patterns and,
    81–85, 91–93
  Firey's theory and, 76–78, 81
  major weaknesses of, 89–91,
    93–94
  problems and assumptions of,
    85–89
Security legislation, 345
Seeley, John R., "The Slum: Its
  Nature, Use, and Users,"
  409–18
Segregated housing for elderly
  persons, 227
Segregation, *see* Ghettos;
  Interracial housing;
  Minority-group housing;
  Negroes
Self-containment, 120–22
Self-liquidation, 6
Selltiz, Claire, 272*n*
  *Studies in the Social Psychology
  of Race and Housing*, 271*n*
Senate
  Subcommittee on Housing,
    *Study of Mortgage Credit*,
    208*n*
  Subcommittee on Housing for
    the Elderly, "Housing for the
    Elderly," 223–26
  Subcommittee on Housing and
    Urban Redevelopment, 240
Servicemen's Readjustment Act,
  338
Settlement houses, 47, 468*n*
  in London, 117
Shaftesbury, 7th Earl of, 5–6
"Shantytowns," 220
Shaw, George Bernard, 246
Sheldon, Henry D., 223
Sheuer-Stevens (redeveloper), 436
Shopping centers, 63, 75, 381
  convenient access to, 90
  European, 115
  first planned, 118

for neighborhood unit, 95, 98,
  103–6, 111, 120, 121, 123
*See also* Business districts;
  Community facilities
Shortage
  of housing, 198, 228
    causing slums, 32
    due to mobility, 176
    future, 13
    history, 7
    sociological analysis, 37
    wartime shortage, 188
  of schools, 37
Siegel, Jack M., 440
Simkhovitch, Mary, 11
Single persons, housing for, 257
  elderly persons, 224, 230
  mobility and, 181–82
  projected future need for, 13, 18
  unattached persons, 217–22
"Six Goals for a Program of
  Low-Income Housing"
  (*Journal of Housing*), 241*n*
Slayton, W., "Urban
  Redevelopment and the
  Urbanite," 179*n*
"Slum Improvement by Private
  Effort" (Buttenheim), 11
"Slumming," 412–13
Slums (blight), 38, 49, 183,
  248–49, 409–19
  aid to families in, 236
  of Boston, 91, 460–64
  clearance of, 50–51, 229, 246,
    252–61
  criteria, 37
  goal of reform, 255–61
  government clearance, 32,
    218–19, 366, 367–68
  history, 4–8, 11–13
  inadequate solution of slum
    problem, 248
  Negro opposition, 46
  segregation impeding, 284–85
  subsidy, 50, 337, 366
  survey indicating need, 395,
    398, 399, 402
  design affecting, 34
  economic strangulation due to,
    428–30
  "exporting" of, 424
  facilities in
    schools, 97
    settlement houses, 47
  high land cost in, 369
  history of, 4–8, 11–13, 20–21
  neighborhood unit scheme
    applied to, 100–1
  population of, 256
    classification, 409–18
    recommendations for relocating
      population, 470–73
    stagnant population, 1–2
  preferred to public housing, 175
  produced by limited market, 32

principal types of, 413*t*
  slum dwellers, 414*t*
  rehabilitation of, 9–10, 209, 401,
    432, 437, 440, 451–57
  renewal reserved for, 442, 470–71
  rent certificates for, 371
  small-scale business in, 250, 417
  social research on, 262–63, 266,
    393
  in theories of urban growth and
    structure, 88*n*
    Firey's theory, 77
    Hoyt's theory, 62, 72, 83–84,
      86
  *See also* Ghettos; Tenements
*Slums and Social Insecurity*
  (Department of Health,
  Education and Welfare), 231*n*
SMA's, 205–6, 210
  of conversions and mergers, 207*t*
  of household formation, 213–15
Smith, Alfred E., 10
Smith, T. Lynn, *The Sociology of
  Rural Life*, 110*n*
Social class
  higher than economic class, 135
  *See also* Low-cost housing;
    Migrant workers;
    Middle-income housing;
    Upper-class districts;
    Working-class housing
*Social Life of a Modern
  Community, The* (Warner
  and Lunt), 86*n*, 87*n*
Social outcasts, 414–15
  *See also* "Homeless men"
"Social Psychology of Housing,
  The" (Merton), 20–29
"Social Questions in Housing and
  Community Planning"
  (Wurster), 30–52
Social reform, *see* Reform
Social research
  aimed at reform, 256, 261
  into community planning, 26,
    28–52
    neighborhood unit formula,
      109–10, 111–14
  into environmental influences,
    261–68
  into housing design, 127–38
  into housing for unattached
    persons, 217, 219
  into interracial housing; *see*
    Interracial housing—social
    research into
  psycho-social research, 20–29,
    265–67, 283–84
  research on Boston's West End,
    458–74
  into public housing, 25, 247–48,
    257–58, 262
  into renewal, 458–74
  into slum population, 409–18
  into standards, 393–94

into urban growth and structure, 98–93
Social Security Act, 239
Social Security Board, 239
"Social Significance of Mobility" (Sullenger), 180
Social system in Firey's theory, 76–77, 80–81
Social Unit movement, 118
Social work
  problems of, 410–11
  among relocating tenants, 472
  welcomed, 452–53
  See also Settlement houses
Sociology of Rural Life, The (Smith), 110n
South
  high-rent neighborhoods in, 72
  higher rate of construction in, 15, 17
  housing expenditures in, 146t, 147–48, 150
  in housing inventory, 207t, 214t
  mobility rate and, 187, 189–90, 271
  racial issue in
    disfranchisement, 282, 297
    effect of rehabilitation, 454
    new Negro communities, 300–1, 302
    nonwhite income, 269
    racial attitudes, 272–74, 296–97
    segregated housing, 44–46, 279, 280, 281, 298–99
South Carolina, 8n
Southern Building Code Congress (SBCC), 303, 375n, 376
Space
  adjustment to, 265
  family size and, 170
  Firey's theories of, 76, 77n, 80
  moving satisfying need for, 185
  open, see Open space
  reduction in, 167
  standards of, 40–41, 229
  use of, 196
    intra-dwelling use, 135–37
    per capita use, 157–58
  See also Environment; Rooms
Spare rooms, 218
Special groups, defined, 227n
Special housing for aged in foreign countries, 225–27
"Speculation in Suburban Lands" (Fisher), 54n
Speeyt v. Morgenthau, 349n
Spending unit, defined, 223
"Sporting crowd" (slum dwellers), 414t, 415, 416
Spring, Bernard P., "Building and Land Use Controls," 373–90
Springfield (Mass.), 69
Stabilizing Construction, 307n
Standards, 233, 391–408
  deficient, 242t, 245t
  economic segregation due to, 44

enforcement of, 238–39, 336, 375–76, 389, 399, 405, 407–8, 420–21, 423, 425, 441, 456
federal research into, 27, 329–31
FHA, 39, 338, 377
history of, 2, 4–5, 13, 32
legislative adherence to, 36
measurement of, 394–403
minimum, defined, 393
neighborhood, 47, 48, 101
reform of, 255–56
renewal and, 418–22, 424–25, 426n, 427
  middle-class standards, 467–68
  recommendations, 471
  rehabilitation, 403–8, 440–41
  slum renewal, 460–64
rising, 13, 19, 91, 196
of sanitary facilities, see Sanitary facilities—standards of
space, 40–41, 229
uniformity and, 39–40
volitional, defined, 393
See also Controls
Stapp, Peyton, 177n
State, Department of, 328
Statistics of Income (Treasury Department), 341n
Stein, Clarence S., 10, 106
  Hillside Homes design of, 230
  Radburn design of, 119, 123
Stevenson, Robert Louis, 24
Stigler, G. J., The Theory of Competitive Price, 80n, 164n
"Stock flow," 197
Stockholm (Sweden), 226
Stores, see Business districts; Shopping centers
Street Corner Society (Whyte), 412–13
Street systems
  narrow, 461, 463
  in neighborhood unit formula
    external streets, 98
    gridiron and specialized, 106, 107t
    internal streets, 100, 106–8
  subdivision control over, 384
  See also Gridiron plan; Road construction
Stressed skin sandwich panel, 328
"Structural Change in the Housebuilding Industry" (Herzog), 317–24
"Structure and Growth of Residential Neighborhoods in American Cities, The" (Hoyt), 53–75
Study of Consumer Expenditures (SCE), 139–52
  income and housing expenditures data from, 145t, 146t, 148t, 149t, 150t, 151t
Study of Mortgage Credit (Senate Subcommittee on Housing), 208n

Study of Saving in the United States, A (Goldsmith), 361
Subcontractors, function of, 310, 316
Subdivision control, 379, 383–87, 389
Subsidy, 174, 247–49, 356–71
  criteria for, 365–67
  direct, 240, 252
  eligibility for, 38
  federal legislation on, 32, 37, 366–67
  flexible, recommended, 471
  history of, 7
  inadequacy of, 235–36
  middle-income, 253–54
  real estate promotion and, 84
  segregation and, 45
  slum clearance through, 50, 337, 366
  tax-exempt, 22, 366, 371
  for urban renewal, 202n, 419, 435
"Subsidy and Housing, The" (Abrams), 365–71
Suburban housing (decentralization), 50, 249
  British, 51; see also "New towns"
  expenditures for, 146t, 147–48
  Hoyt's theory of upper-class, 73, 75, 83
  integration of, 46, 304
  migration to, 36, 44, 49, 189–91, 205, 428, 430, 447–48
  open space standards for, 41
  planned and developed, 117–18
  predicted trend toward, 18–19, 159
Sullenger, T. Earl, "Social Significance of Mobility," 180
Summer, William S., 297
Sunnyside Gardens (N.Y.), 119, 123, 229
Sunset International Petroleum Corp., 324–25
Supply, see Market
Supreme Court decisions
  on restrictive covenants, 113
  on segregation, 45, 280, 281, 282, 299
  on tenement houses, 2n
  on zoning, 3n, 380n, 381, 383
Surplus and filtration rate, 198
Survey maps, 54
Survey of Consumer Expenditures, 1950, 232
"Survey of Consumer Finances" (Federal Reserve Bulletin), 177n, 180, 181
Survey of Current Business (Commerce Department), 322, 361n, 364
Sweden, 8, 42
  housing projects for elderly persons in, 225–26
Syracuse (N.Y.), 189

**T**

Taft, Robert A., 12, 240
Taft-Ellender-Wagner Housing Bill, 394
TAMAP studies, 330
Tarrytown (N.Y.), 431
Taxes, 336, 340–44, 354n, 357, 449–50
  affected by public housing, 174, 342
  in Boston's West End, 465
  British, 6–7
  concessions on, 12
    abatements, 252–53
    concessions reducing rent, 446
    exemptions, 3, 10, 22, 336, 342–43, 366–68, 371
  crowding and, 453
  as housing expenditure, 143
  property value and, 195, 340–42, 349, 423n, 465
  public works and, 344
  before and after redevelopment, 431t
  from residential areas, 14
  from slum districts, 1, 369, 428–29
  zoning based on, 381
Tayback, Matthew, "Housing Environment and Family Life," 261–68
Technological progress, 312–13
  See also Innovation
Tenant organizations, 23, 24–25
  See also Neighborhood associations
Tenement House Commission, 2
Tenements
  five-story, 461
  history of, 2–3, 9
  as immigrant housing, 73, 74
  See also Ghettos; Slums
Tennessee Valley Authority, 335–36
Tenure, 38–39
  affected by federal finance, 347
  average housing expenditure by, 142t, 146t, 152–53
  mobility and, 180t, 181t, 182t, 210
  mortgage payments and, 141–43
  See also Moving; Ownership; Rent
Terrett, Barbara, "Housing and the National Economy," 14–20
Texas A&M College, 328
Theory of Competitive Price, The (Stigler), 80n, 164n
"Theory of Residential Growth and Structure, The" (Rodwin), 75–94
They Went to College, 184
Thorndyke, E. L., 118
Toledo (Ohio), 8

Torrens Acts (England, 1868–82), 6
Town Planning Institute Journal, 118
Town Planning Review (journal), 114n
Trading with the Enemy Act (1917), 337n
Trailers, 207
Transportation, 390
  cost of, 143, 156–57, 195, 351n
  dominating urban design, 116–17
  in Hoyt's theory of urban growth, 58–61, 63–67, 69, 70, 72–73, 75
    critical analysis, 79, 81–83
  integrated, 272
  in neighborhood unit formula, 121
    travel to playgrounds, 98
    travel to school, 96–97
    travel to shopping centers, 98, 105–6
  public, convenience of, 396
  to work, 49, 64
  See also Road construction; Street systems
"Trapped" slum dwellers, 414–16
Treasury Department, 343–44
  Statistics of Income, 341n
Trestrail, Richard, 325
Trusses, 329
Turner, Ralph, 185n
  "Migration to a Medium-sized American City: Attitudes, Motives, and Personal Characteristics Revealed by Open-end Interview Methodology," 184n
TVA, 335–36
Twentieth Century Fund, 109, 228n
Twitchell, Allan A., "An Appraisal Method for Measuring the Quality of Housing," 394–403
Two-story housing, 41

**U**

Unattached persons, 217–22, 416
  defined, 218
"Unfindables" (slum dwellers), 414t, 415–16
Unit Appraisal Form, 396–97
United Nations
  Department of Social Affairs, 42n
  Subcommission on Prevention of Discrimination and Protection of Minorities, 280
United States Housing Corporation, 3, 347n
United States Shipping Board Emergency Fleet Corporation, 347n
U.S. v. Carmack, 349n

United States v. Carolene Products Co., 349n
U.S. v. City of Louisville, 349n
U.S. v. Gettysburg Electric Co., 349n
United States v. 2771.29 Acres of Land, 349n
UNIVAC, 205–6
Unwin, Raymond, 117, 118–19
Upper-class (high-rent) districts, 157, 249
  of Boston, 429t
  controls in, 385–86
  in economically balanced areas, 448
  filtration of, 197
  housing expenditures in, 145t, 148t, 149t, 150t, 151t, 167–68
  Hoyt's analysis of, 65, 67–73, 74
    Firey's critique, 78–79
    Rodwin's critique, 82–85, 86–88, 90–94
  mobility rate and, 183
  recreational facilities for, 101
  redeveloped areas as, 423–24, 427, 432, 464–65
Urban Complex, The, 298n
Urban migration, 36, 187–90, 205, 271
  end of, 2
  future trend of, 19
  of low-income families, 248
  of unattached persons, 218, 220
Urban redevelopment, see Redevelopment
Urban renewal, see Renewal
"Urban Renewal" (McFarland), 428–41
Urban Renewal Administration, 239, 431, 445
Urban Villagers, The (Gans), 458n
"Urbanization of the Negro, The" (Weaver), 298–305
Utilities, see Public utilities
"Utilities and Facilities for New Residential Construction" (McKeever), 384n

**V**

VA, see Veterans Administration
Vacancy ratio, 74, 167–68
  in Boston's West End, 462–63
  filtering and, 200–1
  in furnished rooms, 219
  inventory of, 207–8, 211–12, 213, 215
  in redeveloped areas, 444
Values
  capital, 140–41, 154t, 155, 157
  family, see Family—values of property, see Property values
  related to slums, 409–10, 412
  standards relative to human, 392–93, 467–68

of structures for recent movers,
211t
Veblen, Thorstein, 28
Veiller, Lawrence, 9–11
Venice (Italy), 115
Ventilation, standards of, 2, 5
Vermont, 225
Vertical integration, 317
Vertical urban growth, 62, 64
Veterans Administration (VA),
241, 243t, 248, 344, 353n, 387
insurance program of, 348, 352n
liberal terms offered by, 436
real estate prices influenced by,
338
segregation policy of, 281, 301–3
standards set by, 392
Veterans' Emergency Housing Act
(1946), 337
Veterans' housing
in California, 3, 10
in England, 7
financing of, 335, 338
history of, 12, 32
public, 44, 259
Vienna (Austria), 7
Vinton, Warren Jay, 231
Virginia, 57, 236
See also Alexandria; Richmond
Voluntary Home Mortgage Credit
Program, 280

W

Wagner, Robert F., Sr., 12
Wales, 7
Walkley, Rosabelle,
"Housing Environment and
Family Life," 261–68
Wander, Richard, 290
War housing, 3, 338
British, 6–7
history of, 10, 12, 15, 32
interracial, 271, 280
production of, 243t
research programs for, 346
sale of, 370
for unattached persons, 218, 221
War Production Board, 346
Warner, W. Lloyd, The Social Life
of a Modern Community, 86n,
87n
Washabaugh, Beulah, 212n
Washington (D.C.), 236
growth of, 57, 58, 60–61
high-rent districts, 65–66, 67,
69–71
suburban apartments, 75
history of housing in, 3, 9
interracial housing in, 299–300
redevelopment of, 424n, 444
Georgetown rehabilitation,
437–38, 461
Southwest Redevelopment
Project, 431

study of redevelopment, 401
taxes before and after, 431t
rent-income ratio in, 171t
slums in, 256
zoning of, 383
Water supply, 2, 5, 208–9
Waterfront property, 69–70, 82
"Wayne Township Case, The"
(Haar), 381n
Wealth, residential
comparison of estimates of, 160t
derivation of, 161t
mortgage debt and, 362t
See also Upper-class districts
Weaver, Robert C., "The
Urbanization of the Negro,"
298–305
Webb & Knapp, 325
Welfare recipients, public housing
for, 236–38
Welwyn (England), 2
West
higher rate of construction in, 15,
17
housing expenditures in, 146t,
147–48
in housing inventory, 207t, 214t
migration to, 36, 176, 187,
189–90, 205
minority-group population in, 283
racial issue in, 280
anti-segregation laws, 272
de facto school segregation, 282
interracial housing, 297
segregated housing, 271, 278
zoning, 281
West-Jahoda-Merton study, 295
West Virginia, 8n, 65
See also Charleston
Westgate housing development,
129–30, 131
Wetmore, Louis, 30n
Wheatley Act (England, 1924), 7
Wheaton, William L. C., 30n,
204
"Housing and the National
Economy," 14–20
"Where Shall We Live?"
(Commission on Race and
Housing), 269–86
White, Alfred T., 9
White House rehabilitation, 438
White House Science Advisory
Subcommittee on Housing,
330–31
Whitney, Henry, 247
Whitten, Robert, 99–100
Why Families Move (Rossi), 182,
188
Whyte, William Foote, Street
Corner Society, 412–13
Whyte, William H., Jr., The
Organization Man, 183
Wickens, David L., Residential
Real Estate, 160–61

Williams, Dr. Huntington, "The
Quality of Housing 'Before'
and 'After' Rehabilitation,"
403–8
Wilner, Daniel, "Housing
Environment and Family
Life," 261–68
Windowglass, 11, 383
Windowless dwellings, 2n, 5n
Winnick, Louis, 211, 232
Capital Formation in Residential
Real Estate, 200n, 203n, 357n,
360, 361, 362, 364
The Distribution of Housing
Space, 170
"Facts and Fictions in Urban
Renewal," 441–50
"Family Housing Expenditures:
Elusive Laws and Intrusive
Variances," 139–53
on filtering process, 192–95,
197–98
"The Growth of the Residential
Mortgage Debt," 357–64
Guttentag's critique of, 162–65
Housing Choices and Housing
Constraints, 175n
"Housing: Has There Been a
Downward Shift in Consumers'
Preferences?," 154–62
"Reply," 166–68
"Winnick's Case for a Changing
Attitude toward Housing:
Comment" (Guttentag),
162–65
Wirth, Louis, 111
Wisconsin, University of, 328
Wolff, Reinhold, 209
Wood, Edith Elmer, 10–11
"A Century of the Housing
Problem," 1–8
Wood, Ramsey, "Housing Needs
and Housing Market," 159n
Woodbury, Coleman, 30n
Working-class housing, British, 6–7
See also Migrant workers
Works Progress Administration
(WPA), 349n
credit research by, 345
Division of Social Research,
Urban Housing: A Summary
of Real Property Inventories
1934 to 1956, 177n
World War I, 6–7, 218
emergency powers during, 337
mortgage debt during, 363
World War II, 133, 227n, 302
census during, 345
conversions during, 204
emergency powers during, 335–37
mobility rate during, 176, 180
mortgage debt during, 359, 363
rents during, 367
unattached living arrangements
in, 217–18, 221

World's Fair (1939), 58
WPA, *see* Works Progress
    Administration
Wright, Frank Lloyd, 41
Wright, Henry, 10
    Radburn design of, 119, 123
    Sunnyside Gardens design of, 229
Wurster, Catherine Bauer, 106, 411
    "The Dreary Deadlock of Public
        Housing," 245–51
    "Social Questions in Housing and
        Community Planning," 30–52
Wurster, William W., 30n

**Y**

"Y's," 218
Ylvisaker, Paul, 450
Young, Sir Hilton, 7

**Z**

Zeckendorf, William, 325, 436
Zisook Construction Company
    (Chicago), 439
Zone of transition, 62
Zoning, 89, 328, 338, 366, 379–86,
    388–90, 392
    history of, 3, 5

increase in, 32
industry regulated by, 64, 381,
    382
large areas affected by, 388
in neighborhood unit scheme,
    101, 103–5, 120
as province of states, 349
in rehabilitation program, 452,
    456
segregation by, 44–45, 46, 116,
    123, 281
*Zoning* (Bassett), 103
Zorbaugh, Harvey, *The Gold Coast
    and the Slum*, 411